D1476369

The Zohar

by

Rav Shimon bar Yochai

From The Book of Avraham

with
The Sulam Commentary

by

Rav Yehuda Ashlag

The First Ever Unabridged
English Translation with Commentary

Published by
The Kabbalah Centre International Inc.
Dean Rav S. P. Berg Shlita

Edited and Compiled by
Rabbi Michael Berg

Copyright © 2003

Published by
The Kabbalah Centre International Inc.

155 E. 48th St., New York, NY 10017
1062 S. Robertson Blvd., Los Angeles, CA 90035

Director Rav Berg

First Printing 2001
Revised Edition 2003

Printed in USA

ISBN: 1-57189-092-0

In loving memory
of

Arthur H. Fass

ארתור הירש בן חיים

May this book
open the secrets of the universe,
assist us on our path,
and connect all of us
to the Light.

Karen and Murray

שפע כן חייך
אלהים הייא בו הייא

APPLYING THE POWER OF THE ZOHAR

The Zohar is a book of great mystical power and wisdom. It is Universally recognized as the definitive work on the Kabbalah – and it is also so Much more.

The Zohar is a wellspring of spiritual energy, a fountainhead of metaphysical power that not only reveals and explains, but literally brings blessing, protection, and well-being into the lives of all those who read or peruse its sacred texts. All that is required is worthy desire, the certainty of a trusting heart, and an open and receptive mind. Unlike other books, including the great spiritual texts of other traditions, The Zohar is written in a kind of code, through which metaphors, parables, and cryptic language at first conceal but ultimately reveal the forces of creation.

As electrical current is concealed in wire and cable before disclosing itself as an illuminated light bulb, the spiritual Light of the Creator is wrapped in allegory and symbolism throughout the Aramaic text of the Zohar. And while many books contain information and knowledge, the Zohar both expresses and embodies spiritual Light. The very letters on its pages have the power to bring spiritual wisdom and positive energy into every area of our lives.

As we visually scan the Aramaic texts and study the accompanying insights that appear in English, spiritual power is summoned from above – and worlds tremble as Light is sent forth in response.

It's primary purpose is not only to help us acquire wisdom, but to draw Light from the Upper Worlds and to bring sanctification into our lives. Indeed, the book itself is the most powerful of all tools for cleansing the soul and connecting to the Light of the Creator. As you open these pages, therefore, do not make understanding in the conventional sense your primary goal.

Although you may not have a knowledge of Aramaic, look first at the Aramaic text before reading the English. Do not be discouraged by difficulties with comprehension. Instead, open your heart to the spiritual transformation the Zohar is offering you.

Ultimately, the Zohar is an instrument for refining the individual soul – for removing darkness from the earth – and for bringing well being and blessing to our fellow man.

Its purpose is not only to make us intellectually wise, but to make us spiritually pure.

Torah

Also known as the Five Books of Moses, the Torah is considered to be the physical body of learning, whereas the Zohar is the internal soul. The literal stories of the Torah conceal countless hidden secrets. The Zohar is the Light that illuminates all of the Torah's sublime mysteries.

Beresheet	Genesis
Shemot	Exodus
Vayikra	Leviticus
Bemidbar	Numbers
Devarim	Deuteronomy

Prophets

Amos	Amos
Chagai	Haggai
Chavakuk	Habakkuk
Hoshea	Hosea
Melachim	Kings
Michah	Micah
Nachum	Nahum
Ovadyah	Obadiah
Shmuel	Samuel
Shoftim	Judges
Tzefanyah	Zephaniah
Yechezkel	Ezekiel
Yeshayah	Isaiah
Yirmeyah	Jeremiah
Yoel	Joel
Yonah	Jonah
Zecharyah	Zechariah

Writings

Daniel	Daniel
Divrei Hayamim	Chronicles
Eicha	Lamentations
Ester	Esther
Ezra	Ezra
Nechemiah	Nehemiah
Iyov	Job
Kohelet	Ecclesiastes
Mishlei	Proverbs
Rut	Ruth
Tehilim	Psalms
Sir Hashirim	Songs of Songs

The Ten Sfirot – Emanations

To conceal the blinding *Light* of the Upper World, and thus create a tiny point into which our universe would be born, ten *curtains* were fabricated. These ten *curtains* are called Ten Sfirot. Each successive Sfirah further reduces the emanation of *Light*, gradually dimming its brilliance to a level almost devoid of *Light* – our physical world known as *Malchut*. The only remnant of Light remaining in this darkened universe is a *pilot light* which sustains our existence. This Light is the life force of a human being and the force that gives birth to stars, sustains suns and sets everything from swirling galaxies to busy ant hills in motion. Moreover, the Ten Sfirot act like a prism, refracting the Light into many *colors* giving rise to the diversity of life and matter in our world.

The Ten Sfirot are as follows:

Keter	Crown
Chochmah	Wisdom
Binah	Understanding
Da'at	Knowledge
Zeir Anpin	Small Face, (includes the next six Sfirot):
Chesed	Mercy (Chassadim - plural)
Gvurah	Judgment (Gvurot - Plural)
Tiferet	Splendor
Netzach	Victory (Eternity)
Hod	Glory
Yesod	Foundation
Malchut	Kingdom

The Partzufim - Spiritual forms

One complete structure of the Ten Sfirot creates a *Partzuf* or Spiritual Form. Together, these forces are the building blocks of all reality. As water and sand combine to create cement, the Ten Sfirot

Names of God

As a single ray of white sunlight contains the seven colors of the spectrum, the one Light of the Creator embodies many diverse spiritual forces. These different forces are called *Names of God*. Each Name denotes a specific attribute and spiritual power. The Hebrew letters that compose these Names are the interface by which these varied Forces act upon our physical world. The most common Name of God is the Tetragrammaton (the four letters, *Yud Hei Vav Hei* יהוה). Because of the enormous power that the Tetragrammaton transmits, we do not utter it aloud. When speaking of the Tetragrammaton, we use the term *Hashem* which means, *The Name*.

Adonai, El, Elohim, Hashem, Shadai, Eheyeh, Tzevaot, Yud Hei Vav Hei

People

Er	The son of Noach
Rabbi Elazar	The son of Rabbi Shimon bar Yochai
Rabbi Shimon bar Yochai	Author of the Zohar
Shem, Cham, Yefet	Noach's children
Shet	Seth
Ya'akov	Jacob
Yishai	Jesse (King David's father)
Yitzchak	Isaac
Yosef	Joseph
Yitro	Jethro
Yehuda	Judah

Angels

Angels are distinct energy components, part of a vast communication network running through the upper worlds. Each unique Angel is responsible for transmitting various forces of influence into our physical universe.

Adriel, Ahinael, Dumah (name of Angel in charge of the dead), Gabriel, Kasdiel, Kedumiel, Metatron, Michael, Rachmiel.

---

combine to produce a Spiritual Form [*Partzuf*]. Each of the Spiritual Forms below are therefore composed of one set of Ten Sfirot.

These Spiritual Forms are called:

Atik	Ancient
Atik Yomin	Ancient of Days
Atika Kadisha	Holy Ancient
Atik of Atikin	Ancient of Ancients
Aba	Father
Arich Anpin	Long Face
Ima	Mother
Nukva	Female
Tevunah	Intelligence
Yisrael Saba	Israel Grandfather
Zachar	Male

The Five Worlds

All of the above Spiritual Forms [*Partzufim*] create one spiritual world. There are Five Worlds in total that compose all reality, therefore, five sets of the above Spiritual Forms are required.

Our physical world corresponds to the world of: Asiyah – Action

Adam Kadmon	Primordial Man
Atzilut	Emanation
Briyah	Creation
Yetzirah	Formation
Asiyah	Action

The Five Levels of the soul

Nefesh	First, Lowest level of Soul
Ruach	Second level of Soul
Neshamah	Third level of Soul
Chayah	Fourth level of Soul
Yechidah	Highest, fifth level of Soul

Raphael, Tahariel, Uriel

Nations

Nations actually represent the inner attributes and character traits of our individual self. The nation of Amalek refers to the doubt and uncertainty that dwells within us when we face hardship and obstacles. Moab represents the dual nature of man. Nefilim refers to the sparks of Light that we have defiled through our impure actions, and to the negative forces that lurk within the human soul as a result of our own wrongful deeds.

Amalek, Moab, Nefilim

General

Aba	Father
	Refers to the male principle and positive force in our universe. Correlates to the proton in an atom.
Arvit	The Evening prayer
Chayot	Animals
Chupah	Canopy (wedding ceremony)
Et	The
Avadon	Hell
Gehenom	Hell
Sheol	Hell
	The place a soul goes for purification upon leaving this world.
Ima	Mother
	The female principle and minus force in our universe. Correlates to the electron in an atom.
Kiddush	Blessing over the wine
Klipah	Shell (negativity)
Klipot	Shells (Plural)
Kriat Sh'ma	The Reading of the Sh'ma
Mashiach	Messiah
Minchah	The Afternoon prayer
Mishnah	Study
Mochin	Brain, Spiritual levels of Light
Moed	A designated time or holiday
Negev	The south of Israel
Nukva	Female

Partzuf	Face
Shacharit	The Morning prayer
Shamayim	Heavens (sky)
Shechinah	The Divine presence, The female aspect of the Creator
Tefilin	Phylacteries
The Dinur river	The river of fire
Tzadik	Righteous person
Zion	Another name for Jerusalem
Yisrael	The land of Israel
	The nation of Israel or an individual Israelite
Zohar	Splendor

The Hebrew vowels

Chirik אָ, Cholam אוֹ אֹ, Kamatz אָ, Patach אַ, Segol אֶ, Sh'va אְ, Shuruk אוּ אֻ, Tzere אֵ.

The Twelve Tribes

Asher, Dan, Ephraim, Gad, Issachar, Judah, Levi, Menasheh, Naphtali, Reuben, Shimon, Zebulun

Jewish Holidays

Rosh Hashanah	The Jewish New Year
Yom Kippur	Day of Atonement
Sukkot	Holiday of the Booths
Shmini Atzeret	The day of Convocation
Simchat Torah	Holiday on which we dance with the Torah
Pesach	Passover
Shavout	Holiday of the Weeks

כרך ג

פרשת לך לך, וירא

Vol. III

Lech Lecha, Vayera

A Prayer from The Ari

To be recited before the study of the Zohar

Ruler of the universe, and Master of all masters, The Father of mercy and forgiveness, we thank You, our God and the God of our fathers, by bowing down and kneeling, that You brought us closer to Your Torah and Your holy work, and You enable us to take part in the secrets of Your holy Torah. How worthy are we that You grant us with such big favor, that is the reason we plead before You, that You will forgive and acquit all our sins, and that they should not bring separation between You and us.

And may it be your will before You, our God and the God of our fathers, that You will awaken and prepare our hearts to love and revere You, and may You listen to our utterances, and open our closed heart to the hidden studies of Your Torah, and may our study be pleasant before Your Place of Honor, as the aroma of sweet incense, and may You emanate to us Light from the source of our soul to all of our being. And, may the sparks of your holy servants, through which you revealed Your wisdom to the world, shine.

May their merit and the merit of their fathers, and the merit of their Torah, and holiness, support us so we shall not stumble through our study. And by their merit enlighten our eyes in our learning as it stated by King David, The Sweet Singer of Israel: "Open my eyes, so that I will see wonders from Your Torah" (Tehilim 119:18). Because from His mouth God gives wisdom and understanding.

"May the utterances of my mouth and the thoughts of my heart find favor before You, God, my Strength and my Redeemer" (Tehilim 19:15).

※

Lech Lecha

Names of the articles

1. "Hearken to me, you stout-hearted"

A Synopsis

There are people in our world who are hardhearted, stubborn, and set in their evil and selfish ways. The Zohar describes these people as refusing to change the negative aspects of their natures. They seek not to embrace the path of spiritual transformation and the Light of the Creator. All of us, to a certain degree, possess an aspect of these negative traits.

The Relevance of this Passage

The power available to us through these verses cleanses away negative qualities from our essence and being. The Light flowing through this portion helps to soften our resolve in situations where our stubbornness and ego prevents us from embracing spiritual change. The verses arouse a desire to seek a true connection to the Light of the Creator.

לב. הרהורים מצרים: הארוחה נשירותא.

א. כל כך משאיר וכו', אלא פתח ואמר, משום אלא אאיר כל
הרהורים מצרים. שאם אלא אאיר כל: באו הרבים לעבור
וכו'. לעבור לא, והרהאי שבילי ואורחיתא, ולא מסתכל בהו,
ולבייהו קשין, ולא תבין ואתאבין, לרבונייהו אלא אאיר כל.
ד. לכל כל משאיר וכו', ומתחבר מלאראע בהה אאר, ואלין הרהורים

1. "Get you, out of your country..." (Beresheet 12:1). Rabbi Aba opened the discussion with THIS VERSE AND TO EXPLAIN THE REASON WHY ABRAHAM MERITED THAT THE HOLY ONE, BLESSED BE HE, WOULD SAY THIS TO HIM RATHER THAN TO ANY OTHER PERSON OF HIS TIME. "Hearken to me, you stout-hearted, that are far from righteousness" (Yeshayah 46:12), MEANS how hard are the hearts of the wicked, who see the paths and the ways of Torah, yet do not observe them. THE PATHS ARE THE INTERNAL ASPECTS; THE WAYS ARE THE EXTERNAL ASPECTS. And the hearts of the wicked are stout, as they do not repent and turn back to their Master. THIS IS THE REASON WHY they are called stout-hearted. The verse, "that are far from righteousness," MEANS THAT THEY KEEP THEMSELVES far from Torah; THIS IS WHY THEY REMAIN "FAR FROM RIGHTEOUSNESS."

מִנֵּיהּ, וּבְגִין כָּךְ, אִקְרוּן אַבִּירֵי לֵב. הָרְחוֹקִים מִצְּדָקָה. דְּלָא בָּעָאן לְקָרְבָא לְגַבֵּי קוּדְשָׁא בְּרִיךְ הוּא. בְּגִין כָּךְ, אִינוּן רְחוֹקִים מִצְּדָקָה. כֵּיוָן דְּאִינוּן רְחוֹקִים מִצְּדָקָה, רְחוֹקִים אִינוּן מִשָּׁלוֹם. דְּלֵית לוֹן שָׁלוֹם. דִּכְתִיב אֵין שָׁלוֹם אָמַר ה' לָרְשָׁעִים. מ"ט בְּגִין דְּאִינוּן רְחוֹקִים מִצְּדָקָה.

2. Rabbi Chizkiyah commented ON THE AFOREMENTIONED VERSE: "Since they draw themselves away from the Holy One, blessed be He, therefore they remain far away from Him. And because of this, BECAUSE THEY KEEP FAR AWAY FROM THE HOLY ONE, BLESSED BE HE, they are called stout-hearted. AND THE VERSE TEACHES US THAT they "are far from righteousness." FOR WHAT REASON? BECAUSE they do not wish to come closer to the Holy One, blessed be He, AS THEY ARE STOUT-HEARTED. And because of this, they "are far from righteousness." Because they are far from righteousness, they are also far from peace – they can have no peace. As it is written: "There is no peace, says Hashem, to the wicked" (Yeshayah 48:22). And why is that so? Because they "are far from righteousness," THEY HAVE NO PEACE!

3. תָּא חֲזֵי, אַבְרָהָם בָּעֵי לְקָרְבָא לְקוּדְשָׁא בְּרִיךְ הוּא, וְאִתְקְרַב. הה"ד אָהַבְתָּ צֶדֶק וַתִּשְׂנָא רֶשַׁע. בְּגִין דְּאָהַב צֶדֶק, וְשָׂנָא רֶשַׁע, אִתְקְרַב לִצְדָקָה, וְעַל דָּא כְּתִיב, אַבְרָהָם אוֹהֲבִי. מ"ט אוֹהֲבִי, בְּגִין דִּכְתִיב, אָהַבְתָּ צֶדֶק. רְחִימוּתָא דְּקוּדְשָׁא בְּרִיךְ הוּא, דִּרְחִים לֵיהּ אַבְרָהָם, מִכָּל בְּנֵי דָרֵיהּ, דַּהֲווֹ אַבִּירֵי לֵב, וְאִינוּן רְחוֹקִים מִצְּדָקָה, כְּמָה דְּאִתְּמַר.

3. Come and behold: Abraham indeed succeeded in his desire to get closer to the Holy One, blessed be He. As it is written: "You love righteousness and hate wickedness" (Tehilim 45:8). Because he loved righteousness and hated wickedness, he therefore came closer to righteousness. Therefore, it is written: "Abraham my beloved" (Yeshayah 41:8). Why IS HE "my beloved?" Because it has been said about him, "You love righteousness." This is the love toward the Holy One, blessed be He, whom Abraham loved more than anyone else of his generation, who were "stout-hearted" and "far from righteousness," as has already been explained.

2. Upon what the world exists

A Synopsis

The Zohar discusses our ignorance concerning the pillars that sustain our world, the unseen spiritual forces that give rise to all existence. The Zohar then focuses on another concept concerning the power of midnight. Great importance is attached to spiritual study and work during the hours from midnight to sunrise, when the Light of the Creator is intensified in our physical realm.

The Relevance of this Passage

The increased spiritual power released into the cosmos during the intervening hours of midnight and morning, is made available to us by the words and wisdom that comprise this portion.

4. רַבִּי יוֹסֵי פָּתַח וַאֲמַר, מַה יְּדִידוֹת מִשְׁכְּנוֹתֶיךָ ה' צְבָאוֹת. כַּמָּה אִית לוֹן לִבְנֵי
נָשָׁא, לְאִשְׁתַּדְּלָא בְּקוּדְשָׁא בְּרִיךְ הוּא. דְּכָל בַּר נָשׁ, לָא מַשְׁגַּח וְלָא יָדַע עַל
מַה עָלְמָא קָאֵים. וְאִינוּן לָא מַשְׁגִּיחִין, וְלָא יָדְעֵי בְּמַה קַיְּימָא. וְכַד בְּרָא
קוּדְשָׁא בְּרִיךְ הוּא עָלְמָא, עֲבַד שְׁמַיָּא מֵאֶשָּׁא וּמַיָּא, מְעֹרָבִין כַּחֲדָא
בְּלָא קְפִיאוּ. לְבָתַר קָפִיאוּ בַּאֲוִירָא עִלָּאָה. וְאִינוּן מַיָּא, לְבָתַר
אֲקַדְּרוּ וְאִתְעֲבִידוּ מַיָּא תַּתָּאִין וְתַתָּאֵי, דְּאִינוּן תְּחוֹת הַאי עָלְמָא.

4. Rabbi Yosi opened the discussion by saying: "How lovely are Your dwelling places, Hashem Tzva'ot" (Tehilim 84:2)[1]. How important it is for people to observe the works of the Holy One, blessed be He! All people do not observe and are not aware of what keeps the world in existence. Nor are they aware of what keeps them in existence! THESE TWO SUBJECTS ARE EXPLAINED HERE TO US. When the Holy One, blessed be He, created the world, He made the heaven from fire and water. At first, these elements mingled together without freezing. Only later, by means of the Supernal

---

1. See Glossary for the various names and titles of Hashem and their meanings.

Spirit, did they freeze and solidify. Then, THE HEAVENS, WHICH ARE ZEIR ANPIN, planted the world, THE NUKVA, to be established upon supports, THE THREE COLUMNS OF THE NUKVA. And the supports stand only by the help of the Spirit, WHICH IS THE CENTRAL COLUMN BETWEEN THEM. When that Spirit is gone, the supports are loosened and they quake, and the world is shaken. This is the meaning of, "Who shakes the earth out of its place, and its pillars tremble" (Iyov 9:6). And everything is established upon Torah, for when Yisrael are busy with Torah, THEY ELEVATE MAYIN NUKVIN (LIT. 'FEMALE WATERS') TO ZEIR ANPIN AND NUKVA, AND DRAW THE CENTRAL COLUMN, WHICH IS TORAH. Then the world is established, and the pillars, THE THREE COLUMNS OF ZEIR ANPIN, and the supports, THE THREE COLUMNS OF THE NUKVA, are perfectly situated in their places.

5. תָּא חֲזֵי בְּשַׁעֲתָא דְאִתְּעַר פַּלְגוּת לֵילְיָא, וְקוּדְשָׁא בְּרִיךְ הוּא עָאל לְגִנְתָא דְעֵדֶן, לְאִשְׁתַּעְשְׁעָא עִם צַדִּיקַיָּא. כָּלְהוּ אִילָנִין דִּבְגִנְתָא דְעֵדֶן, מְזַמְּרָן וּמְשַׁבְּחָן קַמֵיהּ. דִּכְתִיב, אָז יְרַנְּנוּ עֲצֵי הַיַּעַר מִלִּפְנֵי ה' וְגו'.

5. Come and behold: When midnight is aroused, and the Holy One, blessed be He, enters the Garden of Eden to enjoy the company of the righteous, all the trees in the Garden of Eden sing and praise Him, as it is written: "Then shall the trees of the forest sing for joy at the presence of Hashem" (I Divrei Hayamim 16:33).

6. וְכָרוֹזָא קָארֵי בְחֵיל, וַאֲמַר, לְכוֹן אָמְרִין קַדִּישִׁין עֶלְיוֹנִין, מָאן מִנְכוֹן, דְּעָיֵיל רוּחָא בְּאוּדְנוֹי, לְמִשְׁמַע. וְעֵינוֹי פְּקָחִין לְמֶחֱמֵי. וְלִבֵּיהּ פָּתוּחַ לְמִנְדַע. בְּשַׁעֲתָא, דְּרוּחָא דְּכָל רוּחִין, אָרִים בְּסִימוּ דְנִשְׁמָתָא, וּמִתַּמָּן, נָפֵיק קָלָא דְּקָלַיָּא, חֵילִין אִתְבַּדַּר לְאַרְבַּע סִטְרֵי עָלְמָא.

6. A crier comes forth and forcefully calls, "You, mighty, holy men! To him among you who has allowed the spirit to enter, and his ears to hear, who has eyes open to see and who has a heart that is open to know! BY THIS CRIER, THE RIGHTEOUS AWAKEN FROM THEIR SLEEP, DELVE TO THE STUDY OF TORAH, AND DRAW THE CENTRAL COLUMN. When the spirit, which is the source of all spirits, arouses the sweetness of the soul, a voice comes from there, which is the source of all voices, and disperses all forces to the four

corners of the world.

7. חַד סָלִיק, לִסְטַר חָד. חַד נָחִית לְהַהוּא סְטַר. חַד עָיֵיל, בֵּין תְּרֵין. תְּרֵין מִתְעַטְּרָן בִּתְלַת. תְּלַת עָיְילֵי בְּחַד. חַד אַפִּיק גְּוְונִין. שִׁית מִנְּהוֹן, לִסְטַר חָד. וְשִׁית מִנְּהוֹן, נָחֲתֵי לְהַהוּא סְטַר. שִׁית עָיְילֵי בִּתְרֵיסָר. תְּרֵיסָר מִתְעָרִין בְּעֶשְׂרִין וּתְרֵין. שִׁית, כְּלִילָן בַּעֲשָׂרָה. עֲשָׂרָה קָאִים בְּחַד.

7. One goes up to one side, TO THE RIGHT OF ZEIR ANPIN, THE SECRET OF THE SOUTH. THE SECOND one descends to the other side, TO THE LEFT SIDE OF ZEIR ANPIN, THE NORTH. Another enters in between the two, BECOMES THE CENTRAL COLUMN OF ZEIR ANPIN, THE SECRET OF THE EAST. IN OTHER WORDS, ZEIR ANPIN IS PLACED BETWEEN THE TWO COLUMNS OF BINAH. AND THESE THREE DIRECTIONS, SOUTH, NORTH, AND EAST, ARE THE SECRET OF CHESED, GVURAH, AND TIFERET OF ZEIR ANPIN. Two are crowned AND SHINE by BECOMING three, CHESED, GVURAH, TIFERET BY THE THIRD, WHICH IS THE CENTRAL COLUMN THAT RECONCILES THEM. And three enter the one, BECAUSE THE CENTRAL COLUMN, WHICH IS THE SECRET OF TIFERET, RECEIVES AND EXPANDS BY ITSELF TO THREE OTHER COLUMNS, NETZACH, HOD AND YESOD. One, WHICH RECONCILES, NAMELY TIFERET OF ZEIR ANPIN, produced colors. IN OTHER WORDS, FROM HIM EMANATED THE SFIROT OF THE NUKVA THAT ARE CALLED 'COLORS'. Six of them—CHESED, GVURAH, TIFERET, NETZACH, HOD AND YESOD, descended to one side, NAMELY TO THE RIGHT, and another six – CHESED, GVURAH, TIFERET, NETZACH, HOD AND YESOD, descended to the other side, NAMELY TO THE LEFT. SO all six – CHESED, GVURAH, TIFERET, NETZACH, HOD AND YESOD – become twelve SFIROT. IN OTHER WORDS, THE SIX SFIROT OF ZEIR ANPIN EXPANDED TO THE NUKVA AND BECAME TWELVE SFIROT, WITH SIX TO HER RIGHT AND SIX TO HER LEFT. The twelve SFIROT EXPAND AND become twenty-two SFIROT. THE six OF ZEIR ANPIN DO NOT BECOME TWELVE HERE, BUT are RATHER included within the ten. THIS IS BECAUSE the ten exist as one.

8. וַוי לְאִינּוּן דְּנַיְימֵי שֵׁינָתָא בְּחוֹרֵיהוֹן, לָא יָדְעֵי וְלָא מִסְתַּכְּלָאן אֵיךְ יְקוּמוּן בְּדִינָא, דְּחוּשְׁבַּן אִתְפְּקַד, כַּד אִסְתְּאַב גּוּפָא, וְנִשְׁמָתָא שַׁטְיָא,

עַל אַנְפֵּי דַאֲוִירָא דְּטִיהֲרָא, וְסָלְקָא וְנַחְתָּא, וְתַרְעִין לָא מִתְפַּתְּחָן, מִתְגַּלְגְּלָן כְּאַבְנִין בְּגוֹ קוּסְפִיתָא. וַוי לוֹן, מַאן יִתְבַּע לוֹן, דְּלָא יְקוּמוּן בְּעִדּוּנָא דָא, בְּגוֹ דוּכְתֵּי דְּעִנּוּגֵי דְּצַדִּיקַיָּא, אִתְפַּקְּדוּן דּוּכְתַּיְיהוּ. אִתְמַסְרוּן בִּידָא דְדוּמָה, נַחֲתֵי וְלָא סַלְקֵי. עֲלַיְיהוּ כְּתִיב, כָּלָה עָנָן וַיֵּלַךְ כֵּן יוֹרֵד שְׁאוֹל לֹא יַעֲלֶה.

8. Woe to those who slumber as sleep covers their eyes sockets – THOSE WHO DO NOT AWAKE FROM THEIR SLEEP TO STUDY TORAH AND DRAW THE CENTRAL COLUMN. THE ILLUMINATION OF THE LEFT COLUMN BLOCKS OFF THE LIGHT NECESSARY FOR THEIR EYESIGHT AND MAKES THEM DROWSY. AS A RESULT, THEY HAVE NO EYES, THAT IS, MOCHIN. THERE IS SLEEP IN THEIR EYE SOCKETS. They do not know and are unable to observe how and in what condition they shall awaken on the Day of Judgment, when they shall be visited upon to settle the account – when the body is defiled and the soul floats on the afternoon air, going up and down, but the gates do not open for it. They are thrown around like the pebbles in the hollow of a sling. Woe to them. Who shall ask about them when they shall not arise to this place of pleasure? In the place where the righteous have pleasure, they shall be missing. They shall be passed on to the angel Dumah, go down TO GEHENOM and not rise. They are described by the words, "As the cloud is consumed and vanishes away, so he who goes down to Sheol shall come up no more" (Iyov 7:9).

9. בְּהַהִיא שַׁעֲתָא אִתְעַר שַׁלְהוֹבָא חַד מִסְּטַר צָפוֹן, וּבָטַשׁ בְּאַרְבַּע סִטְרֵי עָלְמָא, וְנָחִית וּמָטֵי, בֵּין גַּדְפֵּי דְּתַרְנְגוֹלָא. וְאִתְעַר הַהוּא שַׁלְהוֹבָא בֵּיהּ, וְקָרֵי. וְלֵית מַאן דְּאִתְעַר, בַּר אִינּוּן זַכָּאֵי קְשׁוֹט, דְּקַיְימֵי וְאִתְעָרוּ בְּאוֹרַיְיתָא. וּכְדֵין קוּדְשָׁא בְּרִיךְ הוּא, וְכָל אִינּוּן צַדִּיקַיָּיא, דִּבְגוֹ גִּנְתָּא דְּעֵדֶן, צַיְיתֵי לְקָלֵיהוֹן. כְּד"א, הַיּוֹשֶׁבֶת בַּגַּנִּים חֲבֵרִים מַקְשִׁיבִים לְקוֹלֵךְ הַשְׁמִיעִנִי.

9. At that hour, THAT IS, MIDNIGHT, a flame is awakened from the North strikes the four corners of the world, SINCE THE ILLUMINATION OF THE LEFT COLUMN, WHICH IS JUDGMENT, EXPANDS THROUGHOUT THE WORLD. It descends and touches the cock between its wings, WHICH IS THE SECRET OF GABRIEL. As the flame awakens it, it crows. THIS IS THE

SECRET OF THE CRIER MENTIONED BEFORE WITH THE WORDS, "A CRIER COMES FORTH AND FORCEFULLY ANNOUNCES..." But the only ones who awaken to the calling of the cock are the truly righteous, who delve to the study of Torah, DRAWING THE CENTRAL COLUMN. Then the Holy One, blessed be He, together with all the righteous in the Garden of Eden, listen attentively to their voice. As it is written: "You who dwell in the gardens, the companions hearken to your voice: cause me to hear it" (Shir Hashirim 8:13).

3. "Now Hashem said to Abram"

A Synopsis

There is a unique process of preparation that a soul undergoes prior to entering our physical realm. This process consists of promises and commitments made by the soul to the Creator. The soul pledges to embrace the spiritual path of change through Torah and Kabbalah during its lifetime. The specific Torah portion that relates to this passage of Zohar is *Lech Lecha,* which translates into *Go You, Out of Your Country.* The verse concerns God's call to Abraham to leave and go out from his homeland and enter into the Land of Israel. The story is a code and a metaphor concerning the journey of the soul as it leaves the Upper World on its sojourn into our earthly realm.

The Relevance of this Passage

The perpetual pull and tug of the material world is of such magnitude, we forget our true purpose in life as we succumb to the illusions of physical existence. Hence, we need the Light of this portion to reawaken our desire to remain true to our own soul's original commitment to pursue the spiritual path.

סִתְרֵי תּוֹרָה

10. תָּאנָא. בְּתוּקְפָּא דְּהַרְמְנוּ דְמַלְכָּא, אַנְצִיב חַד אִילָנָא רַבָּא וְתַקִּיף. גּוֹ נְטִיעָן עִלָּאִין, נְטִיעַ אִילָנָא דָא. בִּתְרֵיסַר תְּחוּמִין, אִסְתַּחַר. בְּאַרְבַּע סִטְרִין דְּעָלְמָא, פְּרִישָׁא רַגְלֵיה.

Sitrei Torah (Concealed Torah)

10. We have learned that because of the strong desire of the King, WHO IS BINAH, a great and strong tree, WHICH IS ZEIR ANPIN, was planted. GREAT IS THE SECRET OF THE MOCHIN OF CHOCHMAH, AND STRONG IS THE SECRET OF THE MOCHIN OF CHASSADIM. Among the supernal plants, WHICH ARE THE SFIROT OF BINAH, this tree, WHICH IS ZEIR ANPIN, is planted. It turns between twelve borders, and its leg expands to the four winds of the world.

11. ת"ק פַּרְסֵי מַטְלָנוֹי, כָּל רְעוּתִין, דְּאִינוּן פָּרְסִין, בֵּיה תַּלְיָין. כַּד אִתְּעַר הַאי, כֻּלְהוּ מִתְעָרִין בַּהֲדֵיה, לֵית מַאן דְּנָפִיק מֵרְעוּתֵיה. לְבָתַר,

כֻּלְּהוּ בִּרְעוּתָא חֲדָא בַּהֲדֵיהּ.

11. Its journeys were measured at five hundred Persian miles. The desires of these Persian miles, REFERRING TO THEIR WAYS OF BESTOWING ABUNDANCE, come on Him, ON ZEIR ANPIN. So when He awakens, all awaken with Him, and no one is capable of diverting His will. After that, all are united and join His will.

12. קָם מִלְּעֵילָא, נָחִית בְּמַטְלָנוֹי לְגוֹ יַמָּא. מִנֵּיהּ, יַמָּא אִתְמַלְיָא. אִיהוּ מְקוֹרָא דְּכָל מַיִין דְּנָבְעִין. תְּחוֹתֵיהּ מִתְפַּלְּגִין כָּל מֵימוֹי דִּבְרֵאשִׁית. שַׁקְיוּ דְּגִנְתָּא, בֵּיהּ תַּלְיָין.

12. He, ZEIRANPIN, arises from above, AFTER HE HAS RECEIVED MOCHIN FROM BINAH, and descends throughout His journeys to the sea, WHICH IS THE NUKVA. SO, HE GIVES HIS ABUNDANCE TO THE NUKVA. He fills the sea, as He is the source of all the lights that spring IN THE SEA. Underneath Him, all the waters of the Beginning of the Creation are divided. The watering of the Garden, WHICH IS MALCHUT, depends on Him, WHO IS ZEIR ANPIN.

13. כָּל נִשְׁמָתִין דְּעָלְמָא, מִנֵּיהּ פָּרְחִין. נִשְׁמָתִין אִלֵּין עָאלִין בְּגִנְתָּא, לְנָחֲתָא לְהַאי עָלְמָא. נִשְׁמָתָא כַּד נָפְקָא, אִתְבָּרְכָא בְּשֶׁבַע בִּרְכָאן, לְמֶהֱוֵי אַבָּא לְגוּפָא, בְּסְלִיקוּ עִלָּאָה. הה"ד וַיֹּאמֶר ה' אֶל אַבְרָם. הָא נִשְׁמָתָא עִלָּאָה אַבָּא לְגוּפָא בִּסְלִיקוּ דְּדִיּוֹקְנָא עִלָּאָה.

13. All souls of the world come forth from Him, FROM ZEIR ANPIN. These souls enter the Garden, THE NUKVA, and descend into this world IN ORDER TO BE ENCLOTHED IN A BODY. When a soul leaves THERE AND IS ON ITS WAY DOWN TO THIS WORLD, it receives seven blessings so that it may be a father to the body being rightly elevated. Thus, it is written: "Now Hashem said to Abram" (Beresheet 12:1). This is the divine supewnal soul, WHICH IS CALLED ABRAM. IT CONSISTS OF TWO WORDS, AV (lit. 'FATHER') AND RAM (lit. 'SUPERNAL'). It is considered the father of the body and elevates to the level of the divine image, BY THE CHASSIDIM THAT ARE DRAWN AS IT ELEVATES AND REACHES ABA AND IMA.

14. כַּד בַּעְיָא לְנַחֲתָא לְהַאי עָלְמָא, אוֹמֵי לָהּ קוּדְשָׁא בְּרִיךְ הוּא לְמִיטַר פִּקּוּדֵי אוֹרַיְיתָא, וּלְמֶעְבַּד רְעוּתֵיהּ. וּמְסַר לָהּ מְאָה מַפְתְּחָאן דְּבִרְכָאן, דְּכָל יוֹמָא, לְאַשְׁלָמָא לְדַרְגִּין עִלָּאִין, כְּחוּשְׁבַּן לֶךְ לְךָ. דְּהָא כֻּלְּהוּ אִתְמְסַר לָהּ, בְּגִין לְאַתְקָנָא בְּהוּ לְגִנְתָּא, וּלְמִפְלַח לָהּ וּלְנָטְרָא לָהּ. מֵאַרְצְךָ, דָּא גִּנְתָּא דְעֵדֶן.

14. When the soul is ready to descend to this world, the Holy One, blessed be He, makes it swear to perform the precepts of Torah and do His bidding. And He gives each soul one hundred keys of blessings for each and every day, so that it may complete the supernal grades, which reach the numerical value of Lech Lecha (lit. 'Get you out'), WHICH EQUALS ONE HUNDRED. All of them are given to it, TO THE SOUL, so that it may cultivate the Garden, WHICH IS THE NUKVA, to till it and to keep it. "Your country" is the Garden of Eden.

15. וּמוֹלַדְתְּךָ, דָּא גוּפָא, דְּאִתְקְרֵי אִילָנָא דְחַיֵּי, דְּאִיהוּ תְּרֵיסַר שִׁבְטִין עִלָּאִין. וּמִבֵּית אָבִיךָ, דָּא שְׁכִינְתָּא. אָבִיךָ, דָּא קוּדְשָׁא בְּרִיךְ הוּא. שֶׁנֶּאֱמַר גּוֹזֵל אָבִיו וְאִמּוֹ וְאוֹמֵר אֵין פֶּשַׁע וְגוֹ', וְאֵין אָבִיו אֶלָּא קוּדְשָׁא בְּרִיךְ הוּא. וְאֵין אִמּוֹ אֶלָּא כְּנֶסֶת יִשְׂרָאֵל. אֶל הָאָרֶץ אֲשֶׁר אַרְאֶךָּ. דָּא אִיהוּ הַאי עָלְמָא.

(עַד כָּאן סִתְרֵי תּוֹרָה)

15. The verse, "and from your kindred" MEANS from the body, WHICH IS ZEIR ANPIN, that is called 'the Tree of Life'. And it includes the twelve supernal tribes, WHICH ARE THE SECRET OF THE TWELVE BORDERS. THIS PASSAGE INFORMS US THAT THE SOUL IS AN OFFSPRING OF ZEIR ANPIN AND COMES FORTH FROM HIM. THE VERSE "and from your father's house" refers to the Shechinah, WHICH IS CALLED THE HOUSE. "Your father" means the Holy One, blessed be He, WHO IS ZEIR ANPIN. As it is written: "He who steals from his father or his mother, and says it is no transgression..." (Mishlei 28:24). "His father" is none other than the Holy One, blessed be He, and "his mother" is none other than the Congregation of Yisrael, WHICH IS THE NUKVA. The words, "to the land that I will show you," refer to this world, TO WHICH THE SOUL IS SENT.

(End of Sitrei Torah).

16. וַיֹּאמֶר ה' אֶל אַבְרָם. מַה כְּתִיב לְעֵילָּא וַיָּמָת הָרָן עַל פְּנֵי תֶּרַח אָבִיו וְגוֹ'. מַאי אִירְיָא הָכָא, אֶלָּא עַד הַהוּא יוֹמָא, לָא הֲוָה בַּר נָשׁ, דְּמִית בְּחַיֵּי אֲבוֹי, בַּר דָּא. דְּכַד אִתְרְמֵי אַבְרָם לְנוּרָא, אִתְקְטֵיל הָרָן, וּבְגִין דָּא, נָפְקוּ מִתַּמָּן.

16. What is written before the verse, "Hashem said to Abram..."? The words: "And Haran died before his father Terah" (Beresheet 11:28). AND HE ASKS: Of what does he want to inform us BY SAYING "BEFORE" HIS FATHER, TERACH? IF YOU CLAIM THAT "BEFORE" MEANS DURING HIS FATHER'S LIFETIME, this cannot be, for had no other person until that day died during his father's lifetime beside Haran? NEVERTHELESS, IN ALL OTHER INCIDENTS, THE WORD "BEFORE" IS NOT USED. FOR EXAMPLE, WHEN ABEL DIED DURING THE LIFETIME OF ADAM, HIS FATHER, AND WHEN ENOCH, WHO WAS TAKEN BY ELOHIM DURING THE LIFETIME OF JERED, HIS FATHER. AND HE EXPLAINS THAT when Abraham was thrown to the fire, Charan was killed. Because of this, they left UR OF THE CHALDEANS.

4. "...and they left with them from Ur of the Chaldeans"

A Synopsis

The Zohar examines a flickering flame wedded to the wick of a lit candle. Interestingly, a simple wick is able to generate a dazzling flame. Likewise, a simple action on the part of mankind, a single desire to change our ways is all that is required to set aflame the Light of the Creator within our soul. When this Light burns brightly in our life, we draw the strength and power to thoroughly transform our nature.

The Relevance of this Passage

The wonderful analogy concerning the wick and a candle flame is presented by the Zohar to help us arouse the Light of the Creator, giving us the strength to make the necessary spiritual changes in our own life. "One simple action" includes reading these very words, along with the Aramaic text, which ignites resplendent flames of spiritual Light.

17. תָּא חֲזֵי, מַה כְּתִיב, וַיִּקַּח תֶּרַח אֶת אַבְרָם בְּנוֹ וְאֶת לוֹט בֶּן הָרָן וגו'. וַיֵּצְאוּ אִתָּם מֵאוּר כַּשְׂדִּים. וַיֵּצְאוּ אִתָּם. אָתוּ מִבָּעֵי לֵיה. דְּהָא כְּתִיב וַיִּקַּח תֶּרַח וגו'. מַאי, וַיֵּצְאוּ אִתָּם. אֶלָּא, תֶּרַח וְלוֹט, עִם אַבְרָהָם וְשָׂרָה נָפְקוּ, דְּאִינוּן הֲווֹ עִקְּרָא לְמֵיפַק מִגּוֹ אִינוּן חַיָּיבַיָּא. דְּכֵיוָן דְּחָמָא תֶּרַח, דְּאַבְרָהָם בְּרֵיה, אִשְׁתְּזֵיב מִגּוֹ נוּרָא, אִתְהַדַּר לְמֶעְבַּד רְעוּתֵיה דְּאַבְרָהָם, וּבְגִין כָּךְ וַיֵּצְאוּ אִתָּם תֶּרַח וְלוֹט.

17. Come and behold, It is written: "And Terach took Abram, his son, and Lot, the son of Haran...and they left with them from Ur of the Chaldeans" (Beresheet 11:31). HE ASKS: WHY IS IT WRITTEN: "And they left with them," when it should have been written: "with him," NAMELY WITH TERACH? If, as it is written: "And Terach took..." why IS IT THEN WRITTEN: "with them?" BECAUSE Terach and Lot left with Abraham and Sarah, who really wanted to depart from among the wicked. Only after Terach saw that Abraham his son was saved from the fire did he return to follow Avraham's wishes. As a result, Terach and Lot "left with them."

18. וּבְשַׁעְתָּא דִּנְפָקוּ, מַה כְּתִיב, לָלֶכֶת אַרְצָה כְּנַעַן. דִּרְעוּתָא דִּלְהוֹן הֲוָה לְמֵיהַךְ תַּמָּן. מִכָּאן אוֹלִיפְנָא, כָּל מָאן דְּאִתְּעַר לְאִתְדַּכָּאָה,

מְסַיְּיעִין לֵיהּ. תָּא חֲזֵי דְּהָכֵי הוּא. דְּכֵיוָן דִּכְתִיב, לָלֶכֶת אַרְצָה כְּנַעַן,
מִיָּד וַיֹּאמֶר ה' אֶל אַבְרָהָם לֶךְ לְךָ, וְעַד דְּאִיהוּ אִתְּעַר בְּקַדְמֵיתָא, לָא
כְּתִיב לֶךְ לְךָ.

18. And when they left "to go to the land of Canaan" it was because they desired to go there. From this we learn that whoever asks to be purified will be helped. Come and behold that this is so! Because the words, "to go to the land of Canaan," are immediately followed by the words, "Now Hashem said to Abram, 'Get you out'." So before his desire TO GO TO THE LAND OF CANAAN was awakened, it was not yet written: "Get you out." THEREFORE, HE WHO ASKS AND WAKES ON HIS OWN FROM BELOW IS HELPED FROM ABOVE, BECAUSE WITHOUT AWAKENING FROM BELOW THERE IS NO AWAKENING FROM ABOVE.

19. תָּא חֲזֵי. מִלָּה דִּלְעֵילָא לָא אִתְּעַר, עַד דְּאִתְּעַר לְתַתָּא בְּקַדְמֵיתָא,
עַל מַה דְּתִשְׁרֵי הַהִיא דִּלְעֵילָא. וְרָזָא דְּמִלָּה, נְהוֹרָא אוּכְמָא, לָא
אִתְאַחֵיד בִּנְהוֹרָא חִוָּורָא. עַד דְּאִיהִי אִתְּעָרִית בְּקַדְמֵיתָא. כֵּיוָן דְּאִיהִי
אִתְּעָרִית בְּקַדְמֵיתָא. מִיָּד נְהוֹרָא חִוָּורָא שַׁרְיָיא עֲלָהּ.

19. Come and see: Nothing is aroused above before it is first aroused below, so that what is aroused above rests upon it. The secret is that the black flame OF THE CANDLE, WHICH IS THE SECRET OF THE NUKVA, does not hold on to the white flame OF THE CANDLE, WHICH IS THE SECRET OF ZEIR ANPIN, before it is aroused. As soon as it is aroused first, the white flame immediately rests upon it. THIS IS SO BECAUSE THE LOWER ONE HAS TO BE AROUSED FIRST.

20. וְע"ד כְּתִיב אֱלֹקִים אַל דֳּמִי לָךְ אַל תֶּחֱרַשׁ וְאַל תִּשְׁקֹט אֵל. בְּגִין
דְּלָא יִתְפְּסַק נְהוֹרָא חִוָּורָא מֵעָלְמָא, לְעָלְמִין. וְכֵן הַמַּזְכִּירִים אֶת ה' אַל
דֳּמִי לָכֶם. בְּגִין, לְאַתְעָרָא לְתַתָּא, בַּמֶּה דִּישָׁרֵי אִתְּעֲרוּתָא דִּלְעֵילָא. וְכֵן
כֵּיוָן דְּאִתְּעַר בַּר נָשׁ, אִתְּעֲרוּתָא בְּקַדְמֵיתָא, כְּדֵין אִתְּעַר, אִתְּעֲרוּתָא
דִּלְעֵילָא. תָּא חֲזֵי, כֵּיוָן דִּכְתִיב וַיּוֹצֵא אֹתָם מֵאוּר כַּשְׂדִּים וְגוֹ', מִיָּד
וַיֹּאמֶר ה' אֶל אַבְרָם וְגוֹ'.

20. Therefore it is written: "Do not keep silent, Elohim; do not hold your peace, and be still, El" (Tehilim 83:2), so that the white flame will never cease to exist in the world. BECAUSE ELOHIM IS THE SECRET OF THE NUKVA, WHICH IS THE SECRET OF THE BLACK FLAME. SO IF IT DOES NOT HOLD ITS PEACE AND BE STILL AND IF IT NEVER CEASES TO BE AWAKENED FROM BELOW, THEN THE WHITE FLAME, WHICH IS THE SECRET OF ZEIR ANPIN, SHALL ALWAYS REST UPON IT FROM ABOVE. "You who make mention of Hashem, take no rest" (Yeshayah 62:6) so that there will always be awakening from below on which that from above should come and rest upon it. Therefore, when a person first arouses the awakening from below, the awakening from above is aroused. Come and behold, It is written: "and they went out with them from Ur of the Chaldeans." Immediately, "Hashem said to Abram..." THIS MEANS THAT HE RECEIVED HELP FROM ABOVE. THE REASON IS THAT THE LIGHT NEEDS SOMETHING CRUDE FROM BELOW TO CLING ONTO AND THIS CRUDE OBJECT OR ACTION IS ENTIRELY IN THE HANDS OF THE LOWER WORLD.

5. "Get you out," for your sake

A Synopsis

All the supernal forces that govern the various countries and cities of our world are brought to light by the Zohar. Abraham masters the knowledge concerning all these diverse metaphysical intelligences that rule and administer over the cosmos. However, the Creator tells him not to direct his mind towards these supernal matters. Rather, Abraham should focus upon his spiritual work in this physical realm, placing his trust in the Creator regarding the workings of the metaphysical dimension.

The Relevance of this Passage

The ability to trust the Creator above the level of our rational mind and logic, radiates throughout this passage. Often, we mistake the pursuance of otherworldly mystical knowledge for the real spiritual work in this mundane world. This truth is understood through a story concerning the great sage Hillel, who was asked to reveal all the supernal mysteries and secrets of the Torah in the short time that he can remain balanced on one leg. "Love thy neighbor as thyself. All the rest is commentary. Now and go and learn," the sage replied.

21. וַיֹּאמֶר ה' אֶל אַבְרָם לֶךְ לְךָ. אֲמַר ר' אֶלְעָזָר, לֶךְ לְךָ: לְגַרמָךְ, לְאַתְקְנָא גַרמָךְ. לְאַתְקְנָא דַרְגָּא דִילָךְ. לֶךְ לְךָ. לֵית אַנְתְּ כְּדַאי לְמֵיקַם הָכָא, בֵּין חַיָּיבִין אִלֵּין.

21. "Now Hashem said to Abram, Get you out (lit. 'go for you')..." According to Rabbi Elazar, the phrase "Go for you," means "for yourself." IN OTHER WORDS, go out for yourself, to fulfill yourself and complete your grade. "Get you out," for you must not stay here among the wicked.

22. וְרָזָא דְמִלָּה, לֶךְ לְךָ. דְּהָא קוּדְשָׁא בְּרִיךְ הוּא, יָהִיב לֵיהּ לְאַבְרָהָם, רוּחָא דְחָכְמְתָא, וַהֲוָה יָדַע וּמְצָרֵף סִטְרֵי דְיִישׁוּבֵי עָלְמָא, וְאִסְתַּכַּל בְּהוֹ. וְאִתְקַל בְּתִיקְלָא, וְיָדַע חֵילִין דִּי מְמַנָּן עַל סִטְרֵי יִישׁוּבָא.

22. The secret BEHIND THE WORDS "Get you out" is that the Holy One, blessed be He, inspired Abraham with the spirit of wisdom. He knew how to judge the spirits (also winds) of the civilized world. He observed them, weighed them in the scales, and knew how to connect them to the powers entrusted to govern the inhabited places on earth.

23. כַּד מָטָא לְגוֹ נְקוּדָה דְּאֶמְצָעִיתָא דְיִישׁוּבָא, תָּקִיל בְּתִיקְלָא וְלָא הֲוָה סָלֵיק בִּידֵיהּ, אַשְׁגַּח לְמִנְדַּע חֵילָא דִי מְמַנָּא עֲלָהּ, וְלָא יָכִיל לְאִתְדַּבְּקָא בִּרְעוּתֵיהּ.

23. When he reached the middle point of civilization, he weighed it in the scales, but could not reach any conclusion. THIS MEANS THAT HE ELEVATED MAYIN NUKVIN (FEMALE WATERS) IN ORDER TO DRAW DOWN THE SPIRIT OF WISDOM TO THAT PLACE, BUT DID NOT SUCCEED. He tried to see and to know what sort of power governed that place, but could not conceive it.

24. תָּקִיל כַּמָּה זִמְנִין, וְחָמָא, דְּהָא מִתַּמָּן אִשְׁתִּיל כָּל עָלְמָא. אַשְׁגַּח וְצֵרַף וְתָקַל לְמִנְדַּע, וְחָמָא, דְּהָא חֵילָא עִלָּאָה, דַּעֲלָהּ לֵית לֵיהּ שְׁעוּרָא עָמִיק וְסָתִים. וְלָאו אִיהוּ כְּגַוְונֵי דְּסִטְרֵי דַּרְגֵּי דְיִישׁוּבָא.

24. He weighed a few more times before realizing that the whole world sprouts from that place and is established upon it. He observed carefully, and measured, so as to understand the subject, and concluded that the supernal force above it could not be measured, that it is deep and hidden, and that it does not resemble the different parts of the inhabited land.

25. אַשְׁגַּח וְתָקִיל, וְיָדַע, דְּהָא דִּמְהַהִיא נְקוּדָה אֶמְצָעִיתָא דְיִישׁוּבָא, מִנֵּיהּ אִשְׁתִּיל כָּל עָלְמָא, לְכָל סִטְרוֹי. הָכִי נָמֵי יָדַע, דְּהָא חֵילָא דְּשָׁרֵי עֲלָהּ, מִתַּמָּן נָפְקוּ כָּל שְׁאָר חֵילִין, דִּמְמַנָּן עַל כָּל סִטְרֵי עָלְמָא, וְכֻלְּהוּ בֵּיהּ אֲחִידָן. כְּדֵין וַיֵּצְאוּ אִתָּם מֵאוּר כַּשְׂדִּים לָלֶכֶת אַרְצָה כְּנַעַן.

25. He watched attentively, weighed, and realized that the middle point of the inhabited world is the point from which the whole world moves out to all its corners, WHICH MEANS THAT THE POINT GOVERNS ALL THE SFIROT OF ZEIR ANPIN AND ALL THE SFIROT OF NUKVA, WHICH ARE NAMED

THE CORNERS OF THE WORLD, SINCE THE POINT IS PLACED ABOVE THEM. Similarly, he knew the power that now prevails over the point. AS A RESULT, all other powers that govern the corners of the world originate from that point and all THE SFIROT hold to it. Then "they went out with them from Ur of the Chaldeans, to go to the land of Canaan."

26. עוֹד אַשְׁגַּח וְתָקִיל וְצָרֵיף, לְמֵיקַם עַל בְּרִירָא דְמִלָּה, דְּהַהוּא אֲתָר, וְלָא הֲוָה יָדַע, וְלָא יָכִיל לְמֵיקַם עֲלָהּ לְאִתְדַּבְּקָא. כֵּיוָן דְּחָמָא תּוּקְפָּא דְּהַאי אֲתָר, וְלָא יָכִיל לְמֵיקַם עֲלֵיהּ, מִיָּד וַיָּבֹאוּ עַד חָרָן וַיֵּשְׁבוּ שָׁם.

26. He continued to observe, weigh, and examine in an effort to determine the nature of that place, but he was unable to understand it so as to cleave to it. He saw the strength of that place and realized that he could not understand it, and therefore immediately, "they came to Charan, and dwelt there" (Beresheet 11:31).

27. מַאי טַעְמָא דְאַבְרָהָם. אֶלָּא, דְּאִיהוּ הֲוָה יָדַע וְצָרֵיף בְּכָל אִינּוּן שָׁלְטָנִין מְדַבְּרֵי עָלְמָא, בְּכָל סִטְרוֹ דְיִשׁוּבָא. וַהֲוָה תָקִיל וְצָרֵיף אִינּוּן דְּשָׁלְטִין בְּסִטְרֵי דְיִשׁוּבָא מְדַבְּרֵי כֹכְבַיָּא וּמַזָּלֵיהוֹן, מַאן אִינּוּן תַּקִּיפִין, אֵלֵּין עַל אֵלֵּין, וַהֲוָה תָּקִיל כָּל יִשׁוּבֵי דְעָלְמָא, וַהֲוָה סָלִיק בִּידוֹי. כַּד מָטָא לְהַאי אֲתָר, חָמָא תַּקִּיפוּ דַּעֲמִיקִין, וְלָא יָכִיל לְמֵיקַם בֵּיהּ.

27. HE ASKS: Why did Abraham DELAY IN CHARAN AND NOT LEAVE THERE IMMEDIATELY, "TO GO TO THE LAND OF CANAAN," AS IT IS WRITTEN: "AND THEY DWELT THERE"? AND HE ANSWERS: Abraham knew and checked all the governors and rulers of the world that had dominion over the entire civilized world. And he was examining all those who govern and rule over the directions of the world's inhabited land, all those that have dominion over the stars and the constellations. He learned how they exercise their power over one another. In considering all the inhabited places in the world, he did well. But when he reached that place, THE POINT OF MALCHUT, he saw the force of the depths. And he could not withstand it.

28. כֵּיוָן דְּחָמָא קוּדְשָׁא בְּרִיךְ הוּא, אִתְעָרוּתָא דִילֵיהּ, וְתֵיאוּבְתָּא

דִּילֵיהּ, מִיָּד אִתְגְּלֵי עֲלֵיהּ, וַאֲמַר לֵיהּ, לֶךְ לְךָ. לְמִנְדַּע לָךְ, וּלְאִתַקָּנָא גַּרְמָךְ.

28. As soon as the Holy One, blessed be He, noticed his awakening and his passion, He immediately revealed Himself to Abraham and said: "Get you out" in order to learn about and perfect yourself.

29. מֵאַרְצְךָ. מֵהַהוּא סִטְרָא דְּיִשּׁוּבָא דַּהֲוֵית מִתְדַּבַּק בֵּיהּ. וּמִמּוֹלַדְתְּךָ מֵהַהוּא חָכְמָה, דְּאַתְּ מַשְׁגַּח, וְתָקִיל תּוֹלְדָתָא דִּילָךְ, וְרִגְעָא וְשַׁעֲתָא וְזִמְנָא, דְּאִתְיְילִידַת בֵּיהּ, וּבְהַהוּא כּוֹכְבָא, וּבְהַהוּא מַזָּלָא.

29. The words "Your country," AS USED WHEN HE SAID TO HIM, "GET YOU OUT," referred to that side of the inhabited world to which he was attached. THIS IS THE RIGHT SIDE ONLY; THE LEFT SIDE IS NOT INCLUDED. THE WORDS "and from your kindred," MEAN THAT HE TOLD HIM, "GET YOU OUT" from that Wisdom with which you study your horoscope, determined by watching and examining the moment, hour, and time of your birth, and the planet and the sign under which you were born. ALL OF THIS IS RELATED TO THE ILLUMINATION OF THE LEFT SIDE AND IS NOT INCLUDED WITHIN THE RIGHT.

30. וּמִבֵּית אָבִיךָ. דְּלָא תַשְׁגַּח בְּבֵיתָא דַּאֲבוּךְ. וְאִי אִית לָךְ שָׁרְשָׁא לְאִצְלָחָא בְּעָלְמָא, מִבֵּיתָא דַּאֲבוּךְ, בְּגִין כָּךְ לֶךְ לְךָ, מֵחָכְמָה דָּא וּמֵאַשְׁגָּחוּתָא דָּא.

30. The verse, "And from your father's house," MEANS THAT HE TOLD HIM "GET YOU OUT" and never look upon your father's house again, REFERRING TO CHARAN, AND NEVER SEEK TO DISCOVER if the root of your success in the world is from your father's house. Therefore, "Get you out" of this wisdom and this observance.

31. תָּא חֲזֵי. דְּהָכֵי הוּא. דְּהָא נָפְקוּ מֵאוּר כַּשְׂדִּים, וַהֲווֹ בְּחָרָן, אֲמַאי יֵימָא לֵיהּ לֶךְ לְךָ מֵאַרְצְךָ וּמִמּוֹלַדְתְּךָ. אֶלָּא עִקְּרָא דְּמִלְּתָא, כְּמָה דְּאִתְּמָר. אֶל הָאָרֶץ אֲשֶׁר אַרְאֶךָּ. אַרְאֶךָּ, מַה דְּלָא יְכֵילַת לְמֵיקַם עֲלֵיהּ,

וְלָא יְכֵילַת לְמִנְדַּע חֵילָא דְּהַהִיא אַרְעָא, דְּאִיהוּ עָמִיק וְסָתִים.

31. Come and behold: It is indeed so! Because they had already left Ur of the Chaldeans and were in Charan, why should He say to him, "Get you out of your country, and from your kindred?" FOR HE HAS ALREADY LEFT UR OF THE CHALDEANS, WHICH IS HIS COUNTRY AND FAMILY. Therefore, the main point has to be, as previously stated, THAT THE MEANING OF "YOUR COUNTRY" IS THE ILLUMINATION OF THE RIGHT WITHOUT THE LEFT, AND "YOUR KINDRED" IS THE ILLUMINATION OF THE LEFT WITHOUT THE RIGHT. "To the land that I will show you" MEANS THAT "I will show you" what you were not able to conceive – BECAUSE OF THE JUDGMENTS OF THE ILLUMINATION OF THE LEFT – and were not able to know about the power of that land, NAMELY MALCHUT, which is deep and hidden.

6. "And I will make of you a great nation," part one

A Synopsis
All the blessings that Abraham received are explained in the following section of the Zohar. Abraham received these blessings because he let go of his own ego and completely surrendered to the Creator.

The Relevance of this Passage
The intelligence of the body creates an illusion that we are in control of our lives. Nevertheless, anxiety, fear, emotional turmoil, and external chaos continue to be an affliction. When we let go of this illusion and relinquish control, we create a space for the Light of the Creator to enter our existence, removing all darkness. We acquire the power from the blessings that Abraham received, instilling us with the courage to entrust the Creator with control over our life.

32. וְאֶעֶשְׂךָ לְגוֹי גָדוֹל וגו'. וְאֶעֶשְׂךָ, בְּגִין דִּכְתִיב, לֶךְ לְךָ. וַאֲבָרֶכְךָ, בְּגִין דִּכְתִיב, מֵאַרְצְךָ. וַאֲגַדְּלָה שְׁמֶךָ, בְּגִין דִּכְתִיב, וּמִמּוֹלַדְתְּךָ. וֶהְיֵה בְרָכָה, בְּגִין דִּכְתִיב, וּמִבֵּית אָבִיךָ.

32. "And I will make of you a great nation..." (Beresheet 12:2). "And I will make of you" is related to the verse, "Get you out." "And I will bless you" is related to the verse, "from your country." "And make your name great" is related to the verse, "and from your kindred." "And you shall be a blessing" is related to the verse, "and from your father's house."

33. רַבִּי שִׁמְעוֹן אָמַר, וְאֶעֶשְׂךָ לְגוֹי גָדוֹל, מִסְּטְרָא דִּימִינָא. וַאֲבָרֶכְךָ, מִסְּטְרָא דִּשְׂמָאלָא. וַאֲגַדְּלָה שְׁמֶךָ, מִסְּטְרָא דְּאֶמְצָעִיתָא. וֶהְיֵה בְרָכָה, מִסְּטְרָא דְּאַרְעָא דְּיִשְׂרָאֵל. הָא הָכָא כֻּרְסַיָּיא, דְּאַרְבַּע סַמְכִין, דְּכֻלְּהוּ כְּלִילָן בֵּיהּ בְּאַבְרָהָם. מִכָּאן וּלְהָלְאָה, בִּרְכָּאן לְאַחֲרִינֵי, דְּמִתְזְנֵי מֵהָכָא, דִּכְתִיב, וַאֲבָרְכָה מְבָרְכֶיךָ וּמְקַלֶּלְךָ אָאֹר וְנִבְרְכוּ בְךָ כֹּל מִשְׁפְּחֹת הָאֲדָמָה.

33. Rabbi Shimon DISAGREES, AND says that the verse, "And I will make of you a great nation," is THE ILLUMINATION OF the right side; that "and I

will bless you" is THE ILLUMINATION OF the left side; that "and I will make your name great" is THE ILLUMINATION OF the Central Column; and that "and you shall be a blessing" is from the side of the land of Yisrael, FROM THE SIDE OF THE NUKVA, WHICH IS CALLED THE LAND OF YISRAEL. So here is a throne that has four legs, all of which were included in Abraham. THE THREE COLUMNS – CHESED, GVURAH AND TIFERET – ARE THREE LEGS, THE NUKVA IS THE FOURTH LEG. THESE ARE THE FOUR LEGS OF THE UPPER THRONE, WHICH IS BINAH. From here onward, the blessings are for the others who are replenished from here. THIS REFERS TO OTHERS WHO ARE BLESSED FOR HIS SAKE, as it is written: "And I will bless them that bless you and curse them that curse you, and in you shall all families of the earth be blessed."

7. "And from the wicked their light is withheld"

A Synopsis

When one behaves in a negative manner, he immediately disconnects himself from the Light of the Creator. Moreover, negative deeds also block and prevent an individual from receiving any spiritual Light from the righteous souls who are in this world to share their Light with all mankind.

The Relevance of this Passage

Every act of negative behavior can be likened to draping a layer of cloth over a lamp. Life grows progressively darker. We remove these veils from ourselves through the letters and lessons of this section so that we may receive all the Light that is ever-present from the devout souls who dwell among us in our generation.

34. ר׳ אֶלְעָזָר, הֲוָה יָתֵיב קַמֵּיה דְּרַבִּי שִׁמְעוֹן אֲבוֹי, וַהֲוֵי עֲמֵיה, ר׳ יְהוּדָה, וְרַבִּי יִצְחָק, וְרַבִּי חִזְקְיָּה. אָמַר לוֹ ר׳ אֶלְעָזָר לְרַבִּי שִׁמְעוֹן אֲבוֹי, הַאי דִּכְתִיב, לֶךְ לְךָ מֵאַרְצְךָ וּמִמּוֹלַדְתְּךָ. כֵּיוָן דְּכֻלְּהוּ נָפְקוּ לְמֵהַךְ, אֲמַאי לָא אִתְּמָר לֵיה דְּכָלְהוּ יִפְקוּן.

34. Rabbi Elazar was sitting before his father, Rabbi Shimon, together with Rabbi Yehuda, Rabbi Yitzchak, and Rabbi Chizkiyah. Rabbi Elazar asked Rabbi Shimon why is it written: "Get you out of your country, and from your kindred" in the singular? Since they all left UR OF THE CHALDEANS to go to THE LAND OF CANAAN, why was Abraham not told that they all should go?

35. דְּהָא אַף עַל גַּב דְּתֶרַח הֲוָה פָּלַח לע״ז, כֵּיוָן דְּאִתְּעַר בְּאִתְעֲרוּתָא טַב לְמֵיפַק בַּהֲדֵיה דְּאַבְרָהָם, וְהָאמֵינָן קֻדְשָׁא בְּרִיךְ הוּא אִתְרְעֵי בִּתְיוּבְתָּא דְּחַיָּיבַיָּא, וְשָׁרָא לְמֵיפַק, אֲמַאי לָא כְּתִיב לְכוּ לָכֶם. אֲמַאי לְאַבְרָהָם בִּלְחוֹדוֹי לֶךְ לְךָ.

35. Terach was an idol worshipper, but since his desire to leave with Abraham was truly aroused, and, as we have seen, the Holy One, blessed be He, desires that the wicked repent, as Terach started to leave with Abraham, why does it not say, "Go for yourself" in plural? Why does it say "Go for yourself" to Abraham alone?

36. אָמַר לוֹ רִבִּי שִׁמְעוֹן, אִי תֵימָא, דְּתֶרַח כַּד נָפַק, מֵאוּר כַּשְׂדִּים, בְּגִין לְאַהֲדָרָא בִּתְשׁוּבָה הֲוָה, לָאו הָכִי, אֶלָּא כַּד נָפַק, לְאִשְׁתְּזָבָא נָפַק, דַּהֲווֹ כֻּלְּהוּ בְּנֵי אַרְעֵיהּ, בָּעָאן לְמִקְטְלֵיהּ. כֵּיוָן דְּחָזוּ, דְּאִשְׁתְּזֵיב אַבְרָהָם, הֲווֹ אָמְרֵי לֵיהּ לְתֶרַח, אַנְתְּ הוּא דַּהֲוֵית מַטְעֵי לָן, בְּאִלֵּין פְּסִילִין, וּמִגּוֹ דַּחֲלָא דִּלְּהוֹן, נָפַק תֶּרַח, כֵּיוָן דְּמָטָא לְחָרָן, לָא נָפַק מִתַּמָּן לְבָתַר, דִּכְתִיב וַיֵּלֶךְ אַבְרָם כַּאֲשֶׁר דִּבֶּר אֵלָיו ה' וַיֵּלֶךְ אִתּוֹ לוֹט. וְאִילוּ תֶּרַח לָא כְּתִיב.

36. Rabbi Shimon replied that Terach did not leave Ur of the Chaldeans because he wanted to repent and mend his ways, but only to save himself from all the people of his land, who wanted to kill him. Particularly after they saw that Abraham was saved FROM THE FURNACE OF FIRE, they said to Terach, 'You were the one who misled us with these idols,' AND WANTED TO KILL HIM. Because he feared them, Terach left. THEREFORE, when he reached Charan, he stayed, as it is written: "So Abram departed, as Hashem had spoken to him, and Lot went with him" (Beresheet 12:4). Terach is not mentioned in the verse!

37. פָּתַח וְאָמַר, וַיִּמָּנַע מֵרְשָׁעִים אוֹרָם וּזְרוֹעַ רָמָה תִּשָּׁבֵר. הַאי קְרָא אוּקְמוּהָ, אֲבָל, וַיִּמָּנַע מֵרְשָׁעִים אוֹרָם, דָּא נִמְרוֹד וּבְנֵי דָרֵיהּ, דְּנָפַק אַבְרָהָם מִנַּיְיהוּ דַּהֲוָה אוֹרָם. וּזְרוֹעַ רָמָה תִּשָּׁבֵר, דָּא נִמְרוֹד.

37. He opened the discussion by saying: "And from the wicked their light is withheld, and the high arm shall be broken" (Iyov 38:16). This passage has already been explained. Nevertheless, "And from the wicked their light is withheld" applies to Nimrod and the people of his generation, whom Abraham left, since he was "their light"; "the high arm shall be broken" alludes to Nimrod.

38. דָּבָר אַחֵר, וַיִּמָּנַע מֵרְשָׁעִים אוֹרָם, דָּא תֶּרַח וּבְנֵי בֵּיתֵיהּ. אוֹרָם: דָּא אַבְרָהָם. הָאוֹר, לָא כְּתִיב, אֶלָּא אוֹרָם, דַּהֲוָה עִמְּהוֹן. וּזְרוֹעַ רָמָה תִּשָּׁבֵר. דָּא נִמְרוֹד, דַּהֲוָה מַטְעֵי אֲבַתְרֵיהּ, כָּל בְּנֵי עָלְמָא. וּבְגִין כָּךְ כְּתִיב לֶךְ לְךָ. בְּגִין, לְאַנְהָרָא לָךְ, וּלְכָל אִינוּן דְּיִפְּקוּן מִינָךְ, מִכָּאן וּלְהָלְאָה.

38. Another explanation of the verse, "And from the wicked their light is withheld," is that it applies to Terach and his household, and "their light" is Abraham. The verse does not say 'the light,' but "their light," that was among them. THIS REFERS TO ABRAHAM WHO WAS AMONG THEM AND THEN LEFT. "And the high arm shall be broken" applies to Nimrod, who misled the whole world to following him. And this is why it is written: "Get you out," so that the light may shine for you and for all who will descend from now and henceforth.

39. תּוּ פָּתַח וְאָמַר. וְעַתָּה לֹא רָאוּ אוֹר בָּהִיר הוּא בַּשְּׁחָקִים וְרוּחַ עָבְרָה וַתְּטַהֲרֵם. וְעַתָּה לֹא רָאוּ אוֹר, אֵימָתַי, בְּשַׁעְתָּא דַּאֲמַר קֻדְשָׁא בְּרִיךְ הוּא לְאַבְרָהָם לֶךְ לְךָ מֵאַרְצְךָ וּמִמּוֹלַדְתְּךָ וּמִבֵּית אָבִיךָ. בָּהִיר הוּא בַּשְּׁחָקִים. דְּבָעָא קֻדְשָׁא בְּרִיךְ הוּא לְאַדְבָּקָא לֵיהּ לְאַבְרָהָם, בְּהַהוּא אוֹר דִּלְעֵילָא, וּלְאַנְהָרָא תַּמָּן.

39. Furthermore, RABBI SHIMON then discussed the verse, "And now men see not the bright light which is in the clouds; but the wind passes, and cleanses them" (Iyov 37:21). "And now men see not the bright light": when DID THAT HAPPEN? At the time when the Holy One, blessed be He, said to Abraham, "Get you out of your country, and from your kindred, and from your father's house." BECAUSE AFTER ABRAHAM HAD LEFT THEM, THEY WERE NOT ABLE TO SEE THE LIGHT ANYMORE. "The bright light which is in the clouds" ALLUDES TO ABRAHAM, because the Holy One, blessed be He, wished to attach Abraham to the supernal Light and have him shine there.

40. וְרוּחַ עָבְרָה וַתְּטַהֲרֵם. דְּהָא לְבָתַר תָּבוּ בִּתְיוּבְתָּא, תֶּרַח וְכָל בְּנֵי מָאתֵיהּ בְּנֵי מָאתֵיהּ, דִּכְתִיב, וְאֶת הַנֶּפֶשׁ אֲשֶׁר עָשׂוּ בְחָרָן. תֶּרַח: דִּכְתִיב וְאַתָּה תָּבֹא אֶל אֲבוֹתֶיךָ בְּשָׁלוֹם וְגוֹ'.

40. "And the wind passes, and cleanses them" refers to Terach and all the people of his town, all of whom afterwards repented. As it is written: "and the souls that they had made in Charan" (Beresheet 12:5), MEANING THAT THE PEOPLE OF CHARAN REPENTED. The verse, "And you shall come to your fathers in peace" (Beresheet 15:15), INDICATES THAT Terach HAD REPENTED, FOR THE HOLY ONE, BLESSED BE HE, WOULD NOT HAVE SAID THIS TO ABRAHAM OTHERWISE.

8. "And I will make of you a great nation," part two

A Synopsis
At every beginning, at every opening, within every seed-level moment, there are dark forces present whose sole objective is to taint, negatively influence, and curse all that will come after. The Zohar reveals the process by which we can break these curses and remove any negative factors.

The Relevance of this Passage
New projects and new beginnings in our life start out with bountiful optimism and hope. Be that as it may, unseen negative forces often infect the seed level leading to broken dreams and unrealized goals. We receive the power to break our own negative nature and the negative forces around us that try to curse new beginnings in our life.

סִתְרֵי תּוֹרָה

41. וְאֶעֶשְׂךָ לְגוֹי גָדוֹל, הַאי בִּרְכְּתָא חֲדָא. וַאֲבָרֶכְךָ, תְּרֵין. וַאֲגַדְּלָה שְׁמֶךָ, תְּלַת. וֶהְיֵה בְּרָכָה, אַרְבַּע. וַאֲבָרְכָה מְבָרְכֶיךָ, חָמֵשׁ. וּמְקַלֶּלְךָ אָאוֹר, שִׁית. וְנִבְרְכוּ בְךָ כָּל מִשְׁפְּחוֹת הָאֲדָמָה, הָא שְׁבַע. כֵּיוָן דְּאִתְבָּרְכוּ בְּאִלֵּין שְׁבַע בִּרְכָאן, מַה כְּתִיב, וַיֵּלֶךְ אַבְרָם כַּאֲשֶׁר דִּבֶּר אֵלָיו ה'. לְנַחֲתָא לְהַאי עָלְמָא, כְּמָה דְּאִתְפַּקְּדָא.

Sitrei Torah (Concealed Torah)

41. THERE ARE SEVEN BLESSINGS THAT APPEAR IN THIS PASSAGE. One: "And I will make of you a great nation"; two: "and I will bless you"; three: "and make your name great"; four: "and you shall be a blessing"; five: "And I will bless them that bless you"; six: "and curse him that curses you"; and seven: "and in you shall all families of the earth be blessed." And after he received these seven blessings, it is written: "So Abram departed, as Hashem had spoken to him." THIS MEANS THAT HE WENT down to the world, as he was commanded to do.

42. מִיַּד וַיֵּלֶךְ אִתּוֹ לוֹט. דָּא אִיהוּ נָחָשׁ דְּאִתְלַטְיָא, וְאִתְלַטְיָא עָלְמָא

בְּגִינֵיהּ, דְּאִיהוּ קָאֵים לְפִתְחָא, לְאַסְטָאָה לְגוּפָא, וְלָא תִּפְעוֹל נִשְׁמָתָא,
פּוּלְחָנָא דְּאִתְפַּקְּדַת, עַד דְּיַעַבְרוּן עֲלָהּ בְּהַאי עָלְמָא, י"ג שְׁנִין, דְּהָא
מִתְרֵיסַר שְׁנִין וּלְעֵילָא, נִשְׁמָתָא אִתְעָרַת, לְמִפְלַח פּוּלְחָנָא דְּאִתְפַּקְּדַת,
הה"ד וְאַבְרָם בֶּן חָמֵשׁ שָׁנִים וְשִׁבְעִים שָׁנָה. שֶׁבַע וְחָמֵשׁ תְּרֵיסַר אִינוּן.

42. Immediately, "Lot went with him." This is the serpent that was cursed and caused the world to be cursed. THE SCRIPTURES CALL THE SERPENT BY THE NAME LOT, BECAUSE LOT MEANS 'A CURSE' IN ARAMAIC. THE SERPENT WAS CURSED AND BROUGHT CURSES ON THE WORLD. SO HE ACCOMPANIES THE SOUL DURING ITS STAY IN THIS WORLD. And the serpent stands at the opening, in order to mislead the body, AS IT IS WRITTEN: "SIN CROUCHES AT THE DOOR" (BERESHEET 4:7). And this is why the soul will not start fulfilling the mission it was commanded to perform until it has completed thirteen years in this world. Because from the twelfth year onward, the soul is aroused to fulfill its task. Therefore, it is written: "and Abram was seventy five years old" (Beresheet 12:4) – SEVENTY IN REDUCED NUMERICAL VALUE EQUALS SEVEN, and seven and five equals twelve. THEN THE SOUL LEAVES CHARAN, WHICH IS THE KLIPOT, AND IS AROUSED TO SERVE HASHEM AND FULFILL ITS ALLOTTED TASK.

43. וּכְדֵין אִתְחֲזִיאַת נִשְׁמָתָא בְּהַאי עָלְמָא. דְּאִיהִי אַתְיָא מֵחֲמֵשׁ
שְׁנִים, דְּאִינּוּן ת"ק פַּרְסֵי דְּאִילָנָא דְּחַיֵּי. וְשִׁבְעִים שָׁנָה, דָּא אִיהוּ הַהוּא
אִילָנָא מַמָּשׁ, דְּאִיהוּ שְׁבִיעָאָה לְדַרְגִּין, וְשִׁבְעִין שָׁנָה אִתְקְרֵי.

43. And then AFTER TWELVE YEARS, the soul can be seen in this world, because it comes from the "five years," which are the five hundred parasangs of the Tree of Life. IT IS THEN ACKNOWLEDGED AS AN OFFSPRING OF ZEIR ANPIN, WHICH IS CALLED THE TREE OF LIFE, WHICH IS FIVE HUNDRED PARASANGS WALK. "And seventy years" refers to the same tree, which is the seventh among the grades, NAMELY, THE NUKVA, WHICH IS THE SEVENTH SFIRAH AMONG THE SEVEN SFIROT: CHESED, GVURAH, TIFERET, NETZACH, HOD, YESOD AND MALCHUT. AND THEN THE SOUL IS ACKNOWLEDGED AS THE OFFSPRING OF ZEIR ANPIN AND THE NUKVA.

44. כְּדֵין נָפְקַת מֵהַהוּא זוּהֲמָא דְּנָחָשׁ, וְעָאלַת בְּפוּלְחָנָא קַדִּישָׁא, הה״ד, בְּצֵאתוֹ מֵחָרָן, מֵהַהוּא רוּגְזָא וְתוּקְפָּא דְּהַהוּא נָחָשׁ, דַּהֲוָה אַסְטֵי לֵיהּ עַד הַשְׁתָּא לְגוּפָא, וְשָׁלְטָא עֲלוֹי.

44. Then the soul departs from the filth of the serpent and enters to the holy work. And so it is written: "when he departed out of Charan," from the wrath and aggression of the Satan, who until now had ruled over the body by deceiving it.

45. בְּאִילָנָא, שָׁלְטָא עָרְלָה תְּלַת שְׁנִין. בְּבַר נָשׁ, תְּלַת סְרֵי שְׁנִין, דְּאִקְרוּן שְׁנֵי עָרְלָה, כֵּיוָן דְּאַעֲבָרוּ עַל גוּפָא אִינּוּן שְׁנִין, וְאִתְעַבָרַת נִשְׁמָתָא, לְמִפְלַח פּוּלְחָנָא קַדִּישָׁא, פְּקִידַת לְגוּפָא, לִרְעוּתָא טָבָא, לִכְפוֹף לְהַהוּא נָחָשׁ, דְּהָא לָא יָכִיל לְשַׁלְטָאָה כְּמָה דְּהֲוֵי.

45. The Orlah (lit. 'foreskin') rules over the tree for three years, WHICH ARE CALLED THE "ORLAH YEARS." In the human being, the first thirteen years are called the "Orlah years." After the body has lived these years, the soul is aroused to fulfill its holy task. It then receives full control over the body and inspires the goodwill necessary to overcome the serpent. And then the serpent will not be able to control the body as it did before.

46. דִּכְתִּיב, וַיִּקַּח אַבְרָם אֶת שָׂרַי אִשְׁתּוֹ וגו׳, דָּא גוּפָא, דְּאִיהִי לְגַבֵּי נִשְׁמָתָא, כְּנוּקְבָא לְגַבֵּי דְכוּרָא. וְאֶת לוֹט בֶּן אָחִיו, דָּא נָחָשׁ, דְּלָא אֲעֲדֵי כָּל כָּךְ מִן גוּפָא, בְּגִין דִּדְבֵקוּתָא דְּגוּפָא, לָא אַעֲדִיו כָּל כָּךְ מִנֵּיהּ, אֲבָל אִתְעָרוּתָא דְּנִשְׁמָתָא אַלְקֵי לֵיהּ תָּדִיר, וְאַתְרֵי בֵּיהּ, וְאוֹכַח לֵיהּ, וְכָפִיף לֵיהּ, עַל כָּרְחֵיהּ, וְלָא יָכִיל לְשַׁלְטָאָה.

46. As it is written: "And Abram took Sarai his wife..." (Beresheet 12:5). "SARAI HIS WIFE" refers to the body, which in comparison to the soul is like the female toward the male. "And Lot his brother's son" refers to the serpent that does not completely leave the body EVEN AFTER THIRTEEN YEARS, because the clinging of the body is not entirely gone from it. Nevertheless, the arousal of the soul strikes it always, warns and reproves it, and forces it to obey so that it cannot take control any more.

47. וְאֶת כָּל רְכוּשָׁם אֲשֶׁר רָכָשׁוּ, אִלֵּין עוֹבָדִין טָבִין דְּעָבֵיד בַּר נָשׁ,
בְּהַאי עָלְמָא, בְּאִתְעָרוּתָא דְּנִשְׁמָתָא. וְאֶת הַנֶּפֶשׁ אֲשֶׁר עָשׂוּ בְחָרָן.
הַהוּא נֶפֶשׁ, דַּהֲוַת בְּקַדְמֵיתָא בִּדְבֵקוּתָא בְּחַבְרוּתָא דְּהַהִיא עָרְלָה,
בַּהֲדֵי גוּפָא, וְאַתְקִין לָהּ לְבָתַר, דְּהָא לְבָתַר דִּתְלֵיסַר שְׁנִין וּלְעֵילָא,
דְּנִשְׁמָתָא אִתְעָרַת, לְאַתְקְנָא לְגוּפָא, תַּרְוַוייהוּ מִתַּקְּנִין לְהַהוּא נֶפֶשׁ,
דְּמִשְׁתַּתְּפָא בְּתוּקְפָּא דְּנָחָשׁ, וּתְאוּבְתֵּיהּ בִּישָׁא, הה״ד וְאֶת הַנֶּפֶשׁ אֲשֶׁר
עָשׂוּ בְחָרָן.

47. "And all their substance that they had gathered..." refers to the good
deeds that a person performs in this world because of the awakening of the
soul. "And the souls (Nefesh) that they had made in Charan..." REFERS TO
that Nefesh, which at first was attached to the foreskin of the body and
clung to it and which later was amended BY THE NESHAMAH. IT IS
DESCRIBED BY THE WORDS, "AND THE NEFESH THAT THEY HAD MADE
IN CHARAN," WHICH REFER TO THE CRAVING NEFESH, WHICH FEELS
GREAT ATTACHMENT TO THE LUST OF THE BODY AND THE KLIPOT. So
after thirteen years, when the Neshamah is aroused to amend the body, both
THE NESHAMAH AND THE BODY amend that Nefesh that participated in the
harsh JUDGMENTS of the serpent and its evil desires. As it is written: "and
the Nefesh that they had made in Charan..." THE REASON WHY "THEY HAD
MADE" IS WRITTEN IN THE PLURAL IS BECAUSE IT REFERS TO THE
NESHAMAH AND THE BODY, WHICH TOGETHER AMEND THE NEFESH–
THE NESHAMAH BY AWAKENING THE BODY, AND THE BODY BY ITS GOOD
DEEDS.

48. וְעִם כָּל דָּא, נִשְׁמָתָא אַתְקִיפַת בֵּיהּ, בְּהַהוּא נָחָשׁ, לְתַבְּרָא לֵיהּ,
בְּתוּקְפָּא בְּשִׁעְבּוּדָא דִּתְשׁוּבָה, הֲדָא הוּא דִכְתִיב וַיַּעֲבוֹר.

(עד כאן סתרי תורה)

48. With all of this, the Neshamah continues to attack the serpent in order to
break it, so that it will surrender and be enslaved under the influence of
repentance. Therefore, it is written: "And Abram passed through the land to

the place of Shchem" (Beresheet 12:6), BECAUSE SHCHEM IS THE DWELLING PLACE OF THE SHECHINAH. AND THAT IS BECAUSE THE POWER OF THE SERPENT HAS ALREADY BEEN COMPLETELY BROKEN BY THE NESHAMAH.

(End of Sitrei Torah)

9. "So Abram departed, as Hashem had spoken to him…"

A Synopsis

It's explained that every man has angels who accompany him everywhere, recording every single action and deed, large and small. The Final Day of Judgment is then spelled out by the Zohar: The angels come forth during this time and present a list of all our actions, positive and negative, so that we can acknowledge them. The Zohar goes on to declare that no matter how negative a person's actions might become, we should never cast them aside and disregard them.

The Relevance of this Passage

Mankind's nature is to disregard or justify its insensitive and intolerant behavior. Regardless, we are eventually held accountable for all of our actions. An awareness of the gravity and severity of our negative behavior, even the most minute behavioral actions, is imbued into our consciousness by virtue of this passage. This will inspire us to treat others with the same compassion and tolerance that we desire.

49. וַיֵּלֶךְ אַבְרָם כַּאֲשֶׁר דִּבֶּר אֵלָיו ה'. אָמַר רַבִּי אֶלְעָזָר, תָּא חֲזֵי, דְּהָא לָא כְּתִיב וַיֵּצֵא אַבְרָם כַּאֲשֶׁר דִּבֶּר אֵלָיו ה'. אֶלָּא וַיֵּלֶךְ. כד"א לֶךְ לְךָ. דְּהָא יְצִיאָה בְּקַדְמֵיתָא עֲבָדוּ, דִּכְתִיב, וַיֵּצְאוּ אִתָּם מֵאוּר כַּשְׂדִּים לָלֶכֶת אַרְצָה כְּנַעַן. וְהַשְׁתָּא כְּתִיב וַיֵּלֶךְ, וְלָא כְּתִיב וַיֵּצֵא.

49. Rabbi Elazar said, Come and behold, It is not written: "So Abram left, as Hashem had spoken to him," but rather that Abram "departed (lit. 'went') (Heb. vayelech)," as it is written: "Get you out" (Heb. lech lecha). This is so written because they had already left, as it is written: "and they went out with them from Ur of the Chaldeans to go to the land of Canaan." Therefore, it is written: "departed" rather than "left."

50. כַּאֲשֶׁר דִּבֶּר אֵלָיו ה'. דְּאַבְטַח לֵיהּ בְּכָלְהוֹ הַבְטָחוֹת. וַיֵּלֶךְ אִתּוֹ לוֹט, דְּאִתְחַבַּר עִמֵּיהּ, בְּגִין לְמֵילַף מֵעוֹבָדוֹי, וְעִם כָּל דָּא לָא אוֹלִיף כּוּלֵי הַאי. אָמַר רַבִּי אֶלְעָזָר זַכָּאִין אִינוּן צַדִּיקַיָּיא, דְּאוֹלְפֵי אָרְחוֹי דְקֻדְשָׁא בְּרִיךְ הוּא, בְּגִין לְמֵיהַךְ בְּהוֹ, וּלְדָחֲלָא מִנֵּיהּ, מֵהַהוּא יוֹמָא דְּדִינָא,

-32-

דְּזַמִּין בַּר נָשׁ לְמֵיהַב דִּינָא וְחוּשְׁבָּנָא לְקֻדְשָׁא בְּרִיךְ הוּא.

50. "As Hashem had spoken to him..." THIS MEANS according to all the promises He gave him. The words, "and Lot went with him," mean that Lot accompanied Abraham to learn from his behavior. Even so, Lot did not learn much. Rabbi Elazar said: Happy are the righteous who study the ways of the Holy One, blessed be He, in order to follow them and be in awe of Him – in awe of that day of judgment when man will have to account for his deeds before the Holy one, blessed be He.

51. פְּתַח וַאֲמַר, בְּיַד כָּל אָדָם יַחְתּוֹם לָדַעַת כָּל אַנְשֵׁי מַעֲשֵׂהוּ. הַאי קְרָא אוּקְמוּהָ. אֲבָל תָּא חֲזֵי, בְּהַהוּא יוֹמָא, דְּאַשְׁלִימוּ יוֹמוֹי דְּבַר נָשׁ לְאַפְּקָא מֵעַלְמָא, הַהוּא יוֹמָא, דְּגוּפָא אִתְבַּר, וְנַפְשָׁא בָּעְיָא לְאִתְפָּרְשָׁא מִנֵּיהּ. כְּדֵין, אִתְיְיהִיב רְשׁוּ לְבַר נָשׁ לְמֶחֱמֵי, מַה דְּלָא הֲוָה לֵיהּ רְשׁוּ לְמֶחֱמֵי, בְּזִמְנָא דְּגוּפָא שָׁלְטָא, וְקָאִים עַל בּוּרְיֵיהּ.

51. He opened the discussion, saying: "He seals up the hand of every man; that all men whom He has made may know His work." (Iyov 37:7). This passage has already been explained. But come and behold: When the days of man are over and he is about to leave this world, on that day when the body is broken and the soul has to leave it, then that person is permitted to see what he has not been able to see when the body was in control, and he understands things completely.

52. וּכְדֵין קַיְימֵי עֲלֵיהּ תְּלַת שְׁלִיחָן, וְחָשְׁבֵי יוֹמוֹי וְחוֹבוֹי, וְכָל מַה דְּעָבַד בְּהַאי עָלְמָא, וְהוּא אוֹדֵי עַל כֹּלָּא בְּפוּמֵיהּ. וּלְבָתַר הוּא חָתִים עֲלֵיהּ בִּידֵיהּ. הֲדָא הוּא דִכְתִיב, בְּיַד כָּל אָדָם יַחְתּוֹם.

52. Three messengers stand over him and take an account of his days and his sins and all that he has done in this world. And he openly admits everything, and after that he signs it, THE ACCOUNT, with his hand. As it is written: "He seals up the hand of every man..."

53. וּבִידֵיהּ כֻּלְּהוּ חֲתִימִין לְמֵידַן לֵיהּ, בְּהַאי עָלְמָא, עַל קַדְמָאֵי, וְעַל בַּתְרָאֵי, עַל חַדְתֵּי וְעַל עַתִּיקֵי. לָא אִתְנְשֵׁי חַד מִינַּיְיהוּ, הֲהֵ"ד לָדַעַת

כָּל אֲנָשֵׁי מַעֲשֵׂהוּ. וְכָל אִינוּן עוֹבָדִין דַּעֲבַד בְּהַאי עָלְמָא, בְּגוּפָא וְרוּחָא. הָכֵי נָמֵי יָהִיב חוּשְׁבָּנָא בְּגוּפָא וְרוּחָא, עַד לָא יִפּוֹק מֵעָלְמָא.

53. And all DEEDS AND SINS are signed with his hand, so a man can be judged for all of his actions in this world, the early and the recent, the old and the new – not even one of them is forgotten. Therefore, it is written: "that all men whom He has made may know His work." JUST AS all of the actions he committed in this world WERE together in body and in spirit, so he must account FOR THEM WHILE HE IS STILL together in body and spirit, before he leaves this world.

54. תָּא חֲזֵי, כַּמָּה דְּחַיָּיבַיָּא, אַקְשֵׁי קְדַל בְּהַאי עָלְמָא, ה״נ, אֲפִילוּ בְּשַׁעְתָּא דְּבָעֵי לְנַפְקָא מֵהַאי עָלְמָא, אַקְשֵׁי קְדַל. בְּגִין כָּךְ זַכָּאָה הוּא בַּר נָשׁ, דְּיָלִיף בְּהַאי עָלְמָא אָרְחוֹי דְּקֻדְשָׁא בְּרִיךְ הוּא, בְּגִין לְמֵיהַךְ בְּהוּ. וְחַיָּיבָא, אַף עַל גַּב דְּאִסְתַּכַּל בְּהַנֵּי צַדִּיקַיָּיא, אַקְשֵׁי קְדַל, וְלָא בָּעֵי לְמֵילַף.

54. Come and behold: Just as the sinners are stiff-necked in this world, so are they stiff-necked when they are about to leave this world. Therefore, blessed is that person who studies the ways of the Holy One, blessed be He, while in this world, so that he may follow them. But the wicked person, even though he sees these righteous people, stiffens his neck and refuses to learn from them.

55. וּבְגִין כָּךְ אִית לֵיהּ לְצַדִּיקָא, לְמִתְקַף בֵּיהּ, וְאַף עַל גַּב דְּחַיָּיבָא אַקְשֵׁי קְדַל הוּא, לָא יִשְׁבּוֹק לֵיהּ, וְאִית לֵיהּ לְאַתְקְפָא בִּידֵיהּ, וְלָא יִשְׁבּוֹק לֵיהּ, דְּאִי יִשְׁבּוֹק לֵיהּ יְהַךְ וְיַחֲרִיב עָלְמָא.

55. This is why the righteous man must hold on to him and not let go, even though the wicked person "stiffens his neck." The righteous man should hold him tight by the hand and not leave him alone, because if he lets him go, the wicked person will go and destroy the world.

56. תָּא חֲזֵי, מִן אֱלִישָׁע דְּדָחָה לְגֵיחֲזִי. וְכֵן בְּאַבְרָהָם כָּל זִמְנָא דַּהֲוָה

לוֹט בַּהֲדֵיהּ, לָא אִתְחַבַּר בַּהֲדֵי רַשִׁיעַיָא, כֵּיוָן דְּאִתְפְּרַשׁ מִנֵּיהּ, מַה כְּתִיב וַיִּבְחַר לוֹ לוֹט אֶת כָּל כִּכַּר הַיַּרְדֵּן, וּכְתִיב וַיֶּאֱהַל עַד סְדוֹם. מַה כְּתִיב בַּתְרֵיהּ, וְאַנְשֵׁי סְדוֹם רָעִים וְחַטָּאִים לַה׳ מְאֹד.

56. Come and behold: We see examples in the case of Elisha who thrust away Gechazi, and in the case of Abraham and Lot. As long as Lot was with Abraham, Lot did not associate with the wicked. But as soon as he left him, it is written: "Then Lot chose him all the plain of Jordan...and pitched his tent toward Sodom" (Beresheet 13:11-12), followed by "And the men of Sodom were wicked and sinners before Hashem exceedingly" (Ibid. 13). So WE SEE THAT HE DID JOIN THE WICKED!

57. אָמַר רְבִּי אַבָּא, הַאי דַּאֲמַרְתְּ וַיֵּלֶךְ אַבְרָם, וְלָא כְתִיב וַיֵּצֵא אַבְרָם, שַׁפִּיר הוּא. אֲבָל, סוֹפָא דִקְרָא, מַה כְּתִיב, בְּצֵאתוֹ מֵחָרָן. אָמַר רְבִּי אֶלְעָזָר, מֵחָרָן כְּתִיב, וְהַהִיא יְצִיאָה מֵאֶרֶץ מוֹלַדְתּוֹ הֲוַת בְּקַדְמֵיתָא.

57. Rabbi Aba said TO RABBI ELAZAR: You noted that it is written: "Abram went," rather than 'Abram left,' BECAUSE THEY HAD ALREADY LEFT. This is well but at the end of the verse, it is written: "when he departed out of Charan..." SO THE VERSE DOES MENTION LEAVING – EVEN THOUGH HE HAD ALREADY LEFT. Rabbi Elazar responded that it is written "out of Charan," but the main departure was that from the land of his birthplace, which had already occurred. THIS IS NOT THE SAME AS THE DEPARTURE FROM CHARAN THAT IS MENTIONED TOGETHER WITH "GET YOU OUT." SO WE MAY SAY HERE "WHEN HE LEFT CHARAN."

10. "And Abram took Sarai his wife…"

A Synopsis

When a person influences another individual in a positive way, that measure of positive influence is credited for all eternity. Moreover, when the second individual utilizes that same positive influence to then affect others, the positive energy generated is also accrued to the original person. This same principle holds true with all of our negative actions.

The Relevance of this Passage

Our inability to perceive the far-reaching implications of our actions, allows us to behave wantonly and with disregard for others. These verses give us the understanding and enlightenment to foresee all the repercussions associated with our behavior, motivating us to constantly improve our ways through continued spiritual development.

58. וַיִּקַּח אַבְרָם אֶת שָׂרַי אִשְׁתּוֹ. מַהוּ וַיִּקַּח, אֶלָּא, אַמְשִׁיךְ לָהּ בְּמִלֵּי מַעֲלָיְיתָא, בְּגִין דְּלֵית לֵיהּ רְשׁוּ לב"נ לְאַפָּקָא אִתְּתֵיהּ, לְמֵיהַךְ בְּאַרְעָא אָחֳרָא בְּלָא רְעוּתָא דִילָהּ. וְכֵן הוּא אוֹמֵר קַח אֶת אַהֲרֹן. קַח אֶת הַלְוִיִם. וּבְגִין כָּךְ וַיִּקַּח אַבְרָם. מָשִׁיךְ לָהּ בְּמִלִּין, וְאוֹדַע לָהּ אָרְחַיְיהוּ דְּאִינוּן בְּנֵי דָרָא, כַּמָּה בִּישִׁין. וּבְגִין כָּךְ וַיִּקַּח אַבְרָם אֶת שָׂרַי אִשְׁתּוֹ.

58. "And Abraham took Sarai his wife" (Beresheet 12:5). IN THIS VERSE, THE WORD "took" means that Abraham persuaded her to come with soft words, because a man cannot take his wife to another country without her agreement. Similarly, it is written: "Take Aaron" (Bemidbar 20:25) and "Take the Levites" (Bemidbar 3:45). This is why "And Abram took" MEANS THAT he persuaded her with words, telling her how evil were the ways of their generation. Therefore it is written: "And Abram took Sarai his wife."

59. וְאֶת לוֹט בֶּן אָחִיו. מַה חָמָא אַבְרָהָם לְדַבְּקָא עִמֵּיהּ לוֹט. אֶלָּא בְּגִין דְּצָפָה בְּרוּחַ הַקֹּדֶשׁ, דְּזַמִּין לְמֵיפַּק מִנֵּיהּ דָּוִד. וְאֶת הַנֶּפֶשׁ אֲשֶׁר עָשׂוּ בְחָרָן. אִלֵּין גֵּרִים וְגִיּוּרוֹת דְּאַתְקִינוּ נַפְשַׁיְיהוּ, אַבְרָהָם מְגַיֵּיר גּוּבְרִין, וְשָׂרָה מְגַיֶּירֶת נָשִׁין. וּמַעֲלֶה עֲלֵיהוֹן כְּאִלּוּ עַבְדוּ לְהוֹן.

59. Of the verse, "And Lot his brother's son," HE ASKS: What did Abraham see that made him take Lot with him? AND HE REPLIES: He foresaw through the Holy Spirit that David shall issue from him in the future. The words, "and the souls that they had made in Charan," refer to the male and female converts whose souls they amended. Abraham converted the men, while Sarah converted the women. FOR THIS REASON, the verse is written as if they had "made" them.

60. אָמַר רִבִּי אַבָּא אִי הָכֵי, כַּמָּה בְּנֵי נָשָׁא הֲווֹ, אִי תֵּימָא דְּכֻלְּהוּ אֲזָלוּ עֲמֵיהּ. אָמַר רִבִּי אֶלְעָזָר אֵין. וּבְגִין כָּךְ כֻּלְּהוּ בְּנֵי נָשָׁא, דַּהֲווֹ אַזְלִין עֲמֵיהּ, כֻּלְּהוּ אִקְרוּן עַם אֱלֹקֵי אַבְרָהָם. וַהֲוָה מַעֲבַר בְּאַרְעָא, וְלָא הֲוָה דָּחִיל. דִּכְתִיב וַיַּעֲבֹר אַבְרָם בָּאָרֶץ.

60. Rabbi Aba said: If so, then there were a lot of people – REFERRING TO THE CONVERTS. HOW can we say that they all left with him? Rabbi Elazar responded: Indeed so! And because of this, all the people who went with him are called "the people of the Elohim of Abraham" (Tehilim 47:10). And he traveled through the country with no fear, as it is written: "And Abram passed through the land."

61. אָמַר לוֹ ר׳ אַבָּא, אִי הֲוָה כְּתִיב, וְהַנֶּפֶשׁ אֲשֶׁר עָשׂוּ בְחָרָן. הֲוָה אֲמֵינָא הָכֵי, אֶלָּא, וְאֶת הַנֶּפֶשׁ כְּתִיב, אֶת לְאַסְגָּאָה, זְכוּתָא דְּכֻלְּהוּ נַפְשָׁאן, דַּהֲווֹ אָזְלֵי עֲמֵיהּ, דְּכָל מַאן דִּמְזַכֶּה לְאָחֳרָא, הַהוּא זְכוּתָא תַּלְיָא בֵּיהּ, וְלָא אַעֲדֵי מִנֵּיהּ. מְנָלָן, דִּכְתִיב, וְאֶת הַנֶּפֶשׁ אֲשֶׁר עָשׂוּ בְחָרָן. זְכוּתָא דְּאִינּוּן נַפְשָׁן הֲוָה אָזִיל עֲמֵיהּ דְּאַבְרָהָם.

61. Rabbi Aba said to him: If it had been written, 'and souls that they had made in Charan,' then he would have agreed THAT BECAUSE OF THEIR GREAT NUMBERS ABRAHAM HAD NO FEAR WHEN PASSING THROUGH THE LAND. But, he said, it is written: "and the (Heb. *et*) souls," in which the particle *Et* serves as an addition to the merits of those souls that went along with him. IT IS FOR THIS REASON THAT ABRAHAM WAS ABLE TO PASS THROUGH THE LAND WITH NO FEAR. Because he who leads his friend to meritorious conduct benefits always from that conduct and the benefit never leaves him. How do we know this? Because it is written: "And the souls that they had made in Charan." The merit of these souls accompanied Abraham.

62. לֶךְ לְךָ. אָמַר רָבִּי שִׁמְעוֹן, מַאי טַעֲמָא דְּגִלּוּיָא קַדְמָאָה, דְּאִתְגְּלֵי קֻדְשָׁא בְּרִיךְ הוּא עֲלֵיהּ דְּאַבְרָהָם, פָּתַח בְּלֶךְ לְךָ, דְּהָא עַד הָכָא, לָא מַלִּיל עִמֵּיהּ קֻדְשָׁא בְּרִיךְ הוּא, מ"ט פָּתַח לֶךְ לְךָ. אֶלָּא, הָא קָאַמְרוּ, דְּרָמַז בְּחוּשְׁבְּנֵיהּ מְאָה, דְּהָא לִמְאָה שְׁנִין אִתְיְלִיד לֵיהּ בַּר.

62. Of the words "Get you out," Rabbi Shimon asked, when the Holy One, blessed be He, first revealed himself to Abraham, why did He start with 'Get you out'"? Until that time, the Holy One, blessed be He, had not spoken with Abraham. Therefore, why did He start with "Go for yourself"? Because the Hebrew words for "Go for yourself," which are *lech lecha,* have a numerical value of 100. By using these words, the Holy One, blessed by He, gave Abraham a hint that he would have a son in his hundredth year.

63. אֲבָל תָּא חֲזֵי, כָּל מַה דְּעָבִיד קֻדְשָׁא בְּרִיךְ הוּא בְּאַרְעָא, כֹּלָּא רָזָא דְּחָכְמְתָא אִיהוּ, בְּגִין דְּאַבְרָהָם לָא הֲוָה דָּבִיק בֵּיהּ בְּקֻדְשָׁא בְּרִיךְ הוּא, כְּדֵין כִּדְקָא חֲזֵי. אָמַר לֵיהּ לֶךְ לְךָ, וְדָא רֶמֶז לְהַהוּא אֲתַר דְּבָעֵי לְאִתְקָרְבָא בַּהֲדֵיהּ דְּקֻדְשָׁא בְּרִיךְ הוּא, וְאִיהוּ דַּרְגָּא קַדְמָאָה לְאַעֲלָא לְקוּדְשָׁא בְּרִיךְ הוּא, בְּגִין כָּךְ לֶךְ לְךָ.

63. But come and behold: All that the Holy One, blessed be He, performs on earth is done according to Wisdom. Because Abraham was not yet attached to the Holy One, blessed be He, properly, He said to him "Go for yourself." This is a hint for that place and position that Abraham was expected to reach and that would bring him closer to the Holy One, blessed be He. This is why it is written: "Go for yourself." And that is the first grade that Abraham was to attain in coming to the Holy One, blessed be He.

64. וְהַאי דַּרְגָּא לָא יָכִיל אַבְרָהָם לְאִתְאַחֲדָא בֵּיהּ, עַד דְּיֵיעוֹל לְאַרְעָא דְּתַמָּן יְקַבֵּל לֵיהּ לְהַהוּא דַּרְגָּא. כְּגַוְונָא דָא כְּתִיב וַיִּשְׁאַל דָּוִד בַּה׳ לֵאמֹר הַאֶעֱלֶה בְּאַחַת עָרֵי יְהוּדָה, וַיֹּאמֶר ה׳ עֲלֵה. וַיֹּאמֶר אָנָה אֶעֱלֶה, וַיֹּאמֶר חֶבְרוֹנָה. וְכִי כֵּיוָן דְּמִית שָׁאוּל, וּמַלְכוּתָא אִתְחֲזֵי לְדָוִד, אַמַּאי לָא קַבִּיל מַלְכוּתָא מִיָּד עַל כָּל יִשְׂרָאֵל.

64. But Abraham could not reach that grade and hold on to it until he entered the land of Yisrael, because that is where this level is achieved. It was similar with David, about whom it is written: "David inquired of Hashem, saying: Shall I go up to any of the cities of Yehuda? And Hashem said to him, 'Go up.' And David said: Where shall I go up? And Hashem said: 'to Chevron'" (II Shmuel 2:1). Since Saul had died, and David was fit to receive the kingship, why then did he not receive the kingship over Yisrael immediately? WHY DID HE HAVE TO EXERCISE HIS RULERSHIP FOR SEVEN YEARS IN HEBRON?

65. אֶלָּא כֹּלָּא רָזָא דְּחָכְמְתָא אִיהוּ, בְּגִין דְּדָוִד לֵית לֵיהּ לְקַבְּלָא מַלְכוּתָא, אֶלָּא עַד דְּיִתְחַבַּר בַּאֲבָהָן, דְּאִינוּן בְּחֶבְרוֹן, וּכְדֵין בְּהוֹ יְקַבֵּל מַלְכוּתָא. וְעַל דָּא אִתְעַכַּב תַּמָּן שְׁבַע שְׁנִין, בְּגִין דִּיקַבֵּל מַלְכוּתָא כִּדְקָא יָאוֹת, וְכֹלָּא בְּרָזָא דְּחָכְמְתָא וּבְגִין דִּיתַקַּן מַלְכוּתֵיהּ. כְּגַוְונָא דָא, אַבְרָהָם לָא עָאל בְּקִיּוּמָא דְּקוּדְשָׁא בְּרִיךְ הוּא, עַד דְּעָאל לְאַרְעָא.

65. Everything, however, occurs by the secret of Wisdom. David was not ready to receive the kingship until he had connected himself to the Patriarchs buried in Hebron, through whom he was to receive the kingship. Therefore, he remained IN HEBRON for seven years, until he was fit to receive the kingship properly. Thus, everything occurred by the secret of Wisdom so that his kingship would be properly established! The same applies to Abraham; he did not achieve complete fulfillment with the Holy One, blessed be He, until he entered the land of Yisrael.

66. חָמֵי מַה כְּתִיב וַיַּעֲבֹר אַבְרָם בָּאָרֶץ. וַיַּעֲבֹר, וַיֵּלֶךְ מִבָּעֵי לֵיהּ, אֶלָּא, הָכָא הוּא רֶמֶז שְׁמָא קַדִּישָׁא, דְּאִתְחַתִּים בֵּיהּ עָלְמָא, בְּע"ב אַתְוָון, גְּלִיפָן דְּכֻלְּהוּ בִּשְׁמָא דָא. כְּתִיב הָכָא וַיַּעֲבֹר, וּכְתִיב הָתָם וַיַּעֲבֹר ה' עַל פָּנָיו וַיִּקְרָא.

66. See, it is written: "And Abram passed through the land." HE ASKS: WHY DOES THE VERSE READ "passed through (Heb. *vaya'avor*)" instead of 'went'! This is an allusion to the Holy Name – by which the world is sealed – that contains 72 engraved letters, all of which are within that name. *VAYA'AVOR* (*VAV-YUD-AYIN-BET-VAV-RESH*) CONSISTS OF TWO PARTS –

RESH-YUD-VAV (NUMERICALLY=216) AND *AYIN-BET* (=72) – THAT REFER TO THE 216 LETTERS AND 72 NAMES. Thus, it is written in one place, "And...passed through," while it is written in another, "And Hashem passed by (Heb. *vaya'avor*) before him and proclaimed..." (Shemot 34:6) – JUST AS THERE IT IS SPEAKING OF THE HOLY NAME OF *AYIN-BET* (72), SO TOO VAYA'AVOR HERE IS A REFERENCE TO THE HOLY NAME OF *AYIN-BET* (72).

11. "And Abram passed through the land..."

A Synopsis

The Zohar reveals a hidden mystery concerning all the travels of Abraham that are recorded in the Torah. The journeys are not concerned with geographical locations on Earth, but rather with the numerous spiritual levels to which our souls can ascend through personal transformation. The many difficulties associated with battling the angel Satan and the dark side of our nature, are discussed by the Zohar – all of life's processes up to the point of death.

The Relevance of this Passage

Throughout the journey of life, we often veer off the positive track into negativity as we submit to the self-indulgent whims of the physical body and the dark side of our nature. The power of this passage lies in its ability to put us back on a spiritual path, connecting us to the will of our soul.

67. בְּסִפְרָא דְּר' יֵיסָא סָבָא, כְּתִיב הָכָא וַיַּעֲבֹר אַבְרָם בָּאָרֶץ. וּכְתִיב הָתָם אֲנִי אַעֲבִיר כָּל טוּבִי. וְהוּא רֶמֶז לִקְדוּשָׁה דְּאַרְעָא, דְּאָתֵי מֵאֲתַר עִלָּאָה, כִּדְקָא חָזֵי.

67. In the book of Rabbi Yesa Saba (the elder), it states: It is written, "And Abram passed through the land," while elsewhere it is written: "I will make all My goodness pass before you" (Shemot 33:19). JUST AS THERE IT IMPLIES THE ENTIRE GOODNESS OF THE SUPERNAL PLACE, WHICH IS BINAH, SO THE IMPLICATION IS THE SAME HERE–it gives a hint about the holiness of the land, which emanates from a supernal place in all its proper GOODNESS. THIS REFERS TO MALCHUT THAT ENCLOTHES BINAH PROPERLY AND RECEIVES ITS LIGHTS.

68. עַד מְקוֹם שְׁכֶם עַד אֵלוֹן מוֹרֶה. מִסִּטְרָא דָא לְסִטְרָא דָא, כִּדְקָא חָזֵי וְהַכְּנַעֲנִי אָז בָּאָרֶץ. הָא אִתְּמַר, דְּעַד כְּדֵין, שָׁלְטָא חִוְיָא בִּישָׁא דְּאִתְלַטְיָא, וְאַיְיתֵי לְוָוטִין עַל עָלְמָא, דִּכְתִיב כְּנַעַן אָרוּר עֶבֶד עֲבָדִים יִהְיֶה לְאֶחָיו. וּכְתִיב אָרוּר אַתָּה מִכָּל הַבְּהֵמָה וְגו'. וְתַמָּן אִתְקְרִיב אַבְרָהָם לְגַבֵּי קֻדְשָׁא בְּרִיךְ הוּא, מַה כְּתִיב, וַיֵּרָא ה' אֶל אַבְרָם. הָכָא אִתְגְּלֵי לֵיהּ, מַה דְּלָא הֲוָה יָדַע, הַהוּא חֵילָא עֲמִיקָא לְשַׁלְּטָא עַל

-41-

אַרְעָא. וּבְגִין כָּךְ וַיֵּרָא, מַה דַּהֲוָה מִתְכַּסֵּי מִנֵּיהּ.

68. "To the place of Shchem to the plain of Moreh" MEANS from one side to the other side, as was befitting. "And the Can'ani were then in the land," WHICH IS THE SECRET OF THE EVIL SERPENT. It has been explained that at that time the curse of the evil serpent dominated the land, and the world was cursed. As it is written: "Cursed be Canaan; a servant of servants shall he be to his brethren" (Beresheet 9:25), and also "you are cursed above all cattle" (Beresheet 3:14). When Abraham came close to the Holy One, blessed be He, it is written: "And Hashem appeared to Abram" (Beresheet 12:7). Now was revealed to him that which he did not know, because of the profound force that governed the land. Thus appeared to him what had been concealed from him, and he was able to understand it.

69. וּכְדֵין וַיִּבֶן שָׁם מִזְבֵּחַ לַה' הַנִּרְאֶה אֵלָיו, כֵּיוָן דַּאֲמַר לַה', מַהוּ הַנִּרְאֶה אֵלָיו. אֶלָּא הָכָא אִתְגְּלֵי לֵיהּ, הַהוּא דַרְגָּא, דְּשָׁלְטָא עַל אַרְעָא, וְעָאל בֵּיהּ, וְאִתְקַיִּים בֵּיהּ.

69. Then "he built an altar to Hashem, who had appeared to him." Why were the words "who had appeared to him" added? Because here the grade, which was in dominion over the land, appeared to him. He entered it, rose through it, and was established in it.

70. וַיַּעְתֵּק מִשָּׁם הָהָרָה, מִתַּמָּן יָדַע הַר ה'. וְכָלְּהוּ דַרְגִּין דִּנְטִיעִין בְּהַאי אֲתַר, וַיֵּט אָהֳלֹה. בְּהֵ"א כְּתִיב, פָּרִישׁ פְּרִישׁוּ, וְקַבֵּיל מַלְכוּ שְׁמַיָּא, בְּכָלְּהוּ דַרְגִּין דַּאֲחִידָן בֵּיהּ. וּכְדֵין יָדַע דְּקֻדְשָׁא בְּרִיךְ הוּא שַׁלִּיט עַל כֹּלָּא. וּכְדֵין בָּנָה מִזְבֵּחַ.

70. "And he moved from there to the mountain" (Beresheet 12:8), where he recognized the mountain of Hashem and all the grades planted on that place. "And pitched his tent," (Heb. *ohaloh*) WHICH ALLUDES TO THE NUKVA, AS 'OHALOH' IS NOT SPELLED WITH A *VAV* BUT WITH A *HEI*. Thus he spread a curtain and received the kingdom of heaven, along with all the grades that come from it. He then knew that the Holy One, blessed be He, rules over all, and he built an altar.

71. וּתְרֵין מַדְבְּחָן הֲוֹו, בְּגִין דְּהָכָא אִתְגְּלֵי לֵיהּ, דְּהָא קֻדְשָׁא בְּרִיךְ הוּא שַׁלִּיט עַל כֹּלָּא. וְיָדַע חָכְמָה עִלָּאָה, מַה דְּלָא הֲוָה יָדַע מִקַּדְמַת דְּנָא. וּבָנָה תְּרֵין מַדְבְּחָן, חַד לְדַרְגָּא דְּאִתְגַּלְיָא וְחַד לְדַרְגָּא דְּאִתְכַּסְיָא, תָּא חֲזֵי, דְּהָכֵי הֲוָה, בְּקַדְמֵיתָא כְּתִיב, וַיִּבֶן שָׁם מִזְבֵּחַ לַה' הַנִּרְאֶה אֵלָיו וְגו'. וּלְבָתַר כְּתִיב, וַיִּבֶן שָׁם מִזְבֵּחַ לַה' סְתָם, וְלָא כְתִיב הַנִּרְאֶה אֵלָיו. וְכֹלָּא רָזָא דְחָכְמָתָא אִיהוּ.

71. There were actually two altars, because here the Holy One, blessed be He, appeared to him as the ruler over all. He now acquired knowledge of the supernal wisdom, which he had not previously attained. He therefore built two altars – one for the grade that appeared WORLD, and one ALTAR to the grade still hidden. Come and behold: It is written first, "and there he built an altar to Hashem, who had appeared to him," and later just "and there he built an altar to Hashem," without adding "who appeared to him." And all this is according to the secret of Wisdom.

72. וּכְדֵין אִתְעַטַּר אַבְרָהָם מִדַּרְגָּא לְדַרְגָּא, עַד דְּסָלִיק לְדַרְגֵּיהּ, הה"ד וַיִּסַּע אַבְרָם הָלוֹךְ וְנָסוֹעַ הַנֶּגְבָּה. דָּא דָרוֹם, דְּהוּא חוּלָקֵיה דְּאַבְרָהָם. הָלוֹךְ וְנָסוֹעַ. דַּרְגָּא בָּתַר דַּרְגָּא עַד דְּסָלִיק לְדָרוֹם, וְתַמָּן אִתְקַשַּׁר כְּדְקָא יָאוֹת, וְסָלִיק לְדַרְגֵּיהּ לְדָרוֹם.

72. Abraham was then crowned from grade to grade, until he ascended to his own grade. This is the meaning of "And Abram journeyed, going on still toward the Negev." This is the south, BECAUSE HE WANTED TO ATTAIN THE GRADE OF CHESED OF ZEIR ANPIN CALLED SOUTH, Avraham's portion. THIS MEANS HE WAS DESTINED TO BECOME A CHARIOT TO THE SFIRAH OF CHESED OF ZEIR ANPIN, AND HENCE HE IS "going on still," grade after grade, until he reached the south, where he was properly attached, NAMELY, HE FIXED HIMSELF, SO HE COULD HOLD TO THE GRADE OF CHESED PERMANENTLY. HE THEN ascended to the south's grade, THAT IS, HE DESERVED TO BE A CHARIOT OF CHESED OF ZEIR ANPIN CALLED 'SOUTH.'

73. כֵּיוָן דְּאִתְעַטַּר אַבְרָהָם בְּדַרְגּוֹי, בְּאַרְעָא קַדִּישָׁא, וְעָאל בְּדַרְגָּא

קַדִּישָׁא, כְּדֵין מַה כְּתִיב, וַיְהִי רָעָב בָּאָרֶץ. דְּלָא הֲווֹ יָדְעֵי יְדִיעָה, לְקָרְבָא לְגַבֵּי דְקוּדְשָׁא בְּרִיךְ הוּא.

73. After Abraham was crowned with his grades in the Holy Land – THE SECRET OF THE MOCHIN FROM THE REVEALED WORLD, RACHEL, CALLED 'THE HOLY LAND' – and entered the holy grade – THAT IS, THE GRADE OF CHESED, AND THE ASPECT OF THE HIDDEN WORLD, LEAH – then it is written: "And there was famine in the land" (Beresheet 12:10), WHICH MEANS THAT they were not sure how to approach the Holy One, blessed be He, AS IN THE SECRET OF THE VERSE "NOT A FAMINE FOR BREAD, NOR A THIRST FOR WATER, BUT FOR HEARING THE WORDS OF HASHEM" (AMOS 8:11).

74. וַיְהִי רָעָב בָּאָרֶץ. דְּעַד כְּעָן לָא הֲוָה חֵילָא דְעַל אַרְעָא, יָהֵיב תּוּקְפָּא וּמְזוֹנָא עַל אַרְעָא, בְּגִין דְּעַד לָא אִתְקַדְּשַׁת וְלָא קָיְימָא בְּקִיּוּמָא. כֵּיוָן דְּחָמָא אַבְרָהָם, דְּהָא הַהוּא חֵילָא דִמְמַנָּא עַל אַרְעָא, לָא יָהֵיב תּוּקְפָּא וְחֵילָא קַדִּישָׁא כִּדְקָחֲזֵי, כְּדֵין וַיֵּרֶד אַבְרָם מִצְרַיְמָה לָגוּר שָׁם.

74. "And there was famine in the land" because until then the power ruling over the land did not supply the land with strength and nourishment. This occurred because THE NUKVA was not completely built and not PROPERLY established. When Abraham saw that the power appointed over the land did not supply it with might and holy strength as it merited, then "Abram went down to Egypt to sojourn there" (Beresheet 12:10).

75. מְנָא יָדַע אַבְרָהָם. דִּכְתִיב לְזַרְעֲךָ נָתַתִּי אֶת הָאָרֶץ הַזֹּאת. כְּדֵין יָדַע אַבְרָהָם, דְּהָא אַרְעָא לָא אִתְתַּקְנָא בְּתִקּוּנָא קַדִּישָׁא, אֶלָּא בְּדַרְגִּין קַדִּישִׁין, דְּיִפְּקוּן מִנֵּיהּ. וּכְדֵין יָדַע אַבְרָהָם, רָזָא דְחָכְמְתָא, דְּאַרְעָא לָא תִּתַּקַן בִּקְדוּשָׁה, אֶלָּא כִּדְאֲמָרָן.

75. IT IS ASKED: How did Abraham know THAT THE LAND, THE NUKVA, WAS STILL LACKING CORRECTION? From the verse, "To your seed I will give this land." IT DID NOT SAY, 'TO YOU AND YOUR SEED WILL I GIVE

THIS LAND.' Abraham then knew that the only way to amend the land was through the holy grades of his descendants. THEREFORE, IT IS WRITTEN: "TO YOUR SEED I WILL GIVE THIS LAND," AND NOT TO HIMSELF. Abraham then understood the secret of Wisdom, WHEREFORE the land will not be properly mended in holiness, except as we have said, HE THEREFORE WENT DOWN TO EGYPT, FROM THERE TO CORRECT THAT WHICH WAS LACKING.

גִּלָּיוֹן

76. קֻדְשָׁא בְּרִיךְ הוּא רָמִיז חָכְמְתָא עִלָּאָה, בְּאַבְרָהָם וּבְיִצְחָק. אַבְרָהָם דָּא נִשְׁמָתָא לְנִשְׁמָתָא, וְאִיהִי נְשָׁמָה דָּא הִיא שָׂרָה. לוֹט דָּא הוּא נָחָשׁ, וּבַת זוּגֵיהּ דְּהַהוּא סמא"ל. רוּחַ קַדִּישָׁא דָּא יִצְחָק. נֶפֶשׁ קַדִּישָׁא דָּא רִבְקָה. יֵצֶר הָרָע, דָּא רוּחַ הַבְּהֵמָה, וְעַל דָּא אֲמַר שְׁלֹמֹה בְּחָכְמָתֵיהּ, מִי יוֹדֵעַ רוּחַ בְּנֵי הָאָדָם הָעוֹלָה הִיא וגו'. נֶפֶשׁ הַבַּהֲמִית, דָּא נֶפֶשׁ מִסִּטְרָא דְּיֵצֶר הָרָע.

Gilayon (Interpolation)

76. The Holy One, blessed be He, alluded to the supernal Wisdom through Abraham and Isaac; Abraham is the Neshamah of Neshamah, NAMELY THE LIGHT OF CHAYAH. Sarah is the Neshamah, and Lot is the serpent, the spouse of Samael. The holy Ruach is Isaac; the Holy Nefesh is Rivkah. The Evil Inclination is the bestial Nefesh. And concerning this King Solomon said in his wisdom, "Who knows whether the spirit of man goes upwards, and the spirit of the beast goes downwards" (Kohelet 3:21). The bestial Nefesh is the Nefesh that comes from the side of the Evil Inclination.

77. וְעַל דָּא אָמְרוּ דְּאִיהִי נִשְׁמָתָא לְנִשְׁמָתָא, אִתְעֲרַא לְגַבְרָא בְּיִרְאָה וּבְחָכְמְתָא. נִשְׁמָתָא אִתְעֲרַא לְאִינִישׁ בְּבִינָה. הה"ד וַיֹּאמֶר לָאָדָם הֵן יִרְאַת ה' הִיא חָכְמָה וגו'. נִשְׁמָתָא אִתְעֲרֵי בִּתְשׁוּבָה, דְּאִתְקְרֵי בִּינָה, וְאִקְרֵי שָׂרָה. וְרוּחַ הוּא הַקּוֹל וְאִתְקְרֵי דַעַת, וְאִתְעֲרֵי לְאִינִישׁ דִּי סָלִיק קָלֵיהּ בְּאוֹרַיְתָּא וְאִתְקְרֵי תּוֹרָה שֶׁבִּכְתָב, וְנֶפֶשׁ הַשִּׂכְלִית אִתְעָר מִנֵּיהּ עוֹבָדִין טָבִין.

77. And this is what they meant by saying that the Neshamah of Neshamah rests upon a person who feels awe and has Wisdom, MEANING THAT IT IS RECEIVED FROM THE SFIRAH OF CHOCHMAH WITH WISDOM AND AWE. The Neshamah reaches a person in Binah, as it is written: "And to man He said: Behold the fear of Hashem, that is wisdom (Heb. *Chochmah*)" (Iyov 28:28). THEREFORE THE NESHAMAH OF NESHAMAH COMES TO A PERSON ONLY THROUGH AWE AND WISDOM. The Neshamah comes to a person through repentance, which is called 'Binah' and 'Sarah'. The Ruach is called 'the voice', and is also called '*Da'at.*' And this is drawn down to a person who raises his voice in Torah. THE RUACH IS also called the written Torah, and all the positive deeds come from the mental Nefesh.

78. וּבְדוּגְמָא דָא, בָּרָא גוּפָא, מֵאַרְבַּע יְסוֹדוֹת: אֵשׁ, וְרוּחַ, וְעָפָר, וּמַיִם. כְּגַוּוֹנָא דְהוּא נִשְׁמָתָא לְנִשְׁמָתָא, נְשָׁמָה, וְרוּחַ, וְנֶפֶשׁ. מַיִם דָּא דְּכַר, וְדָא הוּא מַיִם מְתִיקֵי דִקְדוּשָׁה, וְאִית מַיִם הַמְאָרְרִים, דְּאִינּוּן יֵצֶר הָרָע. אִית אֶשָּׁא קַדִּישָׁא נוּקְבָא, וְאִית אֶשָּׁא נוּכְרָאָה, אֵשׁ זָרָה. וְעַל דָּא כְּתִיב, וְאַל יָבֹא בְּכָל עֵת אֶל הַקֹּדֶשׁ. דְּאִיהִי נוּקְבָתָא מִן יֵצֶר הָרָע. רוּחַ קַדִּישָׁא אִיהוּ דְּכַר, אִית רוּחַ מְסָאֲבָא, דָּא יֵצֶר הָרָע, שֶׁנֶּאֱמַר כִּי מִשֹּׁרֶשׁ נָחָשׁ יֵצֵא צֶפַע. אִית עָפָר קַדִּישָׁא, וְאִית עָפָר מְסָאֲבָא.

78. In a similar way, the Holy One, blessed be He, created the body from the four elements – namely, Fire, Air, Earth and Water, which correspond to the Neshamah of Neshamah, the Neshamah, the Ruach, and the Nefesh. SO THE NESHAMAH OF NESHAMAH IS THE SECRET OF WATER; THE NESHAMAH IS THE SECRET OF FIRE; THE RUACH IS THE SECRET OF AIR; AND THE NEFESH IS THE SECRET OF EARTH. Water – which is the aspect of the male – REFERS TO THE NESHAMAH OF NESHAMAH THAT COMES FROM CHOCHMAH AND refers to the sweet waters of holiness. The contrasting bitter waters represent the Evil Inclination, WHICH IS THE SECRET OF SAMAEL. The holy fire – which is the aspect of the female – REFERS TO THE NESHAMAH THAT COMES FROM BINAH. IN CONTRAST, there is the foreign fire, to which the words "that he come not at all times to the holy place" (Vayikra 16:2) apply. And this is the female of the Evil Inclination, NAMELY THE SERPENT, WHICH IS THE NUKVA OF SAMAEL. The holy Ruach is the aspect of the Male – SIMILAR TO THE RUACH THAT COMES FROM THE SFIRAH OF *DA'AT.* IT CONTRASTS WITH the unholy

Ruach, which is the Evil Inclination. As it is written: "for out of the serpent's root shall come forth a viper" (Yeshayah 14:29). THIS REFERS TO THE BESTIAL RUACH, WHICH IS CALLED A 'VIPER', AND IS AN OFFSPRING OF THE SERPENT OF THE UNHOLY SIDE, NAMELY BINAH OF THE UNHOLINESS. THIS IS WHY THE VERSE SAYS: "OUT OF THE SERPENT'S ROOT SHALL COME FORTH A VIPER." There is holy Earth, SIMILAR TO THE NEFESH THAT COMES FROM THE LEFT SIDE OF DA'AT. AND IN CONTRAST, there is an Unholy Earth, NAMELY THE BESTIAL NEFESH, WHICH COMES FROM THE EVIL INCLINATION.

79. וְעַל דָּא, נִשְׁמָתָא דְּאִיהִי תְּשׁוּבָה, דִּתְקִיפַת בֵּיהּ בְּהַהוּא נָחָשׁ, לְתַבְּרָא לֵיהּ, בְּשִׁעְבּוּדָא דִּתְשׁוּבָה, וְאַמְשִׁיךְ לֵיהּ לְבָתֵּי כְנֵסִיּוֹת וּלְבָתֵּי מִדְרָשׁוֹת וְאִינּוּן אַרְבַּע יְסוֹדֵי מִתְפַּשְּׁטִין לְכ״ב אַתְוָון, אחה״ע, בומ״ף, גיכ״ק, דטלנ״ת, זסשר״ץ.

עַד כָּאן גִּלְיוֹן.

79. Therefore, the Neshamah, which is repentance, NAMELY BINAH, attacks and overcomes the serpent by the power of enslavement that belongs to repentance. And it drags the serpent to the synagogue and the learning academies. And the four elements THAT ARE THE FOUR ASPECTS OF CHOCHMAH, BINAH, TIFERET AND MALCHUT, expand to 22 letters, THAT COME FROM THE FIVE VOWELS OF ARTICULATION OF THE MOUTH *Aleph-Chet-Hei-Ayin* FROM THE THROAT; *Bet-Vav-Mem-Pe* FROM THE LIPS; *Gimel-Yud-Caf-Kof* FROM THE PALATE; *Dalet-Tet-Lamed-Nun-Tav* FROM THE TONGUE; AND *Zayin-Samech-Shin-Resh-Tzadik* FROM THE TEETH. THESE FIVE VOWELS OF ARTICULATION OF THE MOUTH ARE EQUIVALENT TO KETER, CHOCHMAH, BINAH, TIFERET, AND MALCHUT, WHICH ARE THE FOUR ELEMENTS OF WATER FIRE, AIR, AND EARTH. THIS IS WHY HE SAYS THAT THE FOUR ELEMENTS, WHICH ARE THE SECRET OF THE FIVE VOWELS OF ARTICULATION OF THE MOUTH, EXPAND TO 22 LETTERS.

(End of the Gilayon)

סִתְרֵי תּוֹרָה

80. וַיַּעֲבֹר אַבְרָם בָּאָרֶץ עַד מְקוֹם שְׁכֶם. דָּא בֵּי כְּנִישְׁתָּא, אֲתַר דְּדִיּוּרָא

דִּשְׁכִינְתָּא תַּמָּן, כְּד"א וַאֲנִי נָתַתִּי לְךָ שְׁכֶם אֶחָד. דָּא שְׁכִינְתָּא דְּאִתְחֲזֵי
לֵיהּ, הוֹאִיל וְאִתְקְרֵי צַדִּיק, דְּהָא צֶדֶק לָאו דִּיּוּרָהּ אֶלָּא בַּהֲדֵי צַדִּיק,
וְדָא הוּא עַד מְקוֹם שְׁכֶם. עַד אֵלוֹן מוֹרֶה. אֵלּוּ בָּתֵּי מִדְרָשׁוֹת, דְּאוֹלְפִין
וּמוֹרִים תַּמָּן תּוֹרָה בְּרַבִּים.

Sitrei Torah (Concealed Torah)

80. The verse, "And Abram passed through the land to the place of Shchem," alludes to the synagogue, the place where the Shechinah resides. As it is written: "Moreover I have given to you one portion (Heb. *shchem*)" (Beresheet 48:22), SO SHCHEM is the Shechinah, which is fit for JOSEPH, as he is called 'righteous.' Because righteousness, WHICH IS THE SHECHINAH, does not reside anywhere else but in the righteous, WHO IS JOSEPH. This is the meaning of "to the place of Shchem," REFERRING THE PLACE OF THE SHECHINAH – TO THE SYNAGOGUE. "To the plain of Moreh" alludes to Torah-learning academies, where they teach and instruct Torah to the public.

81. וְהַכְּנַעֲנִי אָז בָּאָרֶץ. כְּדֵין אִתְבַּסַּם וְאִתְתַּקַן יֵצֶר הָרָע בְּגוּפָא בְּעַל
כָּרְחֵיהּ. דְּסַגִּיאִין שְׁמָהָן אִית לֵיהּ, וּבְגִינֵי כָּךְ אִדְכַּר בִּשְׁמָהָן סַגִּיאִין. אָז
בָּאָרֶץ. וַדַּאי וְאִתְכַּפְיָא בְּהַאי, בְּגִין דִּכְדֵין אִיהוּ גּוּפָא, בְּזִמְנָא דְּלָא
אִתְעֲבַר מִנֵּיהּ הַהוּא נָחָשׁ כָּל כָּךְ, בְּגִין דִּבְקוּתָא דְּגוּפָא, כְּדֵין הַכְּנַעֲנִי
אָז בָּאָרֶץ. אַמַּאי אִקְרֵי כְּנַעֲנִי, דְּאַסְחַר גּוּפָא לְדִינִין בִּישִׁין.

81. "And the Cna'ani was then in the land" means that the Evil Inclination was sweetened and amended in spite of itself, in the body WHICH IS CALLED THE LAND. DO NOT BE SURPRISED THAT THE EVIL INCLINATION IS CALLED 'CNA'ANI', because it has many names. "Was then in the land" is certainly against its will, AS IT IS STILL IN THE BODY, WHEN THE SOUL, WHICH IS THE SECRET OF ABRAM, SHINES THROUGH IT. The serpent is not yet completely removed from the body. Therefore, because the body is still attached TO THE SERPENT, the "Cna'ani was then in the land." Why is it called the "Cna'ani?" Because it surrounds (Aramaic aschar) the body with evil judgments. AS THE WORD CNA'ANI MEANS A MERCHANT (HEB. SOCHER), AS IT IS WRITTEN: "HIS TRUTH SHALL BE YOUR SHIELD AND

BUCKLER (HEB. *SOCHERAH*)" (TEHILIM 91:4).

82. וְנִשְׁמָתָא קַיְימָא בְּהַאי עָלְמָא כַּדְקָא יָאוֹת, בְּגִין לְמִזְכֵּי בָּהּ לְבָתַר כַּד נָפְקַת מֵהַאי עָלְמָא, אִי זַכָּאת סַלְקָא לְאַתְרָה דְּנָפְקַת מִתַּמָּן, דִּכְתִיב אֶל מְקוֹם הַמִּזְבֵּחַ אֲשֶׁר עָשָׂה שָׁם בָּרִאשׁוֹנָה, וּכְתִיב אֶל הַמָּקוֹם אֲשֶׁר הָיָה שָׁם אָהֳלֹה בַּתְּחִלָּה. אָהֳלֹה בְּהֵ"א.

82. The soul is properly established in this world, so that we can merit receiving it after it leaves the world. If a soul has merit, it returns to the place from whence it came. As it is written: "To the place of the altar, which he had made there in the beginning" (Beresheet 13:4), and "to the place where his tent (Heb. *ohaloh*) had been at the beginning..." (Ibid. 3). *Ohaloh* is spelled with an additional *Hei*, WHICH REPRESENTS THE SHECHINAH.

83. וְהַשְׁתָּא אִיהִי קַיְימָא בֵּין לְסַלְקָא לְעֵילָא, וּבֵין לְנַחֲתָא לְתַתָּא. בֵּין בֵּית אֵל וּבֵין הָעָי. אִי זַכָּאת, סַלְקָא אֶל מְקוֹם הַמִּזְבֵּחַ אֲשֶׁר עָשָׂה שָׁם וְגוֹ'. מַאן עָשָׂה, וּמַאן מִזְבֵּחַ. אֶלָּא, אֲשֶׁר עָשָׂה שָׁם, דָּא קֻדְשָׁא בְּרִיךְ הוּא. דְּאִיהוּ עָבַד תַּמָּן הַאי מִזְבֵּחַ, וְאַתְקֵין לָהּ עַל תְּרֵיסַר אַבְנִין, לְמִסְפַּר שִׁבְטֵי בְנֵי יַעֲקֹב אֲשֶׁר הָיָה דְבַר ה' אֵלָיו לֵאמֹר יִשְׂרָאֵל יִהְיֶה שְׁמֶךָ וַדַּאי.

83. Now, IN THIS WORLD, it is LOCATED IN THE MIDDLE – between rising upward TO THE PLACE FROM WHENCE IT CAME, and descending downward TO THE PLACE OF PUNISHMENTS. IN OTHER WORDS, between *Bethel*, WHICH IS UP, and *Ay*, WHICH IS DOWN AT THE PLACE OF PUNISHMENTS. If it has merit, it will rise up "to the place of the altar, which he had made..." SO ACCORDING TO THIS, HE ASKS: Who is 'he' who 'had made,' and what is 'the altar'? AND HE REPLIES: "...he had made there" applies to the Holy One, blessed be He, who had made that altar, WHICH IS THE SHECHINAH, and established it upon twelve stones, "according to the number of the tribes of the sons of Jacob, to whom the word of Hashem came, saying, Yisrael shall be your name" (I Melachim 18:31), for sure.

84. וּמִזְבֵּחַ דָּא עָשָׂה שָׁם בָּרִאשׁוֹנָה, כַּד אִתְבְּרֵי עָלְמָא עִלָּאָה טְמִירָא

לְכָל עָלְמִין, וּמִיכָאֵל כַּהֲנָא רַבָּא, קָאֵים וּמַקְרִיב עֲלָהּ, קָרְבְּנִין דְּנִשְׁמָתִין. כֵּיוָן דְּנִשְׁמָתָא סָלְקָא תַּמָּן מַה כְּתִיב, וַיִּקְרָא שָׁם אַבְרָם בְּשֵׁם ה׳. נִשְׁמָתָא קָארֵי תַּמָּן, וְאִצְרִירָא בִּצְרוֹרָא דְחַיֵּי.

84. And this altar, WHICH IS THE SHECHINAH, "he had made there at first," when the upper world, which is concealed from all other worlds, was created. And Michael – THE ANGEL, the High Priest – stands high and sacrifices upon it the offerings of the souls OF THE RIGHTEOUS. And since the soul ascends there and rises up AS AN OFFERING, it is written: "and there Abram called in the name of Hashem" (Beresheet 13:4). The soul calls there IN THE NAME OF HASHEM and is attached to the bundle of life.

85. וְכָל דָּא אִי זַכָּאָה בְּהַאי עָלְמָא, לְאַתְקָנָא גּוּפָא כְּדְקָא יָאוֹת, וּלְאִכַּפְיָא תּוּקְפָא דְּהַהוּא לָטַיָּיא, עַד דְּאִתְפָּרְשָׁא מִנֵּיהּ. מַה כְּתִיב, וַיְהִי רִיב בֵּין רוֹעֵי מִקְנֵה אַבְרָם וּבֵין רוֹעֵי מִקְנֵה לוֹט. דִּבְכָל יוֹמָא וְיוֹמָא, בְּהַאי עָלְמָא, אִינוּן סִיעָן וּמַנְהִיגִין דְּנִשְׁמָתָא, וְאִינוּן סִיעָן וּמַנְהִיגִין דְּיֵצֶר הָרָע, אִינוּן בְּקַטְרוּגָא, מְקַטְרְגִין אִלֵּין בְּאִלֵּין, וְכָל שַׁיְיפִין דְּגוּפָא בְּצַעֲרָא בֵּינַיְיהוּ, בֵּין נִשְׁמָתָא, וְהַהוּא נָחָשׁ, דְּקָא מַגִּיחִין קְרָבָא בְּכָל יוֹמָא.

85. All this happens if THE SOUL merited to amend the body in this world and overcome the power of that cursed being, NAMELY THE EVIL INCLINATION THAT IS CALLED LOT, until it is separated from it. As it is written: "And there was strife between the herdsmen of Avram's cattle (WHICH IS THE SOUL) and the herdsmen of Lot's cattle, (WHICH IS THE EVIL INCLINATION)" (Beresheet 13:7). Because in this world, on each and every day, those camps and rulers from the side of the soul are in strife with the camps and rulers from the side of the body, and they fight with each other – while all the parts of the body are trapped in agony between them, between the soul and the serpent, between those forces that fight each other every day.

86. מַה כְּתִיב, וַיֹּאמֶר אַבְרָם אֶל לוֹט. נִשְׁמָתָא אֲהַדְרָא לְגַבֵּי יֵצֶר הָרָע, וַאֲמַר לֵיהּ אַל נָא תְהִי מְרִיבָה בֵּינִי וּבֵינֶיךָ וּבֵין רוֹעַי וּבֵין רוֹעֶיךָ, סִטְרִין

דִּילִי וְסִטְרִין דִּילָךְ. כִּי אֲנָשִׁים אַחִים אֲנָחְנוּ. יֵצֶר טוֹב וְיִצה"ר קְרֵיבִין דָּא בְּדָא, דָּא לִימִינָא וְדָא לִשְׂמָאלָא.

86. Thus it is written: "And Abram said to Lot" (Beresheet 13:8) that the soul answered the Evil Inclination, "Let there be no strife, I pray you, between me and you, and between my herdsmen and your herdsmen." IN OTHER WORDS, between my camps and your camps "for we are brethren"; because the Good Inclination and the Evil Inclination are close to each other, the one to man's right and the other to his left. THE EVIL INCLINATION IS TO HIS LEFT AND THE GOOD INCLINATION TO HIS RIGHT.

87. הֲלֹא כָל הָאָרֶץ לְפָנֶיךָ הִפָּרֶד נָא מֵעָלַי. סַגִּיאִין חַיָּיבַיָא אִינוּן בְּעָלְמָא, זִיל וְשׁוּט אֲבַתְרַיְיהוּ, וְאִתְפְּרַשׁ מֵעַמִּי. אִם הַשְּׂמֹאל וְאֵימִינָה וְגוֹ'. וְאוֹכַח לֵיהּ, וְאָעֵיק לֵיהּ, בְּכַמָּה קְרָבִין דְּעָבִיד בַּהֲדֵיהּ בְּכָל יוֹמָא, עַד דִּכְתִיב וַיִּפָּרְדוּ אִישׁ מֵעַל אָחִיו.

87. "Is not the whole land before you? Separate yourself, pray you, from me..." (Ibid. 9). There are a lot of wicked men in the world; go and chase after them and leave me alone. "If you will go to the left, then I will go to the right..."; it reproves and annoys it with many fights and arguments every day, until, as it is written: "and they separated themselves the one from the other" (Ibid. 11).

88. כֵּיוָן דְּמִתְפָּרְשִׁין דָּא מִן דָּא, מַה כְּתִיב, אַבְרָם יָשַׁב בְּאֶרֶץ כְּנַעַן. אִתְיַשְּׁבַת נִשְׁמָתָא בְּאִינוּן צַדִּיקַיָּיא, בְּיִשׁוּבָא טַב בִּשְׁלָם. וְלוֹט יָשַׁב בְּעָרֵי הַכִּכָּר, הַהוּא לְטַיָא מְקַטְרְגָא, אָזֵיל לְקַטְרְגָא, וּלְאִתְחַבְּרָא בַּאֲתַר דְּחַיָּיבַיָא תַּמָּן. דִּכְתִיב וַיֶּאֱהַל עַד סְדוֹם. מַה כְּתִיב בַּתְרֵיהּ, וְאַנְשֵׁי סְדוֹם רָעִים וְחַטָּאִים לַה' מְאֹד. תַּמָּן שַׁרְיָא וְשַׁוֵּי דִּיּוּרֵיהּ בֵּינַיְיהוּ, לְאִתְחַבְּרָא בְּהוֹ, לְאַסְטָאָה לוֹן וּלְאוֹבָדָא לוֹן, בְּעוֹבָדִין בִּישִׁין.

88. Since they have separated themselves from each other, it is written: "Abram dwelt in the land of Canaan" (Beresheet 13:12), WHICH MEANS THAT the soul has settled among the righteous in a good and peaceful settlement. "And Lot dwelt in the cities of the plain" MEANS THAT the cursed adversary went to prosecute and join the wicked in their dwellings. As it is written: "and pitched his tent toward Sodom," followed by: "And the men of Sodom were wicked and were sinners before Hashem exceedingly" (Beresheet 13:13). There he dwelt and set his residence among them; he joined them, so that he could deceive them and destroy them by evil deeds.

89. כֵּיוָן דְּאִשְׁתְּאָרַת נִשְׁמָתָא בְּלָא מְקַטְרְגָא, וְאִתְדְּכֵי גּוּפָא מֵהַהוּא זוּהֲמָא, מִיָּד קֻדְשָׁא בְּרִיךְ הוּא אַשְׁרֵי דִּיּוּרֵיהּ בַּהֲדֵיהּ, וְיָרִית אַחְסַנְתָּא עִלָּאָה וְתַתָּאָה, וְאִית לֵיהּ נַיְיחָא בֵּין צַדִּיקַיָּיא, וְהַהוּא לָטְיָא בֵּין אִינּוּן רְשִׁיעַיָּיא, חָטָאן בַּהֲדֵיהּ עַד דְּלָא הֲוָה פּוּרְקָנָא לְחוֹבַיְיהוּ.

89. As the adversary leaves the soul and the body is purified from that defilement, the Holy One, blessed be He, immediately takes up residence beside him, and he inherits the upper and lower portion and is delighted among the righteous. While that cursed one – REFERRING TO LOT – is among the wicked and they sin together with him until finally they cannot be redeemed from their sins.

90. מַה כְּתִיב וַיִּשְׁמַע אַבְרָם כִּי נִשְׁבָּה אָחִיו. וַיִּשְׁמַע אַבְרָם, דָּא נִשְׁמָתָא, דְּאִשְׁתְּאָרַת בְּדִכְיוּ בְּגוּפָא. כִּי נִשְׁבָּה אָחִיו, דָּא יֵצֶר הָרַע, דְּנִשְׁבָּה בֵּין אִינּוּן חַיָּיבַיָּא בְּחוֹבִין סַגִּיאִין. וַיָּרֶק אֶת חֲנִיכָיו יְלִידֵי בֵיתוֹ. אִלֵּין אִינּוּן צַדִּיקַיָּא דְּלָעָאן בְּאוֹרַיְיתָא דְּאִינּוּן שַׁיְיפֵי דְגוּפָא, זְרִיזִין לְמֶיהַךְ בַּהֲדֵיהּ י"ח וּשְׁלֹשׁ מֵאוֹת, אִלֵּין רְמ"ח שַׁיְיפִין דְּגוּפָא, וְשִׁבְעִין דְּרָזָא דְנִשְׁמָתָא, דְּנָפְקָא מִתַּמָּן. בְּכֹלָּא אִזְדְּרַז לְמֵהַךְ תַּמָּן, לְגַבֵּי אִינּוּן חַיָּיבַיָּא, לַאֲתָבָא לוֹן מֵחוֹבַיְיהוֹן.

90. It is then written: "And when Abram heard that his brother was taken captive..." (Beresheet 14:14). "And when Abram heard" refers to the soul which remained purified in the body. "That his brother was taken captive" refers to the Evil Inclination, which was taken captive among the wicked by their innumerable sins. "And he armed his trained servants, born in his own house," means the righteous men who learn Torah and are the limbs of the body. THE LIMBS OF THE BODY ARE LIKENED TO RIGHTEOUS MEN WHO LEARN THE TORAH, armed to join him. They number three hundred and eighteen – 248 limbs of the body and seventy that belong to the secret of the soul. THESE CORRESPOND TO THE SEVEN SFIROT OF ZEIR ANPIN, IN WHICH EACH ONE IS THE NUMBER TEN. The soul comes from THE SEVEN SFIROT OF ZEIR ANPIN. SO 248 PLUS SEVENTY EQUALS THREE HUNDRED AND EIGHTEEN. He was armed with all these to confront those sinners – to make them repent and atone for their sins.

91. מַה כְּתִיב, וַיִּרְדֹּף עַד דָּן. רָדִיף אֲבַתְרַיְיהוּ, וְאוֹדַע לוֹן דִּינָא דְּהַהוּא עָלְמָא, וְעוֹנָשָׁא דְּגֵיהִנֹם, וְלָא יָהִיב דְּמִיכוּ לְעֵינֵיה, בִּימָמָא וּבְלֵילְיָא, עַד דְּאוֹכַח לוֹן לְאִינוּן חַיָּיבִין, וְאָתֵיב לוֹן בִּתְיוּבְתָּא לְגַבֵּי קֻדְשָׁא בְּרִיךְ הוּא. מַה כְּתִיב וַיָּשֶׁב אֶת כָּל הָרְכוּשׁ, אָתֵיב לוֹן בִּתְיוּבְתָּא שְׁלֵימָא כִּדְקָא יָאוֹת.

91. Then, it is written: "and pursued them to Dan (also, judge)." This means he pursued them and told them about the judgment of the World of Truth and the punishment of Gehenom. And he did not allow his eyes to sleep, neither during the day nor at night, until he reproved the sinners and brought them to atone and ask for forgiveness from the Holy One, blessed be He. It is written: "And he brought back all the goods..." (Beresheet 13:16), because he brought them to atone completely for their sins!

92. וְגַם אֶת לוֹט אָחִיו וגו', אֲפִילוּ לְהַהוּא יֵצֶר הָרַע אַתְקִיף בַּהֲדֵיה, עַד דְּאַכְפְּיֵיה בְּעַל כָּרְחֵיה וְאַמְתִיק לֵיה, כִּדְקָא חֲזֵי. כֹּלָּא אָתֵיב בִּתְיוּבְתָּא שְׁלֵימָתָא כִּדְקָא יָאוֹת, בְּגִין דְּלָא אִשְׁתְּכַךְ יְמָמָא וְלֵילְיָא, עַד דְּאוֹכַח לוֹן וּרְדַף לוֹן עַל הַהוּא חוֹבָא דְּחָאבוּ, עַד דְּתָאבוּ בִּתְיוּבְתָּא שְׁלֵימָתָא כִּדְקָחֲזוּ.

92. The words "And also brought again his brother Lot" mean that he even attacked that Evil Inclination, WHICH IS CALLED LOT, until he overcame it by force against its will and weakened it, as should be. He brought them all to wholeheartedly atone for their sins, as should properly be. He reproved and reprimanded them day and night for every single sin they performed, until they repented completely.

93. אַהֲדַרְנָא לְמִלֵּי קַדְמָאֵי דְּפָרְשָׁתָא. כְּתִיב מְצָאוּנִי הַשּׁוֹמְרִים

הַסּוֹבְבִים בָּעִיר וגו', תְּנַן, עָבַד קֻדְשָׁא בְּרִיךְ הוּא, יְרוּשְׁלֵם לְעֵילָא, כְּגַוְונָא דִירוּשְׁלֵם דִּלְתַתָּא, בְּשׁוּרִין, וּמִגְדָּלִין, וּפִתְחִין פְּתִיחִין. וְאִינוּן חוֹמוֹת דְּתַמָּן, אִית עֲלַיְיהוּ נָטְרִין, דְּנָטְרֵי תַּרְעֵי דְּאִינוּן חוֹמוֹת, דִּכְתִיב עַל חוֹמוֹתַיִךְ יְרוּשְׁלַם הִפְקַדְתִּי שׁוֹמְרִים וגו'. וּמִיכָאֵל כַּהֲנָא רַבָּא, עִלָּאָה מִכֻּלְּהוּ נָטְרֵי תַּרְעֵי דְּאִינוּן חוֹמוֹת.

93. Let us return to the first subject of this passage, where it is written: "The watchmen that go about the city found me..." (Shir Hashirim 5:7). We have learned that the Holy One, blessed be He, constructed the celestial Jerusalem, NAMELY BINAH, TO BE just like the terrestrial Jerusalem; NAMELY MALCHUT, with walls, towers, and open gates. And those walls there – THE WALLS IN BINAH AND MALCHUT – have guards stationed upon them. As it is written: "I have set watchmen upon your walls, Jerusalem..." (Yeshayah 62:6). And Michael, the High Priest, is the highest of the gate watchmen.

94. נִשְׁמָה כַּד נָפְקַת מֵהַאי עָלְמָא, אִי זַכָּאת, עָאלַת בְּגִנְתָּא דְעֵדֶן דְּאַרְעָא, דְּנָטַע קֻדְשָׁא בְּרִיךְ הוּא לְרוּחֵיהוֹן דְּצַדִּיקַיָּיא, כְּגַוְונָא דְּהַהוּא גִּנְתָּא דְּעֵדֶן דִּלְעֵילָא, וְתַמָּן כָּל צַדִּיקַיָּא דְּעָלְמָא.

94. When the soul leaves this world, MEANING AS A PERSON DIES, if that person has merit, the soul enters the earthly Garden of Eden, which the Holy One, blessed be He, planted for the spirits of the righteous MEN OF EARTH, WHICH IS MALCHUT. Similarly, He created the Garden of Eden on high, WHICH IS BINAH, where all the righteous people of the world dwell.

95. וְכַד נִשְׁמָתָא נָפְקַת מֵהַאי עָלְמָא, עָאלַת בְּמַעַרְתָּא דְּכַפֶּלְתָּא, דְּתַמָּן אִיהִי פִּתְחָא דְּגַן עֵדֶן. פָּגְעַת בְּאָדָם הָרִאשׁוֹן, וּבְאִינוּן אֲבָהָן דְּתַמָּן, אִי זַכָּאת אִיהִי, חָדָאן בָּה, וּפַתְחִין לָה פִּתְחִין, וְעָאלַת. וְאִי לָא, דַּחְיָין לָה לְבַר. וְאִי זַכָּאת, עָיִילַת לְגִנְתָּא דְּעֵדֶן, כֵּיוָן דְּעָיְילַת, יָתְבָא תַּמָּן בְּגִנְתָּא, וְאִתְלַבְּשַׁת תַּמָּן, בִּלְבוּשָׁא דִּדְיוֹקְנָא דְּהַאי עָלְמָא, וְאִתְעַדְּנַת תַּמָּן.

-54-

95. So when the soul leaves this world, it FIRST enters the cave of Machpelah, where the opening leading to the Garden of Eden is located. Then it meets Adam and the Patriarchs who are there. If the soul is meritorious, they rejoice with it and open all the openings so the soul can enter them. If not, it is pushed outside. If it has merit it enters the Garden and sits there, it clothes itself with a garment in the image of this world and enjoys itself.

12. The three levels: Nefesh, Ruach, and Neshamah

A Synopsis

There are three levels of soul that we can learn to achieve throughout life. We are born into this world with the lowest level of soul. The next two higher levels are attained by way of spiritual accomplishments that we achieve in the course of life.

The Relevance of this Passage

Left to his own devices, man would remain enslaved to the primal urges and impulses of the body, the lowest level of soul. Therefore, the energy of this passage infuses us with the strength to help us climb towards the next level of soul.

96. סִתְרָא דְּסִתְרִין, לַחֲכִימֵי לִבָּא אִתְמְסַר, תְּלַת דַּרְגִּין אִינּוּן, דַּאֲחִידָן דָּא בְּדָא, וְאִלֵּין אִינּוּן: נֶפֶשׁ, רוּחַ, וּנְשָׁמָה. נֶפֶשׁ, אִיהוּ חֵילָא, דְּגוּפָא אִתְבְּנֵי מִנֵּיהּ. דְּכַד בַּר נָשׁ אִתְּעַר בְּהַאי עָלְמָא, לְאִזְדַּוְּוגָא בְּנוּקְבֵיהּ, כָּל שַׁיְיפֵי מִסְתַּכְּמֵי וּמִתְתַּקְנֵי לְאִתְהַנָאָה תַּמָּן, וְהַהוּא נֶפֶשׁ וּרְעוּתָא דִּילֵיהּ, אִסְתַּכַּם בֵּיהּ בְּהַהוּא עוֹבָדָא, וּמָשִׁיךְ לֵיהּ לְהַהוּא נֶפֶשׁ, וְאָעִיל לֵיהּ תַּמָּן בְּהַהוּא זַרְעָא דְּאוֹשִׁיד.

96. The secret of all secrets is passed on to those who are wise in their hearts. There are three levels that are attached to each other, and they are Nefesh, Ruach, and Neshamah. Nefesh is the force from which the body is built. When a man is aroused in this world to mate with his wife, all parts of the body agree on this and are prepared to receive enjoyment from it. Then the Nefesh and the desire of the person indulge willingly in that act. The Nefesh is drawn down and enters the sperm that comes forth.

97. וּמִגּוֹ רְעוּתָא וּמְשִׁיכוּ דְּנַפְשָׁא, דְּמָשִׁיךְ תַּמָּן, אִתְמְשַׁךְ חֵילָא אוֹחֲרָא תַּמָּן, מֵאִינּוּן דַּרְגִּין דְּאִתְקְרוּן אִישִׁים. וְעָאל כֹּלָּא בְּמְשִׁיכוּ דְּהַהוּא זַרְעָא, וְאִתְבְּנֵי מִנֵּיהּ גּוּפָא. וְדָא אִיהוּ חֵילָא קַדְמָאָה תַּתָּאָה, דְּאִינּוּן תְּלַת.

97. From the combination of that desire and the Nefesh, another power is drawn from the levels of the angels, who are called *Ishim* (people). They all

-56-

enter as the sperm flows, and the body is then built and constructed of them. This is the first and lowest power of the three levels.

98. וּבְגִין דְּהַאי נֶפֶשׁ אַקְרִיב, בְּדִבְקוּתָא וִיסוֹדָא דְגוּפָא, קַרְבְּנָא, דְּאִתְקְרֵיב לְכַפְּרָא עַל נִשְׁמָתָא, אִתְיְהִיבַת חוּלְקָא לְאִינוּן דַּרְגִּין דְּאִישִׁים. וּבְגִין דִּמְשִׁיכוּ דְּחוּלְקָא דְּהַהוּא נֶפֶשׁ אָתֵי מִנַּיְיהוּ. וְהַיְינוּ דִּכְתִיב אֶת קַרְבָּנִי לַחְמִי לְאִשַּׁי. בְּגִין דְּהוּא כַּפְּרָה דְּנֶפֶשׁ, נָטְלֵי חוּלְקֵיהוֹן. וְכַד מִית בַּר נָשׁ בְּהַאי עָלְמָא, הַהִיא נֶפֶשׁ לָא אִתְעֲדֵי מִן קַבְרָא לְעָלְמִין. וּבְחֵילָא דָּא, יָדְעֵי מֵתַיָּיא וּמִשְׁתָּעוּ דָּא עִם דָּא.

98. And because the Nefesh offers a sacrifice by attaching itself to the foundation of the body, which is offered as a sacrifice to atone for the Neshamah, then part of it is offered to those grades that are considered as Ishim. Because part of the Nefesh, THE RUACH OF THE NEFESH, is drawn down from them. As it is written: "My offering and my bread for my fire (Heb. *ishai*)..." (Bemidbar 28:2), WHICH MEANS TO THE ISHIM. So, because it is an offering THAT COMES FROM THE POWER of the Nefesh, the Ishim take their part as well. THEIR SHARE IS DETERMINED BY THE AMOUNT ENCLOTHED IN THE NEFESH THAT OFFERS THE SACRIFICE. And when one leaves this world, that Nefesh never leaves the grave. And because of the power OF THIS NEFESH THAT REMAINS IN THE GRAVE, the dead know and talk with each other.

99. רוּחַ, אִיהוּ דְּמְקַיֵּים לַנֶּפֶשׁ בְּהַאי עָלְמָא. וְאִיהוּ מְשִׁיכוּ דְּאִתְעָרוּתָא דְּנוּקְבָא לְגַבֵּי דְכוּרָא, כַּד אִינוּן בְּתֵיאוּבְתָּא חֲדָא, וּכְדֵין אִתְעָרַת לְגַבֵּי דְּכוּרָא בְּתֵיאוּבְתָּא דִּילָהּ, לְהַאי רוּחַ. כְּגַוְונָא דְּנוּקְבָא דִּלְתַתָּא אַשְׁדִּיאַת זַרְעָא בְּתֵיאוּבְתָּא לְגַבֵּי דְכוּרָא. וְסִתְרָא דָּא וְהָרוּחַ תָּשׁוּב אֶל הָאֱלֹקִים אֲשֶׁר נְתָנָהּ.

99. Ruach gives existence to the Nefesh in this world, AS IT DRAWS DOWN THE ABUNDANCE OF LIFE AND PASSES IT ON TO THE NEFESH. THIS IS THE MIDDLE LEVEL OF THE THREE. It is drawn by the arousal of the Nukva OF ATZILUT toward the male OF ATZILUT, when they are in a state of united passion, NAMELY, DURING THE ACT OF MATING. The female is aroused toward the male because of her passion to receive from him the LIGHT OF Ruach, just like a woman in this world who is inseminated by the power of her passion to RECEIVE FROM the man. And this is the secret of the words, "and the spirit (Ruach) shall return to the Elohim who gave it" (Kohelet 12:7). THIS MEANS THAT IT RETURNS TO THE NUKVA, WHICH IS CALLED BY THE NAME OF ELOHIM. AND EVEN THOUGH THE RUACH IS DRAWN FROM ZEIR ANPIN, WHICH IS CALLED YUD HEI VAV HEI, NEVERTHELESS, BECAUSE IT IS THE RESULT OF THE AROUSAL OF THE FEMALE, SHE IS THEN CONSIDERED TO BE THE ROOT CAUSE OF IT. SO AFTER DEATH AND DEPARTURE FROM THE BODY, IT RETURNS TO HER.

100. וְהַאי רוּחַ נָפְקָא מֵהַאי עָלְמָא, וְאִתְפָּרְשַׁת מִנֶּפֶשׁ, עָאל לְגִנְתָּא דְעֵדֶן, דִּבְהַאי עָלְמָא, וְאִתְלַבַּשׁ תַּמָּן גּוֹ אֲוִירָא דְגִנְתָּא. כְּמָה דְמִתְלַבְּשֵׁי מַלְאֲכֵי עִלָּאֵי, כַּד נָחֲתִין לְהַאי עָלְמָא, בְּגִין דְּאִינוּן מֵהַהוּא רוּחַ הֲווֹ, דִּכְתִיב עוֹשֶׂה מַלְאָכָיו רוּחוֹת וגו'.

100. And this Ruach, AFTER A PERSON'S DEATH, leaves this world and is separated from the Nefesh, WHICH REMAINS HOVERING OVER THE GRAVE, and it enters the Garden of Eden of this world. There, it clothes itself with the air of the Garden of Eden, just as the supernal angels do when they come down to this world. Then, they clothe and cover themselves with the air of this world, because they were created from that spirit (Ruach), as it is written: "Who makes the winds (also: spirits) his angels" (Tehilim 104:4).

101. וּבְמִצִיעוּת גִּנְתָּא, אִית עַמּוּדָא חַדָּא, מְרַקְמָא בְּכָל גְּוָונִין. וְהַהוּא רוּחַ, כַּד בָּעֵא לְסַלְקָא, אִתְפַּשַׁט תַּמָּן מֵהַהוּא לְבוּשָׁא, וְעָאל גּוֹ הַהוּא עַמּוּדָא וְסָלִיק לְעֵילָא, גּוֹ הַהוּא אֲתַר דְּנָפְקַת מִנֵּיהּ, כְּדִכְתִיב וְהָרוּחַ תָּשׁוּב וגו'.

101. And in the midst of the Garden, there stands a pillar embroidered with many colors. And when that Ruach wishes to rise up TO THE WORLD OF ATZILUT, it disrobes from that clothing, FROM THE AIR OF THE GARDEN OF EDEN, enters to the pillar, and ascends until it reaches the place from where it came, NAMELY THE NUKVA OF ATZILUT. As it is written: "and the spirit (Ruach) shall return TO THE ELOHIM, WHO GAVE IT."

102. וְנָטִיל לָהּ מִיכָאֵל כַּהֲנָא רַבָּא, וּמַקְרִיב לָהּ קָרְבַּן בּוּסְמִין, קַמֵּי קֻדְשָׁא בְּרִיךְ הוּא, וְיָתְבָא תַּמָּן וּמִתְעַדְּנָא, בְּהַהוּא צְרוֹרָא דְּחַיֵּי, דְּעַיִן לֹא רָאֲתָה אֱלֹקִים זוּלָתְךָ וְגו'. לְבָתַר נָחֲתָא לְגוֹ גִּנְתָּא דְּאַרְעָא, וּמִתְעַדְּנָא בְּכָל עִדּוּנִין, וְאִתְלַבְּשַׁת בְּהַהוּא לְבוּשָׁא, וְיָתְבָא תַּמָּן בְּעִטּוּרָא, עַל חַד תְּרֵין מִכַּמָּה דַּהֲוַת בְּקַדְמֵיתָא.

102. And then, Michael, the High Priest, takes THE RUACH and offers it as a sacrifice of sweet savor to the Holy One, blessed be He, NAMELY ZEIR ANPIN. And it remains there, IN ZEIR ANPIN OF ATZILUT, and enjoys the delicacies of the bundle of Life, WHICH IS DESCRIBED BY THE VERSE, "no eye had ever seen an Elohim, beside You..." (Yeshayah 64:3). Afterwards, it goes down from there and returns to the earthly Garden of Eden. There, it enjoys all the delicacies, clothes itself again with that same clothing, THAT IS, WITH THE AIR OF THE GARDEN OF EDEN, and dwells there crowned with a crown twice as big as the one that it had possessed before IT ROSE UP TO MALE AND FEMALE OF ATZILUT.

103. נְשָׁמָה, הִיא חֵילָא עִלָּאָה עַל כָּל אִלֵּין, וְאִיהִי מֵחֵילָא דִּדְכוּרָא, רָזָא דְּאִילָנָא דְּחַיֵּי. וְדָא סָלְקָא לְעֵילָא מִיָּד. וְכָל הַנֵּי תְּלַת דַּרְגִּין מִתְקַשְּׁרִין כַּחֲדָא דָּא בְּדָא. וְכַד מִתְפָּרְשָׁן, כֻּלְּהוּ סָלְקִין, וְתָבִין לְהַהוּא אֲתַר דְּנָפָקוּ מִנֵּיהּ.

103. The Neshamah is a supernal power high above the other two, NAMELY, THE NEFESH AND THE RUACH. It originates from the power of the male, which is the Tree of Life. THAT IS, ZEIR ANPIN, CALLED 'THE TREE OF LIFE,' DRAWS IT FROM BINAH OF ATZILUT, AND BECAUSE HE DOES SO, HE IS CONSIDERED TO BE ITS ROOT. THIS IS JUST LIKE THE RUACH, WHICH THE NUKVA DRAWS FROM ZEIR ANPIN, AND IS THUS CONSIDERED ITS ROOT. INDEED, THE LIGHT OF ZEIR ANPIN IS CALLED RUACH AND THE LIGHT OF BINAH IS CALLED NESHAMAH. THE NESHAMAH, AFTER MAN'S DEMISE, ascends immediately. IT DOES NOT COME FIRST TO THE EARTHLY GARDEN OF EDEN, AS DOES THE RUACH. RATHER, IT ASCENDS TO ITS ROOT IMMEDIATELY, NAMELY, TO ZEIR ANPIN, WHICH IS ITS ROOT WITH NO REGARD TO ITS DRAWING IT. And these three levels – NEFESH, RUACH, AND NESHAMAH – are attached to one another. When they leave THE BODY, they all rise up and return to the places from which they came.

‏104. כַּד הַאי רוּחָא נָפְקַת מֵהַאי עָלְמָא, וְעָאלַת בְּגוֹ מְעַרְתָּא דְּאָדָם וַאֲבָהָן תַּמָּן, אִינּוּן יָהֲבִין לָה פִּנְקַס סִימָנָא, וְעָאלַת לְגַבֵּי גִּנְתָּא דְּעֵדֶן. קְרִיבַת תַּמָּן וְאַשְׁכָּחַת כְּרוּבִים וְהַהוּא לַהַט הַחֶרֶב הַמִּתְהַפֶּכֶת. אִי זָכָאת, חָמָאן פִּנְקַס סִימָנָא, וּפָתְחִין לָה פִּתְחָא, וְעָאלַת. וְאִי לָא, דַּחְיָין לָה לְבַר.

104. When the Ruach leaves this world and enters the cave of Adam and the Patriarchs, they give it a letter as a sign. Then it goes to the Garden of Eden. When it arrives there, it meets the Cherubs and the flame of the revolving sword. If it is meritorious, then they see the letter, which is the sign, and open the gate for it to enter. If they do not see the letter, they reject it and do not allow it to enter.

‏105. וְיָתְבָא תַּמָּן כָּל הַהוּא זִמְנָא דְּיָתְבָא, מִתְלַבְּשָׁא תַּמָּן בְּדִיּוּקְנָא דְּהַאי עָלְמָא. וּבְרֵישׁ יַרְחֵי וְשַׁבַּתֵּי, כַּד בָּעָאת לְסַלְּקָא, צַדִּיקַיָּיא דִּבְגִנְתָּא דְּעֵדֶן, יַהֲבִין לָה פִּנְקַס סִימָנָא, וְסָלְקַת בְּהַהוּא עַמּוּדָא, וּפָגְעַת בְּאִינּוּן נָטְרֵי חוֹמוֹת יְרוּשָׁלַ͏ם, אִי זָכָאה, פָּתְחִין לָה פִּתְחָא וְעָאלַת. וְאִי לָא, נָטְלִין מִינָה הַהוּא פִּנְקַס וְדַחְיָין לָה לְבַר. תָּבַת לְגִנְתָּא, וְאָמְרָה מְצָאוּנִי הַשֹּׁמְרִים הַסּוֹבְבִים בָּעִיר וְגו'. נָשְׂאוּ אֶת רְדִידִי מֵעָלַי. דָּא אִיהוּ פִּנְקַס סִימָנָא, דְּנָטְלֵי מִנֵּיה, שׁוֹמְרֵי הַחוֹמוֹת, אִלֵּין אִינּוּן נָטְרֵי חוֹמוֹת יְרוּשָׁלַ͏ם.

‏(עַד כָּאן סִתְרֵי תּוֹרָה).

105. And it dwells there some time, sitting and clothing itself in the image of this world. And on the first day of the month and on Shabbat, when it wants to rise TO THE UPPER GARDEN OF EDEN, the righteous men who are in the Garden of Eden give it a letter as a sign. And it ascends through that same pillar, WHICH IS IN THE MIDDLE OF THE LOWER GARDEN OF EDEN, where it meets the watchmen of the walls of Jerusalem. If it is meritorious, they open the gate and it enters. If not, they take the letter away and throw it out. As it is written: "The watchmen that go about the city found me...the keepers of the walls took away my veil from me" (Shir Hashirim 5:7). THE VEIL is the letter given as a sign, which has been taken away from it, by the watchmen of the walls of Jerusalem.

End of Sitrei Torah

13. "And Abram went down to Egypt"

A Synopsis
The Torah presents a story that concerns the patriarch Abraham entering into the land of Egypt. The Zohar reveals that *Egypt* is a code word pertaining to the depths of man's own negativity into which divine sparks of Light have fallen. The great spiritual leaders of history often descended into these negative regions to retrieve and elevate the sparks trapped within the dark recesses of our being.

The Relevance of this Passage
It goes against the grain of man's nature to look inward and reflect upon one's own amoral attributes. Our five senses are steadfastly tuned towards the external environment around us. The introspection and self-scrutiny performed by the sages, serves as a timeless repository of energy available to us through the letters and lessons contained herein. We acquire the inner strength to go deep into one's self and expel the hardhearted qualities from our character.

106. וַיֵּרֶד אַבְרָם מִצְרַיְמָה לָגוּר שָׁם. מ"ט לְמִצְרַיִם. אֶלָּא, בְּגִין דִּשְׁקִיל לְגַן ה'. דִּכְתִיב, כְּגַן ה' כְּאֶרֶץ מִצְרַיִם, דְּתַמָּן שָׁקִיל וְנָחֵית חַד נַהֲרָא, דְּאִיהוּ לִימִינָא, דִּכְתִיב שֵׁם הָאֶחָד פִּישׁוֹן הוּא הַסּוֹבֵב אֵת כָּל אֶרֶץ הַחֲוִילָה אֲשֶׁר שָׁם הַזָּהָב.

106. "And Abram went down to Egypt to sojourn there" (Beresheet 12:10). Why did he go down to Egypt? Because it looked like the garden of Hashem, NAMELY THE GARDEN OF EDEN. As it is written: "like the garden of Hashem, like the land of Egypt..." (Beresheet 13:10). Because a river flows down on the right, as it is written: "The name of the first is Pishon; that is it which encompasses the whole land of Chavilah, where there is gold" (Beresheet 2:11).

107. וְאַבְרָהָם, כֵּיוָן דְּיָדַע, וְעָאל בְּהֵימְנוּתָא שְׁלֵימְתָא, בָּעָא לְמִנְדַּע כָּל אִינוּן דַּרְגִּין, דְּאִתְאַחֲדָן לְתַתָּא. וּמִצְרַיִם הֲוָה נָטִיל מִיָּמִינָא, וּבְגִין כָּךְ, נָחַת לְמִצְרַיִם. וְתָא חֲזֵי, כִּפְנָא לָא אִשְׁתְּכַח בְּאַרְעָא, אֶלָּא כַּד מִסְתַּלְּקֵי רַחֲמֵי מִן דִּינָא.

107. So Abraham achieved knowledge and complete faith, WHICH REFERS TO THE NUKVA OF ZEIR ANPIN, WHICH IS CALLED FAITH. IT WAS CALLED COMPLETE FAITH AFTER IT HAD BEEN COMPLETED BY THE ILLUMINATION OF CHOCHMAH, FROM THE ASPECT OF BINAH THAT RETURNED TO CHOCHMAH. Abraham then wanted to become familiar with all the grades that are attached below. THIS IS A REFERENCE TO THOSE WHO CAN PASS ON THE ABUNDANCE FROM ABOVE DOWNWARDS, WHICH IS THE SECRET OF CHOCHMAH OF THE RIGHT COLUMN. And Egypt came from the right; FROM THE ASPECT OF THE RIVER OF PISHON, WHICH IS THE SECRET OF CHOCHMAH OF THE RIGHT COLUMN. Because of this, he went down to Egypt TO COLLECT ALL THE HOLY SPARKS, FROM THE ASPECT OF CHOCHMAH OF THE RIGHT COLUMN AND GET THEM OUT OF THERE. AFTER ACCOMPLISHING THIS, HE RETURNED TO THE LAND OF YISRAEL. THUS HE WAS FULL AND COMPLETED BY THE MOCHIN OF CHOCHMAH. Come and behold: famine only comes to the land when Mercy leaves Judgment. THIS MEANS WHEN ZEIR ANPIN, WHO IS THE SECRET OF MERCY, DEPARTS FROM THE NUKVA, WHICH IS THE SECRET OF JUDGMENT. BECAUSE THEN THE MATING OF THE MALE AND FEMALE IS DISTURBED, AND FAMINE IS FELT IN THE NUKVA, WHICH IS CALLED THE LAND.

108. וַיְהִי כַּאֲשֶׁר הִקְרִיב לָבֹא מִצְרָיְמָה. אָמַר ר״א, כַּאֲשֶׁר הִקְרִיב, כַּאֲשֶׁר קָרַב, מִבְּעֵי לֵיה, מַאי כַּאֲשֶׁר הִקְרִיב. אֶלָּא כְּדִכְתִיב, וּפַרְעֹה הִקְרִיב, דְּאִיהוּ אַקְרֵיב לְהוּ לְיִשְׂרָאֵל, לִתְיוּבְתָּא. אוֹף הָכָא הִקְרִיב, דְּאַקְרִיב גַּרְמֵיה לְקֻדְשָׁא בְּרִיךְ הוּא, כְּדְקָא יָאוֹת. לָבֹא מִצְרָיְמָה. לְאַשְׁגָּחָא בְּאִינוּן דַּרְגִּין, וּלְאִתְרַחֲקָא מִנַּיְיהוּ, וּלְאִתְרַחֲקָא מֵעוֹבְדֵי מִצְרָיִם.

108. "And it came to pass, when he came (lit. 'caused to come') near to enter to Egypt..." (Beresheet 12:11). Rabbi Elazar said that THE VERSE STATES, "when he caused to come near," whereas it should have stated, 'When he came near.' Why does it say, "when he caused to come near?" This is similar to the verse, "And Pharaoh caused to come close..." (Shemot 14:10), WHICH MEANS that he brought Yisrael to come near to repentance. The same applies here, so "caused to come near" MEANS THAT he brought himself to come near to the Holy One, blessed be He, as should properly be.

"To enter to Egypt," MEANS to observe those grades, LOCATED IN EGYPT, and keep his distance from them, as well as to keep his distance from the worshippers of Egypt.

109. אָמַר רָבִּי יְהוּדָה, תָּא חֲזֵי, בְּגִין דְּנָחַת אַבְרָהָם לְמִצְרַיִם בְּלָא רְשׁוּ, אִשְׁתַּעְבִּידוּ בְּנוֹי בְּמִצְרַיִם, אַרְבַּע מְאָה שְׁנִין, דְּהָא כְּתִיב, וַיֵּרֶד אַבְרָם מִצְרָיְמָה. וְלָא כְּתִיב רֵד מִצְרָיִם, וְאִצְטַעֵר כָּל הַהוּא לֵילְיָא בְּגִינָא דְשָׂרָה.

109. Rabbi Yehuda said, Come and behold: Since he went down to Egypt without consent, his offspring were enslaved in Egypt for four hundred years. As it is written: "and Abram went down to Egypt." It does not say THAT THE HOLY ONE, BLESSED BE HE, TOLD HIM, 'Go down to Egypt!' THEREFORE, he was in misery all that night because of Sarah.

110. וַיֹּאמֶר אֶל שָׂרָה אִשְׁתּוֹ הִנֵּה נָא יָדַעְתִּי כִּי אִשָּׁה יְפַת מַרְאֶה אָתְּ. וְכִי עַד הַהִיא שַׁעֲתָא לָא הֲוָה יָדַע אַבְרָהָם, דְּאִשָּׁה יְפַת מַרְאֶה הֲוַת. אֶלָּא, הָא אוֹקְמוּהָ, דְּעַד הַהִיא שַׁעֲתָא, לָא אִסְתָּכַּל בְּדִיוֹקְנָא דְשָׂרָה, בְּסַגִּיאוּת צְנִיעוּתָא דַּהֲוַת בֵּינַיְהוּ, וְכַד קָרֵיב לְמִצְרַיִם, אִתְגַּלְיָיא אִיהִי, וְחָמָא בָהּ.

110. "And he said to Sarah his wife: 'Behold now, I know that you are a fair woman to look upon'" (Beresheet 12:11). AND HE ASKS: Could it be that until then Abraham did not know that she was a "fair woman to look upon"? AND HE REPLIES: This has already been explained – that until then he did not look upon the image of Sarah, because of their excessive modesty with each other. But when he "came near to enter to Egypt," she revealed herself, and he saw her.

111. דָּבָר אַחֵר בַּמֶּה יָדַע. אֶלָּא עַל יְדָא דְּטוֹרַח אוֹרְחָא, בַּר נָשׁ מִתְבַּזֶּה, וְהִיא קָיְימָא בְּשַׁפִּירוּ דִּילָהּ, וְלָא אִשְׁתַּנֵּי. דָּבָר אַחֵר הִנֵּה נָא יָדַעְתִּי, דְּחָמָא עִמָּהּ שְׁכִינְתָּא. וּבְגִין כָּךְ, אִתְרְחַץ אַבְרָהָם, וַאֲמַר אֲחוֹתִי הִיא.

111. Another explanation for why he knew ONLY THEN THAT SHE WAS A

-64-

FAIR WOMAN TO LOOK UPON is that most people are affected by the hardship of the journey, but Sarah remained beautiful and her appearance did not change. THIS IS HOW HE KNEW MORE THAN EVER THAT SHE IS A FAIR WOMAN TO LOOK UPON. Another explanation of the words, "Behold, now I know..." is that Abraham saw the Shechinah accompanying Sarah, WHICH MEANS THAT HE HAD THE MERIT OF THE REVELATION OF THE SHECHINAH. For this reason, Abraham felt confident and said: "She is my sister."

112. וּמִלָּה דָא אִסְתַּלֵּק, לִתְרֵי גַּוְונִין. חַד כְּמַשְׁמָעוֹ. וְחַד כְּדִכְתִיב אֱמֹר לַחָכְמָה אֲחֹתִי אָתְּ. וּכְתִיב אִמְרִי נָא אֲחֹתִי אָתְּ. וּכְתִיב וְאַתְּ תְּדַבֵּר אֵלֵינוּ. לְמַעַן יִיטַב לִי בַּעֲבוּרֵךְ, כְּלַפֵּי שְׁכִינָה אָמַר, בַּעֲבוּרֵךְ יִיטַב לִי קֻדְשָׁא בְּרִיךְ הוּא. וְחָיְתָה נַפְשִׁי בִּגְלָלֵךְ. בְּגִין דִּבְדָא יִסְתַּלַּק בַּר נָשׁ, וְיִזְכֶּה לְאִסְתַּלְּקָא לְאוֹרְחָא דְחַיֵּי.

112. The phrase, "MY SISTER," has two meanings. The first is literal – NAMELY, THAT YOU ARE MY SISTER. The second is figurative, as in the verse, "Say to wisdom; You are my sister." (Mishlei 7:4). It also is written: "Say, I pray you, you are my sister" (Beresheet 12:13). THE WORD 'YOU' ALLUDES TO THE SHECHINAH. And it is also written: "speak you to us" (Devarim 5:24), WHICH ALSO ALLUDES TO THE SHECHINAH. In addressing the Shechinah, he said: "That it may be well with me for your sake," WHICH MEANS FOR THE SAKE OF THE SHECHINAH, and also "my soul shall live because of you," because, as a result of this, REFERRING TO THE MOCHIN OF CHOCHMAH, a person is elevated up to the path of life, SINCE THE LIGHT OF CHOCHMAH IS CALLED THE LIGHT OF CHAYAH, AS IS ALREADY KNOWN!

113. אִמְרִי נָא אֲחֹתִי וְגוֹ'. ר' יֵיסָא אָמַר, יָדַע הֲוָה אַבְרָהָם דְּכֻלְּהוּ מִצְרָאֵי שְׁטִיפִין אִינּוּן בְּזִמָּה, וְכֵיוָן דְּכָל הַאי יָדַע, אַמַּאי לָא דָחִיל עַל אִתְּתֵיהּ, דְּלָא אַהֲדַר מֵאָרְחָא, וְלָא יֵיעוֹל לְתַמָּן. אֶלָּא בְּגִין דְּחָמָא שְׁכִינְתָּא עִמָּהּ.

113. "Say, I pray you, you are my sister..." Rabbi Yesa said: Abraham knew

that all the Egyptians are lecherous. Since he knew this, how come he was not afraid for his wife and did not return back from this journey and refrain from entering there? AND HE REPLIES: Because he saw that she was accompanied by the Shechinah; THEREFORE HE HAD CONFIDENCE IN HER AND HAD NO FEAR!

14. "And it came to pass, when Abram came to Egypt"

A Synopsis

The Zohar explores the Biblical story in which Sarah, the wife of the patriarch Abraham, is abducted by the King of Egypt. Abraham and Sarah are able to take control over the King, utilizing the tools of the Torah. This event held cosmic significance for future generations. This action of gaining control over the King of Egypt and the negative cosmic forces that he represents, created the means that would be utilized again, five generations later, when the Israelites were freed from bondage in Egypt. The Zohar is demonstrating how man often fails to perceive all the influences and effects that unfold as a result every action we perform.

The Relevance of this Passage

In reality, hardships in life are merely minor interference patterns in comparison to the eternal fulfillment and reality that is ours after we complete our spiritual transformation. We gain the ability to perceive the larger picture when obstacles and difficulties arise in our life. An appreciation for the inevitable consequences that are attached to all of our actions is stimulated within our consciousness.

114. וַיְהִי כְּבֹא אַבְרָם מִצְרָיְמָה וַיִּרְאוּ הַמִּצְרִים אֶת הָאִשָּׁה כִּי יָפָה הִיא מְאֹד. אָמַר רַבִּי יְהוּדָה, בְּתֵיבָה אָעֵיל לָהּ, וּפְתְחוּ לָהּ, לְמֵיסַב מִנָּהּ קוֹסְטוֹנָא. כֵּיוָן דְּאִתְפַּתַּח, הֲוָה נְהוֹרָא, כִּנְהוֹרָא דְּשִׁמְשָׁא, הה"ד כִּי יָפָה הִיא מְאֹד.

114. "And it came to pass, when Abram came to Egypt, the Egyptians beheld the woman that she was very fair" (Beresheet 12:14). Rabbi Yehuda said: He brought her to Egypt in a closed carriage. And the Egyptians opened the carriage to collect taxes from it. But as the carriage was opened, there was light resembling the light of the sun. THIS MEANS THAT THE LIGHT OF SARAH, WHICH IS THE SECRET OF THE MOON, WAS AS STRONG AS THE LIGHT OF THE SUN, ACCORDING TO THE SECRET OF THE "TWO GREAT LIGHTS!" And this is why it is written: "that she was very fair."

115. מַאי מְאֹד. אֶלָּא, דְּחָמוּ בַּתֵּיבָה נְהוֹרָא אָחֲרָא, אַפִּיקוּ לָהּ וְחָמוּ לָהּ, כְּמִלְּקַדְמִין, הה"ד וַיִּרְאוּ אוֹתָהּ שָׂרֵי פַרְעֹה, כֵּיוָן דִּכְתִיב, וַיִּרְאוּ

הַמִּצְרִים אֶת הָאִשָּׁה. מַאי וַיִּרְאוּ אוֹתָהּ שָׂרֵי פַרְעֹה. אֶלָּא דְּאֲפִיקוּ לָהּ,
וְחָמוּ לָהּ, כְּמִלְּקַדְמִין. וּכְדֵין וַיְהַלְלוּ אוֹתָהּ אֶל פַּרְעֹה וְגוֹ'.

115. AND HE ASKS: What DOES THE VERSE ALLUDE TO BY USING THE
WORD 'very'? AND HE REPLIES THAT THE EGYPTIANS saw in the carriage
a different light. They took her out OF THE CARRIAGE, and they saw that
she remained as fair as before, AS FAIR AS SHE WAS IN THE CARRIAGE.
THIS MEANS THAT THE ACTION OF THE EGYPTIANS DID NOT DO HER ANY
DAMAGE. HER BEAUTY WAS NOT CORRUPTED; IT REMAINED AS BEFORE,
AS WHEN SHE WAS IN THE CARRIAGE. Therefore it is written: "The
ministers of Pharaoh saw her." AND SO HE ASKS: Since it is written that
'the Egyptians beheld the woman,' why do I read, 'The ministers of Pharaoh
saw her,' AS THEY TOO WERE EGYPTIANS? AND HE REPLIES: Because
they took her out OF THE CARRIAGE; and saw that she remained AS FAIR as
before – THAT IS, AS SHE WAS IN THE CARRIAGE. And then they
"commended her before Pharaoh, and the woman was taken to Pharaoh's
house."

116. אָמַר רַבִּי יִצְחָק. וַוי לְאִינּוּן חַיָּיבַיָּא דְּעָלְמָא, דְּלָא יָדְעִין וְלָא
מַשְׁגִּיחִין בַּעֲבִידְתֵּיהּ דְּקֻדְשָׁא בְּרִיךְ הוּא, וְאִנּוּן לָא מִסְתַּכְּלֵי דְּכָל מַה
דַּהֲוֵי בְּעָלְמָא, מֵעִם קֻדְשָׁא בְּרִיךְ הוּא אִיהוּ, דְּאִיהוּ יָדַע בְּקַדְמֵיתָא, מַה
דִּלְהֱוֵי בְּסוֹפָא, דִּכְתִיב מַגִּיד מֵרֵאשִׁית אַחֲרִית. וְאִיהוּ אִסְתְּכֵי וַעֲבֵיד
עֲבִידָן בְּקַדְמֵיתָא, בְּגִין לְסַלְּקָא לוֹן, לְבָתַר יוֹמִין.

116. Rabbi Yitzchak said: Woe to those wicked people of the world, as they
do not know and do not observe IN ORDER TO UNDERSTAND that
everything that exists in the world comes from the Holy One, blessed be He.
THIS MEANS THAT HE ALONE HAS DONE, CONTINUES DOING, AND SHALL
DO ALL THE ACTIONS IN THE WORLD. And that He knew from the
beginning what the end shall be, as it is written: "Declaring the end from the
beginning..." (Yeshayah 46:10). And He watches and performs the actions
from the beginning, so that they can later be repeated TO COMPLETION.

117. תָּא חֲזֵי, אִלְמָלֵא דְּאִנְסִיבַת שָׂרַי לְגַבֵּי פַרְעֹה, לָא אִלְקֵי הוּא,
וְאַלְקָאוּתָא דָּא גָּרֵים אַלְקָאוּתָא לְבָתַר כֵּן, דְּיִלְקוּן מִצְרַיִם בְּנִגְעִים

גְדוֹלִים, כְּתִיב הָכָא נְגָעִים גְדוֹלִים, וּכְתִיב הֵתָם וַיִּתֵּן ה' אוֹתוֹת
וּמוֹפְתִים גְדוֹלִים וְרָעִים בְּמִצְרַיִם, מַה לְהַלָן עֶשֶׂר מַכּוֹת, אַף כָּאן עֶשֶׂר
מַכּוֹת. כְּמָה דַעֲבֵיד קֻדְשָׁא בְּרִיךְ הוּא נִסִּין וּגְבוּרָן לְיִשְׂרָאֵל לֵילְיָא, אוֹף
הָכָא עֲבַד לָהּ קֻדְשָׁא בְּרִיךְ הוּא לְשָׂרָה נִסִּין וּגְבוּרָאן לֵילְיָא.

117. Come and behold: Had Sarah not been taken to Pharaoh, he would not
have been plagued. And the result of Pharaoh's plague was another plague,
so the Egyptians suffered great plagues AS YISRAEL LEFT EGYPT. As it is
written: "great plagues" in this passage, and, AS YISRAEL LEFT EGYPT, it is
written: "And Hashem showed signs and wonders, great and sore, upon
Egypt" (Devarim 6:22). HE MAKES AN ANALOGY BETWEEN THE TWO
TIMES WHEN THE WORD "GREAT" IS USED. Because there were ten
plagues, PHARAOH ALSO SUFFERED ten plagues here. And just as the Holy
One, blessed be He, performed miracles and showed His great might during
the night, so here as well, the Holy One, blessed be He, performed miracles
and mighty deeds at night. SO, AS HE WAS INFLICTING THE PLAGUES
UPON PHARAOH, FOR THE SAKE OF SARAH, HE WAS WATCHING AND
OBSERVING THE WAY HE WAS GOING TO REPEAT THEM TO PERFECTION
DURING THE EXODUS OF YISRAEL FROM EGYPT.

118. ר' יוֹסֵי פָּתַח וְאָמַר, וְאַתָּה ה' מָגֵן בַּעֲדִי כְּבוֹדִי וּמֵרִים רֹאשִׁי.
אָמַר דָוִד אַף עַל גַּב דְכָל בְּנֵי עָלְמָא, יֵיתוּן לְאַגָּחָא בִּי קְרָבָא, וְאַתָּה ה'
מָגֵן בַּעֲדִי. תָּא חֲזֵי, כְּתִיב מָגֵן בַּעֲדִי. אָמַר דָוִד לְקֻדְשָׁא בְּרִיךְ הוּא,
רִבּוֹנוֹ שֶׁל עוֹלָם, מִפְּנֵי מָה לָא עַבְדֵי בִּי חֲתִימָה דִבְרָכָה, כְּמָה דְחָתְמֵי
בְּרָכָה בְּאַבְרָהָם, דִּכְתִיב אָנֹכִי מָגֵן לָךְ, וְאָמְרֵי מָגֵן אַבְרָהָם.

118. Rabbi Yosi opened the discussion by saying: "But you, Hashem, are a
shield for me; my glory, and the lifter up of my head" (Tehilim 3:4). David
said: Even if all the people of the world come and make war with me, THEY
WILL NOT BE ABLE TO OVERCOME ME, BECAUSE "You, Hashem, are a
shield for me." Come and behold: It is written: "a shield for me." David said
to the Holy One, blessed be He, Master of the Universe, why is there no
blessing that ends with my name, as there is for Abraham, of whom it is
written: "I am your shield" (Beresheet 15:1) and therefore it is said: 'the
shield of Abraham.' SO WHY DO THEY NOT CONCLUDE A BLESSING WITH

MY NAME, 'THE PROTECTOR OF DAVID'?

119. אָמַר לוֹ קֻדְשָׁא בְּרִיךְ הוּא לְדָוִד, אַבְרָהָם כְּבָר בְּחַנְתִּיו וְצַרְפְתִּיו, וְקָאֵים קַמָּאי בְּקִיּוּמָא שְׁלִים. אָמַר לוֹ דָוִד, א״ה בְּחָנֵנִי ה׳ וְנַסֵּנִי צָרְפָה כִלְיוֹתַי וְלִבִּי. כֵּיוָן דַּעֲבַד הַהִיא מִלָּה דְּבַת שֶׁבַע, אִדְכַּר דָּוִד קַמֵּיה, עַל מַה דַּאֲמַר, אָמַר בָּחַנְתָּ לִבִּי פָּקַדְתָּ לַיְלָה צְרַפְתַּנִי בַל תִּמְצָא זַמּוֹתִי בַל יַעֲבָר פִּי.

119. So the Holy One, blessed be He, answered David, "As for Abraham, I have already tried and tested him, and he resisted THE TEST and was found before me to be wholly steadfast." David said to Him, "Examine me, Hashem, and prove me, purify my kidneys and my heart!" (Tehilim 26:2). But when he became involved in the matter of Bathsheba, David remembered what he had said to the Holy One, blessed be He, and said: "You have proved my heart, You have visited it in the night. You have tried me, but You did find nothing; Let no presumptuous thought pass my lips" (Tehilim 17:3).

120. אָמַר, אֲנָא אֲמִינָא, בְּחָנֵנִי ה׳ וְנַסֵּנִי, וְאַנְתְּ בָּחַנְתָּ לִבִּי. אֲנָא אֲמִינָא צָרְפָה כִלְיוֹתַי, וְאַתְּ צְרַפְתַּנִי, בַּל תִּמְצָא, לָא אַשְׁכַּחַת לִי כְּדְקָא יָאוֹת. זַמּוֹתִי בַּל יַעֲבָר פִּי. מַאן יִתֵּן וְהַאי מִלָּה דְּחֲשָׁבִית, דְּלָא יַעֲבַר לִי פּוּמָאי.

120. He said: I said, "Examine me, Hashem, and prove me," and 'You have examined my heart' BY BATHSHEBA; I said, 'purify my kidneys' and "You have tried me, but You did find nothing." "Let no presumptuous thought pass my lips"; How I wish that the thoughts of my mind would not have been uttered with my mouth AND I WOULD NOT HAVE PROCLAIMED, "EXAMINE ME, HASHEM, AND PROVE ME."

121. וְעִם כָּל דָּא, חָתְמִין בֵּיה בְּרָכָה, דְּקָאַמְרָן מָגֵן דָּוִד. וּבְגִין כָּךְ אֲמַר דָּוִד וְאַתָּה ה׳ מָגֵן בַּעֲדִי כְּבוֹדִי וּמֵרִים רֹאשִׁי, וַדַּאי דַרְגָּא דָּא יְקָרָא דִילִי, דַּאֲנָא מִתְעַטְּרָנָא בֵּיה.

121. But nevertheless, there is a blessing that concludes with the words, "the

Shield of David." For this reason, David said: "But you, Hashem, are a shield for me, my glory, and the lifter of my head." THIS MEANS THAT HE SAID, "This grade OF 'SHIELD' is certainly 'my glory' by which I am crowned."

122. וַיְצַו עָלָיו פַּרְעֹה אֲנָשִׁים וַיְשַׁלְחוּ אוֹתוֹ. תָּא חֲזֵי, קֻדְשָׁא בְּרִיךְ הוּא אִיהוּ מָגֵן לְצַדִּיקַיָּיא, דְּלָא יִשְׁלְטוּן בְּהוֹ בְּנֵי נָשָׁא, וְקֻדְשָׁא בְּרִיךְ הוּא אָגֵין עַל אַבְרָהָם דְּלָא יִשְׁלְטוּן בֵּיה וּבְאִתְּתֵיה.

122. "And Pharaoh commanded his men concerning him; and they sent him away..." (Beresheet 21:20). Come and behold: The Holy One, blessed be He, is the protector of the righteous, who shields them from being ruled by other people. So the Holy One, blessed be He, protected Abraham, so no one could harm him or his wife.

123. תָּא חֲזֵי, שְׁכִינְתָּא לָא אִתְעֲדֵי מִינָּה דְּשָׂרָה, כָּל הַהוּא לֵילְיָא, אָתָא פַּרְעֹה לְמִקְרַב בַּהֲדָהּ, אָתָא מַלְאַךְ וְאַלְקֵי לֵיה, כָּל אֵימַת דַּאֲמָרָה שָׂרָה אַלְקֵי, הוּא מַלְקֵי, וְאַבְרָהָם הֲוָה מַתְקִיף בְּמָארֵיה, דְּהָא שָׂרָה לָא יָכְלִין לְשַׁלְטָאָה עֲלָהּ, הה"ד וְצַדִּיקִים כִּכְפִיר יִבְטָח. וְהָכָא נִסְיוֹנָא הוּא, דְּלָא הִרְהֵר אֲבַתְרֵיה דְּקוּדְשָׁא בְּרִיךְ הוּא.

123. Come and behold: The Shechinah did not leave Sarah at all during that night. When Pharaoh approached her, an angel came and hit him. And whenever Sarah said, "Hit," he hit. All the while Abraham was begging his Master through his prayers, not to allow anyone to harm her. Therefore it is written: "but the righteous are bold (trusting) as a lion" (Mishlei 28:1). Here was a trial by which Hashem tested Abraham, but Abraham had no doubts about the Holy One, blessed be He.

124. אָמַר רָבִּי יִצְחָק, תָּא חֲזֵי, דִּבְגִין כָּךְ לָא פַּקִּיד קוּדְשָׁא בְּרִיךְ הוּא לְנַחֲתָא לְמִצְרַיִם, אֶלָּא הוּא עַצְמוֹ מִגַּרְמֵיה נָחַת, בְּגִין דְּלָא יְהֵא פִּתְחוֹן פֶּה לִבְנֵי עָלְמָא, דַּאֲמַר לֵיה כֵּן, וּלְבָתַר אִצְטַעַר עַל אִתְּתֵיה.

124. Rabbi Yitzchak said, Come and behold: It is because of this that the Holy One, blessed be He, did not command him to go to Egypt. But he went on his own initiative, so that the people of the world would have no reason to say that THE HOLY ONE, BLESSED BE HE, told him to go down to Egypt, and then he was pained for his wife.

125. ר' יִצְחָק פָּתַח וְאָמַר צַדִּיק כַּתָּמָר יִפְרָח כְּאֶרֶז בַּלְבָנוֹן יִשְׂגֶּא צַדִּיק כַּתָּמָר יִפְרָח. מִפְּנֵי מָה אַקִּישׁ צַדִּיק לְתָמָר. מַה תָּמָר, כֵּיוָן דְּגַזְרִין לֵיהּ לָא סָלֵיק עַד זְמַן סַגִּיא, אוֹף הָכֵי צַדִּיק, כֵּיוָן דְּאִתְאֲבֵיד מֵעָלְמָא, לָא סָלֵיק אַחַר תְּחוֹתוֹי עַד זְמַן סַגִּיא.

125. Rabbi Yitzchak opened the discussion by saying, "The righteous shall flourish like the palm tree, he shall grow like the cedar in Lebanon" (Tehilim 92:13). AND HE ASKS: Why are the righteous compared to a palm tree? AND HE ANSWERS: Just as a palm tree, if it is cut down, needs a long time to grow again – AS LONG AS SEVENTY YEARS – SO if the world loses a righteous man, it will take a very long time until another takes his place – AGAIN AS LONG AS SEVENTY YEARS. THESE SEVENTY YEARS ARE THE SECRET OF CHESED, GVURAH, TIFERET, NETZACH, HOD, YESOD AND MALCHUT, EACH OF WHICH EQUALS TEN.

126. כַּתָּמָר יִפְרָח, מַה תָּמָר לָא סָלֵיק אֶלָּא דְּכַר וְנוּקְבָא. אוֹף הָכֵי צַדִּיק, לָא סָלֵיק אֶלָּא דְּכַר וְנוּקְבָא, דְּכַר צַדִּיק, וְנוּקְבָא צְדֶקֶת, כְּגַוְונָא דְּאַבְרָהָם וְשָׂרָה.

126. The words "shall flourish like the palm tree" TEACH US THAT just as a palm tree does not grow unless except as male and female, neither does the righteous person. He does not flourish except as male and female. The male is righteous and the female is righteous, just as Abraham and Sarah were. THEREFORE HE IS COMPLETED AND REACHES PERFECTION ONLY AFTER SEVENTY YEARS HAVE ELAPSED.

127. כְּאֶרֶז בַּלְבָנוֹן יִשְׂגֶּא. מַה אֶרֶז בַּלְבָנוֹן עֶלָּאָה עַל כֹּלָּא, וְכֹלָּא יַתְבֵי תְּחוֹתוֹי, אוֹף הָכֵי צַדִּיק, הוּא עֶלָּאָה עַל כֹּלָּא, וְכֹלָּא יַתְבֵי תְּחוֹתוֹי. וְעָלְמָא לָא קַיְימָא אֶלָּא עַל צַדִּיק חַד, דִּכְתִיב וְצַדִּיק יְסוֹד עוֹלָם. וַעֲלֵיהּ קָאֵים עָלְמָא, וּבְגִינֵיהּ אִסְתְּמִיךְ, וַעֲלֵיהּ אִשְׁתִּיל.

127. " ...he shall grow like the cedar in Lebanon" means that just as a cedar rises high above all the other trees, so the righteous man is above all others, who are situated under him – IN OTHER WORDS, THEY EXIST BECAUSE OF HIM. And the world, WHICH IS THE SECRET OF THE NUKVA, is supported upon one righteous man, as it is written: "the righteous is the foundation of the world" (Mishlei 10:25). So the world, WHICH IS THE NUKVA, rests and is supported by him and is planted on him; BECAUSE OF HIM IT IS WELL SUPPORTED. THIS MEANS THAT HE BESTOWS HIS THREE COLUMNS UPON IT. 'RESTS' IS THE SECRET OF THE RIGHT COLUMN; 'SUPPORTED' IS THE SECRET OF THE LEFT COLUMN; AND 'PLANTED' IS THE SECRET OF THE CENTRAL COLUMN.

128. ר' יְהוּדָה אֲמַר, וְהָא תָּנִינָן, דְּעַל שִׁבְעָה סָמְכִין עָלְמָא קַיְימָא, דִּכְתִיב חָצְבָה עַמּוּדֶיהָ שִׁבְעָה. אָמַר לוֹ ר' יוֹסֵי, הָכֵי הוּא וַדַּאי, אֲבָל כֻּלְּהוּ אָחֳרָנִין בִּשְׁבִיעָאָה קַיְימֵי, דְּאִיהוּ סָמְכָא דְעָלְמָא וְאִיהוּ צַדִּיק. וְדָא אַשְׁקֵי וְרָוֵי עָלְמָא וְזָן כֹּלָּא. וַעֲלֵיהּ כְּתִיב אִמְרוּ צַדִּיק כִּי טוֹב כִּי פְרִי מַעַלְלֵיהֶם יֹאכֵלוּ. וּכְתִיב טוֹב ה' לַכֹּל וְרַחֲמָיו עַל כָּל מַעֲשָׂיו.

128. Rabbi Yehuda said: But we have already learned that the world stands upon seven pillars; WHICH ARE CHESED, GVURAH, TIFERET, NETZACH, HOD, YESOD, AND MALCHUT, AND NOT UPON ONE RIGHTEOUS ALONE, AS RABBI YITZCHAK HAS STATED. As it is written: "she has hewn out her seven pillars" (Mishlei 9:1). Rabbi Yosi told him, It is certainly so! But all the other pillars stand erect because of the seventh pillar, which supports the whole world, and he is CALLED 'the righteous,' NAMELY YESOD OF ZEIR ANPIN. And he refreshes and replenishes the world, WHICH IS THE NUKVA, and nourishes all THE WORLDS. And he is described by the verse, "Say you to the righteous, that it shall be well (also: 'that he is good') with him: for they shall eat the fruit of their doings" (Yeshayah 3:10). And, it is also written: "Hashem is good to all; and his tender mercies are over all his works" (Tehilim 145:9).

129. אָמַר ר' יִצְחָק, הָא כְּתִיב וְנָהָר יוֹצֵא מֵעֵדֶן לְהַשְׁקוֹת אֶת הַגָּן. דָּא הוּא סָמְכָא דְעָלְמָא קָאֵים עֲלֵיהּ, וְאִיהוּ אַשְׁקֵי לְגִנְתָּא, וְגִנְתָּא אִשְׁתַּקֵי

מִנֵּיהּ, וּמִנֵּיהּ עֲבִידָא פֵּירִין. וְכֻלְּהוּ פֵּירִין פָּרְחִין בְּעָלְמָא, וְאִינּוּן קִיּוּמָא דְעָלְמָא, קִיּוּמָא דְאוֹרַיְיתָא, וּמַאן נִינְהוּ, נִשְׁמַתְהוֹן דְּצַדִּיקַיָּיא, דְּאִינּוּן פְּרִי עוֹבָדוֹי דְּקוּדְשָׁא בְּרִיךְ הוּא.

129. Rabbi Yitzchak said: But it is written: "and a river went out of Eden to water the garden," (Beresheet 2:10) WHICH REFERS TO YESOD OF ZEIR ANPIN, WHICH COMES FORTH FROM BINAH THAT RETURNED TO CHOCHMAH, WHICH IS CALLED EDEN. And this is the pillar upon which the world rests; it is the one that waters the garden, WHICH IS THE NUKVA. And the garden is irrigated by it and bears fruits, WHICH ARE THE SOULS OF HUMAN BEINGS. And all the fruits blossom in this world, WHICH IS THE NUKVA, and they maintain of the world and maintain the Torah. AND HE ASKS: Who are THESE FRUITS? AND HE SAYS: They are the souls of the righteous, who are the fruit of the handiwork of the Holy One, blessed be He.

15. The Holy One, blessed be He, delights Himself with the souls of the righteous

A Synopsis

The power of Midnight gives the souls of the living the ability to connect to the righteous souls who have departed our realm and who now dwell in the Garden of Eden. The Creator comes to be with both groups during these mystical hours of the night.

The Relevance of this Passage

Whereas the Torah is an instrument designed for our physical world, the Zohar is a product of the spiritual realm, above the physical elements of time, space, and motion. Accordingly, we can always access the energy aroused during midnight through the sacred words that tell of these mystical secrets.

130. וּבְגִין כָּךְ בְּכָל לֵילְיָא וְלֵילְיָא, נִשְׁמַתְהוֹן דְּצַדִּיקַיָּיא סָלְקֶן, וְכַד אִתְפְּלַג לֵילְיָא, קֻדְשָׁא בְּרִיךְ הוּא אָתֵי לְגִנְתָּא דְעֵדֶן לְאִשְׁתַּעְשְׁעָא בְּהוּ. בְּמַאן. אָמַר רִבִּי יוֹסֵי בְּכֻלְּהוּ. בֵּין אִינּוּן דִּמְדוֹרֵיהוֹן בְּהַהוּא עָלְמָא, בֵּין אִינּוּן דְּיָתְבֵי בִּמְדוֹרֵיהוֹן בְּהַאי עָלְמָא, בְּכֻלְּהוּ מִשְׁתַּעֲשַׁע בְּהוּ קֻדְשָׁא בְּרִיךְ הוּא, בְּפַלְגוּת לֵילְיָא.

130. Because of this, BECAUSE THE SOULS ARE THE FRUIT OF THE HANDIWORK OF THE HOLY ONE, BLESSED BE HE, on each and every night, the souls of the righteous rise up TO THE GARDEN OF EDEN. And at midnight, the Holy one, blessed be He, comes to the Garden of Eden to delight Himself with them. With whom DOES HE DELIGHT HIMSELF? IS IT WITH THE SOULS OF THE LIVING OR THE DECEASED? Rabbi Yosi answers: With them all! With those who dwell in that World OF TRUTH, and with those who dwell in this world. Together, with them all, the Holy One, blessed be He, finds delight at midnight in the Garden of Eden.

131. תָּא חֲזֵי, עָלְמָא דִּלְעֵילָּא, אִצְטְרִיךְ לְאִתְעָרוּתָא דְּעָלְמָא תַּתָּאָה, וְכַד נִשְׁמַתְהוֹן דְּצַדִּיקַיָּיא נָפְקֵי מֵהַאי עָלְמָא, וְסַלְקֵי לְעֵילָּא, כֻּלְּהוּ מִתְלַבְּשֵׁי בִּנְהוֹרָא דִּלְעֵילָּא, בְּדִיּוּקְנָא יְקָר, וּבְהוֹ קֻדְשָׁא בְּרִיךְ הוּא מִשְׁתַּעֲשַׁע, וְתָאִיב לוֹן, דְּאִנְהוּ פְּרִי עוֹבָדוֹי. וְעַל דָּא אִקְרוּן יִשְׂרָאֵל,

דְּאִית לוֹן נִשְׁמָתִין קַדִּישִׁין, בְּגִין לְקֻדְשָׁא בְּרִיךְ הוּא, כְּד"א בָּנִים אַתֶּם
לַה' אֱלֹקֵיכֶם, בָּנִים וַדַּאי, אִיבָּא דְעוֹבָדוֹי.

131. Come and see: The upper world needs to be aroused by the lower world. When the souls of the righteous leave this world and rise up TO THE GARDEN OF EDEN, they are all clothed by the Supernal Light – by a splendid figure. And the Holy One, blessed be He, delights Himself with them and longs for them because they are the fruit of His handiwork. Therefore Yisrael are called "children to the Holy One, blessed be He," because they have acquired holy souls. As it is written: "You are the children of Hashem your Elohim" (Devarim 14:1). Because THE SOULS are definitely the "children" – the fruit – of His Handiwork.

132. אָמַר ר' יֵיסָא, וַאֲפִילוּ אִינוּן דִּבְהַאי עָלְמָא. הָאֵיךְ אָמַר לוֹ, בְּגִין
דִּבְפַלְגוּת לֵילְיָא, כָּל אִינוּן זַכָּאֵי קְשׁוֹט, כֻּלְהוּ מִתְעָרֵי לְמִקְרֵי
בְּאוֹרַיְיתָא, וּלְמִשְׁמַע תּוּשְׁבְּחָן דְּאוֹרַיְיתָא, וְהָא אִתְּמַר, דְּקֻדְשָׁא בְּרִיךְ
הוּא וְכָל אִינוּן צַדִּיקַיָּא דִּבְגוֹ גִּנְתָּא דְעֵדֶן, כֻּלְהוּ צַיְיתִין לְקָלֵיהוֹן,
וְחוּטָא דְחֶסֶד אִתְמְשַׁךְ עֲלַיְיהוּ בִּימָמָא, דִּכְתִיב יוֹמָם יְצַוֶּה ה' חַסְדּוֹ
וּבַלַּיְלָה שִׁירֹה עִמִּי.

132. Rabbi Yesa said: YOU SAY THAT HE even delights himself with those SOULS of this world. How can that be? He replied, Because at midnight, all the truly righteous people awaken to study Torah and recite all the praises of Torah. And we have learned that the Holy One, blessed be He, together with all the righteous who are in the Garden of Eden, all listen attentively to their voices. And during the day, a thread of grace is woven around them. As it is written: "Yet Hashem will command his loving kindness in the daytime, and in the night, His song shall be with me..." (Tehilim 42:9). BECAUSE OF THE SONG AT NIGHT, THEY MERIT HIS LOVING KINDNESS DURING THE DAY.

133. וְעַל דָּא תּוּשְׁבְּחָן דְּסַלְקִין בְּלֵילְיָא קַמֵּיהּ, דָּא תּוּשְׁבַּחְתָּא שְׁלִים.
תָּא חֲזֵי, בְּשַׁעֲתָא דְיִשְׂרָאֵל הֲווֹ סְגִירִין בְּבָתֵּיהוֹן, כַּד קָטַל קֻדְשָׁא בְּרִיךְ
הוּא בְּכוֹרֵיהוֹן דְּמִצְרָאֵי, הֲווֹ אַמְרֵי הַלֵּילָא וְתִשְׁבְּחָן קַמֵּיהּ.

133. Therefore, the praises that rise up before the Holy One, blessed be He, at night, are the most complete. Come and behold: When Yisrael were shut in their houses, while the Holy One, blessed be He, was slaying the firstborns of the Egyptians, they were reciting these praises and psalms before the Holy One, blessed be He.

134. תָּא חֲזֵי דְּדָוִד מַלְכָּא, הֲוָה קָם בְּפַלְגוּת לֵילְיָא, דְּאִי תֵימָא דַּהֲוָה יָתֵיב אוֹ שָׁכֵיב בְּעַרְסֵיה, וַהֲוָה אָמַר שִׁירִין וְתוּשְׁבְּחָן, לָא, אֶלָּא כְּמָה דִּכְתִיב חֲצוֹת לַיְלָה אָקוּם לְהוֹדוֹת לָךְ. אָקוּם: וַדַּאי בַּעֲמִידָה, לְאִתְעַסְּקָא בְּשִׁירִין וְתוּשְׁבְּחָן דְּאוֹרַיְיתָא.

134. Come and behold: King David used to wake up at midnight. And if you might say that he sat or lay down on his bed while reciting these songs and praises, it is not so! Rather, it is as written: "At midnight I will rise to give thanks to You" (Tehilim 119:62). "I will rise" definitely means he stood upright as he was occupied with the songs and praises of Torah.

135. וּבְגִין כָּךְ, דָּוִד מַלְכָּא, חַי לְעָלְמִין, וַאֲפִילוּ בְּיוֹמֵי מַלְכָּא מְשִׁיחָא, אִיהוּ מַלְכָּא. דְּהָא תְּנַן מַלְכָּא מְשִׁיחָא, אִי מִן חַיָּיא הוּא, דָּוִד שְׁמֵיה, וְאִי מִן מֵתַיָּיא הוּא, דָּוִד שְׁמֵיה, וְאִיהוּ הֲוָה אִתְּעַר בְּצַפְרָא עַד לָא יֵיתֵי, דִּכְתִיב עוּרָה כְבוֹדִי עוּרָה הַנֵּבֶל וְכִנּוֹר אָעִירָה שָּׁחַר.

135. And because of to this, BECAUSE HE DELVED TO THE SONGS AND PRAISES OF TORAH, King David lives on forever. Even during the Days of King Messiah, he still remains the king. For we have learned that if Messiah shall be from among the living, David will be his name. And if he shall be from among THE RESURRECTED SOULS OF the deceased, David shall be his name. And he shall arouse the dawn before he arrives. It is written: "Awake, my glory; awake the harp and the lyre; I will awake the dawn" (Tehilim 57:9), BECAUSE HE ALWAYS AROSE TO STUDY TORAH BEFORE THE BREAK OF DAWN!

16. "And Hashem plagued Pharaoh"

A Synopsis

As the Zohar recounts the story of the King of Egypt's abduction and attempted violation of Sarah, we learn that the angels protected her from his amoral advances. Moreover, it is revealed that the Torah story of Avraham's journey into the land of Egypt is a metaphor for battling the highest degrees of negativity and the strongest selfish desires inherent in our nature. Unlike Adam and Noah, who were enticed by the serpent and succumbed to temptation, Abraham faced and overcame the greatest tests of human nature.

The Relevance of this Passage

Avraham's positive action and spiritual strength opened a cosmic window for all mankind. These words open that window in our own lives, allowing Avraham's power and energy to enter.

136. תָּא חֲזֵי, כָּל הַהוּא לֵילְיָא, דִּשְׁרָה הֲוַת לְגַבֵּיהּ דְּפַרְעֹה, אָתוּ מַלְאֲכֵי עִלָּאֵי, לְזַמְרָא לֵיהּ לְקֻדְשָׁא בְּרִיךְ הוּא, בְּשִׁירִין וְתוּשְׁבְּחָן, אָמַר לוֹ קֻדְשָׁא בְּרִיךְ הוּא, כֻּלְּכוּ זִילוּ וַעֲבִידוּ מַכְתְּשִׁין רַבְרְבִין בְּמִצְרַיִם, רְשִׁימוּ לְמַאן דַּאֲנָא זַמִּין לְמֶעְבַּד לְבָתַר. מַה כְּתִיב וַיְנַגַּע ה' אֶת פַּרְעֹה נְגָעִים גְּדוֹלִים וְגוֹ'.

136. Come and behold: Throughout the night that Sarah was with Pharaoh, the supernal angels came to chant songs and praises before the Holy One, blessed be He. The Holy One, blessed be He, said to them, Go all of you and inflict great plagues upon Egypt, so that these plagues will be a sign and an omen of what I will do in the future. As it is written: "And Hashem plagued Pharaoh and his house with great plagues" (Beresheet 12:17).

137. תָּא חֲזֵי, מַה כְּתִיב, וַיִּקְרָא פַרְעֹה לְאַבְרָם וְגוֹ'. מְנָא הֲוָה יָדַע, דְּהָא לָא כְּתִיב הָכָא, כְּמָה דְּאִתְּמַר בַּאֲבִימֶלֶךְ, דִּכְתִיב, וְעַתָּה הָשֵׁב אֵשֶׁת הָאִישׁ כִּי נָבִיא הוּא וְגוֹ', וְהָכָא לָא אָמַר לֵיהּ מִדֵּי.

137. Come and behold, It is written: "And Pharaoh called Abram" (Beresheet 12:18). HE ASKS: How did he know THAT SARAH IS AVRAM'S

WIFE; it is not written here as it is about Abimelech, "Now therefore restore the man's wife, for he is a prophet" (Beresheet 20:7). Here, THE HOLY ONE, BLESSED BE HE, said nothing to Pharaoh!

א138. אָמַר רַבִּי יִצְחָק, הָא כְּתִיב עַל דְּבַר שָׂרֵי אֵשֶׁת אַבְרָם. דְּהָכֵי הֲווֹ אָמְרֵי לֵיהּ, עַל דְּבַר שָׂרֵי אֵשֶׁת אַבְרָם. דְּהָא לָא הֲוָה מְמַלֵּיל עִמֵּיהּ, כְּמָה דִּמְמַלֵּיל בַּאֲבִימֶלֶךְ, אֶלָּא בְּמִלָּה דָא אִתְּמַר, וְלָא יַתִּיר, מַכְתְּשָׁא דָא, עַל דְּבַר שָׂרֵי אֵשֶׁת אַבְרָם אִיהִי, וְלָא הֲוָה מַלֵּיל עִמֵּיהּ, כְּדֵין יָדַע דְּהָא אִתְּתֵיהּ דְּאַבְרָהָם אִיהִי, מִיָּד וַיִּקְרָא פַרְעֹה לְאַבְרָם וַיֹּאמֶר וגו'.

138. Rabbi Yitzchak said: But it is written, "because of Sarai, Avram's wife." For so THE ANGELS said 'because of Sarai, Avram's wife.' Because THE HOLY ONE, BLESSED BE HE, did not speak with him as he did with Abimelech. So only these words were said and no more: This plague is "because of Sarai, Avram's wife." And even this was not said by THE HOLY ONE, BLESSED BE HE, BUT BY THE ANGELS WHO SMOTE HIM. And then he knew that she was Avraham's wife, so it is written: "And Pharaoh called Abram."

139. וַיְצַו עָלָיו פַּרְעֹה אֲנָשִׁים. לָמָּה, בְּגִין דְּלָא יִקְרַב בַּר נָשׁ בְּהוֹ, לְאַבְאָשָׁא לוֹן. וַיְשַׁלְּחוּ אֹתוֹ. לְוָיְיה עֲבָדוּ לֵיהּ, בְּכָל אַרְעָא דְמִצְרַיִם. אָמַר לוֹ קֻדְשָׁא בְּרִיךְ הוּא הָכֵי אַנְתְּ זַמִּין לְמֶעְבַּד לִבְנוֹי, אַתְּ תּוֹזִיף לוֹן מֵאַרְעָךְ, דִּכְתִיב וַיְהִי בְּשַׁלַּח פַּרְעֹה אֶת הָעָם. דְּאוֹזִיף לוֹן מִכָּל אַרְעֵיהּ.

139. "And Pharaoh commanded his men concerning him." HE ASKS: Why did he do so? AND HE SAYS: So that nobody would come near them and harm them. "And they sent him away" means that they prepared an escort, to accompany him through Egypt. The Holy One, blessed be He, said TO PHARAOH, This is what you shall do in the future to his children; you shall escort them out of your land. As it is written: "And it came to pass, when Pharaoh let the people go" (Shemot 13:17) – meaning that he escorted them throughout his entire country.

140. אָמַר רַבִּי אַבָּא, כָּל כָּךְ לָמָּה אִזְדַּמֵּן לֵיהּ לְאַבְרָהָם, וּלְמַאי אִצְטְרִיךְ. אֶלָּא, בְּגִין לְגַדְּלָא שְׁמֵיהּ דְּאַבְרָהָם וְשָׂרָה בְּעָלְמָא, דַּאֲפִילוּ

בְּמִצְרַיִם, דְּאִינּוּן חֲרָשֵׁי עָלְמָא, וְלָא הֲוָה יָכִיל בַּר נָשׁ לְאִשְׁתְּזֵיב מִנַּיְיהוּ, אִתְגַּדַּל אַבְרָהָם, וְאִסְתַּלֵּיק לְעֵילָא, הֲדָא הוּא דִכְתִיב וַיַּעַל אַבְרָם מִמִּצְרַיִם, לְאָן אֲתַר, הַנֶּגְבָּה.

140. Rabbi Aba asked, Why did this happen to Abraham? For what reason did he have to go through it all? AND HE SAID: "So that Abraham and Sarah would achieve great fame in the eyes of the world. So that even in Egypt, which has the greatest magicians from whom nobody can be saved, Abraham was still able to rise high and be elevated. Therefore, it is written: "And Abram went up out of Egypt" (Beresheet 13:1). Where to? "To the Negev," THAT IS, TO HIS PREVIOUS LEVEL.

141. אָמַר רַבִּי שִׁמְעוֹן, תָּא חֲזֵי, כֹּלָּא רָזָא דְחָכְמְתָא אִיהוּ, וְקָא רָמַז הָכָא בְּחָכְמְתָא, וְדַרְגִּין דִּלְתַתָּא, דְּקָא נָחִית אַבְרָהָם לְעוֹמְקַיָּיא דִלְהוֹן, וְיָדַע לוֹן, וְלָא אִתְדַּבַּק בְּהוֹ, וְתָב לְקַמֵּי מָרֵיהּ.

141. Rabbi Shimon said, Come and behold: Everything is in accordance with the secret of Wisdom. The verse here alludes to Chochmah (Wisdom) and grades below – REFERRING TO THE GRADES OF THE EGYPTIANS, WHO DRAW DOWN CHOCHMAH. And Abraham went down to these great depths and knew them all, but did not attach himself to them. Rather, he returned to his Master.

142. וְלָא אִתְפַּתָּא בְּהוֹ, כְּאָדָם, דְּכַד מָטָא לְהַהוּא דַּרְגָּא, אִתְפַּתָּא בְּנָחָשׁ, וְגָרִים מוֹתָא לְעָלְמָא. וְלָא אִתְפַּתָּא כְּנֹחַ, דְּכַד נָחַת וּמָטָא לְהַהוּא דַּרְגָּא, מַה כְּתִיב, וַיֵּשְׁתְּ מִן הַיַּיִן וַיִּשְׁכָּר וַיִּתְגַּל בְּתוֹךְ אָהֳלֹה. אָהֳלֹה כְּתִיב בְּה"א.

142. And he was not enticed by them, as was Adam, who, when he reached that same level, was enticed by the serpent and brought death upon the whole world. And Abraham was not enticed as was Noah, of whom, when he went down to that grade, it is written: "And he drank of the wine and was drunken, and he was uncovered within his tent (Heb. *ohaloh*)" (Beresheet 9:21). *Ohaloh* is spelled with an additional *Hei,* WHICH IS THE SECRET OF 'A STRANGE WOMAN.'

143. אֲבָל בְּאַבְרָהָם מַה כְּתִיב, וַיַּעַל אַבְרָם מִמִּצְרַיִם. דְּסָלִיק וְלָא
נָחִית, וְתָב לְאַתְרֵיה, לְדַרְגָּא עִלָּאָה, דְּאִתְדַּבַּק בֵּיה בְּקַדְמֵיתָא. וְעוֹבָדָא
דָא הֲוָה, בְּגִין, לְאַחֲזָאָה חָכְמְתָא, דְּאִתְקַיַּים בְּקִיּוּמָא שְׁלִים, כִּדְקָא חָזֵי
לֵיה, וְלָא אִתְפַּתָּא, וְקָם בְּקִיּוּמָא וְתָב לְאַתְרֵיה. הַנֶּגְבָּה: דָּא דָּרוֹם,
דַּרְגָּא עִלָּאָה, דְּאִתְאֲחִיד בֵּיה בְּקַדְמֵיתָא, דִּכְתִיב הָלוֹךְ וְנָסוֹעַ הַנֶּגְבָּה.
אוֹף הָכָא הַנֶּגְבָּה, אֲתַר דְּאִתְדַּבַּק בֵּיה בְּקַדְמֵיתָא.

143. But what is written about Abraham? "And Abram went up out of Egypt." That he went up – not down – and returned to his place, to the supernal grade to which he was previously attached. This action came to reveal Wisdom; he deserved to reach full perfection because he was not enticed BY THE EGYPTIANS; rather he remained entirely steadfast and returned to his place. "The Negev" means the south, CHESED OF ZEIR ANPIN. THIS IS the supernal grade to which he first cleaved. As it is written: "And Abram journeyed, going on still toward the Negev" (Beresheet 12:9). So here as well, "to the Negev" MEANS to the grade to which he had previously cleaved.

144. תָּא חֲזֵי, רָזָא דְּמִלָּה, אִי אַבְרָם לָא יֵיחוֹת לְמִצְרַיִם, וְלָא יִצְטָרֵף
תַּמָּן בְּקַדְמֵיתָא. לָא יְהֵא חוּלָק עַדְבֵיה בְּקֻדְשָׁא בְּרִיךְ הוּא. כְּגַוְונָא דָא
לִבְנוֹי, כַּד בָּעָא קֻדְשָׁא בְּרִיךְ הוּא לְמֶעְבַּד לֵיה עַמָּא חֲדָא, עַמָּא שְׁלִים,
וּלְקָרְבָא לוֹן לְגַבֵּיה, אִי לָא נָחֲתוּ בְּקַדְמֵיתָא לְמִצְרַיִם, וְלָא יִצְטַרְפוּן
תַּמָּן, לָא הֲווֹ עַמָּא יְחִידָא דִילֵיה.

144. Come and behold the secret of this matter: Had Abram not gone down to Egypt and been purified, his destiny would not have been attached to the Holy One, blessed be He. And the same thing happened to his children, when the Holy One, blessed be He, wanted to join them to one nation – one perfect and complete nation – and bring them near to Him. Had they not gone to Egypt first and been purified, they would not have become His one nation.

145. כְּגַוְונָא דָא, אִי לָא אִתְיְיהִיבַת אַרְעָא קַדִּישָׁא לִכְנַעַן בְּקַדְמֵיתָא,
וְיִשְׁלוֹט בָּהּ, לָא הֲוַת אַרְעָא חוּלָקֵיה וְעַדְבֵּיה, דְּקֻדְשָׁא בְּרִיךְ הוּא.

וְכֹלָּא רָזָא חֲדָא.

145. In the same manner, had the Holy Land not been given at first to the Cna'anites and had they not ruled over it, then this land would not have been destined to become the portion and lot of the Holy One, blessed be He; it is all the same secret.

17. "With my soul have I desired you in the night"

A Synopsis

Ancient mysteries pertaining to the soul's activities during the night are unveiled by the Zohar. During sleep, people who have made a sincere attempt at spiritual growth and positive change during the day will see their souls elevate to the highest of heights in the spiritual atmosphere during the night. These souls are given a window through which they can perceive the future. Conversely, those who remain spiritually complacent, who have no regard or care for positive deeds and spiritual growth, their souls elevate, but are immediately engulfed by negative forces.

The Relevance of this Passage

When we awaken in the morning, if our soul ascended to great heights during the night, our sense of intuitiveness and foresight is acutely enhanced. We make the right decisions as we are guided by our intuition. If however, our souls are enveloped by negative forces, these entities whisper lies and speak falsehoods to our soul. These words of deception distort a person's reality during the day, so that life appears even more confusing, more chaotic. We find ourselves at the wrong place at the wrong time. Our thoughts, ideas, and decisions lead us down the wrong path. The verses of the Zohar can help us apply our sleep as a powerful tool that can help our soul elevate to great heights during the night.

146. רַבִּי שִׁמְעוֹן הֲוָה אָזִיל בְּאָרְחָא, וַהֲוָה עִמֵּיה ר' אֶלְעָזָר בְּרֵיה, וְרַבִּי אַבָּא וְרַבִּי יְהוּדָה. עַד דַּהֲווֹ אָזְלֵי, אָמַר רָבִּי שִׁמְעוֹן, תַּוְוהְנָא, הֵיךְ בְּנֵי עָלְמָא לָא מַשְׁגִּיחִין, לְמִנְדַע מִלֵּי דְאוֹרַיְיתָא, וְעַל מָה קַיְימֵי. פְּתַח וַאֲמַר, נַפְשִׁי אִוִּיתִיךְ בַּלַּיְלָה אַף רוּחִי בְקִרְבִּי אֲשַׁחֲרֶךָ. הַאי קְרָא אוֹקְמוּהָ, וְאוֹקִימְנָא לֵיה, אֲבָל תָּא חֲזֵי, נַפְשָׁא דְּבַר נָשׁ, כַּד סָלִיק לְעַרְסֵיה, נָפְקַת מִנֵּיה, וְסָלְקָא לְעֵילָא. וְאִי תֵימָא, דְּכֻלְּהוּ סָלְקָאן. לָאו כָּל חַד וְחַד חָמֵי אַפֵּי מַלְכָּא, אֶלָּא נַפְשָׁא סָלְקָא, וְלָא אִשְׁתְּאַר בָּה בַּהֲדֵי גוּפָא, בַּר חַד רְשִׁימוּ דְקִסְטָא דְּחַיּוּתָא דְלִבָּא.

146. Rabbi Shimon was walking along the way, accompanied by his son, Rabbi Elazar, Rabbi Aba, and Rabbi Yehuda. As they were walking, Rabbi Shimon said: I am amazed that the people of this world do not pay attention to the words of Torah or to understanding the reason for their own existence in the world! He opened the discussion by saying: With my soul (Heb. *Nefesh*) have I desired you in the night; with my spirit (Heb. *Ruach*) within me will I seek you early" (Yeshayah 26:9). This verse has already been explained. But come and behold: When a person goes to bed, his Nefesh leaves and mounts on high. And if you say that they all mount on high – REFERRING TO THE OTHER GRADES, RUACH AND NESHAMAH – it is not so! Because not every one sees the face of the King. Only the Nefesh rises up, leaving an impression, in the form of minimum life for the heart, with the body.

147. וְנַפְשָׁא אָזְלָא וּבָעְיָא לְסָלְקָא. וְכַמָּה דַרְגִּין לְדַרְגִּין לְסָלְקָא, שָׁטָאת, וְהִיא אִתְעָרַעַת בְּהַנֵּי קוֹמְרִין טְהִירִין דִּמְסָאֲבוּתָא, אִי הִיא דַכְיָאת, דְּלָא אִסְתָּאֲבַת בִּימָמָא, סָלְקָא לְעֵילָא. וְאִי לָאו דַכְיָאת, אִסְתָּאֲבַת בֵּינַיְיהוּ, וְאִתְדַּבְּקַת בְּהוֹ, וְלָא סָלְקָא יַתִּיר.

147. As the Nefesh leaves THE BODY and wishes to climb. There are many grades to climb. It wanders about and meets with Klipot of the lights of impurity. If the Nefesh is pure and has not been defiled WITH THE BODY during the day, then it rises upward. But if it is impure then it is defiled among THE KLIPOT cleaves onto them, and climbs no further.

148. וְתַמָּן מוֹדָעֵי לָהּ מִלִּין, וְאִיהוּ אִתְדַּבְּקַת מֵאִינּוּן מִלִּין, דִּזְמַן קָרִיב. וּלְזִמְנִין דְּחַיְיכִין בָּהּ, וּמוֹדָעִין לָהּ מִלִּין כְּדִיבִין. וּכְדֵין אָזְלָא כְּהַאי גַּוְונָא כָּל לֵילְיָא, עַד דְּיִתְעַר בַּר נָשׁ, וְתָאבַת לְאַתְרָהּ. זַכָּאִין אִינּוּן צַדִּיקַיָּא, דְּגַלֵּי לוֹן קֻדְשָׁא בְּרִיךְ הוּא, רָזִין דִּילֵיהּ בְּחֶלְמָא, בְּגִין דְּיִסְתַּמְּרוּן מִן דִּינָא. וַוי לְאִינּוּן חַיָּיבֵי עָלְמָא, דִּמְסָאֲבִין גַּרְמַיְיהוּ וְנַפְשַׁיְיהוּ.

148. And there, AMONG THE KLIPOT, they inform the Nefesh about future events, and THE NEFESH cleaves on to them. Sometimes, they scoff with the Nefesh and tell it lies. Thus, in such a manner, it wanders all night until the person wakes up. Then the Nefesh returns to its place IN THE BODY. Happy are the righteous that the Holy One, blessed be He, reveals His secrets to them in their dreams, so that they may protect themselves from

judgment. Woe to those wicked people who defile themselves and their Nefesh.

149. תָּא חֲזֵי, אִינּוּן דְּלָא אִסְתָּאֲבוּ, כַּד סָלְקֵי בְּעַרְסַיְיהוּ, נַפְשָׁא סָלְקָא וְעָאלַת בֵּין כָּל הַנֵּי דַרְגִּין בְּקַדְמֵיתָא, וְסָלְקָא וְלָא אִתְדַּבְּקַת בְּהוּ. וּלְבָתַר אָזְלָא וְשַׁטְאַת, וְסָלְקָא כְּפוּם אוֹרְחָהּ.

149. Come and behold: As for those who have not defiled themselves DURING THE DAY, when they go to bed to sleep the Nefesh rises. At first, it enters among all the grades OF THE KLIPOT, BUT then it rises above them and does not cleave to them. It continues to wander and climb, until it reaches its proper grade.

150. הַהִיא נַפְשָׁא דְּזָכַת לְסָלְקָא, אִתְחֲזִיאַת קַמֵּיהּ דְּסָבַר אַפֵּי יוֹמִין, וְאִתְדַּבְּקַת בִּרְעוּתָא לְאִתְחֲזָאָה בְּתֵיאוּבְתָּא עִלָּאָה, לְמֶחֱמֵי בְּנוֹעַם מַלְכָּא, וּלְבַקְּרָא בְּהֵיכָלֵיהּ. וְדָא הוּא בַּר נָשׁ דְּאִית לֵיהּ חוּלָקָא תָּדִיר בְּעָלְמָא דְּאָתֵי.

150. The Nefesh that deserves to climb high appears before the King and clings passionately to the desire to be seen and to see the pleasantness of the King and visit His palace. Such person shall always have a share in the World to Come.

151. וְדָא הִיא נַפְשָׁא, דִּכְסִיפָא דִּילָהּ, כַּד סָלְקָא, בְּקֻדְשָׁא בְּרִיךְ הוּא, וְלָא אִתְדַּבְּקַת בְּהַנֵּי זִינִין טְהִירִין אַחֲרָנִין, וְהִיא אָזְלַת בָּתַר זִינָא קַדִּישָׁא, בְּאַתְרָא דְּנָפְקַת מִתַּמָּן. וּבְגִין כָּךְ כְּתִיב נַפְשִׁי אִוִּיתִיךְ בַּלַּיְלָה. בְּגִין לְמִרְדַּף בַּתְרָךְ וְלָא לְאִתְפַּתָּאָה בָּתַר זִינָא אַחֲרָא נוּכְרָאָה.

151. This is the Nefesh, who yearns to reach the Holy One, blessed be He, and does not cleave to other kinds of Lights. It follows its own holy kind and seeks the place from which it came – THE SECRET OF THE NUKVA, FROM WHERE IT IS DRAWN OUT AND COMES FORTH. Therefore it is written: "With my soul (Nefesh) have I desired you in the night," so that I may pursue You, CLEAVE TO YOU, and not be tempted by the other idolatrous kinds.

18. Nefesh, Ruach, and Neshamah

A Synopsis
There are three levels to the human soul: Nefesh [lowest level],
Ruach [Middle level], and Neshamah [Highest level of the three].
There is a process that a human being should undergo throughout
the day in order to elevate from the lowest to the highest level.
This process begins with positive spiritual deeds. According to the
Zohar, spiritual deeds are actions that help bring about a dramatic
change in our character. When we align ourselves with negative
people and chaotic situations in life, we ignite self-centered
reactions within ourselves. A spiritual deed is when we rise above
this power of impulse and alter our emotional and behavioral
responses.

The Relevance of this Passage
Attaining higher levels of growth and evolving our own soul is our
ultimate purpose in life, and the strength and inspiration to strive
for these higher levels comes to us through the letters that compose
this passage.

152. תָּא חֲזֵי, נַפְשִׁי: דָּא נֶפֶשׁ דְּאִיהִי שָׁלְטָא בַּלַּיְלָה, וּלְמִרְדַּף בָּתַר
דַּרְגָּא. רוּחַ בַּיּוֹם, דִּכְתִיב נַפְשִׁי אִוִּיתִיךָ בַּלַּיְלָה, דָּא נֶפֶשׁ דְּאִיהִי שָׁלְטָא
בַּלַּיְלָה, אַף רוּחִי בְקִרְבִּי אֲשַׁחֲרֶךָ. דָּא רוּחַ דְּאִיהוּ שָׁלְטָא בִּימָמָא.

152. Come and behold: "My soul (Nefesh)" – this is the one that dominates
at night and pursues its own grade, WHICH IS THE NUKVA OF ZEIR ANPIN,
IN ORDER TO CLEAVE ON TO IT. "My spirit (Ruach)" governs during the
day. As it is written: "With my soul (Nefesh) have I desired you in the
night," this is the Nefesh that rules at night, BECAUSE AT THAT TIME IT
RISES ON HIGH AND IS PRESENTED BEFORE THE KING. "With my spirit
(Ruach) within me will I seek you early" refers to the Ruach, which governs
during the day.

153. וְאִי תֵּימָא, דִּתְרֵין דַּרְגִּין אִינּוּן בִּפְרוּדָא. לָאו הָכֵי, דְּהָא דַּרְגָּא חַד
אִינּוּן, וְאִינּוּן תְּרֵין, בְּחִבּוּרָא חַד. וְחַד עִלָּאָה, דְּשַׁלְטָא עֲלַיְיהוּ,
וְאִתְדְּבַק בְּהוֹ, וְאִינּוּן בֵּיהּ, וְאִתְקְרִיאַת נְשָׁמָה.

153. And if you say THAT NEFESH AND RUACH are two different grades,
-86-

separate from each other, it is not so! They are two combined as one grade. And there is a higher grade that governs them both; it cleaves to them and they to it – and it is called Neshamah.

154. וְכֻלְּהוּ דַּרְגִּין סַלְקָאן בְּרָזָא דְּחָכְמְתָא, דְּכַד מִסְתַּכְּלָן אִלֵּין דַּרְגִּין, יִסְתַּכֵּל בַּר נָשׁ, בְּחָכְמָה עִלָּאָה, וְהַאי נִשְׁמָה עָיֵיל בְּהוּ, וּמִתְדַּבְּקָן בָּה, וְכַד הַאי שָׁלְטָא, כְּדֵין הַהוּא בַּר נָשׁ, אִקְרֵי קָדוֹשׁ, שְׁלִים מִכֹּלָּא, רְעוּתָא חֲדָא לְגַבֵּי קֻדְשָׁא בְּרִיךְ הוּא.

154. All these grades rise in accordance with the secret of the inner Wisdom, because when the grades look at each other, man is able to look upon the Supernal Wisdom and the Neshamah can enter to them – TO THE NEFESH AND THE RUACH, and they cling to it. So when THE NESHAMAH governs, then man is called holy, perfected in all ways and is entirely devoted to the Holy One, blessed be He.

155. נֶפֶשׁ: אִיהוּ אִתְעֲרוּתָא תַּתָּאָה, וְדָא סְמִיכָא בְּגוּפָא, וְזָנַת לֵיהּ, וְגוּפָא אָחִיד בָּהּ, וְהִיא אִתְאַחֲדַת בְּגוּפָא. לְבָתַר אִתְתַּקָּנַת, וְאִתְעֲבִידַת כֻּרְסְיָיא לְאַשְׁרָאָה עֲלָהּ רוּחַ, בְּאִתְעֲרוּתָא דְּהַאי נֶפֶשׁ. דְּאִתְאֲחִידַת בְּגוּפָא, כְּמָה דִּכְתִיב עַד יֵעָרֶה עָלֵינוּ רוּחַ מִמָּרוֹם.

155. The Nefesh rouses from below, WHICH MEANS THAT IT IS LOWEST OF THE LIGHTS NEFESH, RUACH, AND NESHAMAH. Because it is closest to the body and nourishes it, the body clings to it and it to the body. Afterward, THE NEFESH is amended BY THE GOOD DEEDS A PERSON PERFORMS and becomes a throne on which the Ruach dwells. This is because of the awakening of the Nefesh, which is attached to the body. As it is written: "Until the spirit (Ruach) be poured upon us from on high..." (Yeshayah 32:15).

156. לְבָתַר דְּמִתְתַּקְּנֵי תַּרְוַוְיְיהוּ, זְמִינִין לְקַבְּלָא נִשְׁמָה, דְּהָא רוּחַ אִתְעֲבֵיד כֻּרְסְיָיא לְגַבֵּי נִשְׁמָה, לְאַשְׁרָאָה עֲלֵיהּ, וְהַאי נִשְׁמָה, אִיהִי סְתִימָא, עִלָּאָה עַל כֹּלָּא, טְמִירָא דְּכָל טְמִירִין.

156. After both THE NEFESH AND THE RUACH are amended, they are ready

to receive the Neshamah, because the Ruach becomes a throne on which the Neshamah rests. And this Neshamah is high above all and remains concealed, unattainable, and most hidden!

157. אִשְׁתְּכַח, דְּאִית כָּרְסְיָיא לְכָרְסְיָיא, וְכָרְסְיָיא לְגַבֵּי עִלָּאָה עֲלַייהוּ. וְכַד תִּסְתַּכַּל בְּדַרְגִּין, תִּשְׁכַּח רָזָא דְּחָכְמְתָא בְּהַאי מִלָּה. וְכֹלָּא הוּא חָכְמְתָא לְאִתְדַּבְּקָא בְּהַאי גַּוְונָא מִלִּין סְתִימִין.

157. So there is a throne for the throne, BECAUSE THE NEFESH IS A THRONE FOR THE RUACH, WHICH IS ALSO A THRONE, and a throne for the highest level, BECAUSE THE RUACH IS A THRONE FOR THE NESHAMAH, WHICH IS HIGH ABOVE THEM BOTH. And when you study these grades, you find in this subject the secret of Wisdom. IN OTHER WORDS, YOU LEARN HOW THE LIGHT OF CHOCHMAH IS DRAWN BY THE NEFESH, RUACH, AND NESHAMAH. And everything is in accordance with the higher Wisdom, in order to achieve certain mysteries.

158. תָּא חֲזֵי, נֶפֶשׁ אִיהִי אִתְעָרוּתָא תַּתָּאָה, דְּאִתְדַּבְּקָא בֵּיהּ בְּגוּפָא. כְּגַוְונָא דִּנְהוֹרָא דְּבוֹצִינָא, דִּנְהוֹרָא תַּתָּאָה, דְּאִיהִי אוּכְמָא אִתְדַּבְּקַת בִּפְתִילָה, וְלָא אִתְפְּרַשׁ מִנָּהּ, וְלָא אִתְתַּקְנַת אֶלָּא בָּהּ. וְכַד אִתְתַּקְנַת בִּפְתִילָה, אִתְעֲבִידַת כָּרְסְיָיא לִנְהוֹרָא עִלָּאָה חִוָּורָא, דְּשַׁרְיָיא עַל הַהוּא נְהוֹרָא אוּכְמָא.

158. Come and behold: The Nefesh is the awakening factor from below that cleaves to the body. Just like the light of a candle, in which the lowest light, which is black, clings to the wick and exists only through it. So, when THE BLACK LIGHT is improved through AND CLINGS TO the wick, it becomes a throne for the white light above it, BECAUSE THE WHITE LIGHT rests upon the black light. THIS WHITE LIGHT IS EQUIVALENT TO THE LIGHT OF RUACH.

159. לְבָתַר כַּד מִתְתַּקְנָן תַּרְוַויְיהוּ, אִתְעֲבִידַת הַהוּא נְהוֹרָא חִוָּורָא כָּרְסְיָיא לִנְהוֹרָא סְתִימָאָה, דְּלָא אִתְחֲזֵי וְלָא אִתְיְידַע, מַה דְּשַׁרְיָא עַל הַהוּא נְהוֹרָא חִוָּורָא. וּכְדֵין, נְהוֹרָא שְׁלִים. וְכָךְ הוּא בַּר נָשׁ, דְּאִיהוּ

-88-

שְׁלִים בְּכֹלָּא. וּכְדֵין אִקְרֵי קָדוֹשׁ, כְּד"א לִקְדוֹשִׁים אֲשֶׁר בָּאָרֶץ הֵמָּה וְגוֹ'.

159. After they are fixed, THE BLACK LIGHT WITH THE WHITE LIGHT OVER IT, the white light becomes a throne for a concealed light. What rests on the white light, which is neither seen nor known, IS EQUIVALENT TO THE LIGHT OF NESHAMAH. The light is now complete IN SUCH A MANNER THAT THE CANDLE HAS THREE LIGHTS – ONE ON TOP OF THE OTHER. FIRST, A BLACK LIGHT, WHICH IS THE LOWEST OF THEM ALL AND IS ATTACHED TO THE WICK OF THE CANDLE; SECOND, A WHITE LIGHT THAT RESTS ON THE BLACK LIGHT; AND FINALLY, A HIDDEN LIGHT THAT RESTS ON THE WHITE LIGHT. And so a person who reaches perfection in everything ALSO ATTAINS THESE THREE LIGHTS, ONE OVER THE OTHER, AS IS EXPLAINED BY THE LIGHTS OF THE CANDLE, WHICH CORRESPOND TO THE NEFESH, THE RUACH, AND THE NESHAMAH. Then that person is called 'holy,' as it is written: "for holy people who are in the earth..." (Tehilim 16:3).

160. כְּגַוְונָא דָא בְּרָזָא עִלָּאָה. תָּא חֲזֵי בְּשַׁעֲתָא דְעָאל אַבְרָהָם לְאַרְעָא, אִתְחֲזֵי לֵיהּ קֻדְשָׁא בְּרִיךְ הוּא, כְּמָה דְאִתְּמָר, דִּכְתִיב לַה' הַנִּרְאֶה אֵלָיו, וְקַבֵּיל תַּמָּן נֶפֶשׁ וּבָנָה מִזְבֵּחַ לְהַהוּא דַרְגָּא. לְבָתַר הָלוֹךְ וְנָסוֹעַ הַנֶּגְבָּה, דְּקַבֵּיל רוּחַ. לְבָתַר דְּסָלִיק לְאִתְדַּבְּקָא גּוֹ נִשָׁמָה, כְּדֵין וַיִּבֶן שָׁם מִזְבֵּחַ לַה' סְתָם, דָא הִיא נִשָׁמָה, דְּאִיהִי סְתִימָא דְּכָל סְתִימִין.

160. This appears in the same manner, according to the sublime secret, IN THE VERSES BEFORE US. Come and behold: At the time when Abraham came to the land of Yisrael, the Holy One, blessed be He, appeared before him. As we have already stated and as it is written: "to Hashem, who appeared to him" (Beresheet 12:7). There he attained the LIGHT OF Nefesh, and he built an altar for that grade. After this, "he journeyed on still toward the Negev," where he attained the LIGHT OF Ruach. And after that, when he rose to cleave to the LIGHT OF Neshamah, WHICH IS THE SECRET OF BINAH THAT IS CALLED THE "CONCEALED WORLD," IT IS WRITTEN THAT HE simply "built there an altar to Hashem" (Beresheet 13:18). AS IT IS NOT WRITTEN 'TO HASHEM WHO APPEARED TO HIM.' This refers to the Neshamah, which is the most hidden of all. THEREFORE, IT IS NOT

WRITTEN: 'TO HASHEM WHO APPEARED TO HIM' IN RELATION TO THE
NESHAMAH, AS IS WRITTEN FOR THE LIGHT OF NEFESH.

161. לְבָתַר יָדַע דְּבָעֵי לְאִצְטַרְפָא וּלְאִתְעַטְרָא בְּדַרְגִּין, מִיָּד וַיֵּרֶד אַבְרָם
מִצְרָיְמָה, וְאִשְׁתְּזֵיב מִתַּמָּן. וְלָא אִתְפַּתָּא גּוֹ אִינּוּן טְהִירִין, וְאִתְצָרֵיף
וְתָב לְאַתְרֵיה. כֵּיוָן דְּנָחַת וְאִתְצָרֵיף, מִיָּד וַיַּעַל אַבְרָם מִמִּצְרַיִם, סָלִיק
וַדַּאי וְתָב לְאַתְרֵיה, וְאִתְדַּבַּק בִּמְהֵימְנוּתָא עִלָּאָה, דִּכְתִיב הַנֶּגְבָּה.

161. After this, Abraham knew that he should undergo purification and be
crowned with more grades. So immediately, "Abram went down to Egypt,"
where he was saved by not being enticed by the bright lights. As a result, he
was purified, and returned to his place. Since he went down to Egypt and he
was purified, immediately it says "Abram went up out of Egypt." He
assuredly "went up," WHICH MEANS THAT HE ROSE A GRADE, AS HE NOW
MERITED THE LIGHT OF CHAYAH, WHICH IS THE SECRET OF CHOCHMAH
OF THE RIGHT SIDE, and returned to his place, TO THE LAND OF YISRAEL.
And he cleaved to the Supernal Faith, as it is written: "to the Negev,"
WHICH ALLUDES TO THE CHOCHMAH OF THE RIGHT, NAMELY CHESED
THAT RISES UP DURING MATURITY AND BECOMES CHOCHMAH. THERE
ARE FIVE GRADES IN THIS GRADE – NEFESH, RUACH, NESHAMAH,
CHAYAH AND YECHIDAH – AND ABRAHAM NOW MERITED ITS FIRST
GRADES.

162. מִכָּאן וּלְהָלְאָה יָדַע אַבְרָהָם, חָכְמְתָא עִלָּאָה, וְאִתְדַּבַּק בְּקֻדְשָׁא
בְּרִיךְ הוּא, וְאִתְעֲבֵיד יְמִינָא דְּעָלְמָא. כְּדֵין וְאַבְרָם כָּבֵד מְאֹד בַּמִּקְנֶה
בַּכֶּסֶף וּבַזָּהָב. כָּבֵד מְאֹד, בְּסִטְרָא דְּמִזְרָח. בַּמִּקְנֶה, בְּסִטְרָא דְמַעֲרָב.
בַּכֶּסֶף מִסִּטְרָא דְּדָרוֹם. בַּזָּהָב מִסִּטְרָא דְצָפוֹן.

162. From here onward, Abraham acquired the Supernal Wisdom, cleaved
to the Holy One, blessed be He, and became the right of the world. As it is
then written: "And Abram was very rich in cattle, in silver and in gold"
(Beresheet 13:2). "Very rich" from the direction of the east, WHICH IS
TIFERET; "in cattle" from the west, WHICH IS MALCHUT; "in silver" from
the south, WHICH IS CHOCHMAH, and "in gold" from the north, WHICH IS
BINAH.

163. אָתוּ ר' אֶלְעָזָר וְר' אַבָּא וְכָלְהוּ חַבְרַיָּא, וּנְשָׁקוּ יְדוֹי. בָּכָה ר' אַבָּא וַאֲמַר וַוי וַוי כַּד תִּסְתַּלַּק מִן עָלְמָא, מַאן יַנְהִיר נְהוֹרָא דְאוֹרַיְיתָא, זַכָּאָה חוּלְקֵהוֹן דְּחַבְרַיָּיא דְּשָׁמְעִין מִלִּין דְּאוֹרַיְיתָא אִלֵּין מִפּוּמָךְ.

163. Rabbi Elazar, Rabbi Aba, and their companions came and kissed the hands of Rabbi Shimon. Rabbi Aba wept and said: Woe for the time when you shall leave this world. Who shall then light up the light of Torah? Happy is the fate of the companions who have heard these interpretations of Torah coming from your mouth!

19. "And he went on his journeys"

A Synopsis

Abraham the Patriarch attained the highest level of wisdom that a man can achieve. The spiritual process that he endured to acquire this great wisdom is recounted in the following section.

The Relevance of this Passage

According to the Zohar, the wisdom of Kabbalah is not merely information and knowledge that one acquires as an external asset. On the contrary, Kabbalistic wisdom is the very substance of Light, the essence and core of that which it describes. To acquire spiritual wisdom is to, therefore, infuse one's self with spiritual energy. This great Light nurtures and fills our soul through the wisdom and words of this profound portion.

164. אָמַר רַבִּי שִׁמְעוֹן, תָּא חֲזֵי, מַה כְּתִיב, וַיֵּלֶךְ לְמַסָּעָיו. לְמִפְקַד אַתְרֵיהּ וְדַרְגּוֹי. לְמַסָּעָיו. לְמַסָּעוֹ כְּתִיב, מַאן מַסָּעוֹ. דָּא דַרְגָּא קַדְמָאָה, דְּאִתְחֲזֵי לֵיהּ בְּקַדְמֵיתָא, כְּתִיב הָכָא מַסָּעוֹ, וּכְתִיב הָתָם אֶבֶן שְׁלֵמָה מַסַּע נִבְנָה. וְהָא אוֹקִימְנָא, אֶבֶן שְׁלֵמָה וַדַּאי. מַסַּע כְּמָה דְּאִתְּמַר.

164. Rabbi Shimon said, Come and behold: The verse, "And he went on his journeys... (Heb. *lemasa'av*)" (Beresheet 13:3) MEANS that he went to visit his place and his grade. In this verse, *lemasa'av* IS SPELLED WITHOUT THE LETTER *YUD*, INDICATING THE SINGULAR FORM. SO HE ASKS: Which journey? AND HE ANSWERS: This is the first grade that was revealed to him. Here, it is written: "*masa'av* (his journey)"; and in another place thither (Heb. *masa*): "was built of stone made ready before it was brought" (I Melachim 6:7). As we have already explained, assuredly it was "stone made ready (Heb. *shlemah*)" WHICH MEANS THAT THE STONE, WHICH IS MALCHUT, BELONGS TO THE KING TO WHOM THE PEACE (HEB. *SHALOM*) BELONGS. AND KING SOLOMON (HEB. *SHLOMO*) ALLUDES TO THE KING TO WHOM PEACE BELONGS, NAMELY ZEIR ANPIN. SO BY ANALOGY, IN THE FORMER VERSE AS WELL IT REFERS TO THE NUKVA OF ZEIR ANPIN. "*Masa*" has already been explained.

165. וַיֵּלֶךְ לְמַסָּעָיו. כָּל אִינּוּן דַּרְגִּין, דַּרְגָּא בָּתַר דַּרְגָּא, כְּמָה דְּאִתְּמַר. מִנֶּגֶב וְעַד בֵּית אֵל, לְאַתְקָנָא אַתְרֵיהּ, וּלְחַבְּרָא לוֹן בְּיִחוּדָא שְׁלִים.

דְּהָא מִנֶּגֶב וְעַד בֵּית אֵל, אִשְׁתְּכַח רָזָא דְּחָכְמְתָא, כְּדְקָא יָאוֹת.

165. The words, "on his journeys," MEANS THAT HE MOVED ALONG all of these grades, one after the other, as explained, "from the Negev even to Bet El," to firmly establish his place, WHICH IS CHESED, and to unite it WITH BET EL WHICH IS THE NUKVA. Because the secret of Wisdom lies "from the Negev even to Bet El."

166. אֶל הַמָּקוֹם אֲשֶׁר הָיָה שָׁם אָהֳלֹה בַּתְּחִלָּה אָהֳלֹה בְּהֵ"א, מַאן אָהֳלֹה, דָּא בֵּית אֵל, אֶבֶן שְׁלֵמָה כְּדְאֲמָרָן. תּוּ רְשִׁים וַאֲמַר, אֶל מְקוֹם הַמִּזְבֵּחַ אֲשֶׁר עָשָׂה שָׁם בָּרִאשׁוֹנָה. דִּכְתִיב לֵהּ הַנִּרְאֶה אֵלָיו. וּכְדֵין וַיִּקְרָא שָׁם אַבְרָם בְּשֵׁם ה'. כְּדֵין אִתְדַּבַּק בִּמְהֵימְנוּתָא שְׁלֵימָתָא.

166. In the verse, "to the place where his tent (Heb. *ohaloh*) had been at the beginning" (Beresheet 13:3), the word *ohaloh* is spelled with a letter *Hei* (at the end) INSTEAD OF WITH A LETTER *VAV*. THIS IMPLIES THAT *ohaloh* is Bet El, WHICH IS CALLED a "stone made ready," as we have stated, NAMELY THE NUKVA OF ZEIR ANPIN. Furthermore, he states THAT HE REFERS TO THE NUKVA, and says: "To the place of the altar, which he had made there at first..." Of this it says: "to Hashem, who appeared to him," WHICH ALLUDES TO THE SECRET OF THE NUKVA. And then it is written: "And there Abram called in the name of Hashem." Because then he cleaved to the complete faith.

167. תָּא חֲזֵי, בְּקַדְמֵיתָא סָלֵיק מִתַּתָּא לְעֵילָא, דִּכְתִיב וַיֵּרָא ה' אֶל אַבְרָם, וּכְתִיב לֵהּ הַנִּרְאֶה אֵלָיו. וְדָא הוּא דַרְגָּא קַדְמָאָה, כִּדְאֲמָרָן אֶבֶן שְׁלֵמָה. וּלְבָתַר הָלוֹךְ וְנָסוֹעַ הַנֶּגְבָּה. דַּרְגָּא בָּתַר דַּרְגָּא, עַד דְּאִתְעַטַּר בַּדָּרוֹם, חוּלְקֵיהּ וְעַדְבֵּיהּ. לְבָתַר סָתִים מִלָּה, כַּד סָלֵיק, וַאֲמַר לֵהּ סְתָם, דָּא עָלְמָא עִלָּאָה. וּמִתַּמָּן נָטִיל בְּדַרְגִּין, וְנָחֵית מֵעֵילָא לְתַתָּא, וְאִתְדַּבַּק כֹּלָּא בְּאַתְרֵיהּ, כְּדְקָא יָאוֹת.

167. Come and behold: At first, he rose THROUGH THE GRADES from lower to higher, as it is written: "And Hashem appeared to Abram," and "to Hashem who appeared to him." This is the first grade, as we have stated,

WHICH IS THE SECRET OF a "stone made ready," NAMELY, THE GRADE OF NUKVA WHERE 'SEEING' LIES. AND FROM HERE HE ATTAINED THE NEFESH. After this it is written: "going on still toward the south," MEANING THAT HE ROSE grade after grade until he was crowned in the south, WHICH IS CHESED OF ZEIR ANPIN; THIS IS his share and destiny. AND FROM HERE HE REACHED RUACH. After this, as he rose higher, the matter is concealed, and it simply says, "to Hashem," RATHER THAN, "TO HASHEM WHO APPEARED TO HIM." This is the upper world, NAMELY BINAH. AND FROM HERE HE MERITED THE NESHAMAH. He went through further grades, WHICH MEANS THAT HE WENT DOWN TO EGYPT AND WENT UP FROM THERE. THROUGH THIS, HE ACHIEVED THE GRADE OF CHOCHMAH FROM THE RIGHT SIDE, AS CHESED BECAME CHOCHMAH. Afterward he descended from above downward, AS IS EXPLAINED IN THE VERSE, "AND HE WENT ON HIS JOURNEYS..." and everything was properly attached to its place!

168. וְהָכָא כַּד תִּסְתַּכַּל בְּדַרְגִּין, תִּשְׁכַּח רָזָא דְחָכְמְתָא עִלָּאָה, מַה כְּתִיב, וַיֵּלֶךְ לְמַסָּעָיו מִנֶּגֶב, מִסְטְרָא דְיָמִינָא, שֵׁירוּתָא דְעָלְמָא עִלָּאָה, סְתִימָא עֲמִיקָא לְעֵילָא, עַד אֵין סוֹף, וְנָחֵית דַּרְגָּא בָּתַר דַּרְגָּא, מִנֶּגֶב וְעַד בֵּית אֵל מֵעֵילָא לְתַתָּא.

168. Here, as you observe the grades THAT APPEAR IN THE SCRIPTURE, you shall find the secret of the supernal Wisdom (Chochmah) – NAMELY CHOCHMAH OF THE RIGHT SIDE. As it is written: "And he went on his journeys from the Negev." THIS MEANS from the right side, WHICH IS THE SOUTH AND the beginning of the Supernal, NAMELY BINAH, concealed and unfathomed deep, reaching up to the Endless World (Heb. *Ein Sof*). And from there he descended, grade after grade, "from the Negev even to Bet El" (Beresheet 18:8), WHICH IS THE NUKVA.

169. וּכְתִיב, וַיִּקְרָא שָׁם אַבְרָם בְּשֵׁם ה'. אַדְבַּק יְחוּדָא בְּאַתְרֵיה, כִּדְקָא יָאוֹת, דִּכְתִיב, אֶל מְקוֹם הַמִּזְבֵּחַ אֲשֶׁר עָשָׂה שָׁם בָּרִאשׁוֹנָה, מַאי אֲשֶׁר עָשָׂה שָׁם. דְּסָלֵיק לָה מִתַּתָּא לְעֵילָא. וְהַשְׁתָּא נָחֵית בְּדַרְגִּין מֵעֵילָא לְתַתָּא, בְּגִין דְּהוּא לָא תַעֲדֵי מֵאִינוּן דַּרְגִּין עִלָּאִין, וְאִינוּן לָא יַעֲדוּן מִנֵּהּ, וְיִתְיַחֵד כֹּלָּא בְּיִחוּדָא חֲדָא כִּדְקָא יָאוֹת.

169. And it is written: "and there Abram called in the name of Hashem," MEANING THAT he attached Unity in its proper place. As it is written: "To the place of the altar, which he had made there at first." What is THE MEANING OF "which he made there?" IT MEANS THAT FIRST he elevated THE NUKVA from below to the upper grades and now he brought her down through the grades, so that she remains attached to those supernal grades and they remain attached to her, and all become united in one as should be!

170. כְּדֵין אִתְעַטַּר אַבְרָהָם, וַהֲוָה חוּלָק עַדְבֵיה דְּקֻדְשָׁא בְּרִיךְ הוּא וַדַּאי. זַכָּאִין אִינּוּן צַדִּיקַיָּיא, דְּמִתְעַטְּרֵי בֵּיה, בְּקֻדְשָׁא בְּרִיךְ הוּא. וְהוּא, מִתְעַטֵּר בְּהוֹן. זַכָּאִין אִינּוּן בְּעָלְמָא דֵין, וְזַכָּאִין אִינּוּן בְּעָלְמָא דְּאָתֵי. עֲלַיְיהוּ כְּתִיב וְעַמֵּךְ כֻּלָּם צַדִּיקִים לְעוֹלָם יִרְשׁוּ אָרֶץ. וּכְתִיב וְאוֹרַח צַדִּיקִים כְּאוֹר נֹגַהּ הוֹלֵךְ וָאוֹר עַד נְכוֹן הַיּוֹם.

170. Then Abraham was crowned and his destiny surly became connected with the Holy One, blessed be He. Happy are the righteous, who are crowned by the Holy One, blessed be He, and He, in turn, is crowned by them. They are happy in this world, as well as in the World to Come. Of them it is written: "Your people also shall be all righteous: they shall inherit the land for ever" (Yeshayah 60:21), and "But the path of the just is like the gleam of sunlight, that shines ever more brightly until the height of noonday" (Mishlei 4:18).

171. אֲזָלוּ, כַּד מָטוּ בְּחַד בֵּי חֲקַל, יָתְבוּ. פָּתַח ר' שִׁמְעוֹן וְאָמַר, פְּנֵה אֵלַי וְחָנֵּנִי וגו'. הַאי קְרָא אִית לְאִסְתַּכְּלָא בֵּיה, וְהָא אוֹקִימְנָא לֵיה, בְּכַמָּה אֲתָר. אֲבָל בְּהַאי קְרָא, מִלִּין סְתִימִין אִית בֵּיה, פְּנֵה אֵלַי. וְכִי דָּוִד אָמַר פְּנֵה אֵלַי וְחָנֵּנִי.

171. They went along until they reached a field in which they sat down. Rabbi Shimon opened the discussion by saying: "Turn to me and have mercy upon me..." (Tehilim 86:16). This verse should be studied. Even though we have explained it in many places, there is hidden meaning in its passages. HE ASKS: How could it be that David, WHO WAS HUMBLE, should say: "Turn to me and have mercy upon me?"

172. אֶלָּא, בְּגִין דַּרְגָּא דִּילֵיהּ, דְּאִיהוּ אִתְעַטַּר בֵּיהּ קָאָמַר, תְּנָה עֻזְּךָ
לְעַבְדֶּךָ. תְּנָה עֻזְּךָ, דָּא עֹז עִלָּאָה, כִּדְכְתִיב וְיִתֶּן עֹז לְמַלְכּוּ. מַאן מַלְכּוּ.
דָּא מֶלֶךְ סְתָם, מַלְכָּא מְשִׁיחָא. אוּף הָכָא לְעַבְדֶּךָ, דָּא מַלְכָּא מְשִׁיחָא,
כִּדְאָמָרָן מֶלֶךְ סְתָם.

172. AND HE REPLIES: He was referring to his grade, by which he is
crowned. IN OTHER WORDS, HE PRAYED FOR THE SAKE OF THE NUKVA
OF ZEIR ANPIN. In the verse, "give Your strength to your servant," the
words "give Your strength" refer to the supernal strength, WHICH IS
CHOCHMAH. As it is written: "and he shall give strength to his king" (I
Shmuel 2:10). Who is his king? His king, without any specific reference, is
clearly to King Messiah, NAMELY MALCHUT, WHICH IS THE NUKVA OF
ZEIR ANPIN. In this passage, the words "your servant" also refer to
Messiah. As we have stated, the king is mentioned without any reference;
THEREFORE IT ALLUDES TO THE NUKVA.

173. וְהוֹשִׁיעָה לְבֶן אֲמָתֶךָ. וְכִי לָא הֲוָה בְּרֵיהּ דְּיִשַׁי אִיהוּ, עַד דְּאִיהוּ
אָמַר בִּשְׁמָא דְּאִמֵּיהּ, וְלָא בִּשְׁמָא דַּאֲבוֹי. אֶלָּא, הָא אוֹקִימְנָא, דְּכַד
יֵיתֵי בַּר נָשׁ לְקַבֵּל מִלָּה עִלָּאָה לְאִדְכָּרָא, בָּעֵי לְמֶהַךְ בְּמִלָּה דְּאִיהוּ
וַדַּאי. וְעַל דָּא, אַדְכַּר לְאִמֵּיהּ, וְלָא לַאֲבוֹי. וְתוּ, הָא תָּנִינָן דְּדָא מֶלֶךְ
כִּדְקָאָמָרָן.

173. About the verse, "And save the son of Your handmaid" (Tehilim
86:16), HE ASKS: Was he not the son of Jesse? If so, then why did he refer
to himself as the son of his mother and not of his father? AND HE REPLIES:
We have already explained that when a person comes forward to receive
something lofty, he should refer only to things that are absolutely true.
Therefore he mentioned his mother, WHEN HE SAID, "AND SAVE THE SON
OF YOUR HANDMAID," and not his father. And furthermore, we have
already learned that this refers to an unspecified king, as we said. THIS
MEANS THAT HE DID NOT PRAY FOR HIMSELF, BUT FOR THE SAKE OF
THE NUKVA WHICH IS CALLED 'KING' WITH NO FURTHER
QUALIFICATIONS. THIS IS WHY HE MENTIONED HIS MOTHER'S NAME,
WHO PERTAINS TO THE NUKVA, AND NOT HIS FATHER'S NAME!

20. "And there was a strife
between the herdsmen of Avram's cattle"

A Synopsis

When Abraham discovered that Lot, his nephew, was engaged in Idol Worshipping, Abraham knew immediately that he had to disconnect himself completely from Lot. The spiritual principle of this story concerns the influence that our immediate environment exerts upon us. It is incumbent upon all of us to associate with people who are sincere in their desire for spiritual growth. Although our own intentions may be pure, the influences that surround us inevitably affect our way of life.

The Relevance of this Passage

The Kabbalistic definition of *Idol Worshipping* includes much more than simply praying to statues or other false gods. Whenever we allow an external object or situation to control our behavior, our thoughts, or our emotions, we are worshipping an idol. Many people, for example, worship the idol of money. They are disciples and servants to their own businesses. Others are ruled by appearances and the perceptions of those around them. The moment we allow the external world to control our hearts and minds, we are committing the sin of Idol Worshipping. In this portion, freedom from external negative forces and influences is bestowed upon the reader.

174. אֲמַר ר' שִׁמְעוֹן, תָּא חֲזֵי, מַה כְּתִיב, וַיְהִי רִיב בֵּין רֹעֵי מִקְנֵה אַבְרָם, רִב כְּתִיב, חָסֵר יוֹד, דְּבָעָא לוֹט לְמֶהְדַּר לְפוּלְחָנָא נוּכְרָאָה, דְּפָלְחֵי יָתְבֵי אַרְעָא, וְסוֹפֵיהּ דִּקְרָא אוֹכַח, דִּכְתִיב וְהַכְּנַעֲנִי וְהַפְּרִיזִי אָז יוֹשֵׁב בָּאָרֶץ.

174. Rabbi Shimon said, Come and behold, It is written: "And there was strife (Heb. *riv*) between the herdsmen of Avram's cattle." The word *riv* is spelled *Resh Bet* without the letter *Yud*, which means that Lot wanted to return to idol worshipping, which was the custom of the natives. Thus, at the end of the verse, it is written: "and the Cnaani and the Perizi dwelt then in the land." THIS TEACHES US THAT LOT WANTED TO WORSHIP IDOLS AS THEY DID. AND THE REASON WHY IT GIVES *RIV* WITHOUT A *YUD* IS TO POINT TOWARD IDOL WORSHIP. IT FOLLOWS THE SECRET FOUND IN THE VERSE, "AND THE ELDER (HEB. *RAV*) SHALL SERVE THE YOUNGER"

20. "And there was a strife
between the herdsmen of Avram's cattle"

(BERESHEET 25:23). ESAU SAID TO JACOB, "I HAVE ENOUGH (HEB.
RAV - RESH BET)" (BERESHEET 33:9), BUT JACOB SAID TO HIM, "AND
BECAUSE I HAVE ALL (HEB. *KOL*)" (BERESHEET 25:11). THIS IS ALSO
THE SECRET OF THE VERSE, "AND A MIXED MULTITUDE (HEB. *EREV
RAV*) WENT UP ALSO WITH THEM" (SHEMOT 12:38).

175. וּמְנָלָן דְּלוֹט אַהֲדַר לְסָרְחָנֵיהּ, לְפוּלְחָנָא נוּכְרָאָה, דִּכְתִיב, וַיִּסַּע
לוֹט מִקֶּדֶם. מַאי מִקֶּדֶם, מִקַּדְמוֹנוֹ שֶׁל עוֹלָם. כְּתִיב הָכָא, וַיִּסַּע לוֹט
מִקֶּדֶם, וּכְתִיב וַיְהִי בְּנָסְעָם מִקֶּדֶם, מַה לְהַלָּן נְטִילוּ מִקַּדְמוֹנוֹ שֶׁל עוֹלָם
אוּף הָכָא כֵּן.

175. How do we know that Lot reverted to his evil ways of idolatry? We
know is from the verse: "and Lot journeyed from the east (namely: from
yore)" (Beresheet 13:11). And what is the meaning of "yore?" It means
from Him – He who is more ancient than the world. And thus it is written:
"and Lot journeyed from the east," and "it came to pass, as they journeyed
from the east" (Beresheet 11:1). So, because there they journeyed away from
Him – He who is more ancient than the world, it means the same thing here!

176. כֵּיוָן דְּיָדַע אַבְרָהָם, דְּלוֹט לְהָכֵי נָטֵי לִבֵּיהּ. מִיָּד וַיֹּאמֶר אַבְרָם אֶל
לוֹט וגו' הִפָּרֶד נָא מֵעָלַי. לֵית אַנְתְּ כְּדַאי לְאִתְחַבְּרָא בַּהֲדָאי. כְּדֵין
אִתְפְּרַשׁ אַבְרָהָם מִנֵּיהּ, וְלָא בָעָא לְמֵיהַךְ וּלְאִתְחַבְּרָא עִמֵּיהּ, דְּכָל מַאן
דְּיִתְחַבַּר לְחַיָּיבָא, סוֹפֵיהּ לְמֵיהַךְ אֲבַתְרֵיהּ, וּלְאִתְעַנָּשׁ בְּגִינֵיהּ.

176. As soon as Abraham realized that Lot reverted TO IDOLATRY, he spoke
to him: "And Abram said to Lot, separate yourself, I pray you, from me"
(Beresheet 13:8-9) – you are not worthy of associating with me. So
Abraham separated from him and did not want to travel with or deal him
any more, because whoever accompanies a wicked person shall eventually
follow in his steps and be punished because of him.

177. מְנָלָן, מִיהוֹשָׁפָט, דְּאִתְחַבַּר עִם אַחְאָב, וְאִלְמָלֵא זְכוּ דַּאֲבָהָן,
אִתְעֲנַשׁ תַּמָּן, דִּכְתִיב וַיִּזְעַק יְהוֹשָׁפָט. וּכְדֵין אִשְׁתְּזִיב, דִּכְתִיב וַיְסִיתֵם

אֱלֹקִים מִמֶּנּוּ.

177. How do we know this? We know this from Yehoshafat, who associated with Ahab. And had it not been for the merit of his ancestors, Yehoshafat would have been punished because of Ahab. As it is written: "but Yehoshafat cried out..." (II Divrei Hayamim 18:31). Then he was saved, as it is written: "and Elohim moved them to depart from him" (Ibid.)

178. וְעַ״ד לָא בָּעָא אַבְרָם לְמֵיהַךְ בַּהֲדֵיהּ דְּלוֹט. וְעִם כָּל דָּא, לָא בָּעָא לוֹט, לְמֶהֱדַר מִסּוּרְחָנֵיהּ, אֶלָּא וַיִּבְחַר לוֹ לוֹט אֶת כָּל כִּכַּר הַיַּרְדֵּן. וַיִּסַּע לוֹט מִקֶּדֶם. אִתְנְטֵיל מִן קַדְמָאָה דְּעָלְמָא, וְלָא בָּעָא לְאִתְדַּבְּקָא בִּמְהֵימְנוּתָא שְׁלֵימָתָא, כְּאַבְרָהָם.

178. Although Abraham did not want to travel with Lot, Lot still did not want to return from his evil way. As it is written: "Then Lot chose him all the plain of Jordan; and Lot journeyed from the east" (Beresheet 13:11), WHICH MEANS THAT he "journeyed away" from Him – He who is more ancient than the world, and refused to adhere to the true complete Faith, as did Abraham.

179. אַבְרָם יָשַׁב בְּאֶרֶץ כְּנָעַן. לְאִתְדַּבְּקָא בְּאַתְרָא דִּמְהֵימְנוּתָא, וּלְמִנְדַּע חָכְמְתָא, לְאִתְדַּבְּקָא בְּמָארֵיהּ. וְלוֹט יָשַׁב בְּעָרֵי הַכִּכָּר וַיֶּאֱהַל עַד סְדֹם, עִם אִינּוּן חַיָּיבִין דְּעָלְמָא, דִּנְפָקוּ מִגּוֹ מְהֵימְנוּתָא, דִּכְתִיב, וְאַנְשֵׁי סְדוֹם רָעִים וְחַטָּאִים לַה׳ מְאֹד. כָּל חַד אִתְפְּרַשׁ לְאָרְחֵיהּ, כִּדְקָא יָאוֹת. בְּגִין כָּךְ זַכָּאִין אִינּוּן חַבְרַיָּיא, דְּמִשְׁתַּדְּלֵי בְּאוֹרַיְיתָא יְמָמָא וְלֵילְיָא, וְחַבְרוּתָא דִּלְהוֹן בְּקֻדְשָׁא בְּרִיךְ הוּא. וַעֲלַיְיהוּ כְּתִיב וְאַתֶּם הַדְּבֵקִים בַּה׳ אֱלֹקֵיכֶם חַיִּים כֻּלְּכֶם הַיּוֹם.

179. THE LAND OF CANAAN IS THE SECRET OF THE NUKVA, AND, AND IT IS WRITTEN: "Abram dwelt in the land of Canaan" IN ORDER to cleave to the place of the Faith, WHICH IS THE SECRET OF THE NUKVA, and to attain knowledge about the Wisdom of his Master. Lot, however, "dwelt in the cities of the plain, and pitched his tent toward Sodom," WHICH MEANS

20. "And there was a strife between the herdsmen of Avram's cattle"

THAT he became associated with the wicked of the world, who departed from the Faith. They are described by the verse, "But the men of Sodom were wicked and sinners before Hashem exceedingly." Each one departed and went his own way: ABRAHAM TO THE PATH OF HOLINESS, AND LOT TO THE WICKED. Because of this, happy are those freinds, who study Torah day and night, as they cleave to the Holy One, blessed be He. THEY DO AS ABRAHAM DID, AND NOT AS LOT. Of them it is written: "But you that did cleave to Hashem your Elohim are alive every one of you this day" (Devarim 4:4).

21. "And Hashem said to Abram after Lot was separated from him"

A Synopsis

Progressing from the previous section, the Zohar reveals how Abraham the Patriarch prepared and readied himself to receive the Light of the Creator after disconnecting himself from the negative influences of his nephew Lot.

The Relevance of this Passage

This portion illustrates the importance of preparing ourselves, both spiritually and physically, for the Light of Creator to rest upon us. This preparation process is referred to as "building one's Vessel." Without a Vessel, the Light of the Creator cannot be revealed. This important Kabbalistic principle is clarified by an analogy: The sun requires a physical object, a vessel to reflect, and thus, reveal its light. In like manner, the Light of the Creator requires a Vessel in order to illuminate our physical world. These sacred verses assist us in the building of our own Vessel so that spiritual light can illuminate the dark areas of our life.

180. וַה׳ אָמַר אֶל אַבְרָם אַחֲרֵי הִפָּרֶד לוֹט מֵעִמּוֹ וְגו׳. ר׳ אַבָּא פָּתַח וַיָּקָם יוֹנָה לִבְרוֹחַ תַּרְשִׁישָׁה מִלִּפְנֵי ה׳ וְגו׳, וַוי לְמַאן דְּאִסְתַּתַּר מִקַּמֵּי קֻדְשָׁא בְּרִיךְ הוּא, דִּכְתִיב בֵּיהּ הֲלֹא אֶת הַשָּׁמַיִם וְאֶת הָאָרֶץ אֲנִי מָלֵא נְאֻם ה׳. וְהוּא אָתֵי לְמֶעֱרַק מִקַּמֵּיה.

180. "And Hashem said to Abram, after Lot was separated from him..." (Beresheet 13:14). Rabbi Aba opened the discussion by saying: "And Jonah rose up to flee to Tarshish from the presence of Hashem" (Yonah 1:3). Woe to those who hide from the presence of the Holy One, blessed be He, of whom it is written: "I fill the heaven and earth, says Hashem" (Yirmeyah 23:24). AND HE WONDERS, why did Jonah want to flee from the presence OF THE HOLY ONE, BLESSED BE HE?

181. אֶלָּא, כְּתִיב יוֹנָתִי בְּחַגְוֵי הַסֶּלַע בְּסֵתֶר הַמַּדְרֵגָה. יוֹנָתִי: דָּא כְּנֶסֶת יִשְׂרָאֵל. בְּחַגְוֵי הַסֶּלַע: דָּא יְרוּשָׁלַם, דְּאִיהִי סָלְקָא עַל כָּל עָלְמָא. מַה סֶּלַע, אִיהִי עִלָּאָה וְתַקִּיפָא עַל כֹּלָּא, אוֹף יְרוּשָׁלַם אִיהִי עִלָּאָה וְתַקִּיפָא עַל כֹּלָּא. בְּסֵתֶר הַמַּדְרֵגָה: דָּא אֲתָר דְּאִקְרֵי בֵּית קֹדֶשׁ הַקֳּדָשִׁים, לִבָּא דְּכָל עָלְמָא.

181. AND HE REPLIES: In the verse, "My dove (Heb. *yonati*), who are in the clefts of the rock, in the secret places of the cliff" (Shir Hashirim 2:14), "my dove" refers to the Congregation of Yisrael, NAMELY THE SHECHINAH; "in the clefts of the rock" means Jerusalem, that is, the highest place in the world. Just as the rock is more eminent and stronger than everything, so is Jerusalem more eminent and stronger than all. The words, "in the secret places of the cliff" refer to the place that is called the place of the holy of holies, which is the heart of the entire world.

182. וּבְגִּין כָּךְ כְּתִיב בְּסֵתֶר הַמַּדְרֵגָה, בְּגִין דְּתַמָּן הֲוַת שְׁכִינְתָּא מִסְתַּתְּרָא, כְּאִתְּתָא דְּאִיהִי צְנוּעָה לְבַעְלָהּ, וְלָא נָפְקָא מִבֵּיתָא לְבַר. כְּמָה דְּאַתְּ אֲמַר, אֶשְׁתְּךָ כְּגֶפֶן פּוֹרִיָּה בְּיַרְכְּתֵי בֵיתֶךָ וְגו'. כָּךְ כְּנֶסֶת יִשְׂרָאֵל לָא שָׁרְיָיא לְבַר מֵאַתְרָהָא, בְּסִתִּירוּ דְּדַרְגָּא, אֶלָּא בְּזִמְנָא דְגָלוּתָא, דְּאִיהוּ בְּגוֹ גָּלוּתָא, וּבְגִּין דְּאִיהִי בְּגָלוּתָא, שְׁאָר עַמִּין אִית לוֹן טִיבוּ וְשַׁלְוָה יַתִּיר.

182. It is written: "in the secret places of the cliff" OF THE HOLY OF HOLIES because the Shechinah used to hide Herself there, as does a modest wife, who does not show herself out of her house. Just as it is written: "Your wife shall be as a fruitful vine by the sides of your house" (Tehilim 128:3), so the Congregation of Yisrael does not dwell out of its own place, WHICH IS the "secret places of the cliff," except at times of exile. And since it is in exile, then the other nations of the world enjoy greater prosperity and peace THAN YISRAEL.

183. תָּא חֲזֵי, בְּזִמְנָא דְּיִשְׂרָאֵל שָׁרְיָין עַל אַרְעָא קַדִּישָׁא, כֹּלָּא הֲוָה מִתְתַּקַּן כְּדְקָא יָאוֹת, וְכֻרְסְיָיא שְׁלִים עֲלַיְיהוּ, וְעַבְדֵּי פּוּלְחָנָא, וּבְקַע אֲוִירִין דְּעַלְמָא, וְסָלִיק הַהוּא פּוּלְחָנָא לְעֵילָא לְאַתְרֵיהּ, בְּגִין דְּאַרְעָא לָא אִתְתַּקְּנַת לְפוּלְחָנָא, אֶלָּא לְיִשְׂרָאֵל בִּלְחוֹדַיְיהוּ. וּבְגִין כָּךְ, שְׁאָר עַמִּין עעכו"ם, הֲווֹ מִתְרַחֲקֵי, דְּלָא הֲווֹ שָׁלְטִין בָּהּ כִּדְהַשְׁתָּא, בְּגִין דְּלָא אִתְזְנוּ אֶלָּא מִתַּמְצִית.

183. Come and behold: When the nation of Yisrael dwells in the Holy Land, everything is in its place, and the throne, WHICH IS THE NUKVA, is firmly established over them. They worshipped Hashem, WHICH MEANS THAT THEY ELEVATED MAYIN NUKVIN (FEMALE WATERS), and transcended the layers of air of the world. Their service ascended on high to its place TO THE MALE AND THE FEMALE, CAUSING THEM TO MATE WITH EACH OTHER. Because Yisrael alone is suited for the service, other nations were kept afar from the land. They did not rule as they do now. The other nations were nourished only from the residue. IN OTHER WORDS, THE ABUNDANCE THAT YISRAEL DREW DOWN BY THEIR SERVICE WAS ENOUGH TO ALSO NOURISH THE OTHER NATIONS OF THE WORLD. BUT THE MAJORITY OF THE ABUNDANCE WENT TO YISRAEL; THE OTHER NATIONS OF THE WORLD RECEIVED ONLY A RESIDUE OF THIS ABUNDANCE. THIS IS WHY DOMINION WAS GIVEN TO YISRAEL.

184. וְאִי תֵימָא, הָא חָמֵינָן כַּמָּה מַלְכִין הֲווֹ, דְּשַׁלִּיטִין בְּזִמְנָא דְּבֵית הַמִּקְדָּשׁ קַיָּים עַל עָלְמָא. תָּא חֲזֵי, בְּבַיִת רִאשׁוֹן, עַד לָא סָאִיבוּ יִשְׂרָאֵל אַרְעָא, לָא הֲווֹ שַׁלְטִין שְׁאָר עַמִּין עעכו"ם, אֶלָּא, אִתְזְנוּ מִתַּמְצִית, וּבָהּ הֲווֹ שַׁלְטִין, וְלָאו כָּל כָּךְ. כֵּיוָן דְּחָבוּ יִשְׂרָאֵל, וְסָאִיבוּ אַרְעָא, כְּדֵין כִּבְיָכוֹל, דָּחוּ לָהּ לִשְׁכִינְתָּא מֵאַתְרָהּ, וְאִתְקְרָבַת לְדוּכְתָּא אָחֳרָא, וּכְדֵין שַׁלְטִין שְׁאָר עַמִּין, וְאִתְייְהֵיב לוֹן רְשׁוּ לְשַׁלְטָאָה.

184. You may say, 'But we can see that many foreign kings ruled, even when the Temple was still in the world.' Come and behold: During the first Temple, Yisrael had not yet defiled the land. As a result, the other nations did not yet rule completely. Rather, they were nourished from the residue. And because their dominion was nourished by this residue, their rule was not very powerful. But as Yisrael sinned and defiled the land, it was as if they drove the Shechinah from her place to another place. And then, the other nations took control and were allowed to rule.

185. תָּא חֲזֵי, אַרְעָא דְיִשְׂרָאֵל, לָא שַׁלִּיט עֲלָהּ מְמַנָּא אָחֳרָא, בַּר קֻדְשָׁא בְּרִיךְ הוּא בִּלְחוֹדוֹי. וּבְשַׁעֲתָא דְּחָאבוּ יִשְׂרָאֵל, וַהֲווֹ מְקַטְרִין לְטַעֲווֹן אָחֳרָנִין, בְּגוֹ אַרְעָא, כִּבְיָכוֹל אִדְּחְיָיא שְׁכִינְתָּא מֵאַתְרָהּ, וּמָשְׁכֵי וּמְקַטְרֵי לְאִתְקַשְּׁרָא טַעֲווֹן אָחֳרָן גּוֹ שְׁכִינְתָּא, וּכְדֵין אִתְייְהֵיב לוֹן שַׁלְטָנוּתָא, בְּגִין דִּקְטֹרֶת קַטְרָא הוּא לְאִתְקַטְּרָא. וּכְדֵין, שָׁלְטוּ שְׁאָר

עַמִּין, וּבָטְלוּ נְבִיאִים, וְכָל אִינּוּן דַּרְגִּין עִלָּאִין לָא שָׁלְטוּ בְּאַרְעָא.

185. Come and behold: No other Governor rules over the land of Yisrael but the Holy One, blessed be He, alone. So when Yisrael sinned and burned incense to other deities in the land, it is as if the Shechinah was driven from her place. Because the incense attracted other deities, these deities became associates with Yisrael and dominion was handed over to them. Because the incense makes connections, THEY DREW THEIR POWER FROM THE SHECHINAH AND ATTAINED THEIR DOMINION THROUGH HER. Then the other nations ruled, the prophets were no more, and all the supernal grades ceased to rule over the land.

186. וְלָא אַעֲדִיו שָׁלְטָנוּתָא דִּשְׁאָר עַמִּין, בְּגִין דְּאִינּוּן מָשְׁכוּ לִשְׁכִינְתָּא לְגַבַּיְיהוּ. וְעַל דָּא בְּבַיִת שֵׁנִי, הָא שׁוּלְטָנוּתָא מִשְׁאָר עַמִּין, לָא אַעֲדִיו, וְכ"ש בְּגָלוּתָא, דִּשְׁכִינְתָּא בִּשְׁאָר עַמִּין, אֲתַר דִּשְׁאָר מְמַנָּן שָׁלְטִין, וּבְגִין כָּךְ כֻּלְּהוּ יַנְקִין מִן שְׁכִינְתָּא, דְּאִתְקְרִיבַת גַּבַּיְהוּ.

186. And the dominion was not taken away from the other nations, because they drew THE ABUNDANCE OF the Shechinah to themselves. Therefore, during the second Temple, the dominion of the other nations was not withdrawn from them. Even more so at the time of exile, when the Shechinah resided among other nations where other Governors had control. Thus they all draw their power from the Shechinah, who is drawn to them.

187. וְעַל דָּא, בְּזִמְנָא דְּיִשְׂרָאֵל, הֲווֹ שָׁרָאן עַל אַרְעָא, וּפָלְחֵי פּוּלְחָנָא דְקֻדְשָׁא בְּרִיךְ הוּא, שְׁכִינְתָּא הֲוַת צְנוּעָה בֵּינַיְיהוּ, וְלָא נָפְקַת מִגּוֹ בֵּיתָא לְבַר בְּאִתְגַּלְיָיא. וּבְגִין כָּךְ, כָּל אִינּוּן נְבִיאִים דַּהֲווֹ בְּהַהוּא זִמְנָא, לָא נָטְלוּ נְבוּאָה אֶלָּא בְּאַתְרָה כִּדְקָאַמְרָן. וּבְגִין כָּךְ, יוֹנָה הֲוָה עָרַק לְבַר מֵאַרְעָא קַדִּישָׁא, דְּלָא יִתְגְּלֵי עֲלֵיהּ נְבוּאָה, וְלָא יְהַךְ בִּשְׁלִיחוּתָא דְקֻדְשָׁא בְּרִיךְ הוּא.

187. Accordingly, when Yisrael dwelt in the land and performed the services for the Holy One, blessed be He, the Shechinah was hidden modestly among them and did not leave Her home nor appear in public.

Because of this, all the prophets that existed during that time, NAMELY THE TIME WHEN THE TEMPLE STOOD, did not receive their prophecy from outside of Her place, OUTSIDE OF THE LAND OF YISRAEL, as we have stated. Because of this, Jonah fled from the Holy Land. He did not want the prophecy revealed to him, so that he would not be obliged to complete the mission of the Holy One, blessed be He.

188. וְאִי תֵימָא, הָא חָמֵינָן דְּאִתְגַּלְיָיא שְׁכִינְתָּא בְּבָבֶל, דְּאִיהוּ לְבַר. הָא אוֹקִימְנָא, דִּכְתִיב הָיֹה הָיָה, דַּהֲוָה, מַה דְּלָא הֲוָה מִן קַדְמַת דְּנָא, מִיּוֹמָא דְּאִתְבְּנֵי בֵּי מַקְדְּשָׁא, וְהַהִיא נְבוּאָה לְשַׁעֲתָא הֲוַת.

188. You might say, 'But the Shechinah revealed Herself to Ezekiel in Babylon, which is outside of the land of Yisrael!' However, as we have explained, these words, "the word came (Heb. *hayoh hayah*)" (Yechezkel 1:3), refer to an event that never happened before nor since the construction of the Temple. That prophecy was for that time only, TO BRING CONSOLATION TO YISRAEL.

189. וּכְתִיב, עַל נְהַר כְּבָר. נָהָר דִּכְבָר הֲוָה, מִיּוֹמָא דְּאִתְבְּרֵי עָלְמָא, וּשְׁכִינְתָּא אִתְגַּלְיָיא תָּדִיר עֲלֵיהּ, דִּכְתִיב וְנָהָר יוֹצֵא מֵעֵדֶן לְהַשְׁקוֹת אֶת הַגָּן וּמִשָּׁם יִפָּרֵד וְגוֹ'. וְדָא אִיהוּ חַד מִינַּיְיהוּ.

189. And as it is written: "by the river Kevar," WHICH MEANS the river had already (Heb. *kevar*) been there since the creation of the world, and the Shechinah had always appeared there, EVEN BEFORE THE TEMPLE WAS CONSTRUCTED. As it is written: "And a river went out of Eden to water the garden; and from thence it was parted, and branched to four streams" (Beresheet 2:10). The river Kevar is one of these four STREAMS.

190. וְתַמָּן אִתְגַּלְיָיא שְׁכִינְתָּא, לְפוּם שַׁעֲתָא דְּאִצְטְרִיכוּ לָהּ יִשְׂרָאֵל, לְפוּם צַעֲרַיְיהוּ. אֲבָל בְּזִמְנָא אָחֳרָא לָא אִתְגַּלְיָיא, וּבְגִין כָּךְ יוֹנָה, בְּגִין דְּלָא תִשְׁרֵי עֲלוֹי שְׁכִינְתָּא, וְלָא תִתְגְּלֵי עֲלֵיהּ, אֲזַל מֵאַרְעָא קַדִּישָׁא, וַעֲרַק. הה"ד מִלִּפְנֵי ה'. וּכְתִיב כִּי יָדְעוּ הָאֲנָשִׁים כִּי מִלִּפְנֵי ה' הוּא בּוֹרֵחַ.

190. So the Shechinah was revealed there temporarily because of Yisrael's need to be consoled for the misery CAUSED BY THE DESTRUCTION OF THE TEMPLE. But, at other times, the Shechinah did not appear OUTSIDE THE LAND OF YISRAEL. Therefore, Jonah fled, so that the Shechinah would not rest upon or appear before him. He left the Holy Land and fled. This is why it is written: "from the presence of Hashem," and "that the men knew that he fled from the presence of Hashem" (Yonah 1:10).

191. תָּא חֲזֵי כַּמָּה דִּשְׁכִינְתָּא לָא אִתְגַּלְיָא, אֶלָּא בְּאַתְרָא דְּאִתְחֲזֵי לָהּ, אוֹף הָכֵי לָא אִתְחֲזֵי וְלָא אִתְגַּלְיָא, אֶלָּא בְּבַר נָשׁ דְּאִתְחֲזֵי לָהּ. דְּהָא מִן יוֹמָא דְּסָלֵיק עַל רְעוּתֵיהּ דְּלוֹט, לְאִתְהַפְּכָא בְּסֻרְחָנֵיהּ, אִסְתַּלְּקַת רוּחָא קַדִּישָׁא מֵאַבְרָהָם. וְכַד אִסְתַּלַּק לוֹט מִנֵּיהּ, מִיַּד שָׁרָא רוּחַ קוּדְשָׁא בְּדוּכְתֵּיהּ. הֲדָא הוּא דִּכְתִּיב, וַה' אָמַר אֶל אַבְרָם אַחֲרֵי הִפָּרֶד לוֹט מֵעִמּוֹ וְגו'.

191. Come and behold; Just as the Shechinah does not reveal Herself in an inappropriate place, so She does not reveal herself to anyone who is unworthy of Her. So from the time that Lot planned on returning to his evil ways, the Holy Spirit departed from Abraham. And when Lot separated from him, the Holy Spirit came back to rest in its place – NAMELY UPON ABRAHAM. This is why it is written: "And Hashem said to Abram, after Lot was separated from him..."

192. תָּא חֲזֵי, כֵּיוָן דְּחָמָא אַבְרָהָם, דְּלוֹט הֲוָה תָּב לְסֻרְחָנֵיהּ, הֲוָה דָּחִיל אַבְרָהָם, אָמַר דִּילְמָא ח"ו, בְּגִין חַבְרוּתָא דְּדָא, אֲבִידְנָא בְּגִינֵיהּ חוּלָקָא קַדִּישָׁא, דְּאַעֲטַר לִי קֻדְשָׁא בְּרִיךְ הוּא. כֵּיוָן דְּאִתְפְּרַשׁ מִנֵּיהּ, אָמַר לוֹ שָׂא נָא עֵינֶיךָ וּרְאֵה מִן הַמָּקוֹם אֲשֶׁר אַתָּה שָׁם.

192. Come and behold: Abraham saw that Lot returned to his evil habits and was afraid. He said: 'Could it be, heaven forbid, that because I associate with him, I have lost the holy portion that the Holy One, blessed be He, adorned me with!' But as soon as Lot left him, the Holy One, blessed be He, said to him, "Now lift up your eyes, and look from the place where you are."

193. מַאי מִן הַמָּקוֹם אֲשֶׁר אַתָּה שָׁם. דְּאִתְדַּבְּקַת בֵּיהּ בְּקַדְמֵיתָא,

וְאִתְעַטְּרַת בְּהֵימְנוּתָא שְׁלֵימָתָא. צָפוֹנָה, וְנֶגְבָּה, וְקַדְמָה, וְיָמָה. אִלֵּין
אִינוּן מַסָּעָיו, דַּהֲווֹ בְּקַדְמֵיתָא, דִּכְתִיב וַיֵּלֶךְ לְמַסָּעָיו. וּכְתִיב הָלוֹךְ
וְנָסוֹעַ הַנֶּגְבָּה. אִלֵּין דַּרְגִּין עִלָּאִין, דְּאִתְעַטַּר בִּמְהֵימְנוּתָא שְׁלֵימָתָא
בְּקַדְמֵיתָא.

193. AND HE ASKS: What is the meaning of the words, "from the place where you are?" AND HE ANSWERS: They mean from the place to which you have cleaved from the beginning and in which you were adorned by the complete Faith. "Northward, southward, eastward, and westward" are the directions of his first journeys, as it is written: "And he went on his journeys." THIS IS THE SECRET OF NEFESH, RUACH, NESHAMAH, AND CHAYAH. THUS, NORTHWARD IS THE SECRET OF BINAH AND NESHAMAH; SOUTHWARD IS THE SECRET OF CHOCHMAH AND CHAYAH; EASTWARD IS THE SECRET OF TIFERET AND RUACH; WESTWARD IS THE SECRET OF MALCHUT AND NEFESH. And it is written: "going on still toward the Negev"; these are the supernal grades with which he was adorned with the Complete Faith, as at first.

194. וּכְדֵין אִתְבַּשַּׂר, דְּלָא יַעֲדֵי מִנֵּיה וּמִן בְּנוֹי לְעָלְמִין, דִּכְתִיב כִּי אֶת
כָּל הָאָרֶץ אֲשֶׁר אַתָּה רוֹאֶה. מַאי אֲשֶׁר אַתָּה רוֹאֶה. דָּא דַּרְגָּא קַדְמָאָה
דְּאִתְגַּלְיָא לֵיה, כְּד"א לה' הַנִּרְאֶה אֵלָיו. וּבְגִין כָּךְ אֲשֶׁר אַתָּה רוֹאֶה,
בְּגִין דְּדַרְגָּא דָּא קַדְמָאָה, אִתְכְּלִיל מִכֻּלְּהוּ דַּרְגִּין, וְכֻלְּהוּ אִתְחֲזוּן בֵּיה,
וּבְגִין כָּךְ, כִּי אֶת כָּל הָאָרֶץ אֲשֶׁר אַתָּה רוֹאֶה וְגו'.

194. And then he received the good news that they would not depart from him or from his children forever. As it is written: "For all the land which you see, TO YOU WILL I GIVE IT, AND TO YOUR SEED FOR EVER" (Beresheet 13:15). AND HE ASKS: What is the meaning of 'which you see'? AND HE REPLIES: This is the first grade that appeared to him, WHICH IS THE GRADE OF NEFESH. As it is written: 'to Hashem, who appeared to him.' As a result, it is written: 'which you see,' because this first grade, WHICH IS THE NUKVA, includes other grades, and all of the grades appear in it. This is why IT IS WRITTEN: "For all the land which you see ..."

22. "As the apple tree among the trees of the forest"

A Synopsis
The Zohar tells us that Rabbi Elazar and Rabbi Chizkiyah were lodging at an inexpensive inn located in the city of Lod. Kabbalistically, these two great sages are actually occupying a specific spiritual dimension as they discuss the many layers of meaning in Biblical scripture. Specifically, these two spiritual giants are discussing a verse in the Torah that tells of an apple tree in the midst of a forest.

The Relevance of this Passage
As the two mystics explore the various Lights and spiritual forces concealed within the text of the Torah, the letters that form this Kabbalistic story arouses our appreciation for the depth, richness, and spiritual Light contained in each word and verse of the Torah.

195. ר' אֶלְעָזָר אִעֲרַע בְּבֵי אוּשְׁפִּיזָא בְּלוּד, וַהֲוָה עִמֵּיה רַבִּי חִזְקִיָּה. קָם בְּלֵילְיָא לְמִלְעֵי בְּאוֹרַיְיתָא, קָם רַבִּי חִזְקִיָּה גַּבֵּיה, אָמַר לוֹ ר' אֶלְעָזָר, בְּקִיסְטְרָא דְּקוּסְטָא, חַבְרַיָּיא שְׁכִיחֵי.

195. Rabbi Elazar came to an inn in Lod together with Rabbi Chizkiyah. Rabbi Elazar got up during the night to study Torah. Rabbi Chizkiyah stood by him, BECAUSE THE PLACE WAS SMALL. Rabbi Elazar said: The friends always meet in a narrow place. HE MEANT THAT BECAUSE THE FRIENDS STUDY TORAH MUCH OF THE TIME AND WORK ONLY A LITTLE, THEY MEET IN SMALL AND NARROW INNS; THEY HAVE NO MONEY TO RENT LARGE ROOMS.

196. פָּתַח ר' אֶלְעָזָר וְאָמַר, כְּתַפּוּחַ בַּעֲצֵי הַיַּעַר וגו'. כְּתַפּוּחַ, דָּא קֻדְשָׁא בְּרִיךְ הוּא דְּאִיהוּ חָמִיד וּמִתְעַטַּר בִּגְווֹנוֹי, מִכָּל שְׁאָר אִילָנִין, דְּלָא אִית דְּדָמֵי לֵיה. רָשִׁים אִיהוּ מִכֹּלָּא, רָשִׁים הוּא, דְּלֵית אָחֳרָא כְּוָותֵיה.

196. Rabbi Elazar opened the discussion by saying, "As the apple tree among the trees of the forest..." (Shir Hashirim 2:3). "The apple tree" refers to the Holy One, blessed be He, who is precious and decorated by His

colors. HIS COLORS – WHITE, RED, AND GREEN – ARE THE SECRET OF THE THREE COLUMNS OF CHESED, GVURAH, AND TIFERET. His tree has no equal among all the other trees, WHICH REPRESENT THE SEVENTY GOVERNORS WHO IMITATE THE HOLINESS, AS AN APE DOES A MAN. He is distinguished from them all, and there is no one like Him.

197. בְּגִינֵי כָּךְ, בְּצִלּוֹ חִמַּדְתִּי. בְּצִלּוֹ: וְלָא בְּצִלָּא אָחֳרָא. בְּצִלּוֹ: וְלָא בְּצִלָּא דִּשְׁאָר מְמַנָּן. חִמַּדְתִּי, אֵימָתַי, מִן יוֹמָא דַּהֲוָה אַבְרָהָם בְּעָלְמָא, דְּאִיהוּ חָמִיד וְרָחִים לֵיהּ לְקֻדְשָׁא בְּרִיךְ הוּא בְּאַהֲבָה. כְּד"א אַבְרָהָם אוֹהֲבִי. וּפִרְיוֹ מָתוֹק לְחִכִּי, דָּא הוּא יִצְחָק, דְּאִיהוּ אִיבָּא קַדִּישָׁא.

197. Because of this, "I sat down under his shadow with great delight." (Ibid.) The verse reads, "under his shadow," and not under any anyone else's, BECAUSE BEFORE SHE WAS PROPERLY ESTABLISHED AND WELL AMENDED, THE SHECHINAH LAY UNDER THE SHADOW OF THE LEAVES OF THE FIG TREE. SO "UNDER HIS SHADOW" AND NOT UNDER ANY OTHER'S ALLUDES TO THE OTHER SEVENTY GOVERNORS. "With great delight," HE ASKS: Since when? WE CANNOT SAY THAT SHE HAS ALWAYS EXPERIENCED GREAT DELIGHT, PARTICULARLY AFTER THE SIN WHEN SHE WAS UNDER THE INFLUENCE OF THE SEVENTY GOVERNORS!" AND HE SAYS: This is from the day when Abraham came to this world, who loved the Holy One, blessed be He. It is written: "Abraham my beloved" (Yeshayah 41:8), BECAUSE HE FULLY AMENDED THE SHECHINAH AND SHE WAS UNITED AGAIN WITH ZEIR ANPIN." "His fruit was sweet to my taste" refers to Isaac, who is the holy fruit OF ABRAHAM.

198. דָּבָר אַחֵר, בְּצִלּוֹ חִמַּדְתִּי וְיָשַׁבְתִּי, דָּא יַעֲקֹב. וּפִרְיוֹ מָתוֹק לְחִכִּי, דָּא יוֹסֵף הַצַּדִּיק, דַּעֲבַד פֵּירִין קַדִּישִׁין בְּעָלְמָא. וְע"ד כְּתִיב אֵלֶּה תוֹלְדוֹת יַעֲקֹב יוֹסֵף. דְּכָל אִינוּן תּוֹלְדוֹת דְּיַעֲקֹב בְּיוֹסֵף הַצַּדִּיק קַיְימֵי, דַּעֲבֵיד תּוֹלְדוֹת. וּבְגִין כָּךְ, אִקְרוּן יִשְׂרָאֵל, עַל שְׁמָא דְאֶפְרַיִם, דִּכְתִיב הֲבֵן יַקִּיר לִי אֶפְרַיִם וְגוֹ'.

198. Another explanation of the verse, "I sat down under his shadow with great delight," is that it refers to Jacob, WHO IS THE SECRET OF THE CENTRAL COLUMN. "And his fruit was sweet to my taste" refers to Joseph

the righteous, WHO IS THE SECRET OF YESOD, who brought forth holy fruits to the world, NAMELY SOULS. Therefore, it is written: "These are the generations of Jacob: Joseph" (Beresheet 37:2), which shows that all the generations of Jacob are established by Joseph the righteous, WHO IS THE ASPECT OF THE YESOD OF JACOB. And because of this Yisrael is called by the name of Ephraim, as it is written: "Ephraim my dear son" (Yirmeyah 31:19).

199. דָּבָר אַחֵר כְּתַפּוּחַ בַּעֲצֵי הַיַּעַר. דָּא אַבְרָהָם. דְּדָמֵי לֵיהּ לְתַפּוּחַ, דְּסָלֵיק רֵיחִין, וְאִתְרְשִׁים בִּמְהֵימְנוּתָא שְׁלֵימָתָא, עַל כָּל בְּנֵי דָרֵיהּ, וְאִתְרְשִׁים חַד לְעֵילָא, וְאִתְרְשִׁים חַד לְתַתָּא, דִּכְתִיב אֶחָד הָיָה אַבְרָהָם.

199. There is another explanation of the verse "as the apple tree among the trees of the forest" is that the words refer to Abraham, who was like a fragrant apple tree and was distinguished from others of his generation by his complete faith. And he became distinguished as one both above and below. As is written: "Abraham was one" (Yechezkel 33:24).

200. מַאי טַעֲמָא הֲוָה אֶחָד. דְּלָא הֲוָה אָחֳרָא בְּעָלְמָא, דִּי סָלֵיק לִמְהֵימְנוּתָא דְּקֻדְשָׁא בְּרִיךְ הוּא, בַּר אִיהוּ. אָמַר לוֹ ר' חִזְקִיָּה, וְהָא כְּתִיב וְאֶת הַנֶּפֶשׁ אֲשֶׁר עָשׂוּ בְחָרָן. אָמַר לוֹ עַד כְּעַן, אִינוּן לָא הֲווֹ בְּדַרְגִּין עִלָּאִין, דְּאִתְעַטַּר בְּהוֹ אַבְרָהָם.

200. HE ASKS: Why was he 'one'?" AND HE SAYS: Because there was no other then in the world, who had elevated himself by the faith in the Holy One, blessed be He, besides him. Rabbi Chizkiyah said to him: But it is written: "and the souls that they had made in Charan," WHICH MEANS THAT ABRAHAM BROUGHT MEN AND SARAH BROUGHT WOMEN TO BE CONVERTED. SO THERE WERE PEOPLE WITH FAITH IN THE HOLY ONE, BLESSED BE HE, BESIDES HIM! He told him, Nevertheless, they did not reach the supernal grades with which Abraham was adorned!

201. לְבָתַר אָמַר לוֹ, תּוּ שְׁמַעְנָא, דְּלָא אִקְרֵי אַבְרָהָם אֶחָד, עַד דְּאִסְתַּלַּק בְּיִצְחָק וְיַעֲקֹב. כֵּיוָן דְּאִסְתַּלַּק בְּיִצְחָק וְיַעֲקֹב, וַהֲווֹ כֻּלְּהוּ תְּלָתְהוֹן אֲבָהָן דְּעָלְמָא, כְּדֵין אִקְרֵי אַבְרָהָם אֶחָד. וּכְדֵין הוּא תַפּוּחַ

בְּעָלְמָא. רְשִׁים מִכָּל בְּנֵי עָלְמָא. אֲמַר לֵיהּ שַׁפִּיר קָא אֲמַרְתְּ.

201. Later, he said to him: I have also heard that Abraham was not referred to as one, until he became united with Isaac and Jacob. Only after he became associated with Isaac and Jacob and the three were the fathers of the world was Abraham named "one." THIS MEANS THAT ONLY AFTER HE COMBINED ALL THREE COLUMNS TO ONE WAS HE NAMED "ONE"; then he was CALLED the apple tree of the world, WHICH WAS DISTINGUISHED BY ITS THREE COLORS, WHITE, RED, AND GREEN, WHICH ALLUDE TO THE THREE COLUMNS. "Thus, he was distinguished and different from all the people of his generation. He said to him: Well said!

202. דָּבָר אַחֵר, כְּתַפּוּחַ בַּעֲצֵי הַיַּעַר, דָּא קֻדְשָׁא בְּרִיךְ הוּא. כֵּן דּוֹדִי, דָּא קֻדְשָׁא בְּרִיךְ הוּא. בְּצִלּוֹ, דָּא קֻדְשָׁא בְּרִיךְ הוּא. חִמַּדְתִּי וְיָשַׁבְתִּי, בְּיוֹמָא דְּאִתְגְּלֵי קֻדְשָׁא בְּרִיךְ הוּא, עַל טוּרָא דְסִינַי, וְקַבִּילוּ יִשְׂרָאֵל אוֹרַיְיתָא, וַאֲמָרוּ נַעֲשֶׂה וְנִשְׁמַע.

202. A different explanation of the verse, "As the apple tree among the trees of the forest," is that it refers to the Holy One, blessed be He, THE RIGHT COLUMN; "so is my beloved" refers to the Holy One, blessed be He, THE LEFT COLUMN; AND "under his shadow" refers to the Holy One, blessed be He, THE CENTRAL COLUMN. "I sat down...with great delight" refers to the day on which the Holy One, blessed be He, appeared on Mount Sinai, and Yisrael received Torah and said:, "will we do, and obey" (Shemot 24:7). THEN, THE SHECHINAH SAID: "I SAT DOWN...WITH GREAT DELIGHT."

203. וּפִרְיוֹ מָתוֹק לְחִכִּי. אִלֵּין מִלִּין דְּאוֹרַיְיתָא, דִּכְתִיב בְּהוּ וּמְתוּקִים מִדְּבַשׁ וְנוֹפֶת צוּפִים. דָּבָר אַחֵר וּפִרְיוֹ מָתוֹק לְחִכִּי, אִלֵּין נִשְׁמָתְהוֹן דְּצַדִּיקַיָּא, דְּכֻלְּהוּ אִיבָּא דְּעוֹבָדוֹי דְּקוּדְשָׁא בְּרִיךְ הוּא, וְקַיְימֵי עִמֵּיהּ לְעֵילָא.

203. "And his fruit was sweet to my taste" refers to the words of Torah, which are described as "sweeter than honey and the honeycomb" (Tehilim 19:11). According to another explanation, "And his fruit was sweet to my taste" refers to the souls of the righteous, who are all the fruit of the handiwork of the Holy One, blessed be He, and abide with Him above.

204. תָּא חֲזֵי, כָּל נִשְׁמָתִין דְּעָלְמָא, דְּאִינּוּן אִיבָּא דְּעוֹבָדוֹי דְּקֻדְשָׁא בְּרִיךְ הוּא, כֻּלְּהוּ חַד, בְּרָזָא חַד, וְכַד נָחֲתֵי לְעָלְמָא, כֻּלְּהוּ מִתְפָּרְשִׁין, בִּגְוָונִין דְּכַר וְנוּקְבָא, וְאִינּוּן דְּכַר וְנוּקְבָא מְחוּבָּרִין כַּחֲדָא.

204. Come and behold: All the souls in the world, who are the fruit of the handiwork of the Holy One, blessed be He, are one in the same secret. IN THE UPPER WORLD, THEY ARE NOT YET DISTINGUISHED AS MALE AND FEMALE. Only when they descend to the world are their souls separated to male and female. And every soul has a male and female part, united together as one.

205. וְתָא חֲזֵי, תֵּיאוּבְתָּא דְּנוּקְבָא לְגַבֵּי דְכוּרָא, עָבֵיד נָפָשׁ. וּרְעוּתָא דְּתֵיאוּבְתָּא דִּדְכוּרָא, לְגַבֵּי נוּקְבָא, וְאִתְדַּבְּקוּתָא דִּילֵיהּ בָּהּ, אַפֵּיק נָפָשׁ, וְכָלֵיל תֵּיאוּבְתָּא דְּנוּקְבָא, וְנָטֵיל לָהּ. וְאִתְכְּלֵיל תֵּיאוּבְתָּא תַּתָּאָה, בְּתֵיאוּבְתָּא דִּלְעֵילָא, וְאִתְעֲבִידוּ רְעוּתָא חֲדָא, בְּלָא פֵּרוּדָא.

205. Come and behold: The passion of the female to the male brings forth a Nefesh. And the passion of the male towards the female, and his clinging to her, also brings forth a Nefesh, which includes THE NEFESH FROM the passion of the female. Thus the passion of the lower, THE FEMALE, is united with the passion of the upper, THE MALE, and BOTH NEFASHOT become one desire without any separation.

206. וּכְדֵין כָּלֵיל כֹּלָּא נוּקְבָא, וְאִתְעַבְּרַת מִן דְּכוּרָא, וְתֵיאוּבְתִּין דִּתְרְוַויְיהוּ מִתְדַּבְּקָן כַּחֲדָא, וְעַל דָּא, כֹּלָּא כָּלֵיל דָּא בְּדָא. וְכַד נִשְׁמָתִין נָפְקִין, דְּכַר וְנוּקְבָא כַּחֲדָא נָפְקִין.

206. Then the female includes everything within herself BY TAKING BOTH NEFASHOT and becoming pregnant by the male with them. And the passion of both of them conjoins them as one. Therefore, each is included within the other. And when the souls come out, male and female are within them together, as one.

207. לְבָתַר, כֵּיוָן דְּנָחֲתֵי, מִתְפָּרְשָׁן דָּא לְסִטְרָא דָּא, וְדָא לְסִטְרָא דָּא, וְקֻדְשָׁא בְּרִיךְ הוּא מְזַוֵּוג לוֹן לְבָתַר. וְלָא אִתְיְיהֵיב זִוּוּגָא לְאַחֲרָא, אֶלָּא לְקֻדְשָׁא בְּרִיךְ הוּא בִּלְחוֹדוֹי, דְּאִיהוּ יָדַע זִוּוּגָא דִּלְהוֹן לְחַבְּרָא לוֹן כִּדְקָא יָאוֹת.

207. Later, when they descend TO THIS WORLD, they are separated from each other, THE MALE FROM THE FEMALE. Each one turns his way. And the Holy One, blessed be He, mates them again. The key to mating them is given only to the Holy One, blessed be He. Only He knows the proper mate for each to properly reunite them, SO THE MALE AND FEMALE WILL BE OF THE SAME SOUL.

208. זַכָּאָה הוּא בַּר נָשׁ, דְּזָכֵי בְּעוֹבָדוֹי וְאָזֵיל בְּאוֹרַח קְשׁוֹט. בְּגִין דְּאִתְחַבַּר נֶפֶשׁ בְּנֶפֶשׁ, כְּמָה דַּהֲוָה מֵעִיקָרָא. דְּהָא אִי זָכֵי בְּעוֹבָדוֹי, דָּא הוּא בַּר נָשׁ שְׁלִים כִּדְקָא יָאוֹת, וּבְגִין כָּךְ כְּתִיב, וּפִרְיוֹ מָתוֹק לְחִכִּי. דְּהוּא בְּתִקּוּנָא מְבָרַךְ, לְאִתְבָּרְכָא מִנֵּיהּ עָלְמָא, בְּגִין דְּכֹלָּא בְּעוֹבָדִין דְּבַר נָשׁ תַּלְיָא, אִי זָכֵי אִי לָא זָכֵי.

208. Happy is the person who is meritorious in his deeds and walks the Path of Truth, so they will unite one Nefesh with the other, THE MALE WITH THE FEMALE, as they were before THEY CAME TO THIS WORLD. For if he is worthy in deeds, he is a complete man. BUT IF HE IS NOT MERITORIOUS, THAN HE SHALL NOT BE GIVEN HIS SOULMATE. This is why it is written about him, "And his fruit is sweet to my taste." Because this man is blessed with reunion OF MALE AND FEMALE, AS IT SHOULD PROPERLY BE. And the world is blessed by him THROUGH HIS SWEET FRUIT, NAMELY GOODLY CHILDREN, because everything depends on whether a person's actions have been meritorious or not.

209. אָמַר רָבִּי חִזְקִיָּה, הָכֵי שְׁמַעְנָא, דִּכְתִיב מִמֶּנִּי פֶּרְיְךָ נִמְצָא. קֻדְשָׁא בְּרִיךְ הוּא אָמַר לָהּ לִכְנֶסֶת יִשְׂרָאֵל, מִמֶּנִּי וַדַּאי, פֶּרְיְךָ נִמְצָא, פֶּרְיֵי נִמְצָא, לָא כְּתִיב, אֶלָּא פֶּרְיְךָ, הַהוּא תֵּיאוֹבְתָּא דְּנוּקְבָא, דַּעֲבֵיד נֶפֶשׁ, וְאִתְכְּלִיל בְּתוּקְפָּא דִּדְכוּרָא, וְאִתְכְּלִיל נֶפֶשׁ בְּנֶפֶשׁ, וְאִתְעֲבִידוּ חַד,

כְּלִיל דָּא בְּדָא, כִּדְאֲמָרָן. לְבָתַר אִשְׁתְּכָחוּ תַּרְוַויְיהוּ בְּעָלְמָא, וְדָא בְּחֵילָא דִּדְכוּרָא, אִשְׁתְּכַח אִיבָּא דְנוּקְבָא.

209. Rabbi Chizkiyah said: I have heard of the verse, "From me is your fruit found" (Hoshea 14:9). The Holy One, blessed be He, said to the Congregation of Yisrael, WHICH IS THE SHECHINAH, assuredly, "From me assuredly is your fruit found." It is "your fruit," rather than "my fruit," TO TEACH US that the passion of the female forms the Nefesh, which combines with the might of the male, so that the Nefesh OF THE FEMALE is conjoined with the Nefesh OF THE MALE, and they become one, each including the other, as we have already explained. Later, they are separated to two in this world. We see clearly that through the power of the male results the fruit of the female in this world.

210. דָּבָר אָחֵר בְּתֵיאוּבְתָּא דְּנוּקְבָא, אִשְׁתְּכַח אִיבָּא דִּדְכוּרָא, דְּאִי לָאו תֵּיאוּבְתָּא דְּנוּקְבָא לְגַבֵּי דְכוּרָא, לָא אִתְעֲבִידוּ פֵּירִין לְעָלְמִין, הה"ד מִמֶּנִּי פֶּרְיְךָ נִמְצָא.

210. Another explanation OF THE VERSE, "FROM ME IS YOUR FRUIT FOUND" is that the passion of the female, WHENCE THE FEMALE ASPECT OF THE NEFESH COMES, is the source of the fruit of the male, because without the passion of the female to the male, there would not have been any fruit in the world. IN OTHER WORDS, THERE WOULD NOT HAVE BEEN ANY OFFSPRING. Therefore, it is written: "From me is your fruit found!"

23. "And it came to pass in the days of Amrafel"

A Synopsis

Avraham's recognition of the all-encompassing reality of the Creator, is recounted by the Zohar. The Patriarch's step-by-step spiritual process is depicted, beginning with his perception of the rising morning sun. Avraham's soul was profoundly stirred by the underlying cosmic order of our world. This stirring awakened a deep desire to know the ultimate truth, to grasp the supreme Force underlying the physical and metaphysical laws of nature. When Avraham's desire to know the Creator is ignited, only then does the Creator reveal Himself.

The Relevance of this Passage

The act of seeking, in and of itself, is not enough to gain an awareness of the supreme Creator. We must begin to recognize and acknowledge His oneness and direct our efforts along the correct spiritual path. Moreover, our spiritual effort should not be rooted in blind faith; rather, it should take the form of a logical progression of questions and answers, efforts and results, that culminates in a delicate balance of certainty *and* faith. Through this portion, the power of certainty and the desire to seek the ultimate truth are awakened within our soul.

211. וַיְהִי בִּימֵי אמרפל מֶלֶךְ שִׁנְעָר וגו'. רַבִּי יוֹסֵי פָּתַח, מִי הֵעִיר מִמִּזְרָח צֶדֶק יִקְרָאֵהוּ לְרַגְלוֹ וגו'. הַאי קְרָא אוּקְמוּהָ חַבְרַיָיא. אֲבָל הַאי קְרָא בְּרָזָא דְחָכְמְתָא אִיהוּ. דְהָא תָּנִינָן, שִׁבְעָה רְקִיעִין עֲבַד קֻדְשָׁא בְּרִיךְ הוּא לְעֵילָא, וְכֻלְּהוּ לְאִשְׁתְּמוֹדַע יְקָרָא דְקֻדְשָׁא בְּרִיךְ הוּא, וְכֻלְּהוּ קַיְימִין לְאוֹדְעָא רָזָא דִמְהֵימְנוּתָא עִלָּאָה.

211. Rabbi Yosi opened the discussion of the verse, "And it came to pass in the days of Amrafel, king of Shin'ar..." (Beresheet 14:1), with the text, "Who raised up one from the east, whom righteousness met wherever he set his foot..." (Yeshayah 41:2). Although this passage has already been explained, it has another explanation in accordance with the secret of Wisdom. We have learned that the Holy One, blessed be He, created seven firmaments on high, WHICH ARE THE LOWER SEVEN SFIROT OF ATZILUT – CHESED, GVURAH, TIFERET, NETZACH, HOD, YESOD AND MALCHUT. The purpose of them all is to acknowledge the glory of the Holy One,

blessed be He, and they exist to proclaim the secret of the Supernal Faith.

212. תָּא חֲזֵי אִית רְקִיעָא עִלָּאָה סְתִים, לְעֵילָא מִנַּיְיהוּ, דְּאִינוּן שִׁבְעָה, וְדָא הוּא רְקִיעָא דְּדַבַּר לוֹן וְנָהֵיר לוֹן לְכָלְהוּ, וְדָא לָא אִתְיְידַע, וְקַיְימָא בִּשְׁאֶלְתָּא, דְּלָא יְדִיעָא, בְּגִין דְּאִיהוּ סְתִים וְעָמִיק, וְכֹלָּא תְּוָוהִין עֲלֵיהּ, וּבְגִין כָּךְ אִקְרֵי מִי, כְּמָה דְּאוֹקְמוּהָ דִּכְתִיב מִבֶּטֶן מִי יָצָא הַקָּרַח, וְאִתְּמָר. וְהַאי הוּא רְקִיעָא עִלָּאָה, דְּקַיְימָא עַל כָּל אִינוּן שִׁבְעָה.

212. Come and behold: There is a sublime firmament, high above these seven FIRMAMENTS, WHICH IS THE SECRET OF BINAH OF ATZILUT. This firmament guides and illumines all of them. And it is unknowable; THIS REFERS TO ITS UPPER THREE SFIROT, WHICH IS THE SECRET OF ABA AND IMA. It is stated as a question, because it is unknown; THIS REFERS TO ITS LOWER SEVEN SFIROT, WHICH IS THE SECRET OF YISRAEL-SABA AND TEVUNAH. Because it is concealed and so deep, everyone wonders about it. This is why it is called *Mi* (lit. 'who'), REFERRING TO ITS LOWER SEVEN SFIROT, as has been explained. As it is written: "From the womb of whom (Heb. *mi*) came forth the ice" (Iyov 38:29), which was explained. And this is the supernal firmament that stands high above the other seven.

213. וְאִית לְתַתָּא רְקִיעָא, דְּאִיהוּ תַּתָּאָה מִכֻּלְּהוּ וְלָא נָהֵיר. וּבְגִין דְּאִיהוּ תַּתָּאָה דְּלָא נָהֵיר, הַהוּא רְקִיעָא דַּעֲלַיְיהוּ, אִתְחַבַּר בֵּיהּ, וְאִלֵּין תְּרֵין אַתְוָון, כָּלֵיל לוֹן בְּגַוֵּיהּ, וְאִקְרֵי יָם, דְּהַהוּא רְקִיעָא עִלָּאָה, דְּאִקְרֵי מִי.

213. And there is also a firmament down below, NAMELY MALCHUT, which is the lowest of them all, and it does not shine. Since it is the lowest and has no light, the supernal firmament above them, WHICH IS BINAH THAT IS CALLED *MI*, joins with it. THIS MEANS THAT THE SUPERNAL FIRMAMENT, WHICH IS THE SECRET OF *MI* (*MEM-YUD*) DOES NOT ILLUMINATE THE CHOCHMAH TO ANY OF THE LOWER SEVEN FIRMAMENTS, BUT ONLY TO THE LOWEST OF THEM ALL, WHICH IS MALCHUT. And these two letters, *MEM-YUD*, WHICH BELONG TO THE SUPERNAL FIRMAMENT, WHICH IS CALLED *MI*, are included in itself to form a sea (Heb. *yam,* Yud-Mem), of the supernal firmament, which is called *Mi*, A COMOOINATION OF THE LETTERS *MEM* AND *YUD*.

214. בְּגִין דְּכָל אִינּוּן רְקִיעִין אָחֳרָנִין, אִתְעֲבִידוּ נַחֲלִין, וְעָאלִין לְגַבֵּיהּ, וּכְדֵין אִיהוּ יַם עִלָּאָה, וַעֲבַד אִיבִּין וְנוּנִין לִזְנַיְיהוּ, וְעַל דָּא אֲמַר דָּוִד זֶה הַיָּם גָּדוֹל וּרְחַב יָדַיִם שָׁם רֶמֶשׂ וְאֵין מִסְפָּר חַיּוֹת קְטַנּוֹת עִם גְּדוֹלוֹת.

214. Because all of the other firmaments, WHICH ARE ABOVE THE LOWEST FIRMAMENT AND ARE CALLED CHESED, GVURAH, TIFERET, NETZACH, HOD, AND YESOD act as streams and flow to the lowest firmament, it then becomes a supernal sea that produces fruits and fishes in all varieties. THESE ARE THE MOCHIN THAT IT GIVES DOWN TO BRIYAH, YETZIRAH, AND ASIYAH. David described it with the words, "This great and wide sea wherein there are innumerable creeping things, both small and great beasts" (Tehilim 104:25).

215. וְעַל דָּא כְּתִיב מִי הֵעִיר מִמִּזְרָח צֶדֶק יִקְרָאֵהוּ לְרַגְלוֹ. מִי הֵעִיר מִמִּזְרָח דָּא אַבְרָהָם. צֶדֶק יִקְרָאֵהוּ לְרַגְלוֹ, דָּא הוּא רְקִיעָא תַּתָּאָה דְּכָלְהוּ רְקִיעִין, דְּאִתְעֲבִיד יָם. יִתֵּן לְפָנָיו גּוֹיִם. מַאן הַאי. הוּא רְקִיעָא תַּתָּאָה דַּאֲמָרָן, דְּעָבֵיד נוּקְמִין, וְאַפִּיל שָׂנְאִין. וּבְהַאי אִשְׁתַּבַּח דָּוִד וַאֲמַר וְאוֹיְבַי נָתַתָּה לִּי עֹרֶף וּמְשַׂנְאַי אַצְמִיתֵם.

215. On this subject it is written: "Who (Mi) raised up one from the east, whom righteousness met wherever he set his foot..." (Yeshayah 41:2). "Who raised up one from the east" refers to Abraham. ABRAHAM ROUSED UP THE SUPERNAL FIRMAMENT, WHICH IS CALLED MI, TO BRING THE CHOCHMAH DOWN TO THE LOWEST FIRMAMENT, WHICH IS CALLED YAM (YUD-MEM). "whom righteousness met wherever he set his foot" refers to the lowest of all SEVEN firmaments, which has become a sea. Of the verse, "gave the nations before him," HE ASKS: "What is meant by 'before him'?" AND HE SAYS: This is the lowest firmament, as we have said, that takes revenge and overthrows the enemies. David was proud of this and praised it by saying, "You have also given me the necks of my enemies, that I might destroy them that hate me" (Tehilim 18:40).

216. יִתֵּן לְפָנָיו גּוֹיִם. אִלֵּין אִינּוּן עַמִּין דַּהֲוָה רָדִיף עֲלֵיהוֹן אַבְרָהָם, וְקֻדְשָׁא בְּרִיךְ הוּא הֲוָה קָטִיל לוֹן. וּמְלָכִים יַרְדְּ, אִלֵּין מְמַנָּן רַבְרְבָן

-117-

דִּלְעֵילָא. דְּכַד עָבֵיד קוּדְשָׁא בְּרִיךְ הוּא דִּינָא בְּעָלְמָא, בְּכֹלָּא עָבֵיד דִּינָא, בְּעֵילָא וְתַתָּא.

216. "...gave the nations before him" – these are the nations that Abraham put to flight and the Holy One, blessed be He, put to death. "and made him rule over kings" – these are the angels that govern them from above. Because when the Holy One, blessed be He, executes Judgment on the world, He brings it upon all – high above and down below. THIS MEANS; UPON THE NATIONS BELOW AND UPON THEIR GOVERNORS HIGH ABOVE IN THE HEAVENS.

217. יִרְדְּפֵם יַעֲבוֹר שָׁלוֹם אֹרַח בְּרַגְלָיו לֹא יָבוֹא. יִרְדְּפֵם, דָּא אַבְרָהָם. דְּאַבְרָהָם הֲוָה רָדִיף לוֹן וְקַדְשָׁא בְּרִיךְ הוּא הֲוָה עָבַר קַמֵּיה, וְקָטִיל לוֹן. דִּכְתִיב יַעֲבוֹר שָׁלוֹם, דָּא קוּדְשָׁא בְּרִיךְ הוּא דְּאִקְרֵי שָׁלוֹם.

217. The text continues, "He pursued them, and passed on safely." "He pursued them" refers to Abraham. Because Abraham pursued them, and the Holy One, blessed be He, went in front of him and killed them off. As it is written: "and passed on safely (Heb. *shalom*)." This is the Holy One, blessed be He, who is called *shalom*!

218. אֹרַח בְּרַגְלָיו לֹא יָבוֹא. וְכִי סַלְקָא דַעְתָּךְ, דַּהֲוָה אַבְרָהָם אָזִיל בְּגוֹ עֲנָנֵי אוֹ בְּגוֹ סוּסְוָון וּרְתִיכִין. אֶלָּא אֹרַח בְּרַגְלָיו לֹא יָבוֹא, דְּלָא הֲוָה אָזִיל קַמֵּיה דְּאַבְרָהָם, לָא מַלְאָכָא, וְלָא שְׁלִיחָא, אֶלָּא קַדְשָׁא בְּרִיךְ הוּא בִּלְחוֹדוֹי, דִּכְתִיב אֹרַח בְּרַגְלָיו, מַאן רַגְלָיו, אִלֵּין מַלְאָכִין דְּאִינוּן תְּחוֹתוֹי דְּקַדְשָׁא בְּרִיךְ הוּא, כד"א וְעָמְדוּ רַגְלָיו בַּיוֹם הַהוּא וגו'.

218. Of the words, "even by the way that he had not gone with his feet," HE ASKS: Could you ever imagine that Abraham walked through clouds, or mounted upon horses and carriages? BECAUSE IT IS WRITTEN: "BY THE WAY THAT HE HAD NOT GONE WITH HIS FEET!" AND HE REPLIES: "even by the way that he had not gone with his feet" MEANS that neither an angel nor a messenger preceded Abraham, only the Holy One, blessed be He, Himself. It is written: "with his feet." AND HE ASKS: What are 'his feet'? AND HE REPLIES: These are the angels who are beneath the Holy One, blessed be He. As it is written: "And His feet shall stand on that day..." (Zecharyah 14:4), WHICH REFERS TO THE ANGLES THAT ARE CALLED "HIS FEET." SO IN THE VERSE, "HIS FEET" REFER TO THE ANGELS; "HAD NOT GONE" MEANS EVEN BY THE WAY OF ABRAHAM. ONLY THE HOLY ONE, BLESSED BE HE, ACCOMPANIES HIM ON HIS WAY!

219. דָּבָר אַחֵר, מִי הֵעִיר מִמִּזְרָח. תָּא חֲזֵי, בְּשַׁעֲתָא דְּקֻדְשָׁא בְּרִיךְ הוּא אִתְּעַר עָלְמָא, לְאַיְיתָאָה לְאַבְרָהָם, וּלְקָרְבָא לֵיהּ לְגַבֵּיהּ, הַאי אִתְעָרוּתָא, בְּגִין דְּזַמִּין יַעֲקֹב לְמֵיפַּק מִנֵּיהּ, וּלְקַיְּימָא תְּרֵיסַר שִׁבְטִין, כֻּלְּהוּ זַכָּאִין קַמֵּיהּ דְּקֻדְשָׁא בְּרִיךְ הוּא.

219. There is another explanation of the verse, "Who raised up one from the east." Come and behold: When the Holy One, blessed be He, aroused the world, WHICH IS MALCHUT, to bring Abraham closer to Him, this awakening occurred FOR THE SAKE OF JACOB, WHO IS THE SECRET OF THE EAST. Because Jacob was destined to come from Abraham and to bring forth the twelve tribes, which were all righteous before the Holy One, blessed be He.

220. צֶדֶק יִקְרָאֵהוּ לְרַגְלוֹ. דְּקֻדְשָׁא בְּרִיךְ הוּא הֲוָה קָרֵי לֵיהּ תָּדִיר, מִן יוֹמָא דְּאִתְבְּרֵי עָלְמָא, כד"א קוֹרֵא הַדּוֹרוֹת מֵרֹאשׁ. וּבְגִין כָּךְ, צֶדֶק יִקְרָאֵהוּ, וַדַּאי. לְרַגְלוֹ: לְאִתְחַבְּרָא בֵּיהּ בְּפוּלְחָנֵיהּ, וּלְקָרְבָא לֵיהּ לְגַבֵּיהּ. כד"א הָעָם אֲשֶׁר בְּרַגְלֶיךָ.

220. The verse continues, "whom righteousness met wherever he set his foot." The Holy One, blessed be He, called him, REFERRING TO JACOB, always, since the world was created, as the verse says: "calling the generations from the beginning" (Yeshayah 41:4). Therefore, "righteousness," THAT IS MALCHUT, "called," him assuredly! "his foot" MEANS THAT he joined Him in His worship and became closer to Him. As it is written: "and all the people that follow You (lit. 'that are at your feet')" (Shemot 11:8), WHICH MEANS THE PEOPLE WHO CLEAVE ON TO YOU. SO HERE AS WELL, "HIS FOOT" MEANS TO CLEAVE ON TO HIM.

221. דָּבָר אַחֵר מִי הֵעִיר מִמִּזְרָח. דְּמִתַּמָּן שֵׁרוּתָא דִּנְהוֹרָא לְאַנְהָרָא.

בְּגִין, דְּדָרוֹם הַהוּא תּוּקְפָּא דִּנְהוֹרָא דִּילֵיה, מִגּוֹ מִזְרָח אִיהוּ, וְעַל דָּא מִי הֵעִיר הַהוּא נְהוֹרָא דְּדָרוֹם, מִמִּזְרָח. בְּגִין דְּאִיהוּ נָטִיל וְאִתְּזָן בְּקַדְמֵיתָא, וְתֵיאוּבְתָּא דְּהַהוּא רְקִיעָא עִלָּאָה, לְמֵיהַב לֵיה לְמִזְרָח.

221. An alternative explanation of "Who raised up one from the east" is that the light begins to shine from the east. For all the power of the light in the south, WHICH IS CHESED, comes from the east, WHICH IS TIFERET. Therefore, THE VERSE READS, "Who raised up" the light of the south, WHICH IS CHESED, "from the east." THE EAST, BEING TIFERET, RAISED THE LIGHT. Because it, TIFERET, takes and is nourished first, AND AFTERWARD GIVES LIGHT TO THE SIX EXTREMITIES THAT ARE INCLUDED WITHIN TIFERET. AMONG THEM IS THE SOUTH, WHICH IS CHESED. And the desire of the supernal firmament, WHICH IS BINAH, is to give abundance to the east, WHICH IS TIFERET.

222. צֶדֶק יִקְרָאֵהוּ לְרַגְלוֹ. דָּא מַעֲרָב, דְּאִיהוּ קָרֵי לֵיה תָּדִיר וְלָא שָׁכִיךְ. כד"א אֱלֹקִים אַל דֳּמִי לָךְ אַל תֶּחֱרַשׁ וְאַל תִּשְׁקוֹט אֵל. בְּגִין דְּמַעֲרָב אִתְּעַר תָּדִיר לְגַבֵּיה. יִתֵּן לְפָנָיו גּוֹיִם וּמְלָכִים יַרְדְּ. דְּהָא מִנֵּיה קַבֵּיל תּוּקְפָּא לְאַכְנָעָא כָּל אִינּוּן עַמִּין דְּעָלְמָא.

222. The verse "whom righteousness met wherever he set his foot" refers to the west, WHICH IS MALCHUT. It calls on the east, WHICH IS TIFERET, always and does not quiet down. As it is written: "Keep not Your silence, Elohim: do not hold Your peace, and be still, El" (Tehilim 83:2). Because the west, WHICH IS MALCHUT AND IS CALLED ELOHIM, is constantly aroused to Him. "Gave the nations before him and made him rule over kings," because it is from it – FROM THE EAST – that it receives the power to overcome all the nations of the world.

223. רַבִּי יְהוּדָה אֲמַר מִי הֵעִיר מִמִּזְרָח, דָּא אַבְרָהָם. דְּלָא נָטִיל אִתְּעֲרוּתָא לְגַבֵּי קֻדְשָׁא בְּרִיךְ הוּא אֶלָּא מִמִּזְרָח, בְּגִין דְּחַמָּא שִׁמְשָׁא דְּנָפִיק בְּצַפְרָא, מִסִּטְרָא דְמִזְרָח, נָטִיל אִתְּעֲרוּתָא לְנַפְשֵׁיה דְּאִיהוּ קֻדְשָׁא בְּרִיךְ הוּא, אֲמַר דָּא הוּא מַלְכָּא דְּבָרָא יָתִי, פָּלַח לֵיה כָּל הַהוּא יוֹמָא. לְרַמְשָׁא, חָמָא שִׁמְשָׁא דְּאִתְכְּנַשׁ, וְסִיהֲרָא נָהֲרָא. אֲמַר דָּא הוּא

וַדַּאי, דְּשַׁלִּיט עַל הַהוּא פּוּלְחָנָא דִּפְלָחִית כָּל הַאי יוֹמָא, דְּהָא אִתְחֲשַׁךְ קַמֵּיה וְלָא נָהִיר. פָּלַח לֵיה כָּל הַהוּא לֵילְיָא.

223. Rabbi Yehuda said: "Who raised up one from the east?" This is Abraham, who received his awakening to the Holy One, blessed be He, from the east alone. When he saw that the sun rose in the morning from the east, he was awakened to think it is the Holy One, blessed be He. Abraham said OF THE SUN: 'This is the king who created me.' And he worshipped the sun all that day. As evening came, he saw that the sun went down and the moon shone. He said ABOUT THE MOON, 'This must be the one that rules over the worship that he had performed during the day FOR THE SUN. Since the sun has been darkened and shines no more before the moon!' And he worshipped the moon all that night.

224. לְצַפְרָא, חָמָא דְּאָזְלָא חֲשׁוֹכָא, וְאִתְנְהֵיר סִטְרָא דְמִזְרָח, אֲמַר וַדַּאי כָּל אִלֵּין, מַלְכָּא אִית עֲלַיְיהוּ, וְשַׁלִּיט דְּאַנְהִיג לוֹן. כֵּיוָן דְּחָמָא קֻדְשָׁא בְּרִיךְ הוּא, תֵּיאוּבְתָּא דְּאַבְרָהָם לְגַבֵּיה, כְּדֵין אִתְגְּלֵי עֲלוֹי, וּמַלֵּיל עִמֵּיה, דִּכְתִיב צֶדֶק יִקְרָאֵהוּ לְרַגְלוֹ. דְּמַלֵּיל עִמֵּיה, וְאִתְגְּלֵי עֲלֵיה.

224. In the morning, he saw that the moon became dark. As the east lit up, he said: 'There must be a king and ruler over all these, who governs them.' So when the Holy One, blessed be He, saw that Avraham's desire was directed towards Him, He revealed Himself to Abraham and spoke with him. As it is written: "whom righteousness met wherever he set his foot." "RIGHTEOUSNESS" REFERS TO THE HOLY ONE, BLESSED BE HE, WHO CALLED HIM, spoke with him, and revealed Himself to him.

225. רַבִּי יִצְחָק פָּתַח דּוֹבֵר צֶדֶק מַגִּיד מֵישָׁרִים. קֻדְשָׁא בְּרִיךְ הוּא, כָּל מִלּוֹי אִינוּן בְּקוּשְׁטָא, וְעָבֵיד מֵישָׁרִים, בַּמֶּה עָבֵיד מֵישָׁרִים. בְּגִין, דְּכַד בְּרָא קֻדְשָׁא בְּרִיךְ הוּא עָלְמָא, לָא הֲוָה קָאֵים, וַהֲוָה מִתְמוֹטֵט לְהָכָא וּלְהָכָא. אָמַר לוֹ קֻדְשָׁא בְּרִיךְ הוּא לְעָלְמָא, מַה לָךְ דְּאַתְּ מִתְמוֹטֵט. אָמַר לוֹ רִבּוֹנוֹ שֶׁל עוֹלָם, לָא יָכִילְנָא לְמֵיקַם, דְּלֵית בִּי יְסוֹדָא, עַל מַה דְּאִתְקַיַּים.

225. Rabbi Yitzchak opened the discussion by saying: "I speak righteousness, I declare things that are right" (Yeshayah 45:19). All that the Holy One, blessed be He, says is true; all of His actions are just. HE ASKS: How does He act justly? AND HE SAYS: When the Holy One, blessed be He, created the world, it wavered from side to side, unable to stand. The Holy One, blessed be He, said to the world, 'Why are you collapsing?' It answered, 'Master of the Universe, I am unable to stand because I have no foundation to stand upon!'

226. אָמַר לוֹ הָא אֲנָא זַמִּין לְמֵיקָם בָּךְ חַד צַדִּיק, דְּאִיהוּ אַבְרָהָם, דִּי יִרְחֵים לִי. מִיָּד קָאֵים עָלְמָא בְּקִיּוּמֵיהּ, הה״ד אֵלֶּה תּוֹלְדוֹת הַשָּׁמַיִם וְהָאָרֶץ בְּהִבָּרְאָם; אַל תִּקְרָא בְּהִבָּרְאָם אֶלָּא בְּאַבְרָהָם. בְּאַבְרָהָם מִתְקַיֵּים עָלְמָא.

226. THE HOLY ONE, BLESSED BE HE said to the world, 'But I am about to raise within you a righteous man, who is Abraham, who shall love Me!' Immediately, the world stood up and was firmly established. As it is written: "These are the generations of the heavens and of the earth when they were created (Heb. *behibar'am*)" (Beresheet 2:4). Do not read *behibar'am*, but rather, *BeAvraham* (with Abraham) because by Abraham was the world established.

227. אָמַר רַבִּי חִיָּיא, מַגִּיד מֵישָׁרִים. דְּהָא אָתֵיב לֵיהּ עָלְמָא לְקֻדְשָׁא בְּרִיךְ הוּא, הַהוּא אַבְרָהָם זַמִּין הוּא דְּיִפְּקוּן מִנֵּיהּ בְּנִין דְּיַחֲרִיבוּ מַקְדְּשָׁא, וְיוֹקִידוּ אוֹרַיְיתָא. אָמַר לֵיהּ, זַמִּין חַד בַּר נָשׁ לְמֵיפַּק מִנֵּיהּ, דְּאִיהוּ יַעֲקֹב, וְיִפְּקוּן מִנֵּיהּ תְּרֵיסַר שִׁבְטִין, כֻּלְּהוּ זַכָּאִין. מִיָּד אִתְקַיֵּים עָלְמָא בְּגִינֵיהּ הה״ד מַגִּיד מֵישָׁרִים.

227. Rabbi Chiya said: "...I declare things that are right" MEANS that the world answered the Holy One, blessed be He, by saying, 'From this same Abraham, children will come forth who shall destroy the Temple and shall burn the Torah!' THE HOLY ONE, BLESSED BE HE, said to it: 'One man is destined to come from him, who is Jacob. And from him twelve tribes shall come forth, all of them righteous. Immediately the world was established for his sake.' Therefore, it is written: "I declare things that are right," WHICH IS

THE SECRET OF JACOB, WHO IS TIFERET.

228. רַבִּי אֶלְעָזָר אֲמַר, הָא אִתְּעֲרָנָא, וַיְדַבֵּר, וַיַּגֵּד, וַיֹּאמֶר, כָּלְהוּ לְטַעֲמַיְיהוּ מִתְפָּרְשָׁן, וַיְדַבֵּר: אִיהוּ בְּאִתְגַּלְיָא, דַּרְגָּא לְבַר, דְּלָא אִיהוּ דַּרְגָּא פְּנִימָאָה, כְּאִינוּן דַּרְגִּין עִלָּאִין, וְדָא אִיהוּ דוֹבֵר צֶדֶק.

228. Rabbi Elazar said that we have noted here that each one of the terms – "to speak," "to declare," and "to say" – has a meaning of its own. "To speak" means openly, WHICH IS THE SECRET OF MALCHUT AND IS CALLED THE REVEALED WORLD. This is an external, not an internal, grade, as the grades that are higher THAN IT. And this also applies to "speak righteousness," WHICH REFERS TO MALCHUT WHICH IS THE ASPECT OF "SPEAKING."

229. וַיַּגֵּד: אִיהוּ רֶמֶז לְדַרְגָּא פְּנִימָאָה עִלָּאָה, דְּשַׁלְטָאָה עַל דִּבּוּר, וְדָא הוּא מַגִּיד מֵישָׁרִים, מַאן מֵישָׁרִים, דָּא דַּרְגָּא עִלָּאָה דְּיַעֲקֹב שַׁרְיָיא בֵּיהּ. הֲדָא הוּא דִּכְתִיב אַתָּה כּוֹנַנְתָּ מֵישָׁרִים, וּבְגִין כָּךְ מַגִּיד כְּתִיב, וְלָא כְּתִיב דוֹבֵר.

229. "To declare" alludes to the internal and supernal grade, which governs speech THAT IS MALCHUT and this applies also to "declare...right." Who is "right?" This is the supernal grade, where Jacob dwells, NAMELY TIFERET. Hence "You founded things that are right" (Tehilim 99:4). And this is why it says here "declare," rather than "speak." IT SHOWS US THAT THE INTENTION HERE APPLIES TO TIFERET AND NOT TO MALCHUT. AND RABBI ELAZAR HEREBY OFFERS A PROOF FOR WHAT RABBI CHIYA SAID!

230. אֲמַר רַבִּי יִצְחָק, וְהָא כְּתִיב, וַיַּגֵּד לָכֶם אֶת בְּרִיתוֹ. אֲמַר לוֹ הֲכֵי הוּא וַדַּאי אִיהוּ דַּרְגָּא דְּשַׁלְטָא עַל תַּתָּאָה, דְּאִיהוּ דוֹבֵר צֶדֶק. וְכֹלָּא אִיהוּ לְאִסְתַּכְּלָא הָכָא. תָּא חֲזֵי, דְּאַף עַל גַּב דְּדִבּוּר אִיהוּ תַּתָּאָה, לָא תֵּימָא, דְּלָא עִלָּאָה אִיהוּ, אֶלָּא וַדַּאי דִּבּוּר מַלְיָיא אִיהוּ מִכֹּלָּא, וְדַרְגָּא עִלָּאָה אִיהוּ. וְסִימָנֶיךָ כִּי לֹא דָבָר רֵק הוּא מִכֶּם.

230. Rabbi Yitzchak said that it is written: "And He declared to you His covenant" (Devarim 4:13). ACCORDINGLY, IF THE TERM "DECLARE" IS USED WITH THE COVENANT, THEN IT CAN ALSO BE USED WITH RIGHTEOUSNESS! He said to him, "It is surely so" THAT THE TERM "DECLARE" CAN BE USED WITH THE COVENANT, NAMELY WITH YESOD, BECAUSE TIFERET AND THE COVENANT ARE ONE. NEVERTHELESS, YESOD is a grade that is dominant over the lower grade, which is "speak righteousness," SO HERE WE CAN USE THE TERM "DECLARE" AS WELL. And all this should be well examined. Come and behold: Even though we said that the term "speak" is the lowest of them all, do not conclude from this that it is not a high and important GRADE! The term "speak" includes within it all the other GRADES, and is a high grade. And the proof of this appears in the verse, "For it is not a vain thing (speech)" (Devarim 32:47).

231. רַבִּי אֶלְעָזָר, הֲוָה אָזֵיל לְבֵי חֲמוֹי, וַהֲווֹ עִמֵּיה רַבִּי חִיָּיא, וְרַבִּי יוֹסֵי, וְרַבִּי חִזְקִיָּה. אֲמַר רַבִּי אֶלְעָזָר, הָא חָמֵינָא דְּאִתְעֲרוּתָא דִלְעֵילָא לָאו אִיהוּ, אֶלָּא כַּד אִתְעַר לְתַתָּא, דְּהָא אִתְעֲרוּתָא דִלְעֵילָא, בְּתֵיאוּבְתָּא דִלְתַתָּא תַּלְיָיא.

231. Rabbi Elazar was on his way to his father-in-law, accompanied by Rabbi Chiya, Rabbi Yosi, and Rabbi Chizkiyah. Rabbi Elazar said: I see that the awakening from above occurs as a response to awakening from below, because the upper is aroused by the passion and desire of the lower, and depends on it.

24. "Keep not your silence, Elohim"

A Synopsis
The establishment leaders who lived during the time of Abraham want to slay him because he has enlightened the people and led them away from the futility of Idol Worshipping. People like Abraham, who dare to initiate positive change and help others in their spiritual awakening, always encounter opposition from forces who seek to propagate chaos and ignorance for their own personal gain.

The Relevance of this Passage
Throughout human history, any major advancement in civilization was first met with opposition, defiance, and scorn from those who would not benefit by the betterment of the human condition. This spiritual principle holds true in our own personal life. As opportunities for spiritual advancement present themselves to us, there will be obstacles and opposition. This passage gives us protection from the forces that attempt to impede our spiritual progress.

232. פָּתַח וְאָמַר, אֱלֹקִים אַל דֳּמִי לָךְ אַל תֶּחֱרַשׁ וְאַל תִּשְׁקוֹט אֵל. דָּא הוּא אִתְעֲרוּתָא דִלְתַתָּא. בְּגִין לְשַׁלְטָאָה. אָמַר דָּוִד, אֱלֹקִים אַל דֳּמִי לָךְ, לְאִתְעָרָא לְגַבֵּי עִלָּאָה, וּלְאִתְחַבְּרָא גַּבֵּי יְמִינָא.

232. He opened the discussion with the verse, "Keep not Your silence, Elohim: do not hold Your peace, and be still, El" (Tehilim 83:2). This represents the awakening from below; FROM THE NUKVA, to take control. David responded, "Keep not Your silence, Elohim"; from arousing Your desire to the upper, ZEIR ANPIN, and to cling on to the Right, TO HIS CHESED.

233. מַאי טַעֲמָא, בְּגִין כִּי הִנֵּה כִּי אוֹיְבֶיךָ יֶהֱמָיוּן וְגוֹ', כִּי נוֹעֲצוּ לֵב יַחְדָּיו עָלֶיךָ בְּרִית יִכְרוֹתוּ. וּבְגִין כָּךְ, אֱלֹהִים אַל דֳּמִי לָךְ, לְאִתְעָרָא לְגַבֵּי עִילָא, דְּהָא כְּדֵין אִתְעָרַת יְמִינָא, וּקְטִירַת לָהּ בַּהֲדָהּ. וְכַד אִתְקַשְׁרַת בִּימִינָא, כְּדֵין אִתְבַּר שָׂנְאִין, דִּכְתִיב, יְמִינְךָ ה', נֶאְדָּרִי בַּכֹּחַ יְמִינְךָ ה' תִּרְעַץ אוֹיֵב.

233. For what reason? Because "For, lo, Your enemies make a tumult.... For they have consulted together with one consent: they make a covenant against You" (Tehilim 3:6). THE NUKVA IS THE ASPECT OF THE LEFT, WHICH IS THE SECRET OF CHOCHMAH WITHOUT CHASSADIM, AND CHOCHMAH CANNOT SHINE WITHOUT CHASSADIM. THEREFORE ALL THE KLIPOT AND THE ENEMIES OF THE HOLINESS RAISE UP THEIR HEADS. Hence, "Keep not Your silence, Elohim" from awakening toward the upper, ZEIR ANPIN. Because then the right OF ZEIR ANPIN is aroused and attaches Her to itself. WHEN SHE IS ATTACHED TO THE RIGHT – NAMELY WHEN THE CHOCHMAH IN HER IS ENCLOTHED BY THE CHASSADIM OF THE RIGHT – then the enemies are defeated. BECAUSE THE ILLUMINATION OF CHOCHMAH DESTROYS ALL THE ENEMIES OF THE HOLINESS. As it written: "Your right hand, Hashem, has become glorious in power: Your right hand, Hashem, has dashed the enemy in pieces" (Shemot 15:6).

234. וְתָא חֲזֵי, בְּשַׁעֲתָא דְּאִתְחַבָּרוּ כָּל אִינוּן מַלְכִין, לְאַגָּחָא קְרָבָא עֲלֵיהּ דְּאַבְרָהָם, אִתְיָיעֲטוּ לְאַעֲבָרָא לֵיהּ מִן עָלְמָא, וְכֵיוָן דְּשָׁלְטוּ בְּלוֹט, בַּר אֲחוּהּ דְּאַבְרָהָם, מִיָּד אֲזְלוּ, דִּכְתִיב וַיִּקְחוּ אֶת לוֹט וְאֶת רְכוּשׁוֹ בֶּן אֲחִי אַבְרָם וַיֵּלֵכוּ. מ״ט, בְּגִין, דְּדִיּוֹקְנֵיהּ דְּלוֹט הֲוָה דָּמֵי לְאַבְרָהָם, וּבְגִין כָּךְ וַיֵּלֵכוּ, דְּכָל הַהוּא קְרָבָא, בְּגִינֵיהּ הֲוָה.

234. So come and behold: When all those kings joined to make war against Abraham, they consulted one another about how to destroy him. But as soon as they took control over Lot, Avraham's nephew, they immediately left. As it is written: "And they took Lot, Avram's brother's son, and his possessions and departed" (Beresheet 14:12). What was the reason? Lot's image was similar to that of Abraham. As a result, they "departed," AS THEY BELIEVED THEY HAD CAPTURED ABRAHAM, which was the purpose of the war.

235. מַאי טַעֲמָא. בְּגִין, דַּהֲוָה אַבְרָהָם אַפִּיק בְּנֵי עָלְמָא מְפּוּלְחָנָא נוּכְרָאָה, וְאָעִיל לוֹן, בְּפוּלְחָנָא דְּקֻדְשָׁא בְּרִיךְ הוּא. וְתוּ, קַדְשָׁא בְּרִיךְ הוּא אַתְּעַר לוֹן בְּעָלְמָא, בְּגִין לְגַדְלָא שְׁמָא דְּאַבְרָהָם בְּעָלְמָא וּלְקַרְבָא לֵיהּ לְפוּלְחָנֵיהּ.

235. AND HE ASKS: Why DID THEY WANT TO KILL ABRAHAM? AND HE

ANSWERS: Because Abraham took people of this world away from idolatry and brought them to worship the Holy One, blessed be He. THIS IS WHY THEY WANTED TO KILL HIM. In addition, it was the Holy One, blessed be He, who incited them TO FIGHT ABRAHAM, so that Abraham would be brought closer to His way of worship and the name of Abraham would become glorified throughout the world.

236. וְרָזָא דְּמִלָּה, כֵּיוָן דְּאַבְרָהָם אִתְּעַר לְמִרְדַּף אֲבַתְרַיְיהוּ, כְּדֵין אֱלֹקִים אַל דֳּמִי לָךְ, עַד דְּאִתְקַשַּׁר כֹּלָּא בְּאַבְרָהָם, וְכַד אִתְקַשַּׁר כֹּלָּא בְּאַבְרָהָם, כְּדֵין אִתְבָּרוּ כֻּלְּהוּ מַלְכִין מִקַּמֵּיה, כִּדְקָא אֲמָרָן, דִּכְתִיב יְמִינְךָ ה' תִּרְעַץ אוֹיֵב וגו'.

236. And the secret behind this is that when, Abraham pursued them, then IT IS WRITTEN: "Keep not Your silence, Elohim," AS THE NUKVA WAS AROUSED TOWARD ZEIR ANPIN AND ELEVATED MAYIN NUKVIN (FEMALE WATERS) UP TO HIM TO DRAW CHESED, WHICH IS THE SECRET OF THE RIGHT, until all was attached to Abraham, WHO IS THE SECRET OF CHESED OF ZEIR ANPIN. THIS MEANS THAT HER CHOCHMAH WAS CLOTHED BY CHASSADIM AND HER illumination WAS COMPLETED. And when all this was attached to Abraham, then all the kings were defeated before him. As we have previously stated; it is then written: "Your right hand Hashem, has dashed the enemy in pieces."

25. Melchizedek

A Synopsis
Abraham, King David, and the other great spiritual giants of history, devoted their lives to easing the pain of the Shechinah, the collective universal soul that protects and assist us in the physical world. The Shechinah, possessing its own consciousness, experiences the collective pain of humanity when negativity and suffering abound in the world. Similarly, our consciousness and intent to ease the pain of the Shechinah serves to ease the pain of all mankind. Spiritual work cannot be ego-based. We must learn to feel the pain of others and dedicate ourselves to ending their suffering, as well as our own.

The Relevance of this Passage
Many spiritual lessons and benefits radiate throughout these verses. We gain awareness of the global purpose of our existence, which is to diminish and remove our intemperate character traits that separate us from the Light of the Creator. A recognition of the impact that our actions have on both on ourselves and on all mankind, is instilled within our consciousness.

237. וּמַלְכִּי-צֶדֶק מֶלֶךְ שָׁלֵם הוֹצִיא לֶחֶם וָיָיִן. רַבִּי שִׁמְעוֹן פָּתַח וְאָמַר וַיְהִי בְשָׁלֵם סֻכּוֹ וגו'. תָּא חֲזֵי, כַּד סָלֵיק בִּרְעוּתָא דְּקֻדְשָׁא בְּרִיךְ הוּא לְמִבְרֵי עָלְמָא, אַפֵּיק חַד שַׁלְהוֹבָא דְּבוֹצִינָא דְּקַרְדִינוּתָא, וּנְשַׁף זִיקָא בְּזִיקָא, חָשְׁכַאת וְאוֹקִידַת. וְאַפֵּיק מִגּוֹ סִטְרֵי תְּהוֹמָא, חַד טִיף, וְחַבַּר לוֹן כְּחַד, וּבָרָא בְּהוֹ עָלְמָא.

237. "And Melchizedek king of Shalem brought forth bread and wine..." (Beresheet 14:18). Rabbi Shimon opened the discourse, saying, "In Shalem also is set his tabernacle" (Tehilim 76:3). Come and behold: When the Holy One, blessed be He, WHO IS THE SECRET OF BINAH, decided to create the world, WHICH IS THE SECRET OF ZEIR ANPIN THAT IS CALLED THE 'WORLD,' He produced a flame from the Holy illumination. As wind blew wind, THE FLAME darkened and began to burn. And He took out from within an abyss a particular drop, which He joined with the flame. With them, He created the world, WHICH IS ZEIR ANPIN.

238. הַהוּא שַׁלְהוֹבָא סָלֵיק, וְאִתְעַטְּרָא בִּשְׂמָאלָא, וְהַהוּא טִיף סָלֵיק

וְאִתְעַטַּר בְּיָמִינָא, סָלְקוּ חַד בְּחַד, אַחְלִפוּ דּוּכְתַּי, דָּא לְסִטְרָא דָא, וְדָא לְסִטְרָא דָא, דְּנָחֵית סָלֵיק, וּדְסָלֵיק נָחֵית.

238. HE EXPLAINS THAT the flame rose and was crowned by the Left COLUMN OF BINAH. And the drop, WHICH IS THE CENTRAL COLUMN, rose and was crowned by the Right COLUMN OF BINAH. Then they became intertwined – THE RIGHT AND LEFT repeatedly exchanging places with each other. That which had descended now ascended and that which had ascended then descended.

239. אִתְקַטְּרוּ דָּא בְּדָא, נָפֵיק מִבֵּינַיְיהוּ רוּחַ שְׁלִים. כְּדֵין אִינוּן תְּרֵין סִטְרִין, אִתְעֲבִידוּ חַד, וְאִתְיְהֵיב בֵּינַיְיהוּ, וְאִתְעַטְּרוּ חַד בְּחַד. כְּדֵין אִשְׁתְּכַח שְׁלָם לְעֵילָא, וּשְׁלָם לְתַתָּא, וְדַרְגָּא אִתְקַיָּים.

239. BOTH COLUMNS – THE RIGHT AND THE LEFT OF BINAH – combined and a completed Ruach came forth. THIS REFERS TO ZEIR ANPIN, WHO IS CALLED RUACH AND EMANATE FROM THE UNION OF THE TWO COLUMNS. Two sides emerged as one, AND THE RUACH ITSELF was placed in the middle AS THE ASPECT OF THE CENTRAL COLUMN. HENCE, THE RESULT WAS THREE COLUMNS. And they were crowned by one another – THAT IS, ALL THREE COLUMNS OF ZEIR ANPIN WERE CROWNED BY ONE ANOTHER. Then there was perfection above, IN BINAH, and perfection below, IN ZEIR ANPIN. The grade was established, AND THE GRADE OF THE MOCHIN OF ZEIR ANPIN WAS COMPLETED!

240. אִתְעַטְּרַת ה"א בְּוא"ו, וָא"ו בְּה"א, כְּדֵין סַלְקָא ה"א, וְאִתְקַשְׁרָא בְּקִשּׁוּרָא שְׁלִים. כְּדֵין וּמַלְכִּי צֶדֶק מֶלֶךְ שָׁלֵם. מֶלֶךְ שָׁלֵם וַדַּאי, מֶלֶךְ אִיהוּ דְּשַׁלֵּיט בִּשְׁלִימוּ, אֵימָתַי אִיהוּ מֶלֶךְ שָׁלֵם, בְּיוֹמָא דְּכִפּוּרֵי דְּכָל אַנְפִּין נְהִירִין.

240. The FIRST *Hei* OF YUD HEI VAV HEI, WHICH IS BINAH, was crowned by the *Vav,* WHICH IS ZEIR ANPIN. The *Vav* OF YUD HEI VAV HEI, WHICH IS ZEIR ANPIN, in turn, was crowned by the *Hei* OF YUD HEI VAV HEI, WHICH IS BINAH. THEN the SECOND *Hei* OF THE YUD HEI VAV HEI, WHICH IS THE NUKVA OF ZEIR ANPIN TO THE *VAV* OF YUD HEI

VAV HEI, WHICH IS ZEIR ANPIN, rose and became perfectly attached TO HIM, BY RECEIVING FROM HIM THE MOCHIN OF BINAH. Thus, "And Melchizedek king of Shalem (lit. 'perfect')"; and indeed he is a perfect king! THUS, IT IS WRITTEN ABOUT THE SECOND *HEI*, WHICH IS CALLED MELCHIZEDEK: "AND MELCHIZEDEK, KING OF SHALEM," BECAUSE NOW IT IS ASSUREDLY A PERFECT KING. THIS MEANS a king who rules perfectly. He askes: When is THE NUKVA OF ZEIR ANPIN considered to be a perfect king? AND HE ANSWERS: On Yom Kippur, WHEN MALCHUT RISES UP AND ENCLOTHES BINAH, AND when all faces shine – EVEN THE FACE OF THE NUKVA SHINES LIKE THE FACE OF BINAH!

241. וּמַלְכִּי צֶדֶק. דָּא עָלְמָא בַּתְרָאָה. מֶלֶךְ שָׁלֵם, דָּא עָלְמָא עִלָּאָה. דְּאִתְעַטַּר חַד בְּחַד, בְּלָא פְּרוּדָא, תְּרֵין עָלְמִין כַּחֲדָא, וַאֲפִילוּ עָלְמָא תַּתָּאָה, כֹּלָּא חַד מִלָּה אִיהוּ. הוֹצִיא לֶחֶם וָיָיִן, דִּתְרֵין אִלֵּין בֵּיהּ. וְהוּא כֹהֵן לְאֵל עֶלְיוֹן מְשַׁמֵּשׁ עָלְמָא לְקַבֵּל עָלְמָא. וְהוּא כֹהֵן, דָּא יָמִינָא. לְאֵל עֶלְיוֹן, עָלְמָא עִלָּאָה. וּבְגִין כָּךְ, בָּעֵי כַּהֲנָא, לְבָרְכָא עָלְמָא.

241. "And Melchizedek (lit. 'king of justice')" can also be explained as a reference to the last world, NAMELY THE NUKVA OF ZEIR ANPIN, AND "King of Shalem" to the upper world, WHICH IS BINAH. They adorn one another, MEANING THAT THE LOWER WORLD WAS CROWNED BY THE UPPER WORLD, they are inseparable and the two worlds are as one. And even the lower world is entirely one WITH THE UPPER WORLD. WHY? BECAUSE AT THAT TIME THE NUKVA OF ZEIR ANPIN RISES TO CLOTHE BINAH, EVERY LOWER GRADE THAT RISES TO AN UPPER GRADE BECOMES COMPLETELY LIKE IT. THEREFORE, THESE TWO WORLDS, WHICH ARE THE NUKVA AND BINAH, BECOME AS IF THE SAME. "Brought forth bread and wine" indicates that both are included; BREAD ALLUDES TO THE LIGHT OF CHASSADIM FROM THE RIGHT; WINE ALLUDES TO THE ILLUMINATION OF CHOCHMAH FROM THE LEFT. THEREFORE HE "BROUGHT FORTH BREAD AND WINE" TO INFORM US THAT BOTH OF THESE ILLUMINATIONS EXIST NOW IN MELCHIZEDEK, WHICH IS THE SECRET OF THE NUKVA AS SHE ENCLOTHES BINAH. "And he was the priest of the most high El," who served the world that corresponds to another world. "And he was the priest of the most high El" MEANS THAT THE LOWER WORLD SERVES THE UPPER WORLD WITH CHASSADIM.

BECAUSE "the priest" is the right, REFERRING TO THE LIGHT OF CHASSADIM IN THE NUKVA, AND "the most high El" is the upper world, NAMELY BINAH. The priests, therefore, desire to bless the world.

242. תָּא חֲזֵי, בִּרְכָאן נָטֵיל הַאי עָלְמָא תַּתָּאָה, כַּד אִתְחַבַּר בְּכַהֲנָא רַבָּא. כְּדֵין, וַיְבָרְכֵהוּ, וַיֹּאמַר בָּרוּךְ אַבְרָם לְאֵל עֶלְיוֹן. הָכִי הוּא וַדַּאי. כְּגַוְונָא דָּא בָּעֵי כַּהֲנָא לְתַתָּא, לְקַשְּׁרָא קִשְׁרִין, וּלְבָרְכָא הַאי דּוּכְתָּא, בְּגִין דְּיִתְקַשַּׁר בְּיָמִינָא, לְאִתְקַשְּׁרָא תְּרֵין עָלְמִין כְּחַד.

242. Come and behold: This lower world, WHICH IS THE NUKVA, receives blessings when it is attached to the high priest, NAMELY TO THE RIGHT COLUMN OF BINAH THAT IS CALLED "THE HIGH PRIEST." Then, "And blessed him" MEANS THAT AFTER THE NUKVA HAD RECEIVED THE BLESSINGS FROM THE HIGH PRIEST, SHE blessed ABRAHAM. AS IT IS WRITTEN: "and he said: Blessed be Abram of the most high El" (Beresheet 14:19), as it is surely so! The same applies to the priest below IN THIS WORLD. HE SHOULD tie knots, NAMELY TO MEDITATE AS IS EXPLAINED HERE, so as to bless this place, NAMELY THE NUKVA OF ZEIR ANPIN, so that SHE may be attached to CHASSADIM OF the right SIDE OF BINAH. Thus both worlds, THE NUKVA AND BINAH, are united as one!

243. בָּרוּךְ אַבְרָם. רָזָא דְּמִלָּה, תִּקּוּנָא דְּבִרְכָאן אִיהוּ. בָּרוּךְ אַבְרָם, כְּמָה דְּאָמְרִינָן בָּרוּךְ אַתָּה. לְאֵל עֶלְיוֹן, ה' אֱלֹקֵינוּ. קוֹנֵה שָׁמַיִם וָאָרֶץ, מֶלֶךְ הָעוֹלָם. וְהַאי קְרָא, רָזָא דְּבִרְכָאן אִיהוּ. וַיְבָרְכֵהוּ, מִתַּתָּא לְעֵילָא. וּבָרוּךְ אֵל עֶלְיוֹן, מֵעֵילָא לְתַתָּא. וַיִּתֶּן לוֹ מַעֲשֵׂר מִכֹּל. לְאִתְדַּבְּקָא בַּאֲתַר דְּקִשּׁוּרָא אִתְקַשַּׁר לְתַתָּא.

243. "Blessed be Abram." The secret behind this is that this blessing contains the meditations that we are to have whenever we say a blessing. "Blessed be Abram" is similar to the words "Blessed are You," which we recite IN EVERY BLESSING; "of the most high El," WHICH APPEARS HERE, IS SIMILAR TO WHAT WE RECITE IN EVERY BLESSING: "Hashem our Elohim"; "possessor of heaven and earth" IS SIMILAR TO WHAT WE RECITE IN EVERY BLESSING: "the king of the world." So this phrase is the secret of

all the blessings. "And he blessed him, AND SAID: BLESSED BE ABRAM," WHICH IS THE DIRECTION OF THE MEDITATION from below upward. "Blessed be the most high El, WHO HAD DELIVERED THE ENEMIES TO YOUR HANDS" IS THE DIRECTION OF THE MEDITATION from above downward. "And he gave him a tithe of everything" MEANS THAT HE GAVE THE NUKVA A TITHE in order to be attached to that place, where the tie has been made with the world below. THIS IS THE SECRET OF MALCHUT, WHICH FINISHES THE ILLUMINATION OF THE NUKVA, SO AS NOT TO GIVE HOLD TO THE EXTERNALS, AS THE SECRET OF THE TITHE IS THE CONCLUSION OF HER ILLUMINATION.

244. עַד דַּהֲווֹ אָזְלֵי, אִעֲרַע בְּהוֹ ר' יֵיסָא וְחַד יוּדָאי בַּהֲדֵיהּ. וַהֲוָה אָמַר הַהוּא יוּדָאי, לְדָוִד אֵלֶיךָ ה' נַפְשִׁי אֶשָּׂא. לְדָוִד, וְכִי אַמַּאי לָא כְּתִיב, מִזְמוֹר לְדָוִד, אוֹ לְדָוִד מִזְמוֹר.

244. As they were walking, they met Rabbi Yesa and a Jew who was with him. The Jew quoted the verse, "Of David: To you, Hashem, do I lift up my soul" (Tehilim 25:1), AND HE ASKED WHY IS IT WRITTEN "Of David" rather than "A psalm of David" or "To David a psalm?"

245. אֶלָּא, בְּגִין דַּרְגֵּיהּ קָאָמַר לְדָוִד, תּוּשְׁבַּחְתָּא דַּאֲמַר בְּגִינֵיהּ. אֵלֶיךָ ה' נַפְשִׁי אֶשָּׂא. אֵלֶיךָ ה', לְעֵילָּא. נַפְשִׁי: מַאן נַפְשִׁי. דָּא דָּוִד, דַּרְגָּא קַדְמָאָה דְּקָאֲמָרָן. אֶשָּׂא: אֲסַלֵּק. כד"א אֶשָּׂא עֵינַי אֶל הֶהָרִים. בְּגִין, דְּכָל יוֹמוֹי דְּדָוִד, הֲוָה מִשְׁתַּדֵּל לְסַלְקָא דַרְגֵּיהּ, לְאִתְעַטְּרָא לְעֵילָּא, וּלְאִתְקַשְּׁרָא תַּמָּן בְּקִשּׁוּרָא שְׁלִים, כִּדְקָא יָאוֹת.

245. AND HE ANSWERS: It is written 'Of David' because it was meant for his own grade. And the praise that he recited was for his own sake. "To you Hashem, do I lift up my soul" MEANS "To you, Hashem" upward. "My soul (*Nefesh*)." Who is meant by "my *Nefesh*?" David is meant. David is the first grade, as we have stated; NAMELY HE IS MALCHUT, WHICH IS THE FIRST GRADE FROM BELOW UPWARD. "do I lift up" MEANS to elevate, as it is written: "I will lift up my eyes to the hills" (Tehilim 121:1) Because during his entire life, David was always striving to raise his grade TO THAT OF BINAH − to adorn it BY BINAH above and to attach it there in a true and everlasting bond, as it should properly be!

246. כְּגַוְונָא דָא, לְדָוִד בָּרְכִי נַפְשִׁי אֶת ה', בְּגִין דַּרְגֵּיהּ קָאֲמַר, וּמַאי אֲמַר, בָּרְכִי נַפְשִׁי אֶת ה'. אֶת: לְאִתְקַשְּׁרָא בְּקִשּׁוּרָא לְעֵילָא. וְכָל קְרָבַי, מַאן קְרָבַי. אִלֵּין שְׁאָר חֵיוָן בְּרָא, דְּאִקְרוּן קְרָבִים, כְּד"א וּמֵעַי הָמוּ עָלָיו דָּבָר אַחֵר, בָּרְכִי נַפְשִׁי, בְּגִינֵיהּ קָאֲמַר. אֶת ה', דָּא שְׁלִימוּ דְכֹלָּא, אֶת ה' כְּלָלָא דְכֹלָּא.

246. Similarly, "Of David, bless Hashem, my soul (*Nefesh*)" (Tehilim 103:1) was also said for the sake of his own grade. And what did he say? "Bless Hashem, my soul (*Nefesh*)." In this case, the particle *Et* before "Hashem" MEANS to be attached with bonds to the upper GRADE – BINAH. And what is meant by "and all that is within me?" It refers to the other beasts of the fields, NAMELY THE SFIROT OF THE NUKVA, that are called "all that is within me (lit. 'entrails')." As it is written: "and my bowels yearned for him" (Shir Hashirim 5:5) Another explanation of the words "bless ...my soul" is that he said it for the sake of his own grade. "Hashem" is the full perfection of everything – the inclusion of everything. THIS MEANS THAT *ET* IS THE SECRET OF MALCHUT; HASHEM (YUD HEI VAV HEI) IS THE SECRET OF ZEIR ANPIN. SO ET HASHEM ALLUDES TO THE COMPLETE UNISON OF ZEIR ANPIN WITH HIS NUKVA.

247. אָמַר לוֹ רַבִּי אֶלְעָזָר לְרַבִּי יֵיסָא, חֲמֵינָא לָךְ, דְּהָא עִם שְׁכִינְתָּא קָאֲתֵית וְאִתְחַבְּרַת. אָמַר לוֹ, הָכֵי הוּא וַדַּאי, וּתְלַת פַּרְסֵי הוּא דְּאָזֵילְנָא בַּהֲדֵיהּ, וְאָמַר לִי כַּמָּה מִילֵי מַעַלְיָיתָא, וַאֲנָא אֲגִירְנָא לֵיהּ לְיוֹמָא דָא, וְלָא יְדַעְנָא דְּאִיהוּ בּוֹצִינָא דְּנָהֵיר כִּדְחָמֵינָא הַשְׁתָּא.

247. Rabbi Elazar said to Rabbi Yesa: I see that you have come in company with the Shechinah. HE SAID THIS BECAUSE HE SAW THAT THE SHECHINAH RESTED UPON THE JEW. He said to him: Most certainly! I walked with him for three parasangs, and he has told me many goodly matters. And I have hired him to serve me for this day, and did not realize that he is such a shining light as I see now!"

248. אָמַר לוֹ רַבִּי אֶלְעָזָר, לְהַהוּא יוּדָאי, מַה שְּׁמֶךְ, אָמַר לוֹ יוֹעֶזֶר. אָמַר לוֹ יוֹעֶזֶר וְאֶלְעָזָר, יְתִיבָן כַּחֲדָא. יָתְבוּ גַּבֵּי חַד טִנָּרָא בְּהַהוּא חֲקַל. פָּתַח

הַהוּא יוּדָאי וְאָמַר, אָנֹכִי אָנֹכִי הוּא מוֹחֶה פְּשָׁעֶיךָ לְמַעֲנִי וְחַטֹּאתֶיךָ לֹא אֶזְכּוֹר, מַאי טַעֲמָא, תְּרֵי זִמְנֵי, אָנֹכִי אָנֹכִי.

248. Rabbi Elazar asked the Jew, "What is your name?" He answered, "Yoezer." Rabbi Elazar said: Let us sit together, AS OUR NAMES ARE SIMILAR. They sat beside a rock in that field. The Jew opened the discussion, by quoting, "I, even I, am he that blots out your transgressions for my own sake, and will not remember your sins" (Yeshayah 43:25). HE ASKED HIM, "What is the reason for saying 'I... I' twice?"

249. אֶלָּא, חַד בְּסִינַי. וְחַד בְּשַׁעֲתָא דְּבָרָא עָלְמָא. דִּכְתִיב, אָנֹכִי ה' אֱלֹקֶיךָ, דָּא הוּא בְּסִינַי. וְחַד כַּד בָּרָא עָלְמָא, דִּכְתִיב, אָנֹכִי עָשִׂיתִי אֶרֶץ וְאָדָם עָלֶיהָ בָרָאתִי. הוּא בְּגִין לְאַחֲזָאָה, דְּלָא הֲוֵי פְּרוּדָא בֵּין עֵילָא וְתַתָּא.

249. AND HE REPLIED THAT the first "I" was said at Mount Sinai and the second was said during the creation of the world. Thus, at Mount Sinai it is written: "I am Hashem your Elohim" (Shemot 20:2); and at the creation, it is written: "I have made the earth and created man upon it" (Yeshayah 45:12). This shows that there is no separation between above, BINAH, and below, MALCHUT.

250. מוֹחֶה פְּשָׁעֶיךָ. מַעֲבִיר פְּשָׁעֶיךָ לָא כְתִיב, אֶלָּא מוֹחֶה, בְּגִין דְּלָא יִתְחֲזוּן לְעָלְמִין. לְמַעֲנִי. מַאי לְמַעֲנִי, בְּגִין אִינוּן רַחֲמִין דְּתַלְיָין בִּי. דִּכְתִיב כִּי אֵל רַחוּם ה' אֱלֹקֶיךָ וְגוֹ'.

250. HE ASKS: Why does it say "blots out" rather than "removes your transgressions?" AND HE REPLIES: So that they shall never appear again in the world. "For My own sake" – to reveal the compassion that emerges from Me. As it is written: "For Hashem your Elohim is a merciful El" (Devarim 4:31).

251. דָּבָר אַחֵר, מוֹחֶה פְּשָׁעֶיךָ לְמַעֲנִי. תָּא חֲזֵי, חַיָּיבֵי עָלְמָא עָבְדִין פְּגִימוּתָא לְעֵילָא, דְּכַד אִינוּן חוֹבִין סַלְּקִין, רַחֲמִין, וּנְהִירוּ עִלָּאָה,

-134-

וְיַנִּיקוּ דְּבִרְכָּאן, לָא נָחִית לְתַתָּא, וְהַאי דַּרְגָּא לָא נָטִיל בִּרְכָּאן
דִּלְעֵילָא, לְיַנְּקָא לְתַתָּא. וּבְגִין כָּךְ לְמַעֲנִי, בְּגִין דְּלָא יִתְמַנְעוּן בִּרְכָּאן
לְיַנְּקָא לְכֹלָא.

251. Come and behold: Another explanation of the words "blots out your transgressions for My own sake," is that the wicked of the world cause damage. For when their sins rise, mercy and the Supernal Light are lost and blessings cannot descend to this world. So this grade, NAMELY THE NUKVA WHICH IS NAMED "I," does not receive any blessings from above to pass on to the lower beings. THEREFORE, THIS IS CONSIDERED BY HER A DAMAGE, and so She says, "for my own sake," so that blessings will not be withheld from me, to be given to all.

252. כְּגַוְונָא דָּא, רְאוּ עַתָּה כִּי אֲנִי אֲנִי הוּא, לְאַחֲזָאָה דְּלָא הֲוֵי
פְּרוּדָא, בֵּין עֵילָא וְתַתָּא. כְּמָה דְּאִתְּמַר.

252. The same applies to the verse, "See now that I, even I, am He..." (Devarim 32:39), IN WHICH THE FIRST "I" APPLIES TO BINAH AND THE SECOND "I" TO MALCHUT. THIS IS to show that no separation exists between BINAH above and MALCHUT below, as we have already explained.

253. תָּא חֲזֵי, כְּגַוְונָא דָּא, כַּד אִשְׁתַּכָּחוּ זַכָּאִין בְּעָלְמָא, אִתְעָרוּ בִּרְכָּאן
לְעָלְמִין כָּלְּהוּ. כֵּיוָן דְּאָתָא אַבְרָהָם, אִתְעָר בִּרְכָּאן לְעָלְמָא. דִּכְתִיב
וַאֲבָרֶכְךָ. וֶהְיֵה בְּרָכָה, מַאי וֶהְיֵה בְּרָכָה. רְמֵז דְּיִשְׁתַּכְּחוּן בְּגִינֵיהּ
בִּרְכָּאן, לְעֵילָא וְתַתָּא. דִּכְתִיב וְנִבְרְכוּ בְךָ וְגו' וּכְתִיב וַאֲבָרְכָה מְבָרְכֶיךָ.

253. Come and behold: Similarly, when there are righteous people in the world, blessings are sent down to all the worlds. As soon as Abraham arrived, the blessings were sent to the world. As it is written: "and I will bless you, and you shall be a blessing" (Beresheet 12:2). HE ASKS: What is the meaning of, "And you shall be a blessing"? AND HE ANSWERS that because of his merit, blessings shall be abundant on high, IN THE UPPER WORLDS, and down below, IN THE LOWER WORLDS. As it is written: "And in you shall all the families of the earth be blessed," REFERRING TO THE LOWER BEINGS, and "I will bless them that bless you" REFERRING TO THE

UPPER WORLDS. WHEN THEY CONVEY THE BLESSINGS DOWNWARD, THEY ARE BLESSED FIRST, AS IS KNOWN. THIS IS THE SECRET OF "I WILL BLESS THEM THAT BLESS YOU!"

254. אָתָא יִצְחָק, אוֹדַע לְכֹלָּא, דְּאִית דִּין וְאִית דַּיָּין לְעֵילָא, לְאִתְפָּרְעָא מֵרְשִׁיעַיָּא, וְאִיהוּ אִתְּעַר דִּינָא בְּעָלְמָא, בְּגִין דְּיִדְחֲלוּן לֵיהּ לְקֻדְשָׁא בְּרִיךְ הוּא, כָּל בְּנֵי עָלְמָא. אָתָא יַעֲקֹב, וְאִתְּעַר רַחֲמֵי בְּעָלְמָא, וְאַשְׁלִים מְהֵימְנוּתָא בְּעָלְמָא, כִּדְקָא חָזֵי.

254. Isaac arrived and informed everyone that there is judgment and there is a Judge above to punish the wicked. And he awakened judgment on the world, so that all would be in awe of the Holy One, blessed He. Jacob arrived, brought mercy on the world, and perfected the Faith in the world as proper. ABRAHAM DREW CHESED, WHICH IS THE SECRET OF THE RIGHT COLUMN OF THE FAITH, WHICH IS THE SECRET OF THE NUKVA. AND ISAAC DREW FOR HER THE JUDGMENT AND THE SFIRAH OF GVURAH, WHICH IS THE SECRET OF HER LEFT COLUMN. JACOB COMPLETED HER BY DRAWING DOWN MERCY, WHICH IS THE SECRET OF THE CENTRAL COLUMN.

255. בְּיוֹמֵי דְּאַבְרָהָם מַה כְּתִיב, וּמַלְכִּי צֶדֶק מֶלֶךְ שָׁלֵם, דְּאִתְעַטְּרַת כֻּרְסַיָּיא בְּדוּכְתֵּיהּ, וּכְדֵין אִשְׁתְּכַח מֶלֶךְ שָׁלֵם, בְּלָא פְּגִימוּ כְּלָל. הוֹצִיא לֶחֶם וָיָיִן דְּאַפִּיק מְזוֹנִין לְעָלְמִין, כֻּלְּהוּ כִּדְקָא חָזֵי. הוֹצִיא לֶחֶם וָיָיִן, דְּלָא אִתְמְנָעוּ בִּרְכָאן מִכָּלְּהוּ עָלְמִין, הוֹצִיא: כד"א תּוֹצֵא הָאָרֶץ, מִדַּרְגִּין דִּלְעֵילָא אַפִּיק מְזוֹנִין וּבִרְכָאן לְעָלְמִין כָּלְּהוּ.

255. Thus, of the days of Abraham, it is written: "And Melchizedek king of Shalem," since the Throne, THE NUKVA, was crowned in its own place, IN BINAH. Then THE NUKVA, the "king of Shalem" (a perfect king), was completely flawless. THE NUKVA "brought forth bread and wine" to nourish all of the worlds as ought to be. The words "brought forth bread and wine" SHOW THAT the blessings were not withheld from any of the worlds. The words "brought forth" are similar to the phrase "Let the Earth bring forth," (Beresheet 1:24) WHICH REFERS TO THE NUKVA, WHICH BROUGHT nourishment and blessings from the highest levels to all the worlds!

256. וְהוּא כֹהֵן לְאֵל עֶלְיוֹן. דְּאִשְׁתְּכַח כֹּלָא, בִּשְׁלִימוּ עֲלָאָה, כִּדְקָא חֲזֵי. לְאִתְחֲזָאָה כְּמָה דְחַיָּיבַיָא עָבְדֵי פְּגִימוּ בְּעָלְמָא, וּמָנְעֵי בִּרְכָּאן. הָכֵי נָמֵי, בְּגִין זַכָּאִין אַתְיָין בִּרְכָּאן לְעָלְמָא, וּבְגִינַיְיהוּ אִתְבָּרְכָאן כָּל בְּנֵי עָלְמָא.

256. "And he was the priest of the most high El" (Beresheet 14:68) MEANS THAT everything has reached full supernal perfection, as it ought to. THAT REFERS TO THE PERFECTION OF BINAH, WHICH IS CALLED "THE MOST HIGH EL." This teaches us that just as the sinners bring damage upon the world and prevent blessings FROM REACHING IT, so the righteous bring blessings to the world, and for their sake, all the people of the world are blessed as well.

257. וַיִּתֶּן לוֹ מַעֲשֵׂר מִכֹּל. מַאי מַעֲשֵׂר מִכֹּל, מֵאִינוּן בִּרְכָּאן, דְּנָפְקֵי מִכֹּל. בְּגִין דְּאִיהוּ אֲתַר, דְּכָל בִּרְכָּאן דְּנַחֲתֵי לְעָלְמָא, מִתַּמָּן נָפְקֵי. דָּבָר אֲחֵר, וַיִּתֶּן לוֹ מַעֲשֵׂר מִכֹּל. קֻדְשָׁא בְּרִיךְ הוּא יְהַב לֵיהּ מַעַשְׂרָא. וּמַאן אִיהוּ, דָּא דַרְגָּא, דְּכָל פִּתְחִין דִּמְהֵימָנוּתָא, וּבִרְכָּאן דְּעָלְמָא, בֵּיהּ קַיְימֵי. וְאִיהוּ מַעֲשֵׂר, וְאִיהוּ חַד מֵעֲשָׂרָה, וְאִיהוּ עֲשָׂרָה מִמֵּאָה. מִכָּאן וּלְהָלְאָה עָאל אַבְרָהָם, בְּקִיּוּמָא דִלְעֵילָא, כִּדְקָא חֲזֵי. אֲמַר לֵיהּ רַבִּי אֶלְעָזָר שַׁפִּיר קָא אֲמַרְתְּ.

257. What is the meaning of "And he gave him a tithe of all" (Beresheet 14:20), IT MEANS THAT MELCHIZEDEK GAVE HIM those blessings that issue from "all," WHICH IS YESOD. THIS MEANS THAT MELCHIZEDEK, WHO IS THE NUKVA, RECEIVED THE TITHE, WHICH IS THE SECRET OF THE BLESSINGS, FROM YESOD, AND PASSED THEM ON TO ABRAHAM. WHY FROM THE YESOD? Because this is the place from which all blessings that reach the world originate. Another explanation of the words "And he gave him a tithe of all" is that it was the Holy One, blessed be He, who gave Abraham the tithe. And what is the tithe? It is a grade, where all the gates of faith and the blessings of the world are established, it is one out of ten, and ten out of a hundred, NAMELY MALCHUT, WHICH DURING HER IMATURE STATE, HAS NO OTHER SFIRAH BUT KETER. AND THIS SFIRAH IS BUT

ONE OUT OF THE TEN SFIROT OF ZEIR ANPIN. BUT DURING HER STAGE
OF MATURITY, MALCHUT HAS TEN COMPLETE SFIROT, AND THEN SHE
IS "TEN OUT OF A HUNDRED" SFIROT OF ZEIR ANPIN. AND THE HOLY
ONE, BLESSED BE HE, GAVE THIS GRADE TO ABRAHAM. From this point
on, Avraham's existence became firmly established from above, WHICH
MEANS THAT HE MERITED FULL CONCEPTION FOREVER!' Rabbi Elazar
said to him, "You have spoken well!"

258. אָמַר לוֹ ר' אֶלְעָזָר, מַאי עֲבִידְתָּךְ. אָמַר לוֹ קַרְיָנָא דַרְדְּקֵי בְּאַתְרִי,
הַשְׁתָּא אָתָא ר' יוֹסֵי דִּכְפַר חָנִין לְמָתָא, וְסָלִיקוּ לוֹן מִגַּבַּאי, וְאוֹתְבוּ
לוֹן לְגַבֵּיה. וַהֲווֹ יָהֲבִין לִי כָּל בְּנֵי מָתָא אַגְרָא, כְּהַהוּא זִמְנָא דְּדַרְדְּקֵי
הֲווֹ גַּבַּאי. וְאִסְתַּכַּלְנָא בְּנַפְשַׁאי, דְּלָא אִתְחֲזֵי לִי לְאִתְהֲנֵי מִנַּיְיהוּ
לְמַגָּנָא, וַאֲגִירְנָא גַרְמַאי בַּהֲדֵי דְּהַאי חַכִּים. אָמַר רַבִּי אֶלְעָזָר, בִּרְכָאן
דְּאַבָּא אִצְטְרִיכוּ הָכָא.

258. Rabbi Elazar asked him, "What is your job?" He responded, "I teach
children, back home. But when Rabbi Yosi of the village Chanin came to
town, all the children were taken from me and passed on to him.
NEVERTHELESS, the people of my town paid my salary, as they had when
the children were with me. But I searched my soul and found it improper to
benefit from doing nothing. So I offered my services to this wise man,
NAMELY RABBI YESA." Rabbi Elazar said: Here, the blessings of my father
– REFERRING TO RABBI SHIMON BAR YOCHAI – are required.

259. קָמוּ. אָתוֹ קַמֵּיה דְּרַבִּי שִׁמְעוֹן, וַהֲוָה יָתִיב וְלָעֵי כָּל יוֹמָא קַמֵּיה
דְּרַבִּי שִׁמְעוֹן. וְיוֹמָא חַד, הֲוָה עָסִיק בִּנְטִילַת יָדַיִם קַמֵּיה, אָמַר, כָּל
מַאן דְּלָא נָטִיל יְדוֹי כְּדְקָא יָאוֹת, אַף עַל גַּב דְּאִתְעַנַּשׁ לְעֵילָא,
אִתְעַנַּשׁ לְתַתָּא. וּמַאי עוֹנָשֵׁיה לְתַתָּא, דְּגָרִים לֵיה לְגַרְמֵיה מִסְכְּנוּתָא.
כְּמָה דְּעוֹנָשֵׁיה, כָּךְ הָכֵי הוּא זָכֵי, מַאן דְּנָטִיל יְדוֹי כְּדְקָא יָאוֹת. דְּגָרִים
לְגַרְמֵיה בִּרְכָאן דִּלְעֵילָא, דְּשָׁרְיָאן בִּרְכָאן עַל יְדוֹי כְּדְקָא יָאוֹת,
וְאִתְבָּרַךְ בְּעוֹתְרָא.

259. They went before Rabbi Shimon, and THE JEW would sit and study all

day long before Rabbi Shimon. One day, as they were studying the laws concerning the washing of the hands, RABBI SHIMON said: Whoever does not wash his hands properly is punished from above and also below IN THIS WORLD. And what is his punishment below? He brings poverty upon himself. And just as he who washes his hands improperly is punished, so he who washes his hands properly is rewarded ABOVE AND BELOW, bringing the blessings of above on himself. Because the blessings OF ABOVE rest properly on his hands, he is blessed BELOW with wealth.

260. לְבָתַר אַקְדִּים רָבִּי שִׁמְעוֹן, חָמָא לֵיהּ, דְּאַנְטַל יְדוֹי בְּמַיָּא, וְנָטִיל לוֹן, בְּשִׁיעוּרָא סַגְיָיא דְּמַיִין. אָמַר רָבִּי שִׁמְעוֹן מַלֵּא יְדָיו מִבִּרְכוֹתֶיךָ. וְכָךְ הֲוָה, מֵהַהוּא יוֹמָא וּלְהָלְאָה, אִתְעַתַּר, וְאַשְׁכַּח סִימָא, וַהֲוָה לָעֵי בְּאוֹרַיְיתָא, וְיָהֵיב מְזוֹנָא לְמִסְכְּנֵי כָּל יוֹמָא, וַהֲוָה חָדֵי עִמְּהוֹן וּמְסַבַּר לוֹן אַנְפִּין נְהִירִין. קָרָא עֲלֵיהּ רָבִּי שִׁמְעוֹן, וְאַתָּה תָּגִיל בַּה' בִּקְדוֹשׁ וְגוֹ'.

260. At a later time, Rabbi Shimon woke up in time to see the Jew washing his hands with a great quantity of water. Rabbi Shimon said: "Fill his hands with your blessings." And so it was from that day onward, because the Jew became rich and found a treasure, he studied Torah and gave food and nourishment to the poor every day, and was happy and kind to them. As a result, in reference to him, Rabbi Shimon quoted the verse, "And you shall rejoice in Hashem and shall glory in the Holy One of Yisrael" (Yeshayah 41:16).

26. "After these things"
26. "After these things"

A Synopsis
In the material world, the Light of the Creator can only manifest through a physical medium or instrument, which Kabbalah refers to as a Vessel. Just as sunlight requires physical matter to reveal its radiance, spiritual Light requires a Vessel in order to express itself. Though many spiritual traditions teach renunciation of material existence, Kabbalah takes a very different view. Rather than meditating on a mountaintop above the fray and fracas of our daily existence, we must embrace the chaos of life, using it as an opportunity, as a vessel to reveal Light. Spiritual Light ignites in that momentary flash-point of character transformation.

The Relevance of this Passage
Acknowledging and rooting out the negative, dark side of our nature when confronting chaos and conflict, give us the opportunity to effect character change. Moreover, we must initiate the physical actions necessary to transform ourselves, change our world, and reveal the spiritual Light of the Creator. Accordingly, this portion strengthens us so that we successfully confront and transform life's challenges.

261. אַחַר הַדְּבָרִים הָאֵלֶּה הָיָה דְּבַר ה' אֶל אַבְרָם וְגוֹ'. ר' יְהוּדָה פָּתַח אֲנִי לְדוֹדִי וְעָלַי תְּשׁוּקָתוֹ. הָא אוֹקְמוּהָ, אֲבָל בְּאִתְעֲרוּתָא דִלְתַתָּא, אִשְׁתְּכַח אִתְעֲרוּתָא לְעֵילָא, דְּהָא לָא אִתְעַר לְעֵילָא, עַד דְּאִתְעַר לְתַתָּא. וּבִרְכָאן דִּלְעֵילָא לָא מִשְׁתַּכְּחֵי, אֶלָּא בַּמֶה דְּאִית בֵּיה מַמָּשָׁא, וְלָאו אִיהוּ רֵיקַנְיָא.

261. "After these things, the word of Hashem came to Abram..." (Beresheet 15:1). Rabbi Yehuda opened the discourse by quoting, "I am my beloved's, and his desire is toward me" (Shir Hashirim 7:11). As has been explained, this means that awakening below results in awakening above. There can be no awakening from above until there is awakening from below. In addition, blessings from above rest in a place of substance, not in an empty space.

262. מְנָלָן. מֵאֵשֶׁת עוֹבַדְיָהוּ, דַּאֲמַר לָהּ אֱלִישָׁע הַגִּידִי לִי מַה יֶּשׁ לָךְ בַּבָּיִת, דְּהָא בִּרְכָאן דִּלְעֵילָא, לָא שָׁרְיָין עַל פָּתוֹרָא רֵיקַנְיָא, וְלָא בַּאֲתַר

רֵיקָנְיָא. מַה כְּתִיב, וַתֹּאמֶר אֵין לְשִׁפְחָתְךָ כֹל בַּבַּיִת כִּי אִם אָסוּךְ שָׁמֶן. מַאי אָסוּךְ. אֶלָּא אָמַר לוֹ, שִׁיעוּרָא דְּהַאי מִשְׁחָא, לָאו אִיהִי, אֶלָּא כְּדֵי מְשִׁיחַת אֶצְבְּעָא זְעֵירָא.

262. How do we know this? We know this from the wife of Ovadyahu, to whom Elisha said: "Tell me, what have you in the house" (II Melachim 4:2). He asked this because blessings from above do not rest on an empty table, AS WILL BE EXPLAINED ABOUT THE SHEW-BREAD, nor in an empty place, AS IS TOLD OF THE WIFE OF OVADYAHU. "And she said: 'Your handmaid has nothing in the house but a pot of oil'"(Ibid.). AND HE ASKS: What is a pot? AND HE SAYS: There is only enough oil IN THE POT to smear the little finger.

263. אֲמַר לֵה, נַחַמְתָּנִי. דְּהָא לָא יְדַעְנָא, הֵיאַךְ יִשְׁרוֹן בִּרְכָאן דִּלְעֵילָא, בְּדוּכְתָּא רֵיקַנְיָא, אֲבָל הַשְׁתָּא דְּאִית לָךְ שֶׁמֶן, דָּא הוּא אֲתַר, לְאִשְׁתַּכְּחָא בֵּיה בִּרְכָאן. מְנָלָן דִּכְתִיב כַּשֶּׁמֶן הַטּוֹב וגו'. וְסֵיפֵיה מַה כְּתִיב, כִּי שָׁם צִוָּה ה' אֶת הַבְּרָכָה חַיִּים עַד הָעוֹלָם. וּבְאַתְרָא דָּא שָׁרָאן בִּרְכָאן.

263. ELISHA said: You have relieved me. Because I did not know how the blessings of above would rest in an empty place. But now that you have some oil, this is the place where the blessings shall rest. How do we know this? Because it is written: "It is like the precious ointment..." (Tehilim 133:2). And how does the verse end? With the words, "for there Hashem has commanded the blessing, even life for evermore" (Ibid.). SO in this place, NAMELY IN THE OIL, there are blessings.

264. וְאִי תֵימָא כְּטַל חֶרְמוֹן שֶׁיּוֹרֵד עַל הַרְרֵי צִיּוֹן, וְלָא כְתִיב שֶׁמֶן אֶלָּא טַל. אֶלָּא, אִיהוּ שֶׁמֶן, וְאִיהוּ טַל. הַהוּא טַל, אִיהוּ, דְּאַטִּיל קֻדְשָׁא בְּרִיךְ הוּא מִמִּשְׁחָא עִלָּאָה. דְּהַהוּא שֶׁמֶן נָפַק לְסִטְרָא דִּימִינָא.

264. You might think that because in the words, "like the dew of Chermon descending upon the mountains of Zion" (Ibid.), FOLLOWED BY THE WORDS "FOR THERE HASHEM HAS COMMANDED THE BLESSINGS," dew

is mentioned rather than oil. DEW IS THEN THE PLACE FOR THE BLESSING
AND NOT OIL. BUT, HE REPLIES: It is oil and it is dew, MEANING THAT
THEY ARE THE SAME. BECAUSE this dew is what the Holy One, blessed be
He, drew out of the supernal oil, which comes out of the right side.

265. תְּרֵין אִינוּן: יַיִן וְשֶׁמֶן. וְאַזְלוּ לִתְרֵין סִטְרִין, יַיִן לִסְטַר שְׂמָאלָא,
שֶׁמֶן, לִסְטַר יָמִינָא. וּמִסְּטְרָא דְיָמִינָא, נָפְקֵי בִּרְכָּאן לְעָלְמָא, וּמִתַּמָּן
אִתְמְשַׁח מַלְכוּתָא קַדִּישָׁא. וּבְגִין דְּשֶׁמֶן הֲוָה אִתְתַּקַּן לְתַתָּא בְּקַדְמֵיתָא,
שֶׁמֶן אִזְדַּמַּן לְעֵילָא, אֲרִיקוּ דְּבִרְכָּאן.

265. These are two things – wine and oil – and they flow to two sides. Wine
flows to the left and oil to the right. And from the right side all blessings
come forth and descend to this world, and from there, the holy kingdom,
WHICH REFERS TO THE KINGS OF YISRAEL, is anointed. Because oil is
first prepared below, MEANING THAT SHE HAD THE POT OF OIL, WHICH IS
THE SECRET OF THE AWAKENING FROM BELOW, then the oil was available
from above, referring to the flowing of the blessings FROM ABOVE, WHICH
IS THE SECRET OF THE AWAKENING FROM ABOVE, AS IT IS WRITTEN:
"UPON HER SONS, WHO BROUGHT THE VESSELS TO HER; AND SHE
POURED OUT" (II MELACHIM 4:5).

266. תָּא חֲזֵי, מֵאִתְעָרוּתָא דְּהַאי שֶׁמֶן דִּלְעֵילָא, קָאֵי לְאַרְקָא עַל דָּוִד
וּשְׁלֹמֹה, לְאִתְבָּרְכָא בְּנוֹי. מְנָ"ל, דִּכְתִיב, וַיַּעֲמֹד הַשָּׁמֶן. כְּתִיב הָכָא
וַיַּעֲמֹד. וּכְתִיב הָתָם שֹׁרֶשׁ יִשַׁי, אֲשֶׁר עֹמֵד לְנֵס עַמִּים.

266. Come and behold: From the awakening of this oil above, it was poured
on David and Solomon, so that their sons would be blessed. How do we
know this? It is in the verse, "And the oil stopped (lit. 'stood')" (II
Melachim 4:6). THIS IS ANALOGOUS TO WHAT IS written elsewhere, "a root
of Jesse, that stands for a banner of the people..." (Yeshayah 11:10).
BECAUSE THIS VERSE ALLUDES TO DAVID, SOLOMON, AND THEIR
DESCENDANTS, WHO ARE FROM THE ROOT OF JESSE, THEN HERE AS
WELL THE VERSE ALLUDES TO DAVID, SOLOMON, AND THEIR
DESCENDANTS.

267. תָּא חֲזֵי, מְשַׁלְחָן דְּלֶחֶם הַפָּנִים, דְּבִרְכָאן נָפְקִין מִתַּמָּן, וּמְזוֹנָא

לְעָלְמָא, לָא בָעֵי לְאִשְׁתַּכְּחָא רֵיקַנְיָא, אֲפִילוּ רִגְעָא חֲדָא, בְּגִין דְּלָא יִסְתַּלְּקוּן בִּרְכָאן מִתַּמָּן, אוּף הָכֵי לָא מְבָרְכִין עַל שֻׁלְחָן רֵיקַנְיָא, דְּהָא בִּרְכָאן דִּלְעֵילָא, לָא שָׁרְיָין עַל שֻׁלְחָן רֵיקַנְיָא.

267. Come and behold: Just as the table of the shew-bread, from where all the blessings and replenishment of the world come, should not remain empty even for a moment, so that the blessings may not be removed from there, one should never recite blessings over an empty table. The blessings from above will not rest upon an empty table.

268. תָּא חֲזֵי, מַה כְּתִיב אֲנִי לְדוֹדִי וְעָלַי תְּשׁוּקָתוֹ. אֲנִי לְדוֹדִי בְּקַדְמֵיתָא, וּלְבָתַר וְעָלַי תְּשׁוּקָתוֹ. אֲנִי לְדוֹדִי, לְאַתְקָנָא לֵיה דּוּכְתָּא בְּקַדְמֵיתָא, וּלְבָתַר, וְעָלַי תְּשׁוּקָתוֹ.

268. Come and behold, it is then written: "I am my beloved's, and his desire is towards me." First, "I am my beloved's," and then, "his desire is towards me." "I am my beloved's" to prepare a place for him at first BY THE AWAKENING FROM BELOW, and afterwards "his desire is towards me."

269. דָּבָר אַחֵר אֲנִי לְדוֹדִי. דְּהָא תָּנִינָן שְׁכִינְתָּא לָא אִשְׁתַּכְּחַת עִמְּהוֹן דְּחַיָּיבַיָּא, כֵּיוָן דְּאָתֵי בַּר נָשׁ לְאִתְדַּכָּאָה, וּלְמִקְרַב גַּבֵּי דְּקֻדְשָׁא בְּרִיךְ הוּא, כְּדֵין שְׁכִינְתָּא שַׁרְיָא עֲלֵיה. הה"ד אֲנִי לְדוֹדִי בְּקַדְמֵיתָא, וְעָלַי תְּשׁוּקָתוֹ לְבָתַר. אָתֵי בַּר נָשׁ לְאִתְדַּכָּאָה, מְדַכְּאִין לֵיה.

269. Another explanation for "I am my beloved's" is based on the understanding that the Shechinah does not reside among the wicked. As soon as a person desires to purify himself and come close to the Holy One, blessed be He, only then does the Shechinah rest upon him. Therefore it is written: "I am my beloved's" first, and then, "his desire is towards me." Because when a person comes to be purified, he is purified.

270. תָּא חֲזֵי, אַחַר הַדְּבָרִים הָאֵלֶּה, דִּרְדַף אַבְרָהָם בָּתַר אִלֵּין מַלְכִין, וְקָטִיל לוֹן קֻדְשָׁא בְּרִיךְ הוּא, הֲוָה אַבְרָהָם תֹּוהָא, אֲמַר דִּילְמָא ח"ו, גָּרַעְנָא הַהוּא אַגְרָא, דַּהֲוֵינָא אַהֲדַר בְּנֵי נָשָׁא לְגַבֵּי קֻדְשָׁא בְּרִיךְ הוּא,

וְאַחֲדִינָא בְּהוּ, לְקָרְבָא לוֹן לְגַבֵּיה, וְהַשְׁתָּא אִתְקְטִילוּ בְּנֵי נְשָׁא עַל יָדִי. מִיַּד אָמַר לוֹ קֻדְשָׁא בְּרִיךְ הוּא, אַל תִּירָא אַבְרָם אָנֹכִי מָגֵן לָךְ שְׂכָרְךָ הַרְבֵּה וְגו'. אַגְרָא קַבִּילַת עֲלַיְיהוּ, דְּהָא כָּלְהוּ לָא יִזְכּוּן לְעָלְמִין.

270. Come and behold: "After these things," after Abraham pursued the kings, and the Holy One, blessed be He, killed them off, Abraham was wondering if perhaps "I have lost all the reward from bringing people to repent and return to the Holy One, blessed be He, and holding on to them to draw them nearer to Him – since now people were killed by me!" Immediately, the Holy One, blessed be He, said to him: "Fear not, Abram, I am your shield, your reward shall be exceedingly great." You are receiving a reward for them, BECAUSE THEY WERE KILLED, because none of them shall ever be able to improve their behavior.

27. "Hashem came to Abram in a vision"

A Synopsis

The Zohar presents four complex ideas. The first concerns the mysteries of circumcision. Before we can begin to understand any ritual performed in our physical world, we must acquire some understanding of the structure of the Upper Worlds which are the foundation of our physical existence. The Zohar refers to ten dimensions that compose all creation. These dimensions are known as the Ten Sfirot, or Ten Emanations.

The Sfirah of *Yesod* is a reservoir to which all the upper Sfirot pour their various energies. *Yesod* gathers all these elements, blends them, and transfers this great Light to the Sfira of *Malchut*, which is our physical universe. Residing just above *Malchut* in the structure of the Ten Sfirot, *Yesod* acts as the portal through which the awesome forces of Light enter our realm. As the building blocks of all creation, the Ten Sfirot reflect themselves in our world. Thus, we have ten fingers, ten toes, and our numerical system functions on base ten.

The Sfira of *Yesod* correlates to the sexual organ, in which the greatest expression of Light manifests. This great Light is responsible for the miracle of procreation and the pleasure derived from it.

The negative forces in our midst attach themselves to any gateway through which the greatest Light can shine. For this reason, these negative entities are found in the upper world realm of *Yesod*; in our physical realm, negative forces manifest in the human sexual organ. The purpose of the covenant of circumcision is to remove this negative influence from our lives as well as from the worlds above. Circumcision, performed properly with Kabbalistic mediation, removes all negativity from both the child and the world. The act of circumcision brings enormous spiritual benefits to the child, including boosting his immune system. Though small in size, the foreskin contains powerful negative forces, as if it were a nuclear warhead at the tip of a ballistic missile.

The Relevance of this Passage

These specific Aramaic texts emanate spiritual influences that help cleanse and purify the realm of *Yesod* within us, including any negative sexual thoughts, desires or actions. It is these blockages that can prevent us from receiving our full portion of the Light.

271. הָיָה דְּבַר ה' אֶל אַבְרָם בַּמַּחֲזֶה לֵאמֹר. מַאי בַּמַּחֲזֶה. אֶלָּא, בְּהַהוּא חֵיזוּ, דַּרְגָּא דְּכָל דְּיוֹקְנִין אִתְחַזְיָין בֵּיהּ. אָמַר רִבִּי שִׁמְעוֹן תָּא חֲזֵי, עַד לָא אִתְגְּזַר אַבְרָהָם, הֲוָה חַד דַּרְגָּא מַלֵּיל עִמֵּיהּ, וּמַאן אִיהוּ, דָּא מַחֲזֶה, דִּכְתִיב מַחֲזֵה שַׁדַּי יֶחֱזֶה.

271. "The word of Hashem came to Abram in a vision, saying..." HE ASKS: What is meant by a vision? AND HE ANSWERS: This is the mirror, which is the grade in which all images appear. Rabbi Shimon said: Come and behold, before Abraham was circumcised, only one grade spoke to him. And which one was that? It was the 'vision,' NAMELY THE NUKVA. As it is written: "...seeing the vision of Shadai" (Bemidbar 24:16).

272. כֵּיוָן דְּאִתְגְּזַר, הֲווֹ כֻּלְּהוּ דַּרְגִּין שַׁרְיָאן עַל הַאי דַּרְגָּא, וּכְדֵין מַלֵּיל עִמֵּיהּ, הה"ד, וָאֵרָא אֶל אַבְרָהָם אֶל יִצְחָק וְאֶל יַעֲקֹב בְּאֵל שַׁדָּי, וְעַד לָא אִתְגְּזַר, לָא הֲווֹ אִינּוּן דַּרְגִּין שַׁרְיָאן עֲלוֹי לְמַלָּלָא.

272. After Abraham was circumcised, all the grades rested upon that grade, WHICH IS CALLED THE VISION, and then He spoke to him. Hence, it is written: "And I appeared to Abraham," WHO IS THE SECRET OF CHESED, "to Isaac," WHO IS THE SECRET OF GVURAH, "and to Jacob," WHO IS THE SECRET OF TIFERET, "by the name of El Shadai" (Shemot 6:3), WHICH IS THE SECRET OF YESOD AND MALCHUT. ALL THE GRADES, FROM CHESED DOWNWARD, ILLUMINATE IN THE NUKVA. So, before he was circumcised, these grades did not yet speak to him, ONLY THE NUKVA, WHICH IS THE SECRET OF THE "VISION OF SHADAI" ALONE!

273. וְאִי תֵימָא, דְּהָא בְּקַדְמֵיתָא כְּתִיב, וַיֵּרָא ה' אֶל אַבְרָם, וּכְתִיב, וַיִּסַּע אַבְרָם הָלוֹךְ וְנָסוֹעַ הַנֶּגְבָּה. וּכְתִיב וַיִּבֶן שָׁם מִזְבֵּחַ. הָא הָכָא אִינּוּן דַּרְגִּין עִלָּאִין. וְהַשְׁתָּא אֲמָרָן דְּעַד דְּלָא אִתְגְּזַר, לָא הֲווֹ אִינּוּן דַּרְגִּין עִלָּאִין, שַׁרְיָאן עַל הַאי דַּרְגָּא לְמַלָּלָא עִמֵּיהּ.

273. You might say that it is already written: "And Hashem appeared to

Abram," WHICH IS THE LEVEL OF NEFESH, AND "and Abram journeyed, going on still toward the south," WHICH IS RUACH; and "and there he built an altar," WHICH IS NESHAMAH. If here are the supernal grades THAT HE ATTAINED, how can we say that before he was circumcised, the supernal grades did not rest upon that certain grade, in order to speak to him?

274. תָּא חֲזֵי, בְּקַדְמֵיתָא יְהַב קֻדְשָׁא בְּרִיךְ הוּא חָכְמָה לְאַבְרָהָם, לְמִנְדַּע חָכְמָה לְאִתְדַּבְּקָא בֵּיהּ, וְיָדַע רָזָא דִּמְהֵימְנוּתָא, אֲבָל לְמַלָּלָא עִמֵּיהּ, לָא הֲוָה, אֶלָּא הַאי דַרְגָּא תַּתָּאָה בִּלְחוֹדוֹי. כֵּיוָן דְּאִתְגְּזַר, כֻּלְּהוּ דַּרְגִּין עִלָּאִין הֲווֹ שָׁרָאן עַל הַאי דַרְגָּא תַּתָּאָה, בְּגִין לְמַלָּלָא עִמֵּיהּ, וּכְדֵין אִסְתַּלַּק אַבְרָהָם בְּכֹלָּא. כְּמָה דְּאִתְּמָר.

274. AND HE REPLIES, Come and behold: In the beginning; BEFORE HE WAS CIRCUMCISED, the Holy One, blessed be He, gave wisdom to Abraham, NAMELY THE AFOREMENTIONED SUPERNAL GRADES, so that he would know wisdom and would cleave to THE HOLY ONE, BLESSED BE HE. And Abraham did achieve the secret of Faith, but he could not speak to Him, only to the lower grade alone, NAMELY THE NUKVA AS SEEN "THROUGH THE VISION OF SHADAI." But after he was circumcised, then all the supernal grades rested upon this lower grade, in order to speak with him. And then Abraham ascended through all the grades, as has been explained.

275. תָּא חֲזֵי, עַד לָא אִתְגְּזַר בַּר נָשׁ, לָא אִתְאֲחֵיד בִּשְׁמָא דְּקֻדְשָׁא בְּרִיךְ הוּא, כֵּיוָן דְּאִתְגְּזַר, עָאל בִּשְׁמֵיהּ, וְאִתְאֲחֵיד בֵּיהּ. וְאִי תֵימָא אַבְרָהָם, דְּאִתְאֲחֵיד בֵּיהּ, עַד לָא אִתְגְּזַר. הָכֵי הֲוָה, דְּאִתְאֲחֵיד בֵּיהּ וְלָא כְּדְקָא יָאוּת, דְּהָא מִגּוֹ רְחִימוּתָא עִלָּאָה דְּרָחֵים לֵיהּ קֻודְשָׁא בְּרִיךְ הוּא קָרֵיב לֵיהּ.

275. Come and behold: As long as a man is not circumcised, he does not hold on to the Name of the Holy One, blessed be He. As soon as he is circumcised, he enters His Name and is attached to it. And if you say that Abraham was nevertheless attached to Him even before he was circumcised, the response is that he was indeed attached to Him, but not properly. Because of the sublime love that the Holy One, blessed be He, felt toward

Abraham, He brought him closer to Himself, BUT IN SPITE OF ALL THIS, IT WAS NOT AS IT SHOULD PROPERLY BE.

276. לְבָתַר פַּקִיד לֵיהּ, דְּיִתְגְּזַר, וְאִתְיְיהֵיב לֵיהּ בְּרִית. קְשׁוּרָא דְּכֻלְּהוֹ דַּרְגִּין עִלָּאִין. בְּרִית קְשׁוּרָא לְאִתְקַשְּׁרָא כֹּלָּא כַּחֲדָא, לְאִכְלָלָא דָּא בְּדָא, בְּרִית קְשׁוּרָא, דְּכֹלָּא אִתְקְשַׁר בֵּיהּ, וּבְגִין כָּךְ אַבְרָהָם עַד לָא אִתְגְּזַר. מִלּוֹי לָא הֲוָה עִמֵּיהּ, אֶלָּא בַּמַּחֲזֶה. כְּמָה דְּאִתְּמַר.

276. After, THE HOLY ONE, BLESSED BE HE, commanded Abraham to circumcise himself, and presented him with the covenant, WHICH IS YESOD, which is the link to all the supernal grades. The covenant is the bond that links all the grades together, to be included within one another. The covenant is the bond that everything is bound to. And because of this, before Abraham was circumcised, He spoke with him only through the "vision," as we have stated. THE UPPER GRADES WERE MISSING FROM IT, BECAUSE THE COVENANT, WHICH LINKS ALL THE GRADES TOGETHER, WAS MISSING.

277. תָּא חֲזֵי. בְּשַׁעֲתָא דִּבְרָא קֻדְשָׁא בְּרִיךְ הוּא עָלְמָא. לָא אִתְבְּרֵי אֶלָּא עַל בְּרִית. כד"א בְּרֵ"א-שִׁי"ת בָּרָא אֱלֹקִים, וְהַיְינוּ בְּרִית, דְּעַל בְּרִית קַיִּים קֻדְשָׁא בְּרִיךְ הוּא עָלְמָא וּכְתִיב אִם לֹא בְרִיתִי יוֹמָם וָלַיְלָה חֻקּוֹת שָׁמַיִם וָאָרֶץ לֹא שַׂמְתִּי, דְּהָא בְּרִית קְשׁוּרָא אִיהוּ, דְּיוֹמָא וְלֵילְיָא לָא מִתְפָּרְשָׁן.

277. Come and behold: When the Holy One, blessed be He, created the world, He created it based on the covenant. It is written: "In the beginning (Heb. *Beresheet*) Elohim created (Heb. *bara*)" (Beresheet 1:1), WHERE SHEET (ARAM. SIX) refers to the covenant, because by relying upon the covenant, the Holy One, blessed be He, created the world. And it is also written: "If My covenant be not day and night, it were as if I have not appointed the ordinances of heaven and earth" (Yirmeyah 33:25). This is a unifying covenant, which ensures that day and night, WHICH ARE ZEIR ANPIN AND NUKVA, may not be separated.

278. אָמַר רַבִּי אֶלְעָזָר, כַּד בָּרָא קֻדְשָׁא בְּרִיךְ הוּא עָלְמָא, עַל תְּנַאי

הֲוָה, דְּכַד יֵיתוּן יִשְׂרָאֵל, אִם יְקַבְּלוּן אוֹרַיְיתָא יָאוֹת, וְאִם לָאו הֲרֵי
אֲנָא אַהֲדַר לְכוּ, לְתֹהוּ וָבֹהוּ. וְעָלְמָא לָא אִתְקַיֵּים, עַד דְּקַיְימוּ יִשְׂרָאֵל,
עַל טוּרָא דְסִינַי, וְקַבִּילוּ אוֹרַיְיתָא, וּכְדֵין אִתְקַיֵּים עָלְמָא.

278. Rabbi Elazar said: 'When the Holy One, blessed be He, created the world, it was on the condition that if Yisrael will came forth and receiv Torah, all would be well. If Yisrael will not do so, then the world would be returned to chaos. So the world was not firmly established until Yisrael stood at Mount Sinai and received Torah.

A Synopsis
The second idea presented by the Zohar concerns the concept of soul mates. Our success in finding our true soul mate depends on the levels we reach in our spiritual work. If we attain the necessary level of growth, we may merit the appearance of our soul mate in our life.

The Relevance of this Passage
According to Kabbalah, soul mates are two halves of one soul. If two people are soul mates living on opposite ends of the world, circumstances will eventually arise that will lead them across vast continents and oceans in order that they may encounter one another and reunite. The Aramaic words expressing this spiritual truth, assists us towards that end.

279. וּמֵהַהוּא יוֹמָא וּלְהָלְאָה, קַדְשָׁא בְּרִיךְ הוּא בָּרֵי עָלְמִין, וּמָאן
אִינוּן, זִוּוּגִין דִּבְנֵי נָשָׁא. דְּהָא מֵהַהוּא זִמְנָא, קַדְשָׁא בְּרִיךְ הוּא מְזַוֵּוג
זִוּוּגִין, וְאוֹמֵר בַּת פְּלוֹנִי לִפְלוֹנִי, וְאִלֵּין אִינוּן עָלְמִין דְּהוּא בָּרֵי.

279. From that day onward, the Holy One, blessed be He, has been creating worlds. And what are these worlds? They are the matings of human beings. Because ever since that day, the Holy One blessed be He, has been making marriages, by saying: "The daughter of so to so for so and so." These are the worlds He creates, BECAUSE EVERY UNION OF A COUPLE IS CONSIDERED TO BE A WORLD.

סִתְרֵי תּוֹרָה

280. אַחַר הַדְּבָרִים הָאֵלֶּה וְגוֹ'. אִלֵּין פִּתְגָּמֵי אוֹרַיְיתָא, דִּכְתִיב אֶת
הַדְּבָרִים הָאֵלֶּה דִּבֶּר ה' אֶל כָּל קְהַלְכֶם. מַה לְּהַלָּן פִּתְגָּמֵי אוֹרַיְיתָא,
אוֹף הָכָא פִּתְגָּמֵי אוֹרַיְיתָא. בָּתַר דְּאִשְׁתַּדַּל בַּר נָשׁ בְּהַאי עָלְמָא,
בְּדִבְרִים הָאֵלֶּה, קֻדְשָׁא בְּרִיךְ הוּא מְבַשֵּׂר לֵיהּ, וְאַקְדִּים לָהּ לְנִשְׁמָתָא
שְׁלִים, הֲהֲ"ד אַל תִּירָא אַבְרָם אָנֹכִי מָגֵן לָךְ. מִכָּל זַיְינִין בִּישִׁין דְּגֵיהִנֹּם.

Sitrei Torah (Concealed Torah)

280. "After these things." These are the words of Torah, just as "These
words Hashem spoke to all your assembly" (Devarim 5:19) are the words of
Torah. THE MEANING OF THE VERSE IS THAT "After" a person has been
occupied in this world with "these things (lit. 'words')," then the Holy One,
blessed be He, prepares good tidings for the soul and welcomes it. As it is
written: "Fear not, Abram, I am your shield"; I shall shield you from all the
evil aspects in Gehenom."

281. שְׂכָרְךָ הַרְבֵּה מְאֹד. בְּגִין דְּכָל מַאן דְּאִשְׁתַּדַּל בְּאוֹרַיְיתָא בְּהַאי
עָלְמָא, זָכֵי וְאָחְסִין יְרוּתָא אַחְסַנְתָּא בְּעָלְמָא דְּאָתֵי, כְּמָה דִּכְתִיב
לְהַנְחִיל אוֹהֲבַי יֵשׁ. מַאי יֵשׁ. דָּא עָלְמָא דְּאָתֵי. וְאוֹצְרוֹתֵיהֶם אֲמַלֵּא,
בְּהַאי עָלְמָא, מֵעוֹתְרָא וּמִכָּל טִיבוּ דְּעָלְמָא, מַאן דְּאָזֵיל לְיָמִינָא, זָכֵי
לְעָלְמָא דְּאָתֵי. וּמַאן דְּאָזֵיל לִשְׂמָאלָא, הָא עוֹתְרָא בְּעָלְמָא דֵּין.

281. "And your reward shall be exceedingly great," because whoever
studies Torah in this world shall merit and inherit a place in the World to
Come. As it is written: "That I may cause those that love Me to inherit
substance" (Mishlei 8:21). "What is substance?" Substance is "the World to
Come," and "I will fill their treasures" in this world by riches and all
goodness of the world. He who goes to the right shall merit a place in the
World to Come, and he who goes to the left shall merit the riches of this
world.

A Synopsis
The third idea explicated upon by the Zohar concerns the power
associated with the study of Torah. Rabbi Aba helps his student,
Rabbi Yosi, transform his Torah study from a selfish, self-seeking

pursuit, to a process of learning that expresses caring and compassion for the rest of the world.

The benefits of learning Torah are not limited to the traditional concept of acquiring knowledge. Torah study is the sum and substance of spiritual energy itself, and therefore, it reveals enormous spiritual Light both individually and collectively. Our motivation for study should not be selfish desire for knowledge and scholarship. Our purpose should be to reveal and impart Light to others.

The Relevance of this Passage

It is tempting for man to wear the garment of pride as he begins to acquire the knowledge and the secrets of the universe. This discourse helps us accomplish our learning and perform our spiritual work with an intention of sharing combined with deep humility.

282. ר' אַבָּא כַּד אָתָא מֵהָתָם, הֲוָה מַכְרִיז, מַאן בָּעֵי עוֹתְרָא, וּמַאן בָּעֵי אוֹרְכָא דְחַיֵּי בְּעָלְמָא דְאָתֵי, יֵיתֵי וְיִשְׁתַּדַּל בְּאוֹרַיְיתָא. הֲוֹוֹ מִתְכַּנְשִׁין כּוּלֵי עַלְמָא לְגַבֵּיה. רַוָּוק חַד הֲוָה בִּשְׁיבְבוּתֵיה. יוֹמָא חַד אָתָא לְגַבֵּיה, אָמַר לוֹ ר', בָּעֵינָא לְמִלְעֵי בְּאוֹרַיְיתָא, כְּדֵי שֶׁיִּהְיֶה לִי עוֹתְרָא. אָמַר לוֹ הָא וַדַּאי. אָמַר לוֹ מַה שְׁמֶךָ. אָמַר לוֹ יוֹסֵי. אֲמַר לוֹן לְתַלְמִידוֹי דְיִקְרוּן לֵיה ר' יוֹסֵי מָארֵי דְעוֹתְרָא וִיקָרָא. יָתֵיב וְאִתְעַסַּק בְּאוֹרַיְיתָא.

282. After Rabbi Aba returned from BABYLON, he declared that whoever desires to be rich and have a long life in the World to Come should study Torah, and the whole world gathered around him TO STUDY TORAH. There was a bachelor in his neighborhood. One day he said to Rabbi Aba, "Rabbi, I wish to learn Torah so that I may be wealthy." Rabbi Aba responded, "Why of course, YOU SHALL MERIT MUCH WEALTH BY STUDYING TORAH." He asked, "What is your name?" The bachelor responded, "Yosi." Rabbi Aba told his pupils to call the bachelor "Yosi, a man of great wealth and glory." And Yosi delved to the study of Torah.

283. לְיוֹמִין, הֲוָה קָאֵים קַמֵּיה, אָמַר לוֹ ר', אָן הוּא עוֹתְרָא. אָמַר שְׁמַע מִינָהּ, דְּלָא לְשֵׁם שָׁמַיִם קָא עָבֵיד, וְעָאל לְאִדְרֵיה, שְׁמַע חַד קָלָא

דַהֲוָה אָמַר, לָא תַעַנְשֵׁיה, דְּגַבְרָא רַבָּא לִיהֱוֵי. תָּב לְגַבֵּיה, אָמַר לֵיה, תִּיב בְּרִי תִּיב, וַאֲנָא יָהִיבְנָא לָךְ עוֹתְרָא.

283. After a while, as the days passed, Yosi stood before Rabbi Aba and asked, "Rabbi, where is the wealth?" RABBI ABA responded, "I can see that he is not learning for the sake of heaven!" And then he went to his room TO CONSIDER WHAT TO DO WITH YOSI. He then heard a voice that said: Do not punish him, because he shall become a great man! He returned to him and said: Sit down, my son, sit down. And I shall give you wealth.

284. אַדְהָכֵי, אָתָא גַּבְרָא חַד, וּמָאנָא דְּפָז בִּידֵיה, אַפְקֵיה וּנְפַל נְהוֹרָא בְּבֵיתָא. אָמַר לוֹ רַבִּי בָּעֵינָא לְמִזְכֵּי בְּאוֹרַיְיתָא, וַאֲנָא לָא זָכֵינָא, וּבָעֵינָא מָאן דְּיִשְׁתַּדַּל בְּאוֹרַיְיתָא בְּגִינִי. דְּהָא אִית לִי עוֹתְרָא סַגִּי, דְּקָא שָׁבַק לִי אַבָּא, דְּכַד יָתִיב עַל פְּתוֹרֵיה, הֲוָה מְסַדֵּר עֲלֵיה, תְּלֵיסַר כַּסֵּי מֵאלֵין. וּבָעֵינָא לְמִזְכֵּי בְּאוֹרַיְיתָא, וַאֲנָא יָהִיבְנָא עוֹתְרָא.

284. In the meantime, a man appeared with a vessel made of pure gold, He showed it to everyone, and its sparkle lit up the house. He said: Rabbi, I wish to merit Torah. Because I MYSELF have not merited THE UNDERSTANDING OF THE TORAH, I am searching for someone who can learn Torah for my sake. I inherited great wealth from my father, who used to set upon his table thirteen of these cups MADE OF PURE GOLD. I wish to achieve the merit of studying Torah, and I shall give my wealth to achieve it.

285. אָמַר לוֹ לְהַהוּא רַוָוק, תִּשְׁתַּדַּל בְּאוֹרַיְיתָא, וְדָאִיַהֵיב לָךְ עוֹתְרָא, יְהַב לֵיה הַהוּא כַּסָּא דְּפָז. קָרָא עֲלֵיה ר' אַבָּא, לֹא יַעַרְכֶנָּה זָהָב וּזְכוֹכִית וּתְמוּרָתָהּ כְּלִי פָז. יָתִיב וְלָעָא בְּאוֹרַיְיתָא, וְהַהוּא בַּר נָשׁ הֲוָה יָהִיב לֵיה עוֹתְרָא.

285. He said to the bachelor: Study Torah, and this man shall give you wealth! The man gave him the cup of gold. In relation to him, Rabbi Aba said out loud the verse, "Gold and crystal cannot equal it. And the exchange of it shall not be for vessels of fine gold" (Iyov 28:17). The bachelor then sat down and studied Torah, while the other man gave him wealth.

286. לְיוֹמִין עָאל חֲמִידוּ דְאוֹרַיְיתָא בִּמְעוֹי, יוֹמָא חַד הֲוָה יָתִיב, וַהֲוָה בָּכֵי. אַשְׁכְּחֵיה רַבֵּיה דַּהֲוָה בָּכֵי. אָמַר לוֹ עַל מַה קָא בָּכִית. אָמַר לוֹ, וּמַה מַנַּחְנָא חַיֵּי דְעָלְמָא דְאָתֵי, בְּגִין הַאי, לָא בָּעֵינָא אֶלָּא לְמִזְכֵּי לְגַבָּאי. אָמַר לוֹ הַשְׁתָּא ש״מ דְּהָא לְשֵׁם שָׁמַיִם קָא עָבֵיד.

286. As days passed, the desire for the Torah entered his bowels. One day he sat down and cried. His Rabbi found him weeping and said to him, "Why are you weeping?' And he replied, "What am I leaving behind for this WEALTH? The life in the World to Come! I do not want to learn anymore FOR THE SAKE OF THIS MAN. But rather merit Torah for myself." RABBI ABA said: So now I understand that he is doing it for the sake of heaven.

287. קָרָא לֵיה לְהַהוּא גַבְרָא, אָמַר לוֹ טוֹל עוֹתְרָךְ וְהַב לֵיה לְיַתְמֵי וּלְמִסְכְּנֵי, וַאֲנָא יָהֲבְנָא לָךְ חוּלָק יַתִּיר בְּאוֹרַיְיתָא, בְּכָל מַה דַּאֲנַן לָעָאן. אַהֲדַר לֵיה ר׳ יוֹסֵי הַהוּא כַּסָּא דְפָז, וְעַד יוֹמָא לָא אַעֲדֵי שְׁמֵיה וּמִן בְּנוֹי בֶּן פַּזִי, וְהַיְינוּ ר׳ יוֹסֵי בֶּן פַּזִי, וְזָכָה לְכַמָּה אוֹרַיְיתָא, הוּא וּבְנוֹי. דְּלֵית לָךְ אֲגַר טַב בְּעָלְמָא כְּמַאן דְּלָעֵי בְּאוֹרַיְיתָא.

287. He called for that man and said to him, "Take your wealth back and share it with the poor and the orphans. I shall give you a bigger portion in the Torah, from all that we are learning!" Rabbi Yosi returned the cup of gold to him, and to this very day, the name "the son of gold (Heb. ben pazi)" has not been taken away from him or from his children. He became THE FAMOUS Rabbi, Yosi ben Pazi. And he and his sons merited a lot of Torah, because there is no greater reward in the world than to study Torah. AND A RECOMPENSE FOR IT IS NOT NECESSARY. AS IT IS WRITTEN: "GOLD AND CRYSTAL CANNOT EQUAL IT; AND THE EXCHANGE OF IT SHALL NOT BE FOR VESSELS OF FINE GOLD."

A Synopsis

The fourth concept examined by the Zohar concerns the importance and power of the Zohar's Aramaic language. Aramaic is above any invisible negative influences, and this language provides a direct connection to the Creator. Accordingly, when the Creator reveals important wisdom that requires protection from potentially harmful angelic forces, the wisdom is expressed in Aramaic.

Kabbalistically, the Hebrew and Aramaic languages are not merely communication tools for mankind. This instrument of language has many other higher functions, including the direct expression of metaphysical forces in our material world.

The Relevance of this Passage

We live in a world of concealment, where metaphysical forces and spiritual influences remain obscured from the five senses. Inasmuch as mankind has been conditioned to accept only that which the eyes can see, raising our consciousness becomes a considerable and difficult task. The discussion pertaining to Aramaic reinforces our own conviction and connection to the language, elevating our consciousness so that the energy pouring out from the Aramaic letters fills our soul.

288. אַחַר הַדְּבָרִים הָאֵלֶּה הָיָה דְּבַר ה׳ אֶל אַבְרָם בַּמַּחֲזֶה לֵאמֹר וגו'. בְּכָל אֲתַר דִּכְתִיב בְּאוֹרַיְיתָא בַּמַּחֲזֶה, דָּא שְׁמָא דְּאִתְגְּלֵי לַאֲבָהָן, וּמַאן אִיהוּ. שַׁדַּי, שֶׁנֶּאֱמַר וָאֵרָא אֶל אַבְרָהָם אֶל יִצְחָק וְאֶל יַעֲקֹב בְּאֵל שַׁדָּי. כד״א אֲשֶׁר מַחֲזֵה שַׁדַּי יֶחֱזֶה. וְדָא אִיהוּ חֵיזוּ דְּכָל חֶזְוָון עִלָּאִין אִתְחַזְיָין מִגַּוֵּיה, כְּהַאי מַרְאָה, דְּכָל דִּיוֹקְנִין אִתְחַזְיָין בֵּיהּ, וְכֹלָּא חַד. מַרְאָה מַחֲזֵה חַד הוּא, דָּא תַּרְגּוּם, וְדָא לָשׁוֹן הַקּוֹדֶשׁ.

288. "After these things the word of Hashem came to Abram in a vision, saying, 'Fear not, Abram...'" Wherever the words "in a vision" appear in the Torah, it is the one that appeared to the Patriarchs. And what is it? It is Shadai, as it is written: "And I appeared to Abraham, to Isaac, and to Jacob by the name of El Shadai" (Shmot 6:3), and as you may read, "which saw the vision of Shadai" (Bemidbar 24:4). And this is the vision through which all supernal appearances are seen, just as a mirror OF GLASS in which all images are reflected. And vision (Heb. *mar'eh*) and the appearance (Heb. *machazeh*) are the same – one is in Aramaic and the other is in the holy tongue.

289. אָמַר רְבִּי יוֹסֵי, סַגִּיאִין אִינוּן בְּאוֹרַיְיתָא, וְעַל דָּא הֲוָה לֵיהּ רְשׁוּ לְאוּנְקְלוֹס, לְתַרְגֵּם בְּהַהוּא לִישָׁנָא דְּגָלֵי קֻדְשָׁא בְּרִיךְ הוּא בְּאוֹרַיְיתָא.

וְלִישָׁנָא דָא סָתִים אִיהוּ מִגּוֹ מַלְאֲכֵי עִלָּאָה. בְּמֶחֱזֵה, דַּהֲוָה סָתִים
מִמַּלְאֲכֵי עִלָּאֵי דְּלָא יַדְעֵי בְּדָא, כַּד מְמַלֵּיל בֵּיהּ בְּאַבְרָהָם.

289. Rabbi Yosi said: There are many ARAMAIC WORDS in the Torah. Therefore, Onkelos had permission to translate the Torah to the same language that the Holy One, blessed be He, revealed in the Torah. But this language is not understood by the angels above, and they did not recognize it when THE HOLY ONE, BLESSED BE HE, spoke to Abraham.

290. מ״ט, בְּגִין דְּאַבְרָהָם לָא הֲוָה מָהוּל, וַהֲוָה עָרֵל, סָתִים בְּשָׂרָא.
וּבְגִין כָּךְ הֲוָה סָתִים מִנַּיְיהוּ, בְּלִישׁוֹן תַּרְגּוּם. כְּגַוְונָא דָא בִּלְעָם, דִּכְתִיב
אֲשֶׁר מַחֲזֵה שַׁדַּי יֶחֱזֶה. סָתִים הֲוָה מִלָּה מִגּוֹ מַלְאֲכֵי הַשָּׁרֵת, בְּגִין דְּלָא
יְהֵא לוֹן פִּטְרָא, דְּקֻדְשָׁא בְּרִיךְ הוּא מְמַלֵּל בְּהַהוּא עָרֵל מְסָאֲבָא. דְּהָא
מַלְאֲכֵי קַדִּישֵׁי לָאו נִזְקָקִין בְּלִישׁוֹן תַּרְגּוּם.

290. AND HE ASKS: What is the reason, THAT THE HOLY ONE, BLESSED HE, SPOKE WITH ABRAHAM IN A LANGUAGE THAT WAS NOT RECOGNIZABLE BY THE ANGELS? AND HE REPLIES: Because Abraham was not circumcised; his foreskin still covered his flesh. Therefore THE HOLY ONE, BLESSED BE HE, SPOKE in the language of the translation, which is incomprehensible TO THE ANGELS. The same with Bilaam, as it is written: "who sees (Heb. *yechezeh*) the vision of Shadai." The word 'YECHEZEH' is not comprehensible to the ministering angels. So that they have no excuse to complain that the Holy One, blessed be He, is talking with an uncircumcised and impure man. Because the holy angels have no use for the Aramaic translation, THEY WERE UNAWARE THAT THE HOLY ONE, BLESSED BE HE, WAS SPEAKING WITH BILAAM!"

291. אִי תֵימָא דְּלָא יַדְעֵי, וְהָא גַּבְרִיאֵל אוֹלִיף לְיוֹסֵף ע׳ לָשׁוֹן, וְתַרְגּוּם
חַד מֵע׳ לָשׁוֹן הוּא. אֶלָּא מִנְדַּע יַדְעֵי, אֲבָל לָא נִזְקָקִין תְּנַן, דְּלָא חַיְישֵׁי
וְלָא מַשְׁגִּיחִין עֲלֵיהּ, דְּהָא מָאִיס אִיהוּ קַמַּיְיהוּ, מִכָּל שְׁאָר לָשׁוֹן.

291. AND HE ASKS: You say that THE ANGELS do not understand THE LANGUAGE OF THE TRANSLATION, but Gabriel taught Joseph seventy languages and Aramaic was one of them. AND HE REPLIES: They do know the language, but have no use for it. WHICH MEANS THAT they do not care about it and do not pay attention to it, because they dislike this language more than any other language.

292. וְאִי תֵימָא, הוֹאִיל וּמָאִיס אִיהוּ מִמַּלְאֲכֵי עִלָּאֵי, אַמַּאי תִּרְגּוּם אוּנְקְלוֹס אוֹרַיְיתָא בְּהַאי לָשׁוֹן, וְיוֹנָתָן בֶּן עוּזִיאֵל הַמִּקְרָא. אֶלָּא מָאִיס הוּא קַמַּיְיהוּ, וְהָכֵי אִצְטְרִיךְ דְּלֵית קִנְאָה לְמַלְאֲכֵי עִלָּאֵי בַּהֲדַיְיהוּ דְּיִשְׂרָאֵל יַתִּיר, וְעַל דָּא תַּרְגּוּם תּוֹרָה וּמִקְרָא כָּךְ, וְלָאו מָאִיס אִיהוּ, דְּהָא בְּכַמָּה דוּכְתֵּי כָּתַב קֻדְשָׁא בְּרִיךְ הוּא בְּאוֹרַיְיתָא הָכֵי.

292. You may ask, "If it is despised by the angels above, why did Onkelos translate the Torah to that language, and Yonatan ben Uziel the Scriptures?" AND HE REPLIES: It was repulsive only to the angels. And so it should be, so that the angels of above should not envy Yisrael WHEN THEY SAY THE PRAYERS CALLED KEDUSHA DESIDRA. BUT TO US, IT IS NOT DESPICABLE. And this is why they translated Torah and the Scriptures TO THIS LANGUAGE. And it is not despised, because the Holy One, blessed be He, has written it in many places in the Torah USING THIS LANGUAGE.

293. וּבְגִין כָּךְ סָתִים אִיהוּ מִגּוֹ מַלְאֲכֵי עִלָּאֵי קַדִּישֵׁי. וְעַל דָּא אִתְגְּלֵי בֵּיהּ בְּאַבְרָהָם בְּאוֹרַח סָתִים, דְּלָא יִשְׁגְּחוּן בֵּיהּ מַלְאָכִין קַדִּישִׁין, וְלָא יְהֵא לוֹן פִּטְרָא, דְּקוּדְשָׁא בְּרִיךְ הוּא אִתְגְּלֵי עַל בַּר נָשׁ עָרֵל.

293. Because this language is incomprehensible to the holy angels above, the Holy One, blessed be He, revealed Himself to Abraham in this concealed manner, so that the holy angels would not look upon him and have an excuse to accuse the Holy One, blessed be He, for appearing before an uncircumcised man.

294. אֵימָתַי אִתְגְּלֵי לֵיהּ בְּאִתְגַּלְיָא דְּמַלְאֲכֵי עִלָּאֵי, כַּד יָהִיב לֵיהּ בְּרִית קְיָימָא קַדִּישָׁא, דִּכְתִיב וַיְדַבֵּר אִתּוֹ אֱלֹקִים לֵאמֹר. אֱלֹקִים שְׁמָא דְּקוּדְשָׁא, וְלָא כְתִיב בַּמַּחֲזֶה, שְׁמָא בְּאִתְגַּלְיָיא.

294. HE ASKS: When did He openly reveal Himself to him, in front of the

angels of above? AND HE RESPONDS: At the time when He gave him the sign of the Holy covenant. As it is written: "And Elohim talked with him saying..." (Beresheet 17:3). Elohim is a holy name. It is not written: "in a vision," BUT "ELOHIM," WHICH IS a revealed name.

295. לֵאמֹר. מַאי לֵאמֹר, לֵאמֹר וּלְאַכְרְזָא בְּכָל לָשׁוֹן, דְּלָא תְהֵא בְּאִתְכַּסְיָא, לָאו בְּלִישָׁנָא אָחֲרָא, אֶלָּא בְּלִישָׁנָא דְּכֹלָּא מִשְׁתַּעְיָין בָּה, דְּיָכְלֵי לְמֵימַר דָּא לְדָא, וְלָא יָכְלֵי לְקַטְרְגָא וּלְמֵימַר פִּטְרָא, וְעַל דָּא וַיְדַבֵּר אִתּוֹ אֱלֹקִים לֵאמֹר. אֱלֹקִים, וְלָא מַחֲזֶה. בְּגִין דַּהֲוָה מְעַיֵּיל לֵיהּ בִּבְרִית קְיָימָא קַדִּישָׁא, וְקָרֵיב לֵיהּ לְגַבֵּיהּ.

295. AND HE ASKS: What is 'saying'?" AND HE REPLIES: "saying" MEANS to announce and declare in all languages, WHICH THE HOLY ONE, BLESSED BE HE, SPOKE WITH ABRAHAM, so that he was no longer concealed FROM THE ANGELS. He did not speak in any other language – REFERRING TO ARAMAIC – but in a language that all use, so that they were able to talk to each other, and no one would be able to blame or have any pretext. Therefore, "and Elohim talked with him, saying," 'Elohim' and not 'a vision,' as He has brought him to the holy covenant, close to Him.

296. ר' יְהוּדָה אָמַר, בְּגִין כָּךְ אֶת ה' לָא אִתְיְיהַב לֵיהּ עַד דְּאִתְגְּזַר. מ"ט. דְּאִיהִי מַמָּשׁ בְּרִית אִקְרֵי. וְעַל דָּא כֵּיוָן דְּעָאל בִּבְרִית, כְּדֵין אִתְיְיהִיבַת לֵיהּ אָת ה"א. דִּכְתִיב, אֲנִי הִנֵּה בְרִיתִי אִתָּךְ וְהָיִיתָ לְאַב הֲמוֹן גּוֹיִם וְלֹא יִקָּרֵא עוֹד שִׁמְךָ אַבְרָם וְגוֹ'.

296. Rabbi Yehuda said: According to this, the letter *Hei*, WHICH IS THE SHECHINAH, was not given to him, until he was circumcised! Why? Because She is called the actual covenant. Therefore because he entered the covenant, he was given the letter *Hei* IN HIS NAME. As it is written: "As for Me, behold, My covenant is with you, and you shall be a father of many nations. Neither shall your name any more be called Abram..." (Beresheet 17: 4-5).

28. Rabbi Chiya went to visit Rabbi Elazar

A Synopsis

The Zohar offers a story about the travels of Rabbi Chiya and Rabbi Chagai to visit Rabbi Elazar, the son of Kabbalist Rabbi Shimon bar Yochai, author of the Zohar. Kabbalistically, the concept of *travelling* really concerns a spiritual journey of the mind and soul between two sages. As the two mystics embark on their excursion, their discussion of various spiritual matters is intended to attract particular levels of energy into their lives, and ultimately, to raise them to the very spiritual levels they are discussing.

Rabbi Chiya is concerned that his colleague Rabbi Chagai may not be worthy to enter this higher realm, which is symbolized by the mention of Rabbi Elazar. As they begin to approach Rabbi Elazar, who represents the next dimension, Rabbi Chiya suddenly realizes that Rabbi Chagai is actually more worthy than himself. When the two sages reach Rabbi Elazar's home, he does not immediately let them in. He wants to appraise their level of spiritual consciousness. The sages, therefore, wait and sit in silence. After a while, Rabbi Elazar gets up and enters his room. While in his quarters, he hears a voice telling him that the sages are ready and that he should reveal to them all the mysteries and spiritual Light they seek. A study session ensues, and suddenly a great fire encircles Rabbi Elazar. The sages then leave, realizing they are not yet ready to receive the full revelation of spiritual energy that occupies the next realm.

The Relevance of this Passage

Each of us must prepare our own internal vessel in order to continue our growth and spiritual work. The words of this story assist in expanding our vessel and furthering our preparation.

297. אַחַר הַדְּבָרִים הָאֵלֶּה. רַבִּי חִיָּיא הֲוָה אָזִיל לְמֶחֱמֵי לְרַבִּי אֶלְעָזָר, פָּגַע בֵּיהּ רַבִּי חַגַּאי, אָמַר לוֹ הַאי אָרְחָא דִּמְתַקְנָא קַמֵּיהּ דְּמַר, לְאָן אִיהוּ אָזִיל. אָמַר לוֹ לְמֶחֱמֵי לְרַבִּי אֶלְעָזָר. אָמַר לוֹ וַאֲנָא נָמֵי אֵיזִיל בַּהֲדָךְ. אָמַר לוֹ, אִי תֵיכוֹל לְמִסְבַּר סְבָרָא לְמַאי דְּתִשְׁמַע, זִיל. וְאִי לָאו תּוּב אֲבַתְרָךְ. אָמַר לוֹ, לֹא לֵיחוּשׁ מַר לְהַאי, דְּהָא אֲנָא שְׁמַעְנָא כַּמָּה רָזֵי דְאוֹרַיְיתָא, וְיָכֵילְנָא לְמֵיקַם בְּהוֹ.

297. "After these things...": On his way to visit Rabbi Elazar, Rabbi Chiya met Rabbi Chagai. He said to him: This route, which is set before you, sir, where does it lead to? He answered: IT LEADS to my visiting Rabbi Elazar. He said to him: I shall go along with you. He said: If you will be able to understand the wisdom and the reason behind what you will hear, then come along. But if not, then turn back! He said to him, sir, do not worry about this, because I have heard many secrets of Torah, and I was able to understand them.

298. פְּתַח ר' חַגַּאי וַאֲמַר מַאי דִּכְתִיב אֶת קָרְבָּנִי לַחְמִי לְאִשַּׁי וגו'. אֶת קָרְבָּנִי, דָּא קָרְבָּן בִּשְׂרָא, דְּאִתְקְרַב לְכַפָּרָא, דְּמָא עַל דְּמָא, בִּשְׂרָא עַל בִּשְׂרָא, בְּגִין דְּכָל קָרְבָּנִין לָאו מִתְקָרְבִין אֶלָּא עַל בִּשְׂרָא, לְכַפָּרָא עַל בִּשְׂרָא.

298. Rabbi Chagai opened the discussion, saying: This is the meaning of 'My offering, the provision of my sacrifices made by fire...'" (Bemidbar 28:2). "My offering" refers to an offeringof flesh, which is given for atonement; blood OF THE SACRIFICE for the blood OF MAN; flesh OF THE SACRIFICE for the flesh OF MAN. All sacrifices are offered only for the flesh, THAT IS, to atone for the flesh.

299. וְהָכֵי שְׁמַעְנָא, אִי בַּר נָשׁ חָטָא, בְּהֵמָה מַה חָטָאת, דְּקֻדְשָׁא בְּרִיךְ הוּא אָמַר אָדָם כִּי יַקְרִיב מִכֶּם קָרְבָּן וגו'. אַמַּאי. אֶלָּא קֻדְשָׁא בְּרִיךְ הוּא עֲבֵיד רוּחַ בְּנֵי נָשָׁא, וְרוּחַ הַבְּהֵמָה, וְאַפְרֵישׁ דָּא מִן דָּא. וּבְגִין כָּךְ רוּחַ בְּנֵי הָאָדָם הָעוֹלָה הִיא לְמַעְלָה וְרוּחַ הַבְּהֵמָה וגו'. וַדַּאי מִתְפְּרַשׁ דָּא מִן דָּא.

299. And I heard thus: if a man sinned, what is the sin of the animal, that the Holy One, blessed be He, said: "If any man of you bring an offering to Hashem, of the cattle..." (Vayikra 1:2)? AND HE REPLIES: The Holy One, blessed be He, formed the spirit of men and the spirit of animals, and then separated them from each other. Therefore, "the spirit of man goes upwards, and the spirit of the beast goes downwards," (Kohelet 3:21) so they are definitely separated from each other!

300. עַד לָא חָטָא אָדָם, מַה כְּתִיב, וַיֹּאמֶר אֱלֹקִים הִנֵּה נָתַתִּי לָכֶם אֶת כָּל עֵשֶׂב זוֹרֵעַ זֶרַע וגו', וּכְתִיב לָכֶם יִהְיֶה לְאָכְלָה, וְלָא יַתִּיר. כֵּיוָן דְּחָטָא, וְיֵצֶר הָרָע אִשְׁתָּאִיב בְּגוּפָא דִילֵיהּ, וּבְכָל אִינוּן תּוֹלָדִין, עֲבַד בְּהוֹ דִּינָא.

300. Before Adam sinned, it is written: "And Elohim said: Behold, I have given you every herb bearing seed..." (Beresheet 1:29) and "to you it shall be for food" and no more THAN THIS. SO HE WAS NOT PERMITTED TO EAT ANIMALS. But since he had sinned and the Evil Inclination was absorbed to his body and to all of his offspring, He passed His judgment over them; IN OTHER WORDS, HE BROUGHT THE GREAT FLOOD UPON THEM.

301. וּלְבָתַר אָתָא נֹחַ, וְחָמָא דְּהָא גוּפָא אִתְבְּנֵי מֵאַתְרָא דְיֵצֶה"ר אַקְרִיב קָרְבָּן, כְּמָה דְּאַקְרִיב אָדָם, מַה כְּתִיב וַיָּרַח ה' אֶת רֵיחַ הַנִּיחֹחַ וגו'. כִּי יֵצֶר לֵב הָאָדָם רַע מִנְּעוּרָיו. אָמַר קֻדְשָׁא בְּרִיךְ הוּא, מִכָּאן וּלְהָלְאָה, הוֹאִיל וְגוּפָא אִשְׁתָּאִיב מֵהַהוּא יֵצֵה"ר יִתְעַנַּג גוּפָא כְּמָה דְאִתְחֲזֵי לֵיהּ, יֵיכוֹל בִּשְׂרָא. כְּיֶרֶק עֵשֶׂב נָתַתִּי לָכֶם אֶת כֹּל.

301. Later, Noah came and saw that the body is built by the Evil Inclination, so he offered a sacrifice as Adam did. And it is written: "And Hashem smelled a sweet savor...for the impulse of man's heart is evil from his youth." (Beresheet 8:21). The Holy One, blessed be He, said: 'From here onward, because the body is already absorbed by that Evil Inclination, let the body enjoy itself as much as it wants and eat meat.' HE SAID: "even as the green herb have I given you all" (Beresheet 9:3).

302. כַּד אָכִיל בִּשְׂרָא, מֵהַהוּא בִּשְׂרָא אִתְעַנַּג בִּשְׂרָא דִילֵיהּ, וְאִתְעָרַב דָּא בְּדָא, וְאִתְרַבֵּי גוּפָא מִנֵּיהּ, וּמֵהַהוּא עֹנֶג, גוּפָא חָטָא בְּכַמָּה חֲטָאִין. אָמַר קֻדְשָׁא בְּרִיךְ הוּא כַּפָּרָה הוּא עַל גוּפָא בִּשְׂרָא. בִּשְׂרָא אָכִיל, וּבִשְׂרָא אִתְרַבֵּי מִינֵּיהּ, וּבֵיהּ חָטָא, בְּגִין כָּךְ לְכַפָּרָה עַל גוּפֵיהּ בִּשְׂרָא. וּבִשְׂרָא דְּאָכִיל בִּשְׂרָא, עֲבֵיד דְּמָא לְגוּפָא, בְּגִין כָּךְ דָּמָא דְּאִשְׁתְּאַר מֵהַהוּא בִּשְׂרָא לְבַר, אִתְעַתַּד לְכַפָּרָה עַל דְּמָא, דְּאִתְעֲבֵיד מֵהַהוּא בִּשְׂרָא דִילֵיהּ, דִּכְתִיב כִּי הַדָּם הוּא בַּנֶּפֶשׁ יְכַפֵּר.

302. When man eats meat, the flesh of man receives pleasure from that flesh, and they mix together – THE FLESH OF MAN COMBINES WITH THE FLESH OF THE ANIMAL. And the body grows and is built by it. But as a result of the pleasure, WHICH MAN RECEIVED FROM EATING MEAT, his body commits many sins. The Holy One, blessed be He, said: "The meat," REFERRING TO THE MEAT OF THE OFFERING, "shall be atonement for the body." Because one had eaten flesh, and had grown flesh through it IN THE BODY, and by it one had sinned, therefore the meat OF THE OFFERING shall be atonement for the body. So the meat – NAMELY THE FLESH OF THE BODY – that eats meat forms the blood in the body. And because of this, the purpose of the blood that remains outside of the meat OF THE OFFERING is to atone for the blood OF MAN, which was formed by that same meat OF THE ANIMAL. As it is written: "for it is the blood that makes an atonement for the soul" (Vayikra 17:11).

303. כְּתִיב קָרְבָּנִי, וּכְתִיב קָרְבַּנְכֶם, דִּכְתִיב תַּקְרִיבוּ אֶת קָרְבַּנְכֶם, מַה בֵּין הַאי לְהַאי. אֶלָּא קָרְבָּנִי, כְּגוֹן שְׁלָמִים דְּאַתְיָין עַל שָׁלוֹם. קָרְבַּנְכֶם: כְּגוֹן חַטָּאוֹת וַאֲשָׁמוֹת דְּאַתְיָין עַל חֵטְא וְאָשָׁם, בְּגִין כָּךְ אֶת קָרְבָּנִי: בִּשְׂרָא. לַחְמִי: נַהֲמָא וְחַמְרָא. רֵיחַ: דָּא קְטוֹרֶת. נִיחֹחִי: דָּא נַחַת רוּחַ, דְּעָבֵיד כַּהֲנָא בִּרְעוּתָא דִּשְׁמָא קַדִּישָׁא, וְלֵיוָאֵי, בִּרְעוּתָא דְּשִׁיר וְשִׁבְחָה.

303. It is written: "My offering" and "your offering," as it is written: "shall you bring your offering" (Vayikra 1:2). What is the difference between these two phrases? AND HE REPLIES: "My offering" is like peace-offerings that are brought for peace. "Your offering" is like sin or guilt offerings brought to ATONE for sin or guilt. Therefore, "My offering" is meat, "the provision" is bread and wine, "savor" is incense. "Sweet" (Heb. *nichoach*) is satisfaction (Heb. *nachat*) that the priest experiences when meditating on the Holy Name, WHICH HE UTTERS OUT LOUD DURING THE RITUAL OF THE SACRIFICE. And the Levites HAVE THE SAME EXPERIENCE when meditating during the songs and praises, WHICH THEY RECITE DURING THE SACRIFICE.

304. תִּשְׁמְרוּ לְהַקְרִיב לִי בְּמוֹעֲדוֹ. בְּמוֹעֲדוֹ מַאי הֲוֵי, אִי תֵּימָא בְּכָל יוֹמָא בַּבֹּקֶר וּבָעֶרֶב, מַאי אִיהוּ בְּמוֹעֲדוֹ. אֶלָּא מוֹעֲדוֹ, דְּשָׁלְטָא בְּהַהוּא

זִמְנָא רַעֲוָא. רְעוּ דְּאִשְׁתְּכַח לְעֵילָא בְּדַרְגָּא יְדִיעָא. וְעַל דָּא כְּתִיב בְּמוֹעֲדוֹ.

304. Of the verse, "shall you observe to offer to me in their (lit. 'its') due season," HE ASKS: What is meant by "due season?" If you say THAT THE MEANING IS TO OFFER A SACRIFICE every day – morning and evening – why then is it called "its due season?" AND HE REPLIES: "its due season" APPLIES to the desire that rules at that certain moment – NAMELY, THE MOMENT OF THE SACRIFICE. This is the desire that prevails above in that certain grade, WHICH IS THE NUKVA. And for this reason, it is written: 'its due season.'

305. כַּד קָרְבָּן אִתְקְרֵיב, כֻּלָּא נָטְלִין חוּלָקָא, וְאִתְבַּדְּרָן קְלִיפִין לְכָל סִטְרָא, וְיִיחוּדָא אִתְקְרֵיב וְאִתְיַיחַד, וּבוֹצִינִין אִתְנַהֲרִין, וְאִשְׁתְּכַח רַעֲוָא וּרְעוּ בְּכָל עָלְמִין, וְקֻדְשָׁא בְּרִיךְ הוּא אִשְׁתְּכַח בְּרָזָא דְיִחוּדָא חֲדָא כִּדְקָא חֲזֵי. אָתָא ר' חִיָּיא וּנְשָׁקֵיה, אָמַר לֵיה, יָאוֹת אַנְתְּ בְּרִי מִנִּי, לְמֵיהַךְ לְמֶחֱמֵי לֵיה.

305. When an offering is sacrificed, all the worlds receive a part of it, and the Klipot are scattered in all directions. The unison OF THE MALE AND FEMALE grows closer and is completed, and the candles, WHICH ARE THE SECRET OF THE UPPER GRADES, shine. And there is one desire and full companionship in all the worlds. And the Holy One, blessed be He, is in a state of the secret of unity as should properly be. Rabbi Chiya came forward, kissed him, and said: You are more worthy than I to go and see him, REFERRING TO RABBI ELAZAR.

306. אֲזָלוּ, כַּד מָטוֹן לְגַבֵּיה, חָמָא לוֹן יַתְבֵי עַל תַּרְעָא, אָמַר לוֹ לְשַׁמָּשָׁא, זִיל וְאֵימָא לוֹן, הַאי פָּרְסָיָיא דִּתְלַת קַיְימִין, מַהוּ כָּל אֶחָד. אֲמָרוּ לֵיה, זִיל וְאֵימָא לֵיה לְמַר, דְּלָאו לְמַגְּנָא אָמַר דָּוִד מַלְכָּא דְּאִיהוּ רְבִיעָאָה, אֶבֶן מָאֲסוּ הַבּוֹנִים. אָמַר לוֹ זִיל וְאֵימָא לוֹן דְּאָן דְּאָן גָּעֲלוּ בֵּיה בְּדָוִד, דְּאִיהוּ אָמַר אֶבֶן מָאֲסוּ הַבּוֹנִים.

306. They went along. When they reached RABBI ELAZAR, he saw them sitting beside the gate. He said to his attendant, Go and ask them what is the significance OF EACH of the three legs of this throne? They told him: Go and tell our master that it is not in vain that King David, who is the fourth LEG OF THE THRONE, said, "The stone which the builders rejected" (Tehilim 118:22). AND WITH THIS VERSE, THEY GAVE HIM A HINT ABOUT THE THREE COLUMNS THAT PRECEDE DAVID, WHICH ARE CHESED, GVURAH AND TIFERET. He said to him, TO HIS ATTENDANT: Go and tell them, where David was 'rejected' BY THE BUILDERS, that he said, "The stone which the builders rejected?"

307. אַהֲדַר רַבִּי חִיָּיא רֵישֵׁיהּ לְגַבֵּי ר' חַגַּאי, וַאֲמַר לֵיהּ שַׁמְעַת בְּהַאי מִדֵּי. אֲמַר שְׁמַעְנָא, בְּהַאי קְרָא דִּכְתִיב בְּנֵי אִמִּי נִחֲרוּ בִי שָׂמֻנִי וְגוֹ'. דְּהַאי קְרָא שְׁלֹמֹה מַלְכָּא אֲמָרוֹ, וְעַל דָּוִד מַלְכָּא אִתְּמַר, כַּד דָּחוּ לֵיהּ אֲחוֹהִי מִנַּיְיהוּ.

307. Rabbi Chiya turned to Rabbi Chagai and said: Have you heard anything about this? He said: I have heard about the verse that reads "my mother's children were angry with me; they made me the keeper of the vineyards..." (Shir Hashirim 1:6), which King Solomon used to say. It speaks of King David when he was rejected by his brothers.

308. וְתוּ שְׁמַעְנָא, מַאי חָמָא קֻדְשָׁא בְּרִיךְ הוּא לְמֵיהַב מַלְכוּתָא לִיהוּדָה מִכָּל אֲחוֹהִי, אֶלָּא אַתְוָון דִּשְׁמֵיהּ חֲקִיקָן בֵּיהּ, וְקֻדְשָׁא בְּרִיךְ הוּא יְהַב יְקָרָא לִשְׁמֵיהּ, וּבְגִין כָּךְ אַחְסִין מַלְכוּתָא. וְתוּ שְׁמַעְנָא, יְהוּדָה הָא אַתְוָון דִּשְׁמֵיהּ וַדַּאי, ד' לֵיתֵיהּ אֲמַאי. אֶלָּא הָא דָוִד מַלְכָּא, דְּאִתְקַשַּׁר בִּשְׁמֵיהּ מִכָּל בְּנֵי עָלְמָא, דִּכְתִיב, וּבִקְשׁוּ אֶת ה' אֱלֹקֵיהֶם וְאֵת דָּוִד מַלְכָּם וְגוֹ', הָא דָוִד קָשִׁיר בִּשְׁמֵיהּ, תּוּ, דְּאִיהוּ קֶשֶׁר שֶׁל תְּפִלִּין, וַדַּאי ד' דָּוִד מַלְכָּא, וּבְגִין כָּךְ דָּוִד אִתְקַשַּׁר בִּשְׁמֵיהּ.

308. And furthermore, we have heard: What was the reason that the Holy One, blessed be He, gave the kingdom to Judah and not to any of the other brothers? AND HE REPLIES: Because the letters of His Holy name are engraved in him. BECAUSE YUD HEI VAV HEI APPEAR IN THE NAME OF JUDAH (YUD-HEI-VAV-DALET-HEI). So the Holy One, blessed be He,

glorified his name. And this is why he inherited the kingdom. And I have also heard that the name Judah definitely contains the letters of His HOLY Name, but there is no letter *Dalet* IN YUD HEI VAV HEI. AND HE ASKS: Why? AND HE REPLIES: This LETTER *DALET* OF JUDAH represents King David, who is attached to His Name more than all other people of the world. As it is written: "and seek Hashem their Elohim, and David their king" (Hoshea 3:5). So King David is actually attached to His HOLY Name. Furthermore, he is the knot of the Tfilin, AS KING DAVID IS THE SECRET OF THE KNOT OF THE TFILIN OF THE HOLY ONE, BLESSED BE HE. AND THIS IS THE SECRET OF THE NUKVA OF ZEIR ANPIN. So certainly the letter *Dalet* IN JUDAH is King David. And because of this David is attached to His HOLY Name. BECAUSE THE NAME JUDAH INCLUDES YUD HEI VAV HEI, WHICH ALLUDE TO ZEIR ANPIN, AND THE LETTER *DALET*, WHICH ALLUDES TO KING DAVID, WHO IS THE SECRET OF NUKVA OF ZEIR ANPIN.

309. עָאלוּ, כֵּיוָן דְּעָאלוּ יְתִיבוּ קַמֵּיהּ, אִשְׁתִּיק רַבִּי אֶלְעָזָר, וְאִינוּן אִשְׁתִּיקוּ. עָאל ר' אֶלְעָזָר לְאַדְרֵיהּ, שְׁמַע חַד קָלָא דַּהֲוָה אָמַר, זִיל וְאֵימָא לוֹן מַה דְּאִינוּן בָּעְיָין דִּכְשֵׁרִין אִינוּן. אַהֲדַר לְגַבַּיְיהוּ. אָמַר לוֹן, אִית מַאן דְּשָׁמַע מִלָּה לֵימָא לִי. אָמְרוּ לֵיהּ אֲנַן מְחַכָּאן לְאַנְהָרָא מִגּוֹ צַחוּתָא דְּבוֹצִינָא עִלָּאָה וּסְבָרָא נִסְבַּר.

309. They entered. Once they were inside, they sat in front of him. Rabbi Elazar was silent, so they remained silent as well. Rabbi Elazar entered his room, he heard a certain voice there that said: 'Go and tell them what they want, because they are righteous men!' He then returned to them and said: If one of you has heard something, let him say it to me! They responded: We are waiting to shine by the purity of the upper candle, and let us grasp knowledge.

310. פָּתַח וְאָמַר וַה' בְּהֵיכַל קָדְשׁוֹ הַס מִפָּנָיו כָּל הָאָרֶץ. כַּד בָּעֵי קֻדְשָׁא בְּרִיךְ הוּא לְמִבְרֵי עָלְמָא, אִסְתַּכַּל גּוֹ מַחֲשָׁבָה, רָזָא דְּאוֹרַיְיתָא, וְרָשִׁים רְשׁוּמִין, וְלָא הֲוָה יָכִיל לְמֵיקַם עַד דְּבָרָא תְּשׁוּבָה, דְּאִיהִי הֵיכְלָא פְּנִימָאָה עִלָּאָה, וְרָזָא סְתִימָא, וְתַמָּן אִתְרְשִׁימוּ וְאִתְצַיְּירוּ אַתְווָן בְּגָלוּפַיְיהוּ.

310. He opened the discussion with the verse: "But Hashem is in His holy chamber, let all the earth keep silence before Him" (Chavakuk 2:20). When the Holy One, blessed be He, WHO IS THE SECRET OF BINAH, desired to create the world, WHICH IS THE SECRET OF ZEIR ANPIN AND HIS NUKVA, THAT ARE CALLED THE HEAVENS AND THE EARTH, He looked to the thought, WHICH IS THE SECRET OF CHOCHMAH, the secret of the Torah, and took down records. THIS MEANS THAT HE RECORDED, AND DREW THE LIGHT OF CHOCHMAH TO MALE AND FEMALE, but the world was not able to exist. Then He created repentance, which is the sublime and inner chamber, and a guarded secret. And there, IN THE AFOREMENTIONED CHAMBER, the letters, WHICH ARE MALE AND FEMALE, are engraved, WHICH MEANS THAT THEY WERE PREPARED AND MADE WORTHY OF RECEIVING MOCHIN FROM THERE.

311. כֵּיוָן דְּאִתְבְּרֵי דָא, הֲוָה מִסְתַּכַּל בְּהַאי הֵיכָלָא, וְרָשִׁים קַמֵּיהּ צִיּוּרִין דְּכָל עָלְמָא, דִּכְתִיב הַס מִפָּנָיו כָּל הָאָרֶץ. רְשִׁים קַמֵּיהּ רְשׁוּמִין וְצִיּוּרִין דְּכָל עָלְמָא. בָּעֵי לְמִבְרֵי שָׁמַיִם, מָה עֲבַד, אִסְתַּכַּל בְּאוֹר קַדְמָאָה וְאִתְעַטַּף בֵּיהּ, וּבְרָא שָׁמַיִם. דִּכְתִיב עוֹטֶה אוֹר כַּשַּׂלְמָה, וְאַחַר כָּךְ נוֹטֶה שָׁמַיִם כַּיְרִיעָה.

311. As THE CHAMBER was created, He looked to this chamber and drew figures, NAMELY THE MOCHIN that exists in the entire world. This is why it is written: "let all the earth keep silence before Him." He desired to create the heavens, WHICH ARE ZEIR ANPIN. What did He do? He looked upon the First Light, THE FIRST CHAMBER, WHICH IS THE SECRET OF ABA AND IMA, covered Himself with it, and created the heavens. As it is written: "Who covers himself with light as with a garment," and then, "Who stretches out the heavens like a curtain" (Tehilim 104:2).

312. אִסְתַּכַּל לְמֶעְבַּד עָלְמָא תַּתָּאָה, עֲבַד הֵיכָלָא אוֹחֲרָא, וְעָאל בֵּיהּ, וּמִנֵּיהּ אִסְתַּכַּל וְרָשִׁים קַמֵּיהּ כָּל עָלְמִין לְתַתָּא, וּבְרָא לוֹן. הה"ד וַה' בְּהֵיכַל קָדְשׁוֹ הַס מִפָּנָיו כָּל הָאָרֶץ. הַס מִפָּנָיו: ה"ס רְשִׁים קַמֵּיהּ, כָּל נְקוּדִין דְּכָל עָלְמָא, דְּאִינּוּן שִׁתִּין וְחָמֵשׁ, כְּחוּשְׁבַּן ה"ס, שִׁתִּין אִינּוּן, וְחָמֵשׁ אִינּוּן, וְכֻלְּהוּ רְשִׁים קַמֵּיהּ, כַּד בְּרָא עָלְמָא. בְּגִין כָּךְ יְקָרָא

דְּקֻדְשָׁא בְּרִיךְ הוּא לָאו אִיהוּ, אֶלָּא לְאִינּוּן דְּיָדְעִין אָרְחוֹי, וּמְהַכִּין בֵּהּ בְּאוֹרַח קְשׁוֹט, כִּדְקָא יָאוֹת.

312. He studied how to create the lower world, WHICH IS THE NUKVA OF ZEIR ANPIN THAT NEEDS THE LIGHT OF CHOCHMAH, WHICH IS NOT RECEIVED FROM THE FIRST CHAMBER. So He created another chamber and entered to it. And from inside He looked out and drew in front of Himself all the worlds that are below; NAMELY ALL THE QUANTITY OF MOCHIN THAT THEY REQUIRE and created them. Therefore it is written: "But Hashem is in His holy chamber, let all the earth keep silence (Heb. *has*) before Him." *Has* (*Hei-Samech*) is recorded "before him," WHICH MEANS THAT THE NUMERICAL VALUE OF *HEI-SAMECH* IS DRAWN BEFORE HIM, WHICH IS THE NUMBER OF all the "points," WHICH ARE THE SFIROT that exist in every world, WHICH IS THE NUKVA. And they are sixty-five points, a number equivalent to the numerical value of *Hei-Samech*.
Sixty are THE SIX SFIROT – CHESED, GVURAH, TIFERET, NETZACH, HOD AND YESOD, EACH OF WHICH INCLUDES TEN, and five are HALF OF MALCHUT; SHE LACKS THE LAST FIVE – THOSE FROM THE CHEST DOWNWARD. He recorded before Him these sixty-five "POINTS" OF THE NUKVA IN ORDER TO BESTOW ON HER HIS ABUNDANCE when He created the world, WHICH IS THE NUKVA. For this reason, the glory of the Holy One, blessed be He, NAMELY THE SHECHINAH, is destined only to those who know His ways and go along them – in a true manner, as is proper!

313. אַדְהָכֵי דַּהֲוָה מִשְׁתָּעֵי בַּהֲדַיְיהוּ, אָתָא נוּרָא וְאַסְחַר לֵיהּ, וְאִינּוּן יָתְבוּ לְבַר. שָׁמְעוּ חַד קָלָא דַּהֲוָה אָמַר, אִי קַדִּישָׁא, הֱבִיאַנִי הַמֶּלֶךְ חֲדָרָיו, בְּכָל אִינּוּן אִידְרִין, דְּסָבַר דְּאַנְפִּין עוּלֵּימָא קַדִּישָׁא אִתְמְסָרוּ מַפְתְּחָן דִּלְהוֹן בִּידֵיהּ, וְכֻלְּהוּ מְתַקְּנָן לָךְ, וּלְאִינּוּן דִּבְגִינָךְ. וּבְחַיָּיךְ קַדִּישָׁא כָּל חֵילָא דִּשְׁמַיָּא, נָגִילָה וְנִשְׂמְחָה בָּךְ.

313. While he was talking with them, a fire encircled him, and they remained sitting outside. They heard a voice call out, 'O you holy man, "The king has brought me to his chambers"' (Shir Hashirim 1:4) – to all those chambers whose keys have been given to the favored and holy lad, NAMELY MATATRON, WHO IS CALLED "LAD." And all are ready for you and for those who achieve merit through you. And in your life, holy man, all the hosts of the heavens, "we will be glad and rejoice in you!" (Ibid). THIS WAS THE VOICE OF THE SHECHINAH.

314. כַּד חָמוּ אִלֵּין הָכֵי, אִזְדַּעְזְעוּ, וּדְחִילוּ סַגֵּי נָפַל עֲלָיְיהוּ, אָמְרֵי לֵית אֲנַן חַזְיָין לְהַאי, נִפּוֹק מִכָּאן, וְנֶהַךְ לְאוֹרְחִין, יַתְבוּ תַּמָּן כָּל הַהוּא יוֹמָא, וְלָא יָכִילוּ לְמֶחֱמֵי לֵיה, וַאֲמָרוּ לֵית רְעוּתָא דְקֻדְשָׁא בְּרִיךְ הוּא, דְּנֵיתִיב הָכָא, נָפָקוּ מִתַּמָּן וְאַזְלֵי.

314. When these two saw this, they trembled and were overtaken by a great fear. They said: We are not worthy of this. Let us get out of here and go on our way! They sat there that entire day but were unable to see him. Then they said: The Holy One, blessed be He, does not wish us to stay here. They left that place and went away.

29. "Bless Hashem, you angels of His"

A Synopsis
After the awesome experience with Rabbi Elazar, Rabbi Chiya speaks about the giving of the Torah, and how, after the moment of revelation, power over the physical world was placed in the hands of mankind. Prior to the Revelation, the vast network of angels was in control of our physical realm.

The Relevance of this Passage
Our individual deeds and behavior have an accumulated effect on the world as well as on our personal life. The universal responsibility for our actions is stirred within us by this portion.

315. עַד דַּהֲווֹ אָזְלֵי, פְּתַח רַבִּי חִיָּיא וְאָמַר בָּרְכוּ ה' מַלְאָכָיו גִּבּוֹרֵי כֹחַ עוֹשֵׂי דְבָרוֹ וְגוֹ'. זַכָּאִין אִינּוּן יִשְׂרָאֵל מִכָּל שְׁאַר עַמִּין דְּעָלְמָא, דְּקָדְשָׁא בְּרִיךְ הוּא אִתְרְעֵי בְּהוּ מִכָּל שְׁאַר עַמִּין, וַעֲבַד לוֹן חוּלָקֵיהּ וְאַחֲסַנְתֵּיהּ, וְעַל דָּא יָהִיב לוֹן אוֹרַיְיתָא קַדִּישָׁא, בְּגִין דְּכֻלְּהוּ הֲווֹ בִּרְעוּתָא חֲדָא עַל טוּרָא דְּסִינַי וְאַקְדִּימוּ עֲשִׂיָּה לִשְׁמִיעָה.

315. As they were walking along, Rabbi Chiya opened the discussion, saying, "'Bless Hashem, you angels of His, you mighty ones who perform His bidding...'" (Tehilim 103:20). Happy are Yisrael of all the peoples of the world, because the Holy One, blessed be He, chose them from among all the other nations, and He made them His part and portion. This is why He gave them the Holy Torah, since they shared one desire on Mount Sinai. And their "doing" preceded their "hearing," AS THEY SAID, "WILL WE DO" AND THEN THEY SAID, "AND OBEY (LIT. 'HEAR')" (SHEMOT 24:7).

316. כֵּיוָן דְּאַקְדִּימוּ עֲשִׂיָּיה לִשְׁמִיעָה, קְרָא קָדְשָׁא בְּרִיךְ הוּא לְפָמַלְיָא דִילֵיהּ, אָמַר לוֹן, עַד הָכָא הֲוֵיתוּן יְחִידָאִין קַמָּאי בְּעָלְמָא, מִכָּאן וּלְהָלְאָה הָא בְּנֵי בְּאַרְעָא חַבְרִים בַּהֲדַיְיכוּ בְּכֹלָּא. לֵית לְכוּ רְשׁוּ לְקַדְּשָׁא שְׁמִי, עַד דְּיִשְׂרָאֵל יִתְחַבְּרוּן בַּהֲדַיְיכוּ בְּאַרְעָא, וְכֻלְּהוּ תֶּהֱווֹן כַּחֲדָא חַבְרִים לְקַדְּשָׁא שְׁמִי, בְּגִין דְּאַקְדִּימוּ עֲשִׂיָּה לִשְׁמִיעָה, כְּגַוְונָא דְּמַלְאֲכֵי עִלָּאֵי עָבְדֵי בִּרְקִיעָא, דִּכְתִיב בָּרְכוּ ה' מַלְאָכָיו גִּבּוֹרֵי כֹחַ עוֹשֵׂי דְבָרוֹ לִשְׁמֹעַ בְּקוֹל דְּבָרוֹ. עוֹשֵׂי דְבָרוֹ בְּקַדְמֵיתָא, וּלְבָתַר לִשְׁמֹעַ.

316. Because their "doing" preceded their "hearing," the Holy One, blessed be He, called upon His retinue, THE ANGELS; and said to them: 'Until now, you alone have stood before Me. But from now on, My children on earth are your companions in everything. You have no permission to sanctify My Name until Yisrael on earth joins you. And all of you together shall become friends to sanctify My Name.' Because they put "doing" before "hearing," just as the angels do in the heavens above, as it is written: "Bless Hashem, you angels of His, you mighty ones who perform His bidding, hearkening to the voice of His word." "Who perform his bidding" is first; only then is, "hearkening."

317. דָּבָר אַחֵר, בָּרְכוּ ה׳ מַלְאָכָיו. אִלֵּין אִינּוּן צַדִּיקַיָּא בְּאַרְעָא, דְּאִינּוּן חֲשׁוּבִין קַמֵּי קֻדְשָׁא בְּרִיךְ הוּא, כְּמַלְאֲכֵי עִלָּאֵי בִּרְקִיעָא, בְּגִין, דְּאִינּוּן גִּבּוֹרֵי כֹחַ, דְּמִתְגַּבְּרֵי עַל יִצְרֵיהוֹן כִּגְבַר טַב דְּמִתְגַּבֵּר עַל שַׂנְאֵיה. לִשְׁמוֹעַ בְּקוֹל דְּבָרוֹ. דְּזַכָּאן בְּכָל יוֹמָא לְמִשְׁמַע קָלָא מִלְּעֵילָא, בְּשַׁעֲתָא דְּאִצְטְרִיכוּ.

317. Another explanation of the verse "Bless Hashem, you angels of His" is that these are the righteous people on earth, who are important to the Holy One, blessed be He, as the supernal angels in heaven. They are "mighty ones," as they overcome their inclination like a mighty man who overcomes all his enemies, "hearkening to the voice of His word." This means that they have the merit of hearing a voice from heaven every day and every time they need to!

318. הַשְׁתָּא מַאן יָכִיל לְמֵיקַם בַּהֲדַיְיהוּ, דְּאִינּוּן קַדִּישִׁין עֶלְיוֹנִין, זַכָּאִין אִינּוּן דִּיָכְלֵי לְמֵיקַם קַמַּיְיהוּ, זַכָּאִין אִינּוּן דִּיָכְלֵי לְאִשְׁתְּזָבָא מִקַּמַּיְיהוּ, אַשְׁגָּחוּתָא דְּקֻדְשָׁא בְּרִיךְ הוּא עֲלַיְיהוּ בְּכָל יוֹמָא, הֵיךְ אֲנַן יְכִילָן לְמֵיעַל קַמַּיְיהוּ. וְעַל דָּא כְּתִיב אַשְׁרֵי תִּבְחַר וּתְקָרֵב, וּכְתִיב אַשְׁרֵי אָדָם עוֹז לוֹ בָךְ וְגו׳.

(עַד כָּאן סִתְרֵי תוֹרָה)

318. "Now, who is able to be among them – among all those holy and sublime beings? Happy are those who are able to stand before them; Happy

-169-

are those who are able to save themselves from them. The Holy One, blessed be He, supervises them every day; how can we stand before them?" ALL THIS WAS SAID BY RABBI CHIYA IN PRAISE OF RABBI ELAZAR, WITH WHOM THEY COULD NOT STAY. Therefore it is written: "Blessed is the man whom You choose, and cause to approach to You, that he may dwell in your courts" (Tehilim 65:5), and also: "Blessed is the man whose strength is in you" (Tehilim. 84:6).

End of Sitrei Torah

30. "And Abram said, Adonai Hashem Elohim, what will You give me?"

A Synopsis

Abraham cries out to God, lamenting his inability to have children. The Creator explains that all people have certain judgments and decrees hanging over them. These decrees and judgments fall under the influence of the stars and planets. However, God tells Abraham that it is up to him to rise above planetary influences by transforming his very nature. When man changes his internal nature, nature mirrors that action and judgments can be removed. Herein lies the secret behind the name change of Abraham. While he is under the influence of the stars, he is called, Abram אברם. When he undergoes spiritual transformation, the Hebrew letter *Hei* ה is added to his name changing it from Abram to Abraham אברהם.

The Relevance of this Passage

The profound Kabbalistic concept of altering a person's name alphabetically, can be compared to the science of genetic engineering, in which the genetic code of a person is altered in order to reduce predisposition to various diseases and ailments. Interestingly, all DNA is structured and consequently, classified alphabetically. The mysteries contained within this passage give us the power to alter our own spiritual DNA, thereby changing our destiny. By transforming the negative aspects of our nature, we rise above cosmic influences and remove judgments that may be hanging over us.

319. תָּא חֲזֵי, אָנֹכִי מָגֵן לָךְ, דָּא הוּא דַּרְגָּא קַדְמָאָה, דְּאִתְאֲחֵיד בֵּיהּ בְּקַדְמֵיתָא. וַיֹּאמֶר אַבְרָם, אֲדֹנָי ה' מַה תִּתֶּן לִי. אֲדֹנָי: אָלֶף דָּלֶת נוּן יוֹד. אֱלֹקִים יוֹד הֵא וָיו הֵא. אֶלָּא רָזָא דְמִלָּה, חִבּוּרָא דִּתְרֵין עָלְמִין כַּחֲדָא, עַלְמָא תַּתָּאָה, וְעַלְמָא עִלָּאָה.

319. Come and behold: "I am your shield." "I" is the first grade, to which he cleaved at the beginning." "And Abram said, *Adonai Elohim, what will You give me?*" (Beresheet 16:2). YUD HEI VAV HEI IS SPELLED WITH THE VOWELS OF ELOHIM. *Adonai* is spelled *Aleph-Dalet-Nun-Yud,* FULLY SPELLED AS *Aleph-Lamed-final Pe, Dalet-Lamed-Tav, Nun-Vav-Nun, Yud-Vav-Dalet,* WHICH IS THE SECRET OF THE NUKVA; AND YUD HEI VAV

HEI IS WRITTEN WITH THE SAME VOWELS AS Elohim, FULLY SPELLED
Yud-Vav-Dalet, Hei-Yud, Vav-Aleph-Vav, Hei-Yud, WHICH IS THE SECRET
OF BINAH. SO HE FOUND IT DIFFICULT TO UNDERSTAND WHY BOTH
THESE NAMES ARE MENTIONED IN THE SAME VERSE. AND IN
REFERENCE TO THIS HE SAYS: The secret is to unify both the lower and
upper worlds. ADONAI IS THE LOWER WORLD, WHICH IS THE NUKVA,
WHILE YUD HEI VAV HEI, WHICH IS WRITTEN WITH THE SAME VOWELS
AS ELOHIM, IS THE UPPER WORLD, WHICH IS BINAH. AND IN THIS
VERSE BOTH ARE COMBINED TO ONE.

320. מַה תִּתֶּן לִי וְאָנֹכִי הוֹלֵךְ עֲרִירִי. דְּלֵית לִי בַּר, וְאוֹלִיפְנָא דְּכָל מָאן
דְּלֵית לֵיהּ בְּרָא בְּהַאי עָלְמָא, אִקְרֵי עֲרִירִי. כְּד"א עֲרִירִים יִהְיוּ.
וְאַבְרָהָם עַל מָה אֲמַר מִלָּה דָּא, דַּאֲמַר מַה תִּתֶּן לִי, כִּבְיָכוֹל כְּאִילוּ לָא
הֲאֵמִין בֵּיהּ בְּקוּדְשָׁא בְּרִיךְ הוּא.

320. "What will You give me, seeing I go childless" MEANS I have no child.
As we have learned, he who has no child in this world is called childless, as
it is written: "they shall be childless" (Vayikra 20:21). AND HE ASKS: But
why then did Abraham say, 'what will You give me?' It is as if he had no
faith in the Holy One, blessed be He!

321. אֶלָּא, אָמַר לוֹ קֻדְשָׁא בְּרִיךְ הוּא אָנֹכִי מָגֵן לָךְ, בְּהַאי עָלְמָא.
שְׂכָרְךָ הַרְבֵּה מְאֹד, בְּעָלְמָא דְּאָתֵי. מִיָּד אִתְעַר אַבְרָהָם בְּרָזָא
דְּחָכְמְתָא, וַאֲמַר מַה תִּתֶּן לִי, דְּהָא יָדַעֲנָא, דְּלָא קַבֵּיל אֲגַר לְמֵיעַל בֵּיהּ
בְּהַהוּא עָלְמָא, בַּר נָשׁ דְּלָא אוֹלִיד בַּר, וְעַל דָּא אֲמַר מַה תִּתֶּן לִי וְאָנֹכִי
הוֹלֵךְ עֲרִירִי, דְּהָא לָא תִתֶּן לִי דְּלָא זָכִינָא בֵּיהּ. מִכָּאן, דְּבַר נָשׁ דְּלָא
זָכֵי בִּבְנִין בְּהַאי עָלְמָא, לָא זָכֵי בְּהַהוּא עָלְמָא, לַאֲעָלָא גּוֹ פַּרְגּוֹדָא.

321. The Holy One, blessed be He, said to him, "I am your shield" in this
world, "your reward will be very great" in the World to Come. Immediately
then, Abraham was infused with the secret of the Wisdom. He said: "What
will You give me?" Because he knew that if a person has not fathered a son,
he does not receive a reward when he reaches the World to Come. Therefore
he said: "What will You give me, seeing I go childless," as you shall not
give me what I am not worthy of. And from this, WE LEARN that a person

who is not worthy of having children in this world shall not be worthy in the World to Come to be in the presence OF THE HOLY ONE, BLESSED BE HE!

322. וְאַבְרָהָם הֲוָה חָמֵי בְּאִצְטַגְנִינוּת דִּילֵיהּ דְּלָא יוֹלִיד. מַה כְּתִיב וַיּוֹצֵא אוֹתוֹ הַחוּצָה וגו׳. אָמַר לוֹ קֻדְשָׁא בְּרִיךְ הוּא לָא תִסְתַּכַּל בְּהַאי, אֶלָּא בְּרָזָא דִשְׁמִי, יְהֵא לָךְ בַּר. הה״ד כֹּה יִהְיֶה זַרְעֶךָ. רָזָא דִשְׁמָא קַדִּישָׁא, דְּמִתַּמָּן אִתְקַשַּׁר לֵיהּ בְּדָא, וְלָא מִסִּטְרָא אָחֳרָא.

322. And Abraham saw through astrology that he will not have a child. What is written: "And He brought him outside" (Beresheet 15:5). The Holy One, blessed be He, said to him, "Do not look to this – THE WISDOM OF THE STARS – but rather to the secret of My Name, WHICH IS THE NUKVA. "You shall father a son!" This is why it is written: "So (Heb. koh) shall your seed be" (Ibid.). KOH is the secret of the Holy Name, through which a son was born to him; HIS SON DID not COME from the Other Side, WHICH IS OF THE STARS AND CONSTELLATIONS.

323. כֹּה: דְּהוּא תַּרְעָא לִצְלוֹתָא, בָּהּ יִשְׁכַּח בִּרְכָה, בָּהּ יִשְׁכַּח בַּר נָשׁ שְׁאֶלְתֵּיהּ. כֹּה: הַהוּא סִטְרָא דְּאַתְיָיא מִסִּטְרָא דִגְבוּרָה, דְּהָא מִסִּטְרָא דִגְבוּרָה קָא אָתָא יִצְחָק. וְהַהוּא סִטְרָא דִגְבוּרָה כֹּה אִקְרֵי, דְּמִתַּמָּן אַתְיָין אִיבִּין וּפֵירֵי לְעָלְמָא, וְלָא מִסִּטְרָא דִלְתַתָּא, דְּכֹכְבַיָּא וּמַזָּלוֹת.

323. Koh is the gate through which prayers are accepted, WHICH IS THE NUKVA. There the blessing abides; there a person shall fulfill his request! Koh is related to the side of Gvurah, WHICH IS AN ALLUSION TO THE NUKVA, WHICH IS BUILT FROM THE LEFT, WHICH IS GVURAH, because Isaac was born from the side of Gvurah. And the side of Gvurah is called Koh, because it produces all the seeds and fruits that come to the world; THEY COME not from the lower aspect of the stars and constellations.

324. כְּדֵין וְהֶאֱמִין בַּה׳. אִתְדַּבַּק לְעֵילָא, וְלָא אִתְדַּבַּק לְתַתָּא. וְהֶאֱמִין בַּה׳, וְלָא בְּכֹכְבַיָּא וּמַזָּלֵי. וְהֶאֱמִין בַּה׳, דְּאַבְטַח לֵיהּ דְּיַסְגֵּי אַגְרֵיהּ לְעָלְמָא דְּאָתֵי. וְהֶאֱמִין בַּה׳, בְּהַהוּא דַרְגָּא דְּאִתְיְיהֵיב לֵיהּ, דְּמִתַּמָּן יֵיתֵי לֵיהּ זַרְעָא לְאוֹלָדָא בְּעָלְמָא.

324. Then it is written: "And he believed in Hashem," WHICH MEANS THAT he cleaved above and not below. He "believed in Hashem" and not in the stars and the constellations, he believed that his reward in the next world would be great, and he believed in Hashem that from the grade that was given to him, NAMELY *KOH,* he would be able to bring children to the world.

325. וַיַּחְשְׁבֶהָ לוֹ צְדָקָה. וַיַּחְשְׁבֶהָ לוֹ: דְּאַף עַל גַּב דְּאִיהִי דִינָא כְּאִילוּ הִיא רַחֲמֵי הַאי כֹּה. דָּבָר אַחֵר, וַיַּחְשְׁבֶהָ לוֹ צְדָקָה, דְּקָשִׁיר קִשְׁרָא עִלָּאָה בְּתַתָּאָה, לְחַבְּרָא לוֹן כַּחֲדָא.

325. "And he counted it to him for righteousness" (Ibid. 6), he counted it to the name *Koh* as mercy, though it is of judgment. Another meaning of the verse, "and he counted it to him for righteousness," is that he bound the upper, WHICH IS BINAH, with the lower one, WHICH IS THE NUKVA, and combined them as one.

326. תָּא חֲזֵי, הָא אִתְּעָרוּ אַבְרָהָם מוֹלִיד, אַבְרָם אֵינוֹ מוֹלִיד, וְכִי תֵימָא דְּהָא אוֹלִיד יִשְׁמָעֵאל בְּעוֹד דְּאִיהוּ אַבְרָם. אֶלָּא הַהוּא בְּרָא דְּאַבְטַח לֵיהּ קֻדְשָׁא בְּרִיךְ הוּא לָא אוֹלִיד, בְּעוֹד דְּאִיהוּ אַבְרָם, דְּהָא בְּעוֹד דְּאִיהוּ אַבְרָם, אוֹלִיד לְתַתָּא, כֵּיוָן דְּאִתְקְרֵי אַבְרָהָם, וְעָאל בַּבְּרִית, כְּדֵין אוֹלִיד לְעֵילָא, וּבְגִין כָּךְ אַבְרָם אֵינוֹ מוֹלִיד בְּקִשּׁוּרָא עִלָּאָה, אַבְרָהָם מוֹלִיד, כְּמָה דַאֲמָרָן וְאִתְקַשַּׁר לְעֵילָא בְּיִצְחָק.

326. Come and behold: It has been said that 'Abraham,' SPELLED WITH THE LETTER *HEI,* shall father a son, while 'Avram' shall not. If you say that he fathered Ishmael while he was still 'Abram,' THE RESPONSE IS THAT the son promised by the Holy One, blessed be He, was not born while he was 'Abram,' because as long as he was 'Avram' he begot only down below – REFERRING TO ISHMAEL. But once he was called 'Avraham' and entered the covenant, he begot above – IN HOLINESS. Therefore, 'Avram' begets only down below, while 'Avraham' begets in the upper world, as we have stated, because he was attached above to Isaac.

31. "For who is El...and who is a rock, save our Elohim"

A Synopsis

Every human being is a microcosm of the entire universe. Just as every human cell of the body contains the entire genetic code, each of us contains the entire universe within our soul. We are all individual cells of the cosmos. Accordingly, our influence extends throughout the entire universe: Each part contains the whole, and therefore, each part affects the whole. When the Zohar tells us that Adam saw all the souls who would ever come into existence, we are meant to understand that each of us has a definite purpose and role in the world that was known from the moment of creation.

The Relevance of this Passage

Each individual existence has unique importance and purpose in the overall design and development of the universe. Through these passages, true understanding of our power and influence in this world is aroused within us. We gain awareness of the value and magnitude of every action. Moreover, we connect ourselves to our personal mission that was set forth at the moment of creation.

327. וַיְהִי אַבְרָם בֶּן תִּשְׁעִים שָׁנָה וְתֵשַׁע שָׁנִים וגו'. רַבִּי אַבָּא פָּתַח כִּי מִי אֵל מִבַּלְעֲדֵי ה' וּמִי צוּר וגו'. דָּוִד מַלְכָּא אֲמַר הַאי קְרָא כִּי מִי אֵל מִבַּלְעֲדֵי ה'. מָאן הוּא שַׁלִּיטָא אוֹ מְמַנָּא דְּיָכוֹל לְמֶעְבַּד מִדֵּי מִבַּלְעֲדֵי ה', אֶלָּא מַה דְּאִתְפַּקַּד מֵעִם קֻדְשָׁא בְּרִיךְ הוּא, בְּגִין דְּכֻלְּהוּ לָא בִּרְשׁוּתַיְיהוּ קַיְימֵי, וְלָא יָכְלֵי לְמֶעְבַּד מִדֵּי. וּמִי צוּר: וּמַאן אִיהוּ תַּקִּיף דְּיָכוֹל לְמֶעְבַּד תּוּקְפָּא וּגְבוּרָה מִגַּרְמֵיהּ, מִבַּלְעֲדֵי אֱלֹקֵינוּ. אֶלָּא כֻּלְּהוּ בִּידָא דְּקֻדְשָׁא בְּרִיךְ הוּא, וְלָא יָכִיל לְמֶעְבַּד מִדֵּי בַּר בִּרְשׁוּתֵיהּ.

327. "And when Abram was ninety nine years old..." (Beresheet 17:1). In discussing this verse, Rabbi Aba said: "For who is El, save Hashem? And who is a rock, save our Elohim?" (II Shmuel 22:32). King David said this verse, "For who is El, save Hashem?" meaning who is the governor or ruler over things, "save Hashem." EVERYONE DOES what the Holy One, blessed be He commands, as no one can stand on his own or does anything without Hashem. "And who is a rock" – who is strong enough to perform a mighty deed with his own strength – "save our Elohim?" Therefore, everyone is in

the hands of the Holy One, blessed be He, and none can do anything without His permission.

328. דָּבָר אַחֵר, כִּי מִי אֵל מִבַּלְעֲדֵי ה'. דְּקֻדְשָׁא בְּרִיךְ הוּא כֹּלָא בִּרְשׁוּתֵיהּ, וְלָא כְּמַאן דְּאִתְחֲזֵי בְּחֵיזוּ דְּכֹכְבַיָּא וּמַזָּלֵי, דְּכָלְהוּ אַחְזְיָין מִלָּה, וְקֻדְשָׁא בְּרִיךְ הוּא אַחְלַף לֵיהּ לְגַוְונָא אָחֳרָא. וּמִי צוּר זוּלָתִי אֱלֹקֵינוּ. הָא אוּקְמוּהָ, דְּלֵית צַיָּיר כְּמָה דְּקֻדְשָׁא בְּרִיךְ הוּא, דְּאִיהוּ צַיָּיר שְׁלִים, עָבֵיד וְצַיָּיר דְּיוֹקְנָא גּוֹ דְּיוֹקְנָא, וְאַשְׁלִים לְהַהוּא דְּיוֹקְנָא בְּכָל תִּקּוּנֵיהּ, וְאָעֵיל בָּהּ נֶפֶשׁ עִלָּאָה, דְּדָמֵי לְתִקּוּנָא עִלָּאָה, בְּגִין כָּךְ לֵית צַיָּיר כְּקוּדְשָׁא בְּרִיךְ הוּא.

328. According to another explanation of "For who is El, save Hashem?" everything lies in the hands of the Holy One, blessed be He, and not in what is seen in the stars and their signs. The stars may show a particular thing, but the Holy One, blessed be He, changes it to something else. The verse "And who is a rock (Heb. *tzur*), save our Elohim?" has been explained. There is no "portrayer" (Heb. *tzayar*) like the Holy One, blessed be He, who portrays an image within an image, REFERRING TO A FETUS WITHIN HIS MOTHER'S WOMB, completes that image in all its perfection, and inserts to it a heavenly soul that is similar to the Holy One, blessed be He. This is why there is no "portrayer' like the Holy One, blessed be He.

329. תָּא חֲזֵי, מֵהַהוּא זַרְעָא דְּבַר נָשׁ, כַּד אִתְעַר תִּיאוּבְתֵּיהּ לְגַבֵּי נוּקְבֵיהּ, וְנוּקְבֵיהּ אִתְעָרַת לְגַבֵּיהּ, כְּדֵין מִתְחַבְּרָן תַּרְוַוְיְיהוּ כַּחֲדָא, וְנָפַק מִנַּיְיהוּ בַּר חַד, דְּכָלֵיל מִתְּרֵין דְּיוֹקְנִין כְּחַד, בְּגִין דְּקֻדְשָׁא בְּרִיךְ הוּא צַיָּיר לֵיהּ בְּצִיּוּרָא דְּאִתְכְּלִיל מִתַּרְוַוְיְיהוּ. וְעַל דָּא בָּעֵי בַּר נָשׁ לְקֻדְשָׁא גַרְמֵיהּ בְּהַהוּא זִמְנָא, בְּגִין דְּיִשְׁתְּכַח הַהוּא דְּיוֹקְנָא בְּצִיּוּרָא שְׁלִים כִּדְקָא חֲזֵי.

329. Come and behold: when a man and a woman desire each other and join as one, the sperm of man produces a child in whom both of their images are combined. For the Holy One, blessed be He created the child in an image that included both. This is why a person should sanctify himself, at that time, so that this image may be as perfect as should be!'

330. אָמַר רָבִּי חִיָּיא תָּא חֲזֵי, כַּמָּה אִינוּן רַבְרְבִין עוֹבָדוֹי דְּקֻדְשָׁא בְּרִיךְ הוּא, דְּהָא אוּמָנוּתָא וְצִיּוּרָא דְּבַר נָשׁ אִיהוּ כְּגַוְונָא דְּעָלְמָא, וּבְכָל יוֹמָא וְיוֹמָא קֻדְשָׁא בְּרִיךְ הוּא בָּרֵי עָלְמָא, מְזַוֵּוג זִוּוּגִין כָּל חַד וְחַד כְּדְקָא חֲזֵי לֵיהּ, וְהוּא צַיֵּיר דְּיוּקְנֵיהוֹן עַד לָא יֵיתוּן לְעָלְמָא.

330. Rabbi Chiya said, Come and behold: How great are the deeds that the Holy One, blessed be He, performs. Because He creates and portrays human beings in a similar way to THE ART AND PAINTING OF the world. THIS MEANS THAT EVERY HUMAN BEING REFLECTS THE ENTIRE WORLD WITHIN HIMSELF AND THUS IS CALLED A MICROCOSMOS. Every day, the Holy One, blessed be He, creates a world by mating couples, according to their worth. THROUGH THEM, HE CREATES WORLDS. And He forms the images of all offspring, before they come to the world.

331. תָּא חֲזֵי, דְּאָמַר רָבִּי שִׁמְעוֹן, כְּתִיב זֶה סֵפֶר תּוֹלְדוֹת אָדָם. וְכִי סֵפֶר הֲוָה לֵיהּ. אֶלָּא אוֹקְמוּהָ דְּקֻדְשָׁא בְּרִיךְ הוּא אַחֲמֵי לֵיהּ לְאָדָם הָרִאשׁוֹן, דּוֹר דּוֹר וְדוֹרְשָׁיו וְכוּ'. הֵיאַךְ אַחֲמֵי לֵיהּ, אִי תֵימָא דְּחָמָא בְּרוּחַ קוּדְשָׁא, דְּאִינוּן זְמִינִין לְמֵיתֵי לְעָלְמָא. כְּמָאן דְּחָמָא בְּחָכְמְתָא, מַה דְּיֵיתֵי לְעָלְמָא, לָאו הָכֵי. אֶלָּא חָמָא בְּעֵינָא, כֻּלְּהוּ. וְהַהוּא דְּיוּקְנָא דְּזַמִּינִין לְמֵיקָם בֵּיהּ בְּעָלְמָא, כֻּלְּהוּ חָמָא בְּעֵינָא, מ"ט, בְּגִין דְּמִיּוֹמָא דְּאִתְבְּרֵי עָלְמָא, כֻּלְּהוּ נַפְשָׁאן דְּזַמִּינִין לְמֵיקָם בִּבְנֵי נָשָׁא כֻּלְּהוּ קַיְימִין קַמֵּי קֻדְשָׁא בְּרִיךְ הוּא, בְּהַהוּא דְּיוּקְנָא מַמָּשׁ, דְּזַמִּינִין לְמֵיקָם בֵּיהּ בְּעָלְמָא.

331. Come and behold. Rabbi Shimon said that it is written: "This is the book of the generations of Adam" (Beresheet 5:1). AND HE INQUIRES, "Did he actually have a book?" AND HE REPLIES: This has been explained. The Holy One, blessed be He, showed Adam every generation and its leaders. But how did He show him ALL OF THEIR IMAGES? If you say that he saw through the Holy Spirit that they are destined to appear in the world, just like a person who sees through wisdom can tell the future of the world, it is not so! Rather, he saw them all with his eyes; he literally saw the image of their forms in the world with his eyes. AND HE ASKS: Why WAS HE ABLE

TO SEE THEM ALL WITH HIS EYES? AND HE REPLIES: Because since the day the world was created, all the Souls that were to appear in future human beings stand before the Holy One, blessed be He, in the same image and form that they will have in the world.

332. כְּגַוְונָא דָא, כָּל אִינוּן צַדִּיקַיָּיא בָּתַר דְּנָפְקִין מֵהַאי עָלְמָא, כֻּלְּהוֹ נַפְשָׁאן סָלְקָן, וְקָדְשָׁא בְּרִיךְ הוּא אַזְמִין לוֹן דְּיוֹקְנָא אָחֲרָא לְאִתְלַבְּשָׁא בְּהוּ, כְּגַוְונָא דַּהֲווֹ בְּהַאי עָלְמָא, בְּגִין כָּךְ כֻּלְּהוֹ קַיְימִין קַמֵּיה, וְחָמָא לוֹן אָדָם הָרִאשׁוֹן בְּעֵינָא.

332. In the same manner, after all these righteous people depart from this world, their souls rise, and the Holy One, blessed be He, creates for each of them another form in which to be clothed, just as they were clothed and covered while in this world. Therefore, all the souls stand before Him, and so Adam saw them, with his eyes!

333. וְאִי תֵימָא, בָּתַר דְּחָמָא לוֹן, לָא קַיְימֵי בְּקִיּוּמַיְיהוּ. תָּא חֲזֵי כָּל מִלּוֹי דְּקָדְשָׁא בְּרִיךְ הוּא, בְּקִיּוּמָא אִינוּן, וְקָיְימוּ קַמֵּיה עַד דְּנָחֲתוּ לְעָלְמָא, כְּגַוְונָא דָא כְּתִיב כִּי אֶת אֲשֶׁר יֶשְׁנוֹ פֹה וגו'. הָא אוּקְמוּהָ דְּכֻלְּהוֹ בְּנֵי נָשָׁא דְּזַמִּינִין לְמֶהֱוֵי בְּעָלְמָא, כֻּלְּהוֹ אִשְׁתְּכָחוּ תַּמָּן.

333. You might say that after he had seen them, they ceased to exist and disappeared, but all that the Holy One, blessed be He, does, remains in existence. So they stand before Him until their time comes to go down to the world. And according to this, it is written: "But with him that stands here" (Devarim 29:14). And this has been explained – all the human beings, who were destined to appear in the world in the future, were standing there.

334. הָכָא אִית לְאִסְתַּכְּלָא, דְּהָא כְּתִיב, אֶת אֲשֶׁר אֵינֶנּוּ פֹה וגו', וּמַשְׁמַע הַנְהוּ דְּיִפְקוּן מֵאִינוּן דְּקָיְימוּ תַּמָּן, בְּגִין דִּכְתִיב עִמָּנוּ הַיּוֹם, וְלָא כְּתִיב עִמָּנוּ עוֹמֵד הַיּוֹם. אֶלָּא וַדַּאי כֻּלְּהוֹ קָיְימוּ תַּמָּן, אֶלָּא דְּלָא אִתְחֲזוּ לְעֵינָא, בְּגִין כָּךְ כְּתִיב עִמָּנוּ הַיּוֹם, אַף עַל גַּב דְּלָא אִתְחֲזוּן.

334. This should be examined, because it is written: "and also with him that

is not here..." which leads us to conclude that it refers only to those who will be born from those standing there. Therefore, it does not say, "standing with us this day," WHICH WOULD HAVE MEANT THAT THEY WERE STANDING THERE WITH THEM. Instead, it is written: "with us this day," WHICH MEANS THAT THEY ARE NOT WITH THEM! AND HE EXPLAINS, "Assuredly, everyone was standing there, but because they were not seen by the eye, the verse reads "with us this day," WHICH MEANS even though they are unseen. BECAUSE OF THIS, HE COULD NOT SAY "STANDING HERE WITH US THIS DAY."

335. וְאִי תֵימָא, מ"ט לָא אִתְחֲזוּן הָכָא, כְּמָה דְאִתְחֲזוּן לְאָדָם הָרִאשׁוֹן, דְּחָמָא לוֹן עֵינָא בְּעֵינָא, וְהָא הָכָא אִתְחֲזֵי יַתִּיר. אֶלָּא, הָכָא כַּד אִתְיְיהִיבַת אוֹרַיְיתָא לְיִשְׂרָאֵל, חֵיזוּ אָחֲרָא, וְדַרְגִּין עִלָּאִין, הֲווֹ חָמָאן וּמִסְתַּכְּלָאן עֵינָא בְּעֵינָא, וַהֲווֹ תְּאִיבִין לְאִסְתַּכְּלָא וּלְמֶחֱמֵי בִּיקָרָא דְּמָרֵיהוֹן, וּבְגִין כָּךְ חָמוּ יְקָרָא עִלָּאָה דְּקוּדְשָׁא בְּרִיךְ הוּא בִּלְחוֹדוֹי, וְלָא מֵאָחֲרָא.

335. You might say, "What is the reason that they were not seen here – ON MOUNT SINAI – just as they were seen by Adam's own eye. DURING THE GIVING OF THE TORAH, it would have been more proper FOR ALL FUTURE GENERATIONS to be seen?" AND HE REPLIES: Here, when the Torah was given to Yisrael, they were looking at a different mirror, in which they saw the supernal grades eye to eye. And they were craving to look upon the glory of their Master. Therefore they saw the supernal glory of the Holy One, blessed be He, Himself alone, and nothing else besides Him!

336. וְעַל דָּא, כֻּלְּהוּ בְּנֵי נָשָׁא דְּזַמִּינִין לְקַיְימָא בְּעָלְמָא, כֻּלְּהוּ קַיְימֵי קַמֵּי קוּדְשָׁא בְּרִיךְ הוּא, בְּאִינוּן דְּיוֹקְנִין מַמָּשׁ, דְּזַמִּינִין לְקַיְימָא בֵּיהּ, הה"ד גָּלְמִי רָאוּ עֵינֶיךָ וְעַל סִפְרְךָ וְגו'. גָּלְמִי רָאוּ עֵינֶיךָ. מ"ט, בְּגִין דְּדִיוֹקְנָא אָחֲרָא עִלָּאָה הֲוֵי כְּהַאי, וּבְגִין כָּךְ כְּתִיב וּמִי צוּר זוּלָתִי אֱלֹקֵינוּ. מַאן צַיָּיר טַב, דְּצַיָּיר כֹּלָּא כְּקוּדְשָׁא בְּרִיךְ הוּא.

336. Accordingly, all human beings who shall appear in the future in the world stand before the Holy One, blessed be He, clothed in the actual

-179-

images in which they shall eventually appear. Therefore, it is written: "Your eyes did see my unshaped flesh: for in Your book all things are written..." (Tehilim 139:16). What is the reason THAT THE HOLY ONE, BLESSED BE HE, SAW HIS UNSHAPED FLESH? "Because another supernal image THAT WAS STANDING BEFORE HIM – EVEN BEFORE THE WORLD WAS CREATED – was similar to this one. AND THIS IS WHY HE SAW IT. Thus, it is written: "and who is a rock (tzur), save our Elohim? IN OTHER WORDS, who is such a good "portrayer" (tzayar) that he is able to draw everything as does the Holy One, blessed be He!

337. דָּבָר אַחֵר, כִּי מִי אֱלוֹהַּ. דָּא רָזָא דְמִלָּה, דְּהָא אֵל כְּלָלָא הוּא, דְּאִתְכְּלֵיל מִכָּלְהוּ דַּרְגִּין, וְאִי תֵימָא, דְּהָא אֵל אִיהוּ דַּרְגָּא אָחֲרָא, בְּגִין דִּכְתִיב אֵל זוֹעֵם בְּכָל יוֹם. תָּא חֲזֵי, דְּהָא לֵית אֵל מִבַּלְעֲדֵי ה', דְּלָאו אִיהוּ בִּלְחוֹדוֹי, וְלָא אִתְפְּרַשׁ לְעָלְמִין. וְעַל דָּא כְּתִיב כִּי מִי אֵל מִבַּלְעֲדֵי ה' וְגו' וּמִי צוּר וְגו'. דְּהָא צוּר לָאו אִיהוּ בִּלְחוֹדוֹי, אֶלָּא כֹּלָּא חַד, כְּדִכְתִיב וְיָדַעְתָּ הַיּוֹם וַהֲשֵׁבֹתָ אֶל לְבָבֶךָ כִּי ה' הוּא הָאֱלֹקִים וְגו'.

337. Another explanation for "For who is Eloha," is the secret of the matter. THE NUKVA, WHICH IS CALLED El, is inclusive, because it includes all the grades within it – THE GRADES OF THE RIGHT, WHICH ARE CHASSADIM, TOGETHER WITH THE GRADES OF THE LEFT, WHICH ARE GVUROT. You might say that the name El represents a different grade – NOT THE ASPECT OF THE RIGHT – because it is written that, "and an El who has indignation every day" (Tehilim 7:12). HE EXPLAINS, "Come and behold: "For who is El, save Hashem" MEANS THAT THE NUKVA is not separate, BUT IS UNITED WITH YUD HEI VAV HEI (HASHEM), WHO IS ZEIR ANPIN, IN A UNISON THAT is never interrupted." This is described by the words, "For who is El save Hashem, and who is a rock..." because "a rock," WHICH IS THE SECRET OF THE LEFT OF THE NUKVA, is not alone, but everything is one, as it is written: "Know therefore this day, and consider it in your heart, that Hashem He is the Elohim ..." (Devarim 4:39).

32. The vision of Shadai – an ordinary vision

A Synopsis

There are two different levels of connection to the infinite Light and spiritual energy of the Upper Worlds.

"The Vision" מחזה — the lower level

"Yud Hei Vav Hei" יהוה — the higher level

Before he underwent the ritual of circumcision, Abraham could only connect to and experience the level of *The vision*. After circumcision, however, Abraham was able to attain the level of the Yud Hei Vav Hei יהוה.

The Relevance of this Passage

An ability to connect to a higher realm of Light – the level of Yud Hei Vav Hei – is made available to us through forces that are unlocked in this mystical passage. We are drawing upon the purification power of circumcision and Avraham's elevated consciousness to ascend to this exalted realm.

338. תָּא חֲזֵי, עַד לָא אִתְגְּזַר אַבְרָהָם, הֲוָה מְמַלֵּיל עִמֵּיהּ מִגּוֹ מַחֲזֶה בִּלְחוֹדוֹי, כְּמָה דְּאִתְּמַר, דִּכְתִיב הָיָה דְּבַר ה' אֶל אַבְרָם בַּמַּחֲזֶה וְגוֹ'. בַּמַּחֲזֶה: בְּהַהוּא חֵיזוּ דַרְגָּא דְּכָל דְּיוֹקְנִין אִתְחַזְיָין בֵּיהּ, כְּמָה דְּאִתְּמַר. וְהַאי מַחֲזֶה אִיהוּ רָזָא דִּבְרִית.

338. Come and behold: As long as Abraham was not circumcised, the Holy One, blessed be He, spoke to him only through a "vision," WHICH IS THE SECRET OF THE NUKVA WHILE SHE IS AT HER PLACE AND IS DESCRIBED BY THE WORDS, "AND AN EL WHO HAS INDIGNATION EVERY DAY." As we have learned, it is written: "the word of Hashem came to Abram in a vision..." (Beresheet 15:1). The words "in a vision" ALLUDE TO the mirror, NAMELY THE NUKVA, WHICH IS the grade where all the figures, REFERRING TO THE THREE COLUMNS, RIGHT, LEFT, AND CENTRAL, are seen. And this "vision" is the secret of the covenant of circumcision, NAMELY THE NUKVA IN WHICH THE COVENANT SHINES.

339. וְאִי תֵימָא, דִּבְגִין כָּךְ אִקְרֵי מַחֲזֶה, בְּגִין דְּאִיהוּ דַרְגָּא חֵיזוּ דְּכָל דְּיוֹקְנִין אִתְחַזְיָין בֵּיהּ, הָא אֲמָרַתְּ בְּקַדְמֵיתָא, דְּעַד לָא אִתְגְּזַר אַבְרָהָם,

לָא הֲוָה מְמַלֵּיל עִמֵּיה בַּר הַאי דַּרְגָּא, דְּלָא שָׁרָאן עֲלוֹי דַּרְגִּין אָחֳרָנִין, וְהַשְׁתָּא אֲמַרְתְּ בַּמַּחֲזֶה, חֵיזוּ דְּכָל דַּרְגִּין עִלָּאִין, וְהָא עַד לָא אִתְגְּזַר כְּתִיב, הָיָה דְּבַר ה' אֶל אַבְרָם בַּמַּחֲזֶה.

339. AND HE ASKS: How can you say that THE NUKVA is called a vision because it is a grade of a mirror in which all figures appear! Previously, you said that as long as Abraham was not circumcised, the Holy One, blessed be He, spoke to him through the grade OF THE VISION alone, upon which no other grade did dwell. Now you say that 'in a vision' refers to the mirror in which all supernal grades are reflected. And, before Abraham was circumcised, it says, "the word of Hashem came to Abram in a vision.

340. אֶלָּא, הַאי דַּרְגָּא, חֵיזוּ דְּכָל דַּרְגִּין עִלָּאִין אִיהוּ, וּבְחֵיזוּ דְּדַרְגִּין עִלָּאִין אִתַּתְקַן. וְאַף עַל גַּב דִּבְהַהוּא זִמְנָא דְּאַבְרָהָם לָא הֲוָה גְּזִיר, הַאי דַּרְגָּא בְּחֵיזוּ דְּדַרְגִּין עִלָּאִין אִיהוּ, וּבְכָל אִינּוּן גְּוָונִין אִיהוּ קָאִים. וְחֵיזוּ דְּאִינּוּן גְּוָונִין קַיְימֵי תְּחוֹתֵיה, חַד מִיָּמִינָא, גַּוָון חִוָּור. חַד מִשְׂמָאלָא, גַּוָון סוּמָק. חַד דְּכָלִיל מִכָּל גְּוָונִין, וְאִיהוּ חֵיזוּ, דְּכָל גְּוָונִין עִלָּאִין דְּקַיְימֵי עֲלֵיה. וְעַל דָּא בְּהַאי חֵיזוּ קָאִים עֲלֵיה דְּאַבְרָהָם, וּמַלֵּיל עִמֵּיה, וְאַף עַל גַּב דְּלָא אִתְגְּזַר. כֵּיוָן דְּאִתְגְּזַר, מַה כְּתִיב, וַיֵּרָא ה' אֶל אַבְרָם.

340. AND HE REPLIES: This grade, which is definitely the mirror of all the supernal grades, is completed by the mirror of all the supernal grades. Even before Abraham was circumcised, this grade mirrored all of the supernal grades and was completed by the colors OF THE SUPERNAL GRADES. AND ALSO the mirror made of these colors is below Her, BELOW THE NUKVA: white, CHESED, is to the right; red, GVURAH, is to the left; and a third color – GREEN, TIFERET – is composed of all remaining colors. AND TO THE NUKVA THAT IS CALLED A VISION, all the supernal colors – WHITE, RED, AND GREEN – are built on this mirror. Therefore He was reflected in this mirror, which stood upon Abraham, and spoke with him, even though he was not circumcised. As soon as he was circumcised, it is written: 'Hashem appeared to Abram...' (Beresheet 17:1). BECAUSE THE NAME OF YUD HEI VAV HEI BECAME ATTACHED TO HER, MEANING THAT THE ESSENCE OF ALL SUPERNAL GRADES WERE INCLUDED WITHIN HER. THIS WAS NOT TRUE BEFORE ABRAHAM WAS CIRCUMCISED; AT THAT

TIME, ONLY THE THREE COLORS WERE INCLUDED WITHIN HER.

341. תָּא חֲזֵי, מַחֲזֵה שַׁדַּי כְּתִיב בְּבִלְעָם, וּבְאַבְרָהָם כְּתִיב מַחֲזֶה סְתָם, מַה בֵּין הַאי לְהַאי. אֶלָּא, מַחֲזֵה שַׁדַּי, אִלֵּין דַּלְתָּתָא מִנֵּיהּ, וְאִינּוּן חֵיזוּ דִּילֵיהּ. מַחֲזֶה סְתָם, מַחֲזֶה דָּא הוּא ה', דְּכָל דְּיוֹקְנִין עִלָּאִין אִתְחַזְיָין בֵּיהּ, וּבְגִין כָּךְ כְּתִיב בְּאַבְרָהָם, מַחֲזֶה סְתָם, וּבְבִלְעָם מַחֲזֵה שַׁדַּי.

341. Come and behold: In reference to Bilaam, it is written that he saw "the vision of Shadai" (Bemidbar 24:16), but with Abraham, it is written only "in a vision." AND HE ASKS: What is the difference between these two? AND HE REPLIES: The 'vision of the Shadai' refers to THE COLORS below THE NUKVA that are Her mirror. The ordinary 'vision' is the letter *Hei* OF YUD HEI VAV HEI, THE NUKVA, in which all the supernal figures, WHICH ARE THE THREE COLORS, appear. Because of this, it is written 'in a vision' only when referring to Abraham, in the 'vision of Shadai' when referring to Bilaam. HOWEVER, AS ALREADY EXPLAINED, SHE INCLUDES THE THREE COLORS – WHITE, RED, AND GREEN, AND ALSO THE MIRROR COMPOSED OF THESE COLORS UNDERNEATH HER.

342. וְעַל דָּא עַד לָא אִתְגְּזַר אַבְרָהָם, הֲוָה לֵיהּ הַאי דַּרְגָּא כִּדְאֲמָרָן. כֵּיוָן דְּאִתְגְּזַר, מִיָּד וַיֵּרָא ה' אֶל אַבְרָם וְגוֹ'. אִתְחֲזוּן כָּלְּהוּ דַּרְגִּין, עַל הַאי דַּרְגָּא, וְהַאי דַּרְגָּא מַלֵּיל עִמֵּיהּ, כְּדְקָא חָזֵי בִּשְׁלִימוּ. וְאַבְרָהָם אִתְקְטַר מִדַּרְגָּא לְדַרְגָּא, וְעָאל בִּבְרִית קְיָימָא קַדִּישָׁא, כְּדְקָא חָזֵי בִּשְׁלִימוּ.

342. Therefore, before Abraham was circumcised, he reached the grade THAT IS SIMPLY CALLED, "A VISION." Immediately after he was circumcised, however, "Hashem appeared to Abram..." So all the grades OF YUD HEI VAV HEI appeared upon this grade, WHICH IS THE NUKVA, THE ESSENCE OF THESE GRADES. And the grade spoke to him properly, without reservation, BECAUSE THE NUKVA IS THE SECRET OF "SPEAKING." And Abraham clung on to one grade after the other until he became attached to the holy covenant in full perfection, as should properly be!

343. תָּא חֲזֵי, כֵּיוָן דְּאִתְגְּזַר אַבְרָהָם, נָפַק מֵעָרְלָה, וְעָאל בִּקְיָימָא
קַדִּישָׁא, וְאִתְעַטַּר בְּעִטְרָא קַדִּישָׁא, וְעָאל בִּקְיוּמָא, דְּעָלְמָא קָאִים
עֲלֵיהּ, וּכְדֵין אִתְקַיַּים עָלְמָא בְּגִינֵיהּ. בְּגִין דִּכְתִיב אִם לֹא בְּרִיתִי יוֹמָם
וָלַיְלָה חֻקּוֹת שָׁמַיִם וָאָרֶץ לֹא שָׂמְתִּי. וּכְתִיב אֵלֶּה תוֹלְדוֹת הַשָּׁמַיִם
וְהָאָרֶץ בְּהִבָּרְאָם. בְּה"א בְּרָאָם, בְּאַבְרָהָם. וְכֹלָּא בְּרָזָא חֲדָא קָאִים.

343. Come and behold: As Abraham was circumcised, he left THE KLIPAH
OF the foreskin and entered to the holy covenant. He was adorned with the
holy crown and entered the covenant upon which the world is based. Then
the world was firmly established for his sake, as it is written: "If My
covenant be not day and night, it were as if I have not appointed the
ordinances of heaven and earth" (Yirmeyah 33:25). SO IT IS FOR THE SAKE
OF CIRCUMCISION THAT THE WORLD EXISTS. And it is also written:
"These are the generations of heaven and earth when they were created
(Heb. behibar'am)" (Beresheet 2:4). Behibar'am constitutes the letters of
be-hei-bra'am (he created them with Hei). It can also be read beAvraham
(lit. 'with Avraham'). Both are related to the same secret, WHICH IS
CIRCUMCISION. THEREFORE THE WORLD WAS CREATED FOR ABRAHAM
BECAUSE HE HAD ENTERED THE COVENANT OF CIRCUMCISION, WHICH
IS REFERRED TO BY THE VERSE, "IF MY COVENANT BE NOT DAY AND
NIGHT..."

344. וּבְשַׁעֲתָא דְּקֻדְשָׁא בְּרִיךְ הוּא אַחֲמֵי לֵיהּ לְאָדָם, כָּל אִינּוּן דָּרִין
דְּעָלְמָא, וְחָמָא לוֹן כָּל חַד וְחַד, כָּל דָּרָא וְדָרָא, כֻּלְּהוּ קַיְימֵי בְּגִנְתָּא
דְּעֵדֶן, בְּהַהוּא הַיּוֹקְנָא דְּזַמִּינִין לְקַיְימָא בְּהַאי עָלְמָא, וְתָא חֲזֵי, הָא
אִתְּמַר, כֵּיוָן דְּחָמָא לֵיהּ לְדָוִד, דְּלָאו בֵּיהּ חַיִּים כְּלָל, תָּוָה, וְאִיהוּ יָהִיב
לֵיהּ מִדִּילֵיהּ ע' שְׁנִין, בְּגִין כָּךְ הֲווֹ לֵיהּ לְאָדָם, תְּשַׁע מֵאוֹת וּתְלָתִין
שְׁנִין, וְאִינּוּן שַׁבְעִין אִסְתַּלָּקוּ לֵיהּ לְדָוִד.

344. When the Holy One, blessed be He, showed Adam all future
generations of the world, he saw them one by one, one generation after the
other, standing in the Garden of Eden in that same form that they would
have in this world. So come and behold: We have learned that when he saw
that David had no life of his own at all, he stood in wonder and then gave

him 70 years of his own life. Because of this, Adam lived only nine hundred and thirty years; his remaining seventy years were given to David.

345. וּמִלָּה דָּא רָזָא דְּחָכְמְתָא אִיהוּ, דְּדָוִד לֵית לֵיהּ בַּר שַׁבְעִין שְׁנִין, מֵאָדָם קַדְמָאָה, וְכֹלָּא רָזָא דְּחָכְמְתָא אִיהוּ. וְכָל מַה דִּלְתַתָּא כֹּלָּא אִיהוּ בְּרָזָא דִּלְעֵילָא.

345. And this is the secret of Wisdom. The fact that David had only the 70 years given to him by Adam, is in keeping with the higher Wisdom, because everything that occurs below is in accordance with what happens above, IN THE UPPER WORLD.

33. The Holy One, blessed be He, matches couples together

A Synopsis

A discourse on soul mates reveals the mysteries surrounding the male and female aspects of the soul, and the concept of soul mate relationships. When a complete soul enters this physical realm, it does so through the efforts of the angel *Lailah*. During the process of descent, the unified soul separates into male and female halves. If the two halves of the soul embark on a spiritual path during physical existence, they can merit reunification. While the angel *Lailah* is responsible for bringing souls into the physical dimension, it is the Creator Himself who reunites two halves of one soul when the time is right – for only the Creator knows with certainty who are true soul mates.

The Relevance of this Passage

Through this portion, we can merit the appearance of our soul mate in our life and/or strengthen the marital bond with our current partner.

346. וְתָא חֲזֵי, בְּכָל אִינוּן דְּיוֹקְנִין דְּנִשְׁמָתִין דְּעָלְמָא. כֻּלְּהוּ זִוּוּגִין זִוּוּגִין קַמֵּיהּ, לְבָתַר, כַּד אַתְיָין לְהַאי עָלְמָא, קֻדְשָׁא בְּרִיךְ הוּא מְזַוֵּוג זִוּוּגִין. אֲמַר ר' יִצְחָק, קוּדְשָׁא בְּרִיךְ הוּא אָמַר בַּת פְּלוֹנִי לִפְלוֹנִי.

346. Come and behold: All the souls that are destined to come to the world appear before Him, as couples, WHICH MEANS THAT EACH SOUL IS DIVIDED TO A MALE AND FEMALE. Afterward, as they arrive in this world, the Holy One, blessed be He, matches them together. Rabbi Yitzchak said: THE HOLY ONE, BLESSED BE HE, says, 'the daughter of so-and-so to so-and-so.'

347. אָמַר רָבִּי יוֹסֵי, מַאי קָא מַיְירֵי, וְהָא כְּתִיב אֵין כָּל חָדָשׁ תַּחַת הַשֶּׁמֶשׁ. אֲמַר ר' יְהוּדָה, תַּחַת הַשֶּׁמֶשׁ כְּתִיב, שָׁאנֵי לְעֵילָא. אֲמַר רָבִּי יוֹסֵי, מַאי כְּרוֹזָא הָכָא, וְהָא אָמַר ר' חִזְקִיָּה אָמַר רַבִּי חִיָּיא, בְּהַהִיא שַׁעֲתָא מַמָּשׁ, דְּנָפִיק בַּר נָשׁ לְעָלְמָא, בַּת זוּגוֹ אִזְדַּמְּנַת לוֹ.

347. Rabbi Yosi asked: What is the meaning of this? THAT IS, OF THE STATEMENT THAT THE HOLY ONE, BLESSED BE HE, ANNOUNCES WHO

GOES WITH WHOM. HOW CAN THIS BE TRUE SINCE it is written: "and there is nothing new under the sun" (Kohelet 1:9), WHICH MEANS THAT EVERYTHING WAS SETTLED DURING THE CREATION OF THE WORLD. HOWEVER, ACCORDING TO WHAT YOU HAVE SAID, THE ACTION OF MATCHMAKING IS NEW EACH TIME, BECAUSE THE MATCHES MUST BE ANNOUNCED. Rabbi Yehuda said, it is written: "under the sun," yet "above THE SUN," NEW THINGS CAN TAKE PLACE. Rabbi Yosi asked, "Why does He have to make an announcement, since Rabbi Chizkiyah said that Rabbi Chiya said that "at exactly the time a man is born and emerges in the world, his spouse is assigned to him!"

348. אֲמַר רְבִּי אַבָּא, זַכָּאִין אִינוּן צַדִּיקַיָּא, דְּנִשְׁמַתְהוֹן מִתְעַטְּרִין קַמֵּי מַלְכָּא קַדִּישָׁא, עַד לָא יֵיתוֹן לְעָלְמָא, דְּהָכֵי תָּנִינָן, בְּהַהִיא שַׁעֲתָא דְּאַפִּיק קַדְשָׁא בְּרִיךְ הוּא נִשְׁמָתִין לְעָלְמָא, כָּל אִינוּן רוּחִין וְנִשְׁמָתִין, כֻּלְּהוּ כְּלִילָן דְּכַר וְנוּקְבָּא, דְּמִתְחַבְּרָן כַּחֲדָא.

348. Rabbi Aba responded, "Happy are the righteous, whose souls are adorned as they appear before the Holy King, before coming to this world TO ENTER THE BODY. Because we have learned that when the Holy One, blessed be He, sends the souls forth to the world, all of these spirits and souls include a male and a female joined together.

349. וְאִתְמַסְּרָן בִּידָא דְּהַהוּא מְמַנָּא, שְׁלִיחָא דְּאִתְפַּקַּד עַל עִדּוּאֵיהוֹן דִּבְנֵי נָשָׁא, וְלַיְלָה שְׁמֵיהּ. וּבְשַׁעֲתָא דְּנַחֲתִין וְאִתְמַסְּרָן בִּידוֹי, מִתְפָּרְשִׁין. וְלִזְמְנִין דָּא אַקְדִּים מִן דָּא, וְאָחֵית לְהוֹ בִּבְנֵי נָשָׁא.

349. They are handed over to a governor, who is an emissary in charge of human conception and whose name is *Lailah* (Eng. 'Night'). So when they descend to the world and are handed over to that governor, they are separated from each other. Sometimes one precedes the other in coming down and entering the body of a human being.

350. וְכַד מָטָא עִידָן דְּזִוּוּגָא דִּלְהוֹן, קֻדְשָׁא בְּרִיךְ הוּא דְּיָדַע אִינוּן רוּחִין וְנִשְׁמָתִין, מְחַבֵּר לוֹן כִּדְבְקַדְמֵיתָא, וּמַכְרְזָא עֲלַיְיהוּ. וְכַד אִתְחַבְּרָן, אִתְעֲבִידוּ חַד גּוּפָא חַד נִשְׁמָתָא, יְמִינָא וּשְׂמָאלָא כִּדְקָא חָזֵי.

וּבְגִין כָּךְ אֵין כָּל חָדָשׁ תַּחַת הַשָּׁמֶשׁ.

350. When their time to be married arrives, the Holy One, blessed be He, who knows THE MALES AND THE FEMALES OF these spirits and souls, joins them as they were BEFORE THEY CAME DOWN TO THE WORLD. And He announces, THE DAUGHTER OF SO-AND-SO TO SO-AND-SO. When they are joined together, they become one body and one soul – THEY ARE the right and left in proper unison. THE MALE IS THE RIGHT SIDE OF THE BODY AND SOUL; THE FEMALE IS THEIR LEFT SIDE. And because of this, "there is nothing new under the sun," MEANING EVEN THOUGH THE HOLY ONE, BLESSED BE HE, ANNOUNCES, 'THE DAUGHTER OF SO-AND-SO TO SO-AND-SO', THIS IS NOTHING NEW BUT RATHER A RETURN TO HOW THEY WERE BEFORE COMING DOWN TO THIS WORLD. AND SINCE ONLY THE HOLY ONE, BLESSED BE HE, KNOWS THIS, HE THEREFORE ANNOUNCES REGARDING THEM.

351. וְאִי תֵימָא הָא תָּנִינָן, לֵית זְוּוּגָא, אֶלָּא לְפוּם עוֹבָדוֹי וְאָרְחוֹי דְּבַר נָשׁ. הָכֵי הוּא וַדַּאי, דְּאִי זָכֵי, וְעוֹבָדוֹי אִתְכַּשְׁרָן, זָכֵי לְהַהוּא דִּילֵיהּ, לְאִתְחַבְּרָא בֵּיהּ, כְּמָה דְּנָפֵיק.

351. You might say, "But we have learned that a man obtains a mate according to his deeds and ways of behavior!" It is assuredly so! If he is meritorious and his ways are correct, then he deserves his own SOULMATE – to join her AS THEY WERE JOINED when they left THE HOLY ONE, BLESSED BE HE, BEFORE BONDING A BODY.

352. אֲמַר ר' חִיָּיא, מַאן דְּאִתְכַּשְׁרָן עוֹבָדוֹי, בְּאָן אֲתַר יִתְבַּע הַהוּא זְוּוּגָא דִּילֵיהּ. אָמַר לוֹ הָא תָּנִינָן, לְעוֹלָם יִמְכּוֹר אָדָם כו' וְיִשָּׂא בַּת תַּלְמִיד חָכָם. דְּתַלְמִיד חָכָם, פִּקְדוֹנָא דְּמָארֵיהּ, אִתְפַּקְדָן בִּידֵיהּ.

352. Rabbi Chiya asked, "Where should he who performs good deeds look for his soulmate?" He answered, "We have already learned that a man should even sell all his property to marry the daughter of a sage, because the deposit of the Holy One, blessed be He, is handed over to a sage." THEREFORE, HE SHALL SURELY FIND HIS MATE WITH HIM.

353. תָּאנָא בְּרָזָא דְּמַתְנִיתָא, כָּל אִינּוּן דְּאָתוּ בְּגִלְגּוּלָא דְּנִשְׁמָתִין, יָכְלִין לְאַקְדָּמָא בְּרַחֲמֵי זִוּוּגָא דִּלְהוֹן. וְעַל הַאי אִתְּעֲרוּ חַבְרַיָּיא, שְׁמָא יְקַדְמֶנּוּ אַחֵר בְּרַחֲמִים. וְשַׁפִּיר קָאֲמְרוּ, אַחֵר דַּיְיקָא, וְעַל כֵּן קַשִּׁין זִוּוּגִין קַמֵּיהּ דְּקוּדְשָׁא בְּרִיךְ הוּא. וְעַל כֹּלָּא וַדַּאי כִּי יְשָׁרִים דַּרְכֵי ה' כְּתִיב.

353. We have also learned that according to the secret of the Braita, the mating of all souls, which are reincarnated BUT HAVE NO SOULMATES can be performed before their time through mercy. THIS MEANS THAT HE MAY PRECEDE AND MARRY SOMEBODY ELSE'S SOULMATE. THIS IS THE MEANING OF THE WARNING, "WOMEN SHOULD NOT BE MARRIED ON A FEAST DAY, BUT THEY CAN BE BETROTHED, BECAUSE ANOTHER MAN MAY PRECEDE HIM THROUGH MERCY." And what they said is right! The term "another man" is exact. This is the reason why "It is difficult for the Holy, blessed be He, to bring couples together" Above all, assuredly, "the ways of Hashem are right" (Hoshea 14:10), AND ALL THAT HE DOES IS GOOD AND RIGHT.

354. ר' יְהוּדָה שָׁלַח לֵיהּ לְר' אֶלְעָזָר, אָמַר הָא רָזָא דְּמִלָּה יְדַעְנָא, אִינּוּן דְּאָתוּ בְּגִלְגּוּלָא דְּנִשְׁמָתִין, מֵאָן אֲתַר לְהוֹ זִוּוּגָא. שָׁלַח לֵיהּ, כְּתִיב מַה נַּעֲשֶׂה לָהֶם לַנּוֹתָרִים לְנָשִׁים וגו'. וּכְתִיב, לְכוּ וַחֲטַפְתֶּם לָכֶם וגו'. פָּרְשָׁתָא דִּבְנֵי בִנְיָמִין אוֹכַח, וְעַל הַאי תָּנֵינָן, שְׁמָא יְקַדְמֶנּוּ אַחֵר בְּרַחֲמִים.

354. Rabbi Yehuda inquired of Rabbi Elazar, "I am aware of the secret of this subject. THEREFORE I ASK where do those souls that are reincarnated, BUT HAVE NO SOULMATES, find their spouses? He responded, "It is written: 'How shall we do for wives for them that remain?' (Shoftim 21:7), and "you shall catch every man his wife..." (Ibid. 21). Although this passage deals specifically with the sons of Benjamin, IT ACTUALLY DEALS WITH THE REINCARNATED SOULS, WHO MAY PRECEDE THEIR FRIENDS AND TAKE THEIR SOULMATES AWAY FROM THEM THROUGH MERCY. Therefore, as we have learned, "Lest another precede him with Mercy."

355. אָמַר ר' יְהוּדָה הַאי הוּא וַדַּאי, דְּקַשִּׁין זִוּוּגִין קַמֵּי קַדְשָׁא בְּרִיךְ

הוּא. זַכָּאָה חוּלָקְהוֹן דְּיִשְׂרָאֵל, דְּאוֹרַיְיתָא אוֹלִיף לְהוֹ אוֹרְחוֹי דְּקֻדְשָׁא בְּרִיךְ הוּא, וְכָל טְמִירִין וּגְנִיזָא דִּגְנִיזִין קַמֵּיהּ.

355. Rabbi Yehuda said that this is definitely the meaning of "It is difficult for the Holy One, blessed be He, to bring couples together," BECAUSE HE IS OBLIGED TO TAKE FROM ONE AND GIVE TO THE OTHER. Happy is the portion of Yisrael, because the Torah teaches them the ways of conduct of the Holy One, blessed be He, as well as all His secrets and mysteries hidden before Him.

356. וַדַּאי כְּתִיב תּוֹרַת ה' תְּמִימָה וְגוֹ'. זַכָּאָה חוּלָקֵיהּ מַאן דְּיִשְׁתַּדֵּל בְּאוֹרַיְיתָא, וְלָא יִתְפְּרֵשׁ מִינָהּ, דְּכָל מַאן דְּיִתְפְּרַשׁ מֵאוֹרַיְיתָא, אֲפִילוּ שַׁעֲתָא חָדָא, כְּמָה דְּאִתְפְּרַשׁ מֵחַיֵּי דְּעָלְמָא. דִּכְתִיב כִּי הוּא חַיֶּיךָ וְאֹרֶךְ יָמֶיךָ. וּכְתִיב אֹרֶךְ יָמִים וּשְׁנוֹת חַיִּים וְשָׁלוֹם יוֹסִיפוּ לָךְ.

356. Indeed, it is written: "The Torah of Hashem is perfect" (Tehilim 19:8), BECAUSE EVERYTHING APPEARS IN IT. Happy is the portion of him, who studies Torah and is never separated from it. Because whoever abandons the Torah, even for one moment, is separated from eternal life. Therefore, it is written: "For it is your life and length of your days" (Devarim 30:20) and "For length of days and years of life and peace shall they add to you" (Mishlei 3:2).

34. Night and Midnight

A Synopsis
Specific judgments come to our world when the sun sets and night descends. At the stroke of midnight, another transformation occurs as the awesome and compassionate Light of mercy appears in the cosmos. According to the wisdom of the Zohar, whoever delves into the study of Torah during this time of Mercy, after midnight, shall merit a portion in the World to Come.

This mystery is conveyed through a story about Rabbi Aba and Rabbi Ya'akov. The two eminent mystics are traveling through a certain village and they take up lodging at an inn. The inn-keeper has built a complex apparatus that uses water, buckets, and scales to signal the arrival of midnight. These complexities and metaphors within this seemingly simple tale indicate the extreme importance of spiritual study after the stroke of midnight.

The Relevance of this Passage
The compassionate Light of Mercy is aroused through the language that flows through this mystical text of Zohar. This Light helps us merit a share in the World to Come.

357. וַיְהִי אַבְרָם בֶּן תִּשְׁעִים שָׁנָה וגו'. ר' יוֹסֵי פָּתַח, וְעַמֵּךְ כֻּלָּם צַדִּיקִים לְעוֹלָם יִרְשׁוּ אָרֶץ וגו'. זַכָּאִין אִינוּן יִשְׂרָאֵל, מִכָּל שְׁאָר עַמִּין, דְּקֻדְשָׁא בְּרִיךְ הוּא קָרָא לוֹן צַדִּיקִים. דְּתַנְיָא מֵאָה וְעֶשְׂרִין וְחָמֵשׁ אַלְפֵי מָארֵי דְגַדְפִין, דְּאָזְלִין וְטָאסִין כָּל עָלְמָא, וְשָׁמְעִין קָלָא, וְאַחֲדִין לֵיהּ לְהַהוּא קָלָא.

357. "And when Abram was ninety nine years old..." (Beresheet 17:1). Rabbi Yosi opened the discussion by quoting, "Your people also shall be all righteous: they shall inherit the land forever..." (Yeshayah 60:21). Happy is Yisrael above all other nations because the Holy One, blessed be He, called its people righteous. For we have learned that there are 125,000 winged creatures roaming the world ready to hear and receive the voice.

358. כְּמָה דְּתָנִינָן, לֵית לָךְ מִלָּה בְּעָלְמָא, דְּלֵית לָהּ קָלָא, וְאָזְלָא וְטָאסָא בִּרְקִיעָא, וְאַחֲדִין לָהּ מָארֵי דְגַדְפִין וְסָלְקִין הַהוּא קָלָא, וְדַיְינִין לָהּ, הֵן לְטַב, הֵן לְבִישׁ. דִּכְתִיב כִּי עוֹף הַשָּׁמַיִם יוֹלִיךְ אֶת הַקּוֹל וגו'.

358. As we have learned, everything in the world has a voice, which floats and flies in the firmament, where those winged creatures catch it and carry it aloft TO MAYIN NUKVIN (FEMALE WATERS) FOR MALE AND FEMALE, to be judged to good or to evil, as it is written: "For the bird of heaven shall carry the sound and that which has wings shall tell the matter" (Kohelet 10:20).

359. אֵימָתַי דַּיְיִנִין לְהַהוּא קָלָא. רַבִּי חִיָּיא אֲמַר, בְּשַׁעֲתָא דְּבַר נָשׁ שָׁכִיב וְנָאֵים, וְנִשְׁמָתֵיהּ נָפְקַת מִנֵּיהּ, וְהִיא אַסְהִידַת בֵּיהּ בְּבַר נָשׁ, וּכְדֵין דַּיְיִנִין לְהַהוּא קָלָא. הה"ד מִשֹּׁכֶבֶת חֵיקֶךָ שְׁמֹר פִּתְחֵי פִיךָ. מ"ט מִשּׁוּם דְּהִיא אַסְהִידַת בְּבַר נָשׁ. רַבִּי יְהוּדָה אֲמַר, כָּל מַה דְּבַר נָשׁ עָבֵיד בְּכָל יוֹמָא, נִשְׁמָתֵיהּ אַסְהִידַת בֵּיהּ בְּבַר נָשׁ בְּלֵילְיָא.

359. "When do they judge this voice?" IN OTHER WORDS, "WHEN IS THE VOICE CARRIED ALOFT AS MAYIN NUKVIN (FEMALE WATERS) FOR MALE AND FEMALE." Rabbi Chiya answers: When a person goes to bed and sleeps, because at that time, the soul leaves him and testifies about him; that is when the voice is judged. THIS MEANS THAT IT IS ELEVATED TO MAYIN NUKVIN (FEMALE WATERS) IF THE SOUL TESTIFIES IN HIS FAVOR! Therefore, it is written: "keep the doors of your mouth from her that lies in your bosom" (Michah 7:5). Why? Because it is she who testifies against the person. THE WORDS "FROM HER THAT LIES IN YOUR BOSOM" ALLUDE TO THE SOUL. As Rabbi Yehuda says: All that a person does during the day, his soul testifies on him at night.

360. תָּאנָא אֲמַר ר' אֶלְעָזָר, בְּתְחִלַּת שַׁעֲתָא קַמַּיְיתָא בְּלֵילְיָא, כַּד נָשַׁף יְמָמָא, וְעָאל שִׁמְשָׁא, מָארֵי דְּמַפְתְּחָן דִּמְמַנָּן עַל שִׁמְשָׁא, עָאל בִּתְרֵיסַר תַּרְעִין דְּפָתִיחִין בִּימָמָא, בָּתַר דְּעָאל בְּכֻלְּהוּ, כָּל אִינוּן תַּרְעִין סְתִימִין.

360. Rabbi Elazar said, as we have learned: At the beginning of the first hour at night, when the day is blown away and the sun goes down, the keeper of the keys, who is in charge of the sun – MATATRON, THE GOVERNOR OF THE WORLD, WHO DRAWS THE LIGHT OF THE SUN DOWN TO THE WORLD – enters the twelve gates that BELONG TO THE SUN.

THESE GATES are open during the day, WHICH IS THE SECRET OF THE TWELVE HOURS OF DAYLIGHT. After he has passed through all TWELVE GATES, MEANING AFTER THE TWELFTH HOUR IS OVER, then all the gates are closed, MEANING THAT THE DOMINION OF THE DAY HAS ENDED AND THE TIME FOR THE DOMINION OF THE NIGHT HAS COME!

361. כָּרוֹזָא קָאִים, וְשָׁרֵי לְאַכְרְזָא, קָאִים מָאן דְּקָאִים, וְאָחִיד לְאִינּוּן מַפְתְּחָן. בָּתַר דְּסַיֵּים כָּרוֹזָא, כָּל אִינּוּן נְטוּרֵי עָלְמָא מִתְכַּנְּשִׁין וְסָלְקִין, לֵית מָאן דְּפָתַח פִּתְרָא, כֹּלָּא מִשְׁתַּכְּכִין. כְּדֵין דִּינִין דִּלְתַתָּא מִתְעָרִין, וְאָזְלִין וְשָׁאטִין בְּעָלְמָא, וְסִיהֲרָא שָׁארֵי לְאַנְהָרָא.

361. A herald then announces – BECAUSE EVERY CHANGE IS ACCOMPLISHED BY AN ANNOUNCEMENT. Someone rises, THE HERALD, THE ANGEL GABRIEL, WHO holds on to their keys. DURING THE DAY, THE KEYS ARE IN THE HANDS OF MATATRON. THROUGH THESE KEYS, HE DRAWS THE DARKNESS, WHICH IS THE SECRET OF THE ANNOUNCEMENT. After he completes the announcement, all the guardians of the world gather together and ascend FROM THE WORLD. Nobody remains to create an opening TO DRAW DOWN EVEN A TINY LIGHT, because they are all silenced. Then the lower Judgments are aroused. They start to roam the world, and the moon begins to shine.

362. וּמָארֵי דִיבָבָא תָּקְעִין וּמְיַלְלִין, תָּקְעִין תִּנְיָינוּת. כְּדֵין מִתְעָרֵי שִׁירָתָא, וּמְזַמְּרִין קַמֵּי מָארֵיהוֹן, כַּמָּה מָארֵי תְּרֵיסִין קָיְימוּ בְּקִיּוּמַיְיהוּ, וְאִתְעָרִין דִּינִין בְּעָלְמָא, כְּדֵין בְּנֵי נָשָׁא נָיְימִין, וְנִשְׁמָתָא נָפְקַת, וְאַסְהִידַת סַהֲדוּתָא, וְאִתְחַיְּיבַת בְּדִינָא, וְקֻדְשָׁא בְּרִיךְ הוּא עָבֵד חֶסֶד בְּבַר נָשׁ, וְנִשְׁמָתָא תָּבַת לְאַתְרָהּ.

362. And wailers WHICH ARE THE FORCES OF JUDGMENT THAT AROUSE WAILING AND HOWLING IN THE WORLD, cry out loud WITH THE BLOWING OF A TRUMPET. At the second blast, the angels begin to chant and sing before their Master. How many Guardians stand erect TO OFFER PROTECTION FROM JUDGMENTS, and Judgments are aroused in the world. Then as people sleep, their souls leave THEIR BODIES, give testimony, and are sentenced – BECAUSE THERE IS NO RIGHTEOUS PERSON ON EARTH

WHO DOES NOT SIN. But the Holy One, blessed be He, deals mercifully with the human beings and allows the soul to return back IN THE MORNING.

363. בְּפַלְגוּת לֵילְיָא, כַּד צְפּוֹרִין מִתְעָרִין, סִטְרָא דְּצָפוֹן אִתְּעַר בְּרוּחָא, קָם בְּקִיּוּמֵיה, שַׁרְבִיטָא דְּבִסְטַר דָּרוֹם, וּבָטַשׁ בְּהַהוּא רוּחָא, וְשָׁכֵיךְ וְאִתְבַּסָּם, כְּדֵין אִתְּעַר קוּדְשָׁא בְּרִיךְ הוּא בְּנִמוּסוֹי, לְאִשְׁתַּעְשְׁעָא עַם צַדִּיקַיָּא בְּגִנְתָא דְּעֵדֶן.

363. At midnight, when the birds awaken, THAT IS, THE COCKS, a spirit (or wind) rises in the North. THIS REFERS TO THE LEFT COLUMN, WHICH IS THE SECRET OF THE ILLUMINATION OF CHOCHMAH WITHOUT CHASSADIM – THE SECRET OF THE UPPER THREE SFIROT OF RUACH. The scepter then rises in the South, NAMELY IN THE RIGHT COLUMN, WHICH IS THE SECRET OF CHASSADIM, and unites with that spirit OF THE LEFT COLUMN. THUS, THEY ARE INCLUDED WITHIN EACH OTHER, AND THE JUDGMENTS OF THE LEFT COLUMN subside and are mitigated BY CHASSADIM. And the Holy One, blessed be He, is awakened and, as is His wont, delights Himself with the righteous in the Garden of Eden.

364. בְּהַהוּא שַׁעֲתָא, זַכָּאָה חוּלָקֵיה דְּבַר נָשׁ דְּקָאֵים לְאִשְׁתַּעְשַׁע בְּאוֹרַיְיתָא, דְּהָא קַדְשָׁא בְּרִיךְ הוּא, וְכָל צַדִּיקַיָּא דְּבְגִנְתָא דְּעֵדֶן, כֻּלְּהוּ צָיְיתִין לְקָלֵיה. הֲדָא הוּא דִּכְתִיב הַיּוֹשֶׁבֶת בַּגַּנִּים חֲבֵרִים מַקְשִׁיבִים לְקוֹלֵךְ הַשְׁמִיעִנִי.

364. Happy is he who awakens at that time to delight in the Torah, because the Holy One, blessed be He, together with all the righteous in the Garden of Eden listen attentively to his voice. This is why it is written: "You that dwell in the gardens, the companions hearken to your voice, cause me to hear it" (Shir Hashirim 8:13).

365. וְלֹא עוֹד, אֶלָּא דְּקַדְשָׁא בְּרִיךְ הוּא מָשִׁיךְ עֲלֵיה חַד חוּטָא דְּחֶסֶד, לְמֶהֱוֵי נָטִיר בְּעָלְמָא, דְּהָא עִלָּאִין וְתַתָּאִין נָטְרִין לֵיה. הה"ד, יוֹמָם יְצַוֶּה ה' חַסְדּוֹ וּבַלַּיְלָה שִׁירֹה עִמִּי.

365. In addition, the Holy One, blessed be He, draws down upon him a

thread of grace (lit. 'chesed') which earns him protection in this world from both higher and lower beings. Therefore it is written: "Hashem will command His loving kindness (Heb. *Chesed*) in the daytime, and in the night His song shall be with me" (Tehilim 42:9).

366. אָמַר רָבִּי חִזְקִיָּה, כָּל מַאן דְּאִשְׁתַּדַּל בְּהַאי שַׁעֲתָא בְּאוֹרַיְיתָא, וַדַּאי אִית לֵיהּ חוּלָקָא תָּדִיר בְּעָלְמָא דְּאָתֵי. אָמַר ר' יוֹסֵי, מ"ט תָּדִיר. אָמַר לוֹ הָכֵי אוֹלִיפְנָא, דְּכָל פַּלְגוּת לֵילְיָא, כַּד קֻדְשָׁא בְּרִיךְ הוּא אִתְעַר בְּגִנְתָּא דְעֵדֶן, כָּל אִינוּן נְטִיעָן דְּגִינְתָא אִשְׁתַּקְיָין יַתִּיר, מֵהַהוּא נַחֲלָא, דְּאִקְרֵי נַחַל קְדוּמִים, נַחַל עֲדָנִים, דְּלָא פָּסְקוּ מֵימוֹי לְעָלְמִין, כִּבְיָכוֹל הַהוּא דְּקָאֵים וְאִשְׁתַּדַּל בְּאוֹרַיְיתָא, כְּאִילוּ הַהוּא נַחֲלָא אִתְרַק עַל רֵישֵׁיהּ, וְאַשְׁקֵי לֵיהּ, בְּגוֹ אִינוּן נְטִיעָן דְּבְגִנְתָּא דְעֵדֶן.

366. Rabbi Chizkiyah said: Whoever delves to the study of Torah at that hour shall definitely have an eternal share in the World to Come. Rabbi Yosi then asked: What is the meaning of 'eternal'? He answered: This is what I have learned. Every midnight, when the Holy One, blessed be He, enters the Garden of Eden, all the plants – NAMELY THE SFIROT, of the Garden of Eden, WHICH IS THE NUKVA – are watered most generously by the stream that is called the 'ancient stream' and also the 'stream of delight,' WHICH REFERS TO THE SUPERNAL ABA AND IMA, which waters never cease to flow; BECAUSE THE MATING OF ABA AND IMA NEVER STOPS. So, if a person awakens to study Torah, it is as if that stream is poured on his head and he is watered, together with the plants of the Garden of Eden. HE RECEIVES AN ETERNAL PORTION OF THE MOCHIN OF THE WORLD TO COME AS WELL.

367 וְלֹא עוֹד, אֶלָּא הוֹאִיל וְכֻלְּהוּ צַדִּיקַיָּיא, דְּבְגוֹ גִּנְתָּא דְעֵדֶן, צַיְיתִין לֵיהּ, חוּלָקָא שַׁוְיָין לֵיהּ, בְּהַהוּא שַׁקְיוּ דְּנַחֲלָא, אִשְׁתְּכַח דְּאִית לֵיהּ חוּלָקָא תָּדִיר, בְּעָלְמָא דְּאָתֵי.

367. Furthermore, because all the righteous in the Garden of Eden listen to him, they add another portion to that flow of the stream, WHICH ARE THE MOCHIN OF SUPERNAL ABA AND IMA. Therefore he has an eternal portion

in the World to Come, FOR THEY ARE INCLUDED IN THE MOCHIN OF ABA AND IMA.

368. רַבִּי אַבָּא הֲוָה אָתֵי מִטְבֶרְיָה, לְבֵי טְרוֹנְיָא דַּחֲמוֹי, וְר' יַעֲקֹב בְּרֵיהּ הֲוָה עִמֵּיהּ, אִעָרְעוּ בִּכְפַר טַרְשָׁא. כַּד בָּעוּ לְמִשְׁכַּב, אָמַר ר' אַבָּא, לְמָרֵיהּ דְּבֵיתָא, אִית הָכָא תַּרְנְגוֹלָא. אָמַר לוֹ מָארָא דְּבֵיתָא, אַמַּאי. אָמַר לוֹ, בְּגִין דְּקָאֵימְנָא בְּפַלְגוּת לֵילְיָא מַמָּשׁ.

368. Rabbi Aba was traveling from Tiberias to Tronya, where his father-in-law lived, accompanied by his son, Rabbi Ya'akov. When they decided to spend the night in the village of Tarsha, Rabbi Aba asked his landlord, "Is there a cock around here?" The landlord asked, "What do you need a cock for?" Rabbi Aba responded, "Because I awake at midnight exactly! AND I NEED A COCK TO WAKE ME UP.

369. אָמַר לוֹ, לָא אִצְטְרִיךְ, דְּהָא סִימָנָא לִי בְּבֵיתָא, דְּהָדֵין טַקְלָא דְּקַמֵּי עַרְסָאי, מָלֵינָא לֵיהּ מַיָא, וְנָטִיף טִיף טִיף, בְּפַלְגוּת לֵילְיָא מַמָּשׁ, אִתְרָקוּ כֻּלְּהוּ מַיָא, וְאִתְגַּלְגַּל הַאי קִיטְפָא, וְנָהֵים, וְאִשְׁתְּמַע קָלָא בְּכָל בֵּיתָא, וּכְדֵין הוּא פַּלְגוּת לֵילְיָא מַמָּשׁ. וְחַד סָבָא הֲוָה לִי, דַּהֲוָה קָם בְּכָל פַּלְגוּת לֵילְיָא, וְאִשְׁתַּדַּל בְּאוֹרַיְיתָא, וּבְגִינֵי כָךְ, עֲבַד הַאי.

369. THE LANDLORD then said: You do not need THE COCK. I have prepared a signal in the house that indicates midnight, the scales that are before my bed. For this purpose, I fill a vessel with water. The water drips out THROUGH A HOLE IN THE VESSEL so that it empties exactly at midnight. AT THAT MOMENT, ONE SCALE GOES UP WHILE THE OTHER swings downward and roars. IT MAKES NOISE AS IT FALLS. And the sound is heard throughout the house. The signal was created by an old man who once stayed with me and arose at exactly midnight to study Torah.

370. אָמַר ר' אַבָּא, בְּרִיךְ רַחֲמָנָא דְּשַׁדְּרַנִי הָכָא. בְּפַלְגוּת לֵילְיָא נָהֵים, הַהוּא גַּלְגַּלָּא דְקִיטְפָא, קָמוּ רַבִּי אַבָּא וְרַבִּי יַעֲקֹב. שָׁמְעוּ לְהַהוּא גַּבְרָא, דַּהֲוָה יָתִיב בְּשִׁפּוּלֵי בֵּיתָא, וּתְרֵין בְּנוֹי עִמֵּיהּ, וַהֲוָה אָמַר, כְּתִיב חֲצוֹת לַיְלָה אָקוּם לְהוֹדוֹת לָךְ עַל מִשְׁפְּטֵי צִדְקֶךָ, מַאי קָא חָמָא דָוִד, דְּאִיהוּ

אֲמַר חֲצוֹת לַיְלָה, וְלָא בַּחֲצוֹת לַיְלָה. אֶלָּא, וַדַּאי לְקוּדְשָׁא בְּרִיךְ הוּא אֲמַר הָכֵי.

370. Rabbi Aba said: Blessed be HASHEM, the Merciful, who has sent me over here. At midnight, the scale made a noise as it swung down, waking Rabbi Aba and Rabbi Ya'akov. They heard their landlord, who was sitting in a corner of the house with his two sons, say, "It is written: 'Midnight I will rise to give thanks to You because of Your righteous judgments'" (Tehilim 119:62). AND HE ASKED, "What did David see that caused him to say 'Midnight...' instead of "at midnight...?" AND HE REPLIES: Most certainly he was referring to the Holy One, blessed be He, CALLING HIM 'MIDNIGHT.'

371. וְכִי קְדְשָׁא בְּרִיךְ הוּא הָכֵי אִקְרֵי. אֵין, דְּהָא חֲצוֹת לַיְלָה מַמָּשׁ, קְדְשָׁא בְּרִיךְ הוּא אִשְׁתְּכַח, וְסִיעָתָא דִילֵיה, וּכְדֵין הִיא שַׁעֲתָא דְּעָיֵיל בְּגִנְתָּא דְעֵדֶן, לְאִשְׁתַּעְשְׁעָא עִם צַדִּיקַיָּא.

371. AND HE ASKS: Is the Holy One, blessed be He, called so? HE ANSWERED: Yes! Because at midnight exactly, the Holy One, blessed be He, appears with His retinue, and enters the Garden of Eden to delight with the righteous.

372. אֲמַר רַבִּי אַבָּא, לְרַבִּי יַעֲקֹב, וַדַּאי נִשְׁתַּתַּף בִּשְׁכִינְתָּא, וְנִתְחַבַּר כַּחֲדָא, קָרִיבוּ וְיָתִיבוּ עֲמֵיה, אָמְרוּ לֵיה, אֵימָא מִלָּה דְּפוּמָךְ, דְּשַׁפִּיר קָאֲמַרְתְּ. מְנָא לָךְ הַאי. אֲמַר לוֹן, מִלָּה דָא, אוֹלִיפְנָא מִסָּבַאי.

372. Rabbi Aba said to Rabbi Ya'akov, "We shall surely join the Shechinah, so let us join THAT MAN AND HIS SONS." They came closer, sat with him, and said: Say whatever you have to say, for you have spoken well! THEY ASKED HIM: From where do you know all this? He responded: I have learned this from my grandfather.

373. וְתוּ הֲוָה אֲמַר, דְּתִחְלַת שַׁעֲתֵי קַמַּיְיתָא דְּלֵילְיָא, כָּל דִּינִין דִּלְתַתָּא מִתְעָרִין, וְאַזְלִין וְשָׁאטִין בְּעָלְמָא. בְּפַלְגוּת לֵילְיָא מַמָּשׁ, קְדְשָׁא בְּרִיךְ הוּא אִתְּעַר בְּגִנְתָּא דְעֵדֶן, וְדִינִין דִּלְתַתָּא לָא מִשְׁתַּכְּחָן.

373. And he continued: At the first hour of the night all the judgments down below are aroused, THE JUDGMENTS OF MALCHUT WHICH ARE NOT SWEETENED BY BINAH, and fly around the world. Exactly at midnight, however, when the Holy One, blessed be He, enters the Garden of Eden, WHICH IS THE NUKVA, these Judgments disappear and cease to exist.

374. וְכָל נִימוּסִין דִּלְעֵילָא, בְּלֵילְיָא לָא אִשְׁתְּכָחוּ, אֶלָּא בְּפַלְגוּת לֵילְיָא מַמָּשׁ. מְנָלָן. מֵאַבְרָהָם, דִּכְתִיב וַיֵּחָלֵק עֲלֵיהֶם לַיְלָה. בְּמִצְרַיִם, וַיְהִי בַּחֲצִי הַלַּיְלָה. וּבַאֲתָרִין סַגִּיאִין בְּאוֹרַיְיתָא הָכֵי אִשְׁתְּכַח. וְדָוִד הֲוָה יָדַע.

374. And all the pathways of above – NAMELY THE WAYS BY WHICH BINAH SWEETENS THE NUKVA – only occur exactly at midnight. How do we know this? We know this from the verse about Abraham, "And he divided himself against them...(by) night" (Beresheet 14:15). But in Egypt, IT IS WRITTEN: "And it came to pass at midnight" (Shemot 12:29) BECAUSE THE NUKVA WAS THEN SWEETENED BY BINAH AND HER LIGHT WAS REVEALED. And David knew of this, WHICH IS WHY HE SAID: "MIDNIGHT."

375. וּמְנָא הֲוָה יָדַע. אֶלָּא, הָכֵי אָמַר סָבָא, דְּמַלְכוּתָא דִּילֵיהּ בְּהַאי תַּלְיָא. וְעַל דָּא קָאֵים בְּהַהִיא שַׁעֲתָא, וַאֲמַר שִׁירָתָא, וּלְהָכֵי קַרְיֵהּ לְקֻדְשָׁא בְּרִיךְ הוּא חֲצוֹת לַיְלָה מַמָּשׁ אָקוּם לְהוֹדוֹת לָךְ וְגוֹ'. דְּהָא כָּל דִּינִין תַּלְיָין מֵהָכָא, וְדִינִין דְּמַלְכוּתָא מֵהָכָא מִשְׁתַּכְּחִין וְהַהִיא שַׁעֲתָא, אִתְקְטִיר בָּהּ דָּוִד, וְקָם. וַאֲמַר שִׁירָתָא. אָתָא רַבִּי אַבָּא וּנְשָׁקֵיהּ, אָמַר לוֹ וַדַּאי הָכֵי הוּא, בְּרִיךְ רַחֲמָנָא, דְּשַׁדְּרַנִי הָכָא.

375. AND HE ASKED, "How did DAVID know this?" AND HE ANSWERED, so said my grandfather. Because his Kingdom OF DAVID depended on this, ON THE ILLUMINATION OF THE MOCHIN OF MIDNIGHT, David therefore rose at midnight and chanted songs. And so he actually called the Holy One, blessed be He, "Midnight." He also said: "I will rise to give thanks to You..." Then, at that hour, all Judgments stem from here, MEANING ONLY FROM THE NUKVA WHICH IS SWEETENED AT MIDNIGHT, AS THE JUDGMENTS OF THE WORLD BELOW HAVE ALREADY DISAPPEARED. So the Judgments of Malchut are derived only from here, AND NOT FROM ITS UNSWEETENED ASPECT. Therefore, at that hour, David attached himself to it and rose up to chant songs' Rabbi Aba went forward and kissed him. He said: It is assuredly so! Blessed be the Merciful One, who has brought me here.

376. תָּא חֲזֵי, לַיְלָה דִינָא בְּכָל אֲתַר, וְהָא אוֹקִימְנָא מִלָּה, וְהָכֵי הוּא וַדַּאי, וְהָא אִתְעַר קַמֵּי דְּרַבִּי שִׁמְעוֹן. אָמַר הַהוּא יְנוּקָא, בְּרֵיהּ דְּהַהוּא גַּבְרָא, אִי הָכֵי, אַמַּאי כְּתִיב חֲצוֹת לַיְלָה. אָמַר לוֹ, הָא אִתְּמָר, בִּפְלַגּוּת לֵילְיָא, מַלְכוּתָא דִּשְׁמַיָּא אִתְעָרַת. אָמַר אֲנָא שְׁמַעְנָא מִלָּה. אָמַר לוֹ, ר' אַבָּא, אֵימָא בְּרִי טַב דְּהָא מִלָּה דִּפוּמָךְ, קָלָא דְּבוֹצִינָא לֶהֱוֵי.

376. Come and behold: As we have already explained, "night" has always been the time of Judgment; it was discussed in the presence of Rabbi Shimon and is certainly so! The young son of the landlord then asked, "If so, then why is it written: 'Midnight'?" They explained to him, "It is as we have already stated, because the Kingdom of Heaven is awakened at midnight." The son said: I have heard that, but have another explanation! Rabbi Aba then said: Well then, speak up, my son! For your words shall be the voice of the candle, REFERRING TO THE VOICE OF RABBI SHIMON, WHO IS CALLED THE 'LUMINOUS LIGHT.'

377. אָמַר, אֲנָא שְׁמַעְנָא, דְּהָא לַיְלָה דִּינָא דְּמַלְכוּתָא אִיהוּ, וּבְכָל אֲתַר דִּינָא הוּא, וְהַאי דְּקָאָמַר חֲצוֹת, בְּגִין דְּיַנְקָא בִּתְרֵי גַּוְונֵי, בְּדִינָא וְחֶסֶד, וּוַדַּאי פְּלַגּוּתָא קַדְמֵיתָא, דִּינָא הוּא, דְּהָא פְּלַגּוּתָא אָחֳרָא, נְהִירוּ אַנְפָּהָא בְּסִטְרָא דְּחֶסֶד. וְעַל דָּא חֲצוֹת לַיְלָה כְּתִיב וַדַּאי.

377. THE YOUNG SON said: I heard that the night is the time when the Judgment of Malchut is in power. As a result, everywhere THE TERM 'NIGHT' APPEARS, it refers to Judgment. But when the term midnight appears, it is because Malchut is nourished from the two aspects – Judgment and Chesed. So, the first half of the night is the time of Judgment. During the second half, however, the face shines from the aspect of Chesed. This is why it is written: 'Midnight' – THE HALF OF CHESED.

378. קָם רַבִּי אַבָּא, וְשַׁוֵּי יְדוֹי בְּרֵישֵׁיהּ, וּבָרְכֵיהּ, אָמַר וַדַּאי, חֲשִׁיבְנָא

דְּחָכְמְתָא לָא אִשְׁתְּכַח בַּר בְּאִינּוּן זַכָּאֵי דְּזָכוּ בָּהּ. הַשְׁתָּא חָמֵינָא,
דַּאֲפִילוּ יְנוּקֵי בְּדָרָא דְּרַבִּי שִׁמְעוֹן, זָכוּ לְחָכְמְתָא עִלָּאָה. זַכָּאָה אַנְתְּ
רַבִּי שִׁמְעוֹן. וַוי לְדָרָא דְּאַנְתְּ תִּסְתַּלַּק מִנֵּיהּ. יָתְבוּ עַד צַפְרָא, וְאִשְׁתַּדְּלוּ
בְּאוֹרַיְיתָא.

378. Rabbi Aba stood up, placed his hands over his head, and blessed him. He said: I thought that Wisdom was found only among the righteous, who earned it THROUGH PIOUS DEEDS. But now I see that in the generation of Rabbi Shimon, even the young have merited the Supernal Wisdom because of him. Happy are you, Rabbi Shimon. Woe to the generation from which you shall depart. They sat until the morning studying Torah.

379. פָּתַח ר' אַבָּא וְאָמַר, וְעַמֵּךְ כֻּלָּם צַדִּיקִים וְגו'. מִלָּה דָא הָא
אוֹקְמוּהָ חַבְרַיָּיא, מ"ט, כְּתִיב, וְעַמֵּךְ כֻּלָּם צַדִּיקִים, וְכִי כֻּלְּהוּ יִשְׂרָאֵל
צַדִּיקֵי נִינְהוּ. וְהָא כַּמָּה חַיָּיבִין אִית בְּהוֹ בְּיִשְׂרָאֵל, כַּמָּה חַטָּאִין, וְכַמָּה
רְשִׁיעִין, דְּעָבְרִין עַל פִּקּוּדֵי אוֹרַיְיתָא.

379. Rabbi Aba began the discussion with the verse: "Your people also shall be all righteous..." (Yeshayah 60:21). Our friends have already explained this passage. Why is it written: "Your people also shall be all righteous?" How can it be that all the nation of Yisrael is righteous, when there are many wicked people in Yisrael? Many are sinners and transgressors, who disobey the precepts of Torah!

380. אֶלָּא, הָכֵי תָּנָא בְּרָזָא דְּמַתְנִיתִין, זַכָּאִין אִינּוּן יִשְׂרָאֵל, דְּעָבְדִין
קָרְבָּנָא דִּרְעוּתָא לְקַדְשָׁא בְּרִיךְ הוּא, דְּמַקְרִיבִין בְּנַיְיהוּ לִתְמַנְיָא יוֹמִין
לְקָרְבָּנָא, וְכַד אִתְגְּזָרוּ, עָאלוּ בְּהַאי חוּלָקָא טָבָא דְּקַדְשָׁא בְּרִיךְ הוּא,
דִּכְתִיב וְצַדִּיק יְסוֹד עוֹלָם. כֵּיוָן דְּעָאלוּ בְּהַאי חוּלָקָא דְּצַדִּיק, אִקְרוּן
צַדִּיקִים, וַדַּאי כֻּלָּם צַדִּיקִים.

380. But the meaning is found in the secret of the Mishnah. Happy are Yisrael, who voluntarily offer a sacrifice to the Holy One, blessed be He. The sacrifice is the circumcision of their sons eight days after birth. When they are circumcised, they take part in the good portion of the Holy One, blessed be He, as it is written: "The righteous is the foundation (Heb. *yesod*) of the world" (Mishlei 10: 25). As they enter to this portion of the righteous, AS A RESULT OF THEIR CIRCUMCISION, they are the called "righteous." Therefore they are certainly all righteous, BECAUSE NOW THEY ARE ALL CIRCUMCISED, EVEN THE WICKED AMONG THEM. THEREFORE IS WRITTEN: "YOUR PEOPLE ALSO SHALL BE ALL RIGHTEOUS..."

381. וְעַל כֵּן לְעוֹלָם יִירְשׁוּ אָרֶץ. כִּדְכְתִיב פִּתְחוּ לִי שַׁעֲרֵי צֶדֶק אָבֹא בָם. וּכְתִיב זֶה הַשַּׁעַר לַה' צַדִּיקִים יָבֹאוּ בוֹ. אִינּוּן דְּאִתְגְּזָרוּ, וְאִקְרוּן צַדִּיקִים. נֵצֶר מַטָּעַי. נֵצֶר מֵאִינּוּן נְטִיעִין דְּנָטַע קַדְשָׁא בְּרִיךְ הוּא בְּגִנְתָא דְעֵדֶן, הַאי אֶרֶץ חַד מִנַּיְיהוּ, וְעַל כֵּן אִית לְהוּ לְיִשְׂרָאֵל חוּלָקָא טָבָא, בְּעָלְמָא דְּאָתֵי. וּכְתִיב צַדִּיקִים יִירְשׁוּ אָרֶץ. לְעוֹלָם יִירְשׁוּ אָרֶץ. מַהוּ לְעוֹלָם. כְּמָה דְּאוֹקִימְנָא בְּמַתְנִיתָא דִּילָן, וְהָא אִתְּמַר הַאי מִלָּה בֵּין חַבְרַיָּיא.

381. Therefore, "they shall inherit the land for ever" (Yeshayah 60:21). THIS ALLUDES TO THE SHECHINAH THAT IS CALLED "THE LAND." As it is written: "Open to me the gates of righteousness, I will go through them" (Tehilim 118:19) and "This is the gate of Hashem, through which the righteous shall enter" (Ibid. 20). These are those who are circumcised and are called "righteous." "The branch of my plantings" is a branch of the plantings that the Holy One, blessed be He, planted in the Garden of Eden. And this "land" is one of those plantings. THE "PLANTINGS" ARE THE TEN SFIROT OF THE GARDEN OF EDEN, AND MALCHUT OF THEM IS CALLED "THE LAND." Therefore, Yisrael have a goodly portion in the World to Come. As it is written: "The righteous shall inherit the land" (Tehilim 37:29) – "they shall inherit the land forever." AND HE ASKED, "What is "forever?" AND HE SAID: Just as it is explained in our Mishnah and has been settled among the friends.

35. Small Hei and large Hei

A Synopsis
The Zohar presents a very complex metaphysical process that
involves the Hebrew letter *Hei*. Through its shape and sound, the
creative powers of the letter *Hei* ה help determine and influence
our physical world.

The Relevance of this Passage
We develop a greater appreciation of the mystical powers of the
Hebrew letters simply by perusing these verses. A deeper
appreciation automatically amplifies their influence and effectiveness
in each passage of Zohar that we read, learn, or peruse over.

382. וְתָאנָא, מַאי קָא חָמָא קְרָא, דְּלָא אִקְרֵי אַבְרָהָם עַד הַשְׁתָּא.
אֶלָּא, הָכֵי אוֹקִימְנָא, דְּעַד הַשְׁתָּא לָא אִתְגְּזַר, וְכַד אִתְגְּזַר, אִתְחַבַּר
בְּהַאי ה', וּשְׁכִינְתָּא שַׁרְיָא בֵּיה, וּכְדֵין אִקְרֵי אַבְרָהָם.

382. We have already learned the reason why the name Abraham first
occurs only now. We explained that he was not called Abraham until he was
circumcised, because that is when he became attached to the letter *Hei*,
WHICH IS THE SHECHINAH, and the Shechinah rested upon him. Therefore
he was then called Abraham WITH *HEI*!

383. וְהַיְינוּ דִּכְתִיב, אֵלֶּה תוֹלְדוֹת הַשָּׁמַיִם וְהָאָרֶץ בְּהִבָּרְאָם. וְתָאנָא
בְּה' בְּרָאָם. וְתָאנָא בְּאַבְרָהָם. מַאי קָאַמְרֵי, אֶלָּא דָּא חֶסֶד, וְדָא
שְׁכִינְתָּא, וְכֹלָּא נָחִית כַּחֲדָא, וְלָא קַשְׁיָא מִלָּה, וְהַאי וְהַאי הֲוֵי.

383. Therefore it is written: "These are the generations of the heaven and of
the earth when they were created (Heb. *behibar'am*)" (Beresheet 2:4). As
we have learned that "with the letter *Hei*" (*Be-Hei*) "they were created (Heb.
bra'am)." We also learned about the word *beAbraham* (with Abraham),
WHICH CONSISTS OF THE SAME LETTERS AS THE WORD BEHIBAR'AM.
THIS TEACHES US THAT THE WORLD WAS CREATED FOR THE SAKE OF
ABRAHAM. AND HE ASKED, "What are they saying?" IN OTHER WORDS,
"WHY DO THEY DIFFER FROM EACH OTHER IN THE MEANING OF
BEHIBAR'AM? AND HE REPLIED, "One refers to Chesed," SO THE ONE

THAT SAYS THAT BEHIBAR'AM ALLUDES TO ABRAHAM, CHESED, MEANS THAT THE WORLD WAS CREATED BECAUSE OF CHESED. The other refers to the Shechinah, THE OTHER SAYS THAT BEHIBAR'AM, ALLUDES TO THE SHECHINAH BECAUSE THE LETTER *HEI* SIGNIFIES THE SHECHINAH. And there is no contradiction between the two, because they refer to the same meaning, FOR IF THE CHESED EXISTS IN THE WORLD, SO DOES THE SHECHINAH, AND VICE VERSA. THEREFORE, BOTH MEANINGS – CHESED AND THE SHECHINAH – ARE THE SAME. SO THE WORLD WAS CREATED because of the one, CHESED and because of the other, THE SHECHINAH.

384. אָמַר רָבִּי יַעֲקֹב לְר' אַבָּא, הַאי ה' דְּהַבְּרָאָם זְעֵירָא, וְה' דְּהַלָּה' רַבְרְבָא, מַה בֵּין הַאי לְהַאי. אָמַר לוֹ דָּא שְׁמִיטָה וְדָא יוֹבְלָא. וּבְגִין כָּךְ זִמְנִין דְּסִיהֲרָא קַיְימָא בְּאַשְׁלָמוּתָא, וְזִמְנִין בִּפְגִימוּתָא, וּבְאַנְפָּהָא אִשְׁתְּכַח וְאִשְׁתְּמוֹדַע, וְכֹלָּא שַׁפִּיר וְהַאי אִיהוּ בְּרִירָה דְמִלָּה.

384. Rabbi Ya'akov said to Rabbi Aba that the *Hei* in *Behibaram* is small, while the *Hei* in "Do you thus requite Hashem (Hala'Hashem)" (Devarim 32:6) is big! What is the difference between them? He said that the one, THE SMALL *HEI,* is Sabbatical year, NAMELY MALCHUT, while the other, THE LARGE *HEI* is Jubilee, NAMELY BINAH. Because of this, there are times when the moon is full and times when it wanes. WHEN IT IS A GARMENT FOR BINAH, WHICH IS THE LARGE *HEI,* IT IS FULL. BUT BEFORE IT IS A GARMENT FOR BINAH, IT IS A SMALL *HEI.* So THE DIFFERENCE BETWEEN THE SMALL AND LARGE *HEI* can be seen by the phases of the moon. So everything is now clear! This is the clarification of the matter.

36. Essays on circumcision

A Synopsis

Rabbi Aba remains awake all night in anticipation of a circumcision that will take place in the town during the morning. He then accompanies all the townspeople and the family of the child to be circumcised. A lengthy discourse on all the complex secrets and mysteries surrounding circumcision occurs in the Zohar. Circumcision pertains to the purification of the Sfirah of *Yesod* and its counterpart in the physical world, the sexual organ.

The Relevance of this Passage

Circumcision is one of the most powerful cleansing actions available to us, and it is made available by learning these secrets and by meditating upon the words that comprise this portion.

385. אֲמַר רַבִּי אַבָּא, זַכָּאִין אִינוּן יִשְׂרָאֵל, דְּקוּדְשָׁא בְּרִיךְ הוּא אִתְרְעֵי בְּהוֹן, מִכָּל שְׁאָר עַמִּין, וְיָהִיב לוֹן אָת קְיָימָא דָא, דְּכָל מַאן דְּאִית בֵּיהּ הַאי אָת, לָא נָחִית לַגֵּיהִנֹּם, אִי אִיהוּ נָטִיר לֵיהּ, כִּדְקָא יָאוּת, דְּלָא עָיֵיל לֵיהּ בִּרְשׁוּתָא אָחֳרָא, וְלָא מְשַׁקֵּר בִּשְׁמֵיהּ דְּמַלְכָּא, דְּכָל מַאן דִּמְשַׁקֵּר בְּהַאי, כְּמַאן דִּמְשַׁקֵּר בִּשְׁמֵיהּ דְּקוּדְשָׁא בְּרִיךְ הוּא. דִּכְתִיב, בֵּה' בָּגָדוּ כִּי בָנִים זָרִים יָלָדוּ.

385. Rabbi Aba said: Happy are Yisrael, that the Holy One, blessed be He, chose them from among all the other nations to receive the sign of the covenant. Because whoever retains this sign shall not go down to Gehenom as long as he preserves it properly, does not subject it to another power, REFERRING TO A MENSTRUATING WOMAN, A FEMALE SLAVE, A GENTILE WOMAN, OR A PROSTITUTE, and does not lie in the Name of the King. Because if one has lied IN THE NAME, BY THE SIGN OF THE COVENANT, it is as though he has lied in the Name of the Holy One, blessed be He, as it is written: "They have dealt treacherously against Hashem, for they have begotten strange children" (Hoshea 5:7).

386. תּוּ, אֲמַר ר' אַבָּא, בְּזִמְנָא דְּבַר נָשׁ אַסִּיק בְּרֵיהּ, לְאַעֲלֵיהּ לְהַאי בְּרִית, קְרֵי קֻדְשָׁא בְּרִיךְ הוּא לְפַמַלְיָא דִּילֵיהּ, וַאֲמַר, חֲמוּ מַאי בְּרִיָּה עֲבָדִית בְּעָלְמָא. בֵּיהּ שַׁעֲתָא אִזְדַּמַּן אֵלִיָּהוּ וְטָאס עָלְמָא בַּד' טָאסִין,

וְאִזְדְּמַן תַּמָּן.

386. Rabbi Aba continued, "When a man brings his son forth to elevate and initiate him to the covenant, the Holy One, blessed be He, calls upon His retinue, THE ANGELS OF HEAVEN, and declares, 'See what a creature I have made in the world.' At that time, Elijah is invited, flies over the entire world in four crossings, and then appears there."

387. וְעַל דָּא תָּנִינָן דִּבְעֵי בַּר נָשׁ לְתַקְּנָא כָּרְסְיָיא אָחֳרָא לִיקָרָא דִּילֵיהּ, וְיֵימָא דָּא כָּרְסְיָיא דְּאֵלִיָּהוּ, וְאִי לָאו לָא שָׁרֵי תַּמָּן. וְהוּא סָלֵיק, וְאַסְהֵיד קַמֵּי קוּדְשָׁא בְּרִיךְ הוּא.

387. Therefore, we have learned that a man should prepare a chair in honor of Elijah, and should say, "This is the chair of Elijah." If he does not announce this, Elijah will not appear in that place nor ascend and testify about the circumcision before the Holy One, blessed be He.

388. תָּא חֲזֵי, בְּקַדְמֵיתָא כְּתִיב מַה לְּךָ פֹה אֵלִיָּהוּ וְגו'. וּכְתִיב קַנֹּא קִנֵּאתִי לַה' כִּי עָזְבוּ בְרִיתְךָ בְּנֵי יִשְׂרָאֵל וְגו'. אָמַר לוֹ, חַיֶּיךָ בְּכָל אֲתַר דְּהַאי רְשִׁימָא קַדִּישָׁא, יִרְשְׁמוּן לֵיהּ בָּנַי בְּבִשְׂרַיְהוֹן, אַנְתְּ תִּזְדַּמַּן תַּמָּן, וּפוּמָא דְּאַסְהִיד דְּיִשְׂרָאֵל עָזְבוּ, הוּא יַסְהִיד דְּיִשְׂרָאֵל מְקַיְּימִין הַאי קְיָימָא. וְהָא תָּנִינָן, עַל מָה אִתְעֲנַשׁ אֵלִיָּהוּ קַמֵּי קֻדְשָׁא בְּרִיךְ הוּא, עַל דַּאֲמַר דִּלְטוֹרָא עַל בְּנוֹי.

388. Come and behold: It is written first, "What are you doing here, Elijah?" (I Melachim 19:13), and "I have been very jealous for Hashem ...because they have forsaken Your covenant..." (Ibid. 14). THE HOLY ONE, BLESSED BE HE, SAID TO ELIJAH, "As you live, you shall be present in every place that My sons shall imprint this holy sign on their flesh. And the mouth that testified that Yisrael had forsaken the covenant shall now testify that Yisrael observes it!" Thus, we have learned why Elijah was punished by the Holy One, blessed be He – because he accused His sons BY SAYING THAT THE CHILDREN OF YISRAEL "HAVE FORSAKEN YOUR COVENANT."

389. אַדְהָכֵי, הֲוָה אָתֵי נְהוֹרָא, דְּיוֹמָא וַהֲווֹ אָמְרֵי מִלֵּי דְּאוֹרַיְיתָא. קָמוּ

לְמֵיזַל. אָמַר לוֹ הַהוּא גַבְרָא, בַּמֶה דַּעֲסַקְתּוּ בְּהַאי לֵילְיָא, אַשְׁלִימוּ.
אָמְרֵי מַאי הוּא. אָמַר לוֹ דִּתְחֵמוּן לִמְחָר אַנְפּוֹי דְּמָרֵיהּ דִּקְיָימָא, דְּהָא
דְּבֵיתָאי, בָּעָאת בְּעוֹתָא דָא מִנַּיְיכוּ. וּגְזַר קָיָימָא דִּבְרֵי דְּאִתְיְילֵיד לִי,
לִמְחָר לֶיהֱוֵי הִלּוּלָא דִּילֵיהּ. אָמַר רָבִּי אַבָּא, הַאי בְּעוֹתָא דְּמִצְוָה אִיהוּ,
וּלְמֶחֱמֵי אַפֵּי שְׁכִינְתָּא נֵיתִיב.

389. By now, the light of day shone, and they were still studying Torah. As they stood to go, THE LANDLORD said to them, "Complete the subject that you were discussing during the night." They asked, "What subject?" He answered, "Tomorrow you can see the face of the guarantor of the covenant, ELIJAH, because my wife begs you to stay for the celebration of the circumcision of our son." Rabbi Aba responded, "This is an invitation to participate in a commandment, so let us stay!"

390. אוֹרִיכוּ כָּל הַהוּא יוֹמָא, בְּהַהוּא לֵילְיָא, כְּנַשׁ הַהוּא גַבְרָא, כָּל
אִינוּן רְחִימוֹי, וְכָל הַהוּא לֵילְיָא, אִשְׁתַּדְּלוּ בְּאוֹרַיְיתָא, וְלָא הֲוָה מַאן
דְּנָאֵים. אָמַר לוֹ, הַהוּא גַבְרָא בְּמָטוּ מִנַּיְיכוּ, כָּל חַד וְחַד, לֵימָא מִלָּה
חַדְתָּא דְּאוֹרַיְיתָא.

390. They waited all that day. At night, the landlord gathered all his friends together. They studied Torah all that night, and nobody slept. He said to them, "I ask of you all, that each person give a new explanation about the words of the Torah."

391. פָּתַח חַד וַאֲמַר, בִּפְרוֹעַ פְּרָעוֹת בְּיִשְׂרָאֵל בְּהִתְנַדֵּב עָם בָּרְכוּ ה'.
מַאי קָא חָמוּ דְּבוֹרָה וּבָרָק דִּפְתָחוּ בְּהַאי קְרָא. אֶלָּא הָכֵי תָּנֵינָן, לֵית
עָלְמָא מִתְקַיְּימָא, אֶלָּא עַל הַאי בְּרִית, דִּכְתִיב אִם לֹא בְרִיתִי יוֹמָם
וָלַיְלָה וְגו'. דְּהָא שְׁמַיָא וְאַרְעָא עַל דָּא קַיְימִין.

391. One man opened the discussion by saying that it is written: "In time of tumultuous strife (Heb. *pra'ot*) in Yisrael, when the people willingly offered themselves, praise Hashem" (Shoftim 5:2). AND HE ASKED, "Why did Deborah and Barak open their poem with this phrase?" Because, as we have learned, the world cannot exist without this covenant. And it is written: "If My covenant be not day and night, it were as if I had not appointed the ordinances of heaven and earth" (Yirmeyah 33:25), as heaven and earth are established upon it.

392. בְּגִין כָּךְ, כָּל זִמְנָא דְיִשְׂרָאֵל מְקַיְּימִין הַאי בְּרִית, נְמוּסֵי שְׁמַיָא וְאַרְעָא קַיְימִין בְּקִיּוּמַיְיהוּ, וְכָל זִמְנָא דְּח"ו יִשְׂרָאֵל מְבַטְּלִין הַאי בְּרִית, שְׁמַיָא וְאַרְעָא לָא מִתְקַיְּימִין, וּבִרְכָאן לָא מִשְׁתַּכְּחִין בְּעָלְמָא.

392. As a result, as long as Yisrael observe this covenant, the ordinances of heaven and earth continue to exist. But as soon as Yisrael do not heed to this covenant, then the covenant between the heavens and the earth ceases to exist, and no blessings appear in the world.

393. תָּא חֲזֵי, לָא שַׁלִּיטוּ שְׁאָר עַמִּין עַל יִשְׂרָאֵל, אֶלָּא כַּד בְּטִילוּ מִנַּיְיהוּ קְיָימָא דָא. וּמַה בְּטִילוּ מִנַּיְיהוּ. דְּלָא אִתְפָּרְעָן, וְלָא אִתְגַּלְּיָין. וְעַל דָּא כְּתִיב וַיַּעַזְבוּ בְּנֵי יִשְׂרָאֵל אֶת ה' וגו'. וַיִּמְכּוֹר אוֹתָם בְּיַד סִיסְרָא, וַיַּעַזְבוּ אֶת ה' מַמָּשׁ. עַד דַּאֲתַת דְּבוֹרָה, וְאִתְנַדְּבַת לְכָל יִשְׂרָאֵל, בְּמִלָּה דָא, כְּדֵין אִתְכְּנָעוּ שַׂנְאֵיהוֹן תְּחוֹתַיְיהוּ.

393. Come and behold: Other nations ruled over Yisrael only when Yisrael neglected this covenant. And what did they neglect? THEY PERFORMED THE CIRCUMCISION, BUT they did not uncover the corona (Heb. *pri'a*) and reveal the sacred flesh. This is why it is written: "And they forsook Hashem ..." (Shoftim 2:13) and so "He sold them to the hand of Sisra" (I Shmuel 12:9). THEREFORE, THE NATIONS DID NOT RULE OVER YISRAEL UNTIL THEY NEGLECTED THE COVENANT and they actually "forsook Hashem." Then Deborah appeared and volunteered in the name of all Yisrael, for the cause, and then their enemies were subdued.

394. וְהַיְינוּ דְּתָנִינָן, דַּאֲמַר קֻדְשָׁא בְּרִיךְ הוּא לִיהוֹשֻׁעַ, וְכִי יִשְׂרָאֵל אֲטִימִין אִינוּן, וְלָא אִתְפָּרְעוּ וְלָא אִתְגַּלְּיָיא, וְלָא קַיְימִין קְיָימָא דִילִי, וְאַתְּ בָּעֵי לְאַעֲלָא לְהוּ לְאַרְעָא, וּלְאַכְנָעָא שַׂנְאֵיהוֹן. שׁוּב מוֹל אֶת בְּנֵי יִשְׂרָאֵל שֵׁנִית. וְעַד דְּאִתְפָּרְעוּ וְאִתְגַּלְּיָיא הַאי בְּרִית, לָא עָאלוּ לְאַרְעָא,

וְלָא אִתְכְּנָעוּ שַׂנְאֵיהוֹן. אוֹף הָכָא, כֵּיוָן דְּאִתְנַדְבִין יִשְׂרָאֵל, בְּהַאי אָת, אִתְכְּנָעוּ שַׂנְאֵיהוֹן תְּחוֹתַיְיהוּ, וּבִרְכָאן אִתְחֲזַרוּ לְעָלְמָא, הה"ד בִּפְרוֹעַ פְּרָעוֹת בְּיִשְׂרָאֵל בְּהִתְנַדֵּב עָם בָּרְכוּ ה'.

394. This refers to what we have learned about the Holy One, blessed be He, Who said to Joshua, "Yisrael are not circumcised because they did not uncover the sacred flesh. Therefore they do not uphold My covenant. Yet you plan on bringing them to the land of Yisrael and overcoming their enemies. "Circumcise again the children of Yisrael a second time!" (Yehoshua 5:2). And before they uncovered the corona and this covenant was revealed, they did not enter to the land of Yisrael and their enemies were not subdued. So here as well, when Yisrael volunteered to reveal the sign OF THIS COVENANT, their enemies were overcome and blessings returned to the world. Therefore it is written: "In time of tumultuous strife (also: an uncovering of flesh) in Yisrael, when the people willingly offered themselves, praise Hashem."

395. קָם אָחֳרָא, פָּתַח וְאָמַר, וַיְהִי בַדֶּרֶךְ בַּמָּלוֹן וַיִּפְגְּשֵׁהוּ ה' וַיְבַקֵּשׁ הֲמִיתוֹ. לְמַאן לְמֹשֶׁה. אָמַר לוֹ קֻדְשָׁא בְּרִיךְ הוּא, וְכִי אַתְּ אָזִיל לְאַפָּקָא יַת יִשְׂרָאֵל מִמִּצְרַיִם, וּלְאַכְנָעָא מַלְכָּא רַב וְשַׁלִּיטָא, וְאַתְּ אַנְשְׁיֵית מִנָּךְ קְיָימָא, דִּבְרָךְ לָא אִתְגְּזַר, מִיַּד וַיְבַקֵּשׁ הֲמִיתוֹ.

395. Another man stood up and said, as it is written: "And it came to pass on the way in the inn, that Hashem met him, and sought to kill him." (Shemot 4:24) . Whom HAD HE SOUGHT TO KILL? Moses! The Holy One, blessed be He, said to him, "You are about to go and bring Yisrael out of Egypt and overcome a great and powerful ruler, while you neglect a precept – your son is not yet circumcised! Immediately then He "sought to kill him."

396. תָּאנָא, נָחַת גַּבְרִיאֵל בְּשַׁלְהוֹבָא דְּאֶשָּׁא, לְאוֹקְדֵיה, וְאִתְרְמִיז חַד חִיוְיָא מִתּוֹקְדָּא לְשָׁאפָא לֵיה, בְּגַוֵּיה. אֲמַאי חִיוְיָא. אָמַר לוֹ קֻדְשָׁא בְּרִיךְ הוּא, אַתְּ אָזִיל לְקַטְלָא חִיוְיָא רַבְרְבָא וְתַקִּיפָא, וּבְרָךְ לָא אִתְגְּזַר. מִיַּד אִתְרְמִיז לְחַד חִיוְיָא לְקַטְלָא לֵיה.

396. We have learned that Gabriel came down in a flame of fire to burn him.

He appeared as a burning serpent which sought to swallow him. AND HE ASKED, "Why a serpent?" AND HE REPLIED, "The Holy One, blessed be He, said to him, 'You are going to slay a great and mighty serpent, REFERRING TO THE GREAT SEA CRODODILE THAT LIES IN THE RIVERS, WHO IS THE KING OF EGYPT, while your son is not yet circumcised.'" So immediately a serpent was given the intimation to kill MOSES.

397. עַד דְּחָמַת צִפּוֹרָה, וְגָזְרַת לִבְרָהּ, וְאִשְׁתְּזֵיב. הה"ד וַתְּקַח צִפּוֹרָה צֹר. מַהוּ צֹר. אֶלָּא אַסְוָותָא. וּמַאי אַסְוָותָא, דִּכְתִיב וַתִּכְרֹת אֶת עָרְלַת בְּנָהּ דְּנִצְנְצָא בָּהּ רוּחַ קוּדְשָׁא.

397. However, Tziporah understood and circumcised her son, as it is written: "And Tziporah took a flint" (Heb. *tzor*). And what is a tzor? TZOR also MEANS a remedy. And what was the remedy? To "cut off the foreskin of her son" (Ibid. 25). So because the Holy Spirit sparkled within her, MOSES WAS SAVED FROM DEATH.

398. קָם אָחֳרָא וַאֲמַר, וַיֹּאמֶר יוֹסֵף אֶל אֶחָיו גְּשׁוּ נָא אֵלַי וַיִּגָּשׁוּ וַיֹּאמֶר וגו'. וְכִי אַמַּאי קָרֵי לְהוּ, וְהָא קְרִיבִין הֲווֹ גַּבֵּיהּ. אֶלָּא בְּשַׁעֲתָא דַּאֲמַר לוֹן אֲנִי יוֹסֵף אֲחִיכֶם. תְּוָוהוּ, דְּחָמוּ לֵיהּ בְּמַלְכוּ עִלָּאָה. אָמַר יוֹסֵף, מַלְכוּ דָּא, בְּגִין דָּא רֵווֹחְנָא לֵיהּ, גְּשׁוּ נָא אֵלַי. וַיִּגָּשׁוּ, דְּאַחֲזֵי לְהוּ הַאי קְיָימָא דְּמִילָה, אָמַר, דָּא גָּרְמַת לִי מַלְכוּ דָּא, בְּגִין דְּנָטְרִית לָהּ.

398. Another man stood and quoted, "And Joseph said to his brothers, Come near to me, I pray you. And they came near. And he said..." (Beresheet 45:4). AND HE ASKED, "Why did he have to call them, as they were close by?" AND HE REPLIED, "Because when he told them, 'I am Joseph your brother' they were astonished, because they saw him as elevated royalty. So Joseph told them, "I gained this kingdom because of this – REFERRING TO CIRCUMCISION. "Come near to me." They came nearer, and he showed them the sign of the covenant – the circumcision. He said: Because I have preserved the covenant, I have earned this kingdom.

399. מִכָּאן אוֹלִיפְנָא, מַאן דְּנָטִיר לְהַאי אָת קְיָימָא, מַלְכוּ אִתְנַטְרַת לֵיהּ. מְנָלָן, מִבֹּעַז, דִּכְתִיב חַי ה' שִׁכְבִי עַד הַבֹּקֶר. דַּהֲוָה מְקַטְרֵג לֵיהּ

יִצְרֵיהּ, עַד דְּאוֹמֵי אוֹמָאָה, וּנְטִיר לְהַאי בְּרִית, בְּגִין כָּךְ זָכָה דְּנָפְקוּ
מְנֵּיהּ מַלְכִין שַׁלִּיטִין, עַל כָּל שְׁאָר מַלְכִין, וּמַלְכָּא מְשִׁיחָא, דְּאִתְקְרֵי
בִּשְׁמָא דְּקוּדְשָׁא בְּרִיךְ הוּא.

399. From this we have learned that whoever keeps this sign of the covenant, the kingdom will be kept for him. And how do we know this? Another example is Boaz. As it is written: "as Hashem lives, lie down until the morning" (Rut 3:13). Because his lust was aroused and disturbed him until he took an oath – "AS HASHEM LIVES" – and preserved the sign of the covenant. As a result, his sons became kings and rulers over other kings, and the King Messiah, who is called by the name of the Holy One, blessed be He. THEREFORE, KINGSHIP AWAITS HE WHO PRESERVES THE COVENANT FROM DEFILEMENT.

400. פָּתַח אִידָךְ וַאֲמַר, כְּתִיב אִם תַּחֲנֶה עָלַי מַחֲנֶה וְגו'. הָכֵי תָּאנָא,
בְּזֹאת אֲנִי בוֹטֵחַ. מַהוּ בְּזֹאת, דָּא אֶת קָיְימָא, דִּזְמִינָא תָּדִיר גַּבֵּי בַּר
נָשׁ, וְאִתְרְמִיזָא לְעֵילָא, וּבְגִינֵי כָךְ אִתְּמַר בְּזֹאת, כְּמָה דִכְתִיב זֹאת אוֹת
הַבְּרִית. זֹאת בְּרִיתִי. וְכֹלָּא בְּחַד דַּרְגָּא. וְתָאנָא, זֶה וְזֹאת בְּחַד דַּרְגָּא
אִינוּן, וְלָא מִתְפָּרְשָׁן.

400. Another one then quoted, "Though a host should encamp against me..." (Tehilim 27:3). We have learned that "in this (Heb. *zot*) I trust" (Ibid.). What does '*zot* (this)' refer to?" AND HE ANSWERED, "This is the sign of the covenant that always exists in a person and is hinted on high IN MALCHUT CALLED ZOT. Therefore, it is written as *zot*, just as it is also written: "This (Heb. *zot*) is the sign of the covenant" (Beresheet 9:12) and "This (Heb. *zot*) is my covenant" (Yeshayah 59:21). All apply to the same grade. And we have learned, *zeh* (masc. this) and *zot* (fem. this) are both in the same grade and are not separated.

401. וְאִי תֵימָא, אִי הָכֵי הָא שְׁאָר בְּנֵי עָלְמָא, הָכֵי, אַמַּאי דָּוִד
בִּלְחוֹדוֹי, וְלָא אָחֳרָא. אֶלָּא, בְּגִין דַּאֲחִידָא בֵּיהּ, וְאִתְרְמִיזָא בֵּיהּ, וְהוּא
כִּתְרָא דְּמַלְכוּתָא.

401. You might say, "If so, then the other people in the world are the same

AS DAVID, AS THEY CAN SAY 'IN THIS (ZOT) I TRUST.' So why was David the only one to say so, and nobody else as well?" AND HE REPLIED, "Because THE GRADE OF ZOT is attached to DAVID and appears in him, MEANING THAT THE NAME OF DAVID ALLUDES TO MALCHUT and is the Crown of his kingdom.

402. תָּא חֲזֵי, בְּגִין דְּהַאי זֹאת, לָא נָטַר לֵיהּ, דָּוִד מַלְכָּא כַּדְקָא חֲזֵי, מַלְכוּתָא אִתְעֲדֵי מִנֵּיהּ, כָּל הַהוּא זִמְנָא. וְהָכֵי אוֹלִיפְנָא, הַאי זֹאת אִתְרְמִיזָא בְּמַלְכוּתָא דִּלְעֵילָּא, וְאִתְרְמִיזָא בִּירוּשָׁלֵם קַרְתָּא קַדִּישָׁא.

402. Come and behold: Because King David did not preserve ZOT properly, the kingship was taken away from him during all that time THAT HE FOUGHT WITH ABSHALOM, HIS SON. And so we have learned that this Zot is hinted in the upper Kingdom and in the holy city of Jerusalem.

403. בְּהַהוּא שַׁעֲתָא דְּדָוִד עֲבַר עֲלֵיהּ, נָפַק קָלָא וַאֲמַר, דָּוִד בַּמֶּה דְּאִתְקְטַרַת תִּשְׁתְּרֵי. לָךְ טַרְדִּין מִירוּשְׁלֵם, וּמַלְכוּתָא אִתְעֲדֵי מִינָךְ. מנ״ל, דִּכְתִיב הִנְנִי מֵקִים עָלֶיךָ רָעָה מִבֵּיתֶךָ. מִבֵּיתְךָ דַּיְיקָא, וְהָכֵי הֲוָה, בַּמֶּה דַּעֲבַר בֵּיהּ אִתְעֲנַשׁ, וּמַה דָּוִד מַלְכָּא הָכֵי, שְׁאָר בְּנֵי עָלְמָא עַל אַחַת כַּמָּה וְכַמָּה.

403. When David sinned WITH BATHSHEBA, a voice went forth and said: 'David, You are to be disjoined – as you shall be banished from Jerusalem and the kingship shall be taken away from you – from that with which you were united, NAMELY ZOT, WHICH ALLUDES TO MALCHUT AND TO JERUSALEM.' How do we know this? From the verse, "Behold I will raise up evil against you out of your own house" (II Shmuel 12:11). Actually "your own house," HIS OWN HOUSE, WHICH IS THE SECRET OF NUKVA THAT IS CALLED ZOT. AND THE "EVIL" MENTIONED IN THE VERSE REFERS TO HIS SEPARATION FROM HER. And so he was punished for having sinned. BECAUSE HE DID NOT PRESERVE THE GRADE OF ZOT, WHICH IS THE SECRET OF THE COVENANT, HE WAS SEPARATED FROM HER. And if David was punished so, even more so the rest of the world!

404. פָּתַח אִידָךְ וַאֲמַר לוּלֵי ה' עֶזְרָתָה לִי כִּמְעַט שָׁכְנָה דוּמָה נַפְשִׁי.

תָּאנָא. בַּמֶּה זָכָאן יִשְׂרָאֵל, דְּלָא נַחְתֵּי לַגֵּיהִנֹּם, כִּשְׁאָר עַמִּין עכו"ם, וְלָא אִתְמַסְרָן בִּידוֹי דְּדוּמָה, בְּהַאי אָת.

404. Another continued the discussion with the verse, "Unless Hashem had been my help, my soul had soon dwelt in silence (Heb. *Dumah*)" (Tehilim 94:17). We have learned why Yisrael are saved from going down to Gehenom, unlike idol-worshipping nations, and are not handed over to the hands of Dumah, WHO IS THE GOVERNOR OF GEHENOM. They have merit because of the sign OF THE COVENANT.

405. דְּהָכֵי תָּאנָא, בְּשַׁעֲתָא דְּבַר נָשׁ נָפִיק מֵעָלְמָא, כַּמָּה חֲבִילֵי טְהִירִין אִתְפַּקְּדָן עֲלֵיהּ. זְקִיפִין עֵינָא וְחָמָאן הַאי אָת, דְּהוּא קְיָימָא דְּקוּדְשָׁא, אִתְפָּרְשָׁן מִנֵּיהּ. וְלָא אִתְיְיהִיב בִּידוֹי דְּדוּמָה לְנַחְתָּא לַגֵּיהִנֹּם, דְּכָל מַאן דְּאִתְמְסַר בִּידוֹי, נָחִית לַגֵּיהִנֹּם וַדַּאי.

405. Because we have learned that when a person passes from this world, hoards of Klipot fall upon him TO HURT HIM. But when they hold up their eyes and see this sign, which is the sacred covenant, they leave him and he is not handed over to the hands of Dumah to be taken down to Gehenom. Whoever is handed over to his hands shall definitely go down to Gehenom.

406. וּמֵהַאי אָת, דָּחֲלִין עִלָּאִין וְתַתָּאִין, וְדִינִין בִּישִׁין לָא שָׁלְטִין בֵּיהּ בְּבַר נָשׁ, אִי אִיהוּ זָכֵי לְנַטוֹרֵי לֵיהּ, לְהַאי אָת, בְּגִין דְּהוּא אִתְאַחִיד בִּשְׁמָא דְּקוּדְשָׁא בְּרִיךְ הוּא.

406. The upper and lower beings are afraid of this sign and do not inflict evil Judgments on the man who preserves it, because, by doing so, he becomes united with the Name of the Holy One, blessed be He.

407. כֵּיוָן דְּדָוִד מַלְכָּא לָא נָטַר אָת קְיָימָא דָּא כְּדְקָא חָזֵי, אִתְעֲדֵי מִנֵּיהּ מַלְכוּתָא, וְאִתְטְרֵיד מִירוּשָׁלַיִם. מִיַּד דָּחִיל, דְּסָבַר דְּיֵיחֲתוּן לֵיהּ מִיַּד, וְיִמְסְרוּן לֵיהּ בִּידוֹי דְּדוּמָה, וִימוּת בְּהַהוּא עָלְמָא, עַד דְּאִתְבַּשַּׂר בֵּיהּ, דִּכְתִיב גַּם ה' הֶעֱבִיר חַטָּאתְךָ לֹא תָמוּת. בֵּיהּ שַׁעֲתָא פָּתַח וְאָמַר לוּלֵי ה' עֶזְרָתָה לִּי כִּמְעַט שָׁכְנָה דוּמָה נַפְשִׁי.

407. Because David did not preserve this sign of the covenant as he should have, kingship was taken away from him and he was banished from Jerusalem. He was afraid that he would immediately be brought down to be handed over to Dumah and that he would die in the World of Truth WITHOUT MERITING SPIRITUAL LIFE. Then he was given the good news. As it is written: "Hashem also has commuted your sin, you shall not die" (II Shmuel 12:13). At that very moment he exclaimed, "Unless Hashem had been my help, my soul had soon dwelt in silence (Dumah)," MEANING THAT HE WOULD HAVE BEEN HANDED OVER TO THE ANGEL DUMAH.

408. פָּתַח אִידָךְ וַאֲמַר מַאי הַאי דַּאֲמַר דָּוִד וְהַרְאַנִי אוֹתוֹ וְאֶת נָוֵהוּ. מַאן יָכִיל לְמֶחֱמֵי לֵיהּ לְקֻדְשָׁא בְּרִיךְ הוּא. אֶלָּא הָכִי תָּנִינָן, בְּהַהִיא שַׁעֲתָא דְּאִתְגְּזַר עֲלֵיהּ הַהוּא עוֹנָשָׁא, וְדָוִד יָדַע דְּעַל דְּלָא נָטַר הַאי אָת כִּדְקָא יָאוֹת, אִתְעֲנַשׁ בְּהַאי, דְּכֹלָּא כַּחֲדָא אֲחִידָא, וְכֹלָּא מִתְרְמִיז בְּהַאי אָת, וְלָא אִקְרֵי צַדִּיק, מַאן דְּלָא נָטַר לֵיהּ כִּדְקָא יָאוֹת, הֲוָה בָּעֵי בְּעוּתֵיהּ, וַאֲמַר וְהַרְאַנִי אוֹתוֹ וְאֶת נָוֵהוּ.

408. Another one continued the discussion by asking what is meant by the words of David, "and show me both him, and his habitation" (II Shmuel 15:25), for who is able to see the Holy One, blessed be He? AND HE REPLIES, "We have learned that at the moment when ABSHALOM decreed David's punishment, David knew that it was because BY SINING WITH BAT-SHEVA he did not preserve the sign, as he should have. So he was punished in this, IN HAVING HIS KINGDOM TAKEN AWAY FROM HIM, because everything is united as one and everything is alluded to in the sign, MALCHUT OF ABOVE AND JERUSALEM. And one is not a righteous man if he does not preserve the sign properly. For this reason, David prayed and said: "…and show me both him (Heb. *oto*), and his habitation."

409. מַאי אוֹתוֹ. דָּא אָת קְיָימָא קַדִּישָׁא, דְּהָא דָּחִילְנָא דְּאִתְאֲבִיד מִנַּאי. מ"ט. בְּגִין דִּתְרֵין אִלֵּין מַלְכוּתָא וִירוּשְׁלֵם בְּהַאי אֲחִידָן, וּבְגִין כָּךְ תָּלֵי בְּבָעוּתֵיהּ אוֹתוֹ וְאֶת נָוֵהוּ, דְּיִתְהַדַּר מַלְכוּתָא דְּהַאי אָת לְאַתְרֵיהּ. וְכֹלָּא חַד מִלָּה.

409. What is *oto?* It is the sign of the holy covenant (Heb. *ot*), and David was afraid that he had lost it. WHY DID HE THINK THAT HE HAD LOST THE SIGN OF THE COVENANT? Because these two – the kingdom and Jerusalem – are both attached TO THIS SIGN OF THE COVENANT. SO AS THE KINGSHIP WAS TAKEN AWAY FROM HIM AND HE WAS BANISHED FROM JERUSALEM, HE THOUGHT THAT THE SIGN OF THE COVENANT WAS ALSO TAKEN AWAY FROM HIM. Therefore in his prayer he linked "*oto*" and "His habitation" together, BECAUSE *"OTO"* ALLUDES TO THE SIGN THE COVENANT AND "HIS HABITATION" TO MALCHUT. So, he prayed that Malchut (Kingdom) which is attached to this sign (Heb. *ot*), may return to its place – and both subjects are actually the same.

410. פָּתַח אִידָךְ וַאֲמַר וּמִבְּשָׂרִי אֶחֱזֶה אֱלוֹהַּ. מַאי וּמִבְּשָׂרִי, וּמֵעַצְמִי מִבָּעֵי לֵיהּ. אֶלָּא מִבְּשָׂרִי מַמָּשׁ. וּמַאי הִיא. דִּכְתִיב וּבָשָׂר קֹדֶשׁ יַעַבְרוּ מֵעָלָיִךְ. וּכְתִיב וְהָיְתָה בְרִיתִי בִּבְשַׂרְכֶם. דְּתַנְיָא בְּכָל זִמְנָא דְּאִתְרְשִׁים בַּר נָשׁ, בְּהַאי רְשִׁימָא קַדִּישָׁא, דְּהַאי אָת, מִנֵּיהּ חָמֵי לְקֻדְשָׁא בְּרִיךְ הוּא, מִנֵּיהּ מַמָּשׁ, וְנִשְׁמְתָא קַדִּישָׁא אִתְאַחֲדַת בֵּיהּ.

410. Another one then continued with the text: "from my flesh shall I see Eloha" (Iyov 19:26). AND HE ASKS: What is "my flesh"? He should have said 'myself.' AND HE REPLIED THAT "from my flesh" is definitely correct, REFERRING TO YESOD WHICH IS CALLED FLESH, HE SAID: "…SHALL I SEE ELOHA." What is the meaning of "and the holy flesh is passed from you…" (Yirmeyah 11:15), WHICH IS THE SECRET OF THE HOLY COVENANT, and: "and my covenant shall be in your flesh…" (Beresheet 17:13), WHICH APPLIES TO YESOD. We have learned that as long as a man is stamped by the holy imprint of this sign, THAT THIS SIGN OF THE COVENANT IS STAMPED IN HIM AND GUARDS HIM ALWAYS, then from within it he can actually see the Holy One, blessed be He, and the holy soul remains attached to him in the sign of the covenant.

411. וְאִי לָא זָכֵי, דְּלָא נָטִיר הַאי אָת, מַה כְּתִיב מִנִּשְׁמַת אֱלוֹהַּ יֹאבֵדוּ. דְּהָא רְשִׁימוּ דְּקֻדְשָׁא בְּרִיךְ הוּא לָא אִתְנְטִיר. וְאִי זָכֵי וּנְטִיר לֵיהּ, שְׁכִינְתָּא לָא אִתְפְּרַשׁ מִנֵּיהּ.

411. But if he is not deserving, because he did not preserve this sign, what is

written of him? IT IS WRITTEN: "By the breath (or, soul) of Eloha they perish..." (Iyov 4:9), because the imprint of the Holy One, blessed be He, has not been preserved. If he has the merit of preserving it, then the Shechinah shall never depart from him.

412. אֵימָתַי מִתְקַיְימָא בֵּיהּ, כַּד אִתְנְסִיב, וְהַאי אָת עָיֵיל בְּאַתְרֵיהּ, אִשְׁתַּתְּפוּ כַּחֲדָא וְאִקְרֵי חַד שְׁמָא, כְּדֵין חֶסֶד עִלָּאָה שַׁרְיָיא עֲלַיְיהוּ. בְּאָן אֲתַר שַׁרְיָיא. בְּסִטְרָא דִּדְכוּרָא. וּמַאן חֶסֶד. חֶסֶד אֵל, דְּאָתֵי וְנָפַק מֵחָכְמָה עִלָּאָה, וְאִתְעַטַּר בִּדְכוּרָא, וּבְגִין כָּךְ אִתְבַּסְּמַת נוּקְבָּא.

412. AND HE ASKS: When does THE SHECHINAH reside within him? AND HE SAID: When he marries, and this sign enters to its place, TO THE SHECHINAH. Then they are attached together, THE MALE AND THE FEMALE, WHO ARE THE SIGN OF THE COVENANT AND THE SHECHINAH, and are called by one name, and supernal Chesed rests upon them. Where does CHESED rest? It rests at the side of the male. And what is Chesed? It is Chesed IN THE NAME of *El*, that comes forth from the supernal Chochmah and adorns the male as a crown over his head. And by these CHASSADIM, the female is sweetened.

413 תּוּ תָּנֵינָן, אֱלוֹהַּ: הָכֵי הוּא, אֲמַר לוֹ נְהִירוּ דְּחָכְמְתָא. ו' דְּכַר. ה' נוּקְבָּא. אִשְׁתַּתְּפוּ כַּחֲדָא, אֱלוֹהַּ אִקְרֵי. וְנִשְׁמְתָא קַדִּישָׁא מֵהַאי אֲתַר אִתְאַחֲדַת, וְכֹלָּא תַּלְיָא בְּהַאי אָת.

413. And we have learned further (IN EXPLANATION OF THE PREVIOUS PASSAGE) THAT the name Eloha (*El-Vav-Hei*) is interpreted as follows: *El* is the Light of Chochmah, *Vav* is the male, and *Hei* is the female. MALE AND FEMALE are attached together and are called BY ONE NAME, Eloha. So the holy soul clings to this place, and everything depends on the sign OF THE COVENANT.

414. וְעַל דָּא כְּתִיב, וּמִבְּשָׂרִי אֶחֱזֶה אֱלוֹהַּ. דָּא שְׁלִימוּתָא דְּכֹלָּא, מִבְּשָׂרִי מַמָּשׁ, מֵהַאי אָת מַמָּשׁ. וְעַל דָּא זַכָּאִין אִינוּן יִשְׂרָאֵל קַדִּישִׁין, דַּאֲחִידָן בֵּיהּ בְּקֻדְשָׁא בְּרִיךְ הוּא, זַכָּאִין אִינוּן בְּעָלְמָא דֵין, וּבְעָלְמָא

דְּאָתֵי, עֲלַיְיהוּ כְּתִיב וְאַתֶּם הַדְּבֵקִים בַּה' וְגוּ' וּבְגִין כָּךְ חַיִּים כֻּלְּכֶם הַיּוֹם.

414. Hence the words, "from my flesh shall I see Eloha," REFERRING TO THE NAME ELOHA, represent overall completion, because it is "from my flesh," my own – WHICH IS YESOD THAT IS CALLED FLESH – the actual sign of the covenant. Therefore, happy are the holy Yisrael who are united with the Holy One, blessed be He; happy is their portion in this world and the World to Come. Of them, it is written: "You that cleave to Hashem your Elohim are alive every one of you this day" (Devarim 4:4)."

415. אָמַר רִבִּי אַבָּא, וּמַה בְּכָל כָּךְ אַתּוּן חַכִּימִין, וְאַתּוּן יָתְבִין הָכָא, אֲמְרוּ לֵיהּ אִי צִפּוֹרָאָה יִתְעַקְּרוּ מֵאַתְרַיְיהוּ לָא יָדְעִין לְאָן טָאסָן, הה"ד כְּצִפּוֹר נוֹדֶדֶת מִן קִנָּהּ כֵּן אִישׁ נוֹדֵד מִמְּקוֹמוֹ.

415. Rabbi Aba said: You are all so wise, yet you sit here! They said to him: If birds are uprooted from their homes, they shall not know where to fly. As it is written: "As a bird that wanders from her nest, so is a man who wanders from his place" (Mishlei 27:8).

416. וְאַתְרָא דָא זָכֵי לָן לְאוֹרַיְיתָא, וְהַאי אוֹרְחָא דִּילָן. בְּכָל לֵילְיָא, פַּלְגוּתָא אֲנַן נָיְימִין, וּפַלְגוּתָא אֲנַן עָסְקִין בְּאוֹרַיְיתָא. וְכַד אֲנַן קָיְימִין בְּצַפְרָא, רֵיחֵי חַקְלָא, וְנַהֲרֵי מַיָּא, נַהֲרִין לָן אוֹרַיְיתָא, וְאִתְיַישְּׁבַת בְּלִבָּן.

416. So this place, WHERE WE LIVE, has given us the advantage of studying Torah, and also our habit to sleep half the night and to study Torah during the second half. When we rise in the morning, the smell of the fields and water streams illuminates the words of Torah, and they are instilled to our hearts.

417. וְאַתַר דָּא הָא דַּיְינוּהּ לְעֵילָא זִמְנָא חֲדָא, וְכַמָּה סָרְכֵי תְּרֵיסִין, אִסְתַּלְּקוּ בְּהַהוּא דִּינָא, עַל עוֹנְשָׁא דְּאוֹרַיְיתָא, וּכְדֵין אִשְׁתַּדְּלוּתָא דִּילָן יְמָמָא, וְלֵילְיָא בְּאוֹרַיְיתָא הוּא, וְאַתְרָא דָא, קָא מְסַיְּיעָא לָן, וּמַאן

דְּאִתְפְּרַשׁ מִכָּאן כְּמַאן דְּאִתְפְּרַשׁ מֵחַיֵּי עָלְמָא.

417. This place was once punished from above, and many great scholars died because they neglected the study of Torah. Since then, our occupation is studying Torah, day and night, and this place helps us. So whoever leaves this place acts as if he were abandoning eternal life.

418. זָקִיף יְדוֹי רַבִּי אַבָּא, וּבְרֵיךְ לוֹן. יָתְבוּ עַד דְּנָהַר יְמָמָא, בָּתַר דְּנָהַר יְמָמָא, אֲמַרוּ לְאִינּוּן דַּרְדְּקֵי דְּקַמַּיְיהוּ, פּוּקוּ וַחֲמוּ, אִי נָהַר יְמָמָא, וְכָל חַד לֵימָא מִלָּה חַדְתָּא דְאוֹרַיְיתָא, לְהַאי גַּבְרָא רַבָּא.

418. Rabbi Aba raised up his hands, and blessed them. They sat until daylight shone. And after daylight had shone, they told the children who sat in front of them, "Go out and see if day has come." And each one of you should give a new explanation of the Torah to this great man, A REFERENCE TO RABBI ABA!

419. נָפְקוּ וְחָמוּ, דְּנָהַר יְמָמָא, אֲמַר חַד מִנַּיְיהוּ, זַמִּין הַאי יוֹמָא, אֶשָּׁא מִלְּעֵילָא. אֲמַר אָחֳרָא, וּבְהַךְ בֵּיתָא. אֲמַר אָחֳרָא, חַד סָבָא הָכָא, דְּזַמִּין הַאי יוֹמָא לְאִתּוֹקְדָא בְּנוּרָא דָא, אֲמַר ר' אַבָּא, רַחֲמָנָא לִישֵׁזְבָן.

419. They went outside and saw that day had come. One of them said: It is destined that a fire from above shall appear on this day! Another one added: And in this house! Another then said: An old man here is destined to be burned by this fire on this day! Rabbi Aba said: Let the Merciful One save us!

420. תָּוַוה, וְלָא יָכִיל לְמַלְּלָא, אֲמַר קוּטְרָא דְהוּרְמָנָא, בְּאַרְעָא אִתְפָּסַת. וְכָךְ הֲוָה, דְּהַהוּא יוֹמָא, חָמוּ חַבְרַיָּיא, אַפֵּי שְׁכִינְתָּא, וְאִסְתַּחֲרוּ בְּאֶשָּׁא, וְר' אַבָּא אִתְלַהֲטוּ אַנְפּוֹי כְּנוּרָא, מֵחֶדְוָותָא דְאוֹרַיְיתָא.

420. RABBI ABA was astonished and could not speak. Then he said: The secret of the supernal government is grasped on earth, BECAUSE EVEN THE

CHILDREN KNOW HOW TO TELL THE FUTURE. And so it was! On that same day, the friends saw the face of the Shechinah and were surrounded by fire. And Rabbi Aba's face was aflame with the light of the fire from the joy of the Torah.

421. תָּאנָא, כָּל הַהוּא יוֹמָא לָא נָפְקוּ כֻּלְהוּ מִבֵּיתָא, וּבֵיתָא אִתְקַטַּר בְּקִיטְרָא, וַהֲווֹ חַדְתָּאן מִלֵּי בְּגַוַוייְהוּ, כְּאִלּוּ קַבְלוּ הַהוּא יוֹמָא אוֹרַייְתָא, מְטוּרָא דְסִינַי. בָּתַר דְּאִסְתַּלָּקוּ, לָא הֲווֹ יַדְעֵי, אִי הוּא יְמָמָא וְאִי לֵילְיָא. אָמַר רְבִּי אַבָּא, בְּעוֹד דַּאֲנַן קַייְמִין, לֵימָא כָּל חַד מִינָן, מִלָּה חַדְתָּא דְחָכְמְתָא, לְאַקְשְׁרָא טִיבוּ לְמָארֵיה דְּבֵיתָא, מָרֵיה דְהִלּוּלָא.

421. We have learned that all that day, they all did not leave the house, which was enveloped with fire and flame. And the words that were uttered brought happiness among them, as though they received Torah on that day from Mount Sinai. So that when they left that place, they did not know whether it was day or night. Rabbi Aba said: As long as we are here, each of us should say a new word of wisdom, in order to present a fitting return to the landlord, the host of the celebration.

422. פָּתַח חַד וְאָמַר אַשְׁרֵי תִּבְחַר וּתְקָרֵב יִשְׁכֹּן חֲצֵרֶיךָ וגו'. בְּקַדְמֵיתָא חֲצֵרֶיךָ, לְבָתַר בֵּיתֶךָ, וּלְבָתַר הֵיכָלֶךָ. דָּא פְּנִימָאָה מִן דָּא, וְדָא לְעֵילָא מִן דָּא. יִשְׁכֹּן חֲצֵרֶיךָ בְּקַדְמֵיתָא, כְּד"א וְהָיָה הַנִּשְׁאָר בְּצִיּוֹן וְהַנּוֹתָר בִּירוּשָׁלַם קָדוֹשׁ יֵאָמֶר לוֹ.

422. One of them opened the discussion with the verse, "Blessed is the man whom You choose and cause to approach You, that he may dwell in Your courts...; we shall be satisfied with the goodness of Your house, the holy place of Your temple" (Tehilim 65:5). THE VERSE first SAYS: "Your courts," then "Your house," and then "Your temple" – one within the other and one above the other. THIS MEANS THAT MALCHUT HAS THREE GRADES FROM BOTTOM TO TOP, EACH ONE HIGHER THAN THE OTHER. The first is "Your court," WHICH ALLUDES TO THE ASPECTS OF NETZACH, HOD, AND YESOD THAT ARE OUTSIDE OF THE BODY AND ARE CALLED "YOUR COURTS." As it is written: "And is shall come to pass, that he that is left in Zion, and he that remains in Jerusalem, shall be called holy"

(Yeshayah 4:3). BECAUSE THE ESSENCE OF NETZACH, HOD AND YESOD IS YESOD. ZION IS THE INTERNAL ASPECT OF YESOD AND JERUSALEM ITS EXTERNAL ASPECT; BOTH ARE CALLED "COURTS."

423. נִשְׂבְּעָה בְּטוּב בֵּיתֶךָ לְבָתַר, כְּד"א בְּחָכְמָה יִבָּנֶה בָּיִת. הַחָכְמָה יִבָּנֶה בָּיִת, לָא כְתִיב, דְּאִי כְּתִיב הָכֵי הֲוָה מַשְׁמַע דְּחָכְמָה בַּיִת אִקְרֵי, אֶלָּא כְּתִיב בְּחָכְמָה יִבָּנֶה בָּיִת, הַיְינוּ דִכְתִּיב, וְנָהָר יוֹצֵא מֵעֵדֶן לְהַשְׁקוֹת אֶת הַגָּן וְגו'.

423. The verse "We shall be satisfied with the goodness of Your house" comes next, MEANING THAT AFTER THE GRADE OF THE COURT IS COMPLETED, HE THEN MERITS THE GRADE OF THE HOUSE. It is written: "Through wisdom is a house built" (Mishlei 24:3); it is not written: "wisdom will build a house," which would have meant that the wisdom is called a house. Therefore, "Through wisdom is a house built" MEANS THAT WHEN MALCHUT RECEIVES CHOCHMAH, IT IS CALLED A HOUSE. This relates to the verse, "a river went out of Eden to water the garden" (Beresheet 2:10), WHICH IS THE SECRET OF BINAH RETURNING TO CHOCHMAH, AND THE GARDEN IS MALCHUT.

424. קְדוֹשׁ הֵיכָלֶךָ, לְבָתַר, דָּא הוּא שְׁלִימָא דְּכֹלָּא, דְּהָכֵי תָּנִינָן, מַהוּ הֵיכָל. כְּלוֹמַר ה"י כ"ל, הַאי וְהַאי, וְכֹלָּא אִשְׁתְּלֵים כַּחֲדָא.

424. Finally comes "the holy place of Your temple (Heb. heichal)," which is the completion of all. As we have learned, heichal (Hei Yud Caf Lamed) means Hei Kol (Hei Yud Caf Lamed). HE WHO MERITS THIS GRADE IS ASTONISHED AND EXCLAIMS, "HOW WAS ALL (HEB. KOL) THIS REVEALED!" And all here reaches completion, WHICH MEANS THAT EVERYTHING HAS NOW REACHED FULL PERFECTION.

425. רֵישָׁא דִּקְרָא מַה מוֹכַח, דִּכְתִיב אַשְׁרֵי תִּבְחַר וּתְקָרֵב יִשְׁכֹּן חֲצֵרֶיךָ. הַאי מַאן דְּאַקְרִיב בְּרֵיהּ קָרְבָּנָא קַמֵּי קֻדְשָׁא בְּרִיךְ הוּא, רַעֲוָא דְּקֻדְשָׁא בְּרִיךְ הוּא, בְּהַהוּא קָרְבָּנָא, וְאִתְרְעֵי בֵיהּ, וְקָרֵיב לֵיהּ, וְשַׁוֵּי מְדוֹרֵיהּ בִּתְרֵין אַדְרִין, וְאָחִיד לְהַאי וּלְהַאי, דְּאִינוּן תְּרֵין אִתְקַשְּׁרוּ

כַּחֲדָא. דִּכְתִיב יִשְׁכֹּן חֲצֵרֶיךָ. חֲצֵרֶיךָ וַדַּאי תְּרֵי.

425. What does the beginning of the verse teach us? The verse opens, "Blessed is the man whom You choose and cause to approach to You, that he may dwell in Your courts." THIS MEANS THAT whoever offers his son as a sacrifice before the Holy One, blessed be He, CIRCUMCISES HIM, gives something desirable to the Holy One, blessed be, Who then wants him and brings him closer to Himself. There he dwells in the two chambers OF YESOD, WHICH ARE ZION AND JERUSALEM. He clings to both of them, because they are joined as one, as it is written: "that he may dwell in Your courts," "courts" being two!

426. בְּגִינֵי כָךְ, חֲסִידֵי קַדְמָאֵי סָבָאן דְּהָכָא, כַּד מַקְרִיבִין בְּנַיְיהוּ לְקָרְבָּנָא דָא, פָּתְחֵי וְאָמְרֵי, אַשְׁרֵי תִבְחַר וּתְקָרֵב יִשְׁכֹּן חֲצֵרֶיךָ. אִינוּן דְּקַיְימֵי עֲלַיְיהוּ אָמְרֵי, נִשְׂבְּעָה בְּטוּב בֵּיתֶךָ קְדוֹשׁ הֵיכָלֶךָ. לְבָתַר מְבָרֵךְ אֲשֶׁר קב״ו לְהַכְנִיסוֹ בִּבְרִיתוֹ שֶׁל אַבְרָהָם אָבִינוּ. וְאִינוּן דְּקַיְימֵי עֲלַיְיהוּ אָמְרֵי, כְּשֵׁם שֶׁהִכְנַסְתּוֹ לַבְּרִית וכו'.

426. This is why the pious men who lived here in earlier days, the grandfathers of these people, when they offered their sons to this sacrifice OF CIRCUMCISION began by saying, "Blessed is the man whom You choose, and causes to approach to You, that he may dwell in Your courts." Those who were present there said: "We shall be satisfied with the goodness of Your house, of the holy place of Your temple." After this, he would say the blessing, '…who sanctified us with His commandments and commanded us to initiate the child in the covenant of the patriarch Abraham.' And those present responded: 'Just as you have initiated him to the covenant…'

427. וְתָנִינָן, בְּקַדְמֵיתָא לְבָעֵי בַּר נָשׁ רַחֲמִין עֲלֵיהּ, וּלְבָתַר עַל אָחֳרָא, דִּכְתִיב וְכִפֶּר בַּעֲדוֹ בְּקַדְמֵיתָא, וּלְבָתַר וּבְעַד כָּל קְהַל יִשְׂרָאֵל. וַאֲנַן אוֹרְחָא דָא נַקְטִינָן, וְהָכֵי שַׁפִּיר וְחָזֵי לְקַמָּאן.

427. As we have learned, a person should first ask for mercy for himself, and then for another, as it is written: "and he shall make an atonement for himself" at first, and afterward "for all the Congregation of Yisrael"

(Vayikra 16:17). We have chosen this path, which is good and suitable for us. THEREFORE THE HOST OF THE CELEBRATION OF THE CIRCUMCISION SHOULD AT FIRST RECITE VERSES TO ASK FOR MERCY, AND THEN THOSE WHO ARE PRESENT RECITE AFTER HIM.

428. אָמַר רְבִּי אַבָּא, וַדַּאי כָּךְ הוּא וְיָאוֹת מִלָּה, וּמַאן דְּלָא אָמַר הָכֵי, אַפֵּיק גַּרְמֵיה מֵעֲשָׂרָה חוּפוֹת דִּזַמִּין קֻדְשָׁא בְּרִיךְ הוּא לְמֶעְבַּד לְצַדִּיקַיָּא, בְּעָלְמָא דְּאָתֵי, וְכֻלְּהוּ מִתְקַשְׁרָן בְּהַאי. וּבְגִינֵי כָּךְ, עֲשָׂרָה מִלֵּי דִמְהֵימְנוּתָא אִית בְּהַאי קְרָא, אַשְׁרֵי תִּבְחַר וּתְקָרֵב וגו', וְכָל מִלָּה וּמִלָּה חַד חוּפָּה אִתְעֲבֵיד מִנָּה.

428. Rabbi Aba said: "This is definitely well said," REFERRING TO THE VERSE, "BLESSED IS THE MAN WHOM YOU CHOOSE..." He who does not recite this is excluded from under the ten canopies that the Holy One, blessed be He, shall prepare in the future for the righteous men in the World to Come. And everyone should be attached to this VERSE! Therefore this verse contains ten words of faith, "Blessed is the man..." and from each word a canopy is prepared.

429. זַכָּאָה חוּלָקֵיכוֹן בְּעָלְמָא דָא, וּבְעָלְמָא דְּאָתֵי, דְּהָא אוֹרַיְיתָא מִתְקַשְׁרָא בְּלִבַּיְיכוּ, כְּאִילּוּ קַיְימִיתוּ בְּגוּפַיְיכוּ בְּטוּרָא דְסִינַי, בְּשַׁעְתָּא דְאִתְיְהִיבַת אוֹרַיְיתָא לְיִשְׂרָאֵל.

429. Happy are your portions in this world and in the World to Come, as Torah is absorbed into your hearts, as if you were standing yourselves on Mount Sinai at the time when the Torah was given to Yisrael.

430. פָּתַח אִידָךְ וַאֲמַר מִזְבַּח אֲדָמָה תַּעֲשֶׂה לִי וְזָבַחְתָּ עָלָיו אֶת עֹלֹתֶיךָ וְאֶת שְׁלָמֶיךָ וגו'. תָּאנָא, כָּל מַאן דְּקָרֵיב בְּרֵיה לְקָרְבָּנָא דָא, כְּאִילּוּ אַקְרִיב כָּל קָרְבָּנִין דְּעָלְמָא, לְקַמֵּיה דְקֻדְשָׁא בְּרִיךְ הוּא, וּכְאִילּוּ בָּנֵי מַדְבְּחָא שְׁלֵימָתָא קַמֵּיה.

430. Another person began by saying, "An altar of earth you shall make for Me, and shall sacrifice thereon your burnt offerings and your peace offerings..."

(Shemot 20:21). We have learned that whoever offers his son as a sacrifice THROUGH CIRCUMCISION is as deserving as one who has offered all the sacrifices in the world before the Holy One, blessed be He. It is as though he were building a perfect altar to Him!

431. בְּגִינֵי כָךְ, בָּעֵי לְסַדְּרָא מַדְבְּחָא, בְּמָאנָא חַד מַלְיָיא אַרְעָא, לְמִגְזַר עֲלֵיה הַאי קְיָימָא קַדִּישָׁא, וְאִתְחֲשִׁיב קַמֵּי קֻדְשָׁא בְּרִיךְ הוּא, כְּאִילּוּ אַדְבַּח עֲלֵיה עֲלָוָון וְקָרְבָּנִין, עָאנָא וְתוֹרֵי.

431. Thus, the circumcision to this holy covenant should be performed over an altar prepared by using a vessel full of earth. It is considered before the Holy One, blessed be He, as if he had offered sacrifices of sheep and oxen upon the altar.

432. וְנִיחָא לֵיה יַתִּיר מִכֻּלְּהוּ, דִּכְתִיב וְזָבַחְתָּ עָלָיו אֶת עֹלֹתֶיךָ וְאֶת שְׁלָמֶיךָ וְגו'. בְּכָל הַמָּקוֹם אֲשֶׁר אַזְכִּיר אֶת שְׁמִי. מַהוּ אַזְכִּיר אֶת שְׁמִי. דָּא מִילָה, דִּכְתִיב בָּהּ סוֹד ה' לִירֵאָיו וּבְרִיתוֹ לְהוֹדִיעָם.

432. And it, THE CIRCUMCISION, pleases the Holy One, blessed be He, more than all THE OTHER SACRIFICES, as it is written: "and shall sacrifice thereon your burnt offerings and your peace offerings...in every place where I mention My name..." What do the words "I mention My name" mean? They refer to circumcision, as it is written: "The secret of Hashem is with them that fear Him, and He will reveal to them his covenant" (Tehilim 25:14). SO THE COVENANT APPEARS THERE!

433. הַאי מִזְבַּח אֲדָמָה וַדַּאי כְּמָה דַּאֲמִינָא. בַּתְרֵיה מַה כְּתִיב, וְאִם מִזְבַּח אֲבָנִים תַּעֲשֶׂה לִי. רֶמֶז לְגִיּוֹרָא כַּד אִתְגַּיַּיר, דְּאִיהוּ מֵעַם קְשֵׁי קְדַל, וּקְשֵׁי לִבָּא, הַאי אִקְרֵי מִזְבַּח אֲבָנִים.

433. This "altar of earth" is as I have stated. Next, it is written: "And if they make Me an altar of stones" (Shemot 20:22), which is an allusion to the proselyte who comes from a stiff-necked and stony-hearted people. This is what is referred to as an altar of stones.

434. לֹא תִבְנֶה אֶתְהֶן גָּזִית. מָה הוּא. דְּבָעֵי לְאַעֲלָא לֵיה בְּפוּלְחָנָא

דְּקֻדְשָׁא בְּרִיךְ הוּא, וְלָא יִגְזַר יָתֵיהּ, עַד דְּיִנְשֵׁי פּוּלְחָנָא אָחֳרָא דַּעֲבַד עַד הָכָא, וְיַעֲדֵי מִנֵּיהּ הַהוּא קַשְׁיוּ דְלִבָּא.

434. What is the meaning of the verse, "you shall not build it of hewn stones?" (Ibid.) IT MEANS THAT the proselyte should enter to the service of the Holy One, blessed be He, but should not be circumcised until he has forgotten the idol worshipping that he practiced until then and the hardness is removed from his heart.

435. וְאִי אִתְגְּזַר, וְלָא אַעֲדֵי מִנֵּיהּ הַהוּא קַשְׁיָא דְלִבָּא, לְמֵיעַל בְּפוּלְחָנָא קַדִּישָׁא דְּקֻדְשָׁא בְּרִיךְ הוּא, הֲרֵי הוּא כְּהַאי פְּסִילָא דְּאַבְנָא, דְּגָזְרֵי לֵיהּ מֵהַאי גִיסָא, וּמֵהַאי גִיסָא, וְאִשְׁתְּאַר אַבְנָא כִּדְבְקַדְמֵיתָא. בְּגִין כָּךְ לֹא תִבְנֶה אֶתְהֶן גָּזִית. דְּאִי אִשְׁתְּאַר בְּקַשְׁיוּתֵיהּ, כִּי חַרְבְּךָ הֵנַפְתָּ עָלֶיהָ וַתְּחַלֲלֶיהָ, כְּלוֹמַר, הַהוּא גְּזִירוּ דְּאִתְגְּזַר לָא מְהַנְיָא לֵיהּ.

435. Because if he is circumcised before he removes the hardness from his heart in order to join in the holy service of the Holy One, blessed be He, he will be like a statue of stone that is hewn on all sides, but still remains a stone. Because of this, "You shall not build it of hewn stones," because if he still has harshness in his heart, then "you lift up your tool upon it, you have defiled it." This means that the circumcision performed on him serves no purpose.

436. בְּגִינֵי כָךְ, זַכָּאָה חוּלָקֵיהּ דְּמַאן דְּאַקְרִיב הַאי קָרְבָּנָא בְּחֶדְוָותָא בִּרְעוּתָא קַמֵּי קֻדְשָׁא בְּרִיךְ הוּא, וּבָעֵי לְמֶחֱדֵי בְּהַאי חוּלָקָא, כָּל יוֹמָא, דִּכְתִיב וְיִשְׂמְחוּ כָל חוֹסֵי בָךְ לְעוֹלָם יְרַנֵּנוּ וְתָסֵךְ עָלֵימוֹ וְיַעְלְצוּ בְךָ אֹהֲבֵי שְׁמֶךָ.

436. Therefore happy is the fate of he who willingly and joyously offers the sacrifice to the Holy One, blessed be He. And one should rejoice with this person all day long, as it is written: "But let all those that put their trust in You rejoice, let them ever shout for joy, because You defend them, and let those who love Your name be joyful in You" (Tehilim 5:12).

437. פָּתַח אִידָךְ וַאֲמַר, וַיְהִי אַבְרָם בֶּן תִּשְׁעִים שָׁנָה וְתֵשַׁע שָׁנִים וַיֵּרָא
ה' וגו' אֲנִי אֵל שַׁדַּי הִתְהַלֵּךְ לְפָנַי וגו'. הַאי קְרָא אִית לְעַיְינָא בֵּיהּ,
וְקַשְׁיָא בְּכַמָּה אוֹרְחִין, וְכִי עַד הַשְׁתָּא לָא אִתְגְּלֵי לֵיהּ קָדְשָׁא בְּרִיךְ
הוּא לְאַבְרָהָם, אֶלָּא הָאִידְנָא כַּד מָטָא לְהַנֵּי יוֹמִין, וַיֵּרָא ה' אֶל אַבְרָם,
וְלָא קוֹדֶם. וְהָכְתִיב וַיֹּאמֶר ה' אֶל אַבְרָם. וַה' אָמַר אֶל אַבְרָם. וַיֹּאמֶר
לְאַבְרָם יָדוֹעַ תֵּדַע וגו'. וְהָאִידְנָא מָנֵי חוּשְׁבַּן יוֹמִין, וְכַד מָנֵי לְהוּ,
כְּתִיב וַיֵּרָא ה' אֶל אַבְרָם, אִשְׁתְּמַע דְּעַד הַשְׁתָּא לָא אִתְגְּלֵי עֲלוֹי. וְעוֹד
דִּכְתִיב בֶּן תִּשְׁעִים שָׁנָה וְתֵשַׁע שָׁנִים בְּקַדְמֵיתָא שָׁנָה, וּלְבַסּוֹף שָׁנִים.

437. Another one began by saying, "And when Abram was ninety nine years old (lit. 'ninety year and nine years'), Hashem appeared before Abram and said to him, I am El Shadai; walk before, me, and be perfect" (Beresheet 17:1). This passage should be studied carefully, because in many ways it is difficult. Could it be saying that only now, when Abraham reached such an age, did the Holy One, blessed be He, appear for the first time to Abraham? – That "Hashem appeared to Abram," now and never before? But HOW CAN THIS BE, WHEN it has previously been written: "Now Hashem has said to Abram" (Beresheet 12:1), "And Hashem said to Abram" (Beresheet 13:14), "And He said to Abram, know surely..." (Beresheet 15:13). Yet now, as he is counting and calculating the days, it is written: "Hashem appeared to Abram..." which means that until now Hashem did not appear to him. Further, as it is written: "when Abram was ninety year and nine years," it first SAYS "year" and concludes with "years."

438. אֶלָּא הָכֵי תָּאנָא, כָּל אִינוּן יוֹמִין לָא כְּתִיב וַיֵּרָא, מ"ט, אֶלָּא כָּל
כַּמָּה דַּהֲוָה אָטִים וְסָתִים, קָדְשָׁא בְּרִיךְ הוּא לָא אִתְגְּלֵי עֲלֵיהּ כִּדְקָחֲזֵי.
הָאִידְנָא אִתְגְּלֵי עֲלֵיהּ, דִּכְתִיב וַיֵּרָא. מ"ט. מִשּׁוּם דְּבָעָא לְגַלֵּי בֵּיהּ הַאי
אָת כִּתְרָא קַדִּישָׁא.

438. What is the reason that for all the days until now it was not written: "AND HASHEM appeared TO ABRAM?" We have learned that as long as he was uncircumcised and covered, the Holy One, blessed be He, did not appear to him properly. But now He did appear to him properly, as it is written: "And...appeared." For what purpose? To expose in him the sign of

the covenant, which is the holy crown.

439. וְעוֹד דְּבָעָא קָדְשָׁא בְּרִיךְ הוּא לְאַפָּקָא מִנֵּיה זַרְעָא קַדִּישָׁא, וְקַדִּישָׁא לָא לֶהֱוֵי, בְּעוֹד דְּאִיהוּ אָטִים בִּשְׂרָא, אֶלָּא אֲמַר הַשְׁתָּא דְּהוּא בֶּן תִּשְׁעִים שָׁנָה וְתֵשַׁע שָׁנִים, וְזִמְן קָרִיב הוּא דְּיִנְפּוֹק מִנֵּיה זַרְעָא קַדִּישָׁא, לֶהֱוֵי הוּא קַדִּישָׁא בְּקַדְמֵיתָא, וּלְבָתַר יִנְפּוֹק מִנֵּיה זַרְעָא קַדִּישָׁא. בְּגִין כָּךְ מָנֵי יוֹמוֹי בְּהַאי, וְלָא בְּכָל הַנֵּי זִמְנֵי קַדְמֵיתָא.

439. Furthermore, the Holy One, blessed be He, desired to bring forth holy seed from him, and this could not happen as long as Abraham remained with uncovered flesh. So the Holy One, blessed be He, said "Now, that he is ninety year and nine years old, and the time is close for the holy seed to issue from him, MEANING THAT HE IS ALMOST 100 YEARS OLD, let him first become holy, LET HIM FIRST CIRCUMCISE HIMSELF, and after that let the holy seed come forth." This is why his age was counted in this manner now, REFERRING TO THE "NINE YEARS," BECAUSE HE WAS NOW NEAR THE RIGHT AGE TO BEGET HIS CHILD IN COMPLETE PERFECTION, and not at any other time before, REFERRING TO THE OTHER NINETY YEARS, WHEN HE WAS STILL NOT READY TO BEGET HOLY DESCENDANTS. THEREFORE, THESE YEARS ARE DESCRIBED AS "NINETY YEAR" AND NOT "YEARS."

440. תּוּ תִּשְׁעִים שָׁנָה, דְּכָל יוֹמוֹי קַדְמָאֵי לָא הֲווֹ שָׁנִים אֶלָּא כְּחַד שָׁנָה, דְּלָא הֲווֹ יוֹמוֹי יוֹמִין, הַשְׁתָּא דְּמָטָא לְהַאי, שָׁנִים אִינוּן, וְלָא שָׁנָה.

440. Furthermore, THE VERSE SAYS "ninety year" AND NOT YEARS because all the days before HIS CIRCUMCISION were not years. Rather, THEY WERE CONSIDERED AS one year. THIS IS because his days were not considered as days. Only now, as he reached these years, REFERRING TO THE 99TH YEAR, DURING WHICH HE WAS CIRCUMCISED, were they counted as years for him. Therefore they are not counted as a year, BUT RATHER, AS IT IS WRITTEN: "NINE YEARS."

441 וַיֹּאמֶר אֵלָיו אֲנִי אֵל שַׁדָּי. מַאי מַשְׁמַע, דְּעַד הַשְׁתָּא לָא קָאֲמַר

אֲנִי אֵל שַׁדַּי. אֶלָּא הָכֵי תָאנָא, עֲבַד קָדְשָׁא בְּרִיךְ הוּא כְּתָרִין תַּתָּאִין דְּלָא קַדִּישִׁין לְתַתָּא, וְכָל אִינּוּן דְּלָא אִתְגְּזָרוּ יִסְתָּאֲבוּן בְּהוֹן.

441. Of the verse, "and He said to him, I am El Shadai," HE ASKS, "Why has not THE HOLY ONE, BLESSED BE HE said to him until now 'I am El Shadai'." AND HE REPLIES, "Because we have learned that the Holy One, blessed be He, prepared DOWN BELOW lower Crowns, that are not holy. So all those who are uncircumcised are defiled by them."

442. וּרְשִׁימִין בְּהוֹן, וּמַאי רִישׁוּמָא אִית בְּהוֹן דְּאִתְחֲזֵי בְּהוֹ שִׁי"ן דל"ת, וְלָא יַתִּיר, וּבְגִין כָּךְ אִסְתָּאֲבוּן בְּהוֹ, וְאִתְדַּבְּקוּן בְּהוֹ. בָּתַר דְּאִתְגְּזָרוּ, נָפְקִין מֵאַלֵּין, וְעָאלִין בְּגַדְפוֹי דִּשְׁכִינְתָּא, וְאִתְגַּלְיָא בְּהוֹ יוּ"ד רְשִׁימָא קַדִּישָׁא, אָת קְיָימָא שְׁלִים, וְאִתְרְשִׁים בְּהוֹ שַׁדַּ"י, וְאַשְׁתְּלֵים בְּקִיּוּמָא שְׁלִים, וְעַל דָּא כְּתִיב בְּהַאי, אֲנִי אֵל שַׁדַּי.

442. And these LOWER CROWNS have marks! What are these marks? They are the letters *Shin* and *Dalet;* nothing else appears in them. THIS MEANING THAT THE *YUD* IN THE NAME SHADAI IS MISSING FROM THERE. This is why they are defiled by them, and cling on to them – TO THOSE LOWER CROWNS. After they are circumcised, they leave them – THESE LOWER CROWNS – and enter under the wings of the Shechinah, and *Yud*, which is the mark of holiness, is revealed from within them. This is the regular, complete, and proper sign of the covenant. And the name Shadai is imprinted upon those who are circumcised and is completed in full perfection. Therefore, it is written ABOUT ABRAHAM; "I am El Shadai," WHICH WAS NOT WRITTEN BEFORE HE WAS COMMANDED TO PERFORM CIRCUMCISION.

443. הִתְהַלֵּךְ לְפָנַי וֶהְיֵה תָמִים, שְׁלִים, דְּהַשְׁתָּא אַתְ חָסֵר בִּרְשִׁימָא דְּשִׁי"ן וְדל"ת, גְּזַר גַּרְמָךְ, וֶהֱוֵי שְׁלִים, בִּרְשִׁימָא דְּיוּ"ד. וּמַאן דְּאִיהוּ בִּרְשׁוּמָא דָּא, אִתְחֲזֵי לְאִתְבָּרְכָא בִּשְׁמָא דָּא, דִּכְתִיב וְאֵל שַׁדַּי יְבָרֵךְ אוֹתְךָ.

443. In the verse, "walk before me, and be perfect" (Beresheet 17:1),

"PERFECT" MEANS complete. Because until now the letter *YUD* was missing in the mark of *Shin-Dalet*. THEREFORE, THE HOLY ONE, BLESSED BE HE, SAID TO HIM, "Circumcise yourself, and be completed by the mark of the *Yud*," SO THE NAME SHADAI (*SHIN-DALET-YUD*) MAY REACH COMPLETION IN YOU. Because whoever is completed by this mark is worthy of being blessed by this Name, as it is written: "And El Shadai shall bless you..." (Beresheet 28:3).

444. מַהוּ אֵל שַׁדַּי. הַהוּא דִּבְרְכָאן נָפְקָן מִנֵּיהּ, הוּא דְּשַׁלִּיט עַל כָּל כִּתְרִין תַּתָּאִין, וְכֻלָּא מִדַּחַלְתֵּיהּ דָּחֲלִין וּמִזְדַּעְזְעִין, בְּגִין כָּךְ מַאן דְּאִתְגְּזַר, כָּל אִינּוּן דְּלָא קַדִּישִׁין אִתְרַחֲקָן מִנֵּיהּ, וְלָא שָׁלְטִין בֵּיהּ. וְלָא עוֹד אֶלָּא דְּלָא נָחִית לַגֵּיהִנָּם, דִּכְתִיב וְעַמֵּךְ כֻּלָּם צַדִּיקִים וְגוֹ'.

444. AND HE ASKS, "What is the meaning of THE NAME 'El Shadai'?" AND HE ANSWERS, "This is THE NAME from which all the blessings issue. It controls all the lower crowns. And all are in awe and tremble from fear of it. Therefore, all those who are impure stay away from him who has been circumcised and have no control over him. In addition, he is not pulled down to Gehenom, as it is written: "Your people also shall be all righteous..." (Yeshayah 60: 21).

445. אָמַר רִבִּי אַבָּא, זַכָּאִין אַתּוּן בְּעָלְמָא דֵּין וּבְעָלְמָא דְּאָתֵי, זַכָּאָה חוּלָקִי דְּאָתֵינָא לְמִשְׁמַע מִלִּין אִלֵּין מִפּוּמֵיכוֹן, כֻּלְּכוֹ קַדִּישִׁין, כֻּלְּכוֹ בְּנֵי אֱלָהָא קַדִּישָׁא, עֲלַיְיכוּ כְּתִיב זֶה יֹאמַר לַה' אֲנִי וְזֶה יִקְרָא בְּשֵׁם יַעֲקֹב וְזֶה יִכְתֹּב יָדוֹ לַה' וּבְשֵׁם יִשְׂרָאֵל יְכַנֶּה. כָּל חַד מִנְּכוֹן אָחִיד וְאִתְקַשַּׁר בְּמַלְכָּא קַדִּישָׁא עִלָּאָה, וְאַתּוּן רַבְרְבָן מִמַּנָּן תְּרֵיסִין מֵהַהִיא אֶרֶץ, דְּאִקְרֵי אֶרֶץ הַחַיִּים, דְּרַבְרְבָנוֹהִי אָכְלִין מִמַּנָּא דְטַלָּא קַדִּישָׁא.

445. Rabbi Aba said: "Happy is your lot in this world and in the World to Come. Happy is my fate that I have come here and heard these words from your mouths – all of you are holy. You are all the sons of the holy Elohim. Of you it is written: 'One shall say, I am Hashem's, and another shall call himself by the name of Jacob, and another shall subscribe with his hand to Hashem and surname himself by the name of Yisrael' (Yeshayah 44:5). Each of you clings to the holy supernal King and is attached to Him. And

you are ruling governors with shields, from that land that is called the land of the living, WHICH IS THE SECRET OF THE NUKVA THAT ENCLOTHES THE UPPER IMA, where its governors feed on the manna of the sacred dew."

446. פָּתַח אִידָךְ וַאֲמַר אַשְׁרֶיךָ אֶרֶץ שֶׁמַּלְכֵּךְ בֶּן חוֹרִין וְשָׂרַיִךְ בָּעֵת יֹאכֵלוּ. וּכְתִיב אִי לָךְ אֶרֶץ שֶׁמַּלְכֵּךְ נַעַר וְשָׂרַיִךְ בַּבֹּקֶר יֹאכֵלוּ. הַנֵּי קְרָאֵי קַשְׁיָין אַהֲדָדֵי. וְלָא קַשְׁיָין, הַאי דִּכְתִיב אַשְׁרֶיךָ אֶרֶץ, דָּא אֶרֶץ דִּלְעֵילָא, דְּשָׁלְטָא עַל כָּל אִינּוּן חַיִּין דִּלְעֵילָא. וּבְגִין כָּךְ אִקְרֵי אֶרֶץ הַחַיִּים, וַעֲלָהּ כְּתִיב אֶרֶץ אֲשֶׁר ה' אֱלֹהֶיךָ דּוֹרֵשׁ אוֹתָהּ תָּמִיד. וּכְתִיב אֶרֶץ אֲשֶׁר לֹא בְמִסְכֵּנֻת תֹּאכַל בָּהּ לֶחֶם לֹא תֶחְסַר כֹּל בָּהּ. לֹא תֶחְסַר כֹּל בָּהּ דַּיְיקָא. וְכָל כָּךְ לָמָה, מִשׁוּם דִּכְתִיב שֶׁמַּלְכֵּךְ בֶּן חוֹרִין דָּא קֻדְשָׁא בְּרִיךְ הוּא. כְּד"א בְּנִי בְכוֹרִי יִשְׂרָאֵל.

446. Another continued the discussion with "Blessed are you, O land, when your king is a free man and your princes eat in due season..." (Kohelet 10:17). Consider also the previous verse, "Woe to you, land, when your king is a child, and your princes eat in the morning" (Ibid. 16). These two verses do not seem to agree with each other. THE "LAND" REFERS TO THE NUKVA, BUT ONE VERSE SAYS "YOUR KING IS A FREE MAN"; THE OTHER THAT "YOUR KING IS A CHILD!" AND HE SAID: "Indeed they do not CONTRADICT EACH OTHER. "Blessed are you, land" refers to the land above, NAMELY THE NUKVA THAT ASCENDED UPWARD AND ENCLOTHED BINAH, which governs all life on high – IN BINAH. For this reason, it is called the land of the living. Of this land it is written: "land which Hashem your Elohim cares for..." (Devarim 11:12) and "A land in which you shall eat bread without scarceness, you shall not lack anything in it..." (Devarim 8:9). Exactly! "You shall not lack any thing in it" MEANS THAT IT IS NOURISHED BY A NEVER-ENDING UNION. Wherefore all this? Because, as it is written: "your king is the son of a free man." This is the Holy One, blessed be He, WHO IS THE SECRET OF ZEIR ANPIN, as you may read, "Yisrael is my son, My firstborn" (Shemot 4:22).

447. בֶּן חוֹרִין, מַהוּ בֶּן חוֹרִין, כְּד"א יוֹבֵל הוּא קֹדֶשׁ תִּהְיֶה לָכֶם. וּכְתִיב וּקְרָאתֶם דְּרוֹר בָּאָרֶץ. דְּהָא כָּל חֵירוּ מִיּוֹבְלָא קָא אָתֵי, בְּגִין כָּךְ

בֶּן חוֹרִין. וְאִי תֵימָא בֶּן חוֹרִין, וְלָא כְּתִיב בֶּן חֵירוּת. הָכֵי הוּא וַדַּאי, בֶּן חֵירוּת מִיבָּעֵי לֵיהּ.

447. AND HE ASKED, "What is THE MEANING OF the son of a free man?" AND HE ANSWERED, "As you may read, 'For it is the Jubilee, it shall be holy to you...'" (Vayikra 25:12). JUBILEE ALLUDES TO BINAH. And it is further written: "and proclaim liberty throughout all the land..." (Ibid. 10). So all freedom is derived from Jubilee, WHICH IS BINAH, Therefore, WHEN ZEIR ANPIN ATTAINS THE MOCHIN OF BINAH, He is then called "a free man!" AND HE SAID: "You may ask why IS IT WRITTEN 'chorin (masc. a free man)' and not 'cherut (fem. Freedom)?'" AND HE REPLIED, "Definitely, it should be 'a man of freedom!'"

448. אֶלָּא בְּמַתְנִיתָא סְתִימָאָה דִּילָן תָּנֵינָא, כַּד מִתְחַבְּרָן יוּ"ד בְּהֵ' כְּדֵין כְּתִיב וְנָהָר יוֹצֵא מֵעֵדֶן לְהַשְׁקוֹת אֶת הַגָּן. וְלָא תֵימָא כַּד מִתְחַבְּרָן, אֶלָּא מִתְחַבְּרָן וַדַּאי. וּבְגִין כָּךְ בֶּן חוֹרִין כְּתִיב, וְעַל דָּא אַשְׁרֵיךְ אֶרֶץ שֶׁמַּלְכֵּךְ בֶּן חוֹרִין וְשָׂרַיִךְ בָּעֵת יֹאכֵלוּ, בְּחֶדְוָותָא בִּשְׁלִימוּ בִּרְעֵוָּא.

448. IF SO, THEN WHY IS IT WRITTEN: "A FREE MAN?" We have learned the answer in our secret Mishnah. When the *Yud* and the *Hei* are united, it is written: "And a river went out of Eden, WHICH IS ZEIR ANPIN, to water the garden" (Beresheet 2:10). It does not say, "When they are united," but assuredly "they are united." Therefore, it is written: "the son of a free man." This, THEN, is the reason why the verse describes ZEIR ANPIN, "Blessed are you, land, when your king is a free man and your princes eat in due season," NAMELY with pleasure and contentment!

449. אִי לָךְ אֶרֶץ שֶׁמַּלְכֵּךְ נָעַר, הַאי אֶרֶץ דִּלְתַתָּא. דְּתַנֵּינָא כָּל שְׁאָר אַרְעֵי דִּשְׁאָר עַמִּין עכו"ם אִתְיְהִיבוּ לְרַבְרְבִין תְּרֵיסִין דִּמְמַנָּן עֲלַיְיהוּ, וְעֵילָּא מִכֻּלְּהוּ הַהוּא דִּכְתִיב בֵּיהּ, נַעַר הָיִיתִי גַּם זָקַנְתִּי. וְתָאנָא הַאי קְרָא שָׂרוֹ שֶׁל עוֹלָם אֲמָרוֹ. וְעַל דָּא אִי לָךְ אֶרֶץ שֶׁמַּלְכֵּךְ נָעַר. וַוי לְעָלְמָא דְּמִסְּטְרָא דָּא יָנְקָא, וְכַד יִשְׂרָאֵל בְּגָלוּתָא, יַנְקִין כְּמַאן דְּיַנִּיק מֵרְשׁוּתָא אָחֳרָא.

449. The verse "Woe to you, land, when your king is a child" refers to the land down below; NAMELY THE NUKVA THAT IS IN THE WORLD OF BRIYAH, WHO IS THE WIFE OF MATATRON. For we have learned that all the lands that belong to nations that worship the stars and constellations are ruled by the governors. And the highest of them all is he of whom it is written: "I have been young, and now am old" (Tehilim 37:25). And we have also learned that the verse was spoken by the governor of the world, NAMELY MATATRON, WHO IS CALLED "A LAD." Of him it is written: "Woe to the land, when the king is a child." Woe to the world that draws its nourishment from this aspect, NAMELY THE ASPECT OF MATATRON. But when Yisrael are in exile, they draw their nourishment from him, as one who feeds on a stranger BECAUSE YISRAEL ARE SUPPOSED TO DERIVE THEIR SUSTENANCE FROM THE HOLY ONE, BLESSED BE HE, AND NOT FROM MATATRON!

450. וְשָׂרַיִךְ בַּבֹּקֶר יֹאכֵלוּ. וְלָא בְּכוּלֵי יוֹמָא. בַּבֹּקֶר, וְלָא בְּזִמְנָא אָחֳרָא דְּיוֹמָא. דְּתַנְיָא בְּשַׁעֲתָא דְּחַמָּה זוֹרַחַת, וְאַתְיָין וְסַגְדִין לֵיהּ לְשִׁמְשָׁא, רוֹגְזָא תָּלֵי בְּעָלְמָא, בְּשַׁעֲתָא דְּמִנְחָה, רוֹגְזָא תַּלְיָיא בְּעָלְמָא. מַאן גָּרִים הַאי, מִשּׁוּם דְּמַלְכֵּךְ נַעַר, הַהוּא דְּאִקְרֵי נַעַר.

450. The verse says that "your princes eat in the morning" and not during the other hours of the day. The morning IS MENTIONED, and the other times of the day are not. We have learned that when the sun shines AND THE PEOPLE OF THE WORLD bow to the sun, wrath hangs over the world, as it also does at the hour of the afternoon prayer, BECAUSE THAT IS THE TIME OF JUDGMENT. Why is this true? Because "your king is a lad" – he who is called "a lad," NAMELY MATATRON.

451. וְאַתּוּן זַכָּאֵי קְשׁוֹט, קַדִּישֵׁי עֶלְיוֹנִין, בְּנֵי מַלְכָּא קַדִּישָׁא, לָא יַנְקִין מֵהַאי סִטְרָא, אֶלָּא מֵהַהוּא אֲתַר קַדִּישָׁא דִּלְעֵילָּא, עֲלַיְיכוּ כְּתִיב וְאַתֶּם הַדְּבֵקִים בַּה' אֱלֹהֵיכֶם חַיִּים כֻּלְּכֶם הַיּוֹם.

451. And you, truly pious and holy men of above, the sons of the Holy King, do not derive sustenance from that aspect OF MATATRON, but rather from that holy place on high, NAMELY THE NUKVA OF ZEIR ANPIN WHICH IS CALLED THE LAND OF THE LIVING. Of you it is written: "You that cleave to Hashem your Elohim are alive everyone of you this day" (Devarim 4:4).

452. פָּתַח רַבִּי אַבָּא וְאָמַר, אָשִׁירָה נָא לִידִידִי שִׁירַת דּוֹדִי לְכַרְמוֹ וְגוֹ׳
וַיְעַזְּקֵהוּ וַיְסַקְּלֵהוּ וְגוֹ׳. הַנֵּי קְרָאֵי אִית לְאִסְתַּכְּלָא בְּהוּ, אַמַּאי כְּתִיב
שִׁירָה, תּוֹכָחָה מִבְּעֵי לֵיהּ. לִידִידִי, לְדוֹדִי מִבְּעֵי לֵיהּ. כְּמָה דִּכְתִיב
שִׁירַת דּוֹדִי. כֶּרֶם הָיָה לִידִידִי בְּקֶרֶן בֶּן שָׁמֶן. אִסְתַּכְּלָנָא בְּכָל אוֹרַיְיתָא,
וְלָא אַשְׁכַּחְנָא אַתְרָא דְּאִקְרֵי קֶרֶן בֶּן שָׁמֶן.

452. Rabbi Aba then discoursed on the verse, "Now I will sing to my friend a song of my beloved for his vineyard...And he fenced it, and gathered out the stones thereof..." (Yeshayah 5:1-2). These verses should be studied carefully. Why does it read, "a song" rather than "a reprimand?" BECAUSE THESE ARE WORDS OF REPROOF TO YISRAEL. AND FURTHERMORE, IT IS WRITTEN: "to my friend," when it should have been written: "to my beloved," just as it is written: "a song of my beloved!" IN ADDITION, IT IS WRITTEN: "My friend has a vineyard in a very fruitful hill (Heb. *Keren Ben Shemen*)" (Yeshayah 5:1-2). But I have searched the entire Torah and cannot find a place called "Keren Ben Shemen!"

453. אֶלָּא הַנֵּי קְרָאֵי הָא אוּקְמוּהָ חַבְרַיְיא בְּכַמָּה גְּוָונִין, וְכֻלְּהוּ שַׁפִּיר
וְהָכֵי הוּא. אֲבָל אָשִׁירָה נָא לִידִידִי, דָּא יִצְחָק, דַּהֲוָה יְדִיד, וְאִקְרֵי יְדִיד
עַד לָא יִפּוֹק לְעָלְמָא.

453. AND HE REPLIED, "These verses are clarified by the friends in different ways, all of which are good and correct. Nevertheless, "Now will I sing to my friend," refers to Isaac, who was a "friend" and was named "friend" before he even came to this world. THUS WE SAY ABOUT HIM, "HE WHO HAS SANCTIFIED A FRIEND FROM THE WOMB."

454. אַמַּאי יְדִיד. דְּתָנִינָן רְחִימוּ סַגִּי הֲוָה לֵיהּ לְקֻדְשָׁא בְּרִיךְ הוּא בֵּיהּ,
דְּלָא אִתְעֲבִיד, עַד דְּלָא אִתְגְּזַר אַבְרָהָם אֲבוּהָ, וְאִקְרֵי שְׁלִים, וְאִתּוֹסַף
לֵיהּ ה״א לְאַשְׁלָמוּתָא. וְכֵן לְשָׂרָה הַאי ה״א אִתְיְהִיבַת לָהּ.

454. AND HE ASKS, "Why WAS ISAAC CALLED "a friend?" AND HE

ANSWERS, "Because we have learned that the Holy One, blessed be He, bore a great love for Isaac, who was not conceived until Abraham, the patriarch, was circumcised and called 'perfect'." ONLY THEN WAS HE TOLD, "AND BE PERFECT." And the *Hei* was added TO HIS NAME for perfection, as well as to Sarah's name. THEN HE WAS CALLED ABRAHAM AND SHE SARAH!

455. הָכָא אִית לְאִסְתַּכְּלָא, ה' לְשָׂרָה שַׁפִּיר, אֲבָל לְאַבְרָהָם, אַמַּאי ה"א וְלָא יוּ"ד, י' מִבְּעֵי לֵיהּ, דְּהָא הוּא דְּכַר הֲוָה. אֶלָּא רָזָא עִלָּאָה הוּא, סָתִים בִּגְוָון, אַבְרָהָם סָלִיק לְעֵילָא, וְנָטִיל רָזָא מֵה"א עִלָּאָה, דְּאִיהוּ עָלְמָא דִּדְכוּרָא, ה"א עִלָּאָה וְה"א תַּתָּאָה, הַאי תַּלְיָא בִּדְכוּרָא וְהַאי בְּנוּקְבָא וַדַּאי.

455. This should be studied! The *Hei* THAT WAS GIVEN to Sarah is suitable, but why was Abraham given the *Hei* and not the *Yud*. The *Yud* should have been added to his name, because he is a male, AND THE ASPECT OF *YUD* BELONGS TO THE MALE, WHILE THE ASPECT OF THE *HEI* BELONGS TO THE FEMALE! AND HE REPLIES, "There is a sublime secret of a concealed aspect. Abraham rose up and took a secret from the upper *Hei*, BINAH, which is the world of the male. Because of the upper *Hei* and lower *Hei* OF YUD HEI VAV HEI, one relates to the male, NAMELY THE UPPER *HEI*, and one relates to the female, NAMELY THE LOWER *HEI*. SO THE *HEI* THAT ABRAHAM TOOK IS THE UPPER *HEI*, WHICH BELONGS TO THE MALE, NAMELY BINAH.

456. דִּכְתִיב כֹּה יִהְיֶה זַרְעֶךָ. וְתָנָא זַרְעֶךָ, זַרְעֶךָ מַמָּשׁ, דַּהֲוָה שָׁארֵי לְמֵיעַל בְּהַאי קָיָים, וּמַאן דְּשָׁארֵי לְמֵיעַל, בְּהַאי קָיָים עָאל. וּבְגִינֵי כָךְ גִּיּוֹרָא דְּאִתְגְּזַר גֵּר צֶדֶק אִקְרֵי, בְּגִין דְּלָא אָתָא מִגִּזְעָא קַדִּישָׁא דְּאִתְגְּזָרוּ, וְעַל דָּא מַאן דְּעָאל בְּהַאי, שְׁמֵיהּ כְּהַאי.

456. As it is written: "So (Heb. *koh*) shall your seed be" (Beresheet 15:5). And we have learned that "your seed" is actually "your seed!" THIS MEANS THAT *KOH*, WHICH IS MALCHUT, SHALL BE HIS ACTUAL SEED. He started to enter to this covenant, and whoever starts to enter, does actually enter to this covenant, WHICH IS MALCHUT THAT IS CALLED *KOH*. Therefore, a

proselyte who is circumcised is called "a proselyte of righteousness," because he does not come from the "holy seed" that was circumcised AND HE STARTS TO ENTER TO THE COVENANT, AND WHOEVER STARTS ENTERS IN MALCHUT. So whoever enters this, NAMELY MALCHUT THAT IS CALLED "RIGHTEOUSNESS," is called by this name, A PROSELYTE OF RIGHTEOUSNESS.

457. אַבְרָהָם, בְּגִין כָּךְ כְּתִיב בֵּיהּ כֹּה יִהְיֶה זַרְעֶךָ, זַרְעֶךָ מַמָּשׁ, וְאִתְמְסַר לֵיהּ ה״א. אִתְחַבָּרוּ תְּרֵין הַהִי״ן כַּחֲדָא, וְאוֹלִידוּ לְעֵילָא, וּמַאי דְּנָפַק מִנַּיְיהוּ, הוּא יוּ״ד, בְּגִינֵי כָּךְ, יוּ״ד אֶת רֵישָׁא דְּיִצְחָק, דְּכַר. מִכָּאן שָׁארֵי דְּכוּרָא לְאִתְפַּשְּׁטָא, וְעַל דָּא כְּתִיב כִּי בְיִצְחָק יִקָּרֵא לְךָ זָרַע. בְּיִצְחָק, וְלָא בָּךְ. יִצְחָק אוֹלִיד לְעֵילָא, דִּכְתִיב תִּתֵּן אֱמֶת לְיַעֲקֹב. יַעֲקֹב אַשְׁלִים כֹּלָּא.

457. This is why it is written of Abraham. "So (*Koh*) shall your seed be," which means "your seed" exactly. BECAUSE THE TERM *KOH*, WHICH IS THE LOWER *HEI*, NAMELY MALCHUT, SHALL ACTUALLY BE "YOUR SEED." Therefore he was given the *Hei*. AS HE CONTINUES TO EXPLAIN HOW MALCHUT BECOMES HIS "SEED," HE SAYS: The two *Heis*, WHICH ARE BINAH AND MALCHUT, are joined together. AFTER ABRAHAM ROSE TO THE FIRST HEI, THE LOWER HEI, MALCHUT, ROSE UP TO HIM, AND THE TWO JOINED TOGETHER. Then they gave birth up there IN BINAH. And what issues from those, AS THE LEFT COLUMN IS FORMED, is *Yud*. This is why *Yud,* WHICH IS THE ASPECT OF the male, is the first letter of the name of Isaac. From here, the male expands, BECAUSE FROM THE SECRET OF *YUD* THE MALE STARTS TO EXPAND. Because of this, it is written: "for in Isaac shall your seed be called" (Beresheet 21:12). IT SAYS "in Isaac," and not in you. Isaac bore above, as it is written: "You will show truth to Jacob" (Michah 7:20), who completed everything.

458. וְאִי תֵימָא, וְכִי אַבְרָהָם בְּהַאי אִתְאַחֵיד, וְלָא יַתִּיר, וְהָא כְּתִיב חֶסֶד לְאַבְרָהָם. אֶלָּא חוּלָקָא דִּילֵיהּ כָּךְ הוּא, בְּגִין דַּעֲבֵיד חֶסֶד עִם בְּנֵי עָלְמָא, אֲבָל לְאוֹלָדָא, הָכָא אָחִיד, וּמֵהָכָא שָׁארֵי. וְעַל דָּא לָא אִתְגְּזַר אַבְרָהָם, אֶלָּא בֶּן תִּשְׁעִים וְתֵשַׁע שָׁנָה. וְרָזָא דְמִלָּה הָא אִתְיְידַע, וְאוֹקִימְנָא, בְּמַתְנִיתָּא דִילָן.

458. You might claim, "But it was Abraham who was attached to this grade," WHO, IN OTHER WORDS, BECAME INCLUDED IN THE ASPECT OF THE LEFT COLUMN OF ISAAC, and no more! Yet it is written: "Kindness (Chesed) to Abraham" (Michah 7:20), SO HE IS ATTACHED TO THE RIGHT! AND HE REPLIED, "His portion is indeed so, NAMELY CHESED, because he showed kindness to the people of the world. But to beget children, he remained attached to this grade, MEANING THAT HE BECAME INCLUDED WITHIN THE LEFT COLUMN, and from here he begins, BECAUSE THERE IS NO BEGETTING WITHOUT THE ASPECT OF THE ILLUMINATION OF CHOCHMAH, WHICH IS ACHIEVED BY COMBINING THE RIGHT AND LEFT TOGETHER. AND THIS IS THE SECRET OF THE VERSE "IN ISAAC SHALL YOUR SEED BE CALLED," AND NOT IN YOU. This is why Abraham was not circumcised until the age of ninety nine years. And this secret is known and explained in our Mishnah.

459. וּבְגִין כָּךְ יִצְחָק, דִּינָא קַשְׁיָא, נָפַק לְאַחֲדָא לְחוּלְקֵיהּ וּלְאוֹלָדָא וְחֶסֶד אִקְרֵי. וְעַל דָּא יַעֲקֹב אַשְׁלִים כֹּלָּא, מֵהַאי סִטְרָא, וּמֵהַאי סִטְרָא, מִסִּטְרָא דְּאָחִידוּ אַבְרָהָם וְיִצְחָק לְחוּלְקֵיהוֹן לְעֵילָא, הוּא שְׁלֵימוּתָא. מִסִּטְרָא דְּאִתְיְהֵיב לְהוּ לְאוֹלָדָא מִתַּתָּא לְעֵילָא הוּא שְׁלֵימוּתָא. וְעַל דָּא כְּתִיב יִשְׂרָאֵל אֲשֶׁר בְּךָ אֶתְפָּאָר. בֵּיהּ אִתְאֲחִידוּ גְּוָונִין מֵעֵילָא וּמִתַּתָּא.

459. For this, Isaac, who is harsh Judgment, AND IS THE LEFT COLUMN THAT WAS BLOCKED BECAUSE OF THE LACK OF CHASSADIM, came forth to complete his share and beget THE CENTRAL COLUMN, WHICH IS JACOB and is called Chesed. THEN, RIGHT AND LEFT WERE INCLUDED IN EACH OTHER. This is how Jacob completed everything from this side, THE RIGHT SIDE, and from that side, THE LEFT SIDE, from the side where Abraham and Isaac were combined in their portion on high THROUGH JACOB WHO IS THE CENTRAL COLUMN. AND BY THIS, THE CHASSADIM OF THE RIGHT WERE COMPLETED – this is ONE completion – OF JACOB. And from the side that was given the ability to give birth and beget from below upward this is THE SECOND completion FOR JACOB. Therefore it is written: "Yisrael, in whom I will be glorified" (Yeshayah 49:3), BECAUSE in him, IN YISRAEL, were the colors, NAMELY THE LIGHTS, completed from above and below!

460. וְעַל דָּא כְּתִיב הָכָא שִׁירָה, דִּכְתִיב אָשִׁירָה נָא לִידִידִי. שִׁירָה וַדַּאי, דְּהָא אִקְרֵי לְאוֹלָדָא, דְּכַר, דְּהָא אִקְרֵי יָדִיד, עַד לָא יִפּוֹק לְעָלְמָא.

460. This is why it is written "a song" in the verse "Now will I sing to my friend" AND NOT A REPROVAL. This is definitely a song, because he is called to beget a male. HIS MENTION OF "MY FRIEND" ALLUDES TO BEGETTING A MALE, WHO IS ISAAC, THE MOCHIN OF THE LEFT COLUMN OF BINAH, WHICH THE WORLD OF THE MALE. He was call a "friend" before he appeared in the world.

461. וְאִית דְּאָמְרֵי, אָשִׁירָה נָא לִידִידִי דָּא אַבְרָהָם, כְּדְּ"א מַה לִידִידִי בְּבֵיתִי. וְאַבְרָהָם יָרִית יְרוּתָא דְּאַחְסָנַת חוּלָקָא דָא, אֲבָל מַה דַּאֲמִינָא, דְּדָא יִצְחָק הָכֵי הוּא.

461. There are those who say that "Now will I sing to my friend" refers to Abraham, as it is written: "What has my friend to do in my house" (Yirmeyah 11:15), WHICH REFERS TO ABRAHAM. SO MY FRIEND HERE ALSO REFERS TO ABRAHAM. And Abraham inherited the portion of this field, WHICH IS MALCHUT THAT IS CALLED HERE "VINEYARD." AND HE RECITES A SONG OF MY BELOVED FOR HIS VINEYARD. "But," RABBI ABA SAID: "What I have said – that it is Isaac – is indeed so."

462. שִׁירַת דּוֹדִי לְכַרְמוֹ. דָּא קֻדְשָׁא בְּרִיךְ הוּא, דְּאִקְרֵי דּוֹדִי. דִּכְתִיב דּוֹדִי צַח וְאָדוֹם, יְדִידִי אָחִיד בְּדוֹדִי, דְּכַר. וּמִנֵּיהּ אִתְנְטַע כֶּרֶם, דִּכְתִיב, כֶּרֶם הָיָה לִידִידִי.

462. In the verse "A song of my beloved for his vineyard," my beloved refers to the Holy One, blessed be He, who is called "my beloved," as it is written: "My beloved is white and ruddy "(Shir Hashirim 5:10). When my friend is united with my beloved, he is a male. AND THEN, from this WITH THE ILLUMINATION OF THE LEFT COLUMN OF BINAH, he planted a vineyard, WHICH IS MALCHUT AND NUKVA OF ZEIR ANPIN, as it is written: "My beloved has a vineyard" (Yeshayah 5:1), BECAUSE MALCHUT IS CONSTRUCTED BY THE LEFT COLUMN OF BINAH.

463. בְּקֶרֶן בֶּן שָׁמֶן. מַאי בְּקֶרֶן בֶּן שָׁמֶן. אֶלָּא, בַּמֶּה נָפִיק הַאי כֶּרֶם, וּבַמֶּה אִתְנְטַע, חָזַר וְאָמַר בְּקֶרֶן. מַאי קֶרֶן. דִּכְתִיב בְּקֶרֶן הַיּוֹבֵל. בְּקֶרֶן הַיּוֹבֵל שָׁרֵי. וְהַאי קֶרֶן אִתְאַחִיד בְּהַהוּא דְּכַר, דְּאִקְרֵי בֶּן שָׁמֶן.

463. In discoursing on the verse "a very fruitful hill (Heb. *Keren Ben Shemen*)," HE ASKS, "What is *Keren Ben Shemen*? AND HE REPLIED, "This is TO TEACH US how the vineyard came to be and how it was planted!" So he repeated, "by *keren!*" And what is the *keren*? This is, as it is written: "with the ram's horn (lit. 'with the horn *[keren]* of Jubilee')" (Yehoshua 6:5), WHICH ALLUDES TO MALCHUT THAT IS SWEETENED BY BINAH. BECAUSE *KEREN* IS MALCHUT, WHILE THE JUBILEE IS BINAH. And this *Keren* THAT APPEARS HERE has joined this male that is called *Ben Shemen* (lit.'the Son of Oil'), WHICH IS ALSO BINAH. THE VERSE TEACHES US, THAT THE EMERGENCE AND PLANTING OF THE VINEYARD, MALCHUT, WAS BROUGHT ABOUT BY ITS ASCENDING TO BINAH, WHICH IS MALE.

464. מַהוּ בֶּן שָׁמֶן. כְּד"א בֶּן חוֹרִין. וְתַרְוַוייְהוּ חַד מִלָּה, שֶׁמֶן דְּמִתַּמָּן נְגִיד מִשְׁחָא וּרְבוּ, לְאַדְלָקָא בּוֹצִינִין, וּבְגִין כָּךְ בֶּן שָׁמֶן. וְדָא שֶׁמֶן וּרְבוּ נְגִיד וּנְפִיק וְאַדְלִיק בּוֹצִינִין, עַד דְּנָטִיל לֵיהּ, וּכְנֵישׁ לֵיהּ, הַאי קֶרֶן, וְדָא אִקְרֵי קֶרֶן הַיּוֹבֵל. בְּגִינֵי כָּךְ, לֵית מְשִׁיחוּתָא דְּמַלְכוּתָא, אֶלָּא בְּקֶרֶן, וְעַל דָּא אִתְמְשַׁךְ מַלְכוּתָא דְּדָוִד, דְּאִתְמְשַׁח בְּקֶרֶן, וְאִתְאַחִיד בֵּיהּ.

464. HE ASKED, "What is THE MEANING OF '*Ben Shemen'* (the Son of Oil)?' AND HE RESPONDS, "This is the equivalent of the verse "(Heb. *ben* or *bar*) a free man," WHICH MEANS BINAH. And both of them – BEN SHEMEN AND JUBILEE – are the same thing, NAMELY BINAH. AND THIS IS CALLED *Shemen* (oil) because from there, BINAH, the oil and greatness is drawn for the purpose of lighting the candles. Thus, "the son of oil." And this *Keren*, WHICH IS MALCHUT, assembles them all, and this is ALSO CALLED, the *Keren* (horn) of the Jubilee. Therefore, the kingship is anointed only by this horn, and the kingship of THE HOUSE OF David endures because he was anointed with the horn and was attached to it.

465. וַיְעַזְּקֵהוּ, כְּהַאי עִזְקָא דְּאִסְתַּחַר לְכָל סִטְרִין. וַיְסַקְּלֵהוּ, דְּאַעֲדֵי

מִנֵּיהּ וּמֵחוּלָקֵיהּ, כָּל אִינוּן רַבְרְבִין, כָּל אִינוּן תְּרֵיסִין, כָּל אִינוּן כִּתְרִין
תַּתָּאִין, וְהוּא נָסֵיב לֵיהּ לְהַאי כֶּרֶם לְחוּלָקֵיהּ, דִּכְתִיב כִּי חֵלֶק ה' עַמּוֹ
יַעֲקֹב חֶבֶל נַחֲלָתוֹ.

465. The verse continues with the words, "And he fenced it..." AND NOW
HE EXPLAINS THIS VERSE, DESCRIBING HOW THE VINEYARD CAME
FORTH AND WAS BORN BY *KEREN BEN SHEMEN*, OR, IN OTHER WORDS,
BY ASCENDING TO BINAH. SO HE SAID: "And he fenced it," WHICH
MEANS THAT HE RESTRICTED IT AND FENCED IT ALL AROUND, just like a
ring that surrounds it from all directions. "And gathered out the stones
thereof" MEANS THAT he removed all the great ones and all the governors
and the lower crowns from his portion and his vineyard. Then He, NAMELY
BINAH, took the vineyard to be his portion. THIS MEANS THAT IT CLUNG
TO BINAH AND BECAME A PART OF BINAH, as it is written: "For Hashem's
portion is His people; Jacob is the lot of His inheritance" (Devarim 32:9).
BECAUSE AS MALCHUT HAS BECOME A PART OF BINAH, SO YISRAEL
HAS BECOME A PART OF BINAH, BECAUSE THEY ARE ATTACHED TO IT.

466. וַיִּטָּעֵהוּ שׂוֹרֵק, כְּד"א וְאָנֹכִי נְטַעְתִּיךְ שׂוֹרֵק כֻּלֹּה זֶרַע אֱמֶת. כל"ה
כְּתִיב בה"א. מִכָּאן שָׁארֵי אַבְרָהָם לְאוֹלָדָא לְעֵילָא, וּמֵהַאי נָפַק זֶרַע
אֱמֶת. כֻּלֹּה זֶרַע אֱמֶת, וַדַּאי, הַיְינוּ דִּכְתִיב, כֹּה יִהְיֶה זַרְעֶךָ, וְכֹלָּא חַד
מִלָּה. זַכָּאָה חוּלַקְהוֹן דְּיִשְׂרָאֵל, דְּיָרְתוּ יְרוּתָא קַדִּישָׁא דָּא.

466. The verse, "and planted it with the choicest vine" is similar to the verse
"I had planted you a noble vine, an entirely (Heb. *kuloh*) right seed..."
(Yirmeyah 2:21). It is written *kuloh* with the letter *Hei*. SO IT IS AS
THOUGH IT WERE WRITTEN: KOL (ALL) *HEI*, WHICH MEANS ALL OF *HEI*,
WHICH IS MALCHUT. And from this stage Abraham started to beget ISAAC
above. THEREFORE HE SAYS: "and from here the 'right seed' issued –
definitely "an entirely right seed," BECAUSE THE ILLUMINATION OF
CHOCHMAH IS CALLED RIGHT OR TRUTH. And as it is written: "So (*Koh*)
shall your seed be," BECAUSE WHEN THE LEFT COLUMN SHINES IN
MALCHUT, IT IS CALLED *KOH*. Thus, they are the same: "THE CHOICEST
VINE," "THE RIGHT SEED," THE FATHERING OF ISAAC, AND "*KOH* SHALL
YOUR SEED BE." THEY ALL REFER TO THE ILLUMINATION OF THE LEFT

FROM BINAH. Happy is the lot of Yisrael, who receive such a great inheritance.

467. סוֹפֵיהּ דִּקְרָא וַיִּבֶן מִגְדָּל בְּתוֹכוֹ. מַהוּ מִגְדָּל. כְּד"א מִגְדַּל עֹז שֵׁם ה' בּוֹ יָרוּץ צַדִּיק וְנִשְׂגָּב, בּוֹ יָרוּץ צַדִּיק וַדַּאי.

467. The verse continues, "and built a tower in the midst of it." AND HE ASKS, "What is a tower?" AND HE RESPONDS, "This is as it is written: 'The name of Hashem is a strong tower, the righteous runs to it, and is safe'" (Mishlei 18:10). Assuredly, "the righteous runs to it."

468. וְגַם יֶקֶב חָצֵב בּוֹ. דָּא תַּרְעָא דְּצֶדֶק, כְּד"א פִּתְחוּ לִי שַׁעֲרֵי צֶדֶק. מַאי מַשְׁמַע, דְּכָל בַּר יִשְׂרָאֵל דְּאִתְגְּזַר, עַיֵּיל בִּתְרֵוַוייהוּ וְזָכֵי לְתַרְוַוייהוּ.

468. The text, "and also made a winepress therein" refers to the "gate of righteousness," as it is written: "Open to me the gates of righteousness..." (Tehilim 118:19). AND HE ASKS, "What is the meaning OF THE VERSE 'OPEN TO ME THE GATES OF RIGHTEOUSNESS'?" AND HE ANSWERS, "Each person among Yisrael who is circumcised enters and merits them both, THIS IS WHY DAVID PLEADED, "OPEN TO ME THE GATES OF RIGHTEOUSNESS" in order to merit them both.

469. וּמַאן דִּקְרֵיב בְּרֵיהּ לְקָרְבְּנָא דָּא, עַיֵּיל לֵיהּ בִּשְׁמָא קַדִּישָׁא, וְעַל אַת דָּא, מִתְקַיְימִין שְׁמַיָּא וְאַרְעָא. דִּכְתִיב אִם לֹא בְּרִיתִי יוֹמָם וָלַיְלָה חֻקּוֹת שָׁמַיִם וָאָרֶץ לֹא שָׂמְתִּי. וְהַאי מָארֵיהּ דְּהִלּוּלָא דָּא, זָכָה לְכֹלָּא, לְמֶחֱזֵי קוּדְשָׁא בְּרִיךְ הוּא אַנְפִּין בְּאַנְפִּין בְּהַאי יוֹמָא.

469. He who offers his son for the sacrifice OF CIRCUMCISION brings his son to the Holy Name. And the heavens and earth are based upon this sign, as it is written: "If My covenant be not day and night, it were as if I had not appointed the ordinances of heaven and earth" (Yirmeyah 33:25). So our host has merited all this, AND HE HAD THE PRIVILEGE to see the Holy One, blessed be He, face to face on this day.

470. זַכָּאָה חוּלָקָנָא, דְּזָכֵינָא לְהַאי יוֹמָא, וְזַכָּאָה חוּלָקָךְ עִמָּנָא, וְהַאי

בְּרָא דְּאִתְיְילֵיד לָךְ קָרֵינָא עֲלֵיהּ כָּל הַנִּקְרָא בִּשְׁמִי וְגוֹ' יְצַרְתִּיו אַף עֲשִׂיתִיו. וּכְתִיב וְכָל בָּנַיִךְ לִמּוּדֵי ה' וְגוֹ'. אוֹזְפוּהָ לְרַבִּי אַבָּא תְּלַת מִילִין.

470. Happy is our lot that we have merited this day, and happy is your lot together with ours. And upon this boy that is born to you, I pronounce, "Everyone that is called by my name...I have formed him: yea, I have made him" (Yeshayah 43:7), and "And all your children shall be taught of Hashem..." (Yeshayah 54:13). Then he accompanied Rabbi Aba for three miles.

471. אֲמְרוּ לֵיהּ הַאי הַאי מָארֵיהּ דְּהִלּוּלָא אוֹשְׁפִּיזָךְ זָכָה לְכוּלֵּי הַאי, בְּגִין דְּקַיָּים קִיּוּמָא דְּמִצְוָה. אָמַר מַאי הִיא. אָמַר הַהוּא גַבְרָא, דְּבֵיתָאי, אִתַּת אָחִי הֲוָות, וּמִית בְּלָא בְּנִין, וּנְסִיבְנָא לָהּ, וְדָא הוּא בְּרָא קַדְמָאָה דַּהֲוָה לִי מִנָּהּ, וְקָרֵינָא לֵיהּ בִּשְׁמָא דְּאָחִי דְּאִתְפַּטַּר. אָמַר לוֹ מִכָּאן וּלְהָלְאָה קְרֵי לֵיהּ אִידֵי, וְהַיְינוּ אִידֵי בַּר יַעֲקֹב. בָּרֵיךְ לוֹן רַבִּי אַבָּא וְאָזֵיל לְאָרְחֵיהּ.

471. They said to RABBI ABA, "The host who made the ceremony, the owner of your guest house, has merited all this because he performed a precept!" He asked, "What is the precept?" Then that man, THE OWNER OF THE GUESTHOUSE, said: "My wife was the wife of my brother, who died childless. So I married her. And this is the first child that I got from her, and I named him after my dead brother." He said to him, "From now on you shall call him Iddi. He is Iddi the son of Jacob!" Rabbi Aba then blessed them and went on his way.

472. כַּד אָתָא, סְדַר מִלִּין קַמֵּיהּ דְּר' אֶלְעָזָר, וְדָחִיל לְמֵימַר לְר' שִׁמְעוֹן. יוֹמָא חַד הֲוָה קַמֵּיהּ דְּרַבִּי שִׁמְעוֹן, וְאָמַר רַבִּי שִׁמְעוֹן, מַאי דִּכְתִיב וַיִּפֹּל אַבְרָם עַל פָּנָיו וַיְדַבֵּר אִתּוֹ אֱלֹקִים לֵאמֹר אֲנִי הִנֵּה בְרִיתִי אִתָּךְ. מַשְׁמַע דְּעַד דְּלָא אִתְגְּזַר הֲוָה נָפִיל עַל אַנְפּוֹי, וּמַלֵּיל עִמֵּיהּ, בָּתַר דְּאִתְגְּזַר קָאִים בְּקִיּוּמֵיהּ וְלָא דָּחִיל. אֲנִי הִנֵּה בְרִיתִי אִתָּךְ, דְּאַשְׁכַּח גַּרְמֵיהּ גְּזִיר.

472. When he arrived at his destination, he told everything to Rabbi Elazar, but he was afraid to tell it in front of Rabbi Shimon, WHO MIGHT PUNISH THEM FOR REVEALING THE SECRETS. One day, while with Rabbi Shimon, Rabbi Shimon said: "Why is it written: 'And Abram fell on his face and Elohim spoke with him, saying, as for Me, behold My covenant is with you'" (Beresheet 17:3-4). This means that as long as he was not circumcised, he fell on his face when He spoke with him. But after he was circumcised, he stood upright and was not afraid. "As for Me, behold My covenant is with you," MEANING THAT he found himself to be circumcised, AS THE WORDS OF HASHEM AFFECTED HIM AND HE BECAME CIRCUMCISED!

473. אָמַר לוֹ ר' אַבָּא, אִי נִיחָא קַמֵּיהּ דְּמַר דְּלֵימָא קַמֵּיהּ, מֵאִינּוּן מִלֵּי מַעֲלְיָיתָא דִּשְׁמַעֲנָא בְּהַאי, אָמַר לוֹ אֵימָא. אָמַר לוֹ דָּחִילְנָא דְּלָא יִתְעַנְשׁוּ עַל יְדָאי. אָמַר לוֹ ח"ו מִשְּׁמוּעָה רָעָה לֹא יִירָא נָכוֹן לִבּוֹ בָּטוּחַ בַּה'. סָח לֵיהּ עוֹבָדָא, וְסַדֵּר קַמֵּיהּ כָּל אִינּוּן מִלִּין.

473. Rabbi Aba said to him, "I hope it will be pleasing in the eyes of my master for me to say a few of those good things that I have heard about this subject." He said to him: "Speak!" He said to him, "I am afraid that somebody might be punished because of me." Rabbi Shimon said: "Heaven forbid, 'He shall not be afraid of evil tidings, his heart is fixed, trusting in Hashem'" (Tehilim 112:7). Rabbi Aba then told him every thing that had happened.

474. אָמַר לוֹ וְכִי כָּל הַנֵּי מִלֵּי מַעֲלְיָיתָא הֲווֹ טְמִירִין גַּבָּךְ, וְלָא אֲמַרְתְּ לְהוּ. גּוֹזַרְנָא עֲלָךְ דְּכָל תְּלָתִין יוֹמִין אִלֵּין תִּלְעֵי וְתִנְשֵׁי. וְלָא כְתִיב אַל תִּמְנַע טוֹב מִבְּעָלָיו בִּהְיוֹת לְאֵל יָדְךָ לַעֲשׂוֹת. וְכָךְ הֲוָה. אָמַר, גּוֹזַרְנָא, דִּבְאוֹרַיְיתָא, דָּא יִגְלוֹן לְבָבֶל בֵּינֵי חַבְרַיָּיא.

474. Rabbi Shimon said: "Could it be that all these good things were hidden in you and you did not reveal them! I hereby bring a decree upon you that for the next 30 days you shall immediately forget everything you learn! Is it not written: "Withhold not good from them to whom it is due, when it is in the power of your hand to do it" (Mishlei 13.27)? And so it came to be THAT HE FORGOT EVERYTHING HE LEARNED! He, RABBI SHIMON, said: "I bring a decree that they with their learnings; REFERRING TO THE OWNER OF THE GUESTHOUSE AND HIS FRIENDS, be banished to Babylon, where they will stay among the friends THAT LIVE THERE.

475. חֲלַשׁ דַּעְתֵּיהּ דְּרַבִּי אַבָּא, יוֹמָא חַד חָמָא לֵיהּ רַבִּי שִׁמְעוֹן, אָמַר לוֹ טוּפְסְרָא דְּלִבָּךְ בְּאַנְפָּךְ שְׁכִיחַ, אָמַר לוֹ לָא עַל דִּידִי הוּא, אֶלָּא עַל דִּידְהוּ. אָמַר לוֹ ח"ו דְּאִתְעַנָּשׁוּ, אֶלָּא בְּגִין דְּמִלִּין אִתְגַּלְיָין בֵּינַיְיהוּ כָּל כָּךְ, יִגְלוֹן בֵּינֵי חַבְרַיָּיא, יִלְפוּן אִינוּן אָרְחִין, וְאִתְכַּסְיָין מִלִּין בְּגַוַוייְהוּ. דְּהָא מִלִּין לָא אִתְגַּלְיָין אֶלָּא בֵּינָנָא, דְּהָא קֻדְשָׁא בְּרִיךְ הוּא אַסְתְּכִים עִמָּנָא, וְעַל יְדָנָא אִתְגַּלְּיָין מִלִּין.

475. Rabbi Aba's mind became confused. One day, Rabbi Shimon saw him and said: "The reflection of your heart can be seen in your face." RABBI ABA responded, "I am not sorrowful for myself, but for them, AS RABBI SHIMON PUNISHED THEM TO EXILE IN BABYLON. RABBI SHIMON THEN said: "Heaven forbid, that they were punished. Rather, because the secrets were revealed among them so openly, I BROUGHT A DECREE UPON THEM, that they be banished and be among the friends IN BABYLON, where they will learn to conceal and hide the secrets among them. Because the secrets should be revealed only among us, as the Holy One, blessed be He, gave permission to us. So through us only should these things be revealed."

476. אָמַר רַבִּי יוֹסֵי, כְּתִיב אָז יִבָּקַע כַּשַּׁחַר אוֹרֶךְ וְגוֹ'. זַמִּין קֻדְשָׁא בְּרִיךְ הוּא לְאַכְרְזָא עַל בְּנוֹי, וְיֵימָא, אָז יִבָּקַע כַּשַּׁחַר אוֹרֶךְ וַאֲרֻכָתְךָ מְהֵרָה תִצְמָח וְהָלַךְ לְפָנֶיךָ צִדְקֶךָ וּכְבוֹד ה' יַאַסְפֶךָ.

476. Rabbi Yosi said: It is written: "Then shall your light break forth as the morning…" (Yeshayah 58:8). The Holy One, blessed be He, shall in the future declare to His children, "Then shall your light break forth as the morning, and your healing shall spring forth speedily, and your righteousness shall go before you and the glory of Hashem shall be your rearguard."

Vayera

Name of the articles

1. "And Hashem appeared to him"

A Synopsis

There were numerous moments in history when the goal of eternal peace and unending happiness for all mankind was within reach. Both Adam and Noah had the opportunity to cause universal change and bring about endless fulfillment. The Zohar likens the path to permanent peace to the creation and care of a garden. Adam is compared to the force that causes rain water to fall upon and nourish the land, and Noah represents a person who manufactures the tools needed to tend the garden. The appearance of Abraham in our world corresponds to the force that influences the flowers to grow and blossom. Now that Avraham's name includes the additional letter *Hei* ה, signifying the ritual of circumcision, he is now prepared to receive the great Light of the Creator as expressed through the Tetragrammaton יהוה, one of the holy Names of the Creator that radiates His spiritual energy.

The Relevance of this Passage

The path to personal peace is an arduous process that each of us must endure. We can, however, accelerate this process through our connection to this portion. The Light of the Creator fills our soul through the merit and power of Abraham. The energy channeled through our Patriarch nurtures our soul, inspiring us to seek higher levels of spiritual growth. The strength to blossom in all our spiritual endeavors is revealed through the Light of these verses.

١. רַבִּי חִיָּיא פָּתַח, הַנִּצָּנִים נִרְאוּ בָאָרֶץ עֵת הַזָּמִיר הִגִּיעַ וְקוֹל הַתּוֹר נִשְׁמַע בְּאַרְצֵנוּ. הַנִּצָּנִים נִרְאוּ בָאָרֶץ, כַּד בְּרָא קֻדְשָׁא בְּרִיךְ הוּא עָלְמָא, יְהַב בְּאַרְעָא כָּל חֵילָא דְּאִתְחֲזֵי לָהּ. וְכֹלָּא הֲוָה בְּאַרְעָא, וְלָא אֲפִיקַת אִיבִּין בְּעָלְמָא, עַד דְּאִתְבְּרֵי אָדָם, כֵּיוָן דְּאִתְבְּרֵי אָדָם, כֹּלָּא אִתְחֲזֵי בְּעָלְמָא, וְאַרְעָא גַּלִּיאַת אִיבָּהָא, וְחֵילָהָא דְּאִתְפָּקְדוּ בָהּ.

1. Rabbi Chiya opened the discussion: IT IS WRITTEN: "The flowers appeared on the earth, the time of the singing of the birds has come, and the voice of the turtledove is heard in our land" (Shir Hashirim 2:12). "The flowers appeared on the earth," MEANS THAT when the Holy One, blessed be He, created the world, He endowed the earth with appropriate powers, so that everything was in the earth BUT it did not produce any fruit until Adam was created. As soon as Adam was created, everything in the earth became visible, that is, the earth began to reveal the powers and products that were implanted within it. AND THEN IT WAS SAID: "THE FLOWERS APPEAR ON THE EARTH."

2. כְּגַוְונָא דָא, שָׁמַיִם לָא יָהֲבוּ חֵילִין לְאַרְעָא, עַד דְּאָתָא אָדָם. הה"ד, וְכֹל שִׂיחַ הַשָּׂדֶה טֶרֶם יִהְיֶה בָאָרֶץ, וְכָל עֵשֶׂב הַשָּׂדֶה טֶרֶם יִצְמָח, כִּי לֹא הִמְטִיר ה' אֱלֹקִים עַל הָאָרֶץ, וְאָדָם אַיִן לַעֲבֹד אֶת הָאֲדָמָה. אִטַּמָּרוּ כָּל אִינוּן תּוֹלָדִין וְלָא אִתְגַּלְּוּן, וּשְׁמַיָּא אִתְעַכָּבוּ, דְּלָא אַמְטִירוּ עַל אַרְעָא, בְּגִין דְּאָדָם אַיִן, דְּלָא אִשְׁתְּכַח, וְלָא אִתְבְּרֵי, וְכֹלָּא אִתְעַכַּב בְּגִינֵיהּ, כֵּיוָן דְּאִתְחֲזֵי אָדָם, מִיָּד הַנִּצָּנִים נִרְאוּ בָאָרֶץ, וְכָל חַיָּלִין דְּאִתְטַמָּרוּ, אִתְגַּלְּיָאוּ וְאִתְיְהִיבוּ בָהּ.

2. Similarly, the heavens did not give any powers to the earth until humankind appeared, as it is written: "And no plant of the field was yet in the earth, and no herb of the field had yet grown, for Hashem Elohim had not caused it to rain upon the earth, and there was not a man to till the ground" (Beresheet 2:5). All the offspring and products were concealed in the earth. They did not appear, and the heavens were prevented from pouring rain on the earth because humankind did not yet exist. Because it had not yet been created, the revelation of all things was delayed. As soon as humankind appeared, however, "The flowers appeared on the earth," and all the hidden and concealed powers were now revealed.

3. עֵת הַזָּמִיר הִגִּיעַ, דְּאִתְתַּקַּן תִּקּוּנָא דְּתוּשְׁבְּחָן לְזַמְּרָא קַמֵּי קֻדְשָׁא בְּרִיךְ הוּא, מַה דְּלָא אִשְׁתְּכַח עַד לָא אִתְבְּרֵי אָדָם. וְקוֹל הַתּוֹר נִשְׁמַע בְּאַרְצֵנוּ. דָּא מִלָּה דְּקֻדְשָׁא בְּרִיךְ הוּא, דְּלָא אִשְׁתְּכַח בְּעָלְמָא, עַד דְּאִתְבְּרֵי אָדָם, כֵּיוָן דְּאִשְׁתְּכַח אָדָם כֹּלָּא אִשְׁתְּכַח.

3. "...the time of the singing of the birds has come" MEANS THAT a recital was composed of songs and praises to the Holy One, blessed be He. This was not done before humankind was created, "...and the voice of the turtledove is heard in our land." This is the word of the Holy One, blessed be He, which did not exist in the world before humankind was created. But as soon as humankind appeared, everything appeared!

4. בָּתַר דְּחָטָא, כֹּלָּא אִסְתַּלַּק מֵעָלְמָא, וְאִתְלַטְיָא אַרְעָא. הה"ד אֲרוּרָה

הָאֲדָמָה בַּעֲבוּרֶךְ וְגוֹ'. וּכְתִיב כִּי תַעֲבֹד אֶת הָאֲדָמָה לֹא תֹסֵף תֵּת כֹּחָהּ לָךְ וְגוֹ'. וּכְתִיב וְקוֹץ וְדַרְדַּר תַּצְמִיחַ לָךְ.

4. After Adam sinned, everything disappeared from the world, and the earth was cursed, as it is written: "cursed is the earth for your sake" (Beresheet 3:17), "When you till the ground, it shall not henceforth give its strength to you..." (Beresheet 4:12) and "thorns also and thistles it shall bring forth to you" (Beresheet 3:18).

5. אָתָא נֹחַ וְתִקֵּן קַרְדּוּמִין וּפְצִירֵי בְּעָלְמָא. וּלְבָתַר וַיֵּשְׁתְּ מִן הַיַּיִן וַיִּשְׁכָּר וַיִּתְגַּל בְּתוֹךְ אָהֳלֹה. אָתוּ בְּנֵי עָלְמָא וְחָבוּ קַמֵּיהּ דְּקֻדְשָׁא בְּרִיךְ הוּא, וְאִסְתַּלָּקוּ חֵילִין דְּאַרְעָא כְּמִלְקַדְמִין, וַהֲווֹ קַיְימֵי עַד דְּאָתָא אַבְרָהָם.

5. When Noah appeared in the world, he prepared spades and hoes, WHICH MEANS THAT HE PREPARED TOOLS TO TILL THE GROUND. THUS, IT IS WRITTEN OF HIM: "THIS ONE SHALL COMFORT US FROM OUR WORK AND THE TOIL OF OUR HANDS..." (BERESHEET 5: 29). HE SHALL GIVE US TOOLS, SO THAT WE MAY BE FREED FROM PRODUCTION USING OUR BARE HANDS, FOR WHICH WE HAD BEEN DESTINED UNTIL NOW! Afterwards, however, "he drank of the wine, and was drunk; and he was uncovered within his tent" (Beresheet 9: 21). And later, the people of the world sinned before the Holy One, blessed be He. And the powers of the earth disappeared again. THUS, ALL THE IMPROVEMENTS OF NOAH WERE LOST. And so it remained until Abraham appeared.

6. כֵּיוָן דְּאָתָא אַבְרָהָם, מִיָּד הַנִּצָּנִים נִרְאוּ בָאָרֶץ, אִתְתַּקָּנוּ וְאִתְגְּלוּ כָּל חֵילִין בְּאַרְעָא. עֵת הַזָּמִיר הִגִּיעַ, בְּשַׁעֲתָא דַּאֲמַר לֵיהּ קֻדְשָׁא בְּרִיךְ הוּא דְּיִתְגְּזַר, כֵּיוָן דְּמָטָא הַהוּא זִמְנָא, דִּבְרִית, אִשְׁתְּכַח בֵּיהּ בְּאַבְרָהָם, וְאִתְגְּזַר. כְּדֵין אִתְקַיַּים בֵּיהּ, כָּל הַאי קְרָא, וְאִתְקַיַּים עָלְמָא, וּמִלָּה דְּקֻדְשָׁא בְּרִיךְ הוּא הֲוָה בְּאִתְגַּלְיָיא בֵּיהּ, הַה"ד וַיֵּרָא אֵלָיו ה'.

6. As soon as Abraham appeared: "the flowers appeared on the earth." THIS MEANS THAT the powers of the earth were amended and revealed. "The time of the singing of the birds (also: 'pruning') has come," REFERRING TO THE

TIME when the Holy One, blessed be He, told him to circumcise himself. THE TERM 'PRUNING' ALLUDES TO THE REMOVAL OF THE FORESKIN. Thus, the time was ripe for the covenant to appear in Abraham, MEANING when he was circumcised. Only then was the verse, "THE FLOWERS APPEARED..." fulfilled through him, and the word of the Holy One, blessed be He, was revealed openly to him. as it is written: "And Hashem appeared to him," AFTER HE WAS CIRCUMCISED.

7. רַבִּי אֶלְעָזָר פָּתַח, הַאי קְרָא בָּתַר דְּאִתְגְּזַר אַבְרָהָם, דְּעַד לָא אִתְגְּזַר לָא הֲוָה מַלֵּיל עִמֵּיה, אֶלָּא מִגּוֹ דַּרְגָּא תַּתָּאָה, וְדַרְגִּין עִלָּאִין לָא הֲווֹ קַיְימֵי, עַל הַהִיא דַּרְגָּא. כֵּיוָן דְּאִתְגְּזַר, מִיָּד הַנִּצָּנִים נִרְאוּ בָאָרֶץ, אִלֵּין דַּרְגִּין תַּתָּאִין דַּאֲפֵיקַת וְאַתְקֵינַת הַאי דַּרְגָּא תַּתָּאָה.

7. Rabbi Elazar began TO EXPLAIN THAT this verse refers to events after the circumcision of Abraham. Before the circumcision, the Holy One, blessed be He, spoke to him only through the lower grade – SPOKE THROUGH "A VISION," WHICH REFERS TO THE NUKVA WHILE IT IS STILL AT THE STAGE OF THE ILLUMINATION OF THE LEFT SIDE. AS IT IS WRITTEN: "AFTER THESE THINGS THE WORD OF HASHEM CAME TO ABRAM IN A VISION..." The upper grades were not attached to this grade, WHICH MEANS THAT THE UPPER GRADES OF ZEIR ANPIN WERE NOT ATTACHED TO THE NUKVA. As soon as Abraham was circumcised, "the flowers appeared on the earth." These are the lower grades, brought forth and established by the lower grade THAT IS CALLED "A VISION," SO THAT THEY MAY BE UNITED WITH ALL THE UPPER GRADES.

8. עֵת הַזָּמִיר הִגִּיעַ אִלֵּין עַנְפּוֹי דְּעָרְלָה. וְקוֹל הַתּוֹר נִשְׁמַע בְּאַרְצֵנוּ. דָּא קוֹל דְּנָפֵיק מִגּוֹ הַהוּא פְּנִימָאָה דְּכֹלָּא, וְהַהוּא קוֹל נִשְׁמַע, וְדָא קוֹל דְּגָזַר מִלָּה לְמַלָּלָא וְעָבֵיד לָהּ שְׁלִימוּ.

8. "The time of the singing of the birds (also: 'pruning') has come..." ALLUDES TO THE TIME OF PRUNING AND CUTTING OF THE BAD BRANCHES, WHICH ARE the branches of the foreskin, BECAUSE THIS KLIPAH WAS IN CHARGE BEFORE HE WAS CIRCUMCISED. THIS IS ACCORDING TO THE SECRET OF THE VERSE: "A WHISPERER SEPARATES CLOSE FRIENDS" (MISHLEI 16:28). "...and the voice of the turtledove is heard in our land." This is the voice that comes from the innermost aspect of

all. THE VOICE ALLUDES TO ZEIR ANPIN, AND THE INNTERMOST ASPECT OF ALL IS IMA, FROM WHOM ZEIR ANPIN EMANATES AND COMES FORTH. So that voice, ZEIR ANPIN, is heard IN OUR LAND, WHICH IS THE NUKVA – MEANING THAT ZEIR ANPIN MATED WITH THE NUKVA BY THE MAYIN NUKVIN (FEMALE WATERS) THAT WERE ELEVATED THROUGH THE PRECEPT OF CIRCUMCISION. And this is the voice that cuts the word into an utterance. THIS MEANS THAT IT HAS THE ABILITY TO ARTICULATE (LIT. 'CUT THE SPEECH), thereby achieving its perfection.

9. תָּא חֲזֵי, דְּעַד לָא אִתְגְּזַר אַבְרָהָם, לָא הֲוָה עֲלֵיהּ, אֶלָּא הַאי דַרְגָּא כִּדְאֲמָרָן, כֵּיוָן דְּאִתְגְּזַר, מַה כְּתִיב, וַיֵּרָא אֵלָיו ה'. לְמַאן, דְּהָא לָא כְּתִיב, וַיֵּרָא ה' אֶל אַבְרָם. דְּאִי לְאַבְרָם, מַאי שְׁבָחָא הָכָא יַתִּיר, מִבְּקַדְמֵיתָא עַד לָא אִתְגְּזַר, דִּכְתִיב וַיֵּרָא ה' אֶל אַבְרָם.

9. Come and behold: as long as Abraham was not circumcised, only that grade dwelt upon him, as we explained – THAT IS, THE GRADE OF NUKVA WHILE SHE WAS CALLED "A VISION." But after he was circumcised, it is written: "And Hashem appeared to him!" But it is not mentioned to whom, because it is not written: 'And Hashem appeared to Avram'! AND HE ANSWERS: IF IT WERE WRITTEN, 'to Abram,' then what greater sort of praise would there be than that which existed before he was circumcised? Because even then it was written: "And Hashem appeared to Abram" (Beresheet 12: 7).

10. אֶלָּא, רָזָא סְתִימָא אִיהוּ, וַיֵּרָא אֵלָיו ה'. לְהַהוּא דַרְגָּא דְּמַלִּיל עִמֵּיהּ, מַה דְּלָא הֲוָה מִקַּדְמַת דְּנָא, עַד דְּלָא אִתְגְּזַר. דְּהַשְׁתָּא, אִתְגְּלֵי קוֹל, וְאִתְחַבַּר בְּדִבּוּר, כַּד מַלִּיל עִמֵּיהּ.

10. The words: "And Hashem appeared to him" contain a secret. THIS MEANS THAT HE APPEARED TO that grade that spoke to him. IN OTHER WORDS, ZEIR ANPIN, WHICH IS YUD HEI VAV HEI, APPEARED TO HIM, NAMELY TO THE NUKVA. This had not happened before he was circumcised, WHEN THE NUKVA WAS STILL SEPARATED FROM ZEIR ANPIN. And now the voice THAT IS ZEIR ANPIN was revealed and was associated with speech, WHICH IS THE NUKVA, when He spoke with him. THUS, ABRAHAM BENEFITED FROM THE MATING OF MALE AND FEMALE, AND BECAME A CHARIOT FOR BOTH OF THEM. THEREFORE IT IS WRITTEN:

"AND HASHEM APPEARED TO HIM," WHICH ALLUDES TO THE MATING OF MALE AND FEMALE.

11. וְהוּא יוֹשֵׁב פֶּתַח הָאֹהֶל. וְהוּא, וְלֹא גְּלֵי מַאן. אֶלָּא, הָכָא גְּלֵי חָכְמְתָא, דְּכָלְהוֹ דַּרְגִּין שָׁרוּ עַל הַאי דַּרְגָּא תַּתָּאָה, בָּתַר דְּאִתְגְּזַר אַבְרָהָם. תָּא חֲזֵי, וַיֵּרָא אֵלָיו ה'. דָּא הוּא רָזָא דְּקוֹל דְּאִשְׁתְּמַע, דְּאִתְחַבַּר בְּדִבּוּר, וְאִתְגְּלֵי בֵּיהּ.

11. The verse: "and he sat in the tent door" (Beresheet 18:1) says "and he," but does not identify "him." AND HE REPLIES: the verse reveals the wisdom that INDICATES THAT all the grades rested upon that lower grade after Abraham was circumcised. SO THE PHRASE TEACHES US THAT "AND HE," REFERRING TO THE NUKVA, "SAT IN THE TENT DOOR," AS SHE BECAME THE GATEWAY FOR ALL THE GRADES. Come and behold: "And Hashem appeared to him." This is the secret of the voice, NAMELY ZEIR ANPIN, that is heard and attached to the utterance (speech), NAMELY MALCHUT, and revealed through it.

12. וְהוּא יוֹשֵׁב פֶּתַח הָאֹהֶל. דָּא עָלְמָא עִלָּאָה, דְּקָאֵים לְאַנְהָרָא עֲלֵיהּ. כְּחוֹם הַיּוֹם. דְּהָא אִתְנְהֵיר יְמִינָא, דַּרְגָּא דְּאַבְרָהָם אִתְדַּבַּק בֵּיהּ. דָּבָר אַחֵר כְּחוֹם הַיּוֹם. בְּשַׁעֲתָא דְּאִתְקְרִיב דַּרְגָּא לְדַרְגָּא, בְּתֵיאוּבְתָּא דְּדָא לָקֳבֵל דָּא.

12. In the verse: "and he sat in the tent door," THE WORDS, "AND HE" allude to the upper world, NAMELY IMA, that stands over him, REFERRING TO THE NUKVA, to shine upon him. THE NUKVA IS DESCRIBED AS "THE TENT DOOR," BECAUSE SHE HAS BECOME THE GATEWAY FOR THE LIGHTS. THE WORDS, "in the heat of the day," MEAN THAT the right side, WHICH IS CHESED, shone. This is the grade to which Abraham cleaved. Another explanation of "in the heat of the day" IS THAT IT REFERS TO the time when one grade approached another with great passion, AS ZEIR ANPIN APPROACHED THE NUKVA. THEN THEY WERE DESCRIBED BY THE WORDS: "IN THE HEAT OF THE DAY."

13. וַיֵּרָא אֵלָיו. אָמַר רַבִּי אַבָּא, עַד לָא אִתְגְּזַר אַבְרָהָם, הֲוָה אָטִים.

כֵּיוָן דְּאִתְגְּזַר, אִתְגְּלֵי כֹּלָּא, וְשַׁרְיָא עֲלֵיהּ שְׁכִינְתָּא בִּשְׁלִימוּ כִּדְקָא
יָאוֹת. תָּא חֲזֵי. וְהוּא יוֹשֵׁב פֶּתַח הָאֹהֶל. וְהוּא: דָּא עָלְמָא עִלָּאָה, דְּשָׁרֵי
עַל הַאי עָלְמָא תַּתָּאָה, אֵימָתַי, כְּחוֹם הַיּוֹם. בְּזִמְנָא דְּתֵיאוּבְתָּא דְּחַד
צַדִּיק לְמִישְׁרֵי בֵּיהּ.

13. In explaining the words, "appeared to him," Rabbi Aba said that before Abraham was circumcised, he was blocked FROM RECEIVING THE SUPERNAL LIGHTS. As soon as he was circumcised, everything appeared, INCLUDING ALL THE LIGHTS, AS HIS COVER WAS REMOVED. And the Shechinah rested upon him in full perfection, as should properly be. Come and behold. IT IS WRITTEN: "and he sat in the tent door." "He" refers to the upper world, TO BINAH, that rests upon the lower world, WHICH IS THE NUKVA. HE ASKS: When DOES BINAH REST UPON THE NUKVA? AND HE REPLIES: THIS IS WHY THE VERSE CONCLUDES WITH "in the heat of the day" – when the passion of a certain righteous, WHO IS THE YESOD OF ZEIR ANPIN, is aroused to rest IN THE LOWER WORLD, WHICH IS THE NUKVA. THAT IS, WHEN THERE IS A MATING BETWEEN MALE AND FEMALE, THEN THE MOCHIN OF BINAH DWELL WITHIN THE NUKVA.

14. מִיָּד, וַיִּשָּׂא עֵינָיו וַיַּרְא וְהִנֵּה שְׁלֹשָׁה אֲנָשִׁים נִצָּבִים עָלָיו, מַאן
אִינוּן שְׁלֹשָׁה אֲנָשִׁים. אִלֵּין אַבְרָהָם יִצְחָק וְיַעֲקֹב, דְּקַיְימֵי עֲלֵיהּ דְּהַאי
דַרְגָּא, וּמִנַּיְיהוּ יָנִיק וְאִתְּזָן.

14. Immediately AFTER THE MATING OF MALE AND FEMALE WAS COMPLETED, IT IS WRITTEN: "And he lifted up his eyes and looked, and lo, three men stood by him..." (Beresheet 18: 2) AND HE ASKS: Who are these three men? AND HE SAYS: They are Abraham, Isaac, and Jacob – OR CHESED, GVURAH, AND TIFERET OF ZEIR ANPIN THAT ARE NAMED ABRAHAM, ISAAC, AND JACOB. AND HE SAW THEM standing over that grade, WHICH IS THE NUKVA, and from them the Nukva draws sustenance and nourishment.

15. כְּדֵין וַיַּרְא וַיָּרָץ לִקְרָאתָם. דְּתֵיאוּבְתָּא דְּהַאי דַרְגָּא תַּתָּאָה,
לְאִתְחַבְּרָא בְּהוּ, וְחֶדְוָותָא דִּילָהּ, לְאִתְמַשְׁכָא אֲבַתְרַיְיהוּ. וַיִּשְׁתַּחוּ
אַרְצָה. לְאִתְתַּקְּנָא כֻּרְסְיָיא לְגַבַּיְיהוּ.

15. And then: "when he saw them, he ran to meet them," because the passionate desire of the lower grade, WHICH IS THE NUKVA, is to cleave to CHESED, GVURAH, AND TIFERET. And Her joy is to be drawn toward them. SO, ACCORDINGLY, "HE RAN TO MEET THEM" IS SAID ABOUT THE NUKVA THAT WANTED TO CLING TO THEM. THE VERSE CONTINUES, "and bowed himself toward the ground," to become and be formed into a throne for them – SO THAT THE NUKVA BECOMES A THRONE FOR CHESED, GVURAH, AND TIFERET OF ZEIR ANPIN, SO THAT THEY MAY REST UPON HER, AS A PERSON SITS ON A CHAIR.

16. תָּא חֲזֵי, עֲבַד קֻדְשָׁא בְּרִיךְ הוּא לְדָוִד מַלְכָּא, חַד סַמְכָא מִכָּרְסְיָיא עִלָּאָה, כַּאֲבָהָן. וְאַף עַל גַּב דְּאִיהוּ כָּרְסָיָיא לְגַבַּיְיהוּ, אֲבָל, בְּזִמְנָא דְּאִתְחַבָּר בְּהוֹ, אִיהוּ חַד סַמְכָא, לְאִתְתַּקְנָא בְּכָרְסָיָיא עִלָּאָה. וּבְגִין כָּךְ, נָטַל מַלְכוּתָא בְּחֶבְרוֹן, דָּוִד מַלְכָּא, שְׁבַע שְׁנִין, לְאִתְחַבְּרָא בְּהוֹ. וְהָא אִתְּמַר.

16. Come and behold: The Holy One, blessed be He, made King David, WHO IS THE SECRET OF THE NUKVA, one of the legs of the supernal throne, like the patriarchs. AND HE ASKS: Even though She is a throne for THE PATRIARCHS, HOW CAN IT BE SAID THAT SHE WAS SET AT THE SAME LEVEL WITH THE PATRIARCHS TO COMPLETE THE FOURTH LEG OF THE THRONE? AND HE ANSWERS: This is so only when She is united with them for the purpose of being a leg of the supernal throne. King David received the kingdom of Yisrael in Hebron for seven years for this reason – to be united with CHESED, GVURAH, AND TIFERET. This has already been explained.

תּוֹסֶפְתָּא

17. וַיֵּרָא אֵלָיו ה' בְּאֵלוֹנֵי מַמְרֵא. אַמַּאי בְּ אֵלוֹנֵי מַמְרֵא, וְלָא בַּאֲתַר אָחֳרָא. אֶלָּא, בְּגִין דְּיָהִיב לֵיהּ עֵיטָא, עַל גְּזֵירוּ דִּקְנַיְימָא דִּילֵיהּ. בְּשַׁעֲתָא דַּאֲמַר קֻדְשָׁא בְּרִיךְ הוּא לְאַבְרָהָם לְמִגְזַר, אֲזַל אַבְרָהָם לִימָלֵךְ עִם חַבְרוֹי, אֲמַר לֵיהּ עָנֵר, אַנְתְּ בֶּן תִּשְׁעִין שְׁנִין וְאַתְּ מֵעִיק גַּרְמָךְ.

Tosefta (addendum)

17. Of the verse, "And Hashem appeared to him by the terebinths of Mamre" (Beresheet 18:1), HE ASKS: Why by the terebinths of Mamre and not in any other place? AND HE REPLIES: Because Mamre gave him good advice about being circumcised. When the Holy One, blessed be He, told Abraham to circumcise himself, Abraham consulted his friends. Aner told him: You are more than 90 years old, and you shall pain yourself.

18. אָמַר לוֹ מַמְרֵא, דְּכַרְתְּ יוֹמָא דְּרָמוֹ לָךְ כַּשְׂדָּאֵי בְּאַתּוּן דְּנוּרָא. וְהַהוּא כַּפְנָא דַּעֲבַר עַל עָלְמָא, דִּכְתִיב וַיְהִי רָעָב בָּאָרֶץ וַיֵּרֶד אַבְרָם מִצְרַיְמָה. וְאִינוּן מַלְכִין דִּרְדָּפוּ בַּתְרֵיהוֹן, וּמָחִית יַתְהוֹן, וְקָדְשָׁא בְּרִיךְ הוּא שֵׁזְבִינָךְ מִכֻּלָּא, וְלָא יָכִיל בַּר נָשׁ לְמֶעְבַּד לָךְ בִּישׁ. קוּם עֲבֵיד פִּקוּדָא דְּמָרָךְ. אָמַר לוֹ קָדְשָׁא בְּרִיךְ הוּא: מַמְרֵא. אַנְתְּ יְהַבְתְּ לֵיהּ עֵיטָא לְמִגְזַר, חַיֶּיךָ, לֵית אֲנָא מִתְגַּלֵּי עֲלֵיהּ אֶלָּא בְּפַלְטְרִין דִּילָךְ, הה"ד בְּאֵלוֹנֵי מַמְרֵא (עד כָּאן).

18. Mamre, HOWEVER, said to him: Do not forget the day when the Chaldeans threw you into the furnace of fire and famine took over the world, as it is written: "And there was a famine in the land, and Abram went down into Egypt" (Beresheet 12: 10). And you smote all those kings that YOUR MEN pursued. And the Holy One, blessed be He, saved you from them all, so that nobody could do you any harm. So rise and fulfill the precept of your Master. The Holy One, blessed be He, said to MAMRE: You advised him to perform the circumcision. By your life! I shall reveal Myself to him only in your chamber. This is why it is written: "by the terebinths of Mamre."

2. The soul, when it rises from earth to heaven

A Synopsis

The Zohar presents the spiritual significance behind the Torah story and speaks of Abraham sitting under a hot, blazing sun when three people come to visit him. The *blazing sun* is a metaphor for the immense Light of the Creator revealed through the divine instrument of the Tetragrammaton and correspondingly, through the words of the Zohar.

The Relevance of this Passage

The phrase *blazing sun* indicates that an extraordinary amount of spiritual Light is suddenly being revealed in this specific section of the Torah. This concept can be understood through the analogy of a light bulb. A bulb glows at a constant level of illumination. Just before the bulb burns out, however, there is a momentary burst of added light. The Zohar is our instrument to capture the intense spark of Light that is momentarily shining forth in this specific verse of the Torah.

מִדְרָשׁ הַנֶּעֱלָם

19. רַבָּנָן פָּתְחֵי בְּהַאי קְרָא, לְרֵיחַ שְׁמָנֶיךָ טוֹבִים שֶׁמֶן תּוּרַק שְׁמֶךָ וְגו'. ת״ר הַאי נִשְׁמָתָא דְּבַר אֵינָשׁ, בְּשַׁעֲתָא דְּסָלְקָא מֵאַרְעָא לִרְקִיעָא, וְקַיְימָא בְּהַהוּא זִיהֲרָא עִלָּאָה דַּאֲמָרָן, קוּדְשָׁא בְּרִיךְ הוּא מְבַקֵּר לָהּ.

Midrash Hane'elam (Homiletical interpretations on the obscure)

19. The sages began their interpretation of this passage WITH THE VERSE: "Your oils are fragrant. For your flowing oil you are renowned" (Shir Hashirim 1:3). Our sages have taught that when the soul of a human being rises from earth to heaven, REFERRING TO THE TIME WHEN A PERSON SLEEPS AT NIGHT, it stands in the Divine Illumination. The Holy One, blessed be He, visits it.

20. ת״ש. אָמַר רַבִּי שִׁמְעוֹן בֶּן יוֹחָאי, כָּל נִשְׁמָתָא דְּצַדִּיקַיָּיא, כֵּיוָן דְּקַיְימָא בְּאֲתַר שְׁכִינְתָּא יְקָרָא, דְּחֲזְיָא לְמֵיתַב, קוּדְשָׁא בְּרִיךְ הוּא קָרֵי לַאֲבָהָתָא, וַאֲמַר לוֹן, זִילוּ וּבַקְּרוּ לִפְלַנְיָא צַדִּיקָא דְּאָתָא, וְאַקְדִּימוּ לֵיהּ

שְׁלָמָא, מִן שְׁמִי. וְאִינוּן אָמְרִין, מָארֵי עָלְמָא, לָא אִתְחֲזֵי, לְאַבָּא
לְמֵיזַל לְמֵיחֱמֵי לִבְרָא, בְּרָא אִתְחֲזֵי לְמֵיחֲמֵי, וּלְמֶחֱזֵי, וּלְמִתְבַּע לַאֲבוֹי.

20. Come and listen: Rabbi Shimon bar Yochai said: When the soul of a righteous person stands in the place where the Shechinah of His blessed Glory rests – MEANING THAT IT IS WORTHY OF RECEIVING THE ILLUMINATION OF CHOCHMAH, WHICH IS THE SECRET OF 'STANDING UPRIGHT,' and is worthy of sitting by Her, TO RECEIVE THE GARMENT OF CHASSADIM, WHICH IS THE SECRET OF 'SITTING' – The Holy One, blessed be He, WHO IS ZEIR ANPIN, calls upon the patriarchs, WHO ARE CHESED, GVURAH, AND TIFERET, HIS THREE COLUMNS. And He says to them: Go and visit so-and-so, the righteous person who has come, and welcome him in peace in My Name. THIS MEANS THAT THE THREE COLUMNS SHOULD PASS ON THE ILLUMINATION OF THE MATING, WHICH IS CALLED PEACE. THE WORDS "IN MY NAME" REFER TO THE NUKVA. And they claim it is not proper for a father to go and visit his child, but rather the child should seek after his father to see him.

21. וְהוּא קָרֵי לְיַעֲקֹב, וְאָמַר לֵיהּ, אַנְתְּ דַּהֲוָה לָךְ צַעֲרָא דִּבְנִין, זִיל
וְקַבֵּיל פְּנֵי דִּפְלַנְיָא צַדִּיקָא דְּאָתָא הָכָא, וַאֲנָא אֵיזֵיל עִמָּךְ. הה"ד
מְבַקְשֵׁי פָנֶיךָ יַעֲקֹב סֶלָה. מְבַקֵּשׁ לֹא נֶאֱמַר, אֶלָּא מְבַקְשֵׁי. אָמַר רִבִּי
חִיָּיא, מֵרֵישֵׁיהּ דִּקְרָא מַשְׁמַע דִּכְתִיב זֶה דוֹר דּוֹרְשָׁיו וְגו'.

21. The Holy One, blessed be He, then calls upon Jacob and says to him: You, who suffered the sorrow of RAISING children, go and welcome so-and-so, the righteous person who has come here, and I shall go along with you, as it is written: "those who seek your face Jacob, Selah" (Tehilim 24: 6). It does not say "seek" in the singular, but in the plural, BECAUSE IT REFERS TO THE SOULS OF THE RIGHTEOUS WHO JACOB WELCOMES AS THEY SEEK HIS "WELCOME." Rabbi Chiya said: This we understand from the first part of the verse. as it is written: "This is the generation of them that seek him," WHICH TEACHES US THAT THE INTENTION OF THE VERSE ALLUDES TO THE SOULS OF THE RIGHTEOUS, THW SEEKERS NAMELY, THE LEADERS OF THE GENERATION.

22. אָמַר רִבִּי יַעֲקֹב אָמַר רִבִּי חִיָּיא, יַעֲקֹב אָבִינוּ הוּא כִּסֵּא הַכָּבוֹד. וְכֵן
תָּאנָא דְּבֵי אֵלִיָּהוּ, יַעֲקֹב אָבִינוּ הוּא כִּסֵּא בִּפְנֵי עַצְמוֹ, דִּכְתִיב, וְזָכַרְתִּי

אֶת בְּרִיתִי יַעֲקוֹב, בְּרִית כָּרַת קוּדְשָׁא בְּרִיךְ הוּא לְיַעֲקֹב לְבַדּוֹ, יוֹתֵר מִכָּל אֲבוֹתָיו, דַּעֲבֵיד לֵיהּ כֻּסֵּא הַכָּבוֹד בַּר מִן קַדְמָאָה.

22. Rabbi Ya'akov said in the name of Rabbi Chiya: Jacob, the Patriarch, is the Throne of Glory. And the teachings of Elijah also state: Jacob the Patriarch is a Throne by himself, as it is written: "Then will I remember my covenant with Jacob" (Vayikra 26: 42). The Holy One, blessed be He, established a covenant with Jacob alone, more than THE COVENANT HE ESTABLISHED with all his fathers. He made him a Throne of Glory FOR HIS DIVINE PRESENCE TO REST UPON, distinguishing him from his predecessors. AND THE REASON IS THAT HIS FOREFATHERS, WHO ARE ABRAHAM AND ISAAC, ARE NOT ABLE TO SHINE WITHOUT HIM. THEREFORE, HE IN HIMSELF INCLUDES THEIR LIGHTS AS WELL AS HIS OWN, AND THUS BECOMES A THRONE TO HIMSELF.

23. רַבִּי אֱלִיעֶזֶר הֲוָה יָתִיב, וַהֲוָה לָעֵי בְּאוֹרַיְיתָא. אָתָא לְגַבֵּיהּ, ר' עֲקִיבָא, אָמַר לֵיהּ, בְּמַאי קָא עָסִיק מַר. אָמַר לוֹ בְּהַאי קְרָא דִּכְתִיב וְכֻסֵּא כָבוֹד יַנְחִילֵם. מַהוּ כֻּסֵּא כָבוֹד יַנְחִילֵם. זֶה יַעֲקֹב אָבִינוּ, דַּעֲבֵיד לֵיהּ כָּרְסֵי יְקָר בִּלְחוֹדוֹי, לְקַבָּלָא אוּלְפַן נִשְׁמָתָא דְּצַדִּיקַיָּא.

23. Rabbi Eliezer was sitting and studying Torah when Rabbi Akiva arrived. He said to him: Sir, what are you studying? He replies: The passage where it is written: "and to make them inherit the Throne of Glory" (I Shmuel 2:8) — what does "and to make them inherit the Throne of Glory" mean? This is Jacob, the Patriarch for whom he made a Throne of Glory by himself that would receive Torah for the souls of the righteous.

24. וְקוּדְשָׁא בְּרִיךְ הוּא אָזֵיל עִמֵּיהּ, בְּכָל רֵישׁ יַרְחָא וְיַרְחָא. וְכַד חָמֵי נִשְׁמָתָא, יְקָר אַסְפַּקְלַרְיָאה שְׁכִינְתָּא דְמָארֵיהּ, מְבָרְכַת וְסָגְדַת קַמֵּי קוּדְשָׁא בְּרִיךְ הוּא, הה"ד בָּרְכִי נַפְשִׁי וְגו'.

24. And the Holy One, blessed be He, goes with JACOB on the first day of every month. And when the soul sees the glory of the mirror, which is the Shechinah of זאן Master, THEN THE SOUL praises Him and bows down in front of the Holy One, blessed be He. This is THE MEANING OF "Bless Hashem, my soul..." (Tehilim 104:1)

25. אָמַר רַבִּי עֲקִיבָא, קוּדְשָׁא בְּרִיךְ הוּא קָאִים עֲלוֹהִי, וְנִשְׁמָתָא פְּתַח
וַאֲמַר, ה' אֱלֹקַי גָּדַלְתָּ מְאֹד וְגו', כָּל הַפְּרָשָׁה עַד סִיּוּמָא, דְקָאֲמַר יִתַּמּוּ
חַטָּאִים וְגו'. וְעוֹד אָמַר רַבִּי עֲקִיבָא, וְלָא דָא בִּלְחוֹדוֹי, אֶלָּא, מְשַׁבַּחַת
לֵיהּ, עַל גוּפָא דְאִשְׁתָּאַר בְּעָלְמָא דֵין, וַאֲמַר בָּרְכִי נַפְשִׁי אֶת ה' וְכָל
קְרָבַי וְגו'.

25. Rabbi Akiva said: The Holy One, blessed be He, stands over THE SOUL. And the soul begins by saying: "Hashem my Elohim, You are very great...", continuing with all the verses to the end, as the passage reads, "Let the sinners be consumed out of the earth..." (Ibid. 35). Rabbi Akiva continued: As well as this, it praises the Holy One, blessed be He, thanks Him for the body that is left in this world, and says: "Bless Hashem, my soul, and all that is within me, bless His Holy Name" (Tehilim 103: 1). THE WORDS, "ALL THAT IS WITHIN ME," ALLUDE TO THE BODY. AT FIRST, THE SOUL PRAISES AND THANKS THE HOLY ONE, BLESSED BE HE, FOR ITS OWN ACHIEVEMENTS. THEN IT SAYS: "BLESS HASHEM, MY SOUL! HASHEM MY ELOHIM, YOU ARE VERY GREAT." AND THEN IT PRAISES AND THANKS HIM FOR THE BODY, MEANING THAT THE SPLENDOR OF THE SOUL IS DRAWN DOWNWARD TO SHINE UPON THE BODY. AND THEN IT SAYS: "BLESS HASHEM, MY SOUL, AND ALL THAT IS WITHIN ME, BLESS HIS HOLY NAME." THESE PRAISES ARE OFFERED FOR THE LIGHT OF THE BODY.

26. וְקוּדְשָׁא בְּרִיךְ הוּא אָזֵיל. מְנָא לָן הַאי. מֵהַאי קְרָא דִכְתִיב, וַיֵּרָא
אֵלָיו ה' בְּאֵלוֹנֵי מַמְרֵא, זֶה יַעֲקֹב. מַהוּ מַמְרֵא. מִשּׁוּם דְּאַחְסִין מָאתָן
עָלְמִין מֵעֵדֶן, וְהוּא כִּסֵּא. אָמַר רַבִּי יִצְחָק, מַמְרֵא בְּגִימַטְרִיָּא מָאתָן
וְתַמְנִין וְחַד, הֲוָה מָאתָן דְּעֵדֶן, דִכְתִיב וּמָאתַיִם לַנוֹטְרִים אֶת פִּרְיוֹ,
וְתַמְנִין וְחַד, דְּהוּא כִּסֵּא. וּבְגִין כָּךְ אִתְקְרֵי וַיֵּרָא אֵלָיו ה' בְּאֵלוֹנֵי
מַמְרֵא. וְעַל שׁוּם דָּא, נִקְרָא מַמְרֵא.

26. And the Holy One, blessed by He, goes ALONG WITH JACOB. How do we know this? From the passage where it is written: "And Hashem appeared to him by the terebinths of Mamre." This is Jacob, WHO IS CALLED MAMRE. SO THE HOLY ONE, BLESSED BE HE, DID INDEED GO WITH JACOB. AND HE ASKS: Wherefore is the name Mamre? AND HE

ANSWERS: Because Jacob inherited two hundred worlds in Eden, and he is the Throne BECAUSE HE BECAME THE THRONE OF GLORY. And Rabbi Yitzchak explains: The numerical value OF Mamre is 281. So there are the two hundred of Eden WHICH JACOB ATTAINED, as it is written: "and those that guard the fruit thereof two hundred" (Shir Hashirim 8:12), and 81 is the numerical value of *Kise* ('throne'). THUS, MAMRE'S NUMERICAL VALUE OF 281 COMES FROM THE TWO HUNDRED WORLDS OF EDEN, WHICH IS THE SECRET OF CHOCHMAH THAT IS CALLED EDEN, AND FROM THE THRONE, WHICH IS THE SECRET OF CHASSADIM THAT CLOTHE CHOCHMAH. For this reason IT IS SAID: "And Hashem appeared to him by the terebinths of Mamre." And for this reason, JACOB is called Mamre. HE INCLUDES THE ASPECT OF EDEN AND THE ASPECT OF THE THRONE TOGETHER, WHICH ARE THE SECRET OF MAMRE. HENCE "AND HASHEM APPEARED TO HIM."

27. אָמַר רָבִּי יְהוּדָה, מַהוּ בְּאֵלוֹנֵי. ר"ל תּוּקְפוֹי, הה"ד אֲבִיר יַעֲקֹב. וְהוּא יוֹשֵׁב פֶּתַח הָאֹהֶל. הה"ד ה' מִי יָגוּר בְּאָהֳלֶךְ וגו'. כְּחוֹם הַיּוֹם. דִּכְתִיב, וְזָרְחָה לָכֶם יִרְאֵי שְׁמִי שֶׁמֶשׁ צְדָקָה וּמַרְפֵּא בִּכְנָפֶיהָ.

27. Rabbi Yehuda asks: What is the meaning of: "by the terebinths" (Heb. *elonei*)? IF MAMRE IS JACOB, WHY DOES IT SAY "THE TEREBINTHS OF MAMRE?" AND HE ANSWERS: It meant to say 'his might,' as it is written: "by the hands of the mighty one of Jacob" (Beresheet 49:24). THUS, "THE TEREBINTHS OF MAMRE" BEARS RESEMBLANCE TO "THE MIGHTY JACOB," BECAUSE ELONEI MEANS MIGHTY AND STRONG, AND MAMRE IS JACOB. The verse, "and he sat in the tent door" is as it is written: "Hashem, who (Heb. *mi*) shall abide in Your tabernacle (or: 'tent')" (Tehilim 15:1). THIS MEANS THAT THE "TENT DOOR" IS THE SECRET OF THE ILLUMINATION OF THE RIGHT COLUMN, WHICH IS THE SECRET OF THE COVERED CHASSADIM. The verse, "in the heat of the day" is as written: "But to you that fear My name shall the sun of righteousness arise with healing in its wings" (Malachi 3:20). THIS REFERS TO THE ILLUMINATION OF THE LEFT COLUMN. AND THIS IS THE SECRET OF THE ILLUMINATION OF CHOCHMAH WITHOUT CHASSADIM, WHICH IS DESCRIBED AS A 'SUN COMING OUT OF ITS SHEATH' BECAUSE THE LIGHT OF CHOCHMAH DOES NOT SHINE WITHOUT THE SHEATH OF CHASSADIM. AND WHEN IT DOES SHINE WITHOUT CHASSADIM, IT BURNS. ACCORDING TO THE SECRET OF THE VERSE, "IN THE HEAT OF

THE DAY," IS WHEN THE WICKED ARE CONDEMNED BY IT. BUT THE RIGHTEOUS ARE HEALED BY IT BECAUSE THEY ELEVATE THE MAYIN NUKVIN (FEMALE WATERS) AND DRAW DOWN THE CHASSADIM IN ORDER TO CLOTHE CHOCHMAH.

28. אָמַר רַבָּן יוֹחָנָן בֶּן זַכַּאי, בְּהַהִיא שַׁעֲתָא אָזֵיל קוּדְשָׁא בְּרִיךְ הוּא, וּבְגִין דְּשָׁמְעִין אֲבָהָתָא אַבְרָהָם וְיִצְחָק, דְּקוּדְשָׁא בְּרִיךְ הוּא אָזֵיל לְגַבֵּיה, תָּבְעִין מִן יַעֲקֹב לְמֵיזַל עִמְּהוֹן, וּלְאַקְדָּמָא לֵיה שְׁלָם.

28. Rabbi Yochanan ben Zakai said: At that time, WHEN THE SOUL IS AT THE STAGE OF "THE HEAT OF THE DAY," the Holy One, blessed be He, WHO IS ZEIR ANPIN, SHARES HIS ABUNDANCE WITH THE SOUL. And when the Patriarchs, Abraham, Isaac and Jacob, heard the Holy One, blessed be He, REFERRING TO THE ENTIRETY OF ZEIR ANPIN, move towards THE SOUL — MEANING THAT THE PATRIARCHS WERE AWARE THAT THE SOUL WAS IN THE STATE OF "THE HEAT OF THE DAY," AND IN NEED OF THE "PLACE OF THE CLOTHING OF CHASSADIM" — they asks Jacob to go with them and welcome THE SOUL in peace.

29. וְאִינוּן קַיְימִין עֲלוֹהִי. מִמַּאי. דִּכְתִיב, וַיִּשָּׂא עֵינָיו וַיַּרְא וְהִנֵּה שְׁלֹשָׁה אֲנָשִׁים נִצָּבִים עָלָיו. שְׁלֹשָׁה אֲנָשִׁים: אִלֵּין אֲבָהָתָא, אַבְרָהָם יִצְחָק וְיַעֲקֹב, דְּקַיְימִין עֲלוֹהִי, וְחָמוּ עוֹבָדִין טָבִין דְּעָבְדִין. וַיַּרְא וַיָּרָץ לִקְרָאתָם מִפֶּתַח הָאֹהֶל וַיִּשְׁתַּחוּ אָרְצָה. מִשּׁוּם דְּחָמֵי שְׁכִינַת יְקָרָא עִמְּהוֹן. הה"ד, עַל כֵּן עֲלָמוֹת אֲהֵבוּךָ.

29. And ABRAHAM AND ISAAC stand over THE SOUL. THIS MEANS THAT AFTER JACOB SHARED THE ABUNDANCE OF CHASSADIM BY WELCOMING IT WITH PEACE, THE TWO COLUMNS OF ABRAHAM AND ISAAC SHONE UPON IT. As it is written: "And he lifted up his eyes and looked" — REFERRING TO THE SOUL — "and lo, three men stood over him." The "three men" are the patriarchs, Abraham, Isaac, and Jacob, who stood by him, observing the soul and the good deeds it has performed. THIS MEANS THAT THEY EXAMINE THE MAYIN NUKVIN ('FEMALE WATERS') OF THE SOUL AND SHARE WITH IT THE MAYIN DUCHRIN ('MALE WATERS'). "...and when he saw them, he ran to meet them from the tent door, and bowed himself toward the ground," because he saw the Shechinah of His Blessed

Glory with them. Hence, it is written: "...therefore do the young maidens love you" (Shir Hashirim 1:3).

30. דָּבָר אַחֵר, וַיֵּרָא אֵלָיו ה' בְּאֵלוֹנֵי מַמְרֵא. רַבָּנָן פָּתְחֵי בְּהַאי קְרָא, בְּשַׁעַת פְּטִירָתוֹ שֶׁל אָדָם. דְּתַנְיָא, אָמַר רַבִּי יְהוּדָה, בְּשַׁעַת פְּטִירָתוֹ שֶׁל אָדָם, הוּא יוֹם הַדִּין הַגָּדוֹל, שֶׁהַנְּשָׁמָה מִתְפָּרֶדֶת מִן הַגּוּף. וְלֹא נִפְטַר אָדָם מִן הָעוֹלָם, עַד שֶׁרוֹאֶה אֶת הַשְּׁכִינָה. הה"ד, כִּי לֹא יִרְאַנִי הָאָדָם וָחָי. וּבָאִין עִם הַשְּׁכִינָה שְׁלֹשָׁה מַלְאֲכֵי הַשָּׁרֵת, לְקַבֵּל נִשְׁמָתוֹ שֶׁל צַדִּיק. הה"ד וַיֵּרָא אֵלָיו ה' וגו'. כְּחֹם הַיּוֹם. זֶה יוֹם הַדִּין הַבּוֹעֵר כַּתַּנּוּר, לְהַפְרִיד הַנְּשָׁמָה מִן הַגּוּף.

30. Another explanation of: "And Hashem appeared to him by the terebinths of Mamre." The sages began with this verse that speaks of the time of one's demise. We learned that Rabbi Yehuda said that at the time of a person's death, which is the day of the Great Judgment when the soul is separated from the body, no one leaves the world before he sees the Shechinah, as it is written: "...for no man shall see me and live" (Shemot 33: 20). And three ministering angels accompany the Shechinah to welcome the soul of the righteous, as it is written: "And Hashem appeared to him...in the heat of the day." This is the Day of Judgment that burns like a furnace in order to separate the soul from the body.

3. The soul at the time of death

A Synopsis

During sleep and upon death of a righteous individual, the soul travels a certain course as it ascends to the Upper Worlds. If the soul is righteous, it is welcomed to the Upper Worlds by the Patriarchs, specifically Jacob.

The Relevance of this Passage

The return of the soul to its original source is vital. It is through this process that the Creator absorbs the souls, which allows them to be born anew each morning. This otherworldly journey occurs each night, whether or not we are cognizant of it. An individual's degree of awareness, however, and their personal level of spirituality [righteousness] determines the particular course the soul travels and the heights it can attain. The higher the soul ascends is directly proportionate to the measure of Light it receives. This portion awakens a deeper awareness of the Light our soul can achieve if it is righteous, as well as the ability to ascend to greater heights and receive greater revelations of spiritual energy during sleep.

31. וַיִּשָּׂא עֵינָיו וַיַּרְא וְהִנֵּה שְׁלֹשָׁה אֲנָשִׁים. הַמְבַקְּרִים מַעֲשָׂיו מַה שֶּׁעָשָׂה, וְהוּא מוֹדֶה עֲלֵיהֶם בְּפִיו. וְכֵיוָן שֶׁהַנְּשָׁמָה רוֹאָה כָּךְ, יוֹצֵאת מִן הַגּוּף, עַד פֶּתַח בֵּית הַבְּלִיעָה, וְעוֹמֶדֶת שָׁם, עַד שֶׁמִּתְוַדָּה, כָּל מַה שֶּׁעָשָׂה הַגּוּף עִמָּהּ, בָּעוֹלָם הַזֶּה. וְאָז נִשְׁמַת הַצַּדִּיק, הִיא שְׂמֵחָה בְּמַעֲשֶׂיהָ, וּשְׂמֵחָה עַל פִּקְדוֹנָהּ. דְּתָאנָא, אָמַר רַבִּי יִצְחָק, נִשְׁמָתוֹ שֶׁל צַדִּיק מִתְאַוָּה, אֵימָתַי תֵּצֵא מִן הָעוֹלָם הַזֶּה, שֶׁהוּא הֶבֶל, כְּדֵי לְהִתְעַנֵּג בָּעוֹלָם הַבָּא.

31. The verse, "and he lifted up his eyes, and looked, and lo, three men stood by him," refers to those who criticize his behavior and examine his deeds as he confesses them with his mouth. And because the soul sees all this, it leaves the body and reaches the gullet (pharynx), where it remains until it confesses and retells all that the body did together with it in this world. Then the soul of the righteous is happy with what it has done, and is happy with its deposit. We have learned that Rabbi Yitzchak said: The soul of the righteous feels great desire for the moment when it shall leave this world, which is worthless, so that it may enjoy itself in the World to Come!

4. When Rabbi Eliezer became ill

A Synopsis
The Zohar recounts the death of Rabbi Eliezer, the teacher and master of Rabbi Akiva. Rabbi Akiva was the teacher and master of Rabbi Shimon bar Yochai, the author of The Zohar. When a righteous soul departs this world, he reveals his greatest amount of Light and energy. This Light is the total accumulation of his spiritual accomplishments during his lifetime. In addition, the Light that Rabbi Eliezer was unable to reveal during his lifetime, also became manifest at the moment of his passing. Sadly, Rabbi Akiva was not present when his Master left this world. The grief Rabbi Akiva endured was twofold: first for the physical loss of Rabbi Eliezar, and second, for the potential volume of Light that would not be revealed to mankind. It is this unrevealed Light that gives the force of darkness a stronger hold on the world. Rabbi Akiva's pain was for the repercussions of this increased darkness and the suffering mankind would inevitably endure. Kabbalistically, the pain experienced by a devout person serves as a Vessel to draw Light, a counterbalance that arouses the positive energy of the Creator in our physical world.

The Relevance of this Passage
All of our deeds and behavioral actions in this physical realm of existence, bear positive and negative repercussions, both personally and globally. By raising our consciousness towards the importance of positive deeds, and the potential of positive deeds left unfinished, this portion stimulates personal change in order to reveal greater spiritual Light. Our own vessel is expanded by connecting to Rabbi Akiva's pain for the lack of Light in our present world.

32. ת״ר, כְּשֶׁחָלָה רַבִּי אֱלִיעֶזֶר הַגָּדוֹל, הַהוּא יוֹמָא ע״ש הֲוָה, וְאוֹתִיב לִימִינֵיה הוֹרְקְנוֹס בְּרֵיה, וַהֲוָה מְגַלֵּי לֵיה, עֲמִיקְתָא וּמְסַתַּרְתָּא, וְהוּא לָא הֲוָה מְקַבֵּל בְּדַעְתֵּיה מִלַּיָּא, דַּחֲשִׁיב כְּמִטוֹרָף בְּדַעְתֵּיה הֲוָה. כֵּיוָן דְּחָמָא דִּדַעְתָּא דַּאֲבוֹי מִתְיַשְּׁבָא עֲלוֹי, קַבִּיל מִנֵּיה, מְאָה וּתְמַנִין וְתִשְׁעָה רָזִין עִלָּאִין.

32. The sages discussed the time when the great Rabbi Eliezer became ill AND WAS ABOUT TO DIE. The day was Shabbat Eve, and Rabbi Eliezer made his son, Horkenos, sit to his right. He then revealed great and deep secrets to him. But HORKENOS'S mind was not ready to hear him AT FIRST, because he thought that his father's mind was not sufficiently clear. Only after he saw that his father's mind was completely clear did he receive 189 sublime secrets from him.

33. כַּד מָטָא לְאַבְנֵי שַׁיִשׁ, דְּמִתְעָרְבֵי בְּמַיָּא עִלָּאָה, בָּכָה רַבִּי אֱלִיעֶזֶר. וּפָסַק לְמֵימַר, אָמַר, קוּם הָתָם בְּרִי. אָמַר לוֹ אַבָּא לָמָּה. אָמַר לֵיהּ, חֲזֵינָא, דְּאוֹחֵית חֲלָף מִן עָלְמָא. אָמַר לוֹ, זִיל וְאֵימָא לְאִמָּךְ, דְּתִסְתַּלַּק תְּפִלַּאי, בַּאֲתַר עִלָּאָה, וּבָתַר דְּאֶסְתַּלַּק מִן עָלְמָא, וְאֵיתֵי הָכָא לְמֶחֱמֵי לְהוֹן, לָא תִבְכֵּי. דְּאִינוּן קְרִיבִין עִלָּאִין, וְלָא תַתָּאִין. וְדַעְתָּא דְּבַר נָשׁ, לָא יְדַע בְּהוֹ.

33. When he reached THE SECRET OF the marble stones that are mixed with the supernal Waters, Rabbi Eliezer wept and stopped talking. He said: Get up and go over there, my son! He asks him why. He replies: I see that I am soon to pass from the world. Go along and tell your mother that my Tfilin shall disappear and reach a higher place. IN OTHER WORDS, HE GAVE HER A HINT ABOUT HIS APPROACHING DEATH. And after I have departed from this world, I shall come to see them, THE MEMBERS OF THE FAMILY, but they should not cry. Because those above are near, not those below, though the human mind cannot grasp this.

34. עַד דַּהֲווֹ יָתְבֵי, עָאלוּ חַכִּימֵי דָּרָא, לְמִבְקַר לֵיהּ, אוֹלִיט לְהוֹן, עַל דְּלָא אָתוּ לְשַׁמְּשָׁא לֵיהּ. דִּתְנִינָן, גְּדוֹלָה שִׁמּוּשָׁהּ יוֹתֵר מִלִּימוּדָהּ. עַד דְּאָתָא רַבִּי עֲקִיבָא, אָמַר לוֹ, עֲקִיבָא עֲקִיבָא, לָמָּה לָא אָתֵית לְשַׁמְּשָׁא לִי. אָמַר לוֹ רַבִּי לָא הֲוָה לִי פְּנָאי. אַרְתַּח, אָמַר, אֶתְמְהָא עֲלָךְ, אִי תָמוּת מִיתַת עַצְמְךָ. לַטְיֵיהּ, דִּיהֵא קָשֶׁה מִכֻּלְּהוֹן מִיתָתֵיהּ.

34. As they were still sitting, the wise men of the generation came by to visit him. However, he cursed them for not coming to serve him. As we have learned, it is greater to serve the Torah than study it. In the meantime, Rabbi Akiva arrived. He asks: Akiva, Akiva, why have you not come to attend to me? He responded: Rabbi, I had no spare time. He was angry and said: Indeed, I wonder whether you shall die naturally. On that account, he placed a curse on him so that his death would be the worst of them all. THIS MEANS THAT HE PLACED A CURSE ON THE OTHER WISE MEN WHO DID

NOT COME TO SERVE HIM, SO THAT THEY ALSO WOULD NOT DIE NATURALLY. AND HE SAID THAT THE DEATH OF RABBI AKIVA SHALL BE THE CRUELEST OF THEM ALL.

35. בָּכֵי רַבִּי עֲקִיבָא, וַאֲמַר לֵיהּ, רַבִּי, אוֹלִיף לִי אוֹרַיְיתָא. אִפְתַּח פּוּמֵיהּ רַבִּי אֱלִיעֶזֶר, בְּמַעֲשֵׂה מֶרְכָּבָה. אָתָא אֶשָּׁא, וְאַסְחַר לְתַרְוַיְיהוֹן. אָמְרוּ חַכִּימַיָא שמ"ו, דְּלֵית אֲנַן חַזְיָין וּכְדַאִין לְכָךְ, נָפְקוּ לְפִתְחָא דְבָרָא, וְיָתִיבוּ תַּמָּן הֲוָה מַה דַּהֲוָה, וַאֲזַל אֶשָּׁא.

35. Rabbi Akiva wept and said to him: Rabbi, teach Torah to me! Rabbi Eliezer opened his mouth AND, AS HE SPOKE about the works of the divine Chariot, a fire surrounded them both. The wise men said: From this we learn that we are not worthy; nor do we have the privilege TO LISTEN TO THE WORDS OF HIS TEACHINGS. So they sat outside the gate. After everything was over, the fire disappeared.

36. וְאוֹלִיף בְּבַהֶרֶת עַזָּה, תְּלַת מְאָה הֲלָכוֹת פְּסוּקוֹת, וְאוֹלִיף לֵיהּ רי"ו טַעֲמִים, דִּפְסוּקֵי דְּשִׁיר הַשִּׁירִים. וַהֲווֹ עֵינוֹי דְר' עֲקִיבָא, נַחֲתִין מַיָא. וְאִתְחַזַּר אֶשָּׁא כְּקַדְמֵיתָא. כַּד מָטָא לְהַאי פְּסוּקָא סַמְכוּנִי בָּאֲשִׁישׁוֹת רַפְּדוּנִי בַּתַּפּוּחִים כִּי חוֹלַת אַהֲבָה אָנִי. לָא יָכִיל לְמִסְבַּל רַבִּי עֲקִיבָא, וְאָרֵים קָלֵיהּ בִּבְכִיָּיתָא וְגָעֵי, וְלָא הֲוָה מְמַלֵּל מִדְּחִילוּ דִּשְׁכִינְתָּא, דַּהֲוַת תַּמָּן.

36. And he taught THE SECRET of impure white spots (macula) as bright as the snow, 300 halachic rules, and 216 explanations of the verses of Shir Hashirim. Rabbi Akiva's eyes poured with tears like water. Then the fire reappeared AND SURROUNDED THEM BOTH again. When he reached the verse "stay me with flagons, comfort me with apples, for I am sick with love" (Shir Hashirim 2:5). Rabbi Akiva could not bear any more. He raised his voice and burst out bellowing LIKE A BULL. And he could not speak out of fear of the Shechinah that was there.

37. אוֹרֵי לֵיהּ כָּל עֲמִיקְתָּא, וְרָזִין עִלָּאִין, דַּהֲוָה בֵּיהּ בְּשִׁיר הַשִּׁירִים. וְאוֹמֵי לֵיהּ אוֹמָאָה, דְּלָא לִישְׁתַּמֵּשׁ בְּשׁוּם חַד פָּסוּק מִנֵּיהּ. כִּי הֵיכֵי

דְּלָא לִיחֲרֵיב עָלְמָא קוּדְשָׁא בְּרִיךְ הוּא בְּגִינֵיהּ. וְלָא בָּעֵי קַמֵּיהּ
דְּיִשְׁתַּמְּשׁוּן בֵּיהּ בְּרִיְיתֵי, מִסַּגִּיאוּת קְדוּשְׁתָּא דְּאִית בֵּיהּ. לְבָתַר נָפִיק
ר״ע, וְגָעֵי, וְנָבְעִין עֵינוֹי מַיָּא, וַהֲוָה אָמַר וַוי רַבִּי, וַוי רַבִּי, דְּאִשְׁתְּאַר
עָלְמָא יָתוֹם מִנָּךְ. עָאלוּ כָּל שְׁאָר חַבִימַיָּא גַבֵּיהּ, וְשָׁאֲלוּ לֵיהּ, וְאָתֵיב
לְהוֹן.

37. And he taught him all of the deep and sublime secrets that exist in Shir
Hashirim, and made him solemnly swear that he would never use any of
these verses. If he did, then Holy One, blessed be He, would destroy the
world because of him, as it is not His desire that people use it, because of its
supreme holiness. Afterward, Rabbi Akiva left and burst out crying, his eyes
pouring with tears, and said: Woe my teacher, woe my teacher, for the
world is to remain an orphan without you. All the other wise men entered
and stood by him. They asked him questions about Torah and he answered.

38. הֲוָה דָּחִיק לֵיהּ לְר״א, אַפִּיק תְּרֵי דְרוֹעוֹי, וְשַׁוִּינוּן עַל לִבֵּיהּ. פָּתַח
וַאֲמַר, אִי עָלְמָא, עָלְמָא עִלָּאָה חָזְרַת לְאַעֲלָא, וּלְאַגְנְזָא מִן תַּתָּאָה,
כָּל נְהִירוּ וּבוֹצִינָא. וַוי לְכוֹן תְּרֵי דְרָעַי, וַוי לְכוֹן תְּרֵי תּוֹרוֹת,
דְּיִשְׁתַּכְּחוּן יוֹמָא דֵין מִן עָלְמָא. דְּאָמַר רַבִּי יִצְחָק, כָּל יוֹמוֹי דְּר׳
אֱלִיעֶזֶר, הֲוָה נְהִירָא שְׁמַעְתָּא מִפּוּמֵיהּ כְּיוֹמָא דְּאִתְיְהִיבַת בְּטוּרָא
דְסִינַי.

38. Rabbi Eliezer felt confined. He raised both his arms and laid them on his
heart. He said: Woe to the world. The upper world has again concealed and
hidden all light and illumination from the lower WORLD, JUST AS IT WAS
BEFORE HE CAME INTO THE WORLD. Woe to my two arms. Woe to the two
parts of the Torah, as you shall be forgotten by the world on this day. AND
THE ZOHAR STATES that Rabbi Yitzchak said: During the entire lifetime of
Rabbi Eliezer, the Halacha would 'shine from his mouth' as on the day it
was given on mount Sinai.

39. אָמַר אוֹרַיְיתָא גְּמָרִית, וְחָכְמָתָא סְבָרִית, וְשִׁמּוּשָׁא עֲבָדִית. דְּאִלּוּ
יְהוֹן כָּל בְּנֵי אֵינָשָׁא דְּעָלְמָא סוֹפְרִים, לָא יָכְלִין לְמִכְתַּב, וְלָא חַסְרֵי
תַּלְמִידַי מֵחָכְמָתִי, אֶלָּא כְּכוּחְלָא בְּעֵינָא. וַאֲנָא מֵרַבּוֹתַי, אֶלָּא כְּמַאן

דְּשָׁתֵי בְּיַמָּא. וְלָא הֲוָה אֶלָּא לְמֶיהַּן טִיבוּתָא לְרַבּוֹהִי יַתִּיר מִנֵּיהּ.

39. RABBI ELIEZER said: I have learned so much Torah, gaining wisdom and serving SAGES, that even if all the people of the world were to be writers, there would not be enough to write of it. And my pupils have no lack of my wisdom; only as a kohl-pencil (mascara) in the eye, AS MUCH AS A TEARDROP THAT IS SHED BY AN EYE WHEN A DROP OF KOHL ENTERS IT. And I lack very little of the wisdom of my teachers, perhaps only AS MUCH AS a person can drink from the sea. AND THE ZOHAR CONCLUDES that he said this only to show gratitude to his teachers and to hold them in more favor than himself. THIS MEANS THAT WHAT HE HAS OMITTED FROM HIS TEACHERS' WISDOM, WHICH IS AS MUCH AS A PERSON CAN DRINK FROM THE SEA, IS MORE THAN A DROP OF KOHL-PENCIL IN THE EYE, WHICH HE SAID OF HIS STUDENTS' OMISSIONS. THUS, HE SHOWS THAT HE FEELS GRATITUDE TO HIS TEACHERS AND IS GRATEFUL TO THEM MORE THAN TO HIMSELF.

40. וַהֲווֹ שָׁאֲלִין מִנֵּיהּ, בְּהַהוּא סַנְדְּלָא דְּיִבּוּם, עַד דְּנָפַק נִשְׁמָתֵיהּ, וְאָמַר טָהוֹר. וְלָא הֲוָה תַּמָּן ר״ע. כַּד נְפַק שַׁבַּתָּא, אַשְׁכְּחֵיהּ ר' עֲקִיבָא דְּמִית, בָּזַע מָאנֵיהּ, וְגָרִיר כָּל בִּשְׂרֵיהּ, וְדָמָא נָחֵית וְנָגִיד עַל דִּיוֹקְנֵיהּ. הֲוָה צָוַוח וּבְכֵי נְפַק לְבָרָא וְאָמַר שְׁמַיָּא שְׁמַיָּא, אִמְרוּ לְשִׁמְשָׁא וּלְסִיהֲרָא, דִּנְהִירוּתָא דַּהֲוַת נְהֵיר יַתִּיר מִנְּהוֹן, הָא אִתְחַשַּׁךְ.

40. And they were asking him THE LAW of footwear of Yibum (the levirate rite) – IF IT BECOMES DEFILED. As his soul left him, he announced: It is pure. Rabbi Akiva was not there WHEN HE DIED. As the day of Shabbat ended, Rabbi Akiva found him dead. As he ripped his clothes and tore his flesh, the blood started to roll over his beard. He wept and shouted as he stepped outside, and said: Heavens, O heavens, tell the sun and the moon that the light that shone more than they is darkened.

41. אָמַר ר' יְהוּדָה, בְּשָׁעָה שֶׁנִּשְׁמַת הַצַּדִּיק רוֹצָה לָצֵאת, שְׂמֵחָה, וְהַצַּדִּיק בָּטוּחַ בְּמִיתָתוֹ, כְּדֵי לְקַבֵּל שְׂכָרוֹ, הה״ד וַיַּרְא וַיָּרָץ לִקְרָאתָם, בְּשִׂמְחָה, לְקַבֵּל פְּנֵיהֶם. מַאי זֶה מָקוֹם, מִפֶּתַח הָאֹהֶל, כְּדְקָא אָמְרָן. וַיִּשְׁתַּחוּ אָרְצָה לְגַבֵּי שְׁכִינָה.

41. Rabbi Yehuda said: When the soul of a righteous person wishes to leave THE BODY, it feels happy, because the righteous is confident that he shall receive his reward as he dies. Therefore, it is written: "when he saw them, he ran to meet them," REFERRING TO THE THREE ANGELS THAT ACCOMPANIED THE SHECHINAH AS SHE CAME TO RECEIVE HIS SOUL with happiness, as he welcomed THE ANGELS. Where DOES HE WELCOME THEM? As we have learned, at "the tent door," where he "bowed himself toward the ground," toward the Shechinah. THIS MEANS THAT THE SOUL BOWED TO THE SHECHINAH THAT HAD COME TO IT, AS THE SHECHINAH IS CALLED EARTH.

42. ר' יוֹחָנָן פָּתַח וְאָמַר, עַד שֶׁיָּפוּחַ הַיּוֹם וְנָסוּ הַצְּלָלִים סוֹב דְּמֵה לְךָ דוֹדִי לִצְבִי אוֹ לְעֹפֶר הָאַיָּלִים. עַד שֶׁיָּפוּחַ הַיּוֹם וגו', זוֹ אַזְהָרָה לָאָדָם בְּעוֹדוֹ בָּעוֹלָם הַזֶּה, שֶׁהוּא כְּהֶרֶף עַיִן. תָּא חֲזֵי מַה כְּתִיב וְאִלּוּ חָיָה אֶלֶף שָׁנִים פַּעֲמַיִם וגו'. בְּיוֹם הַמִּיתָה, כָּל מַה שֶׁהָיָה, נֶחְשַׁב כְּיוֹם אֶחָד אֶצְלוֹ.

42. Rabbi Yochanan then opened the discussion by quoting: "...until the day breaks, and the shadows flee away...Turn, my beloved, and be you like a roe or a young hart" (Shir Hashirim 2:17). "Until the day break" is a warning for a person who is still in this world; it is like the "blink of the eye." Come and behold: what does it say? "Even if he lived a thousand years twice" (Kohelet 6:6), on the day of his death, it all seems as one day to him.

43. אָמַר רַבִּי שִׁמְעוֹן, נִשְׁמָתוֹ שֶׁל אָדָם מַתְרָה בּוֹ, וְאוֹמֶרֶת, עַד שֶׁיָּפוּחַ הַיּוֹם, וְיִדְמֶה בְּעֵינֶיךָ כְּהֶרֶף עַיִן, בְּעוֹדְךָ בָּעוֹלָם הַזֶּה. וְנָסוּ הַצְּלָלִים: הה"ד כִּי צֵל יָמֵינוּ עֲלֵי אָרֶץ. בְּבַקָּשָׁה מִמְּךָ, סוֹב דְּמֵה לְךָ דוֹדִי לִצְבִי וגו'.

43. Rabbi Shimon said: The soul of a person warns him and says, "Until the day break." And it shall seem to you as the blink of the eye while you are still in this world. The words, "and the shadows flee away" are equivalent to the verse that reads: "because our days upon earth are a shadow" (Iyov 8:9); so I beg of you, "Turn, my beloved, and be you like a roe or a young hart."

44. דָּבָר אַחֵר. עַד שֶׁיָּפוּחַ הַיּוֹם וְגוֹ'. אָמַר רָבִּי שִׁמְעוֹן בֶּן פָּזִי, זוֹ אַזְהָרָה לְאָדָם, בְּעוֹדוֹ בָּעוֹלָם הַזֶּה, שֶׁהוּא כְּהֶרֶף עַיִן. מַה הַצְּבִי קַל בְּרַגְלָיו, אַף אַתָּה הֱיֵה קַל כַּצְּבִי אוֹ כְּעוֹפֶר הָאַיָּלִים, לַעֲשׂוֹת רְצוֹן בּוֹרַאֲךָ, כְּדֵי שֶׁתִּנְחַל הָעוֹלָם הַבָּא, שֶׁהוּא הָרֵי בְּשָׂמִים, הַנִּקְרָא הַר ה', הַר הַתַּעֲנוּג, הָהָר הַטוֹב.

(עַד כָּאן מִדְרָשׁ הַנֶּעֱלָם).

44. There is another explanation for: "Until the day break..." According to Rabbi Shimon ben Pazi, this is a warning for humankind, while still in this world, which is like the blink of the eye. Just as the roe is swift of leg, so you should be as swift as a "roe or a young hart" in performing your Master's wishes, so that you may inherit the World to Come – which is mountains of spices, called "the mountain of Hashem," the mountain of Pleasure, the mountain of Delight.

End of Midrash Hane'elam

5. "And, lo, three men"

A Synopsis

As the white light of the sun refracts into the seven colors of the rainbow, the spiritual Light of the Creator refracts into many "colors" that express all His various attributes. Kabbalistically, physical light is merely a lower frequency of the spiritual Light of the Creator. This infinite, all-inclusive Light of the Creator includes a variety of frequencies and spectrum of colors, ranging from the green blades of grass, to the purple hues of interstellar gases radiating from distant galaxies. Everything in the cosmos represents another color frequency in the spectrum of Creation, including the four kingdoms of inanimate, vegetable, animal, and mankind, as well as intangible forces, such as mercy, judgment, pleasure, truth, and fulfillment. Colors also manifest within angels. The angel Michael, who represents the positive Right Column Force of Sharing, radiates the color white. The angel Gabriel, who represents the Left Column Force of Receiving and the negative principle in our universe, radiates the color red. The angel Raphael represents the Central Column Energy of Balance and illuminates the color green. These three colors illustrate the unique function and role that each angel plays in the ongoing process of creation. Michael is the conduit for the energy of general blessings. Gabriel is the portal through which the force of judgment enters our world. Raphael channels the spiritual energy of healing.

The Relevance of this Passage

The awareness that the Creator manifests His attributes physically, inanimately, and as intangible forces, gives us the opportunity to connect to each of the spiritual frequencies spoken of in this portion. The influence of these forces in our personal life is augmented when we understand their purpose and relevance in the world.

סִתְרֵי תוֹרָה

45. הוּרְמְנוּתָא דְמַלְכָּא, אִתְחֲזֵי בִּתְלַת גְּוָונִין, גַּוָּון חַד, חֵיזוּ דְּאִתְחֲזֵי לְעֵינָא מֵרָחִיק, וְעֵינָא לָא יָכִיל לְקַיְּימָא בִּבְרִירוּ דְּחָזֵי, בְּגִין דְּאִיהוּ מֵרָחוֹק, עַד דְּנָטִיל עֵינָא, חֵיזוּ זְעֵיר, בְּקַמְטוּ דִּילֵיהּ. וְעַל דָּא כְּתִיב מֵרָחוֹק ה' נִרְאָה לִי.

Sitrei Torah (Concealed Torah)

-269-

45. The authority and will of the King, NAMELY THE SHECHINAH, appears in three colors, AND THESE ARE THE THREE COLORS OF THE EYE: WHITE, RED, AND GREEN. One color represents the eye's sight from afar. At this distance, the eye is unable to clearly visualize what it sees until it achieves partial vision by contracting itself. Thus, it is written: "Hashem has appeared from a far to me..." (Yirmeyah 31:2) THIS IS THE SECRET OF THE ILLUMINATION OF THE CENTRAL COLUMN, AS THERE CAN BE NO REVELATION OF THE LIGHTS WITHOUT IT!

‏46. גַּוֶּון תִּנְיָין: חֵיזוּ דְּהַאי עֵינָא, בִּסְתִימוּ דִילֵיהּ, דְּהַאי גַּוֶּון לָא אִתְחֲזֵי לְעֵינָא, בַּר בִּסְתִימוּ זְעֵיר, דְּנָקִיט וְלָא קָיְימָא בִּבְרִירוּ, סָתִים עֵינָא, וּפָתַח זְעֵיר, וְנָקִיט הַהוּא חֵיזוּ, וְגַוֶּון דָּא אִצְטְרִיךְ לְפִתְרוֹנָא, לְקָיְימָא עַל מַה דְּנָקִיט עֵינָא, וְעַל דָּא כְּתִיב מָה אַתָּה רוֹאֶה.

46. The second color represents the eye's sight when the eye is closed. This color is seen by the eye only through a slight shutting, and therefore it is not a clear vision. THE WAY TO SEE is by closing the eye and then opening it a little, to thereby receive this sight. BECAUSE THIS VISION IS NOT CLEAR, it requires interpretation in order to understand what the eye has perceived. Therefore, it is written: "What do you see" (Yirmeyah 1:13)? THIS IS THE SECRET OF THE ILLUMINATION OF THE LEFT COLUMN, WHEN THE LIGHTS ARE STOPPED BECAUSE OF THE LACK OF CHASSADIM.

‏47. גַּוֶּון תְּלִיתָאָה: הוּא זֹהַר אַסְפָּקְלַרְיָאה, דְּלָא אִתְחֲזֵי בֵּיהּ כְּלָל, בַּר בְּגַלְגּוּלָא דְעֵינָא, כַּד אִיהוּ סָתִים בִּסְתִימוּ. וּמְגַלְגְּלִין לֵיהּ בְּגַלְגּוּלָא, וְאִתְחַזְיַאי בְּהַאי גַּלְגּוּלָא, אַסְפָּקְלַרְיָאה דְּנָהֲרָא. וְלָא יָכִיל לְקָיְימָא בְּהַהוּא גַּוֶּון, בַּר דְּחָזֵי זוֹהַר מִנְהֲרָא בִּסְתִימוּ דְּעֵינָא.

47. The third color represents the brilliance of the mirror, which can be seen only when THE EYE is shut and it is rolled backward. As a result of this rolling, the shining mirror is seen. THIS IS THE SECRET OF THE ILLUMINATION OF THE RIGHT COLUMN. But THE EYE is able to absorb this THIRD color only by envisioning the illumination of the brilliance by shutting the eye, WHICH MEANS THE SECOND COLOR IS INCLUDED IN THE FIRST COLOR.

48. וְעַל דָּא כְּתִיב הָיְתָה עָלַי יַד ה'. וְיַד ה' עָלַי חֲזָקָה. וְכֻלְּהוּ מִתְפָּרְשָׁן
מִנְּבִיאֵי קְשׁוֹט. בַּר מֹשֶׁה, מְהֵימָנָא עִלָּאָה, דְּזָכָה לְאִסְתַּכְּלָא לְעֵילָא,
בַּמֶּה דְּלָא אִתְחֲזֵי כְּלָל. עֲלֵיהּ כְּתִיב, לֹא כֵן עַבְדִּי מֹשֶׁה וגו'.

48. Therefore, it is written: "The hand of Hashem was upon me..."
(Yechezkel 37:1) and "but the hand of Hashem was strong upon me"
(Yechezkel 3:14). THIS ABILITY TO SEE BY SHUTTING THE EYE IS
ACCOMPLISHED BY WILL POWER AND IS RELATED TO GVURAH. And all
these are conceived by the true prophets, NAMELY THE FIRST TWO COLORS.
And only Moses, the most faithful, had the ability to see high above to the
point at which THE BRILLIANCE is not seen at all. THIS REFERS TO THE
THIRD COLOR, WHICH IS THE SHINING MIRROR. Of him it is written: "My
servant Moses is not so, who is faithful in all My house" (Bemidbar 12:7).

49. וַיֵּרָא אֵלָיו. אִתְחֲזֵי וְאִתְגְּלֵי לֵיהּ שְׁכִינְתָּא, גּוֹ אִינוּן דַּרְגִּין
דְּאִתְחַבָּרוּ בְּסִטְרוֹי, מִיכָאֵל לְסְטַר יְמִינָא. גַּבְרִיאֵל לְסְטַר שְׂמָאלָא.
רְפָאֵל לְקַמָּא. אוֹרִיאֵל לַאֲחוֹרָא. וְעַל דָּא, אִתְגַּלְיָא עֲלֵיהּ שְׁכִינְתָּא,
בְּהָנֵי אֵלוֹנֵי צוּלְמִין דְּעָלְמָא, בְּגִין לְאַחֲזָאָה קַמַּיְיהוּ בְּרִית קַדְמָאָה
רְשִׁימוּ קַדִּישָׁא, דַּהֲוָה בְּכָל עָלְמָא, בְּרָזָא דִּמְהֵימְנוּתָא.

49. The words "appeared to him" mean that the Shechinah appeared to him
through those grades that are attached to Her own aspects, referring to
Michael on the right side, Gabriel on the left side, Raphael to the front, and
Uriel to the back. This is why the Shechinah appeared to him by the
terebinths (lit. 'among those oak trees'), the shadows of the world, to show
them the first circumcision – the Holy Imprint according to the secret of the
Faith in the whole world.

50. וְהוּא יוֹשֵׁב פֶּתַח הָאֹהֶל. מַאן פֶּתַח הָאֹהֶל. דָּא אֲתַר דְּאִקְרֵי בְּרִית,
רָזָא דִּמְהֵימְנוּתָא. כְּחוֹם הַיּוֹם. דָּא רָזָא דְּאִתְדַּבַּק בֵּיהּ אַבְרָהָם, תּוּקְפָּא
דְּסִטְרָא דִּימִינָא, דַּרְגָּא דִּילֵיהּ.

50. Of the words "and he sat in the tent door," HE ASKS: Where is the tent
door? AND HE ANSWERS: This is the place that is called the covenant,
which is the secret of faith, NAMELY THE NUKVA. The phrase "in the heat of

the day" refers to the secret to which Abraham cleaved, WHICH IS the might of the right side – his own grade.

51. פֶּתַח הָאֹהֶל. רָזָא דְּתַרְעָא דְּצֶדֶק, פִּתְחָא דִּמְהֵימְנוּתָא, דִּכְדֵין עָאל בֵּיהּ אַבְרָהָם, בְּהַהוּא רְשִׁימָא קַדִּישָׁא. כְּחוֹם הַיּוֹם. דָּא צַדִּיק, דַּרְגָּא דְּחִבּוּרָא חֲדָא, דְּעָאל בֵּיהּ מַאן דְּאִתְגְּזַר, וְאִתְרְשִׁים בֵּיהּ, רְשִׁימָא קַדִּישָׁא, דְּהָא אִתְעֲבַר, מֵעָרְלָה, וְעָאל בְּקִיּוּמָא דִּתְרֵין דַּרְגִּין אִלֵּין, דְּאִינּוּן רָזָא דִּמְהֵימְנוּתָא.

51. The "tent door" is the secret of the 'gate of righteousness,' the gateway to the Faith, WHICH IS THE NUKVA AND THE SECRET OF THE JUDGMENTS OF THE NUKVA. AND IT IS CALLED THE GATEWAY because Abraham entered the Holy Imprint OF CIRCUMCISION there. WITHOUT THIS, HE WOULD NOT HAVE ENTERED THE COVENANT. THIS IS WHY IT IS CALLED A GATEWAY. "In the heat of the day" refers to THE ASPECT OF the righteous, the grade of the 'United Oneness,' which is entered and joined by whoever is circumcised and is signed by the Holy Imprint. Because the foreskin has been removed from him, he enters into the illumination of these two grades, THE RIGHTEOUS AND RIGHTEOUSNESS, which are the secret of Faith.

52. וְהִנֵּה שְׁלֹשָׁה אֲנָשִׁים וְגוֹ'. אִלֵּין תְּלַת מַלְאָכִין שְׁלִיחָן, דְּמִתְלַבְּשָׁן בַּאֲוִירָא, וְנָחֲתֵי לְהַאי עָלְמָא, בְּחֵיזוּ דְּבַר נָשׁ. וּתְלַת הֲווֹ, כְּגַוְונָא דִּלְעֵילָּא, בְּגִין דְּקֶשֶׁת לָא אִתְחֲזֵי, אֶלָּא בִּגְוָונִין תְּלָתָא: חִוָּור, וְסוּמָק, וְיָרוֹק. וְהָכֵי הוּא וַדַּאי.

52. The verse, "And, lo, three men," refers to the three angels – messengers who clothe themselves with air and come down to this world in a human image. And they were three, just as there are three above, NAMELY CHESED, GVURAH, AND TIFERET OF ZEIR ANPIN. The rainbow, THE NUKVA, appears only in three colors, white, red, and green. This is exactly LIKE THE THREE COLORS OF CHESED, GVURAH, AND TIFERET OF ZEIR ANPIN.

53. וְאִלֵּין אִינּוּן שְׁלֹשָׁה אֲנָשִׁים, תְּלָתָא גְּוָונִין, גַּוֶון חִוָּור, גַּוֶון סוּמָק, גַּוֶון יָרוֹק. גַּוֶון חִוָּור. דָּא מִיכָאֵל, בְּגִין דְּאִיהוּ סִטְרָא דִּימִינָא. גַּוֶון

סוּמָק: דָּא גַּבְרִיאֵל, סִטְרָא דִשְׂמָאלָא. גָּוֶון יָרוֹק: דָּא רְפָאֵל. וְהַנֵּי אִינּוּן
תְּלַת גַּוְונִין דְּקֶשֶׁת, דְּקֶשֶׁת לָא אִתְחֲזֵי אֶלָּא עִמְּהוֹן, וּבְגִין כָּךְ, וַיֵּרָא
אֵלָיו, גִּלּוּי שְׁכִינָה, בִּתְלַת גַּוְונִין אִלֵּין.

53. And these three people are the three colors, white, red and green. The white color is Michael, because he is on the right side, AS HE COMES FROM CHESED OF ZEIR ANPIN, WHICH IS WHITE. The red color is Gabriel, who is on the left side, AS HE COMES FROM GVURAH OF ZEIR ANPIN, WHICH IS RED. The green color is Raphael, WHO COMES FROM TIFERET OF ZEIR ANPIN, WHICH IS GREEN. And these are the three colors of the rainbow. And the rainbow, WHICH IS THE NUKVA, does not appear and is not seen without them. Therefore, it is written: "appeared to him," BECAUSE the appearance of the Shechinah is SEEN by these three colors. IN OTHER WORDS, THE VERSE "AND, LO, THREE MEN STOOD BY HIM," EXPLAINS THE VERSE "AND HASHEM APPEARED TO HIM." SO, "AND HASHEM APPEARED" MEANS THAT THE SHECHINAH WAS REVEALED TO HIM. AND THIS REVELATION WAS MADE BY THE APPEARANCE OF THE THREE COLORS, OF WHICH THE VERSE CONCLUDES, "AND, LO, THREE MEN STOOD BY HIM" – NAMELY MICHAEL, GABRIEL AND RAPHAEL.

54. וְכֻלְּהוּ אִצְטְרִיכוּ: חַד, לְאַסְיָא מִן הַמִּילָה, וְדָא רְפָאֵל, מָארֵי
דְּאַסְוָון. וְחַד לְבַשְּׂרָא לְשָׂרָה, עַל בְּרָא, וְדָא אִיהוּ מִיכָאֵל. בְּגִין דְּאִיהוּ
אִתְמַנָּא לְיָמִינָא, וְכָל טָבִין וּבִרְכָאן בִּידֵיהּ אִתְמַסְּרָן, מִסִּטְרָא דְיָמִינָא.

54. And each OF THE THREE ANGELS served a different purpose. Raphael, who governs the power to heal, helped Abraham recover from the circumcision. Another, Michael, who came to inform Sarah that she shall bear a son, rules over the right side. All the abundance and the blessings of the right side are handed over to him.

55. וְחַד לַהֲפָכָא לִסְדוֹם, וְדָא אִיהוּ גַּבְרִיאֵל, דְּאִיהוּ לִשְׂמָאלָא. וְאִיהוּ
מְמַנָּא עַל כָּל דִּינִין דְּעָלְמָא, מִסִּטְרָא דִשְׂמָאלָא, לְמֵידַן וּלְמֶעְבַּד עַל
יְדָא דְּמַלְאַךְ הַמָּוֶת, דְּאִיהוּ מָארֵי דְקָטוֹלָא דְּבֵי מַלְכָּא.

55. And Gabriel, who came to overturn Sodom, rules over the left side and is responsible for all Judgments in the world, AS JUDGMENTS COME from the left side. And the execution is done by the Angel of Death, THE KING'S CHIEF BAKER, who executes THE SENTENCES THAT ARE PASSED UNDER GAVRIEL'S RULE.

56. וְכֻלְּהוּ עָבְדוּ שְׁלִיחוּתְהוֹן, וְכָל חַד וְחַד כְּדְקָא חָזֵי לֵיהּ. מַלְאָךְ גַּבְרִיאֵל, בִּשְׁלִיחוּתָא לְנִשְׁמָתָא קַדִּישָׁא, וּמַלְאַךְ הַמָּוֶת בִּשְׁלִיחוּתֵיהּ, לְנַפְשָׁא דְּיֵצֶר הָרָע, וְעִם כָּל דָּא נִשְׁמָתָא קַדִּישָׁא לָא נָפֵיק, עַד דְּחָזֵי שְׁכִינְתָּא.

56. Each and every angel accomplished his mission, as is proper. Gabriel goes on his mission to the holy Neshamah, while the Angel of Death goes on his mission to the Nefesh of the Evil Inclination. In spite of all this, the soul does not leave the body until it sees the Shechinah.

57. כַּד חָמָא לוֹן מִתְחַבְּרָן כַּחֲדָא, כְּדֵין חָמָא שְׁכִינְתָּא בְּגַוְונָהָא, וְסָגִיד. דִּכְתִיב וַיִּשְׁתַּחוּ אָרְצָה. כְּגַוְונָא דְּיַעֲקֹב, שֶׁנֶּאֱמַר וַיִּשְׁתַּחוּ יִשְׂרָאֵל עַל רֹאשׁ הַמִּטָּה לַשְּׁכִינָה.

57. When ABRAHAM saw THE THREE ANGELS join one another, he saw the Shechinah in Her own colors. And he knelt, BECAUSE THE ANGELS ARE THE THREE COLORS OF ZEIR ANPIN IN WHICH THE SHECHINAH CLOTHES HERSELF, As it is written: "...and knelt himself toward the ground." This is similar to what is described of Jacob, of whom it is written: "...and Yisrael knelt himself upon the bed's head" (Beresheet 47:31). THAT IS, HE BOWED to the Shechinah, WHICH IS CALLED THE BED'S HEAD. SO HERE, AS WELL, HE BOWED TO THE SHECHINAH.

58. וּלְגַבֵּי שְׁכִינְתָּא אֲמַר, בִּשְׁמָא אדנ"י, וּלְגַבֵּי צַדִּיק אָדוֹן. דְּהָא כְּדֵין אִקְרֵי אָדוֹן כָּל הָאָרֶץ, כַּד אִתְנַהֲרָא מִצַּדִּיק, וְאִתְנַהֲרָא בְּגַוְונָהָא, דְּהָא בְּגִין דָּא, אִשְׁתְּלִים לְעֵילָא.

58. And he addressed the Shechinah by the name "Adonai," AS HE SAID: "ADONAI ('MY LORDS') IF NOW I HAVE FOUND FAVOR..." (BERESHEET 18:3). IN THE SAME MANNER, the righteous is adressed, WHO IS YESOD OF ZEIR ANPIN, called Adon ('Master'). Then THE SHECHINAH is called

'ADON', "the lord of all the earth" (Yehoshua 3:11), because She is lit up by the righteous, WHO IS CALLED ADON ('MASTER'), and shines in Her colors. THE COLORS ARE DRAWN FROM THE THREE COLUMNS OF ZEIR ANPIN because She reaches perfection on high through them.

59. מֵהָכָא, דְּחֵיזוּ דִּלְתַתָּא, מָשִׁיךְ מְשִׁיכוּ מִלְּעֵילָא, דְּהָא גְּוָונִין אִלֵּין מָשְׁכִין מְשִׁיכָא מִלְּעֵילָא, מֵאִינוּן מְקוֹרִין עִלָּאִין. אדנ"י מָשְׁכָא מִלְּעֵילָא, בְּאִלֵּין תְּלַת גְּוָונִין דְּאִתְלַבַּשׁ בְּהוּ, וּבְהוּ נָטְלָא כָּל מַה דְּנַטְלֵי מִלְּעֵילָא.

59. From this we learn that the "mirror" of below, REFERRING TO THE SHECHINAH, is drawn from BINAH above. These colors, WHICH ARE THE SECRET OF THE THREE ANGELS, acquire the power to draw of the Lights from above – from those supernal sources THAT ARE THE THREE COLUMNS OF BINAH ITSELF.

60. וּבְגִין דְּאִינוּן חֲבוּרָא דִּילָה, וְסָמְכִין דִּילָה, בְּכֹלָּא אִתְּמָר שְׁמָא אדנ"י. דְּהָא שְׁמָא דָא אִתְגְּלֵי לֵיהּ, כָּלִיל בְּרָזִין עִלָּאִין, אִתְגְּלֵי לֵיהּ בְּאִתְגַּלְיָא מַה דְּלָא הֲוָות מִקַּדְמַת דְּנָא, דְּלָא הֲוָה גְּזִיר. וְעַד דְּאִתְגְּזַר לָא בָּעָא קוּדְשָׁא בְּרִיךְ הוּא לְאַפָּקָא מִנֵּיה זַרְעָא קַדִּישָׁא, כֵּיוָן דְּאִתְגְּזַר, מִיָּד נָפַק מִנֵּיה זַרְעָא קַדִּישָׁא.

60. Because they accompany and support Her with everything, She is called Adonai. This name was revealed to ABRAHAM entirely through the secrets of the supernal ones – BY THE LIGHTS OF BINAH. And they appeared to him completely exposed, which did not happen before he was circumcised. Clearly, before he was circumcised, the Holy One, blessed be He, did not wish to issue a holy seed from him. However, as soon as he was circumcised, a holy seed immediately came forth. THAT SEED WAS ISAAC.

61. וּבְגִין כָּךְ, אִתְגְּלֵי עֲלֵיהּ שְׁכִינְתָּא, בְּאִינוּן דַּרְגִּין קַדִּישִׁין. וְהַמַּשְׂכִּילִים יַזְהִירוּ כְּזֹהַר הָרָקִיעַ. זֹהַר: זָהֲרָא דִּזְהָרִין בִּדְלִיקוּ זָהֲרָא. זֹהַר: דְּאַנְהֵיר דְּאַדְלֵיק, וְנָצִיץ לְכַמָּה סִטְרִין.

61. Because of this, BECAUSE OF HIS CIRCUMCISION, the Shechinah

appeared to him in those holy grades, IN KEEPING WITH THE SECRET OF THE VERSE: "And the wise shall shine as the brightness of the firmament..." (Daniel 12:3) THE FIRST brightness is the brilliance that shines when it is lit up. THE SECOND brightness lights up, shines and sparkles in many directions.

62. זֹהַר: סָלִיק וְּנָחֵית. זֹהַר: נָצִיץ לְכָל עֵיבָר. זֹהַר: נָגֵיד וְּנָפֵיק. זֹהַר: דְּלָא פָּסִיק לְעָלְמִין. זֹהַר: דַּעֲבֵיד תּוֹלָדִין.

62. The brightness moves up and then down, shines throughout all aspects, is drawn and comes forth, and never ceases to shine. And the brightness procreates.

63. זֹהַר: טָמִיר וְגָנֵיז, נְצִיצוּ דְּכָל נְצִיצִין וְדַרְגִּין, כֹּלָּא בֵּיה, נָפֵיק וּטְמִיר, סְתִים וְגַלְיָא. חָזֵי וְלָא חָזֵי. סִפְרָא דָא, מַבּוּעָא דְּבֵירָא, נָפֵיק בִּימָמָא, טָמִיר בְּלֵילְיָא, אִשְׁתַּעְשַׁע בְּפַלְגּוּת לֵילְיָא, בְּתוֹלָדִין דְּאַפֵּיק.

63. This brightness, which is hidden and concealed, glows brighter than any sparkle, WHICH MEANS THAT ITS SPARKLE IS GREATER THAN ANY OTHER SPARKLE IN THE WORLDS. And all the grades are located within It. It goes forth and disappears, concealed yet exposed, sees yet does not see. This book, WHICH REFERS TO THE BORDER OR LIMITATION, AS THE HEBREW TERM MEANS BOTH BOOK AND BORDER, is the source of the well, WHICH IS THE NUKVA OF ZEIR ANPIN. It comes out TO SHINE ONLY during the day, BECAUSE ZEIR ANPIN SHINES DURING THE DAY. And It disappears at night, WHEN HE DOES NOT SHINE. And He delights Himself at midnight WITH THE COMPANY OF THE SOULS OF THE RIGHTEOUS THAT ARE the offspring he issued, IN THE GARDEN OF EDEN.

64. זֹהַר: דְּזָהֵיר וְאַנְהֵיר לְכֹלָּא, כְּלָלָא דְּאוֹרַיְיתָא, וְדָא אִיהוּ דְּאִתְחֲזֵי, וְכָל גְּווֹנִין סְתִימִין בֵּיה, וְאִתְקְרֵי בִּשְׁמָא דַאדנ״י. תְּלַת גְּווֹנִין אִתְחֲזֵי לְתַתָּא, מֵהַאי, תְּלַת גְּווֹנִין לְעֵילָא, מֵאִלֵּין עִלָּאִין אִתְמְשַׁךְ כֹּלָּא דְּלָא אִתְחֲזֵי. וְנָצִיץ בִּתְרֵיסַר נְצִיצִין וּזְהִירִין דִּנְצִיצִין מִנֵּיה. תְּלֵיסַר אִינוּן, בְּרָזָא דִשְׁמָא קַדִּישָׁא, וְגוֹ רָזָא דְּאֵין סוֹף, הוי״ה אִקְרֵי.

64. The brightness shines and lights up the entire Torah, WHICH IS THE SECRET OF CHOCHMAH, to all. This is seen, AS IT RECEIVES CHOCHMAH, because all the colors are concealed within It. It is called Adonai. The three colors are seen below it. And three colors are seen above it. Everything is received from the THREE above, AND STILL, they are not seen, BECAUSE THEY DO NOT RECEIVE CHOCHMAH DIRECTLY THEMSELVES. And it sparkles with twelve sparkles and lights that emanate from it. Altogether there are thirteen, ACCORDING TO THE SECRET OF 'ONENESS' THAT INCLUDES THEM ALL, by the secret of the Holy Name, YUD HEI VAV HEI, within the secret of the Endless World (Heb. *Ein-Sof*). THAT WHICH INCLUDES THEM ALL is called Yud Hei Vav Hei, WHILE THE TWELVE GRADES OF THE NUKVA ARE CALLED ADONAI.

65. כַּד אִתְחַבַּר זֹהַר תַּתָּאָה אדנ"י, בְּזֹהַר עִלָּאָה הוי"ה, אִתְעֲבֵיד שְׁמָא סָתִים, דְּבֵיה יָדְעֵי נְבִיאֵי קְשׁוֹט, וּמִסְתַּכְּלָאן לְגוֹ זֹהֲרָא עִלָּאָה, וְדָא יאקדונקי. חֵיזוּ טְמִירִין, דִּכְתִיב כְּעֵין הַחַשְׁמַל מִתּוֹךְ הָאֵשׁ.

65. When the lower brightness, WHICH IS THE BRIGHTNESS OF THE TWELVE CALLED Adonai, joined the upper brightness, WHICH IS ZEIR ANPIN, CALLED Yud Hei Vav Hei, they formed one name through which the true prophets attain THEIR PROPHECIES and look into the supernal brightness. The NAME is *Yud-Aleph-Hei-Dalet-Vav-Nun-Hei-Yud,* WHICH IS A COMBINATION OF YUD HEI VAV HEI AND ADONAI. THROUGH THIS COMBINED NAME, THEY ACHIEVE sublime visions, BECAUSE BY THIS NAME THE VISION OF THE HIDDEN SECRETS CAN BE ACHIEVED, as it is written: "and out of the midst of it, it were the color of electrum out of the midst of the fire" (Yechezkel 1:4).

66. מַתְנִיתִין עִלָּאִין רָמָאִין טָבִין דְּיִמִינָא. תֵּשַׁע נְקוּדִין דְּאוֹרַיְיתָא, נָפְקִין וּמִתְפַּלְּגִין בְּאַתְוָון, וְאַתְוָון בְּהוֹ נָטְלִין מַטְלָנוֹי דַּקִּיקִין בְּרָזֵי. פַּלְטִין אִלֵּין תֵּשַׁע, שַׁלִּיטִין אִינוּן אַתְוָון אַתְוָון, מִנַּיְיהוּ אִתְפַּשְׁטוּ, אִשְׁתְּאָרוּ נְקוּדִין לְאַעֲנָאָה לוֹן. לָא נָטְלִין, בַּר כַּד אִינוּן נָפְקִין.

66. Mishnah: To you who are supernal, great, and good, from the right side, THE FOLLOWING SECRET HAS BEEN SAID: the nine vowels that appear in the Torah are divided by the letters. These letters secretly take short trips. These nine rulers issue these letters, which then expand. The nine vowels

remain intact as so as to have the letters. THE LETTERS move only after THE
VOWELS appear.

‏67. אִלֵּין אִינּוּן בְּרָזָא דְּאֵין סוֹף, כֻּלְּהוּ אַתְוָון מְטַלְלָן בְּרָזָא דְּאֵין סוֹף.
כְּמָה דְּאִינּוּן נָטְלִין לוֹן, הָכֵי נָמֵי אִלֵּין נָטְלֵי אִלֵּין סְתִימִין אַתְוָון, גַּלְיָין וְלָא
גַּלְיָין, הַנֵּי טְמִירִין, עַל מַה דְּשָׁרְיָין אַתְוָון.‏

67. These LETTERS are in accordance with the secret of Ein-Sof and are
under its influence. The sealed letters travel ONLY as much as THE VOWELS
travel. The hidden secrets upon which these letters rest, are both revealed
and not revealed.

‏68. תֵּשַׁע שְׁמָהָן, גְּלִיפָן בְּעֶשֶׂר, וְאִינּוּן: קַדְמָאָה אֶהְיֶה. יוּ"ד ה"א.
אֶהְיֶה אֲשֶׁר אֶהְיֶה. הוי"ה. אֵל. אֱלֹקִים. הוי"ה. צְבָאוֹת. אָדוֹן. שַׁדָּי.‏

68. Nine names are engraved in ten; Ehe'yeh IS KETER; Yud-Hei IS
CHOCHMAH; Ehe'yeh Asher Ehe'yeh IS BINAH; Yud Hei Vav Hei,
WHOSE VOWELS ARE LIKE ELOHIM IS YISRAEL–SABA AND TEVUNAH; El
IS CHESED; Elohim IS GVURAH; Yud Hei Vav Hei IS TIFERET; *Tzva'ot* IS
NETZACH AND HOD; and *Adon* and *Shadai* BOTH REFER TO YESOD.
ADON IS THE CROWN OF YESOD; SHADAI IS YESOD ITSELF.

‏69. אִלֵּין אִינּוּן עֶשֶׂר שְׁמָהָן גְּלִיפָן בְּסִטְרֵייהוֹן. וְכָל הַנֵּי שְׁמָהָן,
אִתְגְּלִיפוּ, וְעָאלִין בְּחַד אֲרוֹן הַבְּרִית, וּמַאן אִיהוּ, שְׁמָא דְּאִתְקְרֵי
אדנ"י. וְדָא אִתְגְּלֵי הַשְׁתָּא לְאַבְרָהָם.‏

69. These ten Names are each engraved according to Its aspect. And all
these Names were engraved and entered the Ark of the Covenant. Which
one is it? It is Adonai, the one that was revealed and appeared AFTER THE
CIRCUMCISION to Abraham. IN OTHER WORDS, THE NAME ADONAI IS
THE SECRET OF THE NUKVA AFTER SHE HAD RECEIVED THE OTHER TEN
NAMES, WHICH ARE ALL THE GRADES OF ATZILUT. BUT BEFORE HE
WAS CIRCUMCISED, HE DID NOT ACHIEVE THE SECRET OF 'SEEING.'
UNTIL THE CIRCUMCISION, HE SAW ONLY THROUGH THE NUKVA,
WITHOUT HER BEING ATTACHED TO THE UPPER GRADES.

‏70. מִיכָאֵל שְׁמָא דִּימִינָא, דְּקָא אָחִיד וּמְשַׁמְּשָׁא לִשְׁמָא דָּא, יַתִּיר‏

מֵאִינּוּן אָחֳרָנִין, בְּכָל אֲתַר דְּרָזָא דְּהַאי שְׁמָא תַּמָּן, מִיכָאֵל תַּמָּן, אִסְתְּלִיק הַאי, מִיכָאֵל אִסְתְּלִיק, אֱלֹקִים בַּהֲדֵי שַׁדַּי.

70. Michael is the name of the right, THAT IS, CHESED, which cleaves to the name ADONAI and serves It more than the other ANGELS. Wherever the secret of the name ADONAI appears, SO DOES Michael. If Michael disappears, so does Elohim, WHICH IS THE NUKVA, together with Shadai, WHICH IS YESOD.

71. בְּקַדְמֵיתָא שְׁלֹשָׁה אֲנָשִׁים, וְאִגְלִימוּ בְּצִיּוּרָא דַּאֲוִירָא, וַהֲווֹ אָכְלֵי, אָכְלֵי וַדַּאי, דְּאֶשָּׁא דִּלְהוֹ אֲכַל וְשֵׁצֵי כֹּלָּא, וְאַעֲבִיד נַחַת רוּחַ לְאַבְרָהָם. אִינּוּן אֶשָּׁא וַדַּאי, וְהַהוּא אֶשָּׁא אִתְכַּסֵּי בְּצִיּוּרָא דַּאֲוִירָא, וְלָא אִתְחֲזֵי, וְהַהוּא מֵיכְלָא אֶשָּׁא מְלַהֲטָא, וְאָכְלָא לֵיהּ, וְאַבְרָהָם מְקַבֵּל נַחַת רוּחַ מֵהַאי.

71. In the beginning, there were three men who were dining while enclothed in an image of air. They most certainly ate, because their fire ate and consumed everything, thus bringing contentment to Abraham. AND HE CLARIFIES THAT they were truly fire. This fire was covered by an image of the air and was not seen. The food that they ate was a burning fire. And they ate it, and Abraham received pleasure from this.

72. כֵּיוָן דְּאִסְתַּלַּק שְׁכִינְתָּא, מַה כְּתִיב, וַיַּעַל אֱלֹקִים מֵעַל אַבְרָהָם, מִיָּד מִסְתַּלַּק בַּהֲדֵיהּ מִיכָאֵל, דִּכְתִיב וַיָּבֹאוּ שְׁנֵי הַמַּלְאָכִים סְדוֹמָה וְגוֹ'. שְׁלֹשָׁה כְּתִיב בְּקַדְמֵיתָא, וְהַשְׁתָּא תְּרֵין, אֶלָּא מִיכָאֵל דְּאִיהוּ יְמִינָא, אִסְתְּלִיק בַּהֲדֵי שְׁכִינְתָּא.

72. As the Shechinah departed, it is written: "and Elohim went up from Abraham" (Beresheet 17:22). So Michael immediately departed with Her, as it is written: "And there came two angels to Sodom..." (Beresheet 19:1). At the beginning, it is written three, but now it reads "two angels." FROM THIS, WE CONCLUDE THAT THE ANGEL Michael, who is to the right, also departed as the Shechinah rose. AND ONLY TWO ANGELS REMAINED.

73. מַלְאָךְ דְּאִתְחֲזֵי לְמָנוֹחַ, נָחַת וְאִיגְלִים בַּאֲוִירָא, וְאִתְחֲזֵי לֵיהּ, וְדָא

-279-

אִיהוּ אוֹרִיאֵל. מַה דְּלָא נָחַת בְּאִלֵּין דְּאַבְרָהָם, נָחַת הָכָא בִּלְחוֹדוֹי, לְבַשְׂרָא לְמָנוֹחַ, דְּאָתֵי מִדָּן.

73. The angel seen by Manoach, who descended and was enclothed by air, is Uriel. He did not come with those angels of Abraham, but came down on his own to inform Manoach, who is a descendant of Dan, THAT HE SHALL HAVE A SON.

74. וּבְגִין דְּלָא חָשִׁיב כְּאַבְרָהָם, לָא כְּתִיב דַּאֲכַל, דְּהָא כְּתִיב אִם תַּעַצְרֵנִי לֹא אוֹכַל בְּלַחְמֶךָ. וּכְתִיב וַיְהִי בַּעֲלוֹת הַלַּהַב מֵעַל הַמִּזְבֵּחַ וַיַּעַל מַלְאַךְ ה' בְּלַהַב הַמִּזְבֵּחַ וגו'. וְהָכָא וַיַּעַל אֱלֹקִים מֵעַל אַבְרָהָם. בְּגִין דְּבֵיהּ אִסְתְּלֵיק מִיכָאֵל, וְאִשְׁתָּאֲרוּ רְפָאֵל וְגַבְרִיאֵל.

74. Because MANOACH is not as important a man as Abraham, it is not written that he (the angel) ate. Rather, it is written: "Though you detain me, I will not eat of your bread..." (Shoftim 13:16) and "For it came to pass, when the flame went up toward heaven...that the angel of Hashem ascended in the flame of the altar..." (Ibid. 20). Here, however, it is written: "and Elohim went up from Abraham"; IT IS NOT WRITTEN THAT THE ANGELS DEPARTED FROM ABRAHAM. THIS IS because Micheal left WITH ELOHIM, while Raphael and Gabriel remained.

75. וַעֲלַיְיהוּ כְּתִיב, שְׁנֵי הַמַּלְאָכִים סְדוֹמָה. בָּעֶרֶב בְּשַׁעֲתָא דְּדִינָא תַּלְיָא עַל עָלְמָא. לְבָתַר אִסְתַּלַּק חַד, וְאִשְׁתְּכַח גַּבְרִיאֵל בִּלְחוֹדֵיהּ. בִּזְכוּתֵיהּ דְּאַבְרָהָם אִשְׁתְּזֵיב לוֹט, וְאִיהוּ אוֹף הָכֵי זָכֵי בְּהוֹ, וְעַל דָּא אָתוּ לְגַבֵּיהּ (ע"ד ס"ת).

75. Of them it is written: "And there came two angels to Sodom at evening." "...at evening..." when Judgment hovers above the world. And afterward, one angel departed, and Gabriel alone remained TO OVERTHROW SODOM. Because of the merit of Abraham, Lot was saved. Therefore, he was also privileged to have the two angels come and visit him.

End of Sitrei Torah

6. "Who shall ascend into the mountain of Hashem"

A Synopsis

When an individual strives to understand his purpose in life and seeks the truth of the Creator, his soul will seek to reunite with the Light of the Creator upon leaving this world. Unfortunately, the vast majority of mankind journeys through this physical world without any inkling of his true purpose, or understanding as to the meaning of his existence. Consequently, a man who directs no effort towards spiritual enlightenment and blindly pursues the material world, will automatically seek the path of negativity when it departs its physical existence. The paths of the spiritual world mirror the pathways we forge in the physical world.

The Relevance of this Passage

There are definite negative blockages within our consciousness that repress our intrinsic desire to seek the meaning of our existence and purpose in life. By helping to remove these impediments, the words and wisdom of this passage stimulate us to pursue the truth of our being. It is a well-known Kabbalistic principle that states, the more we seek to comprehend our purpose and the reality of the Creator, the more spiritual Light we receive.

76. ר' אַבָּא פָּתַח וְאָמַר, מִי יַעֲלֶה בְהַר ה' וּמִי יָקוּם בִּמְקוֹם קָדְשׁוֹ. תָּא חֲזֵי, כָּל בְּנֵי עָלְמָא לָא חָמָאן עַל מָה קָיְימֵי בְּעָלְמָא, וְיוֹמִין אָזְלִין וְסָלְקִין, וְקָיְימֵי קַמֵּי קוּדְשָׁא בְּרִיךְ הוּא, כָּל אִינּוּן יוֹמִין, דִּבְנֵי נָשָׁא קָיְימֵי בְּהוּ בְּהַאי עָלְמָא, דְּהָא כָּלְּהוּ אִתְבְּרִיאוּ וְכָלְּהוּ קָיְימֵי לְעֵילָּא, וּמִנָּלָן דְּאִתְבְּרִיאוּ, דִּכְתִיב יָמִים יוּצָרוּ.

76. Rabbi Aba opened the discussion with the text: "Who shall ascend into the mountain of Hashem? Or who shall stand in His holy place?" (Tehilim 24:3). Come and behold: no man is aware of the reason for his existence in the world. MEN DO NOT SEEK TO KNOW THE PURPOSE OF THEIR LIVES ON EARTH. As the days pass by WITH NO RETURN, they rise up and stand before the Holy One, blessed be He, as they were all created AND HAVE ACTUAL EXISTENCE OF THEIR OWN. How do we know that they were created? Because it is written: "The days were created" (Tehilim 139:16).

77. וְכַד מָטָאן יוֹמִין לְאִסְתַּלְּקָא מֵהַאי עָלְמָא, כָּלְּהוּ קְרֵיבִין קַמֵּי מַלְכָּא עִלָּאָה, הה"ד וַיִּקְרְבוּ יְמֵי דָוִד לָמוּת. וַיִּקְרְבוּ יְמֵי יִשְׂרָאֵל לָמוּת.

77. And when the days depart from this world, they all approach the Supernal King, as it is written: "And the days drew close for David to die" (I Melachim 2:1), "…and the days drew close for Jacob to die" (Beresheet 47:29).

78. בְּגִין דְּכַד בַּר נָשׁ אִיהוּ בְּהַאי עָלְמָא, לָא אַשְׁגַּח וְלָא אִסְתַּכַּל, עַל מַה קַאִים, אֶלָּא כָּל יוֹמָא וְיוֹמָא חָשִׁיב כְּאִילוּ הוּא אָזִיל בְּרֵקַנְיָיא, דְּהָא כַּד נִשְׁמָתָא נָפְקַת מֵהַאי עָלְמָא, לָא יָדְעַת לְאָן אוֹרְחָא סַלְקִין לָהּ, דְּהָא אוֹרְחָא לְסַלְקָא לְעֵילָא לַאֲתַר דְּנְהִירוּ דְּנִשְׁמָתִין עִלָּאִין נָהֲרִין, לָא אִתְיְהֵיב לְכָלְּהוֹן נִשְׁמָתִין, דְּהָא כְּגַוְונָא דְּאִיהוּ אַמְשִׁיךְ עֲלֵיהּ בְּהַאי עָלְמָא, הָכִי אִתְמַשְּׁכַת לְבָתַר דְּנָפֵיק מִנֵּיהּ.

78. When a person is in this world, he is not aware of nor does he look for the reason he was created. For him, every day is considered as if it passes by in emptiness. And when the soul leaves this world, it does not recognize the path through which it is elevated, because the path that leads up, to the place where the luminous sublime souls shine, WHICH IS THE GARDEN OF EDEN, is not shown to all souls. After it departs from him, THE SOUL follows the same way that person followed while in this world.

79. תָּא חֲזֵי, אִי בַּר נָשׁ אִתְמְשִׁיךְ בָּתַר קוּדְשָׁא בְּרִיךְ הוּא וְתֵיאוּבְתָּא דִּילֵיהּ אֲבַתְרֵיהּ בְּהַאי עָלְמָא, לְבָתַר כַּד נָפֵיק מִנֵּיהּ, אִיהוּ אִתְמְשִׁיךְ אֲבַתְרֵיהּ, וְיָהֲבִין לֵיהּ אוֹרַח לְאִסְתַּלְּקָא לְעֵילָא, בָּתַר הַהוּא מְשִׁיכוּ דְּאִתְמְשִׁיךְ בִּרְעוּתָא, כָּל יוֹמָא בְּהַאי עָלְמָא.

79. Come and behold: if a person is drawn after the Holy One, blessed be He, and longs for Him while in this world, then later, when he departs from this world, he also follows THE HOLY ONE, BLESSED BE HE. And he is shown a path to climb that rises upward TO THE PLACE WHERE SOULS SHINE. IN OTHER WORDS, it follows and continues the same path that his desire followed and longed for each day while in this world.

80. אָמַר רָבִּי אַבָּא, יוֹמָא חַד אִעֲרַעְנָא בְּחַד מָתָא, מֵאִינוּן דַּהֲווֹ מִן בְּנֵי קֶדֶם, וְאָמְרוּ לִי מֵהַהִיא חָכְמְתָא דַּהֲווֹ יָדְעִין מִיּוֹמֵי קַדְמָאֵי, וַהֲווֹ אַשְׁכְּחָן סִפְרִין דְּחָכְמְתָא דִּלְהוֹן, וְקָרִיבוּ לִי חַד סִפְרָא.

80. Rabbi Aba said: One day, I came upon a town that belonged to the children of the East. They shared with me a part of the wisdom that they knew from antiquity. Then they searched for books of their own wisdom and gave me one.

81. וַהֲוָה כְּתִיב בֵּיה, דְּהָא כְּגַוְונָא דִּרְעוּתָא דְּבַר נָשׁ אִיכַוֵּין בֵּיה בְּהַאי עָלְמָא, הָכֵי אַמְשִׁיךְ עֲלֵיה רוּחַ מִלְּעֵילָא, כְּגַוְונָא דְּהַהוּא רְעוּתָא דְּאִתְדַּבָּק בֵּיה, אִי רְעוּתֵיה אִיכַוֵּין בְּמִלָּה עִלָּאָה קַדִּישָׁא, אִיהוּ אַמְשִׁיךְ עֲלֵיה לְהַהִיא מִלָּה, מִלְּעֵילָא, לְתַתָּא לְגַבֵּיה.

81. Inside this book, it was written that according to the intention of a person's desire in this world, he draws a spirit from above upon himself similar to the desire that he clung to. If his desire is to achieve something holy and divine, then he draws the same from above and brings it down upon himself.

82. וְאִי רְעוּתֵיה, לְאִתְדַּבְּקָא בְּסִטְרָא אָחֳרָא, וְאִיכַוֵּין בֵּיה, אִיהוּ אַמְשִׁיךְ לְהַהִיא מִלָּה מִלְּעֵילָא לְתַתָּא לְגַבֵּיה. וַהֲווֹ אָמְרֵי דְּעִקָּרָא דְּמִלְּתָא תַּלְיָיא בְּמִלִּין, וּבְעוֹבָדָא, וּבִרְעוּתָא לְאִתְדַּבְּקָא, וּבְדָא אִתְמְשַׁךְ מִלְּעֵילָא לְתַתָּא הַהוּא סִטְרָא דְּאִתְדַּבָּק בָּה.

82. If he wishes to cleave to the Other Side, and is intent upon it, he draws the same from above down and brings it upon himself. They used to say THAT TO DRAW SOMETHING DOWN FROM ABOVE depends mainly on speech, deed, and the wish to cleave to it. This is how that certain side that he cleaves to is drawn down from above.

83. וְאַשְׁכַּחְנָא בֵּיה, כָּל אִינוּן עוֹבָדִין וּפוּלְחָנִין דְּכֹכְבַיָּא וּמַזָּלֵי, וּמִלִּין דְּאִצְטְרִיכוּ לוֹן, וְהָאֵיךְ רְעוּתָא לְאִתְכַּוְונָא בְּהוּ, בְּגִין לְאַמְשָׁכָא לוֹן לְגַבַּיְיהוּ.

83. And I have found IN THAT BOOK all the rites and ceremonies for worshipping the stars and constellations, as well as what is required to worship them and how to direct one's will toward them in order to to draw them closer.

84. כְּגַוְונָא דָא, מַאן דְּבָעֵי לְאִתְדַּבְּקָא לְעֵילָא, בְּרוּחַ קוּדְשָׁא, דְּהָא בְּעוֹבָדָא וּבְמִלִּין, וּבִרְעוּתָא דְּלִבָּא לְכַוְּונָא בְּהַהִיא מִלָּה, תַּלְיָיא מִלְתָא לְאַמְשָׁכָא לֵיהּ לְגַבֵּיהּ, מֵעֵילָא לְתַתָּא, וּלְאִתְדַּבְּקָא בְּהַהִיא מִלָּה.

84. In the same manner, for whoever desirs to cling to the Holy Spirit above, it depends on the act, words, and the intent of the heart, so that he may succeed in drawing it down upon himself so that he may cling to it.

85. וַהֲווֹ אָמְרֵי, כְּמָה דְּבַר נָשׁ אִתְמְשַׁךְ בְּהַאי עָלְמָא, הָכֵי נָמֵי מָשְׁכִין לֵיהּ, כַּד נָפֵיק מֵהַאי עָלְמָא. וּבַמֶּה דְּאִתְדַּבַּק בְּהַאי עָלְמָא, וְאִתְמְשַׁךְ אֲבַתְרֵיהּ, הָכֵי אִתְדַּבַּק בְּהַהוּא עָלְמָא, אִי בְּקוּדְשָׁא בְּקוּדְשָׁא, וְאִי בִּמְסָאֲבָא בִּמְסָאֲבָא.

85. And they were saying: Whatever path a person follows in this world is the path along which he is drawn when he leaves this world. And whatever he clung to and pursued while in this world, he clings to in the World of Truth – if to holiness then to holiness; if to impurity then to impurity.

86. אִי בְּקוּדְשָׁא, מָשְׁכִין לֵיהּ לְגַבֵּי הַהוּא סְטַר, וְאִתְדַּבַּק בֵּיהּ לְעֵילָא, וְאִתְעֲבֵיד מְמַנָּא שַׁמָּשָׁא, לְשַׁמְּשָׁא קַמֵּי קוּדְשָׁא בְּרִיךְ הוּא, בֵּין אִינוּן שְׁאָר מַלְאָכִין. כְּמָה דְּהָכֵי אִתְדַּבַּק לְעֵילָא, וְקָאִים בֵּין אִינוּן קַדִּישִׁין, דִּכְתִיב וְנָתַתִּי לְךָ מַהְלְכִים בֵּין הָעוֹמְדִים הָאֵלֶה.

86. If to holiness, then he is drawn toward that same side OF HOLINESS. He clings to it above, and becomes a serving minister before the Holy One, blessed be He, among all the angels. And so he is attached to the supernal WORLD and stands among those holy beings, as it is written: "then I will give you access among these that stand by" (Zecharyah 3:7).

87. הָכֵי נָמֵי כְּגַוְונָא דָא, אִי בִּמְסָאֲבָא, מָשְׁכִין לֵיהּ לְגַבֵּי הַהוּא סְטַר, וְאִתְעֲבֵיד כְּחַד מִנַּיְיהוּ, לְאִתְדַּבְּקָא בְּהוֹ, וְאִינוּן אִקְרוּן נִזְקֵי בְּנֵי נָשָׁא. וּבְהַהִיא שַׁעֲתָא דְּנָפֵיק מֵהַאי עָלְמָא, נָטְלִין לֵיהּ וְשָׁאֲבִין לֵיהּ בַּגֵּיהִנָּם, בְּהַהוּא אֲתַר דְּדַיְינֵי לוֹן לִבְנֵי מְסָאֲבָא, דְּסָאִיבוּ גַּרְמַיְיהוּ וְרוּחֵיהוּ,

וּלְבָתַר אִתְדַּבַּק בְּהוּ. וְאִיהוּ נִזְקָא, כְּחַד מֵאִינּוּן נִזְקֵי דְעָלְמָא.

87. And so, in the same manner, if HE HAS CLEAVED to impurity WHILE IN THIS WORLD, then he is drawn to the IMPURE side. He becomes one of them and is attached to them. And they are called the 'demons of people.' So when he departs from this world, they take him and cast him into Gehenom – into that place where the impure, who have defiled themselves and their spirits, are judged and punished. He then clings to them, becoming 'a demon', just like the demons of the world.

88. אֲמֵינָא לוֹן, בָּנַי, קְרִיבָא דָא לְמִלִּין דְּאוֹרַיְיתָא, אֲבָל אִית לְכוּ לְאִתְרַחֲקָא מֵאִינּוּן סִפְרִין, בְּגִין דְּלָא יִסְטֵי לְבַּיְיכוּ לְאִלֵּין פּוּלְחָנִין, וּלְכָל אִינּוּן סִטְרִין דְּקָאֲמַר הָכָא, דִּילְמָא חַס וְשָׁלוֹם תִּסְטוּן מִבָּתַר פּוּלְחָנָא דְקוּדְשָׁא בְּרִיךְ הוּא.

88. I said to them: My sons, the sayings of this book are close to the sayings of the Torah. But you should stay away from these books, so that you will not be attracted to those beliefs and all those aspects that are mentioned there. Otherwise, heaven forbid, you may abandon the service of the Holy One, blessed be He!

89. דְּהָא כָּל סִפְרִים אִלֵּין, אַטְעַיִין לוֹן לִבְנֵי נָשָׁא, בְּגִין דִּבְנֵי קֶדֶם חַכִּימִין הֲווֹ, וִירוּתָא דְּחָכְמְתָא דָא, יָרְתוּ מֵאַבְרָהָם, דְּיָהַב לִבְנֵי פִּלַגְשִׁים, דִּכְתִיב וְלִבְנֵי הַפִּלַגְשִׁים אֲשֶׁר לְאַבְרָהָם נָתַן אַבְרָהָם מַתָּנוֹת וַיְשַׁלְּחֵם מֵעַל יִצְחָק בְּנוֹ בְּעוֹדֶנּוּ חַי קֵדְמָה אֶל אֶרֶץ קֶדֶם. וּלְבָתַר אִתְמַשְׁכוּ בְּהַהִיא חָכְמָה לְכַמָּה סִטְרִין.

89. People are led astray because of these books. The people of the east were wise and inherited this wisdom from Abraham, who gave it to the sons of the concubines. As it is written: "But to the sons of the concubines, which Abraham had, Abraham gave gifts, and sent them away from his son, while he yet lived, eastward, to the east country" (Beresheet 25:6). Afterward, they developed their wisdom in many directions.

90. אֲבָל זַרְעָא דְּיִצְחָק חוּלָקָא דְיַעֲקֹב, לָאו הָכֵי, דִּכְתִיב וַיִּתֵּן אַבְרָהָם

אֶת כָּל אֲשֶׁר לוֹ לְיִצְחָק. דָּא חוּלָקָא קַדִּישָׁא דִּמְהֵימְנוּתָא, דְּאִתְדַּבַּק בֵּיהּ אַבְרָהָם. וְנָפַק מֵהַהוּא עַדְבָּא, וּמֵהַהוּא סִטְרָא יַעֲקֹב. מַה כְּתִיב בֵּיהּ וְהִנֵּה ה' נִצָּב עָלָיו. וּכְתִיב וְאַתָּה יַעֲקֹב עַבְדִּי וְגו'. בְּגִינֵי כָךְ בָּעֵי לֵיהּ לְבַר נָשׁ, לְאִתְמַשְּׁכָא בָּתַר קוּדְשָׁא בְּרִיךְ הוּא, וּלְאִתְדַּבְּקָא בֵּיהּ תָּדִיר, דִּכְתִיב וּבוֹ תִדְבָּק.

90. But the seed of Isaac, the portion of Jacob, is not so. As it is written: "And Abraham gave all that he had to Isaac" (Ibid. 5). This is the holy portion of faith that Abraham cleaved to. And from this side and fate did Jacob come. What is written about him? It is written: "And, behold, Hashem stood above him," (Beresheet 28:13) and "But you, Yisrael, are my servant, Jacob..." (Yeshayah 41:8). For this reason, a person should be drawn after the Holy One, blessed be He, and cleave to Him always, as it is written: "and to Him shall you cleave..." (Devarim 10: 20).

91. תָּא חֲזֵי מִי יַעֲלֶה בְהַר ה' וְגו'. וּלְבָתַר אַהֲדַר וּפֵירַשׁ. נְקִי כַפַּיִם. דְּלָא עֲבֵיד בִּידוֹי טוֹפְסָא, וְלָא אִתְתַּקַּף בְּהוֹ בַּמֶּה דְּלָא אִצְטְרִיךְ. וְתוּ, דְּלָא אִסְתָּאַב בְּהוֹ, וְלָא סָאֵיב בְּהוֹ לְגוּפָא, כְּאִינוּן דִּמְסָאֲבִין גַּרְמַיְיהוּ בִּידֵין לְאִסְתָּאֲבָא, וְדָא הוּא נְקִי כַפַּיִם. וּבַר לֵבָב, כְּגַוְונָא דָּא דְּלָא אַמְשִׁיךְ רְעוּתֵיהּ וְלִבֵּיהּ, לְסִטְרָא אַחֲרָא, אֶלָּא לְאִתְמַשְּׁכָא בָּתַר פּוּלְחָנָא דְּקוּדְשָׁא בְּרִיךְ הוּא.

91. Come and behold. It is written: "Who shall ascend into the mountain of Hashem..." (Tehilim 24:3) And after this, he continues to explain that "he that has clean hands." THIS MEANS THAT he has not made an idol with his hands, and his hands did not hold what they should not have held. Furthermore, IT SHOULD BE EXPLAINED THAT THE PHRASE "CLEAN HANDS" MEANS HIS HANDS were not defiled, and he did not defile the body with them, as those who defile themselves with their hands and become impure. This is what "clean hands" means. A "pure heart" is the heart of someone who has not diverted his heart to the Other Side, but rather is drawn after the service of the Holy One, blessed be He!

92. אֲשֶׁר לֹא נָשָׂא לַשָּׁוְא נַפְשִׁי. נַפְשׁוֹ כְּתִיב, נַפְשִׁי קְרִי, וְהָא אוּקְמוּהָ נַפְשִׁי דָּא נֶפֶשׁ דָּוִד, סִטְרָא דִּמְהֵימְנוּתָא. נַפְשׁוֹ דָּא נֶפֶשׁ דְּבַר נָשׁ מַמָּשׁ.

בְּגִין דְּכַד יִפּוֹק מֵהַאי עָלְמָא, וְנַפְשֵׁיה יִסְתַּלַּק בְּעוֹבָדִין דְּכָשְׁרִין, עַל מַה דְּיִתְקַיַּים בְּהוּ, לְמֵיהַךְ בֵּין כָּל אִינוּן קַדִּישִׁין, כד״א אֶתְהַלֵּךְ לִפְנֵי ה' בְּאַרְצוֹת הַחַיִּים. וּבְגִין דְּלָא נָשָׂא לַשָּׁוְא נַפְשִׁי, יִשָּׂא בְרָכָה מֵאֵת ה' וגו'.

92. Of the verse, "who has not lifted up his soul (Nefesh) in vain," observe that it is written "*Nafsho*" ('his soul'), but pronounced "*Nafshi*" ('my soul'). The explanation is that 'my soul' is the soul of David, the aspect of faith WHICH IS THE NUKVA OF ZEIR ANPIN; 'his soul' is actually the soul of a human being. THIS IS THE DIFFERENCE BETWEEN WHAT IS WRITTEN AND HOW IT IS PRONOUNCED. Thus, when a person passes away from this world and his soul (Nefesh) leaves with proper deeds, he will have the privilege of being among all those holy ones, as it is written: "I will walk before Hashem in the land of the living" (Tehilim 116:9). THEREFORE HE SAYS: Because he "has not lifted up his soul in vain...He shall receive the blessing from Hashem..."

7. "And, lo, three men...and they ate"

A Synopsis

A discussion arises as to whether Abraham the Patriarch perceived the three angels, Michael, Gabriel, and Raphael as angelic entities or as physical beings. According to the Zohar, Abraham was able to perceive them as angels by virtue of his circumcision, which removed negativity and elevated his consciousness. The lesson being conveyed concerns the importance of a person's consciousness and its ability to influence perception.

The Relevance of this Passage

Two people often perceive a singular image or event differently because their individual consciousness are on two different levels. Both perceptions are indeed correct; however, one perspective is limited if it remains on a lower level of consciousness, and the other is far-reaching if it occupies a higher level. Achieving transcendence over this physical realm by raising our own consciousness is the intent of this portion. We achieve a heightened sense of awareness, perceiving the true spiritual reality during the day-to-day rigors of physical existence.

93. תָּא חֲזֵי, בָּתַר דְּאִתְגְּזַר אַבְרָהָם, הֲוָה יָתִיב וְכָאִיב, וְקוּדְשָׁא בְּרִיךְ הוּא שָׁדַר לְגַבֵּיה תְּלַת מַלְאָכִין בְּאִתְגַּלְיָא, לְאַקְדְּמָא לֵיהּ שְׁלָם. וְאִי תֵּימָא, דְּהָא בְּאִתְגַּלְיָא, וְכִי מַאן יָכִיל לְמֶחֱמֵי מַלְאָכִין, וְהָא כְּתִיב עוֹשֶׂה מַלְאָכָיו רוּחוֹת וגו'.

93. Come and behold: after Abraham had circumcised himself, he sat down and was in pain. The Holy One, blessed be He, sent him three visible angels to inquire of his well-being. You may wonder how they were visible, for who is able to see angels, as it is written: "Who makes his angels spirits (also, 'winds')" (Tehilim 104:4).

94. אֶלָּא וַדַּאי חָמָא לוֹן, דְּנַחֲתֵי לְאַרְעָא, כְּגַוְונָא דִּבְנֵי נָשָׁא, וְלָא יַקְשֶׁה לָךְ הַאי, דְּהָא וַדַּאי אִינּוּן רוּחִין קַדִּישִׁין, וּבְשַׁעֲתָא דְּנַחֲתֵי לְעָלְמָא, מִתְלַבְּשִׁין בַּאֲוִירֵי וּבִיסוֹדֵי דְּגוֹלְמִין, וְאִתְחֲזוּ לִבְנֵי נָשָׁא מַמָּשׁ, כְּחֵיזוּ דְּיוֹקְנָא דִּלְהוֹן.

94. AND HE REPLIES: He certainly did see them because they came to earth

-288-

in the image of men. And it should not be hard for you to understand because they are definitely holy spirits. But when they come down to this world, they enclothe themselves with the air and the elements of covering and enveloping, until they appear to people exactly in their image.

95. וְתָא חֲזֵי אַבְרָהָם חָמָא לוֹן, כְּחֵיזוּ בְּנֵי נָשָׁא, וְאַף עַל גַּב דַּהֲוָה כָּאִיב מִמִּילָה, נָפַק וְרָהַט אֲבַתְרַיְיהוּ, בְּגִין דְּלָא לְמִגְרַע מַה דַּהֲוָה עָבֵיד מִקַּדְמַת דְּנָא.

95. Come and behold: Abraham saw them in the image of men. And even though he was in pain because of the circumcision, he ran forth to greet them, so that he would not miss anything and would not behave differently than before his circumcision, WHEN HE ALWAYS ACCEPTED AND WELCOMED NEW GUESTS.

96. אָמַר רָבִּי שִׁמְעוֹן וַדַּאי כְּחֵיזוּ דְּמַלְאָכִין חָמָא לוֹן, מִמַּה דִּכְתִיב, וַיֹּאמַר אֲדֹנָי בְּאל״ף דל״ת, שְׁכִינְתָּא הֲוָה אַתְיָא, וְאִלֵּין הֲווֹ סְמִיכִין דִּילָהּ, וְכָרְסְיָיא לְגַבָּהּ, בְּגִין דְּאִינוּן גְּווֹנִין תְּלַת דִּתְחוֹתָא.

96. Rabbi Shimon said: He definitely did see them in the form of angels. THIS CAN BE UNDERSTOOD from the words: "And he said...my lords (Heb. adonai)" with the letters Aleph and Dalet. THESE LETTERS, WHICH FORM THE NAME OF THE SHECHINAH, ARE THE FIRST TWO LETTERS OF THE NAME ADONAI. For it was the Shechinah that was approaching, and these angels were Her supports and throne. They are the three colors – WHITE, RED, AND GREEN – that are under THE SHECHINAH.

97. וְחָמָא הַשְׁתָּא בְּגִין דְּאִתְגְּזַר, מַה דְּלָא הֲוָה חָמֵי מִקַּדְמַת דְּנָא, עַד לָא אִתְגְּזַר, בְּקַדְמֵיתָא לָא הֲוָה יָדַע, אֶלָּא דְּאִינוּן בְּנֵי נָשָׁא, וּלְבָתַר יָדַע דְּאִינוּן מַלְאָכִין קַדִּישִׁין, וְאָתוּ בִּשְׁלִיחוּתָא לְגַבֵּיה. בְּשַׁעֲתָא דְּאָמְרוּ לֵיה אַיֵּ״ה שָׂרָה אִשְׁתָּךְ, וּבִשְׂרוּ לֵיה בְּשׂוֹרַת יִצְחָק.

97. And he saw THAT THEY WERE ANGELS because after he was circumcised, he was able to see what he did not see before he was circumcised. At first, he thought they were human beings. Later, he realized that they were angels on a mission FROM THE HOLY ONE, BLESSED BE

HE. THEY FULFILLED THIS MISSION when they said to him, "Where is Sarah, your wife" (Beresheet 18:9), and informed him about Isaac.

98. אֵלָיו: אַתְוָון נְקוּדוֹת אי"ו, וְסִימָן אי"ו רֶמֶז לְמָה דִּלְעֵילָא, רֶמֶז לְקוּדְשָׁא בְּרִיךְ הוּא. וַיֹּאמֶר הִנֵּה בָאֹהֶל, כְּתִיב הָכָא הִנֵּה בָאֹהֶל, וּכְתִיב הָתָם אֹהֶל בַּל יִצְעָן וְגו'. תָּא חֲזֵי, כֵּיוָן דְּנָקוּד אי"ו, אַמַּאי כְּתִיב לְבָתַר אַיֵּה. אֶלָּא, בְּגִין דְּחִבּוּרָא דִּדְכַר וְנוּקְבָּא כַּחֲדָא, רָזָא דִּמְהֵימָנוּתָא. כְּדֵין אָמַר, וַיֹּאמֶר הִנֵּה בָאֹהֶל, תַּמָּן הוּא קְשׁוּרָא דְּכֹלָּא וְתַמָּן אִשְׁתַּכַּח.

98. In the word, "*Elav* ('to him')," WHICH APPEARS IN THE VERSE "AND THEY SAID TO HIM," the letters with vowels are *Aleph, Yud*, and *Vav*. And this sign, *ayo*, alludes to what is above, implying the Holy One, blessed be He. AND THEY ASKED ABOUT HIM: *AYO* (LIT. 'WHERE IS HE')? And he replies: "Behold, in the tent." THIS MEANS THAT HE WAS ATTACHED TO THE SHECHINAH, BECAUSE here it is written: "in the tent," and there it is written: "a tabernacle (tent) that shall not be taken down..." (Yeshayah 33:20). THUS, IT REFERS TO THE SHECHINAH, JUST AS IN THE LATTER VERSE. Come and behold: Because *ayo* has vowels already, why is it then written: *ayeh* (lit. 'where')? AND HE REPLIES: Because the secret of the Faith is the union of the male and female as one. THIS IS WHY THEY ASKED OF THE HOLY ONE, BLESSED BE HE, "WHERE IS HE (*AYO*)?" AND THEY ASKED OF THE SHECHINAH, "WHERE IS SHE (*AYEH*)?" THIS MEANS THAT THEY AROUSED HIM TO FORM A UNION OF THE HOLY ONE, BLESSED BE HE, WITH HIS SHECHINAH. The verse continues, "And he said: Behold, in the tent," because therein lies the bond of everything – NAMELY THE NUKVA WHO IS CALLED "THE TENT" AND THE HOLY ONE, BLESSED BE HE.

99. אַיֵּה וְגו'. וְכִי לָא הֲווֹ יָדְעֵי מַלְאֲכֵי עִלָּאֵי, דְּשָׂרָה הִנֵּה בָאֹהֶל, אַמַּאי כְּתִיב אַיֵּה. אֶלָּא לָא יָדְעֵי בְּהַאי עָלְמָא, אֶלָּא מַה דְּאִתְמְסַר לְהוֹ לְמִנְדַע. תָּא חֲזֵי, וְעָבַרְתִּי בְּאֶרֶץ מִצְרַיִם אֲנִי ה'. וְכִי כַּמָּה שְׁלִיחִין וּמַלְאָכִין אִית לֵיהּ לְקוּדְשָׁא בְּרִיךְ הוּא, אֶלָּא בְּגִין דְּאִינוּן לָא יָדְעֵי בֵּין טִפָּה דְּבוּכְרָא, לְהַהוּא דְּלָא בּוּכְרָא, בַּר קוּדְשָׁא בְּרִיךְ הוּא בִּלְחוֹדוֹי.

99. Of the question, "Where is she?" HE ASKS: Did the celestial angels not know that Sarah was in the tent? If so, why then is it written THAT THEY ASKED ABOUT HER SAYING, "*Ayeh* ('where?')?" AND HE REPLIES: THE ANGELS have no knowledge of this world, except what is given them to know. Come and behold: "For I will pass through the land of Egypt...I am Hashem" (Shemot 12:12). AND HE ASKS: The Holy One, blessed be He, has so many messengers and angels. WHY DID HE HAVE TO "PASS THROUGH THE LAND OF EGYPT" BY HIMSELF? AND HE REPLIES: Because THE ANGELS do not know how to distinguish between the sperm of a firstborn and that which is not. Only the Holy One, blessed be He, alone knows this.

100. כְּגַוְונָא דָּא, וְהִתְוֵיתָ תָּו עַל מִצְחוֹת הָאֲנָשִׁים. וַאֲמַאי צְרִיכִין. אֶלָּא, בְּגִין דְּאִינּוּן לָא יָדְעֵי, אֶלָּא מַה דְּאִתְמְסַר לוֹן לְמִנְדַּע. כְּגוֹן כָּל אִינּוּן מִלִּין דְּזַמִּין קוּדְשָׁא בְּרִיךְ הוּא לְאַיְיתָאָה עַל עָלְמָא. ומ"ט, בְּגִין דְּקוּדְשָׁא בְּרִיךְ הוּא אַעֲבַר כָּרוֹזָא בְּכָלְהוּ רְקִיעִין, בְּהַהִיא מִלָּה דְּזַמִּין לְאַיְיתָאָה עַל עָלְמָא.

100. This is similar to the text: "and set a mark upon the foreheads of the men..." (Yechezkel 9:4). Why do THE ANGELS need THIS MARK? Because THE ANGELS know only what they are informed of. For example, how do they know all that the Holy One, blessed be He, plans on doing in the world? They know because the Holy One, blessed be He, sends announcements throughout the heavens, informing them of what He is about to perform in the world. THE ANGELS HEAR THESE ANNOUNCEMENTS AND KNOW!

101. כְּגַוְונָא דָּא, בְּשַׁעֲתָא דִּמְחַבְּלָא אִשְׁתְּכַח בְּעָלְמָא, בָּעֵי בַּר נָשׁ לְאִתְכַּסְיָא בְּבֵיתֵיהּ, וְלָא יִתְחֲזֵי בְּשׁוּקָא, בְּגִין דְּלָא יִתְחַבֵּל, כְּדָבָר אַחֵר וְאַתֶּם לֹא תֵצְאוּ אִישׁ מִפֶּתַח בֵּיתוֹ עַד בֹּקֶר. מִנַּיְיהוּ דְּיָכִיל לְאִסְתַּתְּרָא, אֵין, אֲבָל מִקַּמֵּי קוּדְשָׁא בְּרִיךְ הוּא, לָא בָּעֵי לְאִסְתַּתְּרָא, מַה כְּתִיב אִם יִסָּתֵר אִישׁ בַּמִּסְתָּרִים וַאֲנִי לֹא אֶרְאֶנּוּ נְאָם ה'.

101. In the same way, when the Angel of Destruction roams the world, people should hide at home and not be seen at the marketplace. This will prevent the Angel of Destruction from destroying and hurting them. As it is written: "and none of you shall go out of the door of his house until the morning" (Shemot 12:22), because from them – FROM THE ANGELS – we

can and should hide. But there is no need to hide from the Holy One, blessed be He, as it is written: "Can any hide himself in secret places that I shall not see him? Says Hashem" (Yirmeyah 23:24).

102. אַיֵּה שָׂרָה אִשְׁתֶּךָ. דְּלָא בָעוּ לוֹמַר קַמֵּהּ, כֵּיוָן דַּאֲמַר הִנֵּה בָאֹהֶל, מִיָּד וַיֹּאמֶר שׁוֹב אָשׁוּב אֵלֶיךָ כָּעֵת חַיָּה וְהִנֵּה בֵן לְשָׂרָה אִשְׁתֶּךָ וְגוֹ', תָּא חֲזֵי אֹרַח אַרְעָא, דְּעַד לָא אַזְמִין אַבְרָהָם קַמַּיְיהוּ לְמֵיכַל, לָא אָמְרוּ לֵיהּ מִדֵּי, בְּגִין דְּלָא יִתְחֲזֵי דִּבְגִין הַהִיא בְּשׂוֹרָה, קָא אַזְמִין לְהוּ לְמֵיכַל, בָּתַר דִּכְתִיב וַיֹּאכֵלוּ, כְּדֵין אָמְרוּ לֵיהּ הַהִיא בְּשׂוֹרָה.

102. "Where is Sarah, your wife?" HE DID NOT UNDERSTAND WHY THEY ASKED ABOUT HER. WHEN THEY HEARD SHE WAS IN THE TENT, THEY DID NOT ENTER IT TO INFORM HER. INSTEAD, THEY REMAINED OUTSIDE WHILE THEY INFORMED ABRAHAM. AND HE ANSWERS: They did not want to announce THE GOOD NEWS in front of her. So immediately after he said, "Behold, in the tent," it is then written: "he said: I will return and definitely come back to you at this time next year, and, lo, Sarah your wife shall have a son" (Beresheet 18:10). Come and behold: it was very polite and proper that they said nothing to Abraham before he invited them to eat. This way, it did not seem that he invited them to eat because of the good news they brought him. Therefore, only after the verse stated "and they ate," did they inform him about the good news.

103. וַיֹּאכֵלוּ, סָלְקָא דַעְתָּךְ, וְכִי מַלְאֲכֵי עִלָּאֵי אָכְלֵי, אֶלָּא, בְּגִין יְקָרָא דְּאַבְרָהָם, אִתְחֲזֵי הָכִי. אֲמַר ר' אֶלְעָזָר וַיֹּאכֵלוּ וַדַּאי, בְּגִין דְּאִינוּן אֶשָּׁא דְּאָכִיל אֶשָּׁא, וְלָא אִתְחֲזֵי, וְכָל מַה דְּיָהַב לוֹן אַבְרָהָם אָכְלֵי, בְּגִין דְּמִסִּטְרָא דְּאַבְרָהָם אָכְלֵי לְעֵילָא.

103. HE ASKS: IT IS WRITTEN: "and they ate," but do celestial angels eat? AND HE REPLIES: For the sake of Avraham's honor, it seemed AS THOUGH THEY ATE. THIS MEANS THAT THEY MADE IT SEEM AS THOUGH THEY WERE EATING. Rabbi Elazar said: They did actually eat, because they are the "fire that consumes fire." And it is not as though THEY WERE EATING. So they ate everything Abraham offered them, because from the side of Abraham they ate on a supernal level. THIS MEANS THAT THE DRAWING DOWN OF CHASSADIM IS THE SECRET OF 'EATING ON A SUPERNAL

LEVEL,' AND ABRAHAM IS THE SECRET OF CHESED. THEREFORE, EVERYTHING HE OFFERED THEM CAME FROM HIS OWN ATTRIBUTE, FROM THE ATTRIBUTE OF CHESED. AND THEY ATE, JUST AS THEY EAT ABOVE IN THE HEAVENS.

104. תָּא חֲזֵי, כָּל מַה דְּאָכִיל אַבְרָהָם, בְּטַהֲרָה אִיהוּ קָא אָכִיל, וּבְגִין כָּךְ אַקְרֵיב קַמַּיְיהוּ, וְאָכְלֵי, וּנְטִיר אַבְרָהָם בְּבֵיתֵיה דַּכְיָא וּמִסָּאֲבוּתָא, דַּאֲפִילוּ בַּר נָשׁ דְּאִיהוּ מְסָאַב, לָא הֲוָה מְשַׁמֵּשׁ בְּבֵיתֵיה, עַד דַּעֲבֵיד לֵיה טְבִילָה, אוֹ עֲבֵיד לֵיה לְנַטְרָא שִׁבְעָה יוֹמִין, כִּדְקָא חָזֵי לֵיה, בְּבֵיתֵיה, וְהָכֵי הוּא וַדַּאי.

104. Come and behold: everything Abraham ate was according to the rites of purity. And because of this, he served it to the angels, who ate. In his home, he observed the rites of purity so strictly that an impure person could not serve at his home unless he (Abraham) immersed him in a ritual bath IF HE WAS SLIGHTLY IMPURE. Or he made him keep purity properly for seven days at his home, IF HE WAS SEVERELY IMPURE. AFTERWARD, HE IMMERSED HIM.

105. תָּא חֲזֵי כְּתִיב אִישׁ אֲשֶׁר לֹא יִהְיֶה טָהוֹר מִקְּרֵה לָיְלָה וְגו'. מַאי תַּקַּנְתֵּיה, וְהָיָה לִפְנוֹת עֶרֶב יִרְחַץ בַּמָּיִם. אִעֲרַע בֵּיה טוּמְאָה אָחֳרָא, כְּגוֹן זִיבָה, אוֹ סְגִירַת נִדָּה, דַּהֲווֹ תְּרֵי מְסָאֲבוּ, לָא סַגְיָא לֵיה בְּהַהִיא טְבִילָה, בֵּין דְּאִעֲרַע בֵּיה קֶרִי, קוֹדֶם דְּקַבֵּיל טוּמְאָה אָחֳרָא, בֵּין דְּאִעֲרַע בֵּיה לְבָתַר.

105. Come and behold. It is written: "If there be among you any man who is not clean by reason of uncleanliness that chances by night..." (Devarim 23:11) what should he do? The verse continues, "when evening comes on, he shall bathes himself in water..." (Ibid. 12) But if he becomes defiled through any other SEVERE cause, like gonorrhea or leprosy on the impurity of menstrual flow, which include two kinds of defilement, then the ritual immersion FOR CLEANSING HIMSELF FROM THE NOCTURNAL POLLUTION AT EVENING is not sufficient. UNDER THESE CIRCUMSTANCES, HE SHOULD KEEP PURITY FOR SEVEN DAYS. THEN HE SHOULD IMMERSE AGAIN. THERE IS NO DIFFERENCE BETWEEN HE WHO experienced nocturnal pollution before he was defiled with the other kind of defilement and he who was defiled only afterward.

A Synopsis

Abraham and Sarah dedicated their lives to help people make the transformation to a more positive and spiritual way of life. Abraham and Sarah's devotion to this objective aroused genuine miracles of nature.

The Relevance of this Passage

A miracle, a wonder of nature, is essentially a mirror reflecting a profound spiritual change within human nature. Because our natural inclination is self-indulgence at the expense of others, the Light of this passage gives us the strength to overpower our natural tendencies and apportion part of our life to the service of others, exemplified by Abraham and Sarah. When a person dedicates his life to sharing with others, the Creator causes great wonders to be revealed in order to help him toward this pursuit.

106. וְאַבְרָהָם וְשָׂרָה הֲווֹ מְתַקְּנֵי טְבִילָה לְכָלְהוּ, אִיהוּ לְגַבְרֵי וְאִיהִי לְנָשֵׁי. מ"ט אִתְעֲסַק אַבְרָהָם לְדַכָּאָה לִבְנֵי נָשָׁא, בְּגִין דְּאִיהוּ טָהוֹר, וְאִקְרֵי טָהוֹר, דִּכְתִיב מִי יִתֵּן טָהוֹר מִטָּמֵא לֹא אֶחָד. טָהוֹר דָּא אַבְרָהָם דְּנָפַק מִתֶּרַח.

106. Abraham and Sarah prepared ritual baths for every person – he for the men and she for the women. And why was Abraham occupied in purifying other people? Because he is pure and is called pure, as it is written: "Who can bring a pure thing out of an impure? Not one," (Iyov 14:4) where "pure" applies to Abraham, who came out of Terah, WHO IS IMPURE.

107. רַבִּי שִׁמְעוֹן אָמַר, בְּגִין לְתַקָּנָא הַהוּא דַּרְגָּא דְּאַבְרָהָם, וּמַאן אִיהוּ מַיִם. בְּגִין כָּךְ, אַתְקִין לְדַכָּאָה בְּנֵי עָלְמָא בְּמַיָּא. וּבְשַׁעֲתָא דְּאַזְמִין לְמַלְאָכִין, שֵׁירוּתָא דְּמִלּוֹי, מַה כְּתִיב, יוּקַח נָא מְעַט מַיִם. בְּגִין לְאִתְתַּקְּפָא בְּהַהוּא דַּרְגָּא דְּמַיִין שָׁרָאן בָּהּ.

107. Rabbi Shimon said: THIS IS WHY ABRAHAM ENGAGED IN RITUAL IMMERSION – to rectify Avraham's grade. And what is his grade? It is 'waters' – NAMELY CHASSADIM, THAT ARE CALLED 'WATERS'. Because of this, he prepared people to be purified with water. And when he invited the

angels, his first words were as it is written: "Let a little water, I pray you, be fetched..." (Beresheet 18:4) – to strengthen himself with that grade which contains water, NAMELY CHESED.

108. וּבְגִינֵי כָךְ, הֲוָה מְדַכֵּי לְכָל בְּנֵי נָשָׁא מִכֹּלָּא, מִדַכֵּי לוֹן מִסִּטְרָא דַּע״ז, וּמְדַכֵּי לוֹן מִסִּטְרָא דִּמְסָאֲבָא, וְכַמָּה דְּאִיהוּ מְדַכֵּי לְגוּבְרִין, ה״נ שָׂרָה מְדַכְּאַת לְנָשִׁין, וְאִשְׁתַּכָּחוּ כֻּלְּהוּ דְּאַתְיָין לְגַבַּיְיהוּ דָּכְיָין מִכֹּלָּא.

108. This is how he purified people from all sins, including those from the Impure Side and idol worshiping. And just as he purified the men, so did she purify the women. Therefore, all those who came to him were completely purified FROM IDOL WORSHIPING AND DEFILEMENT.

109. תָּא חֲזֵי, אִילָנָא נָטַע אַבְרָהָם, בְּכָל אֲתַר דְּדִיוּרֵיהּ תַּמָּן, וְלָא הֲוָה סָלֵיק בְּכָל אֲתַר כִּדְקָא יָאוֹת, בַּר בְּשַׁעֲתָא דְּדִיוּרֵיהּ בְּאַרְעָא דִּכְנָעַן. וּבְהַהוּא אִילָנָא הֲוָה יָדַע מַאן דְּאִתְאַחִיד בֵּיהּ בְּקוּדְשָׁא בְּרִיךְ הוּא, וּמַאן דְּאִתְאַחִיד בַּע״ז.

109. Come and behold: wherever Abraham lived, he planted a tree. But it did not grow properly in all the places; it only grew properly when he lived in Canaan. And by this tree, he knew who was attached to the Holy One, blessed be He, and who worshiped idols.

110. מַאן דְּאִתְאַחִיד בְּקוּדְשָׁא בְּרִיךְ הוּא, אִילָנָא הֲוָה פָּרֵישׂ עַנְפּוֹי וְחָפֵי עַל רֵישֵׁיהּ וַעֲבֵיד עֲלֵיהּ צִלָּא יָאֶה, וּמַאן דְּאִתְאַחִיד בְּסִטְרָא דַּע״ז, הַהוּא אִילָנָא הֲוָה אִסְתַּלַּק, וְעַנְפּוֹי הֲווֹ סְלִיקִין לְעֵילָא. כְּדֵין הֲוָה יָדַע אַבְרָהָם, וְאַזְהִיר לֵיהּ וְלָא אַעֲדֵי מִתַּמָּן, עַד דְּאִתְאַחִיד בִּמְהֵימְנוּתָא דְּקוּדְשָׁא בְּרִיךְ הוּא.

110. For if a person cleaved to the Holy One, blessed be He, the tree spread out its branches, covered his head, and formed a pleasant shade for him. But if a person was attached to idolatry, the tree raised its branches high. Then Abraham knew THAT HE WORSHIPPED IDOLS. Abraham reprimanded him and did not let him go until he cleaved to faith in the Holy One, blessed be He!

111. וְהָכֵי מַאן דְּאִיהוּ דַּכְיָא, מְקַבֵּל לֵיהּ אִילָנָא. מַאן דְּאִיהוּ מְסָאַב לָא מְקַבֵּל לֵיהּ. כְּדֵין יָדַע אַבְרָהָם וּמְדַכֵּי לוֹן בְּמַיָא.

111. In addition, whoever was pure was accepted by the tree. But whoever was impure was not accepted. Abraham then knew IF A PERSON WAS UNCLEAN. If this was the case, he purified him with water.

112. וּמַעֲיָינָא דְּמַיָיא הֲוָה תְּחוֹת הַהוּא אִילָנָא, וּמַאן דְּצָרִיךְ טְבִילָה, מִיָּד מַיִין סָלְקִין לְגַבֵּיהּ, וְאִילָנָא אִסְתַּלְּקִין עַנְפּוֹי, כְּדֵין יָדַע אַבְרָהָם דְּאִיהוּ מְסָאֲבָא, וּבְעֵי טְבִילָה מִיָּד, וְאִם לָאו, מַיָּא נְגִיבָן, כְּדֵין יָדַע דְּבָעֵי לְאִסְתָּאֲבָא וּלְאִסְתַּמְּרָא שִׁבְעָה יוֹמִין.

112. And there was a spring of water beneath the tree. If a person WHO WAS SLIGHTLY IMPURE needed an immersion, the water immediately rose and the branches of the tree ascended upward. Abraham thus knew that he was impure and had to be immersed in water immediately. But if a person did not need to be cleansed immediately, the spring dried up. Then Abraham knew that he was still impure and needed to wait for seven days.

113. תָּא חֲזֵי, דַּאֲפִילוּ בְּשַׁעֲתָא דְּאַזְמִין לוֹן לַמַּלְאָכִין, אָמַר לוֹן, וְהִשָּׁעֲנוּ תַּחַת הָעֵץ. בְּגִין לְמֶחֱמֵי וּלְמִבְדַּק בְּהוֹ, וּבְהַהוּא אִילָנָא הֲוָה בָּדִיק לְכָל בְּנֵי עָלְמָא, וְרָזָא בְּגִין קוּדְשָׁא בְּרִיךְ הוּא קָא אֲמַר דְּאִיהוּ אִילָנָא דְּחַיֵּי לְכֹלָּא, וּבְגִין כָּךְ, וְהִשָּׁעֲנוּ תַּחַת הָעֵץ, וְלָא תַּחַת עֲבוֹדָה זָרָה.

113. Come and behold: even when he invited the angels, he told them to rest "yourselves under the tree," (Beresheet 18:4) in order to test them. In this way, he examined every person. And the secret is that he said this for the sake of the Holy One, blessed be He, who is THE SECRET OF the Tree of Life for everyone. This is why he TOLD THEM: "and rest yourselves under the tree," WHICH IS THE HOLY ONE blessed be He, and not under idol worshiping.

114. וְתָּא חֲזֵי כַּד חָב אָדָם, בְּעֵץ הַדַּעַת טוֹב וָרָע חָב, דִּכְתִיב וּמֵעֵץ

הַדַעַת וְגוֹ'. וְאִיהוּ בֵּיה חָב, וְגָרַם מוֹתָא לְעָלְמָא. מַה כְּתִיב, וְעַתָּה פֶּן
יִשְׁלַח יָדוֹ וְלָקַח גַם מֵעֵץ הַחַיִּים וְגוֹ'. וְכַד אָתָא אַבְרָהָם, בְּאִילָנָא
אָחֳרָא אַתְקִין עָלְמָא, דְּהוּא אִילָנָא דְּחַיֵּי, וְאוֹדַע מְהֵימְנוּתָא לְכָל בְּנֵי
עָלְמָא.

114. Come and behold: Adam sinned by eating from the Tree of Knowledge of good and evil, as it is written: "But from the tree of knowledge of good and evil..." (Beresheet 2:17). But after he sinned, thereby bringing death upon the entire world, it is written: "and now lest he put forth his hand, and take also of the tree of life, and eat, and live for ever" (Beresheet 3:22). And when Abraham appeared, he ameliorated the world by using another tree, the Tree of Life, to introduce the proper faith to all peoples of the world.

A Synopsis

The sacrifices that occurred inside the ancient temple and the incense that was burned were powerful tools that were used to remove forces of negativity and evil from the entire world. The absence of the physical Temple in our day prevents us from utilizing these instruments. The Zohar, however, explains that the words of the Torah that speak of the sacrifices and incense rouse those same forces of purification into being. Moreover, they transform prosecuting angels into entities that speak only good and favorable words about a person in the Supernal Courts.

The Relevance of this Passage

It was foreseen that a time would come when many physical tools of spirituality would be lost to the ages. The gift of the Torah, the Zohar, and specifically this passage, replenish the spiritual energy lost in the absence of such tools. Accordingly, we can purify negative influences in our own life and the world at large. In addition, we arouse the power to transform decrees of judgment into words of praise on our behalf.

מִדְרָשׁ הַנֶּעֱלָם

Midrash Hane'elam (Homiletical interpretations on the obscure)

115. אָמַר רַבִּי חִיָּיא אָמַר רַב, אִי הֲוֵינָא מִסְתַּכְּלִין בְּפָרָשָׁתָא דָּא,
נִסְתַּכֵּל בְּחָכְמְתָא, אִי עִנְיָינָא דְּנִשְׁמָתָא הִיא, לָאו רֵישָׁא סוֹפָא, וְלָאו

סוֹפָא רֵישָׁא. וְאִי עִנְיָינָא לִפְטִירַת אִינִישׁ מֵעָלְמָא הִיא, נִסְתּוֹר כָּל פַּרְשָׁתָא, אוֹ נוֹקִים פַּרְשָׁתָא בְּהַאי אוֹ בְּהַאי. מַהוּ יוּקַח נָא מְעַט מַיִם וְרַחֲצוּ רַגְלֵיכֶם וגו'. וְאֶקְחָה פַת לֶחֶם וגו'. וַיְמַהֵר אַבְרָהָם הָאֹהֱלָה אֶל שָׂרָה וגו'. וְאֶל הַבָּקָר רָץ אַבְרָהָם וגו'. וַיִּקַּח חֶמְאָה וְחָלָב וגו'.

115. Rabbi Chiya said in the name of Rav: If we look into this passage, we should do so wisely. If THIS PASSAGE DISCUSSES matters of the soul, AS HE STARTED TO EXPLAIN, then there is no connection between the beginning and the end, nor between the end and the beginning. THIS MEANS THAT IT IS HARD TO EXPLAIN THE END OF THE PASSAGE IN RELATION TO THE SOUL, REFERRING TO THE WORDS, "LET A LITTLE WATER, I PRAY YOU, BE FETCHED..." THEREFORE, THE END IS NOT CONNECTED TO THE BEGINNING, AND VICE VERSA. But if THE PASSAGE DISCUSSES the departure of man from this world, let the whole passage deal with this. So either we explain the whole passage in this way or the other WE SHOULD CONTINUE TO EXPLAIN THE MEANING OF, "let a little water, I pray you, be fetched, and wash your feet..." AS WELL AS THE MEANING OF, "And I will fetch a morsel of bread... Abraham hastened into the tent, to Sarah...And Abraham ran to the herd... And he took butter, and milk" (Beresheet 18:4-8).

116. כַּד אָתָא רַב דִּימֵי, אֲמַר, לֹא מָצְאָה הַנְּשָׁמָה תּוֹעֶלֶת לַגּוּף, אִלְמָלֵא מַה שֶׁרָמַז בְּכָאן, רֶמֶז הַקָּרְבָּנוֹת. בָּטְלוּ הַקָּרְבָּנוֹת, לֹא בָּטְלָה הַתּוֹרָה, הַאי דְּלָא אִתְעֲסַק בְּקָרְבָּנוֹת, לִיעֲסַק בַּתּוֹרָה, וְיִתְהֲנֵי לֵיהּ יַתִּיר.

116. When Rabbi Dimi arrived he said: The soul could have no use for the body were it not for the sacrifice-offering implied here THAT APPEAR IN THE VERSES "LET A LITTLE WATER," AND SO ON. Even when the offerings ceased, AS THE TEMPLE WAS DESTROYED, the Torah did not cease to exist. Thus, he can delve in study of the Torah, and it will help him even more than the sacrifices.

117. דַּאֲמַר רַבִּי יוֹחָנָן, כְּשֶׁפֵּירַשׁ הַקּוּדְשָׁא בְּרִיךְ הוּא הַקָּרְבָּנוֹת, אָמַר מֹשֶׁה, רִבּוֹנוֹ שֶׁל עוֹלָם, תֵּינַח בִּזְמַן שֶׁיִּהְיוּ יִשְׂרָאֵל עַל אַדְמָתָם, כֵּיוָן שֶׁיִּגְלוּ מֵעַל אַדְמָתָם מַה יַּעֲשׂוּ, אָמַר לוֹ, מֹשֶׁה, יַעַסְקוּ בַּתּוֹרָה וַאֲנִי מוֹחֵל לָהֶם בִּשְׁבִילָהּ, יוֹתֵר מִכָּל הַקָּרְבָּנוֹת שֶׁבָּעוֹלָם, שֶׁנֶּאֱמַר זֹאת

הַתּוֹרָה לָעוֹלָה לַמִּנְחָה וגו'. כְּלוֹמַר זֹאת הַתּוֹרָה, בִּשְׁבִיל עוֹלָה, בִּשְׁבִיל מִנְחָה, בִּשְׁבִיל חַטָּאת, בִּשְׁבִיל אָשָׁם.

117. Rabbi Yochanan said: When the Holy One, blessed be He, described the sacrificial offerings in detail, Moses said – Master of the universe, this is all right when the children of Yisrael live in their land, but what shall they do when they are exiled from their land? He replies: Moses, let them study Torah, and I shall forgive them, for Its sake, more than for all other sacrifices in the world, as it is written: "This is the Torah of the burnt offering, of the meal offering..." (Vayikra 7:37) This means that the Torah is instead of the burnt offering, instead of the meal offering, instead of the sin offering, and instead of the guilt offering.

118. אָמַר רָבִּי כְּרוּסְפְּדָאי, הַאי מַאן דְּמַדְכַּר בְּפוּמֵיהּ, בְּבָתֵּי כְנֵסִיּוֹת וּבְבָתֵּי מִדְרָשׁוֹת, עִנְיָינָא דְּקָרְבָּנַיָּא וְתִקְרוּבְתָּא, וִיכַוֵּון בְּהוּ, בְּרִית כְּרוּתָה הוּא, דְּאִינּוּן מַלְאֲכַיָּא דְּמַדְכְּרִין חוֹבֵיהּ, לְאַבְאָשָׁא לֵיהּ, דְּלָא יַכְלִין לְמֶעְבַּד לֵיהּ, אֶלָּמְלֵא טִיבוּ.

118. Rabbi Cruspedai said: For whoever utters the phrases of the sacrificial offerings in the synagogues and in academies for the study of Torah, and meditates on them, it is a sealed Covenant that all those angels who mention his sins in order to persecute him can only do him good.

119. וּמַאן יוֹכַח, הַאי פָּרְשָׁתָא יוֹכַח, דְּכֵיוָן דַּאֲמַר וְהִנֵּה שְׁלֹשָׁה אֲנָשִׁים נִצָּבִים עָלָיו, מַהוּ עָלָיו, לְעַיֵּין בְּדִינֵיהּ, כֵּיוָן דְּחָמָא נִשְׁמָתָא דְצַדִּיקַיָּא כָּךְ, מַה כְּתִיב, וַיְמַהֵר אַבְרָהָם הָאֹהֱלָה וגו'. מַהוּ הָאֹהֱלָה. בֵּית הַמִּדְרָשׁ. וּמַהוּ אוֹמֵר מַהֲרִי שְׁלֹשׁ סְאִים, עִנְיַן הַקָּרְבָּנוֹת, וְנִשְׁמָתָא מִתְכַּוְּונָת בְּהוּ, הַה"ד וְאֶל הַבָּקָר רָץ אַבְרָהָם. וּכְדֵין נַיְיחָא לְהוּ, וְלָא יַכְלִין לְאַבְאָשָׁא לֵיהּ.

119. And what proves this to be true? This passage: "And, lo, three men stood by him." What is meant by "stood by him?" It means to judge him and pronounce his sentence. As soon as the soul of the righteous saw this, it is written: "And Abraham hastened into the tent..." What is meant by "into the tent?" This refers to the academy for the study of Torah. And what does he say? He says: "Make ready quickly three measures..." This refers to offerings, to which the soul alludes, as it is written: "And Abraham ran to the herd..." Then they are pleased and appeased, and cannot do him any harm.

120. רַבִּי פִּנְחָס פָּתַח קְרָא, דִּכְתִיב וְהִנֵּה הֵחֵל הַנֶּגֶף בָּעָם, וּכְתִיב וַיֹּאמֶר מֹשֶׁה אֶל אַהֲרֹן קַח אֶת הַמַּחְתָּה וגו'. וּכְתִיב וַתֵּעָצַר הַמַּגֵּפָה. כְּתִיב הָכָא מַהֵר, וּכְתִיב הָתָם מַהֲרִי שְׁלֹשׁ סְאִים. מַה לְּהַלָּן קָרְבָּן לְאִשְׁתֵּזָבָא, אַף כָּאן קָרְבָּן לְאִשְׁתֵּזָבָא.

120. Rabbi Pinchas continued the discussion with the passages: "and, behold, the plague had begun among the people..." (Bemidbar 17:12); "Moses said to Aaron, Take a censer..." (Ibid. 11); "the plague was stayed" (Ibid. 13). WE LEARN THIS THROUGH THE USE OF SIMILAR WORDS. It says here "quickly" IN THE VERSE "AND TAKE IT QUICKLY TO THE CONGREGATION." There it is written: "Make ready quickly three measures." As in the first verse, the word "quickly" here applies to a sacrificial offering as a means of salvation. THIS SUPPORTS THE EXPLANATION OF RABBI CRUSPEDAI.

121. אָמַר רְבִּי פִּנְחָס, זִמְנָא חֲדָא הֲוֵינָא אָזְלֵי בְּאָרְחָא, וַעֲרָעִית בֵּיה בְּאֵלִיָּהוּ, אֲמִינָא לֵיה, לֵימָא לִי מַר מִלָּה דְּמַעֲלֵי לִבְרִיָּיתָא, אָמַר לוֹ, קַיָּים גְּזַר קוּדְשָׁא בְּרִיךְ הוּא, וְעָאלוּ קַמֵּיה כָּל אִלֵּין מַלְאֲכַיָּא, דִּמְמַנָּן לְאַדְכְּרָא חוֹבֵי דְּבַר נָשׁ, דִּי בְּעִדָּנָא דְּיִדְכְּרוּן בְּנֵי אֱנָשָׁא קָרְבָּנַיָּא דְּמַנֵּי מֹשֶׁה, וְשַׁוֵּי לִבֵּיה וּרְעוּתֵיה בְּהוֹ, דְּכָלְּהוּ יִדְכְּרוּן לֵיה לְטַב.

121. Rabbi Pinchas then said: Once, while I was walking, I met Elijah and said to him – Sir, may you say to me something for the well-being of the people. He said to me: The Holy One, blessed be He, signed a covenant with this provision. If the angels who report the transgressions of man enter his presence while human beings simultaneously recite the sacrificial offerings that Moses commanded, and say them with full intention and with all their hearts, then all THE ANGELS will mention their names for good.

122. וְעוֹד בְּעִדָּנָא דְּיֶעֱרַע מוֹתָנָא בִּבְנֵי אֱנָשָׁא, קַיָּימָא אִתְגְּזַר, וְכָרוֹזָא

אַעֲבַר עַל כָּל חֵילָא דִשְׁמַיָּא, דְּאִי יֵיעֲלוּן בְּנוֹהִי בְּאַרְעָא, בְּבָתֵּי כְנֵסִיּוֹת
וּבְבָתֵּי מִדְרָשׁוֹת, וְיֵימְרוּן בִּרְעוּת נַפְשָׁא וְלִבָּא, עִנְיָינָא דִּקְטוֹרֶת בּוּסְמִין,
דַּהֲווֹ לְהוֹ לְיִשְׂרָאֵל, דְּיִתְבַּטַּל מוֹתָנָא מִנַּיְיהוּ.

122. ELIJAH SAID TO ME: Further, there is a signed covenant stating that when there is a plague among people, He sends forth this announcement among all the hosts of the heavens. If the humans enter the synagogues and yeshivahs on earth and recite with all their heart and soul the paragraph of the incense that Yisrael once performed, the plague will stop.

123. אָמַר רִבִּי יִצְחָק בּוֹא וּרְאֵה, מַה כְּתִיב, וַיֹּאמֶר מֹשֶׁה אֶל אַהֲרֹן קַח
אֶת הַמַּחְתָּה וְתֶן עָלֶיהָ אֵשׁ מֵעַל הַמִּזְבֵּחַ וְשִׂים קְטֹרֶת. אָמַר לוֹ אַהֲרֹן
לָמָּה. אָמַר כִּי יָצָא הַקֶּצֶף מִלִּפְנֵי ה׳ וְגו׳. מַה כְּתִיב וַיָּרָץ אֶל תּוֹךְ
הַקָּהָל וְהִנֵּה הֵחֵל הַנֶּגֶף בָּעָם. וּכְתִיב וַיַּעֲמֹד בֵּין הַמֵּתִים וּבֵין הַחַיִּים
וַתֵּעָצַר הַמַּגֵּפָה. וְלָא יָכִיל מַלְאָכָא דִמְחַבְּלָא, לְשַׁלְטָאָה וְנִתְבַּטְּלָא
מוֹתָנָא.

123. Rabbi Yitzchak said: Come and behold. It is written: "And Moses said to Aaron, take a censer and put fire in it from off the altar, and put on incense." Aaron asks him, "Why?" Moses replies: "for the wrath has gone out from before Hashem..." It then says: "and he ran into the midst of the congregation; and behold, the plague had begun among the people...And he stood between the dead and the living; and the plague was stayed." (Bemidbar 17:11-13) Hence, the Angel of Destruction lost his dominion and the "plague was stayed." THUS, IT IS STATED EXPRESSLY THAT THE INCENSE STOPPED THE PLAGUE.

124. ר׳ אַחָא אֲזַל לִכְפַר טַרְשָׁא, אָתָא לְגַבֵּי אוּשְׁפִּיזֵיהּ, לְחִישׁוּ עֲלֵיהוּ
כָּל בְּנֵי מָתָא, אָמְרוּ גַּבְרָא רַבָּא אָתָא הָכָא, נֵזִיל לְגַבֵּיהּ, אָתוֹ לְגַבֵּיהּ,
אָמְרוּ לֵיהּ לָא חָס עַל אוֹבְדָּנָא, אָמַר לְהוֹ מַהוּ. אָמְרוּ לֵיהּ, דְּאִית
שִׁבְעָה יוֹמִין, דְּשָׁארֵי מוֹתָנָא בְּמָאתָא, וְכָל יוֹמָא אִתְתַּקַּף וְלָא אִתְבַּטַּל.

124. Rabbi Acha went to the village of Tarsha, where he stayed at an inn. The people of that village whispered about him, saying: A great man has arrived here; let us go to him. They said to him: Do you not have mercy on us because of the plague? He said to them: What plague? They replied: A plague struck the village seven days ago. And every day that passes, it becomes worse.

125. אֲמַר לְהוּ, נֵיזִיל לְבֵי כְנִישְׁתָּא, וְנִתְבַּע רַחֲמֵי מִן קֳדָם קוּדְשָׁא בְּרִיךְ הוּא. עַד דַּהֲווֹ אָזְלֵי אָתוֹ וַאֲמָרוּ, פְּלוֹנִי וּפְלוֹנִי מִיתוּ, וּפְלוֹנִי וּפְלוֹנִי נָטוּ לָמוּת. אֲמַר לְהוּ רַבִּי אַחָא, לֵית עִתָּא לְקַיְּימָא הָכֵי, דְּשַׁעֲתָא דְחִיקָא.

125. He responded: Let us go to the synagogue and plead for mercy in front of the Holy One, blessed be He. As they were on their way, people came up to them and told them the names of people who had died or were about to die. Rabbi Acha said to them: This is not the time to stand around talking, time presses.

126. אֲבָל אַפְרִישׁוּ מִנְּכוֹן אַרְבְּעִין בְּנֵי נָשָׁא, מֵאִינּוּן דְּזַכָּאִין יַתִּיר, עֲשָׂרָה עֲשָׂרָה לְאַרְבְּעָה חוּלְקִין, וַאֲנָא עִמְּכוֹן, עֲשָׂרָה לְזַוְויָיתָא דְּמָאתָא, וַעֲשָׂרָה לְזַוְויָיתָא דְּמָאתָא, וְכֵן לְאַרְבַּע זַוְויָיתָא דְּמָאתָא, וַאֲמָרוּ בִּרְעוּת נַפְשְׁכוֹן עִנְיָינָא דִקְטֹרֶת בּוּסְמִין, דִּקוּדְשָׁא בְּרִיךְ הוּא יְהַב לְמֹשֶׁה, וְעִנְיָינָא דְקָרְבָּנָא עִמֵּיהּ.

126. Choose forty men from the worthiest among you and divide them into four groups. I shall be among you. Ten men should go to each of the four corners of the city. There, you shall recite, with the might of your souls, the phrases of the incense offering, which the Holy One, blessed be He, handed over to Moses. And you should also recite the phrases of the sacrificial offerings.

127. עֲבָדוּ כֵּן תְּלַת זִמְנִין, וְאַעֲבָרוּ בְּכָל מָאתָא, לְאַרְבַּע זַוְויָיתָא, וַהֲווֹ אָמְרִין כֵּן, לְבָתַר אֲמַר לְהוּ, נֵיזִיל לְאִינּוּן דְּאוֹשִׁיטוּ לְמֵימַת, אַפְרִישׁוּ מְנַיְיכוּ לְבָתֵּיהוֹן, וְאִמְרוּ כְדֵין, וְכַד תְּסַיְּימוּ אִמְרוּן אִלֵּין פְּסוּקַיָּיא וַיֹּאמֶר מֹשֶׁה אֶל אַהֲרֹן קַח אֶת הַמַּחְתָּה וְתֶן עָלֶיהָ אֵשׁ וְגוֹ'. וַיִּקַּח אַהֲרֹן וְגוֹ'. וַיַּעֲמֹד בֵּין הַמֵּתִים וְגוֹ'. וְכֵן עֲבָדוּ וְאִתְבַּטַּל מִנַּיְיהוּ.

127. And so they recited those phrases three times in each of the four corners of the city. He then told them: Let us visit those who are about to die. Choose from among you PEOPLE WHO MAY GO to their houses and recite WHAT WE HAVE SAID. When they finish, say these verses: "And Moses said to Aaron, take a censer... And Aaron took... And he stood between the dead..." (Bemidbar 17:11-13) They followed these instructions, and then THE PLAGUE ceased.

128. שָׁמְעוּ הַהוּא קָלָא דַּאֲמַר, סִתְרָא סִתְרָא קַמַּיְיתָא, אוֹחִילוּ לְעֵילָא, דְּהָא דִינָא דִשְׁמַיָּא לָא אַשְׁרֵי הָכָא, דְּהָא יָדְעֵי לְבַטְּלָא לֵיהּ, חָלַשׁ לְבֵּיהּ דְּרַבִּי אַחָא, אִדְמוֹךְ, שְׁמַע דַּאֲמָרֵי לֵיהּ, כַּד עָבַדְתְּ דָּא, עֲבִיד דָּא, זִיל וְאֵימָא לוֹן דְּיַחְזְרוּן בִּתְשׁוּבָה, דְּחַיָּיבִין אִינּוּן קַמַּאי. קָם וְאַחֲזַר לְהוֹ בִּתְשׁוּבָה שְׁלֵימָתָא, וְקַבִּילוּ עֲלַיְיהוּ דְּלָא יִתְבַּטְּלוּן מֵאוֹרַיְיתָא לְעָלַם, וְאַחֲלִיפוּ שְׁמָא דְּקַרְתָּא, וְקָארוֹן לָהּ מָאתָא מַחְסֵיָא.

128. They heard a voice that said: Secrets, primary secrets have been sweetened above; for the Judgment of heaven does not apply here, because people know how to cancel the Judgment! Rabbi Acha's heart became faint, and he fell asleep. He heard them say to him: As you have done this, go and tell them to repent, because they have sinned before Me! He woke up and made them repent and atone completely for their deeds. And they took it upon themselves never to cease studying Torah. And they changed the name of the village to Mata Machseya ('the village of Mercy'), BECAUSE THE HOLY ONE, BLESSED BE HE, SHOWED MERCY TOWARDS THE VILLAGE.

129. אָמַר רָבִּי יְהוּדָה, לֹא דַּי לָהֶם לַצַּדִּיקִים, שֶׁמְּבַטְּלִין אֶת הַגְּזֵרָה, אֶלָּא לְאַחַר כֵּן, שֶׁמְּבָרְכִין לָהֶם, תֵּדַע לָךְ שֶׁכֵּן הוּא, דְּכֵיוָן שֶׁהַנְּשָׁמָה אוֹמֶרֶת לַגּוּף, מַהֲרִי שְׁלֹשׁ סְאִים וְגו'. וְכָל אוֹתוֹ הָעִנְיָן, וּמְבַטֵּל אֶת הַדִּין, מַה כְּתִיב וַיֹּאמֶר שׁוֹב אָשׁוּב אֵלֶיךָ כָּעֵת חַיָּה. הֲרֵי בְּרָכָה.

129. Rabbi Yehuda said: It is not enough for the righteous to cancel the decree, they must bless them as well. And you should know that it is indeed so! Because the soul says to the body: "Make ready quickly three measures of a fine meal," and other phrases. And so it cancels the sentence of Judgment. And what is then written? And he said: "I will return and definitely come back to you at this time next year." Behold, this is the blessing.

130. כֵּיוָן שֶׁרוֹאִים אוֹתָהּ הַמַּלְאָכִים, שֶׁזֶּה לָקַח עֵצָה לְנַפְשׁוֹ, מַה עוֹשִׂים, הוֹלְכִים אֵצֶל הָרְשָׁעִים, לְעַיֵּן בְּדִינָם, וְלַעֲשׂוֹת בָּהֶם מִשְׁפָּט. הה"ד וַיָּקוּמוּ מִשָּׁם הָאֲנָשִׁים וַיַּשְׁקִיפוּ עַל פְּנֵי סְדוֹם, לִמְקוֹם הָרְשָׁעִים, לַעֲשׂוֹת בָּהֶם מִשְׁפָּט.

130. Now what do the angels do after seeing that this person has taken good advice upon himself? They go to the wicked and examine their cases, in order to judge them, as it is written: "And the men rose up from there, and looked toward Sodom" (Beresheet 18:16) – to the place of the wicked, in order to sentence them.

131. דְּאָמַר רַבִּי יְהוּדָה כָּךְ דַּרְכּוֹ שֶׁל צַדִּיק, כֵּיוָן שֶׁרוֹאֶה שֶׁמְעַיְינִין בְּדִינוֹ, אֵינוֹ מִתְאַחֵר לָשׁוּב וּלְהִתְפַּלֵּל וּלְהַקְרִיב חֶלְבּוֹ וְדָמוֹ לִפְנֵי צוּרוֹ, עַד שֶׁמִּסְתַּלְּקִין בַּעֲלֵי הַדִּין מִמֶּנּוּ.

131. Rabbi Yehuda continued: This is the way of the righteous. As soon as he realizes that the angels are examining his case, he immediately repents, prays, and offers his fat and blood as a sacrifice before his Maker until the persecutor s have gone!

132. דְּכֵיוָן שֶׁאָמַר וַיִּשָּׂא עֵינָיו וַיַּרְא וְהִנֵּה שְׁלֹשָׁה אֲנָשִׁים נִצָּבִים עָלָיו, מַה כְּתִיב בַּנְּשָׁמָה, וַיְמַהֵר אַבְרָהָם הָאֹהֱלָה אֶל שָׂרָה. בְּחִפָּזוֹן וּבִמְהִירוּת, בְּלֹא שׁוּם הַעְכָּבָה, מִיָּד מְמַהֶרֶת הַנְּשָׁמָה אֵצֶל הַגּוּף, לְהַחֲזִירוֹ לְמוּטָב, וּלְבַקֵּשׁ בַּמֶּה שֶׁיִּתְכַּפֵּר לוֹ, עַד שֶׁמִּסְתַּלְּקִין מִמֶּנּוּ בַּעֲלֵי הַדִּין.

132. After saying: "And he lifted up his eyes and looked and, lo, three men stood by him..." – what does it say about the soul? "And Abraham hastened into the tent, to Sarah." He went in a rush, without any delay, as the soul hastens to the body to bring it back to the right path and search for anything that may atone for its sins, until the prosecutors depart from it.

133. ר' אֱלִיעֶזֶר אוֹמֵר, מ"ד וְאַבְרָהָם וְשָׂרָה זְקֵנִים בָּאִים בַּיָּמִים חָדַל

לִהְיוֹת לְשָׂרָה אֹרַח כַּנָּשִׁים. אֶלָּא, כֵּיוָן שֶׁהַנְּשָׁמָה עוֹמֶדֶת בְּמַעֲלָתָהּ, וְהַגּוּף נִשְׁאָר בָּאָרֶץ מִכַּמָּה שָׁנִים, בָּאִים בַּיָּמִים. שָׁנִים וְיָמִים הַרְבֵּה, וְחָדַל לָצֵאת וְלָבֹא וְלַעֲבוֹר אֹרַח כִּשְׁאָר כָּל אָדָם, אִתְבַּשַּׂר לְהַחֲיוֹת הַגּוּף.

133. Rabbi Eliezer says: Why does it say, "Now Abraham and Sarah were old, advanced in days, and the manner of women ceased to be with Sarah" (Beresheet 18:11)? Because the soul preserved its stature and the body remained on earth for all those years, "advanced in days." It is after many years and days that it ceases to come to and fro like other men and it is announced that the body shall be resurrected.

134. מַהוּ אוֹמֵר, אַחֲרֵי בְלוֹתִי הָיְתָה לִּי עֶדְנָה, אַחֲרֵי בְלוֹתִי בֶּעָפָר מֵהַיּוֹם כַּמָּה שָׁנִים, הָיְתָה לִי עֶדְנָה וְחִדּוּשׁ, וַאדֹנִי זָקֵן, שֶׁהַיּוֹם כַּמָּה שָׁנִים, שֶׁיָּצֵאת מִמֶּנִּי, וְלֹא הִפְקִידְנִי.

134. What does it say? "After I am grown old shall I have pleasure" (Ibid. 12). After being wasted in the dust for many years until this day, "shall I have pleasure" and be renewed. "...my lord being old also..." means that it has been many years since you left me, and you have not visited me since.

135. וְקוּדְשָׁא בְּרִיךְ הוּא אָמַר, הֲיִפָּלֵא מֵה' דָּבָר לַמּוֹעֵד. מַהוּ לַמּוֹעֵד. אוֹתוֹ הַיָּדוּעַ אֶצְלִי לְהַחֲיוֹת הַמֵּתִים. וּלְשָׂרָה בֵן. מְלַמֵּד שֶׁיִּתְחַדֵּשׁ כְּבֶן שָׁלֹשׁ שָׁנִים.

135. And the Holy One, blessed be He, said: "Is anything too hard for Hashem? At the time appointed..." (Ibid. 14). What is meant by "the time appointed?" This is the time that is known to me for the resurrection of the dead. "...and Sarah shall have a son," that is, it shall be revived as a three year old.

136. אָמַר רַבִּי יְהוּדָה בְּרַבִּי סִימוֹן, כֵּיוָן שֶׁהַנְּשָׁמָה נִיזוֹנִית מִזִּיוָהּ שֶׁל מַעְלָה, קוּדְשָׁא בְּרִיךְ הוּא אוֹמֵר לְאוֹתוֹ הַמַּלְאָךְ הַנִּקְרָא דּוּמָ"ה, לֵךְ וּבַשֵּׂר לְגוּף פְּלוֹנִי, שֶׁאֲנִי עָתִיד לְהַחֲיוֹתוֹ, לַמּוֹעֵד שֶׁאֲנִי אַחֲיֶה אֶת

הַצַּדִּיקִים לֶעָתִיד לָבֹא. וְהוּא מֵשִׁיב, אַחֲרֵי בְלוֹתִי הָיְתָה לִּי עֶדְנָה. אַחֲרֵי בְלוֹתִי בֶּעָפָר, וְשָׁכַנְתִּי בָּאֲדָמָה, וְאָכַל בִּשָׂרִי רִמָּה, וְגוּשׁ עָפָר, תִּהְיֶה לִּי חִדּוּשׁ.

136. Rabbi Yehuda, the son of Rabbi Simon, said: Because the soul is replenished by the splendor of above, the Holy One, blessed be He, tells the angel Dumah – Go and inform the body of such and such, that I shall resurrect it in the future, at the appointed time, when I shall resurrect the righteous. And it replies: "After I am grown old shall I have pleasure?" After I have waxed in the dust and have dwelt in the soil and worms have eaten my flesh, and I am a clot of earth, shall I be resurrected?

137. קוּדְשָׁא בְּרִיךְ הוּא אוֹמֵר לַנְּשָׁמָה, הה"ד וַיֹּאמֶר ה' אֶל אַבְרָהָם וְגוֹ'. הֲיִפָּלֵא מֵה' דָּבָר לַמּוֹעֵד הַיָּדוּעַ אֶצְלִי, לְהַחֲיוֹת אֶת הַמֵּתִים, אָשׁוּב אֵלֶיךָ אוֹתוֹ הַגּוּף שֶׁהוּא קָדוֹשׁ, מְחוּדָשׁ כְּבָרִאשׁוֹנָה, לִהְיוֹתְכֶם מַלְאָכִים קְדוֹשִׁים. וְאוֹתוֹ הַיּוֹם עָתִיד לְפָנַי לִשְׂמֹחַ בָּהֶם, הה"ד יְהִי כְבוֹד ה' לְעוֹלָם יִשְׂמַח ה' בְּמַעֲשָׂיו.

(ע"כ מדה"נ)

137. The Holy One, blessed be He, says to the soul, as it is written: "And Hashem said to Abraham...Is anything too hard for Hashem? At the time appointed..." (Beresheet 18:13-14) which is known to Me, I will resurrect the dead. I will return to you that same body which is sacred, renewed as before, because you are like the holy angels. And that day shall be merry before Me and I shall rejoice in them, as it is written: "May the glory of Hashem endure forever, let Hashem rejoice in his works..." (Tehilim 104:31).

End of Midrash Hane'elam

8. "And he said I will certainly return to you"

A Synopsis
The Creator informs Abraham, that though barren, his wife, Sarah, will be able to give birth to a child. The Zohar explains that only the Creator Himself possesses the key to childbirth.

The Relevance of this Passage
Whereas man has the power to affect many miracles over nature by changing his own nature, it is only the Creator who can bestow the gift of childbirth. The words that convey this truth allow us to receive and share the energy of childbirth with all of those in need of it.

138. וַיֹּאמֶר שׁוֹב אָשׁוּב אֵלֶיךָ כָּעֵת חַיָּה. אָמַר רָבִּי יִצְחָק, שׁוֹב אָשׁוּב, שׁוֹב יָשׁוּב מִבָּעֵי לֵיהּ, דְּהָא מַפְתְּחָא דָּא לְמִפְקַד עֲקָרוֹת, בִּידָא דְּקוּדְשָׁא בְּרִיךְ הוּא אִיהוּ, וְלָא בִּידָא דִּשְׁלִיחָא אָחֳרָא.

138. "And he said, 'I will certainly return to you at this season...'" (Beresheet 18:10). Rabbi Yitzchak asks: Why is it written: "I will certainly return?" I should have said, 'He will certainly return,' as the key to impregnating barren women is in the hands of the Holy One, blessed be He, and not in the hands of any other messenger.

139. כְּמָה דְּתָנֵינָן, תְּלַת מַפְתְּחוֹת אִינוּן, דְּלָא אִתְמְסָרוּ בִּידָא דִּשְׁלִיחָא, דְּחַיָּה, וּתְחִיַּית הַמֵּתִים, וּגְשָׁמִים. וְהוֹאִיל דְּלָא אִתְמְסָרוּ בִּידָא דִּשְׁלִיחָא, אֲמַאי כְּתִיב שׁוֹב אָשׁוּב. אֶלָּא וַדַּאי קוּדְשָׁא בְּרִיךְ הוּא דַּהֲוָה קָאֵים עֲלַייהוּ, אָמַר מִלָּה, בְּגִין כָּךְ כְּתִיב וַיֹּאמֶר שׁוֹב אָשׁוּב אֵלֶיךָ.

139. As we have learned, there are three keys that were not handed over to any messenger: the keys of life, of the resurrection of the dead, and of the rains. As they were not handed over to any messenger, why is it written "I will certainly return," WHICH MEANS THAT THE ANGEL WILL RETURN "AT THIS TIME" AND VISIT HER? AND HE REPLIES: It is clear that the Holy One, blessed be He, who stood by them said this phrase. This is why it is written: "I will certainly return to you."

150. וְתָא חֲזֵי, בְּכָל אֲתַר דִּכְתִיב וַיֹּאמֶר סְתָם, אוֹ וַיִּקְרָא סְתָם, הוּא
מַלְאָכָא דִּבְרִית, וְלָא אָחֲרָא. וַיֹּאמֶר: דִּכְתִיב וַיֹּאמֶר אִם שָׁמֹעַ תִּשְׁמַע
וְגוֹ'. וַיֹּאמֶר, וְלָא קָאֲמַר מַאן הוּא. וַיִּקְרָא: דִּכְתִיב וַיִּקְרָא אֶל מֹשֶׁה,
וְלָא קָאֲמַר מַאן הֲוָה. אָמַר: דִּכְתִיב וְאֶל מֹשֶׁה אָמַר וְגוֹ'. וְלָא אָמַר
מַאן הֲוָה. אֶלָּא בְּכָל הַנֵי מַלְאָכָא דִּבְרִית הֲוָה. וְכֹלָּא בְּקוּדְשָׁא בְּרִיךְ
הוּא אִתְּמָר. וּבְגִין כָּךְ, כְּתִיב וַיֹּאמֶר שׁוֹב אָשׁוּב אֵלֶיךָ וְגוֹ'. וְהִנֵּה בֵן
וְגוֹ'.

140. Come and behold: wherever it is merely written: "And he said" or "And he called," WITHOUT MENTIONING WHO SAID OR CALLED, it is a reference to the Angel of the Covenant, NAMELY THE SHECHINAH, and no other. "And he said..." appears in the verse "And he said, if you will diligently hearken to the voice..." (Shemot 15:26) but the verse does not mention who said this. It is also written in the verse "And he called upon Moses..." (Vayikra 1:1) but again, it does not say who called. Again, it is written: "And to Moses, he said..." (Shemot 24:1) but it does not say who. In all these places, it is the Angel of the Covenant, NAMELY THE SHECHINAH. And everything has been said in reference to the Holy One, blessed be He, BECAUSE THE SHECHINAH IS THE HOLY ONE, BLESSED BE HE. This is why it is written: "And he said, I will certainly return to you...and, lo, Sarah your wife shall have a son." THUS, THE HOLY ONE, BLESSED BE HE, WHO HAS THE KEY FOR IMPREGNATING BARREN WOMEN IN HIS HANDS, ALONE MAY SAY, "I WILL CERTAINLY RETURN..."

9. "And, lo, Sarah your wife shall have a son"

A Synopsis

When we do not pursue spiritual growth for the purpose of drawing close to The Creator, our true Father, we behave as disrespectful, uncaring children. Therefore, recognizing the Creator as our true Father should be motivation for spiritual growth and transformation.

The Relevance of this Passage

A child cannot truly grow and develop to its fullest without the tenderness, care, and nurturing that a loving parent provides. When we live life without appreciation or comprehension of the Creator, we cannot grow and develop spiritually. The influences of this passage arouse an awareness of the Creator, our true source and origin, along with all the other precious qualities found in children who seek security and comfort from a parent.

141. וְהִנֵּה בֵן לְשָׂרָה אִשְׁתֶּךָ. מ"ט לָא כְּתִיב וְהִנֵּה בֵן לְךָ, אֶלָּא בְּגִין דְּלָא יַחֲשׁוֹב דְּהָא מִן הָגָר אִיהוּ, כְּדִבְקַדְמֵיתָא. רַבִּי שִׁמְעוֹן פָּתַח וְאָמַר, בֵּן יְכַבֵּד אָב וְעֶבֶד אֲדוֹנָיו. בֵּן יְכַבֵּד אָב, דָּא יִצְחָק לְאַבְרָהָם.

141. "And, lo, Sarah your wife shall have a son" (Beresheet 18:10). HE ASKS: Why does the verse not read, 'And, lo, you shall have a son?' AND HE REPLIES: So that he may not assume that he will be born to Hagar as before. Rabbi Shimon opened the discussion by saying: "A son honors his father, and a servant his master" (Malachi 1:6). The words "A son honors his father" refer to Isaac honoring Abraham.

142. אֵימָתַי כַּבֵּד לֵיהּ, בְּשַׁעֲתָא דַּעֲקַד לֵיהּ עַל גַּבֵּי מַדְבְּחָא, וּבְעָא לְמִקְרַב לֵיהּ קָרְבָּנָא, וְיִצְחָק בַּר תְּלָתִין וּשְׁבַע שְׁנִין הֲוָה, וְאַבְרָהָם הֲוָה סָבָא, דְּאִילוּ הֲוָה בָּעִיט בְּרַגְלָא חַד, לָא יָכִיל לְמֵיקַם קַמֵּיהּ, וְאִיהוּ אוֹקִיר לֵיהּ לַאֲבוֹי, וַעֲקַד לֵיהּ כְּחַד אִימְרָא, בְּגִין לְמֶעְבַּד רְעוּתֵיהּ דַּאֲבוֹי.

142. When did he honor him? Isaac was 37 years old when Abraham bound him on the altar and offered him as a sacrifice. Abraham was so old that he could not have countered an attack from Isaac – not even a kick with one foot. But Isaac honored his father, who bound him like a lamb, AND SHOWED NO RESISTANCE, in order to fulfill his father's will.

143. וְעֶבֶד אֲדוֹנָיו: דָּא אֱלִיעֶזֶר לְאַבְרָהָם. כַּד שַׁדַּר לֵיהּ לְחָרָן, וַעֲבַד כָּל רְעוּתֵיהּ דְּאַבְרָהָם, וְאוֹקִיר לֵיהּ, כְּמָה דִכְתִיב וַה' בֵּרַךְ אֶת אֲדוֹנִי וגו'. וּכְתִיב וַיֹּאמֶר עֶבֶד אַבְרָהָם אָנֹכִי. בְּגִין לְאוֹקִיר לֵיהּ לְאַבְרָהָם.

143. An example of a servant honoring his master is Eliezer to Abraham, whom Abraham sent to Charan. There, Eliezer honored Abraham by fulfilling his wishes, as it is written: "And Hashem has blessed my master greatly..." (Beresheet 24:35), as well as "And he said, I am Avraham's servant" (Ibid. 34). He did all of this to show respect to Abraham.

144. דְּהָא בַּר נָשׁ דַּהֲוָה מַיְיתֵי כֶּסֶף וְזָהָב, וְאַבְנֵי יְקָר וּגְמַלִּין, וְאִיהוּ כִּדְקָא יָאוֹת, שַׁפִּיר בְּחֵיזוּ, לָא אָמַר דְּאִיהוּ רְחִימָא דְּאַבְרָהָם, אוֹ קָרִיבָא דִּילֵיהּ. אֶלָּא אָמַר, עֶבֶד אַבְרָהָם אָנֹכִי, בְּגִין לְסַלְּקָא בְּשִׁבְחָא דְּאַבְרָהָם, וּלְאוֹקִיר לֵיהּ בְּעֵינַיְיהוּ.

144. Eliezer is a man who carried silver, gold, precious stones, and camels. He himself was good looking and impressive in appearance. Nevertheless, he did not say that he was a dear friend or a relative of Abraham. Instead, he said, "I am Avraham's servant," in order to raise the esteem of Abraham and make them respect him.

145. וְעַל דָּא בֵּן יְכַבֵּד אָב וְעֶבֶד אֲדוֹנָיו. וְאַתּוּן יִשְׂרָאֵל בָּנַי, קְלָנָא בְּעֵינַיְיכוּ לוֹמַר דַּאֲנָא אֲבוּכוֹן, אוֹ דְּאַתּוּן עֲבָדִין לִי. וְאִם אָב אָנִי אַיֵּה כְּבוֹדִי וגו'. בְּגִין כָּךְ וְהִנֵּה בֵן: דָּא הוּא בֵּן וַדַּאי, וְלָא יִשְׁמָעֵאל. דָּא הוּא בֵּן דְּאוֹקִיר לַאֲבוֹי כִּדְקָא חֲזֵי.

145. Therefore, the verse reads, "A son honors his father, and a servant his master," – but you Yisrael, my children, you are ashamed to say that I am your father or that you are My servants. So "...if then I am a father, where is my honor...?" (Malachi 1:6). Thus, it is written: "And, lo...a son." This is definitely the son, who unlike Ishmael properly honors his father.

146. וְהִנֵּה בֵן לְשָׂרָה אִשְׁתֶּךָ. בֵּן לְשָׂרָה, דִּבְגִינֵיהּ מִיתַת, דְּבִגִינֵיהּ
כְּאִיבַת נַפְשָׁהּ, עַד דְּנַפְּקַת מִינָהּ. וְהִנֵּה בֵן לְשָׂרָה. לְאִסְתַּלְּקָא בְּגִינֵיהּ,
בְּשַׁעֲתָא דְּקוּדְשָׁא בְּרִיךְ הוּא יָתִיב בְּדִינָא עַל עָלְמָא. דִּכְדֵין וַה' פָּקַד
אֶת שָׂרָה וְגו'. דְּהָא מַדְכְּרֵי לְשָׂרָה בְּגִינֵיהּ דְּיִצְחָק. וְעַל דָּא אִיהוּ בֵן
לְשָׂרָה. וְהִנֵּה בֵן לְשָׂרָה. דְּהָא נוּקְבָא נָטְלָא לִבְרָא מִן דְּכוּרָא.

146. "And, lo, Sarah your wife shall have a son," as she died because of
him, WHEN SHE HEARD OF HIM BEING BOUND UPON THE ALTAR. And
because of him, she suffered anguish in her soul until she bore him. "And,
lo, Sarah...shall have a son" MEANS THAT she was exalted on his account
when the Holy One, blessed be He, sat in Judgment on the world – because
at that time, ON ROSH HASHANAH, WHEN ISAAC WAS BORN, "Hashem
visited Sarah..." Clearly, He remembered Sarah for the sake of Isaac. This is
why "Sarah...shall have a son." ANOTHER EXPLANATION OF "And, lo,
Sarah your wife shall have a son" is that BECAUSE the woman receives the
child from the man, THE FEMALE HAS THE CHILD. THEREFORE, THE
VERSE SAYS, "AND, LO, SARAH...SHALL HAVE A SON."

147. וְשָׂרָה שׁוֹמַעַת פֶּתַח הָאֹהֶל וְהוּא אַחֲרָיו. מַאי וְהוּא אַחֲרָיו, וְהִיא
אַחֲרָיו מִבְּעֵי לֵיהּ. אֶלָּא רָזָא אִיהוּ, וְשָׂרָה שׁוֹמַעַת, מַה דַּהֲוָה אֲמַר
פֶּתַח הָאֹהֶל, דָּא דַּרְגָּא תַּתָּאָה פִּתְחָא דִּמְהֵימְנוּתָא. וְהוּא אַחֲרָיו.
דְּאוֹדֵי לֵיהּ, דַּרְגָּא עִלָּאָה. מִן יוֹמָא דַּהֲוַת שָׂרָה בְּעָלְמָא, לָא שָׁמְעַת
מִלָּה דְּקוּדְשָׁא בְּרִיךְ הוּא, בַּר הַהוּא שַׁעֲתָא.

147. "And Sarah heard it in the tent door, which was behind him"
(Beresheet 18:10). AND HE ASKS: What do the words "which was behind
him" mean? Should it not have been written: 'and she was behind him,' AS
IF TO SAY THAT SHE WAS BEHIND THE INFORMING ANGEL? HE REPLIES:
There is a secret here. "And Sarah heard it" REFERS TO the words "tent
door," which correspond to the lower grade, that is, the gate of faith,
NAMELY THE SHECHINAH. "...which was behind him..." MEANS THAT the
upper grade, WHO IS THE HOLY ONE, BLESSED BE HE, confirmed the
declaration. Ever since Sarah came into the world, she did not hear anything
from the Holy One, blessed be He, save at that moment.

148. דָּבָר אַחֵר, דַּהֲוַת יַתְבָא שָׂרָה פֶּתַח הָאֹהֶל, בְּגִין לְמִשְׁמַע מִלִּין,

וְהִיא שָׁמְעַת הַאי מִלָּה דְּאִתְבַּשַּׂר בָּהּ אַבְרָהָם. וְהוּא אַחֲרָיו. אַבְרָהָם,
דַּהֲוָה יָתֵיב אֲחוֹרוֹי דִּשְׁכִינְתָּא.

148. Yet another explanation is that Sarah sat at the "tent door" in order to listen to their words. And she heard the good news that Abraham received. THIS IS WHY IT IS WRITTEN: "AND SARAH HEARD IT IN THE TENT DOOR, which (he) was behind him." IT MEANS THAT Abraham sat behind the Shechinah.

149. וְאַבְרָהָם וְשָׂרָה זְקֵנִים בָּאִים בַּיָּמִים. מַאי בָּאִים בַּיָּמִים. שְׁעוּרִין
דְּיוֹמִין דְּאִתְחֲזֵי כְּדֵין לְהוּ, חַד מֵאָה, וְחַד תִּשְׁעִים, עָאלוּ בְּיוֹמִין,
שְׁעוּרָא דְּיוֹמִין, כִּדְקָא יָאוֹת. בָּאִים בַּיָּמִים. כִּדְבָר אַחֵר כִּי בָא הַיּוֹם,
דְּאָעֲרַב יוֹמָא לְמֵיעַל.

149. "Now Abraham and Sarah were old, advanced in days (lit. 'coming with days')..." (Beresheet 18:11). AND HE ASKS: What is meant by 'coming with days'? AND HE REPLIS: THIS MEANS THAT THEY ARE 'COMING' to the end of their 'days.' Abraham was a hundred years old, and Sarah was ninety. They reached their fill of days, as is proper. 'Coming with days' can be read as 'for the day has come,' WHICH CAN MEAN THAT the day has ended. HERE, AS WELL, "COMING WITH THE DAYS" MEANS THAT THEIR DAYS WERE COMPLETED.

150. חָדַל לִהְיוֹת לְשָׂרָה אֹרַח כַּנָּשִׁים. וְהַהִיא שַׁעֲתָא חָמַאת גַּרְמָהּ
בְּעֶדּוּנָא אָחֳרָא. וּבְגִין כָּךְ אָמְרָה וַאדוֹנִי זָקֵן. דְּהָא אִיהוּ לָא כְּדַאי
לְאוֹלָדָא, בְּגִין דְּאִיהוּ סָבָא.

150. "...and the manner of women ceased to be with Sarah..." At that hour, she suddenly saw herself having "pleasure" again, AS THE "MANNER OF WOMEN" REVIVED WITHIN HER. Thus she said: "...my lord being old also..." meaning that Abraham was too old to be able to beget children. HOWEVER, SHE DID NOT SAY THAT SHE HERSELF WAS TOO OLD.

10. "Her husband is known in the gates"

A Synopsis
Rabbi Yehuda reveals a powerful secret: The Light of the Creator manifests itself in direct proportion to a person's degree of certainty in the reality of the Creator. If we doubt the existence of the Creator, there is no God force in our personal life. It is our consciousness that
creates our existence. For this reason, it is only our absolute conviction and certainty that will bring forth the Creator's existence and influence in our lives, giving us an active role in the process of Creation.

The Relevance of this Passage
All of us are born into this world with varying degrees of doubt in the existence of the Creator. Moreover, the essence of spiritual work and the notion of free will involves removing these layers of uncertainty throughout our life. Doubt, however, is a formidable foe requiring a large measure of certitude and conviction in return. Certainty in the existence of the Creator emerges from this passage, combined with a recognition in the power of our consciousness to influence and shape our reality.

151. ר' יְהוּדָה פָּתַח, נוֹדָע בַּשְּׁעָרִים בַּעֲלָהּ בְּשִׁבְתּוֹ עִם זִקְנֵי אָרֶץ. תָּא חֲזֵי קוּדְשָׁא בְּרִיךְ הוּא אִסְתַּלָּק בִּיקָרֵיהּ, דְּאִיהוּ גָּנִיז וְסָתִים, בְּעִלּוּיָא סַגְיָא. לָאו אִיתֵי בְּעָלְמָא, וְלָא הֲוָה מִן יוֹמָא דְּאִתְבְּרֵי עָלְמָא, דְּיָכִיל לְקַיְּימָא עַל חָכְמָתָא דִּילֵיהּ, וְלָא יָכִיל לְקַיְּימָא בֵּיהּ.

151. Rabbi Yehuda said: "Her husband is known in the gates, when he sits among the elders of the land" (Mishlei 31:23). Come and behold: the Holy One, blessed be He, was exalted in His glory, because He is hidden and greatly elevated. Since the creation of the world, nobody has ever been able to grasp and conceive His entire wisdom. Thus, no one is able to comprehend it.

152. בְּגִין דְּאִיהוּ גָּנִיז וְסָתִים, וְאִסְתַּלָּק לְעֵילָא לְעֵילָא, וְכֻלְּהוּ עִלָּאֵי וְתַתָּאֵי לָא יָכְלִין לְאִתְדַּבְּקָא, עַד דְּכֻלְּהוּ אָמְרִין בָּרוּךְ כְּבוֹד ה' מִמְּקוֹמוֹ. תַּתָּאֵי אָמְרֵי דְּאִיהוּ לְעֵילָא, דִּכְתִיב עַל הַשָּׁמַיִם כְּבוֹדוֹ. עִלָּאֵי אָמְרֵי דְּאִיהוּ לְתַתָּא, דִּכְתִיב עַל כָּל הָאָרֶץ כְּבוֹדֶךָ. עַד דְּכֻלְּהוּ עִלָּאֵי

וְתַתָּאֵי, אָמְרֵי בָּרוּךְ כְּבוֹד ה' מִמְקוֹמוֹ. בְּגִין דְּלָא אִתְיְידַע, וְלָא הֲוָה מַאן דְּיָכִיל לְקַיְימָא בֵּיהּ, וְאַתְּ אֲמַרְתְּ נוֹדָע בַּשְּׁעָרִים בַּעְלָהּ.

152. He is concealed and exalted high above the reach of all the lower and supernal beings. He is so far above that they all proclaim: "Blessed be the glory of Hashem from His place" (Yechezkel 3:12). The people on earth say that THE SHECHINAH is high above, as it is written: "His glory is above the heavens" (Tehilim 113:4), but the supernal beings say that THE SHECHINAH is down below, as it is written: "His glory is over all the earth" (Tehilim 57:12). So that all the supernal and human beings declare: "Blessed be the glory of Hashem from His place," because He is unknowable, and no one is able to grasp Him. Thus, how does one explain the verse: "Her husband is known in the gates"?

153. אֶלָּא וַדַּאי, נוֹדָע בַּשְּׁעָרִים בַּעְלָהּ. דָּא קוּדְשָׁא בְּרִיךְ הוּא. דְּאִיהוּ אִתְיְידַע וְאִתְדַּבַּק, לְפוּם מַה דִּמְשַׁעֵר בְּלִבֵּיהּ, כָּל חַד, כַּמָּה דְּיָכִיל לְאִדַּבְּקָא בְּרוּחָא דְּחָכְמְתָא. וּלְפוּם מַה דִּמְשַׁעֵר בְּלִבֵּיהּ, הָכֵי אִתְיְידַע בְּלִבֵּיהּ. וּבְגִינֵי כָךְ, נוֹדָע בַּשְּׁעָרִים, בְּאִינּוּן שְׁעָרִים. אֲבָל דְּאִתְיְידַע כִּדְקָא יָאוֹת, לָא הֲוָה מַאן דְּיָכִיל לְאִדַּבְּקָא וּלְמִנְדַע לֵיהּ.

153. Most certainly, "Her husband is known in the gates" refers to the Holy One, blessed be He, who is known and conceived according to what each one assumes in his mind and is able to grasp with the Spirit of Wisdom. Thus, he is able to understand according to what he is able to assume. Therefore, it is written: "Her husband is known in the gates (Heb. she'arim)," THAT IS, THOSE ASSUMPTIONS (HEB. SHI'URIM), WHICH EVERYONE FORMS ACCORDING TO HIS OWN MIND, even though full knowledge of Him is far beyond the reach of anyone.

154. רַבִּי שִׁמְעוֹן אָמַר, נוֹדָע בַּשְּׁעָרִים בַּעְלָהּ. מַאן שְׁעָרִים. כְּדָבָר אַחֵר שְׂאוּ שְׁעָרִים רָאשֵׁיכֶם וְהִנָּשְׂאוּ פִּתְחֵי עוֹלָם. וּבְגִין אֵלּוּ שְׁעָרִים, דְּאִינּוּן דַּרְגִין עִלָּאִין, בְּגִינַייְהוּ אִתְיְידַע קוּדְשָׁא בְּרִיךְ הוּא. וְאִי לָא, לָא יָכְלִין לְאִתְדַּבְּקָא בֵּיהּ.

154. Rabbi Shimon asks: "Her husband is known in the gates." What are the gates? They are the same as the gates mentioned in: "Lift up your heads, gates, and lifted them up, you everlasting doors" (Tehilim 24:9). It is through these gates, which are the supernal grades, that the Holy One, blessed be He, is known. For were it not FOR THESE GATES, no one would have been able to commune with Him.

155. תָּא חֲזֵי, דְּהָא נִשְׁמָתָא דְּבַר נָשׁ, לָאו אִיהוּ מַאן דְּיָכִיל לְמִנְדַּע לָהּ, אֶלָּא בְּגִין אִלֵּין שַׁיְיפִין דְּגוּפָא, וְאִינוּן דַּרְגִּין דְּעָבְדִין אוּמָנוּתָא דְּנִשְׁמָתָא, בְּגִין כָּךְ אִתְיְדַע וְלָא אִתְיְדַע. כָּךְ קוּדְשָׁא בְּרִיךְ הוּא, אִתְיְדַע וְלָא אִתְיְדַע. בְּגִין דְּאִיהוּ נִשְׁמָתָא לְנִשְׁמָתָא, רוּחָא לְרוּחָא, גָּנִיז וְטָמִיר מִכֹּלָּא, אֲבָל בְּאִינוּן שְׁעָרִים, דְּאִינוּן פִּתְחִין לְנִשְׁמָתָא אִתְיְדַע קוּדְשָׁא בְּרִיךְ הוּא.

155. Come and behold: even the soul of man cannot be understood directly. It is grasped only through the members of the body, which represent the grades THAT BELONG TO THEM, which reveal the actions of the soul. This is why THE SOUL is conceivable and at the same time inconceivable. IT IS CONCEIVED BY THE MEMBERS OF THE BODY, BUT IS NOT CONCEIVABLE IN ITS OWN ESSENCE. In such a manner, the Holy One, blessed be He, is conceivable and inconceivable. He is the soul to the soul and the spirit to the spirit, hidden and concealed from all. But to he WHO MERITS those gates, NAMELY, THE SUPERNAL GRADES that are the openings of the soul, the Holy One, blessed be He, is made known. SO HE IS CONCEIVABLE BY THE SUPERNAL GRADES, WHICH ARE HIS DOINGS, BUT HE IS INCONCEIVABLE FROM THE ASPECT OF HIS OWN ESSENCE.

156. תָּא חֲזֵי, אִית פִּתְחָא לְפִתְחָא, וְדַרְגָּא לְדַרְגָּא, וּמִנַּיְיהוּ יְדִיעַ יְקָרָא דְּקוּדְשָׁא בְּרִיךְ הוּא. פֶּתַח הָאֹהֶל, דָּא הוּא פִּתְחָא דְּצֶדֶק. כְּדִבָר אַחֵר פִּתְחוּ לִי שַׁעֲרֵי צֶדֶק וְגו'. דָּא פִּתְחָא קַדְמָאָה, לְאָעֲלָא בֵּיהּ, וּבְהַאי פִּתְחָא, אִתְחֲזוּן כָּל שְׁאָר פִּתְחִין עִלָּאִין, מַאן דְּזָכֵי לְהַאי, זָכֵי לְמִנְדַּע בֵּיהּ, וּבְכֻלְּהוּ שְׁאָר פִּתְחִין, בְּגִין דְּכֻלְּהוּ שָׁרָאן עֲלֵיהּ.

156. Come and behold: there is gate upon gate, grade upon grade, through which the glory of the Holy One, blessed be He, is made known. This REFERS TO the "tent door," which is the gate of righteousness, WHICH IS

MALCHUT. Thus, it is written: "Open to me the gates of righteousness" (Tehilim 118:19). And this is the first gate to enter. From this gate, all the other supernal gates can be seen. So whoever enters this gate knows the other gates as well, because they all rest on it.

157. וְהַשְׁתָּא דְּפִתְחָא דָא לָא אִתְיְדַע, בְּגִין דְּיִשְׂרָאֵל בְּגָלוּתָא, וְכֻלְּהוּ פִּתְחִין אִסְתַּלְּקוּ מִנֵּיהּ, וְלָא יָכְלִין לְמִנְדַע וּלְאִתְדַּבְּקָא. אֲבָל בְּזִמְנָא דְּיִפְּקוּן יִשְׂרָאֵל מִן גָּלוּתָא, זְמִינִין כָּלְּהוּ דַּרְגִּין עִלָּאִין, לְמִשְׁרֵי עֲלֵיהּ כִּדְקָא יָאוֹת.

157. But now, this LOWER gate, WHICH IS CALLED THE "TENT DOOR" AND THE "GATE OF RIGHTEOUSNESS" is unknown, because the children of Yisrael are in exile. As a result, all the gates are gone from it. Thus, they are incapable of knowledge and conception. But when Yisrael shall return from exile, all the supernal grades will be destined to dwell upon this gate of righteousness, as should properly be.

158. וּכְדֵין יִנְדְּעוּן בְּנֵי עָלְמָא, חָכְמְתָא עִלָּאָה יַקִּירָא, מַה דְּלָא הֲווֹ יָדְעִין מִקַּדְמַת דְּנָא. דִּכְתִיב וְנָחָה עָלָיו רוּחַ ה' רוּחַ חָכְמָה וּבִינָה רוּחַ עֵצָה וּגְבוּרָה רוּחַ דַּעַת וְיִרְאַת ה'. כָּלְּהוּ זְמִינִין לְאַשְׁרָאָה עַל הַאי פִּתְחָא תַּתָּאָה, דְּאִיהוּ פֶּתַח הָאֹהֶל. וְכָלְּהוּ זְמִינִין לְאַשְׁרָאָה עַל מַלְכָּא מְשִׁיחָא, בְּגִין לְמֵידַן עָלְמָא. דִּכְתִיב וְשָׁפַט בְּצֶדֶק דַּלִּים וגו'.

158. Then, people will have knowledge of the supernal Wisdom, of which they previously knew nothing, as it is written: "And the spirit of Hashem shall rest upon him, the spirit of wisdom and understanding, the spirit of counsel and might, the spirit of knowledge and the fear of Hashem" (Yeshayah 11:2). In the future, all these shall rest upon this lower gate, which is the "tent door," NAMELY MALCHUT. And they shall all rest upon King Messiah to judge the world, as it is written: "But with righteousness shall he judge the poor..." (Ibid. 4)

11. "And he said, 'I will certainly return to you'"

A Synopsis

The Zohar expounds upon the Right Column aspect of Abraham and the Left Column aspect of Isaac in the metaphysical scheme of things. Both the Right and Left Columns of energy are basic building blocks in Creation, similar to the proton and the electron. This spiritual truth is conveyed through the biblical story where Abraham names his son Isaac as opposed to the tradition of the mother naming the child. The story is a metaphor, indicating the importance of the Right and Left Column – the *desire to share* and the *desire to receive*, respectively.

The Relevance of this Passage

Mankind's behavioral actions always embody a particular blend of the Right and Left columns of energy – our ego's *desire to receive* versus our soul's *desire to share*. We develop an awareness of the importance of the actions we take through the Right and Left Column pathways. This allows us to continually seek balance through the process of transforming our *desire to receive for the self alone* into actions of receiving for the sake of sharing with others.

159. בְּגִינֵי כָּךְ, כַּד אִתְבַּשַּׂר אַבְרָהָם, הַאי דַרְגָּא הֲוָה אָמַר, כְּמָה דְאִתְּמָר, דִּכְתִיב וַיֹּאמֶר שׁוֹב אָשׁוּב אֵלֶיךָ כָּעֵת חַיָּה. וַיֹּאמֶר, לָא כְתִיב מַאן הֲוָה, וְדָא הוּא פֶּתַח הָאֹהֶל. וְעַל דָּא, וְשָׂרָה שׁוֹמַעַת, הַאי דַרְגָּא דַּהֲוָה מַלֵּיל עִמֵּיהּ, מַאן דְּלָא הֲוָה שְׁמָעַת מִקַּדְמַת דְּנָא. דִּכְתִיב וְשָׂרָה שׁוֹמַעַת פֶּתַח הָאֹהֶל, דַּהֲוָה מְבַשֵּׂר וַאֲמַר, שׁוֹב אָשׁוּב אֵלֶיךָ כָּעֵת חַיָּה וְהִנֵּה בֵן לְשָׂרָה אִשְׁתֶּךָ.

159. Therefore, it was this grade, NAMELY THE "TENT DOOR," WHICH IS MALCHUT, that informed Abraham OF YITZCHAK'S BIRTH, as we have explained the words: "And he said, I will certainly return to you at this season..." Although it reads, "And he said," it does not say who said. So this is the "tent door," BECAUSE "AND HE SAID" REFERS TO THE SHECHINAH. And Sarah heard this grade, WHICH IS THE "TENT DOOR," from which she had heard nothing before, AS IT WAS SPEAKING WITH ABRAHAM, as it is written: "And Sarah heard it THE WORDS OF the tent door," which declared "I will certainly return to you at this season, and, lo, Sarah your wife shall have a son."

160. תָּא חֲזֵי, כַּמָּה הוּא חֲבִיבוּתָא דְּקוּדְשָׁא בְּרִיךְ הוּא, לְגַבֵּיהּ דְּאַבְרָהָם, דְּהָא לָא נָפַק מִנֵּיהּ יִצְחָק עַד דְּאִתְגְּזַר, לְבָתַר דְּאִתְגְּזַר אִתְבַּשַּׂר בֵּיהּ בְּיִצְחָק, בְּגִין דְּאִיהוּ כְּדֵין זַרְעָא קַדִּישָׁא, וְעַד לָא אִתְגְּזַר, לָאו אִיהוּ זַרְעָא קַדִּישָׁא. וּכְדֵין אִיהוּ, כְּמָה דִּכְתִיב אֲשֶׁר זַרְעוֹ בוֹ לְמִינֵהוּ.

160. Come and behold: the love of the Holy One, blessed be He, for Abraham is so great that Isaac was not born until after Abraham was circumcised. And only after he was circumcised was he informed of Isaac, because only then was the seed holy; before he was circumcised, the seed was not holy. And then it became as it is written: "wherein is its seed after its kind" (Beresheet 1:12), WHICH REFERS TO A KIND AS HOLY AS ABRAHAM.

161. וְתָא חֲזֵי עַד לָא אִתְגְּזַר אַבְרָהָם, הַהוּא זַרְעָא דִּילֵיהּ לָא הֲוָה קַדִּישָׁא, בְּגִין דְּנָפַק בְּגוֹ עָרְלָה, וְאִתְדְּבַק בְּעָרְלָה לְתַתָּא. לְבָתַר דְּאִתְגְּזַר, נָפַק הַהוּא זַרְעָא בְּגוֹ קַדִּישָׁא, וְאִתְדְּבַק בִּקְדוּשָׁה דִּלְעֵילָא, וְאוֹלִיד לְעֵילָא, וְאִתְדְּבַק אַבְרָהָם בְּדַרְגֵּיהּ כִּדְקָא יָאוֹת. תָּא חֲזֵי, כַּד אוֹלִיד אַבְרָהָם לְיִצְחָק, נָפַק קַדִּישָׁא כִּדְקָא יָאוֹת. וְהַאי מַאי אַעֲדוּ, וְאוֹלִידוּ חֲשׁוֹכָא.

161. Come and behold: before Abraham was circumcised, his seed was not holy because it passed through the foreskin and clung to the lower foreskin. But after he was circumcised, his seed issued in holiness and it clung to the holiness of above, and he begot up above. Thus, Abraham clung to his grade, WHICH IS CHESED, properly. Come and behold: when Abraham begot Isaac, he was born holy, as should properly be. So these waters, WHICH ALLUDE TO ABRAHAM WHO IS CHESED, conceived and bore darkness. IN OTHER WORDS, ISAAC, WHO IS THE SECRET OF THE LEFT COLUMN, WAS DARKNESS, BEFORE HE WAS CLOTHED WITH THE CHASSADIM OF ABRAHAM. AFTER HE ISSUED FROM ABRAHAM, HE WAS CLOTHED BY HIS CHASSADIM AND BECAME 'LIGHT.'

162. רַבִּי אֶלְעָזָר שָׁאִיל יוֹמָא חַד, לְרַבִּי שִׁמְעוֹן אֲבוֹי, אָמַר לוֹ הַאי דְּקָרָא לֵיהּ קוּדְשָׁא בְּרִיךְ הוּא יִצְחָק, דִּכְתִיב, וְקָרָאתָ אֶת שְׁמוֹ יִצְחָק,

אֲמַאי, דְּהָא אִתְחֲזֵי דְּעַד לָא נָפַק לְעָלְמָא, קָרָא לֵיהּ יִצְחָק.

162. One day, Rabbi Elazar asks his father, Rabbi Shimon: Why did the Holy One, blessed be He, name him Isaac before he was born, as it is written: "and you shall call his name Isaac?" (Beresheet 17.19). AND WE SHOULD NOT SAY IT WAS BECAUSE SHE SAID "ELOHIM HAS MADE LAUGHTER (HEB. *TZECHOK*) FOR ME..." (BERESHEET 21:6). Because even before he came into the world, the Holy One, blessed be He, called him Isaac, BEFORE REASON WAS GIVEN FOR IT.

163. אָמַר לוֹ הָא הָא אִתְּמַר, דְּאֶשָּׁא נָטַל מַיָּא, דְּהָא מַיָּא מִסִּטְרָא דִּגְבוּרָה קָא אַתְיָין. וְדָא שָׁאִיל, לְלֵוָאֵי דְּאִינּוּן בְּדִיחִין לְהַהוּא סִטְרָא, בְּמָאנֵי זֶמֶר וְתִשְׁבְּחָן, לָקֳבֵיל הַאי סִטְרָא, בְּגִין כָּךְ יִצְחָק אִיהוּ חֶדְוָה, בְּגִין דְּאָתֵי מֵהַהוּא סִטְרָא, וְאִתְדַּבַּק בֵּיהּ.

163. He replies: But we have learned that fire, WHICH IS THE LEFT ASPECT AND GVURAH, received water, WHICH IS THE RIGHT ASPECT AND CHESED, as water came from the aspect of Gvurah. THIS MEANS THAT THE LEFT AND RIGHT WERE COMBINED AND BECAME INCLUDED IN EACH OTHER. THUS, THE LEFT ASPECT BECAME THE ASPECT OF THE WINE THAT GLADDENS ELOHIM AND MAN. And it is required of the Levites, WHO ARE DRAWN FROM THE LEFT COLUMN, that they bring happiness to that side, NAMELY THE LEFT SIDE, with musical instruments and praising songs that correspond to that side. THIS MEANS THAT MUSICAL INSTRUMENTS AND PRAISING SONGS ARE ALSO DRAWN FROM THE LEFT SIDE. And this is why Isaac means laughter and enjoyment; he came from that side, THE LEFT SIDE, and clung to it.

164. תָּא חֲזֵי, יִצְחָק בְּדִיחוּתָא, חֶדְוָה דְּאַחְלַף מַיָּא בְּאֶשָּׁא, וְאֶשָּׁא בְּמַיָּא. וְע"ד אִקְרֵי הָכֵי. וּבְגִין כָּךְ קוּדְשָׁא בְּרִיךְ הוּא קָרֵי לֵיהּ הָכֵי, עַד לָא יִפּוֹק לְעָלְמָא, שְׁמָא דָּא, וְאוֹדַע לֵיהּ לְאַבְרָהָם.

164. Come and behold: Isaac himself is pleasure and laughter because he exchanged water for fire, and fire for water. THUS, THE LEFT AND RIGHT ARE INCLUDED IN EACH OTHER – BECAUSE ISAAC IS THE ASPECT OF THE LEFT, WHICH IS THE FIRE THAT BECAME INCLUDED WITHIN THE WATER,

WHICH IS CHESED AND THE RIGHT ASPECT. THIS CAUSES ALL DELIGHT AND HAPPINESS TO BE DRAWN FROM THE LEFT SIDE. This is why the Holy One, blessed be He, named him ISAAC (LIT. 'HE WILL LAUGH') even before be came into the world, and announced it to Abraham.

165. וְתָא חֲזֵי, בְּכֻלְהוּ אָחֳרָנִין שָׁבַק לוֹן קוּדְשָׁא בְּרִיךְ הוּא, לְמִקְרֵי לוֹן שְׁמָהָן, וַאֲפִילוּ נָשֵׁי הֲווֹ קַרְאַן לִבְנַיְיהוּ שְׁמָהָן, אֲבָל הָכָא לָא שָׁבַק קוּדְשָׁא בְּרִיךְ הוּא לְאִמֵּיהּ, לְמִקְרֵי לֵיהּ שְׁמָא, אֶלָּא לְאַבְרָהָם, דִּכְתִיב וְקָרָאתָ אֶת שְׁמוֹ יִצְחָק, אַנְתְּ וְלָא אָחֳרָא, בְּגִין לְאַחְלָפָא מַיָּא בְּאֶשָּׁא, וְאֶשָּׁא בְּמַיָּא, לְאַכְלְלָא לֵיהּ בְּסִטְרֵיהּ.

165. Come and behold: the Holy One, blessed be He, allowed all children, EXCEPT ISAAC, to be named by their parents. Even women named their children. But here the Holy One, blessed be He, did not allow Yitzchak's mother to name him – only Abraham, as it is written: "and you shall call his name Isaac" (Beresheet 17:19)" – you and no one else, in order to exchange water with fire, and fire with water, WHICH REFERS TO THE INCLUSION OF THE LEFT WITH THE RIGHT AND THE RIGHT WITH THE LEFT, so that Isaac may be included within his side, THE RIGHT SIDE.

12. "And the men rose up from there"

A Synopsis

Before any negative occurrence befalls an individual, the Creator always sends us a gift. This gift is an opportunity to perform a positive action so that we can protect ourselves from any judgments decreed against us. This principle is concealed in the Biblical story of Abraham. The three angels were sent to Abraham by the Creator. When Abraham invites these three angels into his home, it is an act of true kindness. Consider Avraham's situation: He was one hundred years old, it was the third day after his circumcision, which is the most painful day, and the weather was unbearably hot. Nevertheless, Abraham put aside his own self interest and welcomed the three strangers [angels] into his home where he bathed and fed them. This positive action saved the life of Avraham's nephew, Lot, when the cities of Sodom and Gomorra were destroyed.

The Relevance of this Passage

It is human nature to be governed by the primal instinct of self-survival. Yet, it is also uniquely human to put aside one's own needs in consideration of others, albeit, a much more difficult duty to perform. We are empowered with the strength to overcome our natural tendency to be self-absorbed in our own problems. We create the consciousness and awareness to recognize opportunities for sharing. In turn, our positive actions of sharing will give us the ability to overcome or circumvent difficult situations in life.

166. כֵּיוָן דְּאִתְבַּשַּׂר אַבְרָהָם בְּיִצְחָק, מַה כְּתִיב וַיָּקוּמוּ מִשָּׁם הָאֲנָשִׁים וַיַּשְׁקִיפוּ עַל פְּנֵי סְדוֹם. רַבִּי אֶלְעָזָר אָמַר, תָּא חֲזֵי, כַּמָּה אַנְהַג קוּדְשָׁא בְּרִיךְ הוּא טִיבוּ עִם כָּל בְּרִיָּין, וְכָל שֶׁכֵּן, לְאִינּוּן דְּאָזְלֵי בְּאוֹרְחוֹי, דַּאֲפִילּוּ בְּזִמְנָא דְּבָעֵי לְמֵידַן עָלְמָא, אִיהוּ גָּרֵים לְמַאן דְּרָחִים לֵיהּ, לְמִזְכֵּי בְּמִלָּה, עַד לָא יֵיתֵי הַהוּא דִּינָא לְעָלְמָא.

166. After Abraham was told about Isaac, it is written: "And the men rose up from there, and looked toward Sodom" (Beresheet 18:16). Rabbi Elazar said: Come and behold. The Holy One, blessed be He, shows goodness to all beings, but especially to those who follow His path. And even when He decides to judge the world, He arranges for anyone who loves Him to perform a meritorious act before the world is punished.

167. דְּתָנֵינָן, בְּשַׁעֲתָא דְּקוּדְשָׁא בְּרִיךְ הוּא רָחֵים לֵיהּ לְבַר נָשׁ, מְשַׁדַּר לֵיהּ דּוֹרוֹנָא, וּמַאן אִיהוּ מִסְכֵּנָא, בְּגִין דְּיִזְכֵּי בֵּיהּ. וְכֵיוָן דְּזָכֵי בֵּיהּ, אִיהוּ אַמְשִׁיךְ עֲלֵיהּ, חַד חוּטָא דְּחֶסֶד, דְּאִתְמְשַׁךְ מִסְטַר יָמִינָא, וּפָרִישׁ אֲרֵישֵׁיהּ, וּרְשִׁים לֵיהּ, בְּגִין דְּכַד יֵיתֵי דִּינָא לְעָלְמָא, הַהוּא מְחַבְּלָא יִזְדְּהַר בֵּיהּ, וְזָקִיף עֵינוֹי וְחָמָא לְהַהוּא רְשִׁימוּ וּכְדֵין אִסְתַּלַּק מִנֵּיהּ, וְאִזְדְּהַר בֵּיהּ. בְּגִינֵי כָךְ, אַקְדִּים לֵיהּ קוּדְשָׁא בְּרִיךְ הוּא בַּמֶּה דְּיִזְכֵּי.

167. This corresponds to what we have learned. When the Holy One, blessed be He, loves a person, He sends him a present. And what is THAT PRESENT? It is a poor man for whom he can perform a meritorious act. So now that he is meritorious and deserving, the Holy One, blessed be He, draws a cord of grace from the right side upon him. He winds the cord around his head and marks him, so that when Judgment falls on the world, the Angel of Destruction will take notice of him AND NOT HURT HIM. Because he raises his eyes and notices that mark, he avoids him. This is why the Holy One, blessed be He, arranged beforehand to make him meritorious.

168. וְתָא חֲזֵי, כַּד בָּעֵי קוּדְשָׁא בְּרִיךְ הוּא לְאַיְתָאָה דִּינָא עַל סְדוֹם, אַזְכֵּי קוֹדֶם לְאַבְרָהָם, וְשַׁדַּר לֵיהּ דּוֹרוֹנָא לְמִזְכֵּי עִמְּהוֹן, בְּגִין לְשֵׁזָבָא לְלוֹט בַּר אֲחוּהַ מִתַּמָּן, הה"ד וַיִּזְכֹּר אֱלֹקִים אֶת אַבְרָהָם וַיְשַׁלַּח אֶת לוֹט מִתּוֹךְ הַהֲפֵכָה. וְלָא כְתִיב וַיִּזְכֹּר אֱלֹקִים אֶת לוֹט, דְּהָא בִּזְכוּתֵיהּ דְּאַבְרָהָם אִשְׁתְּזֵיב. וּמַאי וַיִּזְכֹּר, דְּדָכִיר לֵיהּ מַאי דְּאַזְכֵּי קוֹדֶם, עִם אִינוּן תְּלַת מַלְאָכִין.

168. Come and behold: when the Holy One, blessed be He, planned to execute Judgment on Sodom, He prepared a meritorious act for Abraham by sending him a present, WHICH REFERS TO THE THREE ANGELS. Because of them, he became deserving. Thereby, he saved Lot, the son of his brother, from destruction. This is why it is written: "and Elohim remembered Abraham, and sent Lot out of the midst of the overthrow," (Beresheet 19:29) and not, 'and Elohim remembered Lot.' As a result of Avraham's meritorious act, he was saved. And "remembered" MEANS THAT He remembered the previous meritorious act that He performed with the three angels.

169. כְּגַוְונָא דָא, בַּר נָשׁ דְּיִזְכֵּי בִּצְדָקָה עִם בְּנֵי נָשָׁא, בְּשַׁעֲתָא דְדִינָא שַׁרְיָא בְּעָלְמָא, קוּדְשָׁא בְּרִיךְ הוּא אַדְכַּר לֵיהּ לְהַהִיא צְדָקָה דַּעֲבַד. בְּגִין דִּבְכָל שַׁעֲתָא דְּזָכֵי בַּר נָשׁ, הָכֵי אַכְתִּיב עֲלֵיהּ לְעֵילָּא, וַאֲפִילּוּ בְּשַׁעֲתָא דְּדִינָא שַׁרְיָא עֲלוֹי, קוּדְשָׁא בְּרִיךְ הוּא אַדְכַּר לֵיהּ, לְהַהוּא טִיבוּ דַּעֲבַד, וְזָכָה עִם בְּנֵי נָשָׁא. כְּדַבָר אַחֵר וּצְדָקָה תַּצִּיל מִמָּוֶת. בְּגִינֵי כָךְ, אַקְדִּים לֵיהּ קוּדְשָׁא בְּרִיךְ הוּא לְאַבְרָהָם, בְּגִין דְּיִזְכֵּי, וְיִשְׁזֵיב לְלוֹט.

169. In the same manner, when harsh Judgment hangs over the world, the Holy One, blessed be He, remembers the charitable deeds that men performed. Every time a person performs a meritorious action, it is noted above. THEREFORE, even when there is harsh judgment on the world, the Holy One, blessed be He, remembers the good that a person has done and has merited through other people. As it is written: "but charity (righteousness) delivers from death" (Mishlei 11:4). According to this, the Holy One, blessed be He, arranged in advance that opportunity for Abraham to perform a meritorious act, so that by his merit Lot would be saved.

170. וַיַּשְׁקִיפוּ עַל פְּנֵי סְדוֹם. תָּא חֲזֵי, וַיָּקוּמוּ מִשָּׁם הָאֲנָשִׁים. מֵהַהִיא סְעוּדָה דְּאַתְקִין לוֹן אַבְרָהָם, וּזְכָה בְּהוּ. אַף עַל גַּב דְּמַלְאָכִין הֲווֹ, זְכָה בְּהוּ, וְכָל הַהוּא מֵיכְלָא, לָא אִשְׁתְּאַר מִנֵּיהּ כְּלוּם בְּגִינֵי דְּאַבְרָהָם, וּלְמִזְכֵּי בֵּיהּ, דְּהָא כְּתִיב וַיֹּאכֵלוּ, בְּאֶשָּׁא דִּלְהוֹן אִתְאֲכֵיל.

170. Come and behold: "And the men rose up from there, and looked toward Sodom." They rose from the meal that Abraham prepared for them, thereby performing a meritorious act. And even though they were angels, WHO DO NOT NEED A MEAL, he nevertheless attained merit because of them. And they purposely left no food over from the meal, so that Abraham would attain merit through the act, as it is written: "and they did eat," as by their fire the food was eaten and consumed.

171. וְאִי תֵימָא, הָא תְּלַת מַלְאָכִין הֲווֹ, הַאי אֶשָּׁא, וְהַאי מַיָּא, וְהַאי רוּחָא. אֶלָּא, כָּל חַד וְחַד כָּלִיל בְּחַבְרֵיהּ, וּבְגִינֵי כָךְ, וַיֹּאכֵלוּ. כְּגַוְונָא דָא וַיֶּחֱזוּ אֶת הָאֱלֹקִים וַיֹּאכְלוּ וַיִּשְׁתּוּ. אֲכִילָה וַדַּאי אָכְלוּ, דְּאִתְּזְנוּ מִן שְׁכִינְתָּא, אוּף הָכָא וַיֹּאכֵלוּ. גָּרְמוּ לְאִתְּזְנָא מֵהַהוּא סִטְרָא דְּאַבְרָהָם

אִתְדְּבַק בֵּיהּ, וּבְגִין כָּךְ, לָא אַשְׁאָרוּ מִמַּה דְּיָהֵיב לוֹן אַבְרָהָם כְּלוּם.

171. You might say: But there were three angels: one of fire, one of water, and one of air. SINCE GABRIEL IS MADE OF FIRE, MICHAEL IS MADE OF WATER, AND RAPHAEL OF AIR, ONLY GABRIEL COULD HAVE CONSUMED THE FOOD WITH HIS FIRE. MICHAEL AND RAPHAEL WERE NOT ABLE TO DO SO, AS THEY ARE NOT MADE OF FIRE. AND HE REPLIES: Each and every one of them includes the others in himself. SO EACH ONE OF THEM WAS MADE OF FIRE, WATER, AND AIR. This is why IT IS WRITTEN ABOUT ALL OF THEM: "and they did eat" – THE FIRE IN EACH OF THEM CONSUMED THE FOOD. Similarly to this, "and they saw Elohim, and did eat and drink" (Shemot 24:11), MEANING that they were indeed nourished from THE SPLENDOR OF the Shechinah, WHICH IS CONSIDERED AS EATING. Thus, in this PASSAGE AS WELL, "and they did eat" MEANS THAT they nourished themselves, THROUGH THEIR EATING, from the side to which Abraham was attached, NAMELY THE RIGHT SIDE, WHICH IS CHASSADIM. And this is why they left nothing from what Abraham offered them – SO THAT THEY COULD DRAW DOWN AS MUCH CHASSADIM AS POSSIBLE.

172. כְּגַוְונָא דָא בָּעֵי לֵיהּ לְבַר נָשׁ, לְמִשְׁתֵּי מֵהַהוּא כַּסָּא דִּבְרָכָה, בְּגִין דְּיִזְכֵּי לְהַהִיא בְּרָכָה דִּלְעֵילָּא. אוּף אִינּוּן אֲכָלוּ, מִמַּה דְּאַתְקִין לוֹן אַבְרָהָם, בְּגִין דְּיִזְכּוּן לְאִתְזָנָא מִסִּטְרָא דְּאַבְרָהָם. דְּהָא מֵהַהוּא סִטְרָא, נָפֵיק מְזוֹנָא לְכֻלְּהוּ מַלְאֲכֵי עִלָּאֵי.

172. On the same principle, one should drink from the cup of benediction, so that by his drinking he will merit the blessing of above. Hence, THE ANGELS also ate from what Abraham had prepared for them, in order to be nourished from the side of Abraham – NAMELY, FROM THE LIGHT OF CHASSADIM, as the sustenance of all the angels above proceeds from that side.

173. וַיַּשְׁקִיפוּ: אִתְעֲרוּתָא דְּרַחֲמֵי לְשֵׁיזָבָא לְלוֹט. כְּתִיב הָכָא וַיַּשְׁקִיפוּ, וּכְתִיב הָתָם הַשְׁקִיפָה מִמְּעוֹן קָדְשְׁךָ. מַה לְּהַלָּן לְרַחֲמֵי, אוּף הָכָא לְרַחֲמֵי.

173. The verse, "and looked toward..." ALLUDES TO the awakening of the quality of Mercy to save Lot. WE LEARN THIS BY COMPARING VERSES. It is written here, "and looked toward," and it is written elsewhere, "Look forth from your Holy habitation" (Devarim 26:15). Because THE LOOKING THERE ALLUDES to Mercy there, it does so here as well.

174. וְאַבְרָהָם הוֹלֵךְ עִמָּם לְשַׁלְּחָם. לְמֶעְבַּד לוֹן לְוָיָה. אָמַר רִבִּי יֵיסָא אִי תֵימָא דְּאַבְרָהָם יָדַע דְּמַלְאָכִין אִינוּן, אַמַּאי אַעֲבֵיד לוֹן לְוָיָה. אֶלָּא אָמַר ר' אֶלְעָזָר, אַף עַל גַּב דַּהֲוָה יָדַע, מַה דַּהֲוָה רָגִיל לְמֶעְבַּד עִם בְּנֵי נָשָׁא, עֲבַד בְּהוֹ, וְאַלְוֵי לוֹן. בְּגִין דְּכָךְ אִצְטְרִיךְ לֵיהּ לְבַר נָשׁ לְמֶעְבַּד לְוָיָה לְאוּשְׁפִּיזִין, דְּהָא כֹּלָּא בְּהַאי תַּלְיָא.

174. "And Abraham went with them to bring them on the way" (Beresheet 18:16), that is, he escorted them. Rabbi Yesa said: If Abraham knew that they were angels, why did he have to escort them? Rabbi Elazar responded: Even though he knew they were angels, he did for them what he was accustomed to do for people. Thus, he escorted them, because it behooves one to escort his guests, since everything depends on this. IN OTHER WORDS, THE PRECEPT OF INVITING GUESTS DEPENDS ON ESCORTING THEM, WHICH IS THE FINAL ACT. AND IT IS NOT CONSIDERED A PRECEPT UNTIL AFTER THE PERSON CONCLUDES IT.

175. וּבְעוֹד דְּאִיהוּ הֲוָה אָזִיל עִמְּהוֹן, אִתְגְּלֵי קוּדְשָׁא בְּרִיךְ הוּא עֲלֵיהּ דְּאַבְרָהָם, דִּכְתִיב וַה' אָמַר הַמְכַסֶּה אֲנִי מֵאַבְרָהָם אֲשֶׁר אֲנִי עֹשֶׂה. וַה': הוּא וּבֵית דִּינֵיהּ, בְּגִין דְּקוּדְשָׁא בְּרִיךְ הוּא הֲוָה אָזִיל עִמְּהוֹן.

175. As he was escorting them, the Holy One, blessed be He, appeared to him, as it is written: "And Hashem said: Shall I hide from Abraham that which I do?" (Ibid. 17) The phrase "And Hashem" APPLIES TO Him and His heavenly court, WHICH IS THE NUKVA, as the Holy One, blessed be He, accompanied them.

176. תָּא חֲזֵי כַּד בַּר נָשׁ עָבֵיד לְוָיָה לְחַבְרֵיהּ, אִיהוּ אַמְשִׁיךְ לִשְׁכִינְתָּא לְאִתְחַבְּרָא בַּהֲדֵיהּ. וּלְמֵהַךְ עִמֵּיהּ בְּאוֹרְחָא לְשֵׁזָבָא לֵיהּ. וּבְגִין כָּךְ בָּעֵי לֵיהּ לְבַר נָשׁ לְלַוּוֵי לְאוּשְׁפִּיזָא, בְּגִין דְּחַבַּר לֵיהּ לִשְׁכִינְתָּא, וְאַמְשִׁיךְ עֲלֵיהּ לְאִתְחַבְּרָא בַּהֲדֵיהּ.

176. Come and behold: when a person escorts his friend, he draws the Shechinah to join him, and walks along with him to protect him. This is the reason why a person should escort his guest; he joins him with the Shechinah and draws the Shechinah to join him.

13. "Shall I hide from Abraham"

A Synopsis
The Creator never allows any intense judgments to rain down upon Creation without first warning the righteous souls who dwell among mankind. This warning offers the righteous the opportunity to take the necessary positive measures to counteract decreed judgments. These righteous souls warn others and create opportunities for people to change their ways.

The Relevance of this Passage
According to the wisdom of Kabbalah, positive actions of sharing are not founded upon the vague concepts of morals, ethics, or codes of right and wrong. Rather, there is a direct dividend to the doer of good deeds. Our charitable actions and positive behavior serve our own spiritual interests, particularly during times of great judgment. We are given the ability to recognize opportunities for sharing and spiritual change when we are preoccupied with our own hardships. An appreciation for the righteous living among us is awakened within our soul, furnishing us with greater protection from any negative events that might be looming over the horizon.

177. בְּגִין כָּךְ וַה׳ אָמַר הַמְכַסֶּה אֲנִי מֵאַבְרָהָם אֲשֶׁר אֲנִי עֹשֶׂה. ר׳ חִיָּיא פָּתַח כִּי לֹא יַעֲשֶׂה ה׳ אֱלֹקִים דָּבָר כִּי אִם גָּלָה סוֹדוֹ אֶל עֲבָדָיו הַנְּבִיאִים. זַכָּאִין אִינּוּן זַכָּאֵי עָלְמָא, דְּקוּדְשָׁא בְּרִיךְ הוּא אִתְרְעֵי בְּהוֹ, וְכָל מַה דְּאִיהוּ עָבֵיד בִּרְקִיעָא, וְזַמִּין לְמֶעְבַּד בְּעָלְמָא, עַל יְדֵי דְּזַכָּאִין עָבֵיד לֵיהּ, וְלָא כַּסֵּי מִנַּיְיהוּ לְעָלְמִין כְּלוּם.

177. Therefore, because of this, THAT IS, BECAUSE HE ESCORTED HIS GUESTS, HE WAS FULLY MERITORIOUS, "and Hashem said: 'Shall I hide from Abraham that which I do?'" Rabbi Chiya opened the discourse with the verse: "For Hashem Elohim will do nothing, until He reveals His secret to His servants the prophets" (Amos 3:7). Blessed are the righteous of the world, that the Holy One, blessed be He, chose them. And all that He has done in the heavens and shall do in the world, He accomplishes through righteous people. And He never hides anything from them.

178. בְּגִין דְּקוּדְשָׁא בְּרִיךְ הוּא בָּעֵי לְשַׁתָּפָא בַּהֲדֵיהּ לְצַדִּיקַיָּא. בְּגִין דְּאִינּוּן אַתְיָין, וּמַזְהֲרִין לִבְנֵי נָשָׁא, לְאָתָבָא מֵחוֹבַיְיהוּ, וְלָא יִתְעַנְּשׁוּן

מִגּוֹ דִּינָא עִלָּאָה, וְלָא יְהֵא לוֹן פִּתְחָא דְפוּמָא לְגַבֵּיהּ. בְּגִינֵי כָּךְ, קוּדְשָׁא בְּרִיךְ הוּא אוֹדַע לוֹן רָזָא, דְּאִיהוּ עָבִיד בְּהוֹ דִּינָא. תּוּ בְּגִין דְּלָא יֵימְרוּן, דְּהָא בְּלָא דִינָא עֲבֵיד בְּהוֹ דִּינָא.

178. For the Holy One, blessed be He, wants the righteous to join Him. This is so that they may warn people and advise them to repent their iniquities so that they will not be punished by celestial punishment, and so that they will have no excuse to complain to Him, SAYING THAT HE DID NOT WARN THEM AND THEY DID NOT KNOW. Therefore, the Holy One, blessed be He, reveals to them the secret that He is about to punish them. He does not want them to be able to claim that He is punishing them without a trial.

179. אֲמַר רַבִּי אֶלְעָזָר, וַוי לוֹן לְחַיָּיבַיָא, דְּלָא יָדְעִין וְלָא מַשְׁגִּיחִין, וְלָא יָדְעִין לְאִסְתַּמְּרָא מֵחוֹבַיְיהוּ. וּמָה קוּדְשָׁא בְּרִיךְ הוּא דִּי כָּל עוֹבָדוֹהִי קְשׁוֹט, וְאוֹרְחָתֵיהּ דִּין, לָא עָבִיד כָּל מַה דַּעֲבֵיד בְּעָלְמָא, עַד דְּגָלֵי לְהוֹ לְצַדִּיקַיָּיא, בְּגִין דְּלָא יְהֵא לוֹן פִּתְחָא דְפוּמָא לִבְנֵי נָשָׁא. גַּבֵּי בְּנֵי נָשָׁא לֹא כ"שׁ דְּאִית לוֹן לְמֶיעֱבַּד מִלַּיְיהוּ דְּלָא יְמַלְלוּן בְּנֵי נָשָׁא סְטִיָא עֲלֵיהוֹן. וְכֵן כְּתִיב וִהְיִיתֶם נְקִיִּים מֵה' וּמִיִּשְׂרָאֵל.

179. Rabbi Elazar said: Woe to the wicked who do not seek TO KNOW, and do not know how to refrain from sin. Hence, the Holy One, blessed be He, whose deeds are just and whose actions are right, never act before He reveals His plans to the righteous, so that other people will have no excuse to complain about Him. SIMILARLY, men should act in a way that prevents other people from uttering accusations against them. Therefore, it is written: "And you shall be clean before Hashem and before Yisrael" (Bemidbar 32:22).

180. וְאִית לוֹן לְמֶיעֱבַּד, דְּלָא יְהֵא לוֹן פִּתְחוֹן פֶּה לִבְנֵי נָשָׁא, וְיִתְרוּן בְּהוֹן, אִי אִינּוּן חָטָאן, וְלָא מַשְׁגְּחֵי לְאִסְתַּמְּרָא, דְּלָא יְהֵא לֵיהּ לְמִדַּת דִּינָא דְּקוּדְשָׁא בְּרִיךְ הוּא, פִּתְחָא דְפוּמָא לְגַבַּיְיהוּ. וּבַמֶּה, בִּתְשׁוּבָה וְעוֹבָדִין דְּכַשְׁרָן.

180. And THE RIGHTEOUS should act accordingly, to prevent other people from complaining ABOUT THE HOLY ONE, BLESSED BE HE, and warn them that if they sin and do not guard themselves, the attribute of Judgment of the Holy One, blessed be He, might have a reason to ACCUSE them. And how may they ESCAPE THIS ATTRIBUTE OF JUDGMENT? By repenting and performing good deeds.

181. תָּא חֲזֵי, וַה' אָמַר הַמְכַסֶּה אֲנִי מֵאַבְרָהָם. אָמַר רַבִּי יְהוּדָה, קוּדְשָׁא בְּרִיךְ הוּא יָהַב כָּל אַרְעָא לְאַבְרָהָם, לְמֶהֱוֵי לֵיהּ אַחֲסָנַת יְרוּתָא לְעָלְמִין. דִּכְתִּיב כִּי אֶת כָּל הָאָרֶץ אֲשֶׁר אַתָּה רֹאֶה לְךָ אֶתְּנֶנָּה וְגוֹ'. וּכְתִיב שָׂא נָא עֵינֶיךָ וּרְאֵה. וּלְבָתַר קוּדְשָׁא בְּרִיךְ הוּא אִצְטְרִיךְ לְאַעֲקָרָא אַתְרִין אִלֵּין. אָמַר קוּדְשָׁא בְּרִיךְ הוּא, כְּבָר יַהֲבִית יַת אַרְעָא לְאַבְרָהָם, וְהוּא אַבָּא לְכֹלָּא, דִּכְתִּיב כִּי אַב הֲמוֹן גּוֹיִם נְתַתִּיךְ. וְלָא יָאוֹת לִי לְמִמְחֵי בְּנִין, וְלָא אוֹדַע לַאֲבוּהוֹן, דְּקָרֵית לֵיהּ אַבְרָהָם אוֹהֲבִי. וּבְגִין כָּךְ אִצְטְרִיךְ לְאוֹדַע לֵיהּ, בְּגִין כָּךְ וַה' אָמַר הַמְכַסֶּה אֲנִי מֵאַבְרָהָם אֲשֶׁר אֲנִי עֹשֶׂה.

181. Come and behold: "And Hashem said: 'Shall I hide from Avraham'." Rabbi Yehuda said: The holy One, blessed be He, has given the entire land to Abraham, as an everlasting heritage, as it is written: "For all the land which you see, to you I give it..." (Beresheet 13:15) as well as, "lift up your eyes and see..." (Ibid. 14). Later, when the Holy One, blessed be He, wanted to uproot and destroy these places, NAMELY SODOM AND GOMORRAH, He said: I have already given the land to Abraham, and he is the father of them all, as it is written: "for a father of a multitude of nations have I made you" (Beresheet 17:5). So it is not fitting for me to smite the children without informing their father whom I have called "Abraham my friend" (Yeshayah 41:8). Therefore, I must inform him. Thus, "And Hashem said: 'Shall I hide from Abraham that which I do?'"

182. אָמַר רַבִּי אַבָּא, תָּא חֲזֵי, עִנְוְתָנוּתָא דְּאַבְרָהָם, דְּאַף עַל גַּב דַּאֲמַר לֵיהּ קוּדְשָׁא בְּרִיךְ הוּא, זַעֲקַת סְדוֹם וַעֲמוֹרָה כִּי רַבָּה. וְעִם כָּל דָּא דְּאוֹרִיךְ עִמֵּיהּ, וְאוֹדַע לֵיהּ, דְּבָעֵי לְמֶעְבַּד דִּינָא בִּסְדוֹם, לָא בָּעָא קַמֵּיהּ לְשֵׁזָבָא לֵיהּ לְלוֹט, וְלָא יַעֲבֵיד בֵּיהּ דִּינָא. מַאי טַעֲמָא, בְּגִין דְּלָא לְמִתְבַּע אַגְרָא מִן עוֹבָדוֹי.

182. Rabbi Aba said: Behold the humility of Abraham, even though the Holy One, blessed be He, said to him: "Because the cry of Sodom and Gomorrah is great" (Beresheet 18:20). Although He delayed Himself by informing Abraham that He wanted to punish Sodom, he did not pray before Him to save Lot from punishment. Why? So that he did not ask for a reward for his deeds.

183. וְעַל דָּא שְׁלַח קוּדְשָׁא בְּרִיךְ הוּא לְלוֹט, וְשֵׁזִיב לֵיהּ, בְּגִינֵיהּ דְּאַבְרָהָם. דִּכְתִיב וַיִּזְכּוֹר אֱלֹקִים אֶת אַבְרָהָם וַיְשַׁלַּח אֶת לוֹט מִתּוֹךְ הַהֲפֵכָה וגו'.

183. Because of this, EVEN THOUGH HE DID NOT ASK FOR IT, the Holy One, blessed be He, sent for Lot and saved him for the sake of Abraham, as it is written: "And Elohim remembered Abraham, and sent Lot out of the midst of the overthrow" (Beresheet 19:29).

184. מַאי אֲשֶׁר יָשַׁב בָּהֵן לוֹט. הָא אִתְּמָר. אֲבָל בְּגִין דְּכֻלְּהוּ חַיָּיבִין, וְלָא אִשְׁתְּכַח מִכֻּלְּהוּ, דְּאִית לֵיהּ מִידֵי דְּזָכוּ, בַּר לוֹט. מִכָּאן אוֹלִיפְנָא, בְּכָל אֲתָר דְּדַיְירִין בֵּיהּ חַיָּיבִין, חָרִיב אִיהוּ.

184. What is meant by "in which Lot dwelt?" WHY WERE THEY NAMED AFTER HIM? This has been explained; it is because they were all wicked and there was nobody among them who was good, save Lot. From this we learn that wherever the wicked stay, that place is doomed to be destroyed. FROM THE VERSE "IN WHICH LOT DWELT," WE LEARN THAT FOR ALL THE OTHER PEOPLE WHO DWELT THERE, IT WAS NOT CONSIDERED TO BE A DWELLING PLACE, BUT RATHER A PLACE OF DESTRUCTION AND DESOLATION UNFIT FOR HABITATION. AND THIS WAS BECAUSE THEY WERE WICKED PEOPLE.

185. אֲשֶׁר יָשַׁב בָּהֵן לוֹט. וְכִי בְּכֻלְּהוּ הֲוָה יָתִיב לוֹט, אֶלָּא בְּגִינֵיהּ הֲווֹ יַתְבֵי, דְּלָא אִתְחָרְבוּ. וְאִי תֵימָא בִּזְכוּתֵיהּ, לָא. אֶלָּא בִּזְכוּתֵיהּ דְּאַבְרָהָם.

185. Of the verse "the cities in which Lot dwelt," HE ASKS: Could it be that Lot lived in all of them? AND HE REPLIES: Because of his presence in those cities, they were not destroyed, and the people were able to dwell there. THIS IS WHY THEY ARE NAMED AFTER HIM. But if you say this was because of the merit of Lot, you are incorrect; it was because of the merit of Abraham.

186. אָמַר רַבִּי שִׁמְעוֹן, תָּא חֲזֵי, דְּשִׁמּוּשָׁא דַּעֲבִיד בַּר נָשׁ לְזַכָּאָה, הַהוּא שִׁמּוּשָׁא, אָגֵין עֲלֵיהּ בְּעָלְמָא. וְלָא עוֹד, אֶלָּא דְּאַף עַל גַּב דְּאִיהוּ חַיָּיבָא, אוֹלִיף מֵאוֹרְחוֹי וַעֲבֵיד לוֹן.

186. Rabbi Shimon said: Come and behold. The service that a person does for the righteous protects him in this world. In addition, even if he is a sinful person, he will learn from the righteous person's behavior and emulate it.

187. תָּא חֲזֵי, דְּהָא בְּגִין דְּאִתְחַבַּר לוֹט בַּהֲדֵיהּ דְּאַבְרָהָם, אַף עַל גַּב דְּלָא אוֹלִיף כָּל עוֹבָדוֹי, אוֹלִיף לְמֶעְבַּד טִיבוּ עִם בְּרִיָּין, כְּמָה דַּהֲוָה עָבֵיד אַבְרָהָם, וְדָא הוּא דְּאוֹתִיב לְכָל אִינּוּן קַרְתֵּי, כָּל הַהוּא זִמְנָא דְּיָתְבוּ, בָּתַר דְּעָאל לוֹט בֵּינַיְיהוּ.

187. Come and behold: as Lot accompanied Abraham, he did not learn all his ways, but he did learn how to show kindness to other people. Thus, as long as Lot dwelt there, the people settled in the cities, which continued to exist. THEREFORE, IT IS WRITTEN: "IN WHICH LOT DWELT."

188. אָמַר רַבִּי שִׁמְעוֹן, תָּא חֲזֵי, דִּשְׁכִינְתָּא לָא אַעֲדֵי מִנֵּיהּ דְּאַבְרָהָם, בְּהַהִיא שַׁעֲתָא דְּקוּדְשָׁא בְּרִיךְ הוּא אֲמַר לֵיהּ, אָמַר לוֹ רַבִּי אֶלְעָזָר, וְהָא שְׁכִינְתָּא הֲוָה מַלִּיל עִמֵּיהּ, דְּהָא בְּדַרְגָּא דָּא אִתְגְּלֵי עֲלֵיהּ קוּדְשָׁא בְּרִיךְ הוּא, דִּכְתִיב וָאֵרָא אֶל אַבְרָהָם אֶל יִצְחָק וְאֶל יַעֲקֹב בְּאֵל שַׁדָּי. אָמַר לֵיהּ הָכֵי הוּא וַדַּאי.

188. Rabbi Shimon said: Behold how the Shechinah stayed with Abraham during the time that the Holy One, blessed be He, was with him. Rabbi Elazar said to him: But it was the Shechinah, Herself, that spoke to him, AND NOT ONLY THE HOLY ONE, BLESSED BE HE ALONE. Because the Holy One, blessed be He, revealed Himself to Abraham through this grade, as it is written: "And I appeared to Abraham, to Isaac, and to Jacob, by the

name of El Shadai" (Shemot 6:3), WHICH IS THE SHECHINAH. IF SO,
THEN WHAT IS THE POINT OF NOTING THE FACT THAT THE SHECHINAH
DID NOT LEAVE ABRAHAM DURING THE TIME WHEN THE HOLY ONE,
BLESSED BE HE, WAS WITH HIM? RABBI SHIMON said: It is certainly so,
AND YOU ARE DEFINITELY RIGHT.

189. וְתָא חֲזֵי מַה כְּתִיב, וַיֹּאמֶר ה' זַעֲקַת סְדֹם וַעֲמֹרָה כִּי רָבָּה.
בְּקַדְמֵיתָא וַה' אָמַר, וּלְבַסּוֹף וַיֹּאמֶר ה' זַעֲקַת סְדוֹם וַעֲמוֹרָה וגו'. דָּא
אִיהוּ דַרְגָּא עִלָּאָה, דְּאִתְגְּלֵי לֵיה עַל דַּרְגָּא תַּתָּאָה.

189. Come and behold. It is written: "And Hashem said (lit. 'And said
Hashem'): 'Because the cry of Sodom and Gomorrah is great...'" At first, IT
IS WRITTEN: "And Hashem said," (Beresheet 18:17) WHICH APPLIES TO
HIM AND HIS HEAVENLY COURT, NAMELY THE SHECHINAH. And later, IT
IS WRITTEN: "And said Hashem: Because the cry of Sodom and Gomorrah
is great," WHICH DOES NOT REFER TO HASHEM ALONE, BUT RATHER TO
the upper grade YUD HEI VAV HEI that appeared to him over the lower
grade, WHICH IS THE SHECHINAH.

מִדְרָשׁ הַנֶּעְלָם

190. וַה' אָמַר הַמְכַסֶּה אֲנִי מֵאַבְרָהָם וגו'. מַה כְּתִיב לְמַעְלָה, וַיָּקוּמוּ
מִשָּׁם הָאֲנָשִׁים וַיַּשְׁקִפוּ עַל פְּנֵי סְדֹם. לַעֲשׂוֹת דִּין בָּרְשָׁעִים, מַה כְּתִיב
אַחֲרָיו הַמְכַסֶּה אֲנִי מֵאַבְרָהָם.

Midrash Hane'elam (Homiletical interpretations on the obscure)

190. "And Hashem said, Shall I hide from Abraham..." What is written
before? "And the men rose up from there, and looked toward Sodom," in
order to punish the wicked. And what is written after? "Shall I hide from
Abraham."

191. אָמַר רָבִּי חִסְדָּא, אֵין הַקוּדְשָׁא בְּרִיךְ הוּא עוֹשֶׂה דִין בָּרְשָׁעִים,
עַד שֶׁנִּמְלָךְ בְּנִשְׁמָתָן שֶׁל צַדִּיקִים, הה"ד מִנִּשְׁמַת אֱלוֹהַ יֹאבֵדוּ, וּכְתִיב
הַמְכַסֶּה אֲנִי מֵאַבְרָהָם. אָמַר הַקוּדְשָׁא בְּרִיךְ הוּא, כְּלוּם יֵשׁ לִי לַעֲשׂוֹת

דִּין בָּרְשָׁעִים, עַד שֶׁאֲמַלֵּךְ בְּנִשְׁמוֹת הַצַּדִּיקִים, וְאוֹמֵר לָהֶם, הָרְשָׁעִים
חָטְאוּ לְפָנַי, אֶעֱשֶׂה בָּהֶם דִּין, דִּכְתִיב וַיֹּאמֶר ה' זַעֲקַת סְדֹם וַעֲמֹרָה כִּי
רָבָּה וְחַטָּאתָם וְגו'.

191. Rabbi Chisda said: The Holy One, blessed be He, does not execute
Judgment on the wicked until He has consulted the souls of the righteous.
This is as it is written: "By the blast (also, 'soul') of Eloha they perish"
(Iyov 4:9), and "Shall I hide from Abraham." The Holy One, blessed be He,
said: How can I punish the wicked without consulting the souls of the
righteous, telling them that the wicked have sinned before Me, and I am
about to punish them. This is as it is written: "And Hashem said: 'because
the cry of Sodom and Gomorrah is great, and because their sin is very
grievous.'"

192. אָמַר רַבִּי אַבָּהוּ, הַנְּשָׁמָה עוֹמֶדֶת בִּמְקוֹמָהּ, וְהִיא יְרֵאָה לְהִתְקָרֵב
אֵלָיו, וְלוֹמַר לְפָנָיו כְּלוּם, עַד שֶׁיֹּאמַר לִמְטַטְרוֹ"ן, שֶׁיַּגִּישֶׁנָּה לְפָנָיו,
וְתֹאמַר מַה שֶׁרְצוֹנָהּ, הה"ד, וַיִּגַּשׁ אַבְרָהָם וַיֹּאמַר הַאַף תִּסְפֶּה צַדִּיק עִם
רָשָׁע חָלִילָה לְךָ וְגו'.

192. Rabbi Abahu said: The soul remains standing in its place and is afraid
to come nearer and say anything to Him until Metatron says he will present
it. Then, it may say what it wants. This is as it is written: "And Abraham
drew near, and said, 'will You also destroy the righteous with the wicked?'"
(Beresheet 18:23) "Far be it from You to do after this manner..." (Ibid. 25).

193. אוּלַי יֵשׁ חֲמִשִּׁים צַדִּיקִים וְגו' הַנְּשָׁמָה פּוֹתַחַת וְאוֹמֶרֶת, רִבּוֹנוֹ שֶׁל
עוֹלָם, שֶׁמָּא נִתְעַסְּקוּ בְּנ' פָּרָשִׁיּוֹת שֶׁל תּוֹרָה, וְאַף עַל פִּי שֶׁלֹּא נִתְעַסְּקוּ
לִשְׁמָהּ, שָׂכָר יֵשׁ לָהֶם לָעוֹלָם הַבָּא, וְלֹא יִכָּנְסוּ לַגֵּיהִנָּם. מַה כְּתִיב
בַּתְרֵיהּ, וַיֹּאמֶר ה' אִם אֶמְצָא בִּסְדֹם חֲמִשִּׁים צַדִּיקִים וְגו'.

193. "Perhaps there are fifty righteous within the city..." (Ibid. 24) Hence,
the soul starts by saying: Master of the universe, they may have learned the
fifty portions of the Torah. And even though they did not learn the portions
for its sake alone, they are still entitled to a reward in the World to Come
and should not be sent to Gehenom. After this, it is written: "And Hashem

said: If I find in Sodom fifty just men within the city..." (Ibid. 26).

194. וְהָא יַתִּיר אִינוּן פַּרְשִׁיּוֹת, נ"ג הֲווֹ. אֶלָּא, אָמַר רַבִּי אַבָּהוּ, חֲמִשָּׁה סְפָרִים הֵם בַּתּוֹרָה, וּבְכָל אֶחָד וְאֶחָד נִכְלָלִים עֲשֶׂרֶת הַדִּבְּרוֹת, עֲשָׂרָה מַאֲמָרוֹת, שֶׁבָּהֶם נִבְרָא הָעוֹלָם, חֲשׁוֹב עֲשָׂרָה בְּכָל חַד מִנְּהוֹן, הוּא חֲמִשִּׁים.

194. He commented: But there are more than fifry portions in the Torah, there are 53. But, as Rabbi Avahu said: Every one of the five books in the Torah includes the Ten Commandments, WHICH IS THE SECRET OF the Ten Divine injunctions (sayings) by which the world was created. Multiply by the five books and you have fifry.

195. עוֹד פּוֹתַחַת הַנְּשָׁמָה וְאוֹמֶרֶת, רִבּוֹנוֹ שֶׁל עוֹלָם, אַף עַל פִּי שֶׁלֹּא נִתְעַסְּקוּ בַּתּוֹרָה, שֶׁמָּא קִבְּלוּ עוֹנְשָׁם, עַל מַה שֶׁחָטְאוּ, בְּב"ד, וְנִתְכַּפֵּר לָהֶם. שֶׁנֶּאֱמַר אַרְבָּעִים יַכֶּנּוּ לֹא יוֹסִיף. וּמִמַּה שֶׁנִּתְבַּיְישׁוּ לִפְנֵיהֶם, דַּיִּם לְהִתְכַּפֵּר לָהֶם, שֶׁלֹּא יִכָּנְסוּ לַגֵּיהִנֹּם. מַה כְּתִיב אַחֲרָיו, לֹא אֶעֱשֶׂה בַּעֲבוּר הָאַרְבָּעִים.

195. The soul goes on, saying: Master of the universe, even though the people did not study the Torah, they may have already been punished for their sins in court and have been forgiven, as it is written: "Forty stripes he may give him, and not exceed..." (Devarim 25:3). And if they have felt ashamed in front of them, this is sufficient for them to be pardoned and not be sent to Gehenom. The following verse says: "I will not do it for the forty's sake" (Beresheet 18:29).

196. עוֹד פּוֹתַחַת וְאוֹמֶרֶת, אוּלַי יֵשׁ שָׁם שְׁלֹשִׁים, אוּלַי יֵשׁ בֵּינֵיהֶם צַדִּיקִים, שֶׁהִשִּׂיגוּ שְׁלֹשִׁים מַעֲלוֹת, הָרְמוּזִים בַּפָּסוּק וַיְהִי בִּשְׁלֹשִׁים שָׁנָה וְהֵם כְּלוּלִים בְּל"ב נְתִיבוֹת. שֶׁהֵם כ"ב אוֹתִיּוֹת, וְוּ"ס. לִפְעָמִים הֵם כְּלוּלִים לִשְׁמוֹנָה.

196. The verse continues: "Perhaps there shall be thirty found there" (Ibid. 30). Maybe there are righteous people among them who have achieved the thirty attributes indicated in the verse: "Now it came to pass in the thirtieth year"

(Yechezkel 1:1), and that are included within the 32 paths, which are formed by the 22 Hebrew letters and the ten Sfirot. The latter, at times, are counted as eight.

197. עוֹד פּוֹתַחַת וְאוֹמֶרֶת, אוּלַי יִמָּצְאוּן שָׁם עֶשְׂרִים, שֶׁמָּא יִגְדְּלוּ בָּנִים לְתַלְמוּד תּוֹרָה, וְיֵשׁ לָהֶם שָׂכָר, לַעֲשֶׂרֶת הַדִּבְּרוֹת, שְׁתֵּי פְּעָמִים בְּכָל יוֹם, דְּאָמַר ר׳ יִצְחָק כָּל הַמְגַדֵּל בְּנוֹ לְתַלְמוּד תּוֹרָה, וּמוֹלִיכוֹ לְבֵית רַבּוֹ, בַּבֹּקֶר וּבָעֶרֶב, מַעֲלֶה עָלָיו הַכָּתוּב כְּאִלּוּ קִיֵּם הַתּוֹרָה, ב׳ פְּעָמִים בְּכָל יוֹם. מַה כְּתִיב, וַיֹּאמֶר לֹא אַשְׁחִית בַּעֲבוּר הָעֶשְׂרִים.

197. It speaks further: "Perhaps there shall be twenty found there..." (Beresheet 18:31) Perhaps they will raise sons to study the Torah, thereby receiving their reward of the Ten Commandments, twice every day. This is according to Rabbi Yitzchak, who said: He who educates his son in the Torah and takes him to the house of his Rabbi (teacher) in the morning and in the evening is described by the words of the Torah as though he has performed the entire Torah twice a day. What does it say? "And he said: "I will not destroy it for the twenty's sake" (Ibid.).

198. עוֹד פּוֹתַחַת וְאוֹמֶרֶת, אוּלַי יִמָּצְאוּן שָׁם עֲשָׂרָה. אוֹמֶרֶת רִבּוֹנוֹ שֶׁל עוֹלָם, שֶׁמָּא הָיוּ מֵאוֹתָם הָעֲשָׂרָה הָרִאשׁוֹנִים שֶׁל בֵּית הַכְּנֶסֶת, שֶׁנּוֹטֵל שָׂכָר כְּנֶגֶד כּוּלָם, שֶׁבָּאִים אַחֲרֵיהֶם, מַה כְּתִיב וַיֹּאמֶר לֹא אַשְׁחִית בַּעֲבוּר הָעֲשָׂרָה.

198. It goes on: "Perhaps ten shall be found there..." (Ibid. 32). It says: Master of the universe, maybe they were among the first ten who arrived at the synagogue. If so, they have earned the reward of all the people who came in after them. Then, it is written: "I will not destroy it for the sake of the ten."

199. כָּל זֶה יֵשׁ לְנִשְׁמַת הַצַּדִּיק, לוֹמַר עַל הָרְשָׁעִים, כֵּיוָן שֶׁלֹּא נִמְצָא בְּיָדָם כְּלוּם, מַה כְּתִיב, וַיֵּלֶךְ ה׳ כַּאֲשֶׁר כִּלָּה לְדַבֵּר אֶל אַבְרָהָם. וְאַבְרָהָם שָׁב לִמְקוֹמוֹ. מַהוּ לִמְקוֹמוֹ. לְמָקוֹם מַעֲלָתוֹ הַיְדוּעָה.

199. The soul of the righteous has all this to say for the sinners. And because they have nothing, it is written: "And Hashem went His way, as

soon as he left speaking to Abraham, and Abraham returned to his place" (Beresheet 18:33). What is "to his place?" It is the place of his well-known grade.

200. אָמַר רַבִּי, מִצְוָה לוֹ לְאָדָם לְהִתְפַּלֵּל עַל הָרְשָׁעִים, כְּדֵי שֶׁיַּחְזְרוּ לְמוּטָב. וְלֹא יִכָּנְסוּ לַגֵּיהִנֹּם. דִּכְתִיב וַאֲנִי בַּחֲלוֹתָם לְבוּשִׁי שָׂק וְגוֹ'. וְאָמַר רַבִּי, אָסוּר לוֹ לְאָדָם לְהִתְפַּלֵּל עַל הָרְשָׁעִים שֶׁיִּסְתַּלְּקוּ מִן הָעוֹלָם, שֶׁאִלְמָלֵא סִלְקוֹ הַקּוּדְשָׁא בְּרִיךְ הוּא לְתֶרַח מִן הָעוֹלָם, כְּשֶׁהָיָה עוֹבֵד עֲבוֹדָה זָרָה, לֹא בָּא אַבְרָהָם אָבִינוּ לָעוֹלָם, וְשִׁבְטֵי יִשְׂרָאֵל לֹא הָיוּ, וְהַמֶּלֶךְ דָּוִד, וּמֶלֶךְ הַמָּשִׁיחַ, וְהַתּוֹרָה, לֹא נִתְּנָה, וְכָל אוֹתָם הַצַּדִּיקִים, וְהַחֲסִידִים, וְהַנְּבִיאִים, לֹא הָיוּ בָּעוֹלָם. אָמַר ר' יְהוּדָה, כֵּיוָן שֶׁרוֹאֶה הַקּוּדְשָׁא בְּרִיךְ הוּא, שֶׁלֹּא נִמְצָא בָּרְשָׁעִים כְּלוּם, מִכָּל אוֹתָם הָעִנְיָינִים, מַה כְּתִיב, וַיָּבֹאוּ שְׁנֵי הַמַּלְאָכִים סְדוֹמָה וְגוֹ'.

200. Rabbi said: It is behooves for a person to pray for the sinners so that they may repent and not enter Gehenom, as it is written: "But as for me, when they were sick, my clothing was sackcloth..." (Tehilim 35:13). And Rabbi continued: A person should never pray that the sinners may leave the world. Because had the Holy One, blessed be He, taken Terah out of this world for worshipping idols, Abraham would have never come into the world; the tribes of Yisrael would not have existed, nor would King David or King Messiah; the Torah would not have been given; and none of the righteous and pious men, with all the prophets, would have been in the world. Rabbi Yehuda said: Because the Holy One, blessed be He, sees that the sinners have nothing from all that was mentioned above, it is written: "And there came two angels to Sodom..." (Beresheet 19:1)

14. "I will go down now, and see"

A Synopsis

The literal Torah story states that the Creator came down to see the cities of Sodom and Gomorrah before they were destroyed. Kabbalistically, these stories signify the energy of the Creator shifting from the frequency of mercy into one of judgment. The Creator Himself, however, never stands in judgment of us. It is our own actions that determine which frequency of energy we draw down upon ourselves. The analogy of electrical energy helps convey the Zohar's principle. We can utilize electrical energy to light and power entire cities, or we can place our finger in a wall socket and electrocute ourselves. The nature of the energy has never changed. It was our free will as to how we connected into this energy, that changed.

The Relevance of this Passage

We generate an awareness of the consequences attached to all our behavioral actions, along with the understanding that the Creator is not at fault for the hardships we endure in life. By knowing that all our actions influence the amount of Light we receive, we are inspired to seize control over how we interact with the World and, in turn, how the World interacts with us.

201. אֵרְדָה נָא וְאֶרְאֶה הַכְּצַעֲקָתָה הַבָּאָה אֵלַי עָשׂוּ כָּלָה. לְמַאן קָאֲמַר. אִי תֵימָא לְאִינוּן מַלְאָכִין, מַאן חָמָא מַלִּיל עִם דָּא, וּפַקִּיד לְדָא. אֶלָּא, לְאַבְרָהָם קָאֲמַר, דִּבִרְשׁוּתֵיה קַיְימִין אִינוּן אַתְרֵי. דָּבָר אָחֳר, לְאִינוּן מַלְאָכִין.

201. "I will go down, and see whether they have done (Heb. *asu*) altogether according to the cry of it, which has come to me... (Beresheet 18:21) HE ASKS: To whom did He, THE HOLY ONE, BLESSED BE HE, say: "YOU SHOULD DESTROY," BECAUSE THE ZOHAR EXPLAINS THIS VERSE AS IF *ASU* WAS IN THE IMPERATIVE MODE, THEREBY SAYING 'DESTROY!' If you say THAT HE ADDRESSED these angels by saying, 'DESTROY,' who has ever seen the like, that He spoke with ABRAHAM while commanding THE ANGELS? Rather, He addressed Abraham, saying, "DESTROY," because all those places were under his supervision. Another explanation IS THAT HE ADDRESSED those angels SAYING, "DESTROY."

202. מַה דְּאִתְּמָר לְאַבְרָהָם, מַה טַעֲמָא עָשׂוּ, עָשָׂה מִבָּעֵי לֵיהּ, מַאי עָשׂוּ, אֶלָּא דָא אַבְרָהָם, וּשְׁכִינְתָּא לָא אַעֲדֵי מִנֵּיהּ. מַה דְּאִתְּמָר לְמַלְאָכִין, בְּגִין דַּהֲווֹ זְמִינִין תַּמָּן, וַהֲווֹ מִשְׁתַּכְּחִין לְמֶעְבַּד דִּינָא, וְעַל דָּא עָשׂוּ.

202. AND HE ASKS: If He addressed Abraham, SAYING, "DESTROY (ASU)," why IS IT WRITTEN IN THE PLURAL instead of the singular, namely, "destroy (aseh)." AND HE RESPONDS: HE SAID THIS BECAUSE HE ADDRESSED BOTH Abraham and the Shechinah that had never left him. THIS IS WHY HE SAID: "DESTROY (ASU)." HE THEN SAID THAT WE NEED TO CLARIFY what we said about His address to the angels, SAYING, "DESTROY." FOR IT LOOKS AS IF THE HOLY ONE, BLESSED BE HE, TALKED TO ABRAHAM WHILE COMMANDING THE ANGELS. AND HE EXPLAINED: THIS IS SO, because THE ANGELS stood by waiting to execute Judgment. And this is why HE SAID "destroy" in the plural.

203. דָּבָר אַחֵר עָשׂוּ, כְּתַרְגּוּמוֹ עֲבָדוּ. וְכִי לָא הֲוָה יָדַע קוּדְשָׁא בְּרִיךְ הוּא, דְּאִיהוּ אֲמַר אֵרְדָה נָא וְאֶרְאֶה, וְהָא כֹּלָּא אִתְגְּלֵי קַמֵּיהּ. אֶלָּא, אֵרְדָה נָא מִדַּרְגָּא דְּרַחֲמֵי, לְדַרְגָּא דְּדִינָא, וְהַיְינוּ יְרִידָה. וְאֶרְאֶה: רְאִיָּה דָא הִיא לְאַשְׁגָּחָא עֲלֵיהוֹן, בְּמַאן דִּינָא יָדִין לוֹן.

203. Another explanation of "asu" is, translated from the Aramaic, "they have worshipped," WHICH REFERS TO THE PEOPLE OF SODOM. HE ASKS: But did not the Holy One, blessed be He, know, that He had to go down? Is not everything revealed before Him? AND HE RESPONDS: But "I will go down" MEANS to descend from the grade of Mercy to the grade of Judgment, and the phrase "And see" means to determine suitable punishments.

204. אַשְׁכְּחָן רְאִיָּה לְטַב, וְאַשְׁכְּחָן רְאִיָּה לְבִישׁ. רְאִיָּה לְטַב: דִּכְתִיב וַיַּרְא אֱלֹקִים אֶת בְּנֵי יִשְׂרָאֵל וַיֵּדַע. רְאִיָּה לְבִישׁ: דִּכְתִיב אֵרְדָה נָא וְאֶרְאֶה. לְאַשְׁגָּחָא עֲלַיְיהוּ בְּדִינָא, וְעַל דָּא אֲמַר קוּדְשָׁא בְּרִיךְ הוּא, הַמְכַסֶּה אֲנִי מֵאַבְרָהָם.

204. We have learned that there is seeing for good and seeing for evil.

Seeing for the good is illustrated in the verse, "And Elohim looked upon the children of Yisrael..." (Shemot 2:25). Seeing for evil is illustrated in the verse, "I will go down now and see," in order to choose their punishments. This is what the Holy One blessed be He, meant by asking "Shall I hide from Abraham?"

15. "Abraham shall surely become"

A Synopsis

In every generation there is a circle of righteous souls living among us. Through their spiritual actions and presence in this physical existence, they literally uphold and sustain our world. Their positive energy balances out all the negative actions committed by self-centered and unspiritual people among us. This prevents the scales of judgment from tipping too far over to the side of negativity, which would cause great destruction in the world. Interestingly, these great souls often conceal their true identity and appear to us as mirrors of ourselves in the form of difficult people in our lives. They reflect all the negative traits that we ourselves possess but fail to recognize.

The Relevance of this Passage

Protection from negative influences is bestowed upon us through the merit of righteous people, past and present. We achieve the self-restraint and judgment to consider difficult people in our lives as reflections of our own negative traits. The wisdom and inspiration to change ourselves, instead of always trying to change others, emerges through the letters that form this passage.

205. וְאַבְרָהָם הָיוֹ יִהְיֶה לְגוֹי גָּדוֹל וְעָצוּם. מַאי טַעְמָא בִּרְכָה דָא הָכָא. אֶלָּא, בְּגִין לְאוֹדְעָא דַּאֲפִילוּ בְּשַׁעֲתָא דְּקוּדְשָׁא בְּרִיךְ הוּא יָתִיב בְּדִינָא עַל עָלְמָא, לָא אִשְׁתַּנֵּי. דְּהָא יָתִיב בְּדִינָא עַל דָּא, וּבְרַחֲמֵי עַל דָּא, וְכֹלָּא בְּרִגְעָא חֲדָא וּבְשַׁעֲתָא חֲדָא.

205. Of the verse, "Seeing that Abraham shall surely become a great and mighty nation..." (Beresheet 18:18) HE ASKS: Why does this blessing appear here? AND HE RESPONDS: To teach us that even when the Holy One, blessed be He, sits in Judgment on the world, He is unchanging. Because He displays Judgment to one and Mercy to the other. And all this happens simultaneously. SO WHILE HE DISPLAYED JUDGMENT TOWARD SODOM, HE SHOWED MERCY TOWARDS ABRAHAM AND BLESSED HIM BY SAYING: "ABRAHAM SHALL SURELY BECOME A GREAT AND MIGHTY NATION."

206. אָמַר רָבִּי יְהוּדָה, וְהָא כְתִיב וַאֲנִי תְפִלָּתִי לְךָ ה' עֵת רָצוֹן. זְמְנִין דְּאִיהוּ עֵת רָצוֹן, וְזִמְנִין דְּלָאו אִיהוּ עֵת רָצוֹן. זְמְנִין דְּשָׁמַע, וְזִמְנִין

דְּלָא שָׁמַע. זִמְנִין דְּאִשְׁתְּכַח, וְזִמְנִין דְּלָא אִשְׁתְּכַח. דִּכְתִיב דִּרְשׁוּ ה׳
בְּהִמָּצְאוֹ קְרָאוּהוּ בִּהְיוֹתוֹ קָרוֹב.

206. Rabbi Yehuda then said: But it is written, "But as for me, my prayer is
to You, Hashem, in an acceptable time" (Tehilim 69:14). THIS SHOWS
THAT some times are acceptable, while other times are not. So there are
times when He listens TO THE PRAYER and times when He does not; there
are times when He is present, and times when He is not. This corresponds to
what is written: "Seek Hashem while He may be found, call upon Him
while he is near" (Yeshayah 55:6). THUS, WE CAN CONCLUDE THAT
THERE ARE TIMES WHEN HE IS NOT PRESENT AND CANNOT BE FOUND,
NAMELY, DURING THE TIME OF JUDGMENT. IF THIS IS TRUE, HOW CAN
YOU SAY THAT WHILE HE SITS IN JUDGMENT ON ONE, HE SITS IN
MERCY ON THE OTHER?

207. אָמַר ר׳ אֶלְעָזָר, כָּאן לְיָחִיד, כָּאן לְצִבּוּר. כָּאן לַאֲתַר חָד, וְכָאן
לְכוּלֵי עָלְמָא. בְּגִינֵי כָּךְ בָּרִיךְ לֵיהּ לְאַבְרָהָם דְּאִיהוּ שָׁקִיל כְּכָל עָלְמָא,
דִּכְתִיב אֵלֶּה תוֹלְדוֹת הַשָּׁמַיִם וְהָאָרֶץ בְּהִבָּרְאָם. וְתָנֵינָן בְּאַבְרָהָם.

207. Rabbi Elazar said that the verses sometimes refer to individuals and
sometimes refer to the entire community. FOR THE INDIVIDUAL IT
CHANGES ACCORDING TO THE TIMES. FO THE ENTIRE COMMUNITY,
HOWEVER, HE ALWAYS DISPLAYS MERCY, EVEN WHEN HE SITS IN
JUDGMENT. Here it applies to one place, while there it applies to the whole
world, TO WHICH HE ALWAYS SHOWS MERCY AND NEVER CHANGES.
This is why He blessed Abraham AT THE TIME WHEN JUDGMENT WAS
EXECUTED ON SODOM. Abraham is considered as the whole world,
because it is written: "These are the generations of the heaven and the earth
when they were created (Heb. *Behibar'am*)" (Beresheet 2:4) and we have
learned THAT *BEHIBAR'AM* CONTAINS THE LETTERS OF *BeAbraham* ('with
Abraham'). THEREFORE, HE WAS CONSIDERED AS THE WHOLE WORLD.

208. יִהְיֶה. בְּגִימַטְרִיָּא שְׁלֹשִׁים. הָכֵי תָּנֵינָן, תְּלָתִין צַדִּיקִים, אַזְמִין
קוּדְשָׁא בְּרִיךְ הוּא, בְּכָל דָּרָא וְדָרָא לְעָלְמָא. כְּמָה דְּאַזְמִין לְאַבְרָהָם.

208. The numerical value of the letters in *yihyeh* ('shall...become') is 30.
And we have learned that the Holy One, blessed be He, arranged for each

generation to have thirty righteous men, just as Abraham had for his generation. THIS MEANS, AS IT IS WRITTEN: "THESE ARE THE GENERATIONS OF THE HEAVEN AND THE EARTH WHEN THEY WERE CREATED (BEHIBAR'AM)," WHICH IS THE COMBINATION OF THE LETTERS BEAVRAHAM, FOR WHOSE SAKE THE WORLD WAS CREATED. AND HE SAYS: THERE ARE THIRTY RIGHTEOUS MEN IN EACH AND EVERY GENERATION, FOR WHOSE SAKE THE WORLD WAS CREATED, AS IT WAS CREATED FOR THE SAKE OF ABRAHAM.

209. פָּתַח וְאָמַר, מִן הַשְּׁלֹשִׁים הֲכִי נִכְבָּד וְאֶל הַשְּׁלֹשָׁה לֹא בָא וגו'. מִן הַשְּׁלֹשִׁים הֲכִי נִכְבָּד, אֵלֶּין אִינּוּן תְּלָתִין צַדִּיקִים, דְּאַזְמִין קוּדְשָׁא בְּרִיךְ הוּא לְעָלְמָא, וְלָא יְבַטֵּל לוֹן מִנֵּיהּ. וּבְנָיָהוּ בֶּן יְהוֹיָדָע, כְּתִיב בֵּיהּ מִן הַשְּׁלֹשִׁים הֲכִי נִכְבָּד. אִיהוּ חַד מִנַּיְיהוּ. וְאֶל הַשְּׁלֹשָׁה לֹא בָא. דְּלָא שָׁקִיל לִתְלָתָא אָחֲרָנִין, דְּעָלְמָא קָאִים עֲלַיְיהוּ.

209. He opened with the verse: "He was more honorable than the thirty, but he attained not to the first three..."(II Shmuel 23:23). "He was more honorable than the thirty" refers to the thirty righteous men whom the Holy One, blessed be He, had called upon to come into this world in every generation so the world will not remain without them. And of Benaiah, the son of Jehoida, it is written: "He was most honorable among the thirty," as he was one of them, "but he attained not to the first three" because he is not of equal importance as the first three, upon whom the world is established.

210. וְאֶל הַשְּׁלֹשָׁה לֹא בָא. לְמֶהֱוֵי בְּמִנְיָינָא כְּחַד מִנַּיְיהוּ. בְּאִינּוּן תְּלָתִין זַכָּאִין, זָכָה לְמֵיעַל בְּחוּשְׁבְּנָא, אֲבָל וְאֶל הַשְּׁלֹשָׁה לֹא בָא, דְּלָא זָכָה לְאִתְחַבְּרָא בְּהוֹ וּלְמֶהֱוֵי עִמְּהוֹן בְּחוּלָקָא חֲדָא. יִהְיֶה: כְּמָה דְּתָנִינָן, תְּלָתִין הֲוָה. וּבְגִין כָּךְ, קוּדְשָׁא בְּרִיךְ הוּא בָּרְכֵיהּ, בְּאִינּוּן תְּלָתִין צַדִּיקִים.

210. Thus, "but he attained not to the first three" MEANS THAT HE IS NOT EQUAL TO THE THREE UPON WHOM THE WORLD IS ESTABLISHED. He was not counted as one of them. He deserved to be included among the thirty righteous men, but he was not on a level with "the first three," and was not privileged to be associated with them as an equal. "Yihyeh

('shall...become')," as we have learned, is numerically equal to thirty, and for that the Holy One, blessed be He, blessed him so that HE COULD BECOME EQUAL TO ALL the 30 righteous people.

16. "Whether they have done altogether according to the cry of it"

A Synopsis

The negativity and spiritual darkness that enveloped the cities of Sodom and Gomorrah was so intense that outsiders refused to step foot within the city boundaries. The wisdom being distilled concerns a self-awareness of the dark side of our own nature. When we associate with negative people, we inevitably fall into their negative sphere of influence, because our own negative side ignites and ultimately dominates us, leading us down a path of darkness. We are to avoid negative people out of concern for our own dark side. This kind of inner reflection and self-awareness is a prerequisite for spiritual development.

The Relevance of this Passage

Perhaps the greatest deception the angel Satan ever devised was convincing the rational mind that he doesn't really exist. This artful deception extends to the dark side of our own nature. An awareness of our own negative character traits begins to emerge in our consciousness so that we can uproot them and transform our nature. This self-recognition further helps to protect us from external negative influences.

211. תָּא חֲזֵי, אָמַר לֵיהּ קוּדְשָׁא בְּרִיךְ הוּא לְאַבְרָהָם, זַעֲקַת סְדוֹם וַעֲמוֹרָה כִּי רָבָּה, דְּהָא סַלֵּיקַת קָדָמַי, מַה דְּאִינוּן עָבְדִין לְכָל עָלְמָא, דְּכָל עָלְמָא מָנְעֵי רַגְלַייהוּ דְּלָא לְמֵיעַל בִּסְדוֹם וַעֲמוֹרָה. דִּכְתִיב פָּרַץ נַחַל מֵעִם גָּר הַנִּשְׁכָּחִים מִנִּי רָגֶל דַּלוּ מֵאֱנוֹשׁ נָעוּ. פָּרַץ נַחַל מֵעִם גָּר: פִּרְצָה הֲוָה פָּרִיץ נַחַל, לְאִינוּן בְּנֵי עָלְמָא דְּעָאלוּ לְתַמָּן, דְּכָלְהוּ, דְּחָמָאן לְמַאן דַּהֲווֹ יַהֲבֵי, לְמֵיכַל וּלְמִשְׁתֵּי לְבַר נָשׁ אָחֳרָא, שַׁדְיָין לֵיהּ בְּעוֹמְקָא דְּנַהֲרָא, וְאִיהוּ דְּנָטֵיל לֵיהּ הָכֵי נָמֵי.

211. Come and behold: The Holy One, blessed be He, said to Abraham, "the cry of Sodom and Gomorrah is great," because their conduct towards other people has reached Me. As a result of this conduct, the whole world avoids setting foot in Sodom and Gomorrah. Thus, it is written: "he breaks open a water course in place far from inhabitants, forgotten by foot travellers; they are dried up, they are gone away from men" (Iyov 28:4). "He breaks open a water course in place far from inhabitants" MEANS THAT "the water course," WHICH ALLUDES TO SODOM, "break open" for all the inhabitants of the

-344-

world who entered there. Because if any of them saw somebody give food or drink to a stranger, they cast him into the deep river, along with the person who received the food and drink.

212. וְעַל דָּא כָּלְהוּ בְּנֵי עָלְמָא, הֲווֹ נִשְׁכָּחִים מִנִּי רָגֶל, דְּמָנְעֵי רַגְלַיְיהוּ לָא לְמֵיעַל תַּמָּן, וּמַאן דְּעָאל, דַּלּוּ מֵאֱנוֹשׁ נָעוּ, דַּהֲווֹ דָּלֵי גּוּפָא בְּכַפְנָא, לָא הֲווֹ יַהֲבֵי לֵיהּ לְמֵיכַל וּלְמִשְׁתֵּי, וְאִשְׁתַּנֵּי דְּיוֹקְנַיְיהוּ מִשְׁאָר בְּנֵי עָלְמָא דִּכְתִיב דַּלּוּ מֵאֱנוֹשׁ נָעוּ. כְּתִיב הָכָא נָעוּ. וּכְתִיב הָתָם נָעוּ מַעְגְּלוֹתֶיהָ. הָכִי נָמֵי הֲווֹ סָטָאן מַעְגְּלִין וְאוֹרְחִין, דְּלָא לְמֵיעַל תַּמָּן. וַאֲפִילּוּ עוֹפֵי שְׁמַיָּא הֲווֹ מָנְעֵי לְמֵיעַל תַּמָּן, דִּכְתִיב נָתִיב לֹא יְדָעוֹ עָיִט וְגוֹ'. וּבְגִינֵי כָּךְ, כּוּלֵּי עָלְמָא הֲווֹ צָוְוחִין עַל סְדוֹם וְעַל עֲמוֹרָה, וְעַל כָּלְהוּ קַרְתֵּי, דְּכָלְהוּ כְּגַוְונָא חֲדָא הֲווֹ.

212. This is why all people of the world were "forgotten by foot travellers," that is, they avoided setting foot in there. And whoever did enter, "they are dried up, they are gone away," WHICH MEANS THAT they dried the STRENGTH OF THEIR bodies with hunger by not giving them anything to eat nor to drink. As a result, they no longer looked like human beings, as it is written: "they are dried up, they are gone away" (Iyov 28:4). Here, it is written: "they are gone away," and elsewhere it is written: "her paths wander" (Mishlei 5:6). IN BOTH VERSES, IT MEANS THAT "HER PATHS WANDER" AND CANNOT BE FOUND. "THEY ARE GONE" MEANS THAT they avoided the routes of convoys and other paths in order not to enter there. Even the birds in the sky stopped themselves from entering there, as it is written: "There is a path which no bird of prey knows..." (Iyov 28:7). And because of all this, the entire world cried out against Sodom and Gomorrah and against all the cities, which were considered all the same.

213. זַעֲקַת סְדוֹם וַעֲמוֹרָה כִּי רָבָּה, אָמַר לוֹ אַבְרָהָם, אֲמַאי. אֲמַר לֵיהּ, וְחַטָּאתָם כִּי כָבְדָה מְאֹד. בְּגִינֵי כָּךְ, אֵרְדָה נָא וְאֶרְאֶה הַכְּצַעֲקָתָהּ. הַכְּצַעֲקָתָם מִבָּעֵי לֵיהּ, דְּהָא כְּתִיב זַעֲקַת סְדוֹם וַעֲמוֹרָה, וּתְרֵי קַרְתֵּי הֲווֹ, אֲמַאי הַכְּצַעֲקָתָהּ. אֶלָּא הָא אֲקִמוּהָ.

213. "The cry of Sodom and Gomorrah is great," Abraham asks the Holy One, blessed be He: Why? He answers: "because their sin is very grievous."

And this is why "I will go down now, and see whether...according to the cry of it." AND HE SAID: It should have been said, 'according to the cry of them,' because it is written: "the cry of Sodom and Gomorrah." Thus, there were two cities. If so, why does it say, "the cry of it" IN THE SINGULAR? AND HE ANSWERED: "This has already been clarified."

214. תָּא חֲזֵי בְּסִטְרָא דִתּוֹתֵי קָלָא דְּבַרְדָּא, סָלְקִין קוּטְרֵי, כָּלְּהוּ בְּכִתְפָּא. מִתְכַּנְּשֵׁי בְּחַד טִיף, וְעָאלִין בְּגוֹ נוּקְבֵי דִתְהוֹמָא רַבָּא אִתְעֲבִידוּ חָמֵשׁ בְּחַד. חַד אִיהוּ כַּד אִיכָּא צְלִילִין, קָלִין, דְּכָלְּהוּ אִתְעֲבִידוּ חַד. קָלָא דְּסָלֵיק מִתַּתָּא, עָאל בֵּינַיְיהוּ, וְאִתְמַשְׁכוּ כְּחַד.

214. Come and behold: from the side underneath the sound of hailstones, all the tangles of the shoulder rise and are gathered into one drop, which then enters the holes of the great abyss, where five become one. When their voices are clear, they unite as one. Then, a voice from below enters among them and becomes one with them.

215. וְהַהוּא קָלָא סָלְקָא וְנַחְתָּא, תָּבְעָא דִינָא לְאִתְמַשְׁכָא לְתַתָּא. כַּד הַאי קָלָא סָלְקָא לְמִתְבַּע דִּינָא, כְּדֵין אִתְגְּלֵי קוּדְשָׁא בְּרִיךְ הוּא לְאַשְׁגָּחָא בְּדִינָא.

215. For that voice goes up and down, demanding that Judgment be drawn down. So when this voice rises to demand justice, the Holy One, blessed be He, reveals Himself to ensure justice is done.

216. אֲמַר רַבִּי שִׁמְעוֹן, הַכְּצַעֲקָתָהּ. מַאן הַכְּצַעֲקָתָהּ, דָּא גְּזֵרַת דִּינָא, דְּתָבְעָא דִינָא כָּל יוֹמָא. דְּהָכֵי תָּנִינָן כַּמָּה שְׁנִין קַיְימָא גְּזֵרַת דִּינָא, וְתָבְעָא מִקַּמֵּי קוּדְשָׁא בְּרִיךְ הוּא, עַל דְּזַבִּינוּ אֲחוֹי דְּיוֹסֵף לְיוֹסֵף. בְּגִין דִּגְזֵרַת דִּינָא, צָוְוחַת עַל דִּינָא, וְעַל דָּא, הַכְּצַעֲקָתָהּ הַבָּאָה אֵלָי.

216. Rabbi Shimon then said: IT IS WRITTEN, "according to the cry of it." To whom does this cry belong? AND HE REPLIES: This is the decree of Judgment that demands justice every day. SO THE PHRASE, "THE CRY OF IT" REFERS TO IT (judgment). As we have learned, for many years the Decree of Judgment demanded from the Holy One, blessed be He, THE

PENALTY FOR what the brothers of Joseph had done when they sold him. The Decree of Judgment cried out aloud for justice TO BE REVEALED. This is why IT IS WRITTEN: "according to the cry of it, which has come to me." IT REFERS TO THE CRY OF THE DECREE OF JUDGMENT.

217. מַה הַבָּאָה אֵלַי, דָּא הוּא רָזָא, כִּדְבָר אַחַר בָּעֶרֶב הִיא בָאָה וּבַבֹּקֶר הִיא שָׁבָה. וְדָא הוּא הַבָּאָה אֵלַי תָּדִיר. כְּגַוְונָא דָא, קֵץ כָּל בָּשָׂר בָּא לְפָנַי. וְהָא אִתְּמַר. עָשׂוֹ כָלָה הָא אִתְּמַר.

217. AND HE ASKS: What is MEANT BY THE PHRASE, "which has come to me?" AND HE RESPONDS: There is a secret here. As you may read, "In the evening she would return (lit. 'comes'), and in the morning she would return..." (Ester 2:14). The words "which has come to me" are written in the present tense to indicate a repeated action. Similarly the verse, "The End of all Flesh has come before me" (Beresheet 5:13) is also written in the present tense. The phrase "then destroy" has already been explained.

17. "Will You also destroy the righteous with the wicked?"

A Synopsis

A discussion takes place concerning Abraham, Noah, and Moses, specifically their role in protecting mankind. Three distinct levels of selfless love for others are exemplified through these three great spiritual leaders. Noah built the Ark and did all that God had commanded of him, but his efforts and concern ended there, as he did not continue to fight and lobby on behalf of mankind. Abraham took the cause of his fellow man a step further when he argued with the Creator in an effort to save Sodom and Gomorrah. However, once Abraham realized that the argument was lost, he accepted it. Moses, on the other hand, never gave up the fight for his fellow man even when all hope was lost, offering his own life in exchange for saving the entire nation.

The Relevance of this Passage

Spiritual complacency can cause the noblest person to fall to lower levels of being. Therefore, spiritual evolvement may be compared to the endeavor of climbing up a downward moving escalator. One must constantly progress forward against opposing forces. The moment we stand still, anywhere along the journey, we immediately begin to regress. The Light of this passage inspires us to continually grow spiritually so that we evolve a consciousness of true caring, self-sacrifice, and unconditional love for others. Through selfless love we protect all mankind and ourselves.

218. וַיִּגַּשׁ אַבְרָהָם וַיֹּאמַר הַאַף תִּסְפֶּה צַדִּיק עִם רָשָׁע. אָמַר ר' יְהוּדָה מַאן חָמָא אַבָּא דְּרַחֲמָנוּתָא כְּאַבְרָהָם. תָּא חֲזֵי, בְּנֹחַ כְּתִיב וַיֹּאמֶר אֱלֹקִים לְנֹחַ קֵץ כָּל בָּשָׂר בָּא לְפָנַי וגו'. עֲשֵׂה לְךָ תֵּבַת עֲצֵי גֹפֶר. וְאִשְׁתִּיק, וְלָא אָמַר לֵיהּ מִידֵי, וְלָא בָּעָא רַחֲמֵי. אֲבָל אַבְרָהָם, בְּשַׁעֲתָא דַּאֲמַר לֵיהּ קוּדְשָׁא בְּרִיךְ הוּא, זַעֲקַת סְדוֹם וַעֲמוֹרָה כִּי רָבָּה וגו'. אֵרְדָה נָא וְאֶרְאֶה וגו'. מִיָּד כְּתִיב וַיִּגַּשׁ אַבְרָהָם וַיֹּאמַר הַאַף תִּסְפֶּה צַדִּיק עִם רָשָׁע.

218. "And Abraham drew near, and said: Will You also destroy the righteous with the wicked?" (Beresheet 18:23). Rabbi Yehuda says: Who has met a father as merciful as Abraham? Come and behold. In regard to Noah, it is written: "And Elohim said to Noah: The End of all Flesh has come before Me... Make you an ark of gopher wood" (Beresheet 6:13-14).

And he remained silent and did not beg for mercy, while as soon as the Holy One, blessed be He, said to Abraham "the cry of Sodom and Gomorrah is great...I will go down now, and see," it is written: "And Abraham drew near, and said: Will You also destroy the righteous with the wicked?"

219. אָמַר רַבִּי אֶלְעָזָר אוּף אַבְרָהָם, לָא עָבַד שְׁלִימוּ כַּדְקָא יָאוֹת. נֹחַ לָא עֲבֵיד מִידֵי, לָא הַאי וְלָא הַאי. אַבְרָהָם תָּבַע דִּינָא כַּדְקָא יָאוֹת, דְּלָא יְמוּת זַכָּאָה עִם חַיָּיבָא. וְשָׁאֲרֵי מֵחַמְשִׁים, עַד עֲשָׂרָה, עָבַד וְלָא אַשְׁלֵים, דְּלָא בְּעָא רַחֲמֵי בֵּין כָּךְ וּבֵין כָּךְ, דְּאָמַר אַבְרָהָם לָא בָּעֵינָא לְמִתְבַּע אֲגַר עוֹבָדוֹי.

219. Rabbi Elazar said: Even Abraham did not act perfectly, as he should have done, but Noah did nothing. HE DID NOT ASK FOR MERCY ON BEHALF OF THE RIGHTEOUS, AS ABRAHAM DID, OR ON BEHALF OF THE SINNERS, AS MOSES DID. Abraham demanded a proper judgment so that the righteous would not perish with the sinners. He started with fifty righteous people and eventually descended to ten. Then, he stopped. He did not plead for Mercy in any case, WHETHER THERE WERE RIGHTEOUS PEOPLE OR NOT. This is because Abraham said: I do not want to demand any reward for my actions, MEANING THAT HE DID NOT BELIEVE THAT HE DESERVED ANY REWARD FOR ASKING TO FREE SINNERS FROM THEIR PUNISHMENT.

220. אֲבָל מַאן עָבַד שְׁלִימוּ כַּדְקָא יָאוֹת דָּא מֹשֶׁה. דְּכֵיוָן דְּאָמַר קוּדְשָׁא בְּרִיךְ הוּא סָרוּ מַהֵר מִן הַדֶּרֶךְ וְגו'. עָשׂוּ לָהֶם עֵגֶל מַסֵּכָה וַיִּשְׁתַּחֲווּ לוֹ. מִיָּד מַה כְּתִיב וַיְחַל מֹשֶׁה אֶת פְּנֵי ה' אֱלֹקָיו וְגו'. עַד דְּאָמַר וְעַתָּה אִם תִּשָּׂא חַטָּאתָם וְאִם אַיִן מְחֵנִי נָא מִסִּפְרְךָ אֲשֶׁר כָּתַבְתָּ. וְאַף עַל גַּב דְּכֻלְּהוּ חָטוּ, לָא זָז מִתַּמָּן, עַד דְּאָמַר לֵיהּ סָלַחְתִּי כִּדְבָרֶךְ.

220. The one who acted perfectly was Moses. Because as soon as the Holy One, blessed be He, said to him, "they have turned aside quickly from the way...they have made them a molten calf, and have worshiped it," (Shemot 32:8) it is written: "And Moses besought Hashem his Elohim..." (Ibid. 11) And the verse continues until he said, "Yet now, if You will forgive their sin–and if not, blot me, I pray You, out of Your book which You have written" (Ibid. 32). And even though they had all sinned, he did not budge

from there until He told him: "I have pardoned according to your word" (Bemidbar 14:20). THERE IS A SECTION MISSING HERE THAT MUST HAVE BEEN OVERLOOKED AS THIS PASSAGE WAS COPIED. AND THIS IS THE CORRECT VERSION: We have discussed and learned that he did not budge from there until the Holy One, blessed be He, forgave Yisrael, as it is written: "And Hashem reconsidered the evil which he thought to do to his people" (Shemot 32:14), and "I have pardoned according to your word." THIS MUST BE THE CORRECT VERSION FOR IT IS IMPOSSIBLE FOR THE ZOHAR NOT TO MENTION THE PARDON FOR THE SIN OF THE CALF AND TO READ, "I HAVE PARDONED ACCORDING TO YOUR WORD" (BEMIDBAR 14:20), WHICH WAS SAID ABOUT THE SPIES.

221. אֲבָל אַבְרָהָם לָא אַשְׁגַּח אֶלָּא אִי אִי אִשְׁתְּכַח בְּהוֹ זַכַּאי, וְאִם לָאו לָא. וְעַל דָּא לָא הֲוָה בְּעָלְמָא בַּר נָשׁ, דְּיָגֵין עַל דָּרֵיה, כְּמֹשֶׁה, דְּאִיהוּ רַעְיָא מְהֵימְנָא.

221. But Abraham considered only whether there might have been any righteous among them. And because there were not ANY RIGHTEOUS AMONG THEM, he did not PRAY FOR ANY OF THEM. This is why there has never been a person in the world who protected his generation as has Moses, the Faithful Shepherd.

222. וַיִּגַּשׁ אַבְרָהָם וַיֹּאמַר, אַתְקִין גַּרְמֵיה לְמִתְבַּע דָּא. אוּלַי יִמָּצְאוּן שָׁם חֲמִשִּׁים. שָׁרָא מֵחֲמִשִּׁים, דְּאִיהוּ שֵׁירוּתָא לְמִנְדַּע, עַד עֲשָׂרָה, דְּאִיהוּ עֲשִׂירָאָה, סוֹפָא דְּכָל דַּרְגִּין.

222. "And Abraham drew near, and said..." means that he prepared himself before beseeching, "Perhaps there are fifty righteous..." He started with 50, which is the beginning of Knowledge, until he descended to ten, which is the number of the last of all grades.

223. אָמַר ר' יִצְחָק עַד עֲשָׂרָה, אֵלֵּין עֲשָׂרָה יוֹמִין, דְּבֵין רֹאשׁ הַשָּׁנָה לְיוֹם הַכִּפּוּרִים. בְּגִין כָּךְ שָׁרָא מֵחֲמִשִּׁים עַד עֲשָׂרָה. וְכֵיוָן דִּמְטָא לַעֲשָׂרָה, אֲמַר, מִכָּאן וּלְתַתָּא לָאו הוּא אֲתַר דְּקַיְימָא בִּתְשׁוּבָה, בְּגִינֵי כָךְ לָא נָחַת לְתַתָּא מֵעֲשָׂרָה.

223. Rabbi Yitzchak said: Abraham stopped at the number ten, which represents the ten days between between Rosh Hashana and Yom Kippur, DURING WHICH THE TEN SFIROT OF MALCHUT ARE PREPARED TO ASCEND TO BINAH. This is why he started TO PLEAD for the fifty, but stopped at ten. THESE SYMBOLIZE THE TEN SFIROT OF MALCHUT, WHICH ARE CORRECTED DURING THE TEN DAYS OF REPENTANCE. As he reached ten, he said: From here downward, MALCHUT IS NOT SWEETENED BY BINAH, WHICH IS ALSO CALLED 'REPENTENCE'. Therefore, he concluded that this was not a place for repantance, and he he did not CONTINUE IMPLORING AND reducing the number under ten.

18. "And the two angels came to Sodom"

A Synopsis
During a discussion concerning the two angels who executed the decree of destruction upon the cities of Sodom and Gomorrah, the Zohar expounds upon the protective power of the Torah through its study. The Torah is called the Tree of Life. Kabbalistically, the Tree of Life is a realm of pure order and serenity. It is the origin of all human happiness, well-being, and contentment. The Torah becomes the Tree of Life by virtue of our consciousness and certainty in its powers. Our awareness is the mechanism that activates the Tree of Life forces.

The Relevance of this Passage
As a lamp requires electrical current before it can illuminate a darkened room, Kabbalistic tools, such as the Torah, are in need of spiritual current in order to become active. Spiritual current is the stuff of consciousness and certainty. We develop a true sense of appreciation and certitude in the power of the Torah and the Tree of Life energy that radiates through its verses.

224. וַיָּבֹאוּ שְׁנֵי הַמַּלְאָכִים סְדוֹמָה בָּעֶרֶב וְגוֹ'. אָמַר ר' יוֹסֵי, תָּא חֲזֵי, מַה כְּתִיב לְעֵילָא, וַיֵּלֶךְ ה' כַּאֲשֶׁר כִּלָּה לְדַבֵּר אֶל אַבְרָהָם. דְּהָא כֵּיוָן דְּאִתְפְּרַשׁ שְׁכִינְתָּא מֵאַבְרָהָם, וְאַבְרָהָם תָּב לְאַתְרֵיה, כְּדֵין וַיָּבֹאוּ שְׁנֵי הַמַּלְאָכִים סְדוֹמָה בָּעֶרֶב, דְּהָא חַד אִסְתַּלַּק בִּשְׁכִינְתָּא, וְאִשְׁתְּאָרוּ אִינוּן תְּרֵין.

224. "And the two angels came to Sodom at evening..." (Beresheet 19:1). Rabbi Yosi said, Come and behold: It is written: "And Hashem went His way, as soon as He had left speaking to Abraham..." (Beresheet 18:33). As the Shechinah had departed from Abraham, and Abraham returned to his place, then "the two angels came to Sodom at evening..." There were only two angels because one had departed with the Shechinah.

225. כֵּיוָן דְּחָמָא לוֹט לוֹן, רָהַט בַּתְרַיְיהוּ. מַאי טַעֲמָא, וְכִי כָּל אִינוּן דַּהֲווֹ אַתְיָין, אִיהוּ אָעֵיל לוֹן לְבֵיתֵיה, וְיָהֵיב לוֹן לְמֵיכַל וּלְמִשְׁתֵּי, וּבְנֵי מָתָא הֵיךְ לָא קַטְלִין לֵיה, דְּהָא לִבְרַתֵּיה עָבְדוּ דִינָא.

225. As Lot saw them, he ran after them. Why? He invited everyone who

came to his city into his house and offered them food and drink. If so, then how come the people of his own town did not kill him, as they did his daughter.

226. וּמַאי הוּא, דִּבְרַתֵּיהּ דְּלוֹט, יַהֲבַת פִּתָּא דְּנַהֲמָא לְחַד עַנְיָא, יָדְעוּ בָהּ, שָׁפוּהָ דוּבְשָׁא, וְאוֹתְבוּהָ בְּרֵישׁ אִיגְרָא, עַד דַּאֲכָלוּהָ צְרָעֵי.

226. For what reason was she killed? The daughter of Lot offered a piece of bread to a poor man. As soon as the townspeople found out, they covered her with honey and put her on the roof until she was stung to death by bees.

227. אֶלָּא בְּגִין דַּהֲוָה בְּלֵילְיָא, חָשִׁיב דְּלָא יִסְתַּכְּלוּן לֵיהּ בְּנֵי מָתָא, וְעִם כָּל דָּא, כֵּיוָן דַּאֲעָלוּ לְבֵיתָא, אִתְכְּנָשׁוּ כֻּלְּהוּ, וְאַסְחֲרוּ לְבֵיתָא.

227. AND HE REPLIES: Because it was at night, Lot thought that the townspeople would not see him. Nevertheless, as soon as they entered his house, the townspeople gathered and surrounded the house.

228. אָמַר רִבִּי יִצְחָק, אַמַּאי רָהַט לוֹט אֲבַתְרַיְיהוּ, דִּכְתִיב וַיַּרְא לוֹט וַיָּרָץ לִקְרָאתָם. ר' חִזְקִיָּה וְר' יֵיסָא. חַד אָמַר, דְּיוֹקְנָא דְּאַבְרָהָם חָמָא עִמְּהוֹן. וְחַד אָמַר שְׁכִינְתָּא אַתְיָא עֲלַיְיהוּ. כְּתִיב הָכָא וַיַּרְא לוֹט וַיָּרָץ לִקְרָאתָם, וּכְתִיב הָתָם וַיָּרָץ לִקְרָאתָם מִפֶּתַח הָאֹהֶל. מַה לְהַלָּן חָמָא שְׁכִינְתָּא, אוֹף הָכָא חָמָא שְׁכִינְתָּא.

228. Rabbi Yitzchak asks: Why did Lot run after the angels?, as it is written: "and Lot seeing them rose up to meet them..." Rabbi Chizkiyah or Rabbi Yesa, one responded that he saw the image of Abraham among them; the other said that he saw the Shechinah resting upon them. AND HE DREW AN ANALOGY. It is written here, "and Lot seeing them rose up to meet them," and elsewhere, "and when he saw them he ran to meet them from the tent door..." (Bereshet 18:2). So, just as he saw the Shechinah there, he saw the Shechinah here as well.

229. וְעַל דָּא, וַיַּרְא לוֹט וַיָּרָץ לִקְרָאתָם, וַיֹּאמֶר הִנֶּה נָא אֲדֹנַי בָּאָלֶ"ף דָּלֶ"ת נו"ן יו"ד. סוּרוּ נָא, גְּשׁוּ נָא מִבָּעֵי לֵיהּ, מַאי סוּרוּ נָא. אֶלָּא

לְאַהֲדָרָא לוֹן סַחֲרָנֵיה דְּבֵיתָא, בְּגִין דְּלָא יֶחֱמוּן לוֹן בְּנֵי מָתָא, וְלָא יֵעֲלוּן בְּאוֹרַח מֵישָׁר לְבֵיתָא, וּבְגִין כָּךְ, סוּרוּ נָא.

229. This is the reason why "Lot seeing them run to meet them...And he said, 'Behold now, my lords (Heb. *adonai*),'" spelled with *Aleph, Dalet, Nun* and *Yud,* THAT IS, THE NAME OF THE SHECHINAH. IN OUR SCRIPTURES IT IS NOT WRITTEN: 'AND HE RAN TO MEET THEM,' BUT RATHER, "ROSE UP TO MEET THEM." ACCORDING TO THE ZOHAR, THE WORDS "ROSE TO MEET THEM" MEAN THAT HE ROSE UP AND RAN TO MEET THEM. OTHERWISE, IT SHOULD HAVE BEEN WRITTEN: 'HE ROSE UP BEFORE THEM.' The verse continues, "turn in, I pray you." HE ASKS: WHY IS IT WRITTEN, "turn in, I pray you," when it should have been written, 'draw near, I pray you.' What is MEANT BY "turn in?" AND HE RESPONDS: He did not want them to enter the house in the regular way, so his townspeople would not see them. This is why HE SAID, "turn in, I pray you."

230. ר' חִזְקִיָּה פָּתַח כִּי הוּא לִקְצוֹת הָאָרֶץ יַבִּיט תַּחַת כָּל הַשָּׁמַיִם יִרְאֶה. כַּמָּה אִית לוֹן לִבְנֵי נָשָׁא, לְאִסְתַּכְּלָא בְּעוֹבָדוֹי דְּקוּדְשָׁא בְּרִיךְ הוּא, וּלְאִשְׁתַּדְּלָא בְּאוֹרַיְיתָא יְמָמָא וְלֵילֵי, דְּכָל מָאן דְּאִשְׁתַּדַּל בְּאוֹרַיְיתָא, קוּדְשָׁא בְּרִיךְ הוּא אִשְׁתַּבַּח בֵּיה לְעֵילָא, וְאִשְׁתַּבַּח בֵּיה לְתַתָּא, בְּגִין דְּאוֹרַיְיתָא, אִילָנָא דְּחַיֵּי אִיהִי, לְכָל אִינוּן דְּעָסְקִין בָּה, לְמֵיהַב לוֹן חַיִּין בְּעָלְמָא דֵּין, וּלְמֵיהַב לוֹן חַיִּין בְּעָלְמָא דְּאָתֵי.

230. Rabbi Chizkiyah began the discussion by saying: IT IS WRITTEN, "For He looks to the ends of the earth, and sees under the whole heaven" (Iyov 28:24). How important it is for all human beings to observe the works of the Holy One, blessed be He, and to study Torah day and night. He who studies the Torah is glorified by the Holy One, blessed be He, on high and down below, because the Torah is the Tree of Life for all those who occupy themselves in it. It grants them life in this world and offers them life in the World to Come.

231. תָּא חֲזֵי כִּי הוּא לִקְצוֹת הָאָרֶץ יַבִּיט. לְמֵיהַב לוֹן מְזוֹנָא, וּלְסַפְּקָא לוֹן מִכָּל מַה דְּאִצְטְרִיכוּ, בְּגִין דְּאִיהוּ אַשְׁגַּח בָּה תָּדִיר, דִּכְתִיב תָּמִיד

עֵינֵי ה׳ אֱלֹקֶיךָ בָּה מֵרֵשִׁית הַשָּׁנָה וְעַד אַחֲרִית שָׁנָה.

231. Come and behold: IT IS WRITTEN, "For He looks to the end of the earth" in order to supply them with food and provide for their needs. THE "EARTH" IS MALCHUT; "ENDS OF THE EARTH" REFERS TO ALL THAT ISSUES FROM HER, because it is He who takes care of Her always. As it is written: "The eyes of Hashem your Elohim are always upon it, from the beginning of the year to the end of the year" (Devarim 11:12).

232. בְּגִין דְּאֶרֶץ דָּא, מַה כְּתִיב בָּה, מִמֶּרְחָק תָּבִיא לַחְמָה. וּלְבָתַר אִיהִי יָהֲבַת מְזוֹנָא וְטַרְפָּא, לְכָל אִינּוּן חֵיוָן בָּרָא, דִּכְתִיב וַתָּקָם בְּעוֹד לַיְלָה וַתִּתֵּן טֶרֶף לְבֵיתָהּ וְחֹק לְנַעֲרוֹתֶיהָ.

232. It is written of this earth, NAMELY MALCHUT: "she brings her food from afar" (Mishlei 31:14). And then, "She" provides the beasts of the fields, WHICH ARE THE ANGELS OF THE WORLDS BRIYAH, YETZIRAH, AND ASIYAH, with food and sustenance, as it is written: "She rises also while it is yet night, and gives meat to her household and a portion to her maidens" (Ibid. 15).

233. וְעַל דָּא כִּי הוּא לִקְצוֹת הָאָרֶץ יַבִּיט תַּחַת כָּל הַשָּׁמַיִם יִרְאֶה. לְכֻלְּהוּ בְּנֵי עָלְמָא, לְמֵיהַב לוֹן מְזוֹנָא וְסִפּוּקָא, לְכָל מַה דְּאִצְטְרִיךְ כָּל חַד וְחַד, דִּכְתִיב, פּוֹתֵחַ אֶת יָדֶךָ וּמַשְׂבִּיעַ לְכָל חַי רָצוֹן.

233. This is why IT IS WRITTEN: "for He looks to the ends of the earth, and sees under the whole heaven," ALLUDING to all the people in the world, in order to supply them with food and provisions, each and every one according to his needs, as it is written: "You open your hand, and satisfy the desire of every living thing" (Tehilim 145:16).

234. דָּבָר אַחֵר כִּי הוּא לִקְצוֹת הָאָרֶץ יַבִּיט. לְאִסְתַּכְּלָא עוֹבָדוֹי דְּבַר נָשׁ, וּלְאַשְׁגָּחָא בְּכָל מַה דְּעַבְדֵי בְּנֵי נָשָׁא בְּעָלְמָא. תַּחַת כָּל הַשָּׁמַיִם יִרְאֶה. מִסְתַּכֵּל וְחָמֵי לְכָל חַד וְחַד.

234. There is another explanation OF THE VERSE: "for He looks to the ends of the earth," which IS THAT He observes the makings of man and watches closely over what people are doing in the world. He "sees under the whole heaven," which means that He watches and keeps an eye on each and every person.

235. תָּא חֲזֵי כֵּיוָן דְּחָמָא קוּדְשָׁא בְּרִיךְ הוּא, עוֹבְדִין דִּסְדוֹם וַעֲמוֹרָה, שַׁדַּר לוֹן לְאִינוּן מַלְאָכִין, לְחַבָּלָא לִסְדוֹם. מַה כְּתִיב, וַיַּרְא לוֹט, חָמָא לִשְׁכִינְתָּא, וְכִי מַאן יָכִיל לְמֶחֱמֵי שְׁכִינְתָּא, אֶלָּא, חָמָא זָהֲרָא חַד דְּנָהֵיר, דְּקָא סַלְקָא עַל רֵישַׁיְיהוּ. וּכְדֵין וַיֹּאמֶר הִנֵּה נָא אֲדֹנַי בְּאָלֶ"ף דָּלֶ"ת, כְּמָה דְאִתְּמַר. וּבְגִין שְׁכִינְתָּא, הַהוּא נְהִירוּ דְּנָהֵיר, קָאֲמַר סוּרוּ נָא אֶל בֵּית עַבְדְּכֶם.

235. Come and behold: as a result of the Holy One, blessed be He seeing the actions of Sodom and Gomorrah, He sent forth those angels to destroy Sodom. It is written: "and Lot seeing..." WHICH MEANS THAT he was "seeing" the Shechinah. AND HE ASKS: "But who can possibly see the Shechinah?" AND HE REPLIES: He saw a light shining and rising high above their heads. And then he said: "Behold now, Adonai (Eng. 'my master')," spelled with Aleph and Dalet WHICH IS THE NAME OF THE SHECHINAH. Thus, for the sake of the Shechinah, NAMELY that certain illumination that shone UPON THEIR HEADS, he said, "turn in, I pray you, into your servant's house..."

236. וְלִינוּ וְרַחֲצוּ רַגְלֵיכֶם. לָא עֲבַד הָכֵי אַבְרָהָם, אֶלָּא בְּקַדְמֵיתָא אָמַר וְרַחֲצוּ רַגְלֵיכֶם, וּלְבָתַר וְאֶקְחָה פַת לֶחֶם וגו'. אֲבָל לוֹט אָמַר, סוּרוּ נָא אֶל בֵּית עַבְדְּכֶם וְלִינוּ. וּלְבָתַר וְרַחֲצוּ רַגְלֵיכֶם וְהִשְׁכַּמְתֶּם וַהֲלַכְתֶּם לְדַרְכְּכֶם. בְּגִין דְּלָא יִשְׁתְּמוֹדְעוּן בְּהוּ בְּנֵי נָשָׁא.

236. The verse continues, "and sleep and wash your feet..." but Abraham did not do so. Rather, he said at first, "wash your feet," and only later, "And I will fetch a morsel of bread." Lot, however, said, "turn in, I pray you, into your servant's house, and tarry all night," and then, "and wash your feet, and you may rise up early, and go your ways." And this was to prevent other people from knowing about them. IF OTHER PEOPLE HAPPENED TO KNOW ABOUT THEM AND APPROACHED THEM, THEY COULD CLAIM THAT THEY

HAD JUST ARRIVED A SHORT WHILE AGO, AS THEY HAD NOT EVEN
WASHED THEIR FEET FROM THE DUST OF THE JOURNEY.

237. וַיֹּאמְרוּ לֹא כִּי בָרְחוֹב נָלִין. בְּגִין דְּכָךְ הֲווֹ עָבְדֵי אוֹרְחִין דְּעָאלִין
תַּמָּן, לָא הֲוָה בַר נָשׁ דְּיִכְנוֹשׁ לוֹן לְבֵיתָא, וְעַל דָּא, אָמְרוּ לֹא כִּי
בָרְחוֹב נָלִין, מַה כְּתִיב וַיִּפְצַר בָּם מְאֹד וגו'.

237. "And they said, 'No, but we will abide in the street all night,'" because
that was the practice in these cities – GUESTS SLEPT IN THE STREET
BECAUSE no person invited them to his house. This is why they said, "we
will abide in the street." And then it is written: "and he pressed upon them
greatly" (Beresheet 19:3).

238. תָּא חֲזֵי, כַּד קוּדְשָׁא בְּרִיךְ הוּא עָבֵיד דִּינָא בְּעָלְמָא, שְׁלִיחָא חֲדָא
עָבֵיד לֵיהּ, וְהַשְׁתָּא חָמֵינָן תְּרֵי שְׁלוּחֵי, אֲמַאי, וְכִי לָא סַגֵּי בְּחַד. אֶלָּא
חַד הֲוָה, וּמַה דַּאֲמַר תְּרֵי, חַד הֲוָה לְאַפָּקָא לֵיהּ לְלוֹט, וּלְשֵׁזָבָא לֵיהּ,
וְחַד לְמֵיהְפַּךְ לְקַרְתָּא, וּלְחַבָּלָא אַרְעָא, וּבְגִין כָּךְ אִשְׁתְּאַר חַד.

238. Come and behold: when the Holy One, blessed be He, executes
Judgment on the world, one messenger performs it. But now, DURING THE
OVERTHROW OF SODOM, we see two messengers, AS IT IS WRITTEN: "AND
TWO ANGELS CAME TO SODOM." Is not one angel sufficient? AND HE
REPLIES: "There indeed was only one; the scriptures mentions two because
one came to save Lot, while the other came to overthrow the city and
destroy the land. Therefore, there was only one assigned TO OVERTHROW
SODOM.

19. The Garden of Eden and Gehenom

A Synopsis

Man is constantly tested by his own negative inclination in order to provide him with the opportunity to exercise free will. Man activates free will the moment he resists his natural selfish tendencies. The righteous people of this world are those who have conquered their negative natures and subjugated all Evil Inclinations. It is upon their merit that our physical world is sustained. A man who conquers his own negative nature and ego is far stronger and far greater than the man who conquers armies or builds empires.

The Zohar explains that the Garden of Eden and Hell exist both in our physical realm and in the Supernal Worlds. The true righteous dwell in the Garden of Eden above, while the most wicked of men dwell in the lower realm of Hell. There is a story in the Talmud that Hell on Earth was discovered and visited by a great sage some 2000 years ago. This sage stormed the gates of Hell and stole away the knife from the Angel of Death. The Creator explained to the sage that the system of Hell is a necessary process in order to help cleanse the souls of the wicked so that they, too, may be able to partake in the world-to-come. The Creator, therefore, called for the sage to return the knife.

The Relevance of this Passage

The Garden of Eden is not only a long sought-after paradise located in some remote island in the world-to-come, but it is also a state-of-mind that we experience in the here and now. We connect ourselves to the Garden of Eden on Earth, arousing tranquillity, happiness, and inner peace in our soul. We begin to sense and grasp the significance of the hardships that strike in our personal life. During difficult times, when life feels like Hell on Earth, afflictions have a cleansing effect on our soul. Awareness and acceptance of this spiritual truth accelerates the process, and trying times pass more quickly.

מִדְרָשׁ הַנֶּעֱלָם

239. רַבִּי פָּתַח, בְּהַאי קְרָא, וְאֵלֶּה הַגּוֹיִם אֲשֶׁר הִנִּיחַ ה' לְנַסּוֹת בָּם אֶת יִשְׂרָאֵל. אָמַר רַבִּי, חֲזֵי הֲוֵית בְּהַהוּא עָלְמָא, וְלֵית עָלְמָא קָאִים, אֶלָּא בְּאִינּוּן דְּשַׁלִּיטִין עַל רְעוּתָא דְּלִבְּהוֹן. שֶׁנֶּאֱמַר עֵדוּת בִּיהוֹסֵף שָׁמוֹ וגו'.

אָמַר רַב יְהוּדָה, לָמָּה זָכָה יוֹסֵף לְאוֹתָהּ הַמַּעֲלָה וְהַמַּלְכוּת, בִּשְׁבִיל
שֶׁכָּבַשׁ יִצְרוֹ. דְּתָנֵינָן כָּל הַכּוֹבֵשׁ אֶת יִצְרוֹ, מַלְכוּתָא דִשְׁמַיָּא אָחֵיל
עֲלֵיהּ.

Midrash Hane'elam (Homiletical interpretations on the obscure)

239. Rabbi opened the discussion by quoting the verse: "Now these are the nations which Hashem left, to test Yisrael by them..." (Shoftim 3:1). Rabbi said: I have been looking into that world, NAMELY THE ETERNAL WORLD, and saw that the world can exist only because of righteous people who have control over the desire of their hearts. As it is written: "this he ordained in Yehosef for a testimony..." (Tehilim 81:6). Rabbi Yehuda then said: Why did Joseph merit that high grade and kingdom? The answer is because he overcame his lust. As we have learned, the heavenly Kingdom awaits he who overcomes his lustful desires.

240. דַּאֲמַר ר' אַחָא, לֹא בָּרָא הַקּוּדְשָׁא בְּרִיךְ הוּא לַיצה"ר, אֶלָּא
לְנַסּוֹת בּוֹ בְּנֵי אָדָם. וּמִי בָּעֵי קוּדְשָׁא בְּרִיךְ הוּא לְנַסּוּתָא בִּבְנֵי נָשָׁא.
אֵין. דַּאֲמַר ר' אַחָא, מנ"ל, מִדִּכְתִיב כִּי יָקוּם בְּקִרְבְּךָ נָבִיא וְגוֹ'. וּבָא
הָאוֹת וְהַמּוֹפֵת וְגוֹ'. כִּי מְנַסֶּה ה' אֱלֹקֵיכֶם וְגוֹ'.

240. As Rabbi Acha has said: The Holy One, blessed be He, has created the Evil Inclination solely for the purpose of trying humanity. And does the Holy One, blessed be He, intend on trying humanity? Yes. How do we know this? From the verse: "If there arise among you a prophet or a dreamer of dreams...And the sign or the wonder came to pass...For Hashem your Elohim tests you..." (Devarim 13:1-3)

241. וּלְמָה בָּעֵי נַסּוּתָא, דְּהָא כָּל עוֹבָדוֹי דְּבַר נָשׁ אִתְגְּלֵי קַמֵּיהּ, אֶלָּא
שֶׁלֹּא לָתֵת פִּתְחוֹן פֶּה לִבְנֵי אָדָם, רְאֵה מַה כְּתִיב וְלוֹט יוֹשֵׁב בְּשַׁעַר
סְדוֹם דַּהֲוָה יָתֵיב לְנַסּוּתָא לִבְרִיָּיתָא. אָמַר רַבִּי יִצְחָק, מַאי דִּכְתִיב
וְהָרְשָׁעִים כַּיָּם נִגְרָשׁ וְגוֹ'. אֲפִילוּ בִּשְׁעַת דִּינוֹ שֶׁל רָשָׁע הוּא מֵעִיז פָּנָיו,
וַאֲזַי הוּא בְּרִשְׁעָתוֹ קַיָּים, רְאֵה מַה כְּתִיב טֶרֶם יִשְׁכָּבוּ וְגוֹ'.

241. And why does He intend on trying it, as all the deeds of humankind are well known to Him? So as that humankind should have no excuse to complain. See what is written: "and Lot sat in the gate of Sodom," WHICH MEANS that he was sitting and reproving the people. Rabbi Yitzchak asks: What is the verse: "But the wicked are like the troubled sea..." (Yeshayah 57:20)? Even when the wicked is on trial, he shows insolence and confirms his guilt. As it is written: "But before they lay down..." (Beresheet 19:4).

242. אָמַר ר' יִצְחָק, כְּשֵׁם שֶׁבָּרָא קוּדְשָׁא בְּרִיךְ הוּא גַּן עֵדֶן בָּאָרֶץ, כָּךְ בָּרָא גֵּיהִנֹּם בָּאָרֶץ. וּכְשֵׁם שֶׁבָּרָא גַּן עֵדֶן לְמַעְלָה, כָּךְ בָּרָא גֵּיהִנֹּם לְמַעְלָה. גַּן עֵדֶן בָּאָרֶץ, דִּכְתִיב וַיִּטַּע ה' אֱלֹקִים גַּן בְּעֵדֶן וְגוֹ'. גֵּיהִנֹּם בָּאָרֶץ, דִּכְתִיב אֶרֶץ עֵפָתָה כְּמוֹ אֹפֶל וְגוֹ'.

242. Rabbi Yitzchak continued: Just as the Holy One, blessed be He, created the Garden of Eden upon earth, so did He create Gehenom as well. And just as He created the Garden of Eden above, so did He create Gehenom there. The earthly Garden of Eden is referred to in the verse: "And Hashem Elohim planted a garden eastward in Eden..." (Beresheet 2:8) and earthly Gehanom is referred to in the verse: "A land of gloom, as darkness itself..." (Iyov 10:22)

243. גַּן עֵדֶן לְמַעְלָה, דִּכְתִיב וְהָיְתָה נֶפֶשׁ אֲדוֹנִי צְרוּרָה בִּצְרוֹר הַחַיִּים אֶת ה' אֱלֹקֶיךָ. וּכְתִיב וְהָרוּחַ תָּשׁוּב אֶל הָאֱלֹקִים אֲשֶׁר נְתָנָהּ. גֵּיהִנֹּם לְמַעְלָה דִּכְתִיב וְאֵת נֶפֶשׁ אֹיְבֶיךָ יְקַלְעֶנָּה בְּתוֹךְ כַּף הַקָּלַע.

243. There is a Garden of Eden above, as is written: "but the soul of my lord shall be bound in the bundle of life with Hashem your Elohim..." (I Shmuel 25:29) and, "and the spirit shall return to Elohim who gave it" (Kohelet 12:7). And there is a Gehenom above, as it is written: "and the souls of your enemies, these shall he sling out, as out of the hollow of a sling" (I Shmuel 25:29).

244. גַּן עֵדֶן לְמַטָּה כִּדְקָאֲמָרָן. גַּן עֵדֶן לְמַעְלָה, לְנִשְׁמָתָן שֶׁל צַדִּיקִים גְּמוּרִים, לִהְיוֹת נִזּוֹנִין מֵאוֹר הַגָּדוֹל שֶׁל מַעְלָה. גֵּיהִנֹּם לְמַטָּה, לְאוֹתָם הָרְשָׁעִים שֶׁלֹּא קִבְּלוּ בְּרִית מִילָה, וְלֹא הֶאֱמִינוּ בְּהַקּוּדְשָׁא בְּרִיךְ הוּא

וְדָתוֹ, וְלֹא שָׁמְרוּ שַׁבָּת, וְאֵלּוּ הֵם עכו"ם, שֶׁנִּדּוֹנִים בָּאֵשׁ, שֶׁנֶּאֱמַר מֵהָאֵשׁ יָצָאוּ וְהָאֵשׁ תֹּאכְלֵם וגו'. וּכְתִיב וְיָצְאוּ וְרָאוּ בְּפִגְרֵי הָאֲנָשִׁים וגו'.

244. The Garden of Eden below is as we have said. The Garden of Eden above is for the souls of the completely righteous, so that they may be replenished by the Great Light of above. Gehenom down below is for those wicked who refused to perform circumcision, did not believe in the Holy One, blessed be He, nor in His religion, and did not keep the Shabbat. And these are those who worship the stars and constellations, and who are condemned with fire. As it is written: "and they came out from fire, and fire shall devour them..." (Yechezkel 15:7) and, "And they shall go forth, and look upon the carcasses of the men..." (Yeshayah 66:24)

245. גֵּיהִנֹּם לְמַעְלָה, לְאוֹתָם פּוֹשְׁעֵי יִשְׂרָאֵל שֶׁעָבְרוּ עַל מִצְוֹת הַתּוֹרָה, וְלֹא חָזְרוּ בִּתְשׁוּבָה, שֶׁדּוֹחִים אוֹתָם לַחוּץ, עַד שֶׁיְּקַבְּלוּ עוֹנְשָׁם. וְהוֹלְכִים וְסוֹבְבִים כָּל הָעוֹלָם, שֶׁנֶּאֱמַר סָבִיב רְשָׁעִים יִתְהַלָּכוּן.

245. The Gehenom above is for those sinners of Yisrael who have transgressed the precepts of Torah, and have not repented. They are rejected and stay outside until they are punished. And they wander around the whole world, as it is written: "The wicked walk on every side..." (Tehilim 12:9)

246. וְשָׁם נִדּוֹנִים שְׁנֵים עָשָׂר חֹדֶשׁ לְאַחַר כֵּן, מְדוֹרָם עִם אוֹתָם שֶׁקִּבְּלוּ עָנְשָׁם בְּמוֹתָם כָּל אֶחָד וְאֶחָד כְּפִי הַמָּקוֹם הָרָאוּי לוֹ. וְהָרְשָׁעִים שֶׁל עכו"ם, נִדּוֹנִים תָּמִיד בָּאֵשׁ וּבַמַּיִם, וְשׁוּב אֵינָם עוֹלִים, שֶׁנֶּאֱמַר וְאִשָּׁם לֹא תִכְבֶּה.

246. And they are sentenced to stay there for twelve months. Later, they reside with those who received their punishment at their death, each to a place according to what he deserves. The sinners who worship the stars and the constellations are constantly punished by fire and water, and they never emerge again, as it is written: "neither shall their fire be quenched" (Yeshayah 66:24).

247. מִשְׁפַּט הָרְשָׁעִים בַּגֵּיהִנֹּם, כְּמָה דִּכְתִיב, וַה' הִמְטִיר עַל סְדֹם וְעַל

עֲמֹרָה גָּפְרִית וָאֵשׁ וגו'. וְשׁוּב אֵינָם עוֹלִים, וְלֹא יָקוּמוּ לְיוֹם הַדִּין, שֶׁנֶּאֱמַר אֲשֶׁר הָפַךְ ה' בְּאַפּוֹ וּבַחֲמָתוֹ, בְּאַפּוֹ: בָּעוֹלָם הַזֶּה. וּבַחֲמָתוֹ: בָּעוֹלָם הַבָּא.

247. The sinners are sentenced in Gehenom according to what is written: "Then Hashem rained upon Sodom and upon Gomorrah brimstone and fire..." (Beresheet 19:24). And they never emerged from there and shall not rise for the Day of Judgment, as it is written: "which Hashem overthrew in His anger, and in His wrath" (Devarim 29:22). "In His anger" refers to this world; "and in His wrath" refers to the World to Come.

248. אָמַר ר' יִצְחָק לְהַאי גַּוְונָא אִית גַּן עֵדֶן לְמַעְלָה, וְאִית גַּן עֵדֶן לְמַטָּה. אִית גֵּיהִנֹּם לְמַטָּה, וְאִית גֵּיהִנֹּם לְמַעְלָה. אָמַר ר' יַעֲקֹב, הָרְשָׁעִים שֶׁקִּלְקְלוּ בְּרִית מִילָה שֶׁבָּהֶם, וְחִלְּלוּ שַׁבָּת בְּפַרְהֶסְיָא, וְחִלְּלוּ אֶת הַמּוֹעֲדוֹת, וְשֶׁכָּפְרוּ בַּתּוֹרָה, וְשֶׁכָּפְרוּ בִּתְחִיַּית הַמֵּתִים, וְכַדּוֹמֶה לָהֶם, יוֹרְדִים לַגֵּיהִנֹּם שֶׁלְּמַטָּה, וְנִדּוֹנִים שָׁם וְשׁוּב אֵינָם עוֹלִים.

248. Rabbi Yitzchak said: In keeping with what I have explained, there is a Garden of Eden above and another below; there is a Gehenom below and another above. Rabbi Ya'akov said: The wicked who have defiled their circumcision, desecrated the Shabbat in public, desecrated the festivals, and have rejected the Torah, the resurrection of the dead, and so on, all shall enter Gehenom below. They shall be punished there and shall never rise up again.

249. אֲבָל יָקוּמוּ לְיוֹם הַדִּין, וְיָקוּמוּ לִתְחִיַּית הַמֵּתִים, וַעֲלֵיהֶם נֶאֱמַר וְרַבִּים מִישֵׁנֵי אַדְמַת עָפָר יָקִיצוּ אֵלֶּה לְחַיֵּי עוֹלָם וגו'. וַעֲלֵיהֶם נֶאֱמַר וְהָיוּ דֵרָאוֹן לְכָל בָּשָׂר. מַה דֵרָאוֹן, דַּי רָאוֹן, שֶׁהַכֹּל יֹאמְרוּ דַּי בִּרְאִיָּיתָם, וְעַל הַצַּדִּיקִים שֶׁבְּיִשְׂרָאֵל נֶאֱמַר, וְעַמֵּךְ כֻּלָּם צַדִּיקִים וגו'.

(ע"כ מדרה"נ).

249. But they shall rise on the Day of Judgment and for the resurrection of the dead. They are described by the words: "And many of them that sleep in the dust of the earth shall awake, some to everlasting life, and some to shame and everlasting contempt" (Daniel 12:2). And they are also described by the words, "and they shall be abhorrent to all flesh" (Heb. *dera'on*) (Yeshayah 66:24). What is *dera'on*? *Dai-Ra'on*, WHICH MEANS that all shall say, *Dai* ('enough') - *Ra'on* ('of seeing them') – THEY SHALL HAVE HAD ENOUGH OF SEEING THEM. But of the righteous in Yisrael, it is said: "Your people shall also be all righteous..." (Yeshayah 60:21).

End of Midrash Hane'elam

20. "And Hashem rained upon Sodom"

A Synopsis

The various levels of judgment that occur in Hell are expounded upon by the sages of the Zohar. These judgments were expressed in our physical world during the time of Sodom and Gomorrah and the time of Noah and the flood. The implements of water, fire, and brimstone were used to bring about judgment during these times of intense negativity. The Zohar reveals that the 72 Names of G-d, along with the angels who are connected to each particular sequence of Hebrew Letters that form the 72 Names, were the conduits by which the force of judgment expressed itself in our physical realm.

The Relevance of this Passage

The 72 Names of God is an ancient formula encoded in the Torah passage that tells the story of the parting of the Red Sea. This instrument emits both merciful and judgmental forces into our world. Through this passage of Zohar we arouse the protection and positive aspects from the 72 Names and the corresponding angels, thereby removing negative elements and judgments from our life.

250. וַה׳ הִמְטִיר עַל סְדֹם וְעַל עֲמֹרָה וְגוּ׳, ר׳ חִיָּיא פָּתַח, הִנֵּה יוֹם ה׳ בָּא אַכְזָרִי וְגוּ׳. הִנֵּה יוֹם ה׳ בָּא, דָּא בֵּי דִינָא לְתַתָּא. בָּא: כְּמָה דְאִתְּמָר הַבָּאָה אֵלַי, בְּגִין דְּלָא עָבֵיד דִּינָא, עַד דְעָאל, וְנָטִיל רְשׁוּ, כְּגַוְונָא דָא, קֵץ כָּל בָּשָׂר בָּא לְפָנַי.

250. Next is the verse: "And Hashem rained upon Sodom and upon Gomorrah..." Rabbi Chiya opened the discussion with the verse: "Behold, the day of Hashem comes, cruel both with wrath and fierce anger..." (Yeshayah 13:9) "Behold, the day of Hashem comes" alludes to the earthly Courthouse, WHICH REFERS TO THE JUDGMENTS THAT ISSUE FROM MALCHUT, DURING THE TIME WHEN SHE IS AT THE STAGE OF ILLUMINATION FROM THE LEFT, BEFORE BEING COMBINED WITH THE CENTRAL COLUMN, WHICH IS CALLED THE DECREE OF JUDGMENT. "Comes" is as explained IN REFERENCE TO THE PHRASE, "WHICH HAS COME TO ME," WHICH MEANS THAT SHE ALWAYS COMES AT THE BEGINNING OF EVERY UNION. "Which has come to me" is so because it does not execute Judgment before it enters and receives permission. The same is explained by the verse, "The End of all Flesh has come before Me,"

WHICH MEANS THAT IT CAME TO ASK FOR PERMISSION.

251. דָּבָר אַחֵר הִנֵּה יוֹם ה' בָּא. דָּא הוּא מְחַבְּלָא לְתַתָּא, כַּד נָטִיל נִשְׁמְתָא. בְּגִינֵי כָּךְ אַכְזָרִי, וְעֶבְרָה, לְשׁוּם הָאָרֶץ לְשַׁמָּה. דָּא סְדוֹם וַעֲמוֹרָה, וְחַטָּאֶיהָ יַשְׁמִיד מִמֶּנָּה. אִלֵּין יַתְבֵי אַרְעָא.

251. Another explanation of "Behold, the day of Hashem comes" is that it refers to the Saboteur of Below, NAMELY THE ANGEL OF DEATH, when he takes the soul away. This is why THE VERSE CALLS HIM "cruel both with wrath...to lay the land desolate," ALLUDING TO Sodom and Gomorrah, WHICH WERE THROWN OVER AND DESERTED. The phrase, "and he shall destroy the sinners thereof out of it," REFERS TO those who inhabited that land.

252. מַה כְּתִיב בַּתְרֵיהּ, כִּי כֹכְבֵי הַשָּׁמַיִם וּכְסִילֵיהֶם וגו'. דְּהָא מִן שְׁמַיָּא אַמְטַר עֲלֵיהוֹן אֶשָּׁא, וְאַעֲבַר לוֹן מִן עָלְמָא. לְבָתַר מַה כְּתִיב, אוֹקִיר אֱנוֹשׁ מִפָּז וגו'. דָּא אַבְרָהָם, דְּקוּדְשָׁא בְּרִיךְ הוּא סָלֵיק לֵיהּ, עַל כָּל בְּנֵי עָלְמָא.

252. After this, it is written: "For the stars of heaven and the constellations thereof..." (Yeshayah 13:10) because it was from the heavens that He rained fire down on them and wiped them out of the world. Then, it is written: "I will make men more rare than fine gold..." (Ibid. 12). This is Abraham, whom the Holy One, blessed be He, raised up and cherished more than any other person in the world.

253. ר' יְהוּדָה אוֹקִים לוֹן לְהָנֵי קְרָאֵי בְּיוֹמָא דְּאִתְחָרַב בֵּי מַקְדְּשָׁא, דִּבְהַהוּא יוֹמָא, אִתְחַשְּׁכוּ עִלָּאֵי וְתַתָּאֵי, וְאִתְחַשְּׁכָן שְׁמַיָּא וְכֹכְבַיָּא. ר' אֶלְעָזָר, מוֹקִים לְהָנֵי קְרָאֵי, בְּיוֹמֵי דְּיוֹקִים קוּדְשָׁא בְּרִיךְ הוּא לִכְנֶסֶת יִשְׂרָאֵל מֵעַפְרָא, וְהַהוּא יוֹמָא, יִתְיְדַע לְעֵילָא וְתַתָּא, דִּכְתִיב וְהָיָה יוֹם אֶחָד הוּא יִוָּדַע לַה'. וְהַהוּא יוֹמָא, יוֹמָא דְּנוּקְמָא אִיהוּ, דְּזַמִּין קוּדְשָׁא בְּרִיךְ הוּא לְנַקְמָא מִשְּׁאָר עַמִּין עוֹבְדֵי עכו"ם.

253. Rabbi Yehuda related these verses to the day when the Temple was destroyed. On that day, both the celestial and earthly beings darkened, along with the stars and heavens. Rabbi Elazar explained these verses as follows: The day on which the Holy One, blessed be He, shall raise the Congregation of Yisrael up from the dust, NAMELY AT THE TIME OF REDEMPTION, shall be known on high and down below. As it is written: "But it shall be one day which shall be known to Hashem..." (Zecharyah 14:7). And on that day, the Holy One, blessed be He, shall take revenge on the idol worshippers.

254. וְכַד קוּדְשָׁא בְּרִיךְ הוּא יַעֲבֵיד נוּקְמִין בִּשְׁאָר עַמִּין עעכו"ם, כְּדֵין אוֹקִיר אֱנוֹשׁ מִפָּז. דָּא מַלְכָּא מְשִׁיחָא, דְּיִסְתַּלֵּק וְיִתְיַיקַר עַל כָּל בְּנֵי עָלְמָא, וְכָל בְּנֵי עָלְמָא יִפְלְחוּן וְיִסְגְּדוּן קַמֵּיה, דִּכְתִיב לְפָנָיו יִכְרְעוּ צִיִּים וְגו', מַלְכֵי תַרְשִׁישׁ וְגו'.

254. So when the Holy One, blessed be He, takes revenge on the worshipers of the planets and constellations, it shall be said: "I will make men more rare than fine gold." This is King Messiah, who shall rise up over all peoples of the world and be so honored that all of humanity will bow before him and obey him. This is as it is written: "They that dwell in the wilderness shall bow before him...the kings of Tarshish...shall bring presents..." (Tehilim 72:9-10).

255. תָּא חֲזֵי, אַף עַל גֵּב דִּנְבוּאָה דָא, אִתְּמָר עַל בָּבֶל, בְּכֹלָּא אִתְּמָר. דְּהָא חָמֵינָן בְּהַאי פַּרְשָׁתָא, דִּכְתִיב כִּי יְרַחֵם ה' אֶת יַעֲקֹב. וּכְתִיב וּלְקָחוּם עַמִּים וֶהֱבִיאוּם אֶל מְקוֹמָם.

255. Come and behold: even though this prophecy – REFERRING TO THE VERSES THAT READ "BEHOLD, THE DAY OF HASHEM..." AND "I WILL MAKE MAN..." – was said specifically about Babylon AS WRITTEN, 'THE BURDEN OF BABYLON' (YESHAYAH 13:1), it is said NEVERTHELESS about everything. It is also written in this same passage: "For Hashem will have mercy on Jacob...And the people shall take them, and bring them to their place..." (Yeshayah 14:1-2). IT SEEMS THAT THE SAGES OF THE ZOHAR HAD A DIFFERENT SECTIONING OF THE BIBLE, BECAUSE IN OUR BOOKS, THESE VERSES APPEAR IN THE FOLLOWING CHAPTER.

256. וַה' הִמְטִיר עַל סְדוֹם. דָּא דַּרְגָּא דְּבֵי דִינָא לְתַתָּא, דְּנָטִיל רְשׁוּ מֵעֵילָּא. ר' יִצְחָק אָמַר דַּעֲבֵיד דִּינָא בְּרַחֲמֵי. דִּכְתִיב, מֵאֵת ה' מִן

הַשָּׁמָיִם. בְּגִין לְאִשְׁתַּכְּחָא, דִּינָא בְּרַחֲמֵי, וְאִי תֵּימָא מַאי רַחֲמֵי הָכָא,
דִּכְתִיב, וַיְהִי בְּשַׁחֵת אֱלֹקִים אֶת עָרֵי הַכִּכָּר וַיִּזְכֹּר אֱלֹקִים אֶת אַבְרָהָם
וְגוֹ', וּלְבָתַר נָפְקוּ מִנֵּיהּ תְּרֵין אוּמִין שְׁלֵמִין, וְזָכָה דְּנָפֵיק מִנֵּיהּ דָּוִד
וּשְׁלֹמֹה מַלְכָּא.

256. The phrase, "Then Hashem rained upon Sodom," refers to the level of the earthly Courthouse, which is granted permission from above. Rabbi Yitzchak said that the Judgment was executed with Mercy, as it is written: "from Hashem out of heaven," FOR THE NAME YUD HEI VAV HEI IMPLIES MERCY. This is so that Judgment will be mixed with Mercy. You might ask: What Mercy is there here? HE REPLIES: As it is written: "And it came to pass, when Elohim destroyed the cities of the plain, that Elohim remembered Abraham..." (Beresheet 19:29). And after this, two whole nations issued from LOT. And he had the honor of being the great ancestor of David and King Solomon.

257. חֲמֵי מַה כְּתִיב וַיְהִי כְּהוֹצִיאָם אוֹתָם הַחוּצָה וַיֹּאמֶר וְגוֹ'. תָּא חֲזֵי
בְּשַׁעֲתָא דְּדִינָא שָׁרֵי בְּעָלְמָא, הָא אִתְּמָר דְּלָא לִיבְּעֵי לְבַר נָשׁ
לְאִשְׁתַּכְּחָא בְּשׁוּקָא, בְּגִין דְּכֵיוָן דְּשַׁרְיָא דִּינָא, לָא אַשְׁגַּח בֵּין זַכָּאָה
וְחַיָּיבָא, וְלָא בָּעֵי לְאִשְׁתַּכְּחָא תַּמָּן. וְהָא אִתְּמָר דִּבְגִין כָּךְ אִסְתִּים נֹחַ
בַּתֵּיבָה, וְלָא יַשְׁגַּח בְּעָלְמָא בְּשַׁעֲתָא דְּדִינָא יִתְעֲבֵיד. וּכְתִיב וְאַתֶּם לֹא
תֵצְאוּ אִישׁ מִפֶּתַח בֵּיתוֹ עַד בֹּקֶר. עַד דְּיִתְעֲבֵיד דִּינָא. וּבְגִין כָּךְ וַיֹּאמֶר
הִמָּלֵט עַל נַפְשְׁךָ אַל תַּבִּיט אַחֲרֶיךָ וְגוֹ'.

257. See what is written: "And it came to pass, when they had brought them outside abroad, that he said: ESCAPE FOR YOUR LIFE" (Beresheet 19:17). Come and behold: we have learned that when Judgment hangs over the world, people should not be at the marketplace. This is because when Judgment comes, it does not distinguish between the righteous and the wicked. Therefore, one should not be there. And it has been explained that this is why Noah hid in the ark and did not look upon the world as judgment was executed. And so it is written: "and none of you shall go out of the door of his house until the morning" (Shemot 12:22), THAT IS, until judgment is executed. And this is why it is written: "Escape for your life, look not behind you..."

258. ר' יִצְחָק וְר' יְהוּדָה הֲווֹ אָזְלֵי בְּאָרְחָא. אָמַר ר' יְהוּדָה לְר' יִצְחָק, דִּינָא דַּעֲבֵיד קוּדְשָׁא בְּרִיךְ הוּא בַּמַּבּוּל, וְדִינָא דִּסְדוֹם, תַּרְוַויְיהוּ דִּינִין דְּגֵיהִנֹּם הֲווֹ. בְּגִין דְּחַיָּיבֵי גֵּיהִנֹּם, אִתְדָּנוּ בְּמַיָּא וּבְאֶשָּׁא.

258. As they were walking, Rabbi Yehuda said to Rabbi Yitzchak: The Judgment that the Holy One, blessed be He, executed at the Great Flood and the Judgment of Sodom were both Judgments of Gehenom, because the sinners in Gehenom are punished by water and fire.

259. אָמַר ר' יִצְחָק, סְדוֹם בְּדִינָא דְּגֵיהִנֹּם אִתְדָּן, דִּכְתִיב, וַה' הִמְטִיר עַל סְדוֹם וְעַל עֲמֹרָה גָּפְרִית וָאֵשׁ מֵאֵת ה' מִן הַשָּׁמָיִם. דָּא מִסִּטְרָא דְּמַיָּא וְדָא מִסִּטְרָא דְּאֶשָּׁא. דָּא וְדָא הוּא דִּינָא דְּגֵיהִנֹּם, וְחַיָּיבִין דְּגֵיהִנֹּם בִּתְרֵין דִּינִין אִלֵּין אִתְדָּנוּ.

259. Rabbi Yitzchak responded that Sodom was sentenced by the Judgment of Gehenom, as it is written: "Then Hashem rained upon Sodom and upon Gomorrah brimstone and fire from Hashem out of heaven." One was punished with the aspect of water; the other with the aspect of fire; and both are the punishments of Gehenom. The sinners in Gehenom are punished with both these aspects of Judgment BECAUSE THERE IS THE 'GEHENOM OF SNOW,' WHICH IS WATER, AND THERE IS THE 'GEHENOM OF FIRE.'

260. אָמַר לוֹ, דִּינָא דְּחַיָּיבֵי דְּגֵיהִנֹּם, תְּרֵיסַר יַרְחֵי, וְקוּדְשָׁא בְּרִיךְ הוּא סָלִיק לוֹן מִגֵּיהִנֹּם, וְתַמָּן מִתְלַבְּנִין, וְיָתְבִין לְתַרְעָא דְּגֵיהִנֹּם וְחָמָאן אִינּוּן חַיָּיבִין דְּעָאלִין, וְדָנִין לוֹן תַּמָּן, וְאִינּוּן תָּבְעֵי רַחֲמֵי עֲלַיְיהוּ. וּלְבָתַר, קוּדְשָׁא בְּרִיךְ הוּא חַיֵּיס עֲלַיְיהוּ, וְאָעֵיל לוֹן לְדוּכְתָּא דְּאִצְטְרִיךְ לוֹן. מֵהַהוּא יוֹמָא וּלְהָלְאָה, גּוּפָא אִשְׁתְּכַךְ בְּעַפְרָא, וְנִשְׁמָתָא יַרְתָא אַתְרָהּ כִּדְחָזֵי לָהּ.

260. He said to him: The sinners are sentenced to twelve months in Gehenom, WHERE THEY ARE CLEANSED, THAT IS PURIFIED. LATER, the Holy One, blessed be He, raises them from Gehenom and makes them sit at its gates watching other sinners enter and receive punishment. And they ask for Mercy for them. And after this, the Holy One, blessed be He, is merciful

to them. HE RAISES THEM UP AND AWAY FROM THE GATES OF
GEHENOM, bringing them to the place required for them. From that day
onward, the body rests in the dust while the soul inherits its appropriate
place.

261. תָּא חֲזֵי, דְּהָא אִתְּמָר, דַּאֲפִילוּ אִינּוּן בְּנֵי טוֹפָנָא, לָא אִתְּדָנוּ, אֶלָּא
בְּאֶשָׁא וּמַיָּא. מַיָּיא קְרִירָן נַחֲתֵי מִלְּעֵילָא, וּמַיָּיא רְתִיחָן סַלְּקֵי מִתַּתָּא
כְּאֶשָׁא. וְאִתְּדָנוּ בִּתְרֵי דִּינִין, בְּגִין דְּדִינָא דִּלְעֵילָא, הָכֵי הֲוָה, בְּגִין כָּךְ
בִּסְדוֹם גָּפְרִית וָאֵשׁ.

261. Come and behold: we have learned that even the generation of the
Great Flood was punished with fire and water only. Cold water came down
from above and boiling water from below, FROM THE BOTTOM OF THE
EARTH, as fire. So they were punished by the two Judgments, because the
Judgment of above is executed WITH TWO KINDS OF JUDGMENT: WATER
AND FIIRE. And this is why there was brimstone and fire in Sodom –
BECAUSE THE BRIMSTONE COMES FROM WATER, AS IS KNOWN.

262. אָמַר לוֹ, אִי יְקוּמוּן לְיוֹם דִּינָא, אָמַר לוֹ הָא אִתְּמָר. אֲבָל אִלֵּין
דִּסְדוֹם וַעֲמוֹרָה, לָא יְקוּמוּן, וּקְרָא אוֹכַח, דִּכְתִיב גָּפְרִית וָמֶלַח שְׂרֵפָה
כָל אַרְצָהּ לֹא תִזָּרַע וְלֹא תַצְמִיחַ וְגוֹ'. אֲשֶׁר הָפַךְ ה' בְּאַפּוֹ וּבַחֲמָתוֹ.
אֲשֶׁר הָפַךְ ה': בְּעָלְמָא דֵּין. בְּאַפּוֹ: בְּעָלְמָא דְּאָתֵי. וּבַחֲמָתוֹ: בְּזִמְנָא
דְּזַמִּין קוּדְשָׁא בְּרִיךְ הוּא לַאֲחָיַיא מֵתַיָּיא.

262. He asks him: Will THE PEOPLE OF SODOM rise IN THE FUTURE for
the Day of Judgment? He responded: We have already learned this. Those
PEOPLE of Sodom and Gomorrah will not rise FOR JUDGMENT IN THE
FUTURE DURING THE RESURRECTION OF THE DEAD. This is proven by
the verse: "And that the whole land there is of brimstone, and salt, and
burning...which Hashem overthrew in His anger, and in His wrath"
(Devarim 29:22). "Which Hashem overthrew" means in the present world;
"in His anger" means in the World to Come; and "in His wrath" means at
the time when the Holy One, blessed be He, shall resurrect the dead.

263. אָמַר לוֹ תָּא חֲזֵי, כַּמָּה דְּאַרְעָא דִּלְהוֹן אִתְאֲבֵיד לְעָלַם וּלְעָלְמֵי

עָלְמַיָא, הָכֵי נְמֵי אִתְאֲבִידוּ אִינוּן, לְעָלַם וּלְעָלְמֵי עָלְמַיָא. וְתָא חֲזֵי,
דִּינָא דְּקוּדְשָׁא בְּרִיךְ הוּא, דִּינָא לָקֳבֵל דִּינָא, אִינוּן לָא הֲוָה תַּיְיבִין
נַפְשָׁא דְּמִסְכְּנָא, בְּמֵיכְלָא וּבְמִשְׁתַּיָּא, אוֹף הָכֵי קוּדְשָׁא בְּרִיךְ הוּא לָא
אֲתֵיב לוֹן נַפְשַׁיְיהוּ לְעָלְמָא דְּאָתֵי.

263. He said to him: "Come and behold. Just as their land was destroyed forever, so were they destroyed forever. Behold, the Judgment of the Holy One, blessed be He, is Judgment for Judgment, NAMELY, A JUST RETRIBUTION. Just as they did not revive the soul of the poor with food or with drink, so in the same way, the Holy One, blessed be He, does not give their soul back to them in the World to Come.

264. וְתָא חֲזֵי, אִינוּן אִתְמַנְעוּ מִצְדָקָה, דְּאִקְרֵי חַיִּים, אוֹף קוּדְשָׁא בְּרִיךְ
הוּא, מָנַע מִנַּיְיהוּ חַיִּים, בְּעָלְמָא דֵין, וּבְעָלְמָא דְּאָתֵי. וְכַמָּה דְּאִינוּן
מָנְעוּ אוֹרְחִין וּשְׁבִילִין מִבְּנֵי עָלְמָא, ה״ן קוּדְשָׁא בְּרִיךְ הוּא מָנַע מִנַּיְיהוּ
אוֹרְחִין וּשְׁבִילִין דְּרַחֲמֵי, לְרַחֲמָא עֲלַיְיהוּ בְּעָלְמָא דֵין, וּבְעָלְמָא דְּאָתֵי.

264. Come and behold: they refrained from giving charity, which is called life. Thus, the Holy One, blessed be He, withheld life from them in this world and in the World to Come. And just as they blocked the pathways and routes for other people, so did the Holy One, blessed be He, block the pathways and routes of mercy from them, so that they could not receive Mercy in this world or in the World to Come.

265. ר' אַבָּא אָמַר, כֻּלְּהוּ בְּנֵי עָלְמָא יְקוּמוּן, וִיקוּמוּן לְדִינָא. וַעֲלַיְיהוּ
כְּתִיב וְאֵלֶּה לַחֲרָפוֹת וּלְדֵרְאוֹן עוֹלָם. וְקוּדְשָׁא בְּרִיךְ הוּא מָארֵי דְרַחֲמִין
אִיהוּ, כֵּיוָן דְּדָן לְהוּ בְּהַאי עָלְמָא, וְקַבִּילוּ דִּינָא, לָא אִתְדָּנוּ בְּכֻלְּהוּ
דִּינִין.

265. Rabbi Aba then said: All the people of the world will rise AT THE RESURRECTION OF THE DEAD and be judged. But of THE PEOPLE OF SODOM, it is said: "and some to shame and everlasting contempt" (Daniel 12:2). Yet the Holy One, blessed be He, is merciful. Because He punished them in this world and they accepted His punishment, they shall not be punished in the future with all Judgments, BUT ONLY WITH A FEW OF THEM.

266. אָמַר רַבִּי חִיָּיא כְּתִיב וַיְשַׁלַּח אֶת לוֹט מִתּוֹךְ הַהֲפֵכָה וְגו'. מַהוּ בַּהֲפֹךְ אֶת הֶעָרִים אֲשֶׁר יָשַׁב בָּהֵן לוֹט. אֶלָּא, בְּכֻלְּהוּ עֲבַד דִּיּוּרֵיהּ לוֹט, דִּכְתִיב וְלוֹט יָשַׁב בְּעָרֵי הַכִּכָּר וַיֶּאֱהַל עַד סְדוֹם. וְלָא קַבִּילוּ לֵיהּ, בַּר דְּמֶלֶךְ סְדוֹם קַבִּיל לֵיהּ בִּסְדוֹם, בְּגִינֵיהּ דְּאַבְרָהָם.

266. Rabbi Chiya said that it is written: "and sent Lot out of the midst of the overthrow..." AND HE ASKS: What is MEANT BY "when He overthrew the cities in which Lot dwelt," SINCE HE DWELT ONLY IN ONE OF THEM? AND HE REPLIES: Lot did dwell in all of them. As it is written: "and Lot dwellt in the cities of the plain and pitched his tent toward Sodom" (Beresheet 13:12). But nobody accepted him in Sodom, except for the King of Sodom, for the sake of Abraham, WHO RETURNED HIS PEOPLE AND THE GOODS THAT HE HAD LOST DURING THE WAR OF THE FOUR KINGS.

סִתְרֵי תּוֹרָה

267. תּוֹסֶפְתָּא. קְטוּרֵי רָמָאי, הוֹרְמְנֵי דִּבְדוֹרֵי, חַכִּימִין, בְּסָכְלְתָנוּ יִסְתַּכְּלוּן לְמִנְדַע, בְּשַׁעֲתָא דְּרֵישָׁא חִוְּרָא אַתְקֵין כָּרְסְיָיא, עַל גַּב סָמְכִין דְּאַבְנִין דְּמַרְגְּלִיטָן טָבָן.

Sitrei Torah (Concealed Torah)

267. Tosefta (Addendum). Sublime Connections, NAMELY THOSE RIGHTEOUS PEOPLE WHOSE NEFESH, RUACH AND NESHAMAH ARE CONNECTED AND ATTACHED TO THE GREATNESS OF THE HOLY ONE, BLESSED BE HE: Governors who shatter THE POWERS OF THE OTHER SIDE, the Wise in understanding, look to know. The White Head, NAMELY ARICH ANPIN WHOSE HAIR IS LIKE PURE SHEAF, prepares the Throne, WHICH IS AN ALLUSION TO BINAH, and sets it upon pillars of precious stones and gems – WHICH IS A REFERENCE TO CHESED, GVURAH AND TIFERET OF ZEIR ANPIN AND THE NUKVA, WHICH ARE THE FOUR 'LEGS' OF THE THRONE, WHICH IS BINAH.

268. בֵּין אִינּוּן אַבְנִין, אִית חַד מַרְגְּלִיטָא, שַׁפִּירָא בְּחֵיזוּ, יָאָה בְּרֵיוָא,

קוּמְטְרָא דְּקִיטָרָא, דִּמְלַהֲטָא בְּעֵ' גְּוָונִין, אִינּוּן ע' גְּוָונִין מְלַהֲטָן לְכָל סְטַר.

268. Among these stones, there is a particular gem. THIS IS A REFERENCE TO THE NUKVA OF ZEIR-ANPIN, which is beautiful and glamorous; it is the place where the smoke and fire gather and glow through seventy aspects. THIS REFERS TO THE DECREE OF JUDGMENT, WHICH IS THE ILLUMINATION OF THE LEFT SIDE IN THE NUKVA, BEFORE IT IS INCLUDED WITHIN THE RIGHT. THEN SHE IS A PLACE OF JUDGMENT ACCORDING TO THE SECRET OF A 'BURNING FIRE AND HOT STEAM OF THE FURNACE.' These seventy aspects glow in all directions, THAT IS, TO ALL 'FOUR WINDS' (DIRECTIONS) OF THE WORLD, WHICH ARE NAMED CHOCHMAH, BINAH, TIFERET, AND MALCHUT.

269. אִלֵּין ע', מִתְפָּרְשָׁאן מִגּוֹ ג' גְּוָונִין. אִלֵּין זִיקִין, בְּזִיקִין דִּנְצִיצִין לְד' סִטְרֵי עָלְמָא, הָכָא אִיתָא זִיקָא תַּקִּיפָא, דִּסְטַר שְׂמָאלָא, דְּאִתְאַחֵיד בִּשְׁמַיָא. אִינּוּן גְּוָונִין שַׁבְעִין, דִּינָא יָתֵיב וְסִפְרִין פְּתִיחוּ.

269. These seventy ASPECTS issue from the three colors, WHICH ARE WHITE, RED, AND GREEN, WHILE THE COLOR OF MALCHUT, WHICH IS BLACK, DOES NOT APPEAR THERE. These sparks ARE INCLUDED within the sparks that sparkle in the four directions of the world. A strong spark lies to the left side, which clings to the heavens, NAMELY ZEIR ANPIN. The Judgments that are in these seventy aspects are modified, and the books are open, AS IF TO SAY THAT EVEN THOUGH THE BOOKS IN WHICH THE JUDGMENTS (OR 'SENTENCES') ARE WRITTEN ARE OPEN AND SEEN BY ALL, THE JUDGMENT IS NEVERTHELESS MODIFIED AND DOES NOT EXECUTE ANY PUNISHMENT.

270. מֵהָכָא נָפְקֵי גִּירִין, וְסַיְיפִין, וְרוֹמְחִין, וְאֶשָׁא דְּקוּסְטְרָא. וְאִתְאַחֵיד אֶשָׁא תַּקִּיפָא, דְּנָפְקָא מִשְּׁמַיִם בֵּיהּ, וְכַד אִתְאַחַד אֶשָׁא עִלָּאָה, בְּאִלֵּין דִּלְתַתָּא, לֵית מַאן דְּיָכִיל לְאִתְבַּר רוּגְזָא וְדִינָא.

270. From here the Arrows, Swords, Spears, and the Fire of the Tower go forth. And a strong Fire comes out of the heavens, ZEIR ANPIN clinging to it, NAMELY, TO THE NUKVA. Thus, when the upper Fire, NAMELY THE

JUDGMENTS OF ZEIR ANPIN, clings to the lower Fire, NAMELY THE SEVENTY JUDGMENTS OF THE NUKVA, no one can cancel the wrath and Judgment THAT BELONG TO THE JUDGMENTS OF THE NUKVA.

271. עַיְינִין לַהֲטִין כְּטִיסִין דְּנוּרָא, נְחֵית בְּהוּ לְעָלְמָא. וַוי מַאן דְּאִעְרַע בֵּיה, חֲגִיר חַרְבִין, אִיהוּ חַרְבָּא שְׁנָנָא בִּידֵיה, לָא חָיֵיס עַל טַב וְעַל בִּיש, דְּהָא פְּסָקָא דְּאִינוּן שִׁבְעִין, בִּרְשׁוּ דְּאִתְאַחִיד הַהוּא סִטְרָא דִשְׁמַיָּא, נְחֵית בִּידָא שְׂמָאלָא.

271. ZEIR ANPIN comes down to the world with the eyes glowing like the fiery flames of fire, THAT IS, WITH EYES GLOWING WITH FIRE, ACCORDING TO THE SECRET OF THE VERSE, "I WILL GO DOWN NOW, AND SEE..." Woe to he who shall run into Him when He is armed with Swords. THIS REFERS TO THE JUDGMENTS, WHICH ARE CALLED 'SWORDS.' He has a sharp Sword in His hand and has pity on neither the good nor the bad. The verdict of those seventy COLORS comes down by the left hand, with permission granted by the Unison to which that 'Side of the Heavens' is attached.

272. בְּכַמָּה דִּינִין אִתְהַפֵּךְ, בְּכַמָּה גְּוָונִין הֲפוֹךְ בְּכָל יוֹמָא, אִיהוּ אִקְרֵי כֶּרֶם זֶלֶת, דְּמִתְקָנָא לְגַבֵּי בְּנֵי אָדָם. כָּל גְּוָונִין דִּכְלֵי זַעֲמוֹ דְּקוּדְשָׁא בְּרִיךְ הוּא, בֵּיה אִתְחֲזְיָין. וְאִינוּן יָתְבִין בְּרוּמֵי דְעָלְמָא, וּבְנֵי נָשָׁא בְּסִכְלוּתָא דִּלְהוֹן, לָא מַשְׁגִּיחֵי בְּהוֹן.

272. He changes into many kinds of Judgment. Every day He changes into many colors. THIS MEANS THAT THEY RECEIVE A DIFFERENT SHAPE EACH TIME. It happens when offensive speech is exalted and collected cheaply among the rulers of men. All sorts of Judgments appear in the 'Vessel of Wrath' of the Holy One, blessed be He. And THESE JUDGMENTS remain at the top of the world, while human beings, because of their ignorance, are not aware of them.

273. גָּפְרִית וָאֵשׁ, הַתּוּכָא דְמַיָּא וְאֶשָּׁא, דְּמִתְהַתְּכֵי מִן שְׁמַיָּא אִתְאַחֲדוּ דָא בְּדָא, וְנַחַת עַל סְדוֹם. וַוי לְחַיָּיבַיָא דְּלָא מַשְׁגִּיחִין עַל יְקָרָא דְמָארֵיהוֹן.

273. "Brimstone and fire" REFERS TO the waste of water and fire that have been drawn from the heavens, combined together, and released upon Sodom. Woe to the wicked, who do not pay attention for the glory of their Master.

274. עֲשָׂרָה שְׁמָהָן, גְּלִיפָן בְּהוּרְמְנוּתָא דְמַלְכָּא, עֲשַׂר אִינוּן, וְסָלְקִין לְחוּשְׁבַּן סַגִּי. שִׁבְעִין גְּוָונִין, מְלַהֲטֵי לְכָל סְטַר. נַפְקֵי מִגּוֹ שְׁמָהָן דְּאִתְגְּלִיף רָזָא דְע' שְׁמָהָן דְּמַלְאָכַיָּא. דְּאִינוּן בְּרָזָא דִשְׁמַיָּא.

274. Ten Names are engraved by the King's authority. THE TEN NAMES REFER TO THE TEN SFIROT; there are ten SFIROT, AS EXPLAINED IN SEFER YETZIRAH (THE BOOK OF FORMATION); TEN EXACTLY, NOT NINE OR ELEVEN. NEVERTHELESS, THEY ALSO add up to a greater number, WHICH IS A REFERENCE TO THE 72 NAMES. THIS CAN BE EXPLAINED FURTHER. These seventy colors that glow in all directions derive from these Names, THAT IS, FROM THE 72 NAMES. AND THESE SEVENTY COLORS WERE ENGRAVED and formed into the secret of the seventy Names of the angels, which are the secret of the heavens.

275. וְאִינוּן: מִיכָאֵל, גַּבְרִיאֵל, רְפָאֵל, נוּרִיאֵל. קָמַץ: קְדוּמִיאֵל, מלכיאל, צדקיאל. פַּתָּח: פדאל, תומיאל. חסדיאל. צֵרֵי: צוריאל, רזיאל, יופיאל. סֶגּוֹל: סטוטריה, גזריאל, ותריאל, למאל. חִרְק: חזקיאל, רְהְטִיאֵל, קדשיאל. שְׁבָא: שמעאל, ברכיאל, אהיאל. חֹלָם: חניאל, להדיאל, מחניאל. שֻׁרֶק: שמשיאל, רהביאל, קמשיאל. שֻׁרֶק: שמראל, רהטיאל, קרשיאל.

275. And they are Michael, Gabriel, Raphael, Nuriel. Kamatz (a vowel): Kedumiel, Malkiel, Tzadkiel. Patach (a vowel): Pedael, Tumiel, Chasdiel. Tzere (a vowel): Tzuriel, Raziel, Yofiel. Segol (a vowel): Stuteriyah, Gazriel, Vatriel, Lamael. Chirik (a vowel): Chazkiel, Rehatiel, Kadshiel. Sh'va (a vowel): Shemael, Barchiel, Ahiel. Cholam (a vowel): Chaniel, Lahadiel, Machniel. Shuruk (a vowel): Shamshiel, Rehaviel, Kamshiel. Shuruk (a vowel) called melafum. Shemar'el, Rehatiel, Karshiel.

276. אהניאל. ברקיאל. גדיאל. דומיאל. הדריאל. ודרגזיה. זהריאל.

חניאל. טהריאל. יעזריאל. כרעיאל. למדריאל. מלכיאל. נהריאל.
סניה. ענאל. פתחיאל. צוריאל. קנאל. רמיאל. שעריאל. תבכיאל.

276. Ahaniel, Barkiel, Gadiel, Dumiel, Hadriel, Vadergaziyah, Zahariel, Chaniel, Tahariel, Ya'azriel, Kariel, Lamdiel, Malkiel, Nehariel, Saniyah, Anael, Patchiel, Tzuriel, Kanael, Remiel, Sha'ariel, Tavkiel.

277. תפוריא. שכניאל. רנאל. קמריה. צוריה. פסיסיה. עיריאל.
סמכיאל. נריאל. מדוניה. לסניה. כמסריה. יריאל. טסמסיה. חניאל.
זכריאל. ודריאל. הינאל. דנבאל. גדיאל. בדאל. אדירירון. אדני עַל
כֻּלְהו.

277. Tefuriya, Shachniel, Renael, Kamriyah, Tzuriyah, Psisiyah, Iriel, Samchiel, Neriel, Madoniyah, Lasniyah, Kamsariyah, Yeriel, Tasmasiyah, Chaniel, Zachriel, Vadriel, Hinael, Denabael, Gadiel, Bedael, Adiriron. Adonai is above them all.

278. כַּד מִתְחַבְּרָן כֻּלְהו כַּחֲדָא, בְּרָזָא חֲדָא, בְּחֵילָא עִלָּאָה, כְּדֵין אִקְרֵי
וידוד, כֹּלָּא בִּכְלָלָא חֲדָא. מֵאֵת יי׳ מִן הַשָּׁמַיִם, שְׁמָא קַדִּישָׁא,
דְּאִתְגְּלַף בְּע׳ שְׁמָהָן אָחֲרָנִין, רָזָא דִשְׁמַיָם. וְאִלֵּין אִינוּן שִׁבְעִין,
דְּשָׁלְטִין עַל אִלֵּין ע׳ דִּינִין, רָזָא דְוַיְהו״ה, וְאִלֵּין שִׁבְעִין שְׁמָהָן
בִּקְדוּשָׁה יהו״ה שָׁמַיִם.

278. When they are all joined together as one, in one secret, by the power of the Almighty, NAMELY ZEIR ANPIN, then He is called *Vav*-Yud Hei Vav Hei, WHICH MEANS THAT all are united as one. THIS REFERS TO ZEIR ANPIN AND THE NUKVA TOGETHER WITH THE SEVENTY ANGELS BELOW HER. The phrase, "from Hashem out of heaven" REFERS TO the Holy Name that is engraved with the other seventy Names of the secret of the heavens – WHICH ALLUDE TO ZEIR-ANPIN, WHICH IS THE NAME OF 72 THAT ARE IN THE MOCHIN OF ZEIR-ANPIN, WHILE IN ESSENCE IT INCLUDES SEVENTY. So these are the seventy OF ZEIR ANPIN that control the seventy Judgments OF THE NUKVA THAT GLOW IN ALL DIRECTIONS. They are the secret of *Vav-Yud-Vav-Hei-Hei*. And these seventy names of holiness, NAMELY THE MOCHIN OF ZEIR ANPIN, ARE THE SECRET OF Yud Hei Vav

Hei WITHOUT THE LETTER *VAV*, CALLED the "heavens."

279. אִלֵּין נָטְלִין מֵאִלֵּין, וְידוּד נָטִיל מֵאֵת ידוד, דָּא מִן דָּא. וְאִלֵּין תַּלְיָין מֵאִלֵּין, תַּתָּאִין בְּעִלָּאִין, וְכֹלָּא קְשׁוּרָא חֲדָא. וּבְהַאי קוּדְשָׁא בְּרִיךְ הוּא אִשְׁתְּמוֹדַע בִּיקָרֵיה. שָׁמַיִם דְּאִינוּן ע׳, רָזָא ידוד, דָּא אִיהוּ, בְּרָזָא דְשַׁבְעִין וּתְרֵין שְׁמָהָן, וְאִלֵּין אִינוּן דְּנָפְקֵי מִן וַיִּסַּע, וַיָּבֹא, וַיֵּט.

279. These SEVENTY JUDGMENTS WITHIN THE NUKVA receive from those SEVENTY NAMES OF ZEIR ANPIN. *Vav*-Yud Hei Vav Hei, WHICH INCLUDES SEVENTY JUDGMENTS, receives from Yud Hei Vav Hei, WHICH IS THE SECRET OF THE SEVENTY NAMES WITHIN ZEIR ANPIN, the one from the other. So these are dependent on those, WHICH MEANS THAT the lower beings, WHICH ARE THE SEVENTY JUDGMENTS, ARE DEPENDENT on the upper ones, WHICH ARE THE SEVENTY NAMES OF ZEIR ANPIN. They are all connected together AND THEY ALL SHINE SIMULTANEOUSLY. And thus, the Holy One, blessed be He, appears in His glory. AS WE HAVE STATED the heavens have a numerical value of seventy and the secret of Yud Hei Vav Hei WITHOUT THE LETTER *VAV* is the secret of the 72 names derived from the three verses, "and he went...and he came...and he stretched out," (Shemot 14:19-21) WHICH APPEAR IN THE PORTION OF THE PARTING OF THE RED SEA.

280. וה״ו, יל״י, סי״ט, על״ם, מה״ש, לל״ה, אכ״א, כה״ת, הז״י, אל״ד, לא״ו, הה״ע. חֵלֶק רִאשׁוֹן יז״ל, מב״ה, הר״י, הק״ם, לא״ו, כל״י, לו״ו, פה״ל, נל״ך, יי״י, מל״ה, חה״ו. חֵלֶק שֵׁנִי נת״ה, הא״א, יר״ת, שא״ה, רי״י, או״ם לכ״ב, וש״ר, יח״ו, לה״ח, כו״ק, מנ״ד. חֵלֶק שְׁלִישִׁי אנ״י, חע״ם, רה״ע, יי״ז, הה״ה, מי״ך, וו״ל, יל״ה, סא״ל, ער״י, עש״ל, מי״ה. חֵלֶק רְבִיעִי וה״ו, דנ״י, החַ״ש, עמ״ם, ננ״א, ני״ת, מב״ה, פו״י, נמ״מ, יי״ל, הר״ח, מצ״ר. חֵלֶק חֲמִישִׁי ומ״ב, יה״ה, ענ״ו, מח״י, דמ״ב, מנ״ק, אי״ע, חב״ו, רא״ה, יב״מ, הי״י, מו״ם. חֵלֶק שִׁי: בשכמל״ו

280. *Vav-Hei-Vav, Yud-Lamed-Yud, Samech-Yud-Tet, Ayin-Lamed-Mem, Mem-Hei-Shin, Lamed-Lamed-Hei, Aleph-Caf-Aleph, Caf-Hei-Tav, Hei-Zayin-Yud, Aleph-Lamed-Dalet, Lamed-Aleph-Vav, Hei-Hei-Ayin.*
First part: *Yud-Zayin-Lamed, Mem-Bet-Hei, Hei-Resh-Yud, Hei-Kof-Mem,*

Lamed-Aleph-Vav, Caf-Lamed-Yud, Lamed-Vav-Vav, Pei-Hei-Lamed, Nun-Lamed-Caf, Yud-Yud-Yud, Mem-Lamed-Hei, Chet-Hei-Vav.

Second part: Nun-Tav-Hei, Hei-Aleph-Aleph, Yud-Resh-Tav, Shin-Aleph -Hei, Resh-Yud-Yud, Aleph-Vav-Mem, Lamed-Caf-Bet, Vav-Shin-Resh, Yud-Chet -Vav, Lamed-Hei-Chet, Caf-Vav-Kof, Mem-Nun-Dalet.

Third part: Aleph-Nun-Yud, Chet-Ayin-Mem, Resh-Hei-Ayin, Yud-Yud- Zayin, Hei-Hei-Hei, Mem-Yud-Caf, Vav-Vav-Lamed, Yud-Lamed-Hei, Samech-Aleph -Lamed, Ayin-Resh-Yud, Ayin-Shin-Lamed, Mem-Yud-Hei.

Fouth part: Vav-Hei-Vav, Dalet-Nun-Yud, Hei-Chet-Shin, Ayin-Mem-Mem, Nun-Nun-Aleph, Nun-Yud-Tav, Mem-Bet-Hei, Pei-Vav-Yud, Nun -Mem-Mem, Yud-Yud-Lamed, Hei-Resh-Chet, Mem-Tzadi-Resh.

Fifth part: Vav-Mem-Bet, Yud-Hei-Hei, Ayin-Nun-Vav, Mem-Chet-Yud, Dalet -Mem-Bet, Mem-Nun-Kof, Aleph-Yud-Ayin, Chet-Bet-Vav, Resh-Aleph -Hei, Yud-Bet-Mem, Hei-Yud-Yud, Mem-Vav-Mem.

The sixth part 'Blessed is the Name of His glorious kingdom Forever and ever.

281. וְאִלֵּין אִינוּן שִׁבְעִין שְׁמָהָן, דְּשַׁלְטִין עַל שִׁבְעִין דַּרְגִּין תַּתָּאִין, רָזָא וִידוד. אִלֵּין שִׁבְעִין שְׁמָהָן ידוד, רָזָא דְּאִקְרֵי שָׁמַיִם, שִׁבְעָא רְקִיעִין אִינוּן, דְּסַלְקִין לְשִׁבְעִין שְׁמָהָן, שְׁמָא קַדִּישָׁא, וְדָא אִיהוּ וַידוד הִמְטִיר, מֵאֵת ידוד מִן הַשָּׁמָיִם.

281. And these are the seventy names that control the seventy lower grades, WHICH ARE the secret of Vav-Yud Hei Vav Hei, TOGETHER WITH THE LETTER VAV. And these are the seventy names, WHICH ARE THE SECRET OF Yud Hei Vav Hei WITHOUT THE LETTER VAV, ACCORDING TO the secret of the "heavens," NAMELY ZEIR ANPIN. There are seven firmaments, WHICH CORRESPOND TO THE SEVEN SFIROT OF ZEIR ANPIN THAT ARE CALLED THE "HEAVENS." EACH INCLUDES TEN, THEREBY adding up to the seventy names of the Holy Name YUD HEI VAV HEI. And this IS THE SECRET OF THE VERSES, "And Hashem (Vav-Yud Hei Vav Hei) rained," – WHICH IS THE SECRET OF THE SEVENTY JUDGMENTS OF THE NUKVA, AND "from Hashem out of heaven" – WHICH IS THE SECRET THAT IS CALLED SEVENTY NAMES INCLUDED WITHIN THE HOLY NAME YUD HEI VAV HEI.

282. סִתְרָא דְּסִתְרִין לַחֲכִימִין אִתְמְסַר, שְׁמָא דָּא דְּאִקְרֵי שָׁמַיִם, מִנֵּיהּ אִתְבְּרֵי סִתְרָא, דְּאִקְרֵי אָדָם. חֻשְׁבַּן שַׁיְיפֵי גוּפָא, דְּאִינוּן חוּשְׁבַּן מָאתָן

וְאַרְבְּעִין וּתְמַנְיָא שַׁיְיפִין.

282. A very deep secret was passed on to the wise in relation to this name that is called 'the heavens.' From this secret, the sublime mystery that is called man was created, and the number of a person's body parts is 248.

283. חֻשְׁבַּן אַתְווֹהִי מָאתָן וְשִׁית סְרֵי, שְׁמָא דָא דְּאִיהוּ רָזָא וְסִתְרָא כְּלָלָא דְּכָל אוֹרַיְיתָא, בְּכ"ב אַתְוָון וְעֶשֶׂר אֲמִירָן, בְּגִין דְּהָא שְׁמָא דָא, מָאתָן וְשִׁית סְרֵי אַתְוָון, וּתְלָתִין וּתְרֵין שְׁבִילִין דְּאִתְכְּלִילָן בֵּיהּ, הָא מָאתָן וְאַרְבְּעִין וּתְמַנְיָא שַׁיְיפִין דְּגוּפָא.

283. The number of letters IN THE 72 NAMES adds up to 216. EACH NAME HAS THREE LETTERS; THREE TIMES 72 EQUALS 216. This Name OF THE 72 NAMES is the secret and most sublime mystery; it is the essence of the Torah. And IT IS INCLUDED in the 22 letters and the ten 'Sayings,' THEIR NUMERICAL VALUE IS 32, WHICH IS ALSO THE SECRET OF THE 32 PATHS OF WISDOM. Therefore, this name is composed of 216 letters and 32 pathways, which total 248 together. And these are the 248 parts of the body.

284. רָזָא דְּאִקְרֵי אָדָם, דְּשַׁלִּיט עַל כֻּרְסְיָיא, רָזָא דְּשַׁבְעִין דִּלְתַתָּא, וְסִתְרָא דָא, דִּכְתִיב וְעַל דְּמוּת הַכִּסֵּא דְּמוּת כְּמַרְאֵה אָדָם עָלָיו מִלְמַעְלָה, וְדָא הוּא סִתְרָא דִּכְתִיב וַיְיָ' הִמְטִיר עַל סְדוֹם וְגו'. מֵאֵת יי' מִן הַשָּׁמָיִם. וְכֹלָּא חַד, וּמִלָּה חֲדָא, וְסִתְרָא חֲדָא, לַחֲכִימֵי לִבָּא אִתְמְסַר זַכָּאָה חוּלָקֵהוֹן בְּעָלְמָא דֵין וּבְעָלְמָא דְּאָתֵי.

284. This is the secret OF WHY ZEIR ANPIN IS called 'Man', who rules over the Throne, WHICH IS the secret of the lower seventy, WHICH REFERS TO THE SEVENTY KINDS OF JUDGMENT AND THE SEVENTY ANGELS THAT ISSUE FROM THEM. THESE ARE CALLED THE 'THRONE.' And this is the secret of what is written: "and upon the likeness of the throne was the likeness as the appearance of a man above upon it" (Yechezkel 1:26). THIS IS ZEIR ANPIN, WHO IS CALLED 'MAN'. HE IS ABOVE ON THE THRONE, WHICH IS THE SECRET OF THE NUKVA AND HER SEVENTY KINDS OF JUDGMENT. And this is the secret of what is written: "Then (And) Hashem rained upon Sodom," WHICH ALLUDES TO THE NUKVA AND HER SEVENTY

KINDS OF JUDGMENT, WHICH IS THE SECRET OF THE THRONE. The phrase, "from Hashem out of heaven" REFERS TO THE SECRET OF ZEIR ANPIN, WHO IS ABOVE UPON THE THRONE. And everything belongs to the same issue and the same secret. This has been passed on to those wise men at heart. Happy are they in this world and in the World to Come.

285. סְדוֹם גְּזַר דִּינָא דִּלְהוֹן, עַל דְּמָנְעוּ צְדָקָה מִנַּיְיהוּ, כִּדְבָר אַחֵר וְיַד עָנִי וְאֶבְיוֹן לֹא הֶחֱזִיקָה. וּבְגִין כָּךְ, דִּינָא לָא הֲוָה, אֶלָּא מִן שָׁמַיִם, צְדָקָה וְשָׁמַיִם כֹּלָּא חַד, וּכְתִיב כִּי גָדוֹל מֵעַל שָׁמַיִם חַסְדֶּךָ, וּבְגִין דְּתַלְיָא צְדָקָה בַּשָּׁמַיִם, דִּינָא הוּא מִשָּׁמַיִם, דִּכְתִיב מֵאֵת יי' מִן הַשָּׁמָיִם.

285. As for Sodom, its people were punished because they refrained from giving charity. As it is written: "neither did she strengthen the hand of the poor and needy" (Yechezkel 16:49). And this is why the Judgment upon them came solely from heaven – because "charity" and "heaven" are one. As it is written: "For your kindness is great above the heavens" (Tehilim 108:5), INDICATING THAT "CHARITY" AND "KINDNESS" ARE BOTH DRAWN FROM THE HEAVENS ABOVE. Because charity depends on the heavens, their Judgment is also drawn down from the heavens, as it is written: "from Hashem out of heaven."

286. דִּינָא דְּיִשְׂרָאֵל מֵהַאי אֲתַר, דִּכְתִיב וַיִּגְדַּל עֲוֹן בַּת עַמִּי מֵחַטַּאת סְדוֹם. וְאִקְרֵי יְרוּשְׁלֵם, אֲחוֹת לִסְדוֹם, כִּדְבָר אַחֵר הִנֵּה זֶה הָיָה עֲוֹן סְדוֹם אֲחוֹתֵךְ, וְדִינְהוֹן הֲוָה מִן שְׁמַיָּא, דִּינָא חֲדָא כִּסְדוֹם, עַל דְּמָנְעוּ צְדָקָה מִנַּיְיהוּ. בַּר דְּדָא אִתְהַפָּךְ, וְדָא אִתְחָרַב, דָּא אִית לָהּ תְּקוּמָה, וְדָא לֵית לָהּ תְּקוּמָה (ע"כ ס"ת).

286. The Judgment upon Yisrael comes from that place as well, REFERRING TO THE HEAVENS, as it is written: "For the iniquity of the daughter of my people is greater than the sin of Sodom" (Eichah 4:6), where Jerusalem is called the 'Sister of S'dom'. As it is written: "Behold, this was the iniquity of your sister Sodom" (Yechezkel 16:49). And THIS IS WHY their Judgment came upon them from the heavens – the same Judgment as fell on Sodom –

because they refused to give charity. The only difference is that one was overthrown, NAMELY SODOM, while the other, JERUSALEM, was destroyed. The second shall be reconstructed, REFERRING TO JERUSALEM, while the other, SODOM, shall not.

End of Sitrei Torah

21. "But his wife looked back"

A Synopsis

The Zohar divulges the spiritual significance of a Biblical story about Lot and his wife. In the literal story, Lot's wife is turned into a pillar of salt when she turns to look behind her husband. In reality, she looked into the face of the Angel of Destruction. The Angel of Destruction can only wreak havoc and devastation when we look him in the face.

The Relevance of this Passage

Our five senses restrict us to a narrow, limited view of reality. We journey through life wearing blinders. Consequently, we stumble into negative circumstances that create upheaval and turmoil. We receive assistance from the Creator, enlightening our consciousness to His spiritual direction. This assistance guides and protects us so that we never come face-to-face with destructive entities at anytime in our life.

287. וַתַּבֵּט אִשְׁתּוֹ מֵאַחֲרָיו, מֵאַחֲרֶיהָ מִבָּעֵי לֵיהּ, אֶלָּא מִבָּתַר שְׁכִינְתָּא, ר׳ יוֹסֵי אָמַר, מִבַּתְרֵיהּ דְּלוֹט, דִּמְחַבְּלָא אָזִיל אֲבַתְרֵיהּ, וְכִי אֲבַתְרֵיהּ אָזִיל, וְהָא הוּא שַׁדַּר לֵיהּ, אֶלָּא בְּכָל אֲתַר דַּהֲוָה אָזִיל לוֹט, אִתְעַכַּב מְחַבְּלָא לְחַבְּלָא, וְכָל אֲתַר דְּאָזִיל כְּבַר, וְשָׁבִיק לַאֲחוֹרֵיהּ, הֲוָה מְהַפֵּךְ לֵיהּ מְחַבְּלָא.

287. Of the verse, "But his wife looked back from behind him" (Beresheet 19:26), he asks: Why is it written "from behind him" rather than 'From behind her,' namely, behind the Shechinah. AND Rabbi Yosi replies: "from behind him" MEANS from behind Lot, as the Angel of Destruction went behind him. AND HE ASKS: How could THE ANGEL OF DESTRUCTION have followed behind him after sending him away? AND HE REPLIES: The Angel of Destruction refrained from destroying any place where Lot went. But the Angel of Destruction overthrew the place from which he had departed.

288. וּבְגִין כָּךְ, אָמַר לֵיהּ, אַל תַּבֵּט אַחֲרֶיךָ, דְּהָא אֲנָא אֲחַבֵּל בַּתְרָךְ, וְעַל דָּא כְּתִיב, וַתַּבֵּט אִשְׁתּוֹ מֵאַחֲרָיו. וַחֲמַת מְחַבְּלָא, כְּדֵין וַתְּהִי נְצִיב מֶלַח. דְּהָא בְּכָל זִמְנָא דִּמְחַבְּלָא, לָא חָמֵי אַנְפּוֹי דְּבַר נָשׁ, לָא מְחַבֵּיל

לֵיהּ, כֵּיוָן דְּאִתְתֵּיהּ אַהֲדָרַת אַנְפָּהָא, לְאִסְתַּכְּלָא אֲבַתְרֵיהּ, מִיָּד וַתְּהִי נְצִיב מֶלַח.

288. This is why THE ANGEL OF DESTRUCTION said to him, "Look not behind you," because everything behind you I will destroy. Therefore, it is written: "But his wife looked from behind him," and saw the Angel of Destruction. As a result, "she became a pillar of salt." As long as the Angel of Destruction does not see a person's face, he does not destroy them. But as Lot's wife did turn her face back to look "from behind him," she immediately "became a pillar of salt."

22. "A land in which you shall eat bread without scarceness"

A Synopsis

The power emanating from the Land of Israel is the source of all spiritual energy for the entire world. Whenever we pray, our thoughts and consciousness should be directed towards the Land of Israel so that we connect ourselves to this fountainhead of spiritual nourishment.

The Relevance of this Passage

There are many regions on the planet that emit powerful spiritual forces. These geographical locations are the portals through which the Light of the Upper Worlds enters into the physical dimension. The Land of Israel is the energy centre and source for the entire world and for this reason, it has remained front and center on the world stage for millennia. This passage creates a powerful conduit, connecting our souls to the Land of Israel and ultimately, the Creator, the source of all spiritual nourishment.

289. רַבִּי אֶלְעָזָר וְרַבִּי יוֹסֵי, הֲווֹ קַיְימֵי יוֹמָא חַד, וְעָסְקֵי בְּהַאי קְרָא, אֲמַר רַבִּי אֶלְעָזָר, כְּתִיב אֶרֶץ אֲשֶׁר לֹא בְמִסְכֵּנוּת תֹּאכַל בָּה לֶחֶם לֹא תֶחְסַר כֹּל בָּה. הַאי בָּה בָּה, תְּרֵי זִמְנֵי, אֲמַאי. אֶלָּא הָא אִתְּמָר, דְּקוּדְשָׁא בְּרִיךְ הוּא, פָּלִיג כָּל עַמִּין וְאַרְעָאן לִמְמַנָּן שְׁלִיחָן, וְאַרְעָא דְיִשְׂרָאֵל, לָא שַׁלִּיט בָּה מַלְאָכָא, וְלָא מְמַנָּא אָחֳרָא, אֶלָּא אִיהוּ בִּלְחוֹדוֹי, בְּגִין כָּךְ אָעֵיל לְעַמָּא דְּלָא שַׁלִּיט בְּהוֹ אָחֳרָא, לְאַרְעָא דְּלָא שַׁלִּיט בָּה אָחֳרָא.

289. Rabbi Elazar and Rabbi Yosi were standing one day and discussing this passage. Rabbi Elazar said: It is written, "A land in which (lit. 'which in it') you shall eat bread without scarceness; you shall not lack anything in it..." (Devarim 8:9). Why are the words "in it" repeated twice? It has already been stated that the Holy One, blessed be He, divided all the peoples and the lands according to appointed Messengers. But the land of Yisrael has no angel or Governor controlling it, only THE HOLY ONE, BLESSED BE HE alone. This is why He brought the people over whom no one rules, EXCEPT THE HOLY ONE, BLESSED BE HE, to the land over which no one rules, EXCEPT THE HOLY ONE, BLESSED BE HE.

290. תָּא חֲזֵי, קוּדְשָׁא בְּרִיךְ הוּא, יָהִיב מְזוֹנָא תַּמָּן בְּקַדְמֵיתָא, וּלְבָתַר

לְכָל עָלְמָא. כָּל שְׁאָר עַמִּין עכו״ם בְּמִסְכֵּנוּת, וְאַרְעָא דְּיִשְׂרָאֵל לָאו
הָכֵי, אֶלָּא אֶרֶץ יִשְׂרָאֵל אִתְּזָן בְּקַדְמֵיתָא, וּלְבָתַר כָּל עָלְמָא.

290. Come and behold: the Holy One, blessed be He, supplied THE LAND
OF YISRAEL with provisions and food first, and then to the rest of the world.
So all the other nations that worship planets and constellations "eat in
scarceness," while in the land of Yisrael it is not so – because the land of
Yisrael is nourished first and only then the rest of the world, WHICH FEEDS
ON THE LEFTOVERS.

291. וּבְגִין כָּךְ אֶרֶץ אֲשֶׁר לֹא בְמִסְכֵּנוּת תֹּאכַל בָּהּ לֶחֶם. אֶלָּא בַּעֲתִירוּ,
בִּסְפּוּקָא דְכֹלָּא. תֹּאכַל בָּהּ, וְלָא בַּאֲתַר אָחֳרָא. בָּהּ בִּקְדִישׁוּ דְּאַרְעָא.
בָּהּ שַׁרְיָא מְהֵימְנוּתָא עִלָּאָה. בָּהּ שַׁרְיָא בִּרְכְתָא דִּלְעֵילָא, וְלָא בַּאֲתַר
אָחֳרָא.

291. This is why IT IS WRITTEN: "A land which in it you shall eat bread
without scarceness," in which you shall eat in abundance. Thus, "in it you
shall eat," but only "in it," and not in any other place. Thus, "in it"
ALLUDES TO the holiness of the land; "in it" the supernal Faith resides, "in
it" rests the blessing from above, but only "in it" and in no other place.
HENCE, THE VERSE MENTIONS "IN IT" TWICE, ALLUDING TO ALL THAT IS
DESCRIBED ABOVE.

292. תָּא חֲזֵי כְּתִיב כְּגַן יי׳ כְּאֶרֶץ מִצְרַיִם. עַד הָכָא לָא אִתְיְדַע, גַּן יי׳
אִי הוּא אֶרֶץ מִצְרַיִם, וְאִי אִיהוּ אֶרֶץ סְדוֹם, וְאִי אִיהוּ גַּן יי׳, דְּאִקְרֵי גַּן
עֵדֶן. אֶלָּא, כְּגַן יי׳ דְּאִית בֵּיהּ סְפּוּקָא, וְעֵדוּנָא דְּכֹלָּא, הָכֵי נָמֵי הֲוָה
סְדוֹם, וְהָכֵי נָמֵי מִצְרַיִם. מַה גַּן יי׳, לָא אִצְטְרִיךְ בַּר נָשׁ לְאַשְׁקָאָה לֵיהּ,
אוּף מִצְרַיִם לָא אִצְטְרִיךְ אָחֳרָא לְאַשְׁקָאָה לֵיהּ, בְּגִין דְּנִילוּס אִיהוּ
אַסֵּיק, וְאַשְׁקֵי לְכָל אַרְעָא דְמִצְרַיִם.

292. Come and behold: it is written, "as the garden of Hashem, like the land
of Egypt, AS YOU COME TO TZOAR" (Beresheet 13:10). AND HE ASKS: It is
still not clear FROM THE VERSE if Egypt or Sodom is "as the garden of
Hashem," or if the "garden of Hashem" is the garden that is called the

Garden of Eden? AND HE REPLIES: Actually, THE PHRASE "as the garden of Hashem," WHICH IS THE GARDEN OF EDEN AND which is full of abundance and pleasure for all, refers to Sodom and Egypt. Just as the garden of Hashem did not require irrigation, neither did Egypt, which was irrigated by the river Nile.

293. תָּא חֲזֵי מַה כְּתִיב וְהָיָה אֲשֶׁר לֹא יַעֲלֶה מֵאֵת מִשְׁפְּחוֹת הָאָרֶץ אֶל יְרוּשָׁלֵם וְגוֹ'. דָּא הוּא עוֹנָשָׁא דִּלְהוֹן, דְּאִתְמְנַע מִנְּהוֹן מִטְרָא, מַה כְּתִיב, וְאִם מִשְׁפַּחַת מִצְרַיִם לֹא תַעֲלֶה וְלֹא בָאָה וְגוֹ'. חָמֵי דְּלָא כְּתִיב, וְלֹא עֲלֵיהֶם יִהְיֶה הַגֶּשֶׁם, בְּגִין דְּלָא נָחִית מִטְרָא לְמִצְרַיִם, וְלָא אִצְטַרְכָן לֵיהּ, אֶלָּא עוֹנָשָׁא דִּלְהוֹן מַה הוּא, דִּכְתִיב וְזֹאת תִּהְיֶה הַמַּגֵּפָה אֲשֶׁר יִגּוֹף ה' אֶת כָּל הַגּוֹיִם וְגוֹ'. בְּגִין דְּמִצְרַיִם לָא צְרִיכִין לְמִטְרָא, אוֹף סְדוֹם, מַה כְּתִיב בֵּיהּ, כִּי כֻלָּהּ מַשְׁקֶה, כָּל עֲדוּנִין דְּעָלְמָא הֲווֹ בָהּ, וְעַל דָּא לָא בָעָאן דִּבְנֵי נָשָׁא אָחֲרָנִין יִתְעַדְּנוּן בָּהּ.

293. Come and behold: it is written, "And whosoever does not come up of all the families of the earth to Jerusalem..." (Zecharyah 14:17) – would be punished by having rain withheld. But "if the family of Egypt does not go up, and does not come Jerusalem" (Ibid. 18), it is not written that "upon them shall be no rain," because it usually does not rain in Egypt, and the people there are in no need of it. So what is their punishment? It is as the verse continues, "this shall be the plague, with which Hashem will smite the nations..."(Ibid.), since the Egyptians don't need rain. Sodom, as well, was "well watered everywhere..." (Beresheet 13:10) WHICH MEANS THAT it had all the worldly pleasures and delights. For they did not want any other person to share these delights or receive these pleasures there, THE PEOPLE DID NOT RECEIVE ANY GUESTS.

294. רַבִּי חִיָּיא אֲמַר, אִינּוּן הֲווֹ חַיָּיבִין מִגַּרְמַיְיהוּ, וּמְמוֹנְהוֹן, דְּכָל בַּר נָשׁ דְּאִיהוּ צַר עֵינָא לְגַבֵּי מִסְכֵּנָא, יָאוֹת הוּא דְּלָא יִתְקַיַּים בְּעָלְמָא. וְלֹא עוֹד, אֶלָּא דְּלֵית לֵיהּ חַיִּים לְעָלְמָא דְּאָתֵי. וְכָל מַאן דְּאִיהוּ וַותְרָן לְגַבֵּי מִסְכֵּנָא יָאוֹת הוּא דְּיִתְקַיַּים בְּעָלְמָא, וְיִתְקַיַּים עָלְמָא בְּגִינֵיהּ, וְאִית לֵיהּ חַיִּים וְאוֹרְכָא דְּחַיֵּי לְעָלְמָא דְּאָתֵי.

294. Rabbi Chiya said: THE PEOPLE OF SODOM were wicked because of

themselves and their possessions AND NOT BECAUSE OF THEIR FERTILE LAND. THIS IS TRUE, BECAUSE THEY REFUSED TO GIVE CHARITY. A person who is stingy with the poor is not worthy of continued existence in the world. In addition, he has no life in the World to Come. But whoever is goodhearted towards the needy is worthy of existence in the world, and the world exists because of his merit. He shall have life and longevity in the World to Come.

23. "And Lot went up out of Tzoar"

A Synopsis

There are no coincidences in life. No matter how accidental or random an event may appear to be, there is always an existing and underlying order and root cause. For example, Lot is taken advantage of by his daughters. He gets drunk with wine and his daughters engage in an incestuous relationship with their father. The Zohar explains that the wine corresponds to negative Left Column energy in this specific situation because it was used for immoral purposes. Remarkably, King David's ancestry is rooted in this incestuous relationship, and from the House of King David, will emerge the Messiah. A profound lesson of life is distilled through this controversial chain of events. Kabbalistically, the spiritual and physical worlds are perfectly balanced – the greater the force of negativity, the greater potential for revelation of a positive force. The Messiah is destined to generate the greatest possible spiritual Light in this world and therefore, the Messiah must emerge from the lowest and darkest realm. A union between Lot and his wife cannot be considered darkness, so this relationship could not plant the seed of the Messiah. Incest is considered the lowest and darkest form of union and therefore, it can also be transformed into the highest and brightest form of spiritual Light.

The Relevance of this Passage

The flaming light of a candle holds no genuine value or worth when measured against the brilliant radiance of the sun. Though, in a darkened room, a single flame assumes great importance and significance. We are born into a world of darkness so that our spiritual efforts achieve significance and illumination. Constant striving against our dark side bestows value and worth upon our positive attributes. Awareness and recognition of the importance of confronting our dark side and transforming our negative characteristics into positive attributes, arise through the words and wisdom of these verses.

295. וַיַּעַל לוֹט מִצּוֹעַר וַיֵּשֶׁב בָּהָר הוּא וּשְׁתֵּי בְנוֹתָיו עִמּוֹ וגו'. מַאי טַעְמָא. בְּגִין דְּחָמָא דַּהֲוָה קָרֵיב לִסְדוֹם, וְאִסְתַּלַּק מִתַּמָּן.

295. "And Lot went up out of Tzoar, and dwelt in the mountain and his two daughters with him..." (Beresheet 19:30). HE ASKS: Why DID HE GO UP OUT OF TZOAR? AND HE REPLIES: Because he noticed that Tzoar was close to Sodom. That is why he left there.

296. רַבִּי יִצְחָק פָּתַח וְהוּא מְסִבּוֹת מִתְהַפֵּךְ בְּתַחְבּוּלֹתָו לְפָעֳלָם וגו'. קוּדְשָׁא בְּרִיךְ הוּא, מְסַבֵּב סִבּוּבִין דְּעָלְמָא, וְאַיְיתֵי קוּמְרִין טְהִירִין, לְמֶעְבַּד עוֹבָדוֹי וּלְבָתַר מְהַפֵּךְ לוֹן, וְעָבֵיד לוֹן בְּגַוְונָא אָחֳרָא.

296. Rabbi Yitzchak then began the discussion by quoting: "And it is turned around and about by His councels, that they may do whatsoever He commands them..." (Iyov 37:12). THIS MEANS THAT the Holy One, blessed be He, arranges events in the world and creates destructive lights to accomplish His actions. And afterward, He turns them around again and again in different ways.

297. וּבַמֶּה בְּתַחְבּוּלוֹתָיו, עָבֵיד תַּחְבּוּלִין, וּמְסַבֵּב סִבּוּבִין, לַאֲפָכָא לוֹן, וְלָאו כְּאִינּוּן קַדְמָאֵי. לְפָעֳלָם, בְּגִין פְּעָלָם דִּבְנֵי נָשָׁא, כְּמָה דְּאִינּוּן עָבְדִין עוֹבָדִין, הָכֵי מְהַפֵּךְ לוֹן. כֹּל אֲשֶׁר יְצַוֵּם עַל פְּנֵי תֵבֵל אָרְצָה. בְּגִין דְּעוֹבָדִין דִּבְנֵי נָשָׁא, מְהַפֵּךְ לְאִינּוּן מְסִבּוֹת, בְּכָל מַה דְּאִיהוּ פַּקִיד לוֹן עַל פְּנֵי תֵבֵל וגו'.

297. HE ASKS: And with what DOES HE TURN THEM AROUND? AND HE REPLIES: THIS IS DONE by His councels, THAT IS, THE HOLY ONE, BLESSED BE HE, plans schemes and invents reasons to turn things around, so that they are completely changed and are not similar to what they seemed to be previously. "...that they may do..." refers to the doings of people and the ways in which they accomplish their deeds. This is how He turns things around AND CHANGES THE ACTIVITIES OF THE DESTRUCTIVE LIGHTS. And "whatsoever He commands them upon the face of the world in the earth" MEANS THAT events change because the activities of people change, thereby turning around those same activities that THE HOLY ONE, BLESSED BE HE, commands them to accomplish upon earth. AND THEY ARE CHANGED INTO MANY DIFFERENT FORMS IN THE WORLD, ALL ACCORDING TO THE QUALITY OF THE ACTIVITIES OF THE PEOPLE. WITH THESE WORDS, RABBI YITZCHAK BEGAN THE DISCUSSION TO UNDERSTAND THE ISSUE OF AMON AND MOAB, AND HOW THEY WERE FORMED AS A RESULT OF A CORRUPT ACTION, AND HOW ALL THE KINGS OF JUDAH ISSUED FROM THEM, EVEN KING MESSIAH.

298. רַבִּי אֶלְעָזָר אֲמַר, וְהוּא מְסִבּוֹת מִתְהַפֵּךְ. הַקוּדְשָׁא בְּרִיךְ הוּא

מְסַבֵּב סְבוּבִין, וְאַיְיתֵי, עוֹבָדִין בְּעָלְמָא לְאִתְקַיְימָא, וּלְבָתַר דַּחֲשִׁיבוּ
בְּנֵי נָשָׁא דְּיִתְקַיְימוּן אִינוּן עוֹבָדִין, קוּדְשָׁא בְּרִיךְ הוּא מְהַפֵּךְ לוֹן
לְאִינוּן עוֹבָדִין, מִכְּמָה דַּהֲווֹ בְּקַדְמֵיתָא.

298. Rabbi Elazar said: "And it is turned around and about by His schemes..." This means that the Holy One, blessed be He, guides the course of events and causes certain actions to be performed in the world. As soon as the people are convinced that events are stable, the Holy One, blessed be He, turns them "around and about" and completely changes them again. HERE, RABBI ELAZAR DISAGREES WITH RABBI YITZCHAK'S EXPLANATION THAT IN THE BEGINNING THE ACTIVITIES WERE DISRUPTED BY DESTRUCTIVE LIGHTS, BUT LATER WERE TURNED "AROUND AND ABOUT" AND AMENDED BY THE HOLY ONE, BLESSED BE HE. RABBI ELAZAR EXPLAINS THAT IN THE BEGINNING THEY WERE GOOD AND WORTHY OF EXISTING IN THE WORLD, BUT WERE EVENTUALLY CORRUPTED BY THE DOINGS OF THE PEOPLE. AS A RESULT, THE HOLY ONE, BLESSED BE HE, TURNED THEM "AROUND AND ABOUT" FOR THE BETTER, IF THE PEOPLE REPENT AND ATONE FOR THEIR MISDOINGS.

299. בְּתַחְבּוּלוֹתָיו. בְּתַחְבּוּלָתוֹ כְּתִיב, כְּהַאי אוּמָנָא דְּעָבֵיד מָאנִין
דְּחַרְסָא, בְּעוֹד דְּהַהִיא טִיקְלָא, אִסְתַּחֲרַת קַמֵּיהּ, חָשִׁיב לְמֶעְבַּד כְּגַוְונָא
דָא, עָבֵיד. חָשִׁיב לְמֶעְבַּד כְּגַוְונָא אָחֳרָא, עָבֵיד. מְהַפֵּךְ מָאנָא דָא
לְמָאנָא דָא, בְּגִין דְּהַהוּא טִיקְלָא אִסְתַּחֲרַת קַמֵּיהּ.

299. The word, "by His councels" is spelled without a *Yud*, WHICH INDICATES THE SINGULAR FORM, and could be compared to a potter who shapes vessels from clay. As long as the stone wheel is still revolving, he can fashion the pot according to his taste and even change its shape. This is possible only while the pots are still turning.

300. כָּךְ קוּדְשָׁא בְּרִיךְ הוּא, מְהַפֵּךְ עוֹבָדוֹי, דְּאִיהוּ עָבֵיד. בְּתַחְבּוּלָתוּ
חָסֵר יו״ד, וּמַאן אִיהוּ, דָא בֵּי דִינָא לְתַתָּא, דְּאִיהוּ טַקְלָא, דְּאִסְתַּחֲרַת
קַמֵּיהּ, וְעַל דָּא, מְהַפֵּךְ מָאנִין, מִמָּאנָא דָא, לְמָאנָא אָחֳרָא.

300. Similarly, the Holy One, blessed be He, turns His actions "around and about by His councel(s)," minus the *Yud*, WHICH IS THE SINGULAR FORM.

But what is "HIS COUNCEL?" His councel is the lower court of Judgment, THAT IS, THE NUKVA OF ZEIR ANPIN, which corresponds to the pots of clay turning in front of the potter. And he changes them from one vessels to another.

301. וְכָל דָּא כְּפִי פָּעֲלָם דִּבְנֵי נָשָׁא, אִי מְטִיבִין בְּנֵי נָשָׁא עוֹבָדֵיהוֹן, הַהוּא טַקְלָא דְּסַחֲרָא, אַסְחָרַת לוֹן לְיָמִינָא, וּכְדֵין אִתְעֲבִידוּ עוֹבָדִין בְּעָלְמָא, לְאוֹטָבָא לוֹן כִּדְקָא יָאוֹת. וְטִיקְלָא אַסְחָרַת תָּדִיר, וְלָא שָׁכִיךְ, בְּהַהוּא סִטְרָא דְּיָמִינָא, וְעָלְמָא מִתְגַּלְגְּלָא בֵּיה.

301. And all is done to reflect people's actions. THE HOLY ONE, BLESSED BE HE, CHANGES THE FORM OF THE VESSELS in accordance with the actions of people. If the people perform good deeds, the clay pots revolve to the right, WHICH IS CHESED. If their actions benefit humanity, CHASSADIM AND ALL GOODNESS WILL BE DRAWN DOWN INTO THE WORLD. As long as the stone wheel turns to the right, events will be positive. The world will revolve with it AND RECEIVE THE DOINGS AND ACTIONS FROM THE RIGHT COLUMN, WHICH IS CHESED.

302. אָתוּ בְּנֵי נָשָׁא לְאַבְאָשָׁא תַּחְבּוּלָתוּ, דְּאַסְחַר תָּדִיר, וַהֲוָה קַיְימָא בְּאַסְחָרוּתָא דְּיָמִינָא, קוּדְשָׁא בְּרִיךְ הוּא אַסְחַר לֵיה בְּסִטְרָא דִּשְׂמָאלָא, וּמְהַפֵּךְ מְסִבּוֹת וּמָאנִין, דַּהֲווֹ בְּקַדְמֵיתָא, לְהַהוּא סְטַר שְׂמָאלָא.

302. But, if people intend to sin, then the Holy One, blessed be He will direct "His councel," WHICH IS THE NUKVA that constantly moves and which was revolving to the right, to turn around and revolve to the left. And He turn the objects and the vessels, which were to the right, to the left.

303. וּכְדֵין טַקְלָא אַסְחָרָא, וְאִתְעֲבִידוּ עוֹבָדִין בְּעָלְמָא, לְאַבְאָשָׁא לוֹן לִבְנֵי נָשָׁא. וְטַקְלָא אַסְחַר לְהַהוּא סִטְרָא, עַד דִּבְנֵי נָשָׁא תָּיְיבִין לְאוֹטָבָא עוֹבָדֵיהוֹן. וְטַקְלָא קַיְימָא בְּעוֹבָדִין דִּבְנֵי נָשָׁא. וְעַל דָּא בְּתַחְבּוּלָתוּ לְפָעֳלָם וְלָא קַיְימָא תָּדִיר.

303. As a result, the stone wheels change direction and become actions that will hurt humankind. And these stone wheels keep turning in that direction

– TO THE LEFT – until people perform good deeds again. So the direction in which the stone wheels turn depends on the actions of humankind. THEREFORE, IT IS WRITTEN: "AND IT IS TURNED AROUND AND ABOUT BY HIS COUNCELS THAT THEY MAY DO WHATSOEVER HE COMMANDS THEM," because the "councel," WHICH IS THE SECRET OF THE STONE WHEELS, depends upon the actions OF HUMANKIND. And it never stands still; IT CONSTANTLY REVOLVES EITHER TO THE RIGHT OR TO THE LEFT.

304. תָּא חֲזֵי, קוּדְשָׁא בְּרִיךְ הוּא גָּרַם סְבוּבִין וְעוֹבָדִין בְּעָלְמָא, בְּגִין לְמֶעְבַּד כֹּלָּא כְּדְקָא יָאוּת. וְכֹלָּא נָפְקָא מֵעִקָּרָא וְשָׁרְשָׁא דִּלְעֵילָּא. אַקְרֵיב אַבְרָהָם לְגַבֵּיה, נָפַק מִנֵּיה יִשְׁמָעֵאל, דְּלָא הֲוָה אַבְרָהָם גְּזִיר, כַּד נָפַק מִנֵּיה, בְּגִין דְּאִיהוּ לְתַתָּא, וְלָא אִשְׁתְּלִים בְּאָת קְיָימָא קַדִּישָׁא.

304. Come and behold: the Holy One, blessed be He, has created all the events and actions necessary to accomplish everything properly. And everything comes down AND IS DRAWN INTO THE WORLD from the main source and root above. THE HOLY ONE, BLESSED BE HE, brought Abraham to be close to Him. He then begot Ishmael, who was born before Abraham was circumcised. Thus, Ishmael was born down below and was not perfected by the sign of the Covenant.

305. לְבָתַר קוּדְשָׁא בְּרִיךְ הוּא סַבֵּב סְבוּבִין בְּתַחְבּוּלוֹתָיו, וְאִתְגְּזַר אַבְרָהָם, וְעָאל בַּבְּרִית, וְאִשְׁתְּלִים בִּשְׁמֵיה, וְאִקְרֵי אַבְרָהָם, וְה' עִלָּאָה אַעֲטָרַת לֵיה, בְּרָזָא דְּמַיִם מֵרוּחַ.

305. Later on, the Holy One, blessed be He, guided the course of events by His councel, and Abraham was circumcised and joined the Covenant. His name was completed, and he was called Abraham, WITH THE ADDITION OF THE *Hei*. So the first *Hei* OF THE HOLY NAME, YUD HEI VAV HEI, WHICH IS BINAH, became his crown, according to the secret of deriving water from air.

306. כֵּיוָן דְּרָזָא אִשְׁתְּלִים, וְאִתְגְּזַר, נָפַק מִנֵּיה יִצְחָק, וַהֲוָה זַרְעָא קַדִּישָׁא, וְאִתְקַשַּׁר לְעֵילָּא, בְּרָזָא דְּאֵשׁ מִמַּיִם, וְעַל דָּא כְּתִיב, וְאָנֹכִי נְטַעְתִּיךְ שׂוֹרֵק כֻּלֹּה זֶרַע אֱמֶת. וְלָא אִתְקַשַּׁר בְּהַהוּא סִטְרָא אָחֳרָא.

306. As soon as this secret was perfected and Abraham was circumcised, Isaac was born to him. He was a "Holy Seed" and was attached up above according to the secret of deriving fire from water. And so it is written: "Yet I had planted you a noble vine, wholly a right seed..." (Yirmeyah 2:21). Hence, he was not related to the Other Side, WHICH REFERS TO THE LEFT SIDE ALONE. INSTEAD, HE WAS INCLUDED WITHIN THE RIGHT SIDE.

307. תָּא חֲזֵי, לוֹט נָפְקוּ מִנֵּיה, וּמִבְּנָתֵיה תְּרֵין אוּמִין, מִתְפָּרְשָׁן, וְאִתְקְשָׁרוּ בְּהַהוּא סִטְרָא, דְּאִתְחֲזֵי לוֹן, וְעַל דָּא קוּדְשָׁא בְּרִיךְ הוּא מְסַבֵּב סְבוּבִין, וּמְגַלְגֵּל גִּלְגּוּלִין בְּעָלְמָא, דְּיִתְעֲבֵיד כֹּלָא כִּדְקָא יָאוֹת, וְיִתְקַשַּׁר כֹּלָא בְּאַתְרֵיה.

307. Come and behold: two separate nations came forth from Lot and his daughters, which were attached to the side that was appropriate for them, NAMELY THE OTHER SIDE. This is why the Holy One, blessed be He, manipulates events and turns things around in the world; He wants everything to be well arranged and related to its place IN HOLINESS. THIS MEANS THAT EVERYTHING SHOULD BE CAREFULLY ARRANGED AND PROPERLY PLANNED TO ENSURE THE PROPER ISSUING OF THE KINGS OF JUDAH AND KING MESSIAH. THIS IS THE MEANING OF THE VERSE, "AND IT IS TURNED AROUND AND ABOUT BY HIS COUNCEL(S) THAT THEY MAY DO WHATSOEVER HE COMMANDS THEM."

308. תָּא חֲזֵי, יָאוֹת הֲוָה לְלוֹט, דְּקוּדְשָׁא בְּרִיךְ הוּא יָפֵיק מִנֵּיה וּמֵאִתְּתֵיה, תְּרֵין אוּמִין אִלֵּין, אֶלָּא בְּגִין לְאִתְקַשְׁרָא בְּאַתְרַיְיהוּ, דְּאִתְחֲזֵי לְהוֹ. וְאִתְעֲבִידוּ מִגּוֹ יֵינָא, וְהַהוּא יֵינָא, אִזְדַּמַּן לְהוֹן בְּמְעַרְתָּא, הַהִיא לֵילְיָא, וְדָא הוּא רָזָא דְּאִתְעֲבִידוּ, כְּמָה דְאַתְּ אָמֵר וַיַּשְׁקֵ מִן הַיַּיִן וַיִּשְׁכָּר. וְהָא אִתְּמַר וְאוֹקְמוּה.

308. Come and behold: Lot was worthy of having the Holy One, blessed be He, produce these two nations from his union with his wife. But in order to attach them to their predestined place, HE PRODUCED THEM FROM HIS DAUGHTERS. AND THIS was achieved with the help of wine, AS IT IS WRITTEN: "AND THEY MADE THEIR FATHER DRINK WINE" (BERESHEET 19:33). This wine, which is the secret explanation of their actions, was prepared ESPECIALLY for them and was found on that specific night in the cave. IF THERE HAD BEEN NO WINE, THESE TWO NATIONS WOULD NOT HAVE COME INTO THE WORLD. Therefore, it is written: "And he drank of the wine, and was drunk" (Beresheet 9:21), and this has already been explained.

309. תָּא חֲזֵי, מוֹאָב וְעַמּוֹן, אִינוּן קָרָאן לוֹן שְׁמָהָן, מוֹאָב מֵאָב. ר' יוֹסֵי אָמַר, בְּכִירָה בַּחֲצִיפוּ אָמְרָה, מוֹאָב מֵאַבָּא הוּא. וְהַצְעִירָה גַּם הִיא יָלְדָה בֵן וַתִּקְרָא שְׁמוֹ בֶּן עַמִּי. בִּצְנִיעוּ, אָמְרָה בֶּן עַמִּי, בַּר עַמִּי, וְלָא אָמְרָה מִמָּאן הֲוָה.

309. Come and behold: they called their sons Moab and Amon. SHE CALLED HIM Moab, BECAUSE HE WAS Me-av (lit. 'from father'). Rabbi Yosi said: The elder daughter cried out boldly – Mo-av, he is born from my father! "And the younger daughter also bore a son, whom she called Ben-Ami (lit. 'the son of my people')," in a cryptic way (Beresheet 19:38) but she did not declare who fathered him.

310. תָּא חֲזֵי, בְּקַדְמֵיתָא כְּתִיב, וְלָא יָדַע בְּשִׁכְבָה וּבְקוּמָהּ. בוּא"ו, וְנָקוּד עַל וא"ו, בְּגִין דְּסִיּוּעָא דִּלְעֵילָּא הֲוָה אִשְׁתְּכַח בְּהַהוּא עוֹבָדָא, דְּזַמִּין מַלְכָּא מְשִׁיחָא לְנָפְקָא מִנֵּיהּ, וּבְגִין כָּךְ, אִשְׁתְּלִים הָכָא בוּא"ו. וּבְאַחֲרָא, כְּתִיב וּבְקֻמָהּ חָסֵר וי"ו בְּגִין דְּלָא נְפַק מִינָהּ חוּלְקָא לְקוּדְשָׁא בְּרִיךְ הוּא, כְּהַאי אַחֲרָא, וְעַל דָּא כְּתִיב בְּהַאי אַחֲרָא קַשִׁישָׁא, וּבְקוּמָהּ בוּא"ו מָלֵא, וְנָקוּד עֲלָהּ.

310. Come and behold. Of the elder daughter, it is written: "and he perceived not when she lay down, nor when she arose" (Ibid. 33). The phrase, "when she arose" is spelled with a Vav with a dot above it. This indicates that there was help from above in performing that action, which was to ultimately result in the birth of Messiah. Of the younger daughter, however, it is written: "nor when she arose" (Ibid. 35), without a Vav, because her issue was not for the sake of the Holy One, blessed be He. This is why when writting "when she arose," about the elder sister, there is a dot over the Vav. EVEN THOUGH THE YOUNGER DAUGHTER ALSO PRODUCED KINGS – NAAMAH THE AMMONITE WAS KING SOLOMON'S WIFE AND THE MOTHER OF RECHAV'AM – NEVERTHELSS KING DAVID, CERTAINLY, IS THE MOST IMPORTANT OF ALL, AS HE IS MESSIAH.

311. ר' שִׁמְעוֹן אֲמַר לָא יָדַע, דִּזַמִּין קוּדְשָׁא בְּרִיךְ הוּא לְאוֹקְמָא מִינָהּ, דָּוִד מַלְכָּא וּשְׁלמֹה, וְכָל שְׁאָר מַלְכִין, וּמַלְכָּא מְשִׁיחָא. תּוּ וּבְקוּמָהּ דִּכְתִיב בְּרוּת, וַתָּקָם בְּטֶרֶם יַכִּיר אִישׁ אֶת רֵעֵהוּ וגו'. וּבְהַהוּא יוֹמָא הֲוָה לָהּ קִימָה וַדַּאי אִתְחַבַּר עִמָּהּ בֹּעַז, לְהָקִים שֵׁם הַמֵּת עַל נַחֲלָתוֹ, וְאִתָּקַם מִנָּהּ כָּל הַנֵּי מַלְכִין וְכָל עִלּוּיָא דְיִשְׂרָאֵל. וְלֹא יָדַע בְּשִׁכְבָהּ, דִּכְתִיב וַתִּשְׁכַּב מַרְגְּלוֹתָיו עַד הַבֹּקֶר. וּבְקוּמָהּ, דִּכְתִיב וַתָּקָם בטרום (בְּטֶרֶם) יַכִּיר אִישׁ אֶת רֵעֵהוּ וגו'. בְּגִין כָּךְ וּבְקוּמָהּ נָקוּד וא"ו.

311. Rabbi Shimon then said: THE MEANING OF THE VERSE, "HE PERCEIVED NOT WHEN SHE LAY DOWN, NOR WHEN SHE AROSE" IS THAT he did not know that the Holy One, blessed be He, intended to raise from her King David and KING Solomon, and all the other kings, along with Messiah. Furthermore, THE PHRASE, "when she arose" is ANALOGOUS TO what was said of Rut: "and she rose up before one could discern another" (Rut 3:14). And on that day, she certainly had an issue, because Boaz mated with her to preserve the name of the dead and his lineage. Thus, all these kings and all the noble men in Yisrael were raised through her. ACCORDING TO ANOTHER EXPLANATION, "and he perceived not when she lay down" RESEMBLES THE WORDS, "And she lay at his feet until the morning." It is written: "when she arose" and, "she rose up before one could discern another..." This is WHY "when she arose" IS SPELLED with a *Vav* with a dot above it. THE DIFFERENCE BETWEEN THIS EXPLANATION AND THE FIRST ONE IS THAT HERE HE EXPLAINED THE VERSE, "AND HE PERCEIVED NOT WHEN SHE LAY DOWN" AS WELL. IN THE FIRST EXPLANATION HE DID NOT EXPLAIN THIS VERSE.

312. תָּא חֲזֵי, עִנְוְתָנוּתָא דְאַבְרָהָם, דְּהָא אֲפִילוּ בְּקַדְמֵיתָא, כַּד בָּעָא קוּדְשָׁא בְּרִיךְ הוּא לְמֶעְבַּד דִּינָא בִּסְדוֹם, לָא בָעָא מִנֵּיהּ רַחֲמֵי עַל לוֹט, לְבָתַר דִּכְתִיב, וַיַּרְא וְהִנֵּה עָלָה קִיטֹר הָאָרֶץ כְּקִיטֹר הַכִּבְשָׁן. לָא תָבַע עֲלֵיהּ דְּלוֹט, וְלָא אֲמַר עֲלֵיהּ לְקוּדְשָׁא בְּרִיךְ הוּא כְּלוּם, אוּף הָכֵי קוּדְשָׁא בְּרִיךְ הוּא, לָא אֲמַר לֵיהּ מִדֵּי, בְּגִין דְּלָא יַחֲשֵׁב אַבְרָהָם דְּקוּדְשָׁא בְּרִיךְ הוּא גָּרַע מִזְּכוּתֵיהּ כְּלוּם.

312. Come and behold: see how modest Abraham was. From the beginning,

when the Holy One, blessed be He, determined to execute His Judgment on Sodom, ABRAHAM PLEADED FOR MERCY, BUT he did not plead for Mercy for Lot. Later, when it is written: "and, lo, the smoke of the country went up as the smoke of a furnace" (Beresheet 19:28), Abraham still did not intercede for Lot and said nothing to the Holy One, blessed be He, in Lot's favor. And the Holy One, blessed be He, did not mention anything to him, so that Abraham would not think that the Holy One, blessed be He, had drawn on Avraham's merits BECAUSE OF THAT.

313. וְאִי תֵימָא, דְּאַבְרָהָם לָא הֲוָה חָשִׁיב לֵיהּ לְלוֹט בְּלִבֵּיהּ כְּלוּם, הָא מְסַר נַפְשֵׁיהּ, לְמֵיהַךְ לְאַגָּחָא קְרָבָא, בַּחֲמִשָּׁה מַלְכִין תַּקִּיפִין, כד"א וַיִּשְׁמַע אַבְרָם כִּי נִשְׁבָּה אָחִיו וגו'. וּכְתִיב וַיֵּחָלֵק עֲלֵיהֶם לַיְלָה. וּכְתִיב וַיָּשֶׁב אֵת כָּל הָרְכֻשׁ וְגַם אֶת לוֹט אָחִיו וּרְכֻשׁוֹ הֵשִׁיב וגו'. אֲבָל בִּרְחִימוּתָא דִּרְחִים לְקוּדְשָׁא בְּרִיךְ הוּא, וְחָמָא עוֹבָדוֹי דְּלוֹט, דְּלָא כַשְׁרָן כִּדְקָא יָאוֹת, לָא בָּעָא אַבְרָהָם, דְּבְגִינֵיהּ יִשְׁבּוֹק קוּדְשָׁא בְּרִיךְ הוּא כְּלוּם מִדִּילֵיהּ, וּבְגִינֵי כָּךְ, לָא תָּבַע עֲלֵיהּ רַחֲמֵי, לָא בְּקַדְמֵיתָא וְלָא בְּסוֹפָא.

313. We know that Abraham cared about Lot because Abraham risked his life for Lot by waging war against four powerful kings. As it is written: "And when Abram heard that his brother was taken captive...And he divided himself against them...by night...And he brought back all the goods, and also brought back his brother Lot, and his possessions" (Beresheet 14:14-16). However, because of AVRAHAM'S love for the Holy One, blessed be He, and because he knew of Lot's misconduct, he did not ask that the Holy One, blessed be He, overlook Lot's actions. Thus, he did not plead for Mercy on Lot's account – neither in the beginning, nor in the end.

A Synopsis

Beginning with paragraph 314 and onward, we find what is known as *midrash hane'elam* – "hidden explanations." These hidden explanations of the Zohar appear primarily in the first few sections of *Genesis*. This particular section explains that the story of Lot and his daughters is a parable referring to man and his Evil Inclination. The Zohar explains how the Evil Inclination always catches us and how we can protect ourselves from it.

מִדְרָשׁ הַנֶּעֱלָם

314. וַיַּעַל לוֹט מִצּוֹעַר וגו'. אָמַר רַבִּי אַבָּהוּ, בֹּא וּרְאֵה מַה כְּתִיב בַּיֵּצֶר הָרָע, תֵּדַע לְךָ, שֶׁאֵינוֹ מִתְבַּטֵּל לְעוֹלָם מִבְּנֵי אָדָם, עַד אוֹתוֹ זְמָן, דִּכְתִיב וַהֲסִרֹתִי אֶת לֵב הָאֶבֶן וגו'. שֶׁאַף עַל פִּי שֶׁרוֹאֶה בְּנֵי אָדָם נִדּוֹנִין בַּגֵּיהִנֹּם, הוּא בָּא וְחוֹזֵר לוֹ אֵצֶל בְּנֵי אָדָם, הֲדָא הוּא דִכְתִיב וַיַּעַל לוֹט מִצּוֹעַר. מִצַּעֲרָה שֶׁל גֵּיהִנֹּם, מִשָּׁם עוֹלֶה לְפַתּוֹת בְּנֵי אָדָם.

Midrash Hane'elam (Homiletical interpretations on the obscure)

314. "And Lot went up out of Tzoar." Rabbi Avahu said: Behold what is written about the Evil Inclination. You should know that it will always exist in human beings until that time, of which it is written: "and I will take away the stony heart out of your flesh" (Yechezkel 36:26). And even though it sees human beings punished in Gehenom, it returns again in people. This is as it is written: "And Lot went up out of Tzoar," that is, out of the agony (Heb. *tza'ar*) of Gehenom. From there, he goes up to seduce people.

315. אָמַר רַבִּי יְהוּדָה, שָׁלֹשׁ הַנְהָגוֹת, יֵשׁ בָּאָדָם: הַנְהָגַת הַשֵּׂכֶל וְהַחָכְמָה, וְזוֹ הִיא כֹּחַ הַנְּשָׁמָה הַקְּדוֹשָׁה. וְהַנְהָגַת הַתַּאֲוָה, שֶׁהִיא מִתְאַוָּה בְּכָל תַּאֲוֹת רָעוֹת, וְזֶהוּ כֹּחַ הַתַּאֲוָה. וְהַהַנְהָגָה, הַמַּנְהֶגֶת לִבְנֵי אָדָם, וּמְחַזֶּקֶת הַגּוּף, וְהִיא נִקְרֵאת נֶפֶשׁ הַגּוּף. אָמַר רַב דִּימֵי, זֶהוּ כֹּחַ הַמַּחֲזִיק.

315. Rabbi Yehuda said: There are three directing powers in people. One is the directing power of the mind and wisdom, which is the power of the Holy Neshamah. Next is the directing power of lust, which craves all kinds of evil desires. And finally, the directing power that controls human beings in their behavior and strengthens the body. This is called the Nefesh of the body, of which Rabbi Dimi said: This is the Maintaining Power.

316. אָמַר רַבִּי יְהוּדָה, בֹּא וּרְאֵה, לְעוֹלָם אֵין יֵצֶר הָרָע שׁוֹלֵט, אֶלָּא בְּאֵלּוּ ב' כֹּחוֹת אִלֵּין דַּאֲמָרָן: נֶפֶשׁ הַמִּתְאַוָּה, הִיא הָרוֹדֶפֶת אַחַר יֵצֶר הָרָע לְעוֹלָם, מַשְׁמַע, דִּכְתִיב וַתֹּאמֶר הַבְּכִירָה אֶל הַצְּעִירָה אָבִינוּ זָקֵן.

נֶפֶשׁ הַמִּתְאַוָּה, הִיא מְעוֹרֶרֶת אֶת הָאַחֶרֶת, וּמְפַתָּה אוֹתָהּ, עִם הַגּוּף, לְהִדָּבֵק בַּיֵּצֶר הָרָע, וְהִיא אוֹמֶרֶת, לְכָה נַשְׁקֶה אֶת אָבִינוּ יַיִן וְנִשְׁכְּבָה עִמּוֹ. מַה יֵּשׁ לָנוּ בָּעוֹלָם הַבָּא, נֵלֵךְ וְנִרְדּוֹף אַחַר יֵצֶר הָרָע, וְאַחַר תְּשׁוּקַת חֶמְדַּת הָעוֹלָם הַזֶּה, וּמַה עוֹשׂוֹת, שֶׁתֵּיהֶן מַסְכִּימוֹת לְהִדָּבֵק בּוֹ, מַה כְּתִיב וַתַּשְׁקֶיןָ אֶת אֲבִיהֶן יַיִן. מִתְפַּטְּמוֹת, לְהִתְעוֹרֵר לַיֵּצֶר הָרָע, בַּאֲכִילָה וּבִשְׁתִיָּה.

316. Rabbi Yehuda said: Come and behold. The Evil Inclination has control over the last two powers. The lusting Nefesh always follows the Evil Inclination. We learn this from what is written: "And the firstborn said to the younger, Our father is old..." (Beresheet 19:31) The lusting Nefesh arouses the other and seduces it through the body to cleave to the Evil Inclination. And it says: "Come, let us make our father drink wine, and we will lie with him." What is for us in in the World to Come? Let us pursue the Evil Inclination and the lustful pleasures of this world. So what did they do? They agreed to cling to it. Thus, it is written: "And they made their father drink wine." They feed ravenously in order to arouse themselves and reach the Evil Inclination through food and drink.

317. וַתָּקָם הַבְּכִירָה וַתִּשְׁכַּב אֶת אָבִיהָ. כְּשֶׁאָדָם שׁוֹכֵב עַל מִטָּתוֹ בַּלַּיְלָה, נֶפֶשׁ הַמִּתְאַוָּה הִיא הַמְעוֹרֶרֶת לַיֵּצֶר הָרָע, וּמְהַרְהֶרֶת בּוֹ, וְהוּא דָבֵק בְּכָל הִרְהוּר רָע, עַד שֶׁמִּתְעַבֶּרֶת מְעַט שֶׁמֵּבִיא בְּלֵב הָאָדָם, אוֹתָהּ הַמַּחֲשָׁבָה הָרָעָה, וּדְבֵקָה בּוֹ, וַעֲדַיִין יֵשׁ בְּלִבּוֹ, וְלֹא נִגְמַר לַעֲשׂוֹתָהּ, עַד שֶׁזֹּאת הַתַּאֲוָה, מְעוֹרֶרֶת לְכֹח הַגּוּף כְּמִתְּחִלָּה, לְהִדָּבֵק בַּיֵּצֶר הָרָע, וְאָז הוּא תַּשְׁלוּם הָרָעָה, הַהַ״ד וַתַּהֲרֶיןָ שְׁתֵּי בְנוֹת לוֹט מֵאֲבִיהֶן.

317. "...and the firstborn went in, and lay with her father" (Ibid. 33). When a person lies in bed at night, the lusting Nefesh arouses the Evil Inclination. It clings to it until he cling to every evil thought, and it conceives a little, which brings that evil thought into the heart of man. And it clings to it and remains in the heart without being fulfilled, until that lustful desire arouses the power of the body, as it did at first, to cling to the Evil Inclination. And then evil is achieved, as it is written: "Thus were both the daughters of Lot with child by their father" (Ibid. 36).

318. אָמַר רַבִּי יִצְחָק, מֵעוֹלָם אֵין יֵצֶר הָרָע מִתְפַּתֶּה, אֶלָּא בַּאֲכִילָה וּשְׁתִיָּה, וּמִתּוֹךְ שִׂמְחַת הַיַּיִן, אָז שׁוֹלֵט בָּאָדָם. בַּצַּדִּיק, מַה כְּתִיב בֵּיהּ, צַדִּיק אֹכֵל לְשֹׂבַע נַפְשׁוֹ. וְאֵינוּ מִשְׁתַּכֵּר לְעוֹלָם, דְּאָמַר רַבִּי יְהוּדָה, הַאי צוּרְבָּא מֵרַבָּנָן, דְּמַרְוֵי, קָרֵינָא עֲלֵיהּ, נֶזֶם זָהָב בְּאַף חֲזִיר. וְלֹא עוֹד, אֶלָּא שֶׁמְּחַלֵּל שֵׁם שָׁמַיִם. מִנְהַג הָרְשָׁעִים מַהוּ, וְהִנֵּה שָׂשׂוֹן וְשִׂמְחָה. הַיַּיִן אָז שׁוֹלֵט בָּאָדָם, הָרֹג בָּקָר וְשָׁחֹט צֹאן וְגוֹ'. עֲלֵיהֶם אָמַר הַכָּתוּב הוֹי מַשְׁכִּימֵי בַבֹּקֶר שֵׁכָר יִרְדֹּפוּ וְגוֹ'. כְּדֵי לְעוֹרֵר לַיֵּצֶר הָרָע, שֶׁאֵין יֵצֶר הָרָע מִתְעוֹרֵר אֶלָּא מִתּוֹךְ הַיַּיִן, הֲדָא הוּא דִכְתִיב וַתַּשְׁקֶיןָ אֶת אֲבִיהֶן יַיִן.

318. Rabbi Yitzchak said: The Evil Inclination can be seduced only by eating and drinking, and by the merriment of wine. Then it controls humankind. As for the righteous, what is written of him? It is written: "The righteous eats to the satisfying of his soul" (Mishlei 13:25), and never becomes drunk. As Rabbi Yehuda said: A Torah scholar who gets drunk is described as "A jewel of gold in a swine's snout" (Mishlei 11:22). And as well as that, he desecrates the Celestial Name. How do sinners behave? It is written: "And behold joy and gladness..." (Yeshayah 22:13). At this stage, wine takes over a person, "slaying oxen, and killing sheep, eating flesh and drinking wine" (Ibid.). Of them the Scriptures say: "Woe to them that rise up early in the morning, that they may follow strong drink..." (Yeshayah 5:11) to arouse the Evil Inclination, as this inclination is not aroused without wine. Therefore, it is written: "And they made their father drink wine."

319. אָמַר רַבִּי אַבָּהוּ, מַה כְּתִיב וְלֹא יָדַע בְּשִׁכְבָהּ וּבְקוּמָהּ. כְּלוֹמַר, יֵצֶר הָרָע אֵינוּ מַשְׁגִּיחַ בָּהּ, בְּשִׁכְבָהּ בָּעוֹלָם הַזֶּה, וּבְקוּמָהּ לָעוֹלָם הַבָּא, אֶלָּא מִתְעוֹרֵר עִם כֹּחַ הַגּוּף, לַעֲבוֹד תַּאֲוָתוֹ בָּעוֹלָם הַזֶּה. דְּאָמַר ר' אַבָּהוּ, בְּשָׁעָה שֶׁנִּכְנָסִין הָרְשָׁעִים בַּגֵּיהִנֹּם, מַכְנִיסִים לַיֵּצֶר הָרָע, לִרְאוֹת בָּהֶן, הֲדָא הוּא דִכְתִיב, וְלוֹט בָּא צֹעֲרָה, לְצַעֲרָה שֶׁל גֵּיהִנֹּם, וּנְפַק לֵיהּ מִתַּמָּן, לְנַסוּתָא לִבְרִיָּיתָא, כִּדְקָאַמְרָן. הֲדָא הוּא דִכְתִיב, וַיַּעַל לוֹט מִצּוֹעַר, מִצַּעֲרָה שֶׁל גֵּיהִנֹּם.

319. Rabbi Avahu then said: It is written that, "he perceived not when she

lay down, nor when she arose." This means that the Evil Inclination is not aware of its lying down in this world, nor of its rising up to the World to Come. It is aroused through the power of the body to accomplish its lustful desires in this world. As Rabbi Avahu said: When the sinners enter into Gehenom, the Evil Inclination is brought there to see them. As it is written: "when Lot entered into Tzoar (Heb. *tza'ar*, 'agony')" (Beresheet 19:23), that is, into the agony of Gehenom. And from there it rises to seduce people. Therefore, it is written: "And Lot went up out of Tzoar," out of the agony of Gehenom.

320. וַיֵּשֶׁב בָּהָר, אָמַר ר' יִצְחָק, מַשְׁמַע דִּכְתִיב בָּהָר, מְלַמֵּד שֶׁהוּא שָׁם מוֹשָׁבוֹ, בִּמְקוֹם הָר, גּוּף שֶׁהוּא חָרֵב כָּהָר, דְּלֵית בֵּיהּ טִיבוּתָא, וּב' בְּנוֹתָיו עִמּוֹ. אֵלּוּ הַב' כֹּחוֹת, דַּאֲמָרָן. כִּי יָרֵא לָשֶׁבֶת בְּצוֹעַר, יִרְאָה וַחֲרָדָה נוֹפֶלֶת עָלָיו בְּשָׁעָה שֶׁרוֹאֶה צַעַר גֵּיהִנֹּם, שֶׁמְּצַעֲרִין לָרְשָׁעִים, וְחוֹשֵׁב שֶׁשָּׁם יִדּוֹן, כֵּיוָן שֶׁרוֹאֶה שֶׁאֵינוֹ נִדּוֹן שָׁם, יוֹצֵא וְהוֹלֵךְ לְפַתּוֹת בְּנֵי אָדָם אַחֲרָיו.

320. "...and dwelt in the mountain..." (Ibid. 30) Rabbi Yitzchak said: What we learn from the words, "in the mountain" is that this is the dwelling place of Lot and his two daughters, who are the two forces mentioned before. In the mountain means in the body, which is as wasted as a mountain that has no goodness in it. Because "he feared to dwell in Tzoar" (Ibid. 30), fear and anxiety overtook him, as he saw the agony of Gehenom and the misery of the wicked. And it thinks it will be punished there. However, as soon as it realizes that it shall not be punished there, the Evil Inclination goes out and seeks to seduce human beings to follow it.

321. רַב הוּנָא כַּד הֲוָה דָּרִישׁ, לְאַזְדַּהֲרָא לִבְנֵי אָדָם, הֲוָה אֲמַר לְהוּ, בָּנַי, אִסְתַּמָּרוּ מִשְׁלִיחָא שֶׁל גֵּיהִנֹּם, וּמַאן הוּא, זֶהוּ יֵצֶר הָרָע, שֶׁהוּא שָׁלִיחַ שֶׁל גֵּיהִנֹּם.

321. Rabbi Huna discussed this subject in an effort to warn people. He would say to them: My children, beware of the 'messenger from Gehenom'. And who is this messenger? It is the Evil Inclination, which is the 'messenger from Gehenom'.

322. רַבִּי אַבָּא אָמַר, מַאי דִּכְתִיב לַעֲלוּקָה שְׁתֵּי בָנוֹת הַב הַב. אֵלּוּ

שְׁתֵּי בְנוֹת לוֹט דַּאֲמָרָן, שֶׁהִיא נֶפֶשׁ הַמִּתְאַוָּה, וְנֶפֶשׁ הַמִּשְׁתַּתֶּפֶת בַּגּוּף, הָרוֹדֶפֶת אַחַר יֵצֶר הָרָע לְעוֹלָם. אָמַר ר' יְהוֹשֻׁעַ, כְּתִיב הָכָא בְּלוֹט, כִּי יָרֵא לָשֶׁבֶת בְּצוֹעַר, וּכְתִיב הָתָם לַעֲלוּקָה שְׁתֵּי בָנוֹת הַב הַב. יָרֵ"א בְּגִימַטְרִיָּא הוּא עֲלוּקָ"ה. אָמַר ר' יִצְחָק, אִי יָרֵא הוּא, לְמַאי אָתֵי לְמִטְעֵי בְּרִיָּיתָא, אֶלָּא כָּךְ כָּל עוֹשֵׂה עַוְלָה, כְּשֶׁרוֹאֶה הָרָע, מִתְיָרֵא לְפִי שָׁעָה, מִיָּד חוֹזֵר לְרִשְׁעָתוֹ, וְאֵינוֹ חוֹשֵׁשׁ לִכְלוּם, כָּךְ יֵצֶר הָרָע, בְּשָׁעָה שֶׁרוֹאֶה דִּין בָּרְשָׁעִים, יָרֵא, כֵּיוָן שֶׁיּוֹצֵא לַחוּץ, אֵינוֹ חוֹשֵׁשׁ כְּלוּם.

322. Rabbi Aba then asks: Why is it written, "The leech has two daughters, crying: Give, give" (Mishlei 30:15)? These refer to the two daughters of Lot, who correspond to the lusting Nefesh and the Nefesh that takes part in the body and constantly pursues the Evil Inclination. Rabbi Yehoshua said: About Lot, it is written, "he feared to dwell in Tzoar." It is also written there that "the leech has two daughters, crying: Give, give." The numerical value of 'feared' equals that of 'leech.' Rabbi Yitzchak said: If he was afraid, why then does the Evil Inclination come to misguide people? But, this is indeed the way of the wicked. When he sees evil, his fear lasts only a moment. He then immediately returns to his wicked ways and fears nothing. Similarly, when the Evil Inclination sees the wicked being punished, it is afraid. But as soon as it leaves, it fears nothing."

323. רַבִּי אַבָּא אָמַר, מַ"ד וַתֹּאמֶר הַבְּכִירָה אֶל הַצְּעִירָה אָבִינוּ זָקֵן. מַאי אָבִינוּ זָקֵן. זֶהוּ יֵצֶר הָרָע, שֶׁנִּקְרָא זָקֵן, שֶׁנֶּאֱמַר זָקֵן וּכְסִיל. שֶׁהוּא זָקֵן, שֶׁנּוֹלַד עִם הָאָדָם, דִּתְנִינָן, אָמַר רַבִּי יְהוּדָה אָמַר רַבִּי יוֹסֵי, אוֹתָהּ נֶפֶשׁ הַמִּתְאַוָּה, אוֹמֶרֶת לָאַחֶרֶת, אָבִינוּ זָקֵן, נִרְדּוֹף אַחֲרָיו, וְנִדְבַּק בּוֹ, כִּשְׁאָר כָּל הָרְשָׁעִים שֶׁבָּעוֹלָם. וְאִישׁ אֵין בָּאָרֶץ לָבֹא עָלֵינוּ, אֵין אִישׁ צַדִּיק בָּאָרֶץ, וְאֵין אִישׁ שַׁלִּיט עַל יִצְרוֹ, הַרְבֵּה רְשָׁעִים בָּאָרֶץ, לֵית אֲנַן בִּלְחוֹדָנָא חַיָּיבִין, נַעֲשֶׂה כְּדֶרֶךְ כָּל הָאָרֶץ, שֶׁהֵם חַיָּיבִים, שֶׁעַד הַיּוֹם דֶּרֶךְ כָּל הָאָרֶץ הוּא. לְכָה נַשְׁקֶה אֶת אָבִינוּ יַיִן, נִשְׂמַח בָּעוֹלָם הַזֶּה, נֹאכַל וְנִשְׁתֶּה, וְנִרְוֶה חַמְרָא, וְנִדְבַּק בְּאָבִינוּ, בְּיצָה"ר, וְנִשְׁכְּבָה עִמּוֹ. וְרוּחַ הַקֹּדֶשׁ צֹוַוחַת וְאוֹמֶרֶת, גַּם אֵלֶּה בַּיַּיִן שָׁגוּ וּבַשֵּׁכָר תָּעוּ.

323. Rabbi Aba said: In reference to the verse, "And the firstborn said to the younger, Our father is old..." what is "our father is old"? This alludes to the Evil Inclination, that is called 'old', as it is written: "an old and foolish king" (Kohelet 4:13). It is old because it is born together with person. As we have learned, Rabbi Yehuda said: Rabbi Yosi said that the lusting Nefesh says to the other one – Our father is old, so let us follow him and cling to him, like all the other wicked people in the world. "...and there is not a man in the earth to come to us" means that there is no righteous person upon earth, and there is no one who has control over his lustful desires. So there are many sinners in the world and we therefore will not be the only guilty ones. Let us do as all the people on earth do – let us sin, since until now this is the way all people on earth conduct themselves. "Let us make our father drink wine," let us be happy in this world by eating and drinking and getting drunk. We will then cling to our "father," namely the Evil Inclination, and "we will lie with him." And the Holy Spirit cries out loud and says: "But they also have erred through wine and through strong drink are out of the way..." (Yeshayah 28:7)

324. אָמַר רַבִּי יְהוּדָה, תָּא חֲזֵי, מַה כְּתִיב, וַתַּשְׁקֶיןָ אֶת אֲבִיהֶן יָיִן. דֶּרֶךְ הָרְשָׁעִים לִטְעוֹת אַחֲרֵי הַיַּיִן, לְפַנֵּק לְיִצה״ר וּלְעוֹרְרוֹ, וְעַד שֶׁהוּא שָׂמֵחַ בְּשִׁכְרוּתוֹ, שׁוֹכֵב עַל מִטָּתוֹ, מִיָּד וַתָּקָם הַבְּכִירָה, וַתִּשְׁכַּב אֶת אָבִיהָ. הִיא מְזוּמֶּנֶת עִמּוֹ, וּמִתְאַוָּה וּמְהַרְהֶרֶת בְּכָל הִרְהוּרִים רָעִים, וְיֵצֶר הָרַע מִתְחַבֵּר עִמָּהּ וְנִדְבַּק בָּהּ, וְאֵינוּ מַשְׁגִּיחַ בָּהּ מַה הוּא מִמֶּנָּהּ. בְּשִׁכְבָהּ וּבְקוּמָהּ. בְּשִׁכְבָהּ בָּעוֹלָם הַזֶּה. וּבְקוּמָהּ לֶעָתִיד לָבֹא. בְּשִׁכְבָהּ, בָּעוֹלָם הַבָּא, כְּשֶׁתִּתֵּן דִּין וְחֶשְׁבּוֹן. וּבְקוּמָהּ, לְיוֹם הַדִּין, דִּכְתִיב וְרַבִּים מִיְּשֵׁנֵי אַדְמַת עָפָר יָקִיצוּ וגו'. בְּשׁוּם עִנְיָן מֵאֵלּוּ, אֵין מַשְׁגִּיחַ בָּהּ יֵצֶר הָרַע, אֶלָּא דָבֵק בָּהּ, וְהִיא נִדְבֶּקֶת בּוֹ, וּלְאַחַר כֵּן, מְעוֹרֶרֶת לְאַחֲרָא, לְאַחַר שֶׁהַהִרְהוּר גָּדוֹל, נִדְבַּק בַּיֵּצֶר הָרַע, בָּאָה הָאַחֶרֶת, וְנִדְבֶּקֶת בּוֹ.

324. Rabbi Yehuda then said: Come and behold. It is written: "And they made their father drink wine" (Beresheet 19:33). The way of the wicked is to go astray by drinking wine, to indulge the Evil Inclination with pleasures and arouse it until it rejoices in drunkenness and lies in its bed. Immediately then, "the firstborn went in and lay with her father"; she joins him and begins to imagine all kinds of bad thoughts. The Evil Inclination joins her and clings to her, and ceases to be aware of her or of what it does to her "when she lay down" in this world or, "when she arose" to the World to Come. "…when she lay down…" in the World to Come, she will account for her deeds and be judged for them. And "When she arose" for the Day of Judgment, it is written: "And many of them that sleep in the dust of the earth shall awake" (Daniel 12:2). Here the Evil Inclination has no perception at all, so it clings to her, and she clings to it. Later, she arouses the other. Thus, after the great thought is attached to the Evil Inclination, the other one comes and clings to it.

325. וַתַּשְׁקֶיןָ אֶת אֲבִיהֶן יָיִן. כְּמוֹ כֵן, לְעוֹרֵר לַיֵּצֶר הָרָע, וְנִדְבֶּקֶת בּוֹ, וַאֲזַי תַּשְׁלוּם הָרָעוֹת לַעֲשׂוֹת, וּמִתְעַבְּרוֹת שְׁתֵּיהֶן, מִיֵּצֶר הָרָע, הֲדָא הוּא דִכְתִיב, וַתַּהֲרֶיןָ שְׁתֵּי בְנוֹת לוֹט מֵאֲבִיהֶן. עַד שֶׁיָּצָא לַפּוֹעַל מַעֲשֵׂיהֶן, זוֹ יוֹלֶדֶת רִשְׁעָתָהּ, וְזוֹ יוֹלֶדֶת רִשְׁעָתָהּ, וְכֵן דַּרְכָּם שֶׁל רְשָׁעִים, בְּעִנְיָן זֶה, עִם יֵצֶר הָרָע, עַד שֶׁהוֹרֵג לָאָדָם וּמוֹלִיכוֹ לַגֵּיהִנֹּם וּמַכְנִיסוֹ שָׁם, וְאַחַ"כ עוֹלֶה מִשָּׁם לְפַתּוֹת לִבְנֵי אָדָם, כְּמוֹ כֵן. וּמִי שֶׁמַּכִּיר בּוֹ, נִצּוֹל מִמֶּנּוּ, וְאֵינוֹ מִתְחַבֵּר עִמּוֹ.

325. "And they made their father drink wine" (Beresheet 19:35), to arouse the Evil Inclination and cling to it. And then they fulfilled their evil thoughts through action, and they both became pregnant to the Evil Inclination. As it is written: "Thus were both the daughters of Lot with child by their father" (Idib. 36). Now that their deeds are done, each one "bears its evil." This is the way of the wicked. They interact with the Evil Inclination until it kills them, and then drags them down into Gehenom, where it leaves them. Afterward, it goes out to seduce more people, as has been explained. So he who recognizes its ways is saved from it and never joins it.

326. אָמַר רַבִּי יִצְחָק, מָשָׁל לְמָה הַדָּבָר דּוֹמֶה, לְכַת לִסְטִים, שֶׁהָיוּ אוֹרְבִים בַּדְּרָכִים, לִגְזוֹל וְלַהֲרוֹג לִבְנֵי אָדָם, וּמַפְרִישִׁים מֵהֶם אֶחָד, שֶׁיּוֹדֵעַ לְהָסִית לִבְנֵי אָדָם וּלְשׁוֹנוֹ רַךְ, מֶה עָבִיד, מַקְדִּים וְהוֹלֵךְ לְקַבְּלָם, וְנַעֲשָׂה כְּעֶבֶד לִפְנֵיהֶם, עַד שֶׁמַּאֲמִינִים הַטִּפְּשִׁים בּוֹ, וּבוֹטְחִים בְּאַהֲבָתוֹ וּבְשִׂיחָתוֹ, וּשְׂמֵחִים עִמּוֹ, וּמוֹלִיכְכֶם בְּחֵלֶק דְּבָרָיו, בְּאוֹתוֹ הַדֶּרֶךְ שֶׁהַלִּסְטִים שָׁם, כֵּיוָן שֶׁמַּגִּיעַ עִמָּהֶם לְשָׁם הוּא הָרִאשׁוֹן שֶׁהוֹרֵג בָּם, לְאַחַר שֶׁנְּתָנָם בְּיַד הַלִּסְטִים לְהָרְגָם, וְלָקַחַת מָמוֹנָם וְאִינוּן צֻוְוחִין

וְאָמְרִין, וַוי דַּאֲצֵיתְנָא לְדֵין וְלִרְכִּיכָא דִּלִישָׁנֵיהּ, לְאַחַר שֶׁהָרְגוּ אֵלֶּה, עוֹלֶה מִשָּׁם וְיוֹצֵא לְפַתּוֹת לִבְנֵי אָדָם, כְּמִתְּחִלָּה. הַפִּקְחִים מָה הֵם עוֹשִׂים, כְּשֶׁרוֹאִים לָזֶה, יוֹצֵא לִקְרָאתָם וּמְפַתֶּה לָהֶם, מַכִּירִין בּוֹ, שֶׁהוּא צוֹדֶה אֶת נַפְשָׁם וְהוֹרְגִים אוֹתוֹ, וְהוֹלְכִים בְּדֶרֶךְ אַחֶרֶת. כָּךְ הוּא יֵצֶר הָרָע, יוֹצֵא מִכַּת הַלִּסְטִים, עוֹלֶה מִגֵּיהִנֹּם לְקַבְּלָא דִּבְנֵי נָשָׁא, וּלְפַתּוֹת לָהֶם בְּחֵלֶק מֶתֶק דְּבָרָיו, הֲדָא הוּא דִכְתִיב, וַיַּעַל לוֹט מִצוֹעַר וַיֵּשֶׁב בָּהָר וְגוֹ'. כְּמוֹ לִסְטִים, לֶאֱרוֹב לִבְנֵי אָדָם, מַה עוֹשֶׂה, עוֹבֵר לִפְנֵיהֶם, וְהַטִּפְּשִׁים מַאֲמִינִים בּוֹ וּבְאַהֲבָתוֹ, שֶׁהוּא הוֹלֵךְ לְפַתּוֹתָם, וְעוֹבֵד לָהֶם כְּעֶבֶד, שֶׁנּוֹתֵן לָהֶם נָשִׁים יָפוֹת אֲסוּרוֹת, נוֹתֵן לָהֶם בְּנֵי אָדָם לְהָרַע, מְפָרֵק מֵהֶם עוֹל תּוֹרָה, וְעוֹל מַלְכוּת שָׁמַיִם. הַטִּפְּשִׁים רוֹאִים כָּךְ, בּוֹטְחִים בְּאַהֲבָתוֹ, עַד שֶׁהוֹלֵךְ עִמָּהֶם, וּמוֹלִיכְכֶם בְּאוֹתוֹ דֶּרֶךְ שֶׁהַלִּסְטִים שָׁם, בְּדֶרֶךְ גֵּיהִנֹּם, אֲשֶׁר אֵין דֶּרֶךְ לִנְטוֹת יָמִין וּשְׂמֹאל, כֵּיוָן שֶׁמַּגִּיעַ עִמָּהֶם לְשָׁם, הוּא הָרִאשׁוֹן שֶׁהוֹרֵג לָהֶם, וְנַעֲשָׂה לָהֶם מַה"מ, וּמַכְנִיסָן לְגֵיהִנֹּם, וּמוֹרִידִין לְהוֹן מַלְאֲכֵי חַבָּלָה, וְאִינוּן צָוְוחִין וְאָמְרִין, וַוי דַּאֲצֵיתְנָא לְדֵין, וְלָא מְהַנְיָא לוֹן. לְאַחַר כֵּן עוֹלֶה מִשָּׁם, וְיוֹצֵא לְפַתּוֹת לִבְנֵי אָדָם. הַפִּקְחִין כְּשֶׁרוֹאִין אוֹתוֹ, מַכִּירִים אוֹתוֹ, וּמִתְגַּבְּרִים עָלָיו, עַד שֶׁשּׁוֹלְטִין עָלָיו, וְסָאטִין מִזֶּה הַדֶּרֶךְ, וְלוֹקְחִין דֶּרֶךְ אַחֶרֶת לְהִנָּצֵל מִמֶּנּוּ.

326. Rabbi Yitzchak said: This is similar to the example of a group of bandits that prepares ambushes along the roads to rob and kill people. They choose one person from among them, who knows how to deceive other men with soft words. What does he do? He first goes among the intended victims to welcome and serve them until the foolish among them trust him – his affection and his way of speech – and rejoice with him. He leads them on with his soothing words, so that they follow the route along which the other bandits are hiding. And as soon as they reach the hiding place, he is the first to kill them. The other bandits come, kill them, and take their money. While the victims shout and cry: Woe to us for listening to him, NAMELY TO THE EVIL INCLINATION, and to his soothing words. After they are killed, he emerges and goes to deceive other people, as before. What do those who are clever do? When they see him coming to seduce them, they recognize him as the one who ambushes their souls. So they kill him and travel a different route. This is the way of the Evil Inclination. It emerges from among the group of bandits, that is, it leaves Gehenom to welcome people and seduces them with its sweet tongue. As it is written: "And Lot went up out of Tzoar, and dwelt in the mountain," just like the bandits did, to prey on people. What does it do? It walks in front of them. And the fools have faith in it and in its love, through which it deceives them. It serves them as a slave who supplies them with beautiful, forbidden women. It allows people to be bad, and frees them from the commitments of Torah and the yoke of the Heavenly Kingdom. The fools see all this and trust in its love, accept its guidance, and follow it along the same path where the bandits are hidden, the path to Gehenom, along which there is no way of turning to the right or to the left. And as soon as it arrives with them at that place, it is the first to kill them and become the Angel of Death for them. Then it makes them enter Gehenom and brings them down to the Angels of Destruction. And they cry out, saying: Woe to us for listening to it – NAMELY, TO THE EVIL INCLINATION – but their cries serve no purpose. REPENTANCE AND REMORSE ARE ONLY EFFECTIVE DURING ONE'S LIFETIME, NOT AFTER DEATH. Afterward, the Evil Inclination leaves Gehenom and goes to seduce other people. The clever, who immediately recognize it, will overcome it until they have full control over it. Then they choose a different route to save themselves.

327. רַב יוֹסֵף כַּד הֲוָה נָחִית לְבָבֶל, חָמָא אִינוּן רַוָּוקַיָּא, דַּהֲווֹ עַיְילֵי וְנָפְקֵי בֵּינֵי נָשֵׁי שַׁפִּירִין, וְלָא חָטָאן, אָמַר לוֹן לָא מִסְתְּפוּ אֵלֵין מִיצה"ר, אָמְרוּ לֵיהּ, לָא מִקּוֹנְדְרִיטוֹן בִּישָׁא קָאֲתֵינָא, מִקְדוּשָׁתָא דְּקַדִּישָׁא אִתְגַּזַּרְנָא, דְּאָמַר רַב יְהוּדָה אָמַר רַב, צָרִיךְ אָדָם לְקַדֵּשׁ עַצְמוֹ בִּשְׁעַת תַּשְׁמִישׁ, וְנָפְקֵי מִנֵּיהּ בְּנֵי קַדִּישֵׁי, בְּנֵי מַעֲלֵי, דְּלָא מִסְתְּפוּ מִיצה"ר. שֶׁנֶּאֱמַר וְהִתְקַדִּשְׁתֶּם וִהְיִיתֶם קְדוֹשִׁים.

327. Rabbi Yosef traveled to Babylon where he saw young lads WHO WERE NOT YET MARRIED. They walked freely among beautiful women and did not commit any sin. He asks them: Are you not afraid of the Evil Inclination? They answered: We do not come from a mixture of good and bad, but were hewn out of the Holy of the Holies. THIS MEANS THAT THEIR PARENTS HAD NO EVIL THOUGHTS AT THE TIME OF THEIR MATING, WHEN THE YOUNG LADS WERE 'HEWN OUT' OF THEM. BECAUSE THEY HAD ONLY HOLY THOUGHTS, THE YOUNG LADS WERE NOT AFRAID OF THE

EVIL INCLINATION. As Rabbi Yehuda said that Rav said: A person should sanctify himself during sexual intercourse in order to produce holy children, sons with holy attributes who have no fear of the Evil Inclination. This is according to the verse: "Sanctify yourselves therefore, and be holy" (Vayikra 20:7).

328. ר' אַבָּא אֲמַר, מַאי דִכְתִיב וְאֶת שַׁבְּתוֹתַי קַדֵּשׁוּ, אֶלָּא אֵין עוֹנָתָן שֶׁל תָּא חֲזֵי, אֶלָּא מִשַּׁבָּת לְשַׁבָּת, וּמַזְהַר לְהוּ, דְּהוֹאִיל דְּתַשְׁמִישׁ הַמִּטָּה דְּמִצְוָה הוּא, קַדֵּשׁוּ. כְּלוֹמַר, קַדְּשׁוּ עַצְמְכֶם בְּשַׁבְּתוֹתַי, בְּהַהוּא תַּשְׁמִישׁ דְּמִצְוָה אָמַר רַב יְהוּדָה אָמַר רַב, הַאי מַאן דְּעָיֵיל לְקַרְתָּא, וְחָמֵי נַשֵׁי שַׁפִּירָן יַרְכִּין עֵינוֹי, וְיֵימָא הָכִי סָךְ סָפָאן, אִיגְזַר אִיגְזַרְנָא קַרְדִּינָא תְּקִיל פּוּק פּוּק, דַּאֲבוֹי קַדִּישָׁא דְּשַׁבַּתָּא הוּא. מ״ט דַּחֲמִימוּת דְּאָרְחָא שָׁלַט בֵּיהּ, וְיָכִיל יצה״ר לְשַׁלְטָא עֲלוֹי.

(עַד כָּאן מִדְרַשׁ הַנֶּעֱלָם).

328. Rabbi Aba asks: What is MEANT BY THE VERSE: "And hallow My Shabbatot...(Heb. plural)" (Yechezkel 20:20)? THIS MEANS that the 'mating period' of the sages are timed every Shabbat. And he warns them that because sexual intercourse is a precept, 'hallow' means that you should sanctify yourselves during 'My Shabbatot (Heb. plural)' through the precept of mating. Rav Yehuda said that Rav said: Whoever arrives at a city and sees nice women should lower his eyes and say – Look how I have been 'hewn' from highly important parents. You dangerous obstacle – WHICH IS A REFERENCE TO THE KLIPAH THAT CAUSES THE THOUGHT OF WOMEN – get out, get out OF ME. As he is a 'holy fruit' of Shabbat, WHICH MEANS THAT HE WAS BORN FROM A MATING DURING SHABBAT, THE KLIPAH HAS NO CONTROL OVER HIM. SO HE ASKS: Why then SHOULD HE WHISPER THESE PHRASES AS HE ENTERS THE CITY? AND HE ANSWERS: BECAUSE the heat OF THE HARDSHIP of traveling overcomes him. So the Evil Inclination might also overcome him.

End of Midrash Hane'elam

24. Amon and Moab

A Synopsis

The original Serpent in the Garden of Eden ate fruits from the tree, which is also interpreted as drinking wine. Through this action, two negative energy forces came into existence – [do not pronounce] *malcon*, and *peor*. The Zohar expounds upon these two negative forces and how they manifest into our world to influence man. The two children born from an incestuous relationship between Lot and his two daughters were the physical manifestation of these two forces. King David, who is a descendant of these offspring, used this tremendous negativity as a tool to take control over the two negative forces. According to the laws of spirituality, in order to attain genuine control over any situation or force, one must have some connection to it. It was destined that King David be seeded with this negativity because he was ingrained with the spiritual strength necessary to take control over it. The moment man seizes control over any negative aspect of his nature, for example, the trait of jealousy, he immediately influences and minimizes the force of jealousy in the entire world. The envy that lurks within in the hearts of all men is rooted in one source. This principle holds true for all negative qualities.

The Relevance of this Passage

Mankind's natural instinct is to treat multiple symptoms, as opposed to curing the one underlying and unseen cause. All of our negative traits are rooted in one source. We gain control over our own negativity and reactive impulses and their source and origin by virtue of this passage. Moreover, we connect ourselves to any negativity that we came into contact with at prior times in our life and take control over and diminish the root of these forces as well.

סִתְרֵי תּוֹרָה

329. וַיַּעַל לוֹט מִצּוֹעַר וגו', מִגּוֹ הוּרְמְנוּתָא דְמַלְכָּא, אִתְפְּרָשָׁא מִסְּטְרָא דִּימִינָא, חַד הַתּוּבָא דִּקְטוֹרָא דְּגוּלְפָא, מִתְדַּבְּקָא בְּגוֹ הַתּוּבָא דְּדַהֲבָא, מִסְּטְרָא דִּשְׂמָאלָא, בְּגוֹ מְסָאֲבוּ, דִּיּוּרֵיה. וְאִתְעֲבֵיד קְטוֹרָא חֲדָא דְּאִילָנָא.

Sitrei Torah (Concealed Torah)

329. "And Lot went up out of Tzoar..." Because of the desire of the King, a

bit of refuse, which bears an engraved image, is separated from the right side and clings to the refuse of the gold that comes from the left side. And it resides within the 'unholiness,' which was shaped into the image of the tree.

330. כַּד בָּעָא יִצְחָק לְאִתְעָרָא בְּעָלְמָא, בְּתוּקְפֵיה דְּדִינָא קַשְׁיָא, אִתְתַּקַּף, וּפָרֵישׁ דַּרְגִּין מִקִּיּוּמַיְיהוּ, וְאִתְתַּקַּף אַבְרָהָם, וּפָרֵישׁ הַהוּא דִּקְטוֹרָא חֲדָא דְּאִילָנָא, מִגּוֹ הַהוּא מְסָאֲבוּ.

330. When Isaac, WHO IS THE LEFT COLUMN OF HOLINESS, wanted to rise up in the world, by the might of the harsh Judgment, he overcame the grades OF THE LEFT AND severed them from their sustenance. THIS IS HOW THE RIGHT COLUMN, CALLED Abraham, became strong. He therefore separated that figure from the Unholiness.

331. הַהוּא נָחָשׁ קַדְמָאָה, עָאל בְּאִנְבֵּיה דְּהַהוּא אִילָנָא, וְאִיהוּ חַמְרָא דִּשָּׁתָא, וְאוֹלִיד תְּרֵין דַּרְגִּין, קְטוּרִין דָּא בְּדָא. וְאִינּוּן דַּרְגִּין דְּסָחֲרָן בִּסְטַר מְסָאֲבוּ, חַד אִקְרֵי מַלְכּוֹ"ם, וְחַד אִקְרֵי פְּעוֹ"ר.

331. The primordial Serpent penetrated the fruits of that Tree, this being the wine that it drank. And it begot two grades that are interrelated and surround the side of Unholiness. One is called Malcom, and the other Peor.

332. דָּא עֵיטָא דְּאִתְכַּסְיָא, וְדָא עֵיטָא דְּאִתְגַּלְיָא. פְּעוֹר דְּאִתְגַּלְיָא אִיהוּ, וְכָל עוֹבָדוֹי בְּאִתְגַּלְיָא, מַלְכּוֹ"ם דְּאִתְכַּסְיָא אִיהוּ, וְכָל עוֹבָדוֹי בְּאִתְכַּסְיָא. מֵאִלֵּין תְּרֵין אִתְפָּרְשָׁן זִינִין סַגִּיאִין לִזְנַיְיהוּ, וְסָחֲרָן יַמָּא רַבָּא, וּלְכָל אִלֵּין סִטְרֵי מְסָאֲבוּ, וְכָל חַד וְחַד שָׁף לְדוּכְתֵּיה.

332. One is a hidden advice. The other is an open advice. AND HE EXPLAINED THAT Peor is revealed, and all its actions, ITS DEEDS, are performed in the open. Malcom, in contrast, is hidden, and all its actions, ITS DEEDS, are secretive. These kinds of Unholy elements were separated and went forth, surrounding the Great Sea, WHICH IS THE NUKVA, and each and every aspect of impurity turns towards its place.

333. כְּגַוְונָא דָּא אִיהוּ לְתַתָּא, לוֹט אִתְפְּרַשׁ מֵאַבְרָהָם, וְשַׁוֵּי דִּיּוּרֵיה

בְּאַנְשֵׁי סְדוֹם, כַּד אִתְּעַר דִּינָא בְּהוּ, אִדְכַּר לְאַבְרָהָם, וּשְׁלַח לֵיהּ מִתַּמָּן,
וְאִתְפְּרֵישׁ מִנַּיְיהוּ.

333. In the same manner, WHAT OCCURS IN THE UPPER WORLDS HAPPENS WITH THE SOULS down below. Lot, WHO IS THE REFUSE OF THE RIGHT, separated himself from Abraham and dwelt among the people of Sodom, WHO ARE THE REFUSE OF THE GOLD THAT COMES FROM THE LEFT. AND HE ACHIEVED COMPLETION FROM THEM, AS IS EXPLAINED IN THE UPPER WORLDS. When the Judgment was aroused and they were overthrown, THE HOLY ONE, BLESSED BE HE, remembered Abraham, and saved LOT. Thus, Lot was separated from THE UNHOLINESS OF SODOM AND RETURNED TO THE HOLY SIDE.

334. יַיִן אַשְׁקִיאוּ לֵיהּ בְּנָתֵיהּ, וְאוֹלִידוּ בְּהוּ תְּרֵין אוּמִּין, חַד אִקְרֵי
עַמּוֹן, וְחַד אִקְרֵי מוֹאָב, חַד בְּאִתְגַּלְיָא, וְחַד בְּאִתְכַּסְיָא. עַמּוֹן דַּרְגָּא
דִּילֵיהּ מִלְכּוֹ"ם, עֵיטָא דְּאִתְכַּסְיָא, מוֹאָב דַּרְגָּא דִּילֵיהּ פְּעוֹ"ר, כֹּלָּא
בְּאִתְגַּלְיָא.

334. His daughters made him drink wine, WHICH IS THE SECRET OF THE PRIMORDIAL SERPENT, and they bore him two nations. One was named Amon, which is hidden, and the other Moab, which is revealed. The grade of Amon is THE IDOL Malcom, the adviser of concealment. The grade of Moab is Peor, which is completely revealed.

335. כְּגַוְונָא דָּא בְּנָתֵיהּ, דָּא אָמְרַת בֶּן עַמִּי, בְּרָא אִית לִי מֵעַמִּי, וְלָא
אָמְרַת מִמַּאן הוּא, בְּגִין כָּךְ, אִיהוּ הֲוָה בְּאִתְכַּסְיָא. דָּא אָמְרַת מוֹאָב,
מֵאָב הוּא דְּנָא, מֵאַבָּא אוֹלִידַת לֵיהּ, דַּרְגָּא דִּילֵיהּ פְּעוֹ"ר מִלָּה
בְּאִתְגַּלְיָא.

335. His daughters behaved similarly. One said, "Ben-Ami (lit. 'son of my people') I have a son from my nation," but she did not name the father. This is why he is related to the concealed aspect. The other daughter said, "Moab he came from my father (Me'av). I have borne a son from my father." Thus, this son's grade is Peor, the unconcealed aspect.

336. וּבְתְרֵין אִלֵּין, אָחִיד דָּוִד מַלְכָּא לְבָתַר, מִן מוֹאָב אָתַת רוּת, וּנְפַק מִנָּהּ דָּוִד מַלְכָּא. מִן עַמּוֹן אִתְעַטַּר דָּוִד מַלְכָּא, בְּהַאי עֲטָרָא, דְּאִיהִי סַהֲדוּתָא לְזַרְעָא דְּדָוִד, דִּכְתִיב וַיִּתֵּן עָלָיו אֶת הַנֵּזֶר וְאֶת הָעֵדוּת. וְהַאי הֲוַת מִן מַלְכֹּם, דַּרְגָּא דִּבְנֵי עַמּוֹן, דִּכְתִיב וַיִּקַּח אֶת עֲטֶרֶת מַלְכָּם.

336. King David was attached to both AMON AND MOAB, because Rut issued from Moab and King David from her. And David was enthroned by the crown of Amon, which was a testimony to the seed of David. As it is written: "And he brought forth the king's son, and put the crown upon him, and gave him the testimony" (II Melachim 11:12). This crown came from Malcom, which is the grade of the children of Amon, as it is written: "And he took their king's (Heb. *malcam*) crown" (II Shmuel 12:30).

337. מַלְכֹּם, דַּרְגָּא דִּבְנֵי עַמּוֹן הוּא, דִּכְתִיב וַתְּהִי עַל רֹאשׁ דָּוִד, וּמִתַּמָּן הֲוָה סַהֲדוּתָא לִבְנוֹי לְעָלְמִין, וּבָהּ אִשְׁתְּמוֹדַע מַאן דְּאִיהוּ מִן בְּנוֹי דְּדָוִד דְּאִתְחֲזֵי לְמַלְכָּא וַדַּאי, דְּאָמְרִין מִן דָּוִד הוּא. דַּאֲפִילוּ אִתְיְלִיד בְּהַהוּא יוֹמָא, יָכִיל הֲוָה לְמִסְבַּל הַהִיא עֲטָרָא עַל רֵישֵׁיהּ, דַּהֲוַת מִשְׁקַל כִּכַּר זָהָב, וְאֶבֶן יְקָרָה הֲוַת. וּבַר נָשׁ אָחֳרָא לָא יָכִיל לְמִסְבְּלָא. וְדָא הוּא דִּכְתִיב בְּיוֹאָשׁ וַיִּתֵּן עָלָיו אֶת הַנֵּזֶר וְאֶת הָעֵדוּת.

337. Malcom is the grade of the children of Amon. As it is written: "and it was set on David's head" (II Shmuel 12:30). And from then on, it became an everlasting testimony for his sons after him. Through it, it became evident who are of the sons of David and worthy of kingship. IF HE WAS ABLE TO BEAR THE CROWN UPON HIS HEAD, then they said that he is certainly from the seed of David. Even on the day he was born, he was already able to bear the weight of the crown upon his head, though it was heavy with gold and a precious stone. Others, WHO WERE NOT FROM DAVID'S SEED, could not bear it. Therefore, it is written about Yoash: "and he put the crown upon him, and gave him the testimony."

338. וּבְתְרֵין דַּרְגִּין אִתְאֲחִיד דָּוִד מַלְכָּא, וְאִינּוּן תּוּקְפָא דְּמַלְכוּתֵיהּ, לְאִתְתַּקְּפָא עַל שְׁאָר עַמִּין, דְּאִי לָא אִתְכְּלִיל בְּסִטְרָא דִּלְהוֹן, לָא יָכִיל לְאִתְתַּקְּפָא עֲלַיְיהוּ, כָּל דַּרְגִּין דִּשְׁאָר עַמִּין כְּלִילָן בֵּיהּ בְּדָוִד,

לְאִתְגַּבְּרָא וּלְאִתְתַּקְפָא עֲלַיְיהוּ.

338. King David was attached to both of these grades. They are the might of his kingdom. Through them, he was able to overcome all other nations. If he had not been included within their aspects, he would not have been able to overcome them. So all the grades of all the other nations of the world were included within David, so that he could overcome them.

339. וַיַּעַל לוֹט מִצּוֹעַר וַיֵּשֶׁב בָּהָר. כְּתִיב לַעֲלוּקָה שְׁתֵּי בָנוֹת הַב הַב. אִלֵּין שְׁתֵּי בָנוֹת דְּיֵצֶר הָרָע, דְּאִינּוּן מִתְעָרִין לֵיהּ, לְשַׁלְּטָא בְּגוּפָא. חֲדָא אִיהִי נֶפֶשׁ, דְּאִתְרְבִיאַת תָּדִיר בְּגוּפָא. וְחֲדָא אִיהִי נֶפֶשׁ, דְּכְסִיפַת בְּתִיאוֹבְתִּין בִּישִׁין, וּבְכָל כְּסוּפִין בִּישִׁין דְּהַאי עָלְמָא. דָּא אִיהִי בְּכִיר"ה וְדָא אִיהִי צְעִיר"ה.

339. "And Lot went up out of Tzoar, and dwelt in the mountain." It is written: "The leech hath two daughters, crying: Give, give..." (Mishlei 30:15). These are the two daughters of the Evil Inclination who arouse the Evil Inclination to rule the body. One is the Nefesh that constantly grows within the body; the other is the Nefesh that lusts after evil desires of this world. The latter is the firstborn, while the former, THE FIRST ONE, is the younger.

340. וְיצֶה"ר לָא אִתְחַבָּר תָּדִיר, אֶלָּא בִּתְרֵין אִלֵּין, בְּגִין לְפַתָּאָה לִבְנֵי נָשָׁא וּבְגִין דִּיהֵמְנוּן לֵיהּ לְאוֹבָדָא לְהוֹ, לַאֲתַר גִּירִין דְּמוֹתָא, וְיִפְלְחוּן לֵיהּ. כד"א עַד יְפַלַּח חֵץ כְּבֵדוֹ.

340. The Evil Inclination always clings to both of these SOULS in order to seduce human beings and make them trust it, SO THAT IT MAY lead them to the place WHERE THEY ARE SHOT BY the 'Arrows of Death' and torn into shreds, as it is written: "Till a dart strike through his liver..." (Mishlei 7:23).

341. לְלִסְטִים דִּמְקַפְּחֵי בְּטוּרַיָּא, וּטְמִירוּ גַרְמַיְיהוּ בַּאֲתַר דְּחֵיל דְּטוּרַיָּא, וְיָדְעִין דְּהָא בְּנֵי נָשָׁא אִתְטַמְּרָן גַּרְמַיְיהוּ, לְמֵיהַךְ בְּאִינּוּן דּוּכְתֵּי, מָה עָבְדֵי, בְּרִירוּ מִנַּיְיהוּ הַהוּא דַּחֲדִידָא בְּלִישָׁנֵיהּ מִכֹּלָּא, הַהוּא דְּיָדַע

-410-

לְמִפְתֵּי בְּנֵי נָשָׁא, וְיִפּוֹק מִבֵּינַיְיהוּ, וִיתֵיב בְּאוֹרַח מֵישָׁר, דְּכָל בְּנֵי עָלְמָא עָבְרִין תַּמָּן, כֵּיוָן דְּמָטָא לְגַבַּיְיהוּ, שָׁרֵי לְאִתְחַבְּרָא תַּמָּן.

(עַד כָּאן סִתְרֵי תּוֹרָה).

341. AND THIS IS SIMILAR to those thieving bandits in the mountains who hide in a frightening spot to which most people refrain from traveling. How do they bring people to that place? They choose from among them the one who has the sharpest tongue, one who knows how to tempt people. This one leaves them and travels on the main path TO THE PLACE through which all people pass. As soon as he arrives there and meets them, NAMELY, THE INHABITANTS OF THE WORLD, he joins them. HE PULLS THEM INTO HIS NET AND BRINGS THEM TO THAT EVIL SPOT WHERE THE OTHER BANDITS WAIT TO ROB AND MURDER THEM. THIS IS HOW THE EVIL INCLINATION WORKS. IT SEDUCES HUMAN BEINGS AND PERSUADES THEM TO HAVE FAITH IN IT, WHILE IT BRINGS THEM TO THE PLACE OF THE "ARROWS OF DEATH."

End of Sitrei Torah

25. "She is my sister"

A Synopsis

Before Abraham goes down into the land of Egypt, he attaches himself to the divine presence known as the *Shechinah*. The word *Egypt* is a code for negativity and darkness. The spiritual principle concealed in this story can be revealed by analogy. If a person lowers himself into a deep, darkened pit, filled with deadly snakes, to retrieve a great treasure, he first secures himself to a powerful rope to ensure a safe retreat. The rope becomes his lifeline as he enters into a dangerous environment. Abraham attached himself to the force called *Shechinah* before he entered into the pit of negativity [Egypt] so that he would maintain a lifeline to the Creator.

The Relevance of this Passage

There are moments in life when negative situations consume us. Without supernal assistance, we fall prey to the traps and lures set up by the forces of negativity. We are building for ourselves a secure lifeline to the Creator for those difficult moments in life when we stumble and fall into negativity.

342. וַיִּסַּע מִשָּׁם אַבְרָהָם אַרְצָה הַנֶּגֶב. כָּל מַטְלָנוֹי הֲווֹ לִסְטְרָא דְּדָרוֹמָא, יַתִּיר מִסִּטְרָא אָחֳרָא, בְּגִין דְּהָא בְּחָכְמְתָא עֲבַד, לְאִתְדַּבְּקָא בִּדְרוֹמָא.

342. "And Abraham journeyed from there toward the south country" (Beresheet 20:1). All of Avraham's journeys were to the south, WHICH IS CHESED, rather than in any other direction. He planned wisely, so that he would be attached to the south.

343. וַיֹּאמֶר אַבְרָהָם אֶל שָׂרָה אִשְׁתּוֹ אֲחוֹתִי הִיא. תָּנִינָן לָא לִיבָּעֵי לֵיהּ לְבַר נָשׁ לְסַמְכָא עַל נִיסָא, וְאִי קוּדְשָׁא בְּרִיךְ הוּא אַרְחֵישׁ נִיסָא לְבַר נָשׁ, לָא אִית לֵיהּ לְסַמְכָא עַל נִיסָא זִמְנָא אָחֳרָא, בְּגִין דְּלָאו בְּכָל שַׁעֲתָא וְשַׁעֲתָא אִתְרְחֵישׁ נִיסָא.

343. "And Abraham said of Sarah his wife, She is my sister..." (Beresheet 20:2). We have learned that a person should not rely on miracles. If the Holy One, blessed be He, performs a miracle for somebody, he should not

rely on a miracle another time, because miracles do not simply occur at any given time.

344. וְאִי יֵיעוֹל בַּר נָשׁ גַּרְמֵיהּ בַּאֲתַר דְּנִזְקָא אִשְׁתְּכַח לְעֵינָא, הָא פָּקַע כָּל זְכוּתֵיהּ דַּעֲבַד בְּקַדְמֵיתָא, וְאוֹקְמוּהָ. כד״א קָטֹנְתִּי מִכֹּל הַחֲסָדִים וּמִכָּל הָאֱמֶת וגו'. וְאַבְרָהָם כֵּיוָן דְּסָלֵיק מִמִּצְרַיִם, וְאִשְׁתְּזֵיב זִמְנָא חֲדָא, הַשְׁתָּא אַמַּאי אָעֵיל גַּרְמֵיהּ בְּצַעֲרָא כְּקַדְמֵיתָא, וַאֲמַר אֲחוֹתִי הִיא.

344. A person who knowingly puts himself in danger may use up all of his merits, because, as it is written: "I am unworthy of the least of all the mercies, and of all the trust..." (Beresheet 32:11). AND HE ASKS: If Abraham knew that his emergence from Egypt was a miracle, why did he put himself into difficulty again by saying, "She is my sister?"

345. אֶלָּא אַבְרָהָם לָא סָמִיךְ עַל גַּרְמֵיהּ כְּלוּם, וְחָמָא שְׁכִינְתָּא תָּדִיר בְּדִיּוּרָהּ דְּשָׂרָה, וְלָא אַעֲדֵי מִתַּמָּן, וּבְגִין דַּהֲוַת תַּמָּן, אַסְמֵיךְ אַבְרָהָם וַאֲמַר אֲחוֹתִי הִיא, כְּמָה דִכְתִיב אֱמֹר לַחָכְמָה אֲחֹתִי אָתְּ, וּבְגִין כָּךְ אֲמַר אֲחוֹתִי הִיא.

345. AND HE REPLIES: Abraham did not rely on himself at all, but saw the Shechinah dwelling constantly in Sarah's residence, from which She never moved. And because THE SHECHINAH was there, Abraham relied on Her and said, "She is my sister," as it is written: "Say to Wisdom, You are my sister" (Mishlei 7:4). THIS MEANS THAT THE SHECHINAH IS ALSO CALLED WISDOM. Therefore he said, "She is my sister."

346. וַיָּבֹא אֱלֹקִים אֶל אֲבִימֶלֶךְ וגו'. וְכִי קוּדְשָׁא בְּרִיךְ הוּא אָתָא לְגַבַּיְיהוּ דְּרַשִׁיעַיָּא, כְּמָה דִכְתִיב וַיָּבֹא אֱלֹקִים אֶל בִּלְעָם. וַיָּבֹא אֱלֹקִים אֶל לָבָן. אֶלָּא הַהוּא מְמַנָּא שְׁלִיחָא דְּאִתְפַּקְדָּא עֲלַיְיהוּ הֲוָה, בְּגִין דְּכֻלְּהוּ כַּד עָבְדֵי שְׁלִיחוּתָא, נַטְלֵי שְׁמָא דָּא, וּמִסִּטְרָא דְּדִינָא קָא אַתְיָין. וְעַל דָּא, וַיָּבֹא אֱלֹקִים אֶל אֲבִימֶלֶךְ בַּחֲלוֹם הַלַּיְלָה וַיֹּאמֶר לוֹ הִנְּךָ מֵת עַל הָאִשָּׁה אֲשֶׁר לָקַחְתָּ וגו'.

346. "But Elohim came to Abimelech..." HE ASKS: Could it be that the Holy One, blessed be He, visits the wicked, as it is written: "and Elohim came to Bilaam" (Bemidbar 22:9) and "Elohim came to Laban" (Beresheet 31:24)? AND HE REPLIES: This was only a Governor, a messenger who was in charge over them, as EVERY NATION HAS A CELESTIAL GOVERNOR. When ANGELS complete their missions, WHICH THEY RECEIVE FROM HASHEM, they are called by the holy name ELOHIM, because they represented the aspect of Judgment AND THE NAME ELOHIM IS AN INDICATION OF JUDGMENT. This is why it is written: "But Elohim came to Abimelech, in a dream by night, and said to him, Behold, you are but a dead man for the woman which you have taken" (Beresheet 20:3), REFERRING ONLY TO THE ANGEL THAT GOVERNS HIS NATION AND NOT TO THE HOLY ONE, BLESSED BE HE.

347. רַבִּי שִׁמְעוֹן פָּתַח וְאָמַר שְׂפַת אֱמֶת וגו'. שְׂפַת אֱמֶת תִּכּוֹן לָעַד. דָּא אַבְרָהָם, דְּכָל מִלּוֹי בְּקַדְמֵיתָא וּבְסוֹפָא הֲווֹ בֶּאֱמֶת. וְעַד אַרְגִּיעָה לְשׁוֹן שָׁקֶר. דָּא אֲבִימֶלֶךְ.

347. Rabbi Shimon opened the discourse with the verse: "The language of truth shall be established forever..." (Mishlei 12:19) This refers to Abraham, whose words were always truthful. The phrase, "but a lying tongue is but for a moment" (Ibid.), however, refers to Abimelech.

348. בְּאַבְרָהָם נֶאֱמַר, וַיֹּאמֶר אַבְרָהָם אֶל שָׂרָה אִשְׁתּוֹ אֲחֹתִי הוּא. דָּא בְּקַדְמֵיתָא, דַּאֲמַר בְּגִין שְׁכִינְתָּא דַּהֲוַת עִמָּהּ דְּשָׂרָה, אֲחוֹתִי הִיא, וְאַבְרָהָם בְּחָכְמְתָא עֲבַד.

348. Of Abraham it is written: "And Abraham said of Sarah his wife, She is my sister." This is similar to what he said IN EGYPT, when he said to the Shechinah that accompanied Sarah, "She is my sister." SO TWICE ABRAHAM SAID, "SHE IS MY SISTER," AND REFERRED TO THE SHECHINAH WHEN HE SAID IT. And Abraham did EVERYTHING wisely.

349. מ"ט, בְּגִין דְּאַבְרָהָם, מִסִּטְרָא דִּימִינָא אִיהוּ, אֲמַר אֲחוֹתִי הִיא וְרָזָא, כד"א אֱמֹר לַחָכְמָה אֲחֹתִי אָתְּ. וְעַל דָּא, אַבְרָהָם קָרָא לָהּ תָּדִיר אֲחוֹתִי, בְּגִין דְּאִתְדַּבַּק בַּהֲדָהּ, וְלָא יִתְעַדּוּן דָּא מִן דָּא לְעָלְמִין.

349. HE ASKS: WHY IS THE SHECHINAH CALLED SISTER? AND HE RESPONDS: Because Abraham is related to the right side, he said, "She is my sister." And the secret corresponds to what is written: "my sister, my love, my dove, my undefiled" (Shir Hashirim 5:2). And Abraham always called Her "my sister" because he cleaved to Her and they were never separated.

350. לְסוֹף מַה כְּתִיב, וְגַם אָמְנָה אֲחֹתִי בַת אָבִי הוּא אַךְ לֹא בַת אִמִּי. וְכִי הָכֵי הֲוָה. אֶלָּא, כֹּלָּא בְּגִין שְׁכִינְתָּא קָאֲמַר, אֲחוֹתִי הִיא בְּקַדְמֵיתָא, דִּכְתִיב אֱמֹר לַחָכְמָה אֲחֹתִי אָתְּ. וּלְבָתַר וְגַם אָמְנָה. מַאי וְגַם, לְאִתּוֹסְפָא, עַל מַה דְּקָאֲמַר בְּקַדְמֵיתָא. אֲחוֹתִי בַת אָבִי הִיא. בְּרַתֵּיהּ דְּחָכְמָה עִלָּאָה, וּבְגִין כָּךְ אִתְקְרֵי אֲחוֹתִי, וְאִתְקְרֵי חָכְמָה. אַךְ לֹא בַת אִמִּי. מֵאֲתַר דְּשֵׁירוּתָא דְּכֹלָּא, סְתִימָא עִלָּאָה. וְעַל דָּא, וַתְּהִי לִי לְאִשָּׁה. בְּאַחְוָה בַּחֲבִיבוּתָא, דִּכְתִיב וִימִינוֹ תְחַבְּקֵנִי. וְכֹלָּא רָזָא דְּחָכְמְתָא אִיהוּ.

350. In the end, it is written: "And yet indeed she is my sister, she is the daughter of my father, but not the daughter of my mother" (Beresheet 20:12). SO HE ASKS: Was IT REALLY SO? WAS SHE NOT THE DAUGHTER OF CHARAN? AND HE REPLIES: Everything that he said was a reference to the Shechinah. "She is my sister," that he said in the beginning is similar to, "Say to Wisdom, You are my sister." And he concluded, "And yet indeed." What is MEANT BY "And"? It expands THE EXPLANATION with: "she is my sister, the daughter of my father," WHICH MEANS THAT THE SHECHINAH is a daughter of the supernal Chochmah, WHICH IS THE SUPERNAL ABA AND IMA, BOTH OF WHICH ARE CALLED ABA. This is why THE SHECHINAH is called his 'Sister' and 'Wisdom', but not, AS STATED IN THE PRECEDING PARAGRAPH, "the daughter of my mother." THIS MEANS THAT "MY MOTHER" IS DRAWN from the place where everything begins and where everything is concealed, WHICH IS ARICH ANPIN. FROM ARICH ANPIN, THE SECRET OF BINAH THAT RETURNS TO BECOME CHOCHMAH IS DRAWN. BINAH BECOMES ENCLOTHED BY YISRAEL–SABA AND TENUVAH, COLLECTIVELY CALLED IMA. SO THE SHECHINAH HERE IS NOT A "DAUGHTER," BUT RATHER A "MOTHER" HERSELF, AS SHE ENCLOTHES HER. Therefore, BECAUSE SHE IS THE ASPECT OF THE LEFT, FROM THE SIDE OF THE MOTHER, "she became my wife" in fondness and affection as expressed in the verse, "and his right hand embraces me" (Shir

Hashirim 8:3). SHE LONGS FOR THE CHASSADIM OF THE RIGHT, SO THAT HER CHOCHMAH MAY BE ENCLOTHED BY THE CHASSADIM. All this is according to the secret of Wisdom.

351. תָּא חֲזֵי, בְּקַדְמֵיתָא כַּד נַחֲתוּ לְמִצְרַיִם, הָכֵי קָאֲמַר, בְּגִין לְאִתְדַּבְּקָא בְּגוֹ מְהֵימְנוּתָא, וְקָרָא לָהּ אֲחוֹתִי, בְּגִין דְּלָא יִטְעוּן גּוֹ אִינּוּן דַּרְגִּין דִּלְבַר. אוּף הָכָא אֲחוֹתִי, בְּגִין דְּלָא אִתְעֲדֵי מִגּוֹ מְהֵימְנוּתָא, כִּדְקָא יָאוּת.

351. Come and behold: when they first went down to Egypt, he said, "SHE IS MY SISTER" in order to cleave to the Faith. Therefore, he called Her "my sister," so that they would not be mistaken and follow those grades outside HOLINESS. So here as well, WITH ABIMELECH, he said, "my sister" in order not to be diverted from the proper Faith.

352. דְּהָא אֲבִימֶלֶךְ, וְכָל אִינּוּן יָתְבֵי אַרְעָא, הֲווֹ אַזְלֵי בָּתַר פּוּלְחָנָא נוּכְרָאָה, וְאִיהוּ אִתְדַּבַּק גּוֹ מְהֵימְנוּתָא, וּבְגִין כָּךְ, עָאל לְתַמָּן, וְאָמַר אֲחוֹתִי, מָה אָחוֹת לָא אִתְפְּרַשׁ מֵאָחָא לְעָלְמִין, אוּף הָכָא. דְּהָא אִתְּתָא יְכֵילַת לְאִתְפְּרָשָׁא, אֲבָל אָחוֹת לָא אִתְפְּרַשׁ, דְּהָא תְּרֵין אַחִין לָא יָכְלִין לְאִתְפְּרָשָׁא, לְעָלְמִין וּלְעָלְמֵי עָלְמִין.

352. This is because Abimelech and all the inhabitants of the land followed idolatry, while ABRAHAM cleaved to the Faith. So when he entered there, he said OF THE SHECHINAH, "She is my sister." Just as a sister can never be separated from a brother, so here as well, ABRAHAM WAS ATTACHED TO THE SHECHINAH IN SUCH A MANNER THAT THEY COULD NEVER BE SEPARATED. Although a wife can be separated FROM HER HUSBAND, a sister can never be separated FROM HER BROTHER, because two siblings can never ever be separated.

353. וּבְגִין כָּךְ אֲמַר אַבְרָהָם אֲחוֹתִי הִיא, דְּהָא כֻּלְּהוֹן הֲווֹ לְהוּטִין גּוֹ טָהֳרֵי כֹּכְבַיָּא וּמַזָּלֵי, וּפַלְחֵי לוֹן, וְאַבְרָהָם הֲוָה מִתְדַּבַּק גּוֹ מְהֵימְנוּתָא, וְאָמַר אֲחוֹתִי, דְּלָא נִתְפְּרַשׁ לְעָלְמִין. וְסִימָנֵיךְ וְלַאֲחוֹתוֹ הַבְּתוּלָה. דְּאִתְּמַר לְכֹהֵן, אַתְרָא דְּאַבְרָהָם שַׁרְיָא בֵּיהּ.

-416-

353. Thus Abraham said, "She is my sister." Everybody was enthusiastic about running after and worshipping the lights of the stars and constellations, but Abraham cleaved to the Faith and said ABOUT THE SHECHINAH, "She is my sister," and we shall never be separated from each other. You may derive this FROM THE WORDS: "And for his sister a virgin" (Vayikra 21:3), which has been said about the priest, but signifies the place where Abraham, WHO IS THE RIGHT COLUMN AND CHESED, resides. THE SHECHINAH IS CALLED HIS "VIRGIN SISTER" BECAUSE, FROM THE ASPECT OF THE RIGHT SIDE, THE SHECHINAH IS CALLED BOTH A "SISTER" AND A "DAUGHTER."

354. כְּתִיב אֶת יי' אֱלֹהֶיךָ תִּירָא אֹתוֹ תַעֲבֹד וּבוֹ תִדְבָּק וּבִשְׁמוֹ תִשָּׁבֵעַ. הַאי קְרָא אוּקְמוּהָ. אֲבָל תָּא חֲזֵי, לַיי' אֱלֹהֶיךָ תִּירָא, לָא כְּתִיב, אֶלָּא אֶת יי', מַאי אֶת, דָּא דַרְגָּא קַדְמָאָה, אֲתַר דַּחֲלָא דְקוּדְשָׁא בְּרִיךְ הוּא, וּבְגִין כָּךְ כְּתִיב תִּירָא, דְּתַמָּן בָּעֵי בַּר נָשׁ לְדַחֲלָא קַמֵּי מָארֵיה, בְּגִין דְּאִיהוּ דִינָא.

354. It is written: "You shall fear Hashem your Elohim, Him you shall serve, and to Him you shall cleave, and swear by his Name" (Devarim 10:20). This phrase has already been explained, but nevertheless, come and behold. It is not written: 'Hashem (to Hashem) your Elohim you shall have fear,' USING THE DATIVE CASE, but only "fear (*et*) Hashem." So what does THE ACCUSATIVE PARTICLE *Et* mean? It refers to the first grade OF THE TEN SFIROT, COUNTING UPWARD, NAMELY THE NUKVA, WHICH IS the region of fear of the Holy One, blessed be He. Therefore, it is written: "You shall fear," because there, IN THE NUKVA, a person should fear his Master, as She represents Judgment.

355. וְאוֹתוֹ תַעֲבֹד. דָּא דַרְגָּא עִלָּאָה, דְּקַיְימָא עַל הַאי דַרְגָּא תַּתָּאָה, וְלָא מִתְפָּרְשָׁאן לְעָלְמִין, אֶת וְאוֹתוֹ, דָּא בְּדָא דְּבֵקִין, וְלָא אִתְפָּרְשָׁן. מַאי וְאוֹתוֹ. דָּא אֲתַר בְּרִית קַדִּישָׁא. אוֹת לְעָלְמִין, דְּהָא פּוּלְחָנָא לָא שַׁרְיָא בְּאֶת, וְלָאו אִיהוּ לְמִפְלַח, אֶלָּא לְמִדְחַל, אֲבָל פּוּלְחָנָא אִיהוּ לְעֵילָא, וּבְגִין כָּךְ וְאוֹתוֹ תַעֲבֹד.

355. "And him (Heb. *oto*) you shall serve" alludes to the upper grade, NAMELY YESOD OF ZEIR ANPIN, which resides above this lower grade,

WHICH IS THE NUKVA, and they are never separated from each other. THESE TWO WORDS, *Et* ('the') and *Oto* ('him') cleave to each other and are never separated. SO HE ASKS: What does "*Oto*" mean? AND HE ANSWERS: This is the region of the Holy Covenant, an everlasting sign (Heb. *ot*) THAT REFERS TO YESOD, because no worshipping is done in *Et* ('the'), which does not pertain to service, but to fear. But service is above IN YESOD OF ZEIR ANPIN, WHICH IS NAMED *OTO*. And this is why IT IS WRITTEN: "him (Heb. *oto*) you shall serve."

356. וּבוֹ תִדְבָּק. בַּאֲתַר דְּאִיהוּ דְּבֵקוּתָא לְאִתְדַּבְּקָא, דְּאִיהוּ גוּפָא, דְּשַׁרֵי בְּאֶמְצָעִיתָא. וּבִשְׁמוֹ תִּשָּׁבֵעַ, אֲתַר שְׁבִיעָאָה דְּדַרְגִּין. וְסִימָנֵיךְ וְאֶת דָּוִד מַלְכָּם אֲשֶׁר אָקִים לָהֶם.

356. The phrase, "and to Him you shall cleave" refers to the region where cleaving occurs, which is the center of the body, NAMELY IN THE CENTRAL COLUMN, WHICH IS TIFERET AND LIES BETWEEN THE TWO ARMS, WHICH ARE CHESED AND GVURAH, WHO REPRESENT THE TWO COLUMNS – LEFT AND RIGHT. The words, "and swear (Heb. *tishave'a*) by His name" refer to the seventh (Heb. *sheva*) region among the grades, NAMELY THE NUKVA, WHICH IS RELATED TO THE SECRET OF SHABBAT. And this is learned from the verse: "and David their king, whom I will raise up for them" (Yirmeyah 30:9).

357. בְּגִין כָּךְ אִתְדַּבַּק אַבְרָהָם בִּמְהֵימְנוּתָא, כַּד נָחַת לְמִצְרַיִם, וְכַד אֲזַל לְאַרְעָא דִּפְלִשְׁתִּים. לְבַר נָשׁ, דְּבָעֵא לְנַחֲתָא גוֹ גוּבָא עֲמִיקָא, דְּחֵיל דְּלָא יָכִיל לְסַלְּקָא מִגוֹ גוּבָא, מָה עֲבַד, קָשַׁר חַד קִשְׁרָא דְּחֶבֶל לְעֵילָא מִן גּוּבָא, אָמַר, הוֹאִיל דְּקַשִׁירְנָא קִשְׁרָא דָא, מִכָּאן וּלְהָלְאָה אֵעוּל תַּמָּן. כָּךְ אַבְרָהָם, בְּשַׁעֲתָא דְּבָעָא לְנַחֲתָא לְמִצְרַיִם, עַד לָא יֵיחוּת תַּמָּן, קָשַׁר קִשְׁרָא דִּמְהֵימְנוּתָא בְּקַדְמֵיתָא, לְאִתְתַּקְּפָא בֵּיהּ, וּלְבָתַר נָחַת.

357. This is how Abraham cleaved to the Faith. THIS IS AN ALLUSION TO THE SECRET OF THE SHECHINAH AT THE GRADE OF 'SISTER', when he went down to Egypt and when he went to the land of the Philistines. This is similar to a person who plans to descend into a deep pit, but is afraid that he

may not be able to climb back out. What does he do? He fastens a rope high above the pit, and says to himself: Now that I have tied this knot, I will enter the pit. Similarly, before Abraham went to Egypt, he secured himself with the knot of Faith. Only after this was secure did he travel to Egypt.

358. אוֹף הָכֵי נָמֵי, כַּד עָאל לְאַרְעָא דִּפְלִשְׁתִּים. בְּגִין כָּךְ שְׂפַת אֱמֶת תִּכּוֹן לָעַד. וְעַד אַרְגִּיעָה לְשׁוֹן שָׁקֶר, דָּא אֲבִימֶלֶךְ, דַּאֲמַר בְּתוֹם לְבָבִי וּבְנִקְיוֹן כַּפַּי. וְכַד אֲהַדְרוּ לֵיהּ, מַה כְּתִיב, גַּם אָנֹכִי יָדַעְתִּי כִּי בְתָם לְבָבְךָ עָשִׂיתָ זֹאת וְלָא כְתִיב נִקְיוֹן כַּפַּיִם.

358. And he did the same when he entered the land of the Philistines. This is why it is written: "The language of truth is established forever, but a lying tongue is but for a moment" (Mishlei 12:19). THIS APPLIES TO Abimelech, who said: "In the integrity of my heart and the innocency of my hands have I done this" (Beresheet 20:5). But ELOHIM answers him by saying: "I know that you did this in the simplicity of your heart" (Ibid. 6). He did not say, 'and innocence of your hands,' AS ABIMELECH CLAIMED. THUS, ABIMELECH LIED WHEN HE SAID, "AND THE INNOCENCY OF MY HANDS," AND THIS IS WHY IT IS WRITTEN OF HIM: "BUT A LYING TONGUE IS BUT FOR A MOMENT."

359. וְעַתָּה הָשֵׁב אֵשֶׁת הָאִישׁ כִּי נָבִיא הוּא. ר' יְהוּדָה פָּתַח וַאֲמַר, רַגְלֵי חֲסִידָו יִשְׁמֹר וְגוֹ'. חֲסִידוּ כְּתִיב, חַד, וְדָא אַבְרָהָם, דְּקוּדְשָׁא בְּרִיךְ הוּא נָטִיר לֵיהּ תָּדִיר, וְלָא אַעֲדֵי נְטִירוּ מִנֵּיהּ לְעָלְמִין. וּמַה דַּאֲמַר רַגְלֵי, דָּא אִתְּתֵיהּ, דְּקוּדְשָׁא בְּרִיךְ הוּא שַׁדַּר שְׁכִינְתֵּיהּ עִמָּהּ, וְנָטַר לָהּ תָּדִיר.

359. "Now, restore to the man his wife, for he is a prophet" (Beresheet 20:7). Rabbi Yehuda began the discussion with the verse, "He guards the feet of his pious ones (Heb. chasidav)..." (I Shmuel 2:9). Chasidav is spelled WITHOUT THE LETTER YUD, WHICH INDICATES THAT THE VERSE APPLIES to one PIOUS MAN. And this is Abraham, who is always protected by the Holy One, blessed be He, as He never removed His protection from over him. It is written, "He guards the feet" BECAUSE "THE FEET" allude to AVRAHAM'S wife, along with whom, in order to guard her, the Holy One, blessed be He, sent His Shechinah.

360. דָּבָר אַחֵר רַגְלֵי חֲסִידָיו יִשְׁמֹר. חַד, דָּא אַבְרָהָם, דְּקוּדְשָׁא בְּרִיךְ

הוּא אָזֵיל עִמֵיהּ תָּדִיר, בְּגִין דְּלָא יֵיכְלוּן לְנַזְקָא לֵיהּ. וּרְשָׁעִים בַּחֹשֶׁךְ יִדַּמּוּ. אִלֵּין אִנּוּן מַלְכִין. דְּקָטַל קוּדְשָׁא בְּרִיךְ הוּא בְּהַהוּא לֵילְיָא, דִּרְדַף בַּתְרַיְיהוּ.

360. Another explanation of the verse: "He guards the feet of his pious ones" IS THAT CHASIDAV IS WRITTEN WITHOUT THE LETTER *YUD*, WHICH IMPLIES One. That one was Abraham, who was always accompanied by the Holy One, blessed be He, so that nobody could harm him. "...and the wicked shall be silent in darkness..." refers to the kings whom the Holy One, blessed be He, had slain during that night that Abraham pursued them.

361. הה״ד בַּחֹשֶׁךְ יִדַּמּוּ, דָּא לֵילְיָא, דְּאִתְקַשַּׁר בַּחֲשׁוֹכָא, וְקָטַל לוֹן, וְאַבְרָהָם רָדִיף, וְלֵילְיָא קָטִיל לוֹן, הה״ד וַיֵּחָלֵק עֲלֵיהֶם לַיְלָה הוּא וַעֲבָדָיו וַיַּכֵּם. וַיֵּחָלֵק עֲלֵיהֶם לַיְלָה, דָּא קוּדְשָׁא בְּרִיךְ הוּא דְּפָלֵיג רַחֲמֵי מִן דִּינָא, בְּגִין לְמֶעְבַּד נוּקְמִין לְאַבְרָהָם, וּבְגִין כָּךְ וּרְשָׁעִים בַּחֹשֶׁךְ יִדַּמּוּ. וַיַּכֵּם, וַיַּכּוּם מִבָּעֵי לֵיהּ. אֶלָּא, דָּא קוּדְשָׁא בְּרִיךְ הוּא. כִּי לֹא בְכֹחַ יִגְבַּר אִישׁ. דְּאִיהוּ וֶאֱלִיעֶזֶר, הֲווֹ בִּלְחוֹדַיְיהוּ.

361. Therefore, it is written: "shall be silent in darkness," WHICH MEANS the night, NAMELY THE NUKVA. Abraham pursued the kings, and the night, as it became united with the darkness, slew the kings. Thus, it is written: "And he divided himself against them, he and his servants, by night (lit. 'And the night divided upon them) and smote them" (Beresheet 14:15). Therefore, the phrase, "And the night divided upon them" refers to the Holy One, blessed be He, who separated Judgment from Mercy, in order to avenge Abraham. Thus, IT IS WRITTEN: "and the wicked shall be silent in darkness...and (he) smote them." It should have been written: 'and (they) smote them' IN THE PLURAL, BECAUSE ABRAHAM AND HIS SERVANTS SMOTE THEM. But of course, it was the Holy One, blessed be He, WHO REALLY SMOTE THEM, "for by strength shall no man prevail" (I Shmuel 2:9), as he was alone there with Eliezer. THE NUMERICAL VALUE OF ELIEZER IS 318 AND ABRAHAM HAD 318 SERVANTS, WHICH ARE MENTIONED IN THE SCRIPTURES.

362. ר' יִצְחָק אֲמַר, וְהָא תָּנִינָן בַּאֲתַר דְּנִזְקָא שְׁכִיחַ, לָא יִסְמוֹךְ בַּר נָשׁ

עַל נִיסָּא, וְלָא הֲוָה אֲתַר דִּנְזְקָא אִשְׁתְּכַח כְּהַאי, דְּאַבְרָהָם אֲזִיל בָּתַר
חֲמִשָּׁה מַלְכִין לְמִרְדַּף בַּתְרַיְיהוּ, וְלָאֲגָחָא קְרָבָא. אָמַר ר' יְהוּדָה כַּד
אֲזִיל אַבְרָהָם לְהַאי, לָא אֲזַל לַאֲגָחָא קְרָבָא, וְלָא סָמַךְ עַל נִיסָּא, אֶלָּא
צַעֲרָא דְלוֹט, אַפְקֵיהּ מִבֵּיתֵיהּ, וְנָטִיל מָמוֹנָא לְמִפְרַק לֵיהּ, וְאִי לָאו,
דִּימוּת בַּהֲדֵיהּ גּוֹ שִׁבְיֵהּ. כֵּיוָן דִּנְפַק חָמָא שְׁכִינְתָּא דִּנְהֲרָא קַמֵּיהּ, וְכַמָּה
חֵילִין סָחֲרָנֵיהּ, בְּהַהִיא שַׁעֲתָא רָדַף בַּתְרַיְיהוּ וְקוּדְשָׁא בְּרִיךְ הוּא קָטִיל
לוֹן, הֲדָא הוּא דִכְתִיב וּרְשָׁעִים בַּחֹשֶׁךְ יִדַּמּוּ.

362. Rabbi Yitzchak said: But we have learned that where harm is expected, a person should not depend on a miracle to save him. And there is no place more dangerous than that into which Abraham pursued the four kings to wage war against them. WHY, THEN, DID HE RELY ON A MIRACLE TO HAPPEN? Rabbi Yehuda responded: Abraham did not set out with the intention of waging war, nor did he rely on the occurrence of a miracle. Rather, he left his house because of the distress of Lot, whom he planned to ransom and free. And had he not been able to free him, he would have died with him in captivity. But as soon as he began his journey, he saw the Shechinah shining in front of him and armies OF ANGELS surrounding him. At that time, he started to pursue them while the Holy One, blessed be He, slew them. This is why it is written: "and the wicked shall be silent in darkness."

363. ר' שִׁמְעוֹן אָמַר, רָזָא אִיהוּ, רַגְלֵי חֲסִידָיו יִשְׁמֹר, דָּא אַבְרָהָם. וְכַד
נָפַק אִשְׁתַּתַּף יִצְחָק בַּהֲדֵיהּ, וְנָפְלוּ קַמֵּיהּ, וְאִי לָאו דְּאִשְׁתַּתַּף יִצְחָק
בַּהֲדֵיהּ דְּאַבְרָהָם, לָא אִשְׁתְּצִיאוּ, הה"ד וּרְשָׁעִים בַּחֹשֶׁךְ יִדַּמּוּ. כִּי לֹא
בְכֹחַ יִגְבַּר אִישׁ. אַף עַל גַּב דְּחֵילָא אִשְׁתְּכַח תָּדִיר בְּיָמִינָא, אִי לָא הֲוָה
בְּסִטְרָא דִשְׂמָאלָא, לָא אִתְדַּחְיָין קַמֵּיהּ.

363. Rabbi Shimon said: There is a secret hidden in the verse, "He guards the feet of his pious," who is Abraham. When Abraham set out TO WAGE WAR ON THE KINGS, Isaac joined him. And they fell before him. If Isaac had not joined Abraham, he would not have been able to slay them, as it is written: "and the wicked shall be silent in darkness." "...by strength shall no man prevail." Even though strength always lies with the right, WHICH IS ABRAHAM, if THE RIGHT was not included within the left side, WHICH IS

ISAAC, then THE KINGS would not have retreated before him.

364. דָּבָר אַחֵר רַגְלֵי חֲסִידָיו יִשְׁמֹר, בְּשַׁעֲתָא דְּבַר נָשׁ רָחִים לֵיהּ לְקוּדְשָׁא בְּרִיךְ הוּא, קוּדְשָׁא בְּרִיךְ הוּא רָחִים לֵיהּ, בְּכָל מַה דְּאִיהוּ עָבֵיד, וְנָטֵיר אָרְחוֹי, כד"א יְיָ' יִשְׁמָר צֵאתְךָ וּבוֹאֶךָ מֵעַתָּה וְעַד עוֹלָם.

364. Another explanation of the verse, "He guards the feet of his pious ones" is that when a person loves the Holy One, blessed be He, the Holy One, blessed be He, returns that love by guarding all that he does and his journeys. As it is written: "Hashem shall preserve your going out and your coming in from this time forth and even for evermore" (Tehilim 121:8).

365. תָּא חֲזֵי כַּמָּה חֲבִיבוּתֵיהּ דְּאַבְרָהָם, לְגַבֵּי קוּדְשָׁא בְּרִיךְ הוּא, דִּבְכָל אֲתַר דַּהֲוָה אָזֵיל, לָא הֲוָה חָיֵיס עַל דִּילֵיהּ כְּלוּם, אֶלָּא, בְּגִין לְאִתְדַּבְּקָא בֵּיהּ בְּקוּדְשָׁא בְּרִיךְ הוּא, וּבְגִין כָּךְ רַגְלֵי חֲסִידָיו יִשְׁמֹר. וְדָא הִיא אִתְּתֵיהּ, דִּכְתִיב וַאֲבִימֶלֶךְ לֹא קָרַב אֵלֶיהָ. וּכְתִיב כִּי עַל כֵּן לֹא נְתַתִּיךָ לִנְגֹּעַ אֵלֶיהָ.

365. Come and behold: observe how much Abraham loved the Holy One, blessed be He. Wherever he went, he had no regard for his possessions at all. All his thoughts were directed toward cleaving to the Holy One, blessed be He, alone. Therefore, the verse "He guards the feet of his pious" alludes to his wife, BECAUSE HIS FEET ALLUDE TO HIS WIFE, about whom it is written: "Now Abimelech had not come near her" (Beresheet 20:4), and also, "therefore I did not allow you to touch her" (Ibid. 6).

366. בְּפַרְעֹה מַה כְּתִיב, וַיְנַגַּע יְיָ' אֶת פַּרְעֹה וגו' עַל דְּבַר. אִיהִי אָמְרָה, וְקוּדְשָׁא בְּרִיךְ הוּא הֲוָה מָחֵי, וּבְגִין כָּךְ רַגְלֵי חֲסִידָיו יִשְׁמֹר. וּרְשָׁעִים בַּחֹשֶׁךְ יִדַּמּוּ, אִלֵּין פַּרְעֹה וַאֲבִימֶלֶךְ, דְּקוּדְשָׁא בְּרִיךְ הוּא עָבַד בְּהוּ דִּינִין בְּלֵילְיָא. כִּי לֹא בְכֹחַ יִגְבַּר אִישׁ. מַאן אִישׁ, דָּא אַבְרָהָם, דִּכְתִיב וְעַתָּה הָשֵׁב אֵשֶׁת הָאִישׁ וגו'.

366. About Pharaoh, it is written: "And Hashem plagued Pharaoh, and his house with great plagues" (Beresheet 12:17). SARAH spoke out directly to

the Holy One, blessed be He, ASKING HIM TO SMITE, and He smote. It is written: "He guards the feet of the pious (ones), and the wicked are silent in darkness," BECAUSE it was Pharaoh and Abimelech on whom the Holy One, blessed be He, inflicted Judgments at night – BY DARKNESS. Who is the "man" referred to in the verse: "for by strength shall no man prevail? " This man is Abraham, as it is written: "Now therefore, restore the man his wife..." (Beresheet 20:7)

26. "And the Satan standing at his right to prosecute him"

A Synopsis

The negative angel, Satan, stands on the right side of the High Priest Joshua, who has just been thrown into a pit of fire. Kabbalistically, the right side signifies the attribute of mercy, and fire signifies the concept of severe judgment. In this story, the angel Satan tells the Creator that if He is going to show mercy upon Joshua, then He should be obligated to save all the people who were with Joshua, even though they are unworthy. In other words, Satan is cleverly implying that the Creator cannot possibly save Joshua because of these special circumstances. Nonetheless, the Creator emancipates Joshua. The spiritual lesson of this story is as follows: During a time of intense judgment, the righteous can still be saved amidst all the upheaval and destruction. According to the Kabbalah, another example of the Creator performing the difficult task of concurrently emitting the forces of mercy and judgment, was during the splitting of the Red Sea, when the Israelites crossed over to safety while the Egyptians were drowning.

The Relevance of this Passage

Both wicked and righteous people dwell among us and their behavioral actions have an appropriate effect on the state of the world. By mending our own ways and choosing the path of spirituality, we are securely connected, by this section, to the Creator's attributes of mercy during times of severe judgment.

367. וַיְיָ׳ פָּקַד אֶת שָׂרָה כַּאֲשֶׁר אָמַר וְגוֹ׳. רַבִּי חִיָּיא, פָּתַח וְאָמַר, וַיַּרְאֵנִי אֶת יְהוֹשֻׁעַ הַכֹּהֵן הַגָּדוֹל עוֹמֵד לִפְנֵי מַלְאַךְ יי׳ וְהַשָּׂטָן עוֹמֵד עַל יְמִינוֹ לְשִׂטְנוֹ. הַאי קְרָא אִית לְאִסְתַּכְּלָא בֵּיה. וַיַּרְאֵנִי אֶת יְהוֹשֻׁעַ הַכֹּהֵן הַגָּדוֹל, דָּא יְהוֹשֻׁעַ בֶּן יְהוֹצָדָק. עוֹמֵד לִפְנֵי מַלְאַךְ יי׳, מַאן מַלְאַךְ יי׳. דָּא אֲתַר צְרוֹרָא דְּנִשְׁמָתֵיה דְּצַדִּיק צְרִירָא בֵּיה, וְכָל אִינּוּן נִשְׁמָתִין דְּצַדִּיקַיָּא קַיְימִין תַּמָּן, וְדָא הוּא מַלְאַךְ יי׳.

367. "And Hashem visited Sarah as He had said..." (Beresheet 21:1) Rabbi Chiya opened the discussion with the verse: "And he showed me Joshua the High Priest standing before the angel of Hashem, and the Satan standing at his right to prosecute him" (Zecharyah 3:1). This passage should be studied carefully. "And he showed me Joshua the High Priest" refers to Joshua, the son of Yehotzadak. In the phrase, "standing before the angel of Hashem,"

who is the "angel of Hashem"? It is the region THAT IS CALLED the Bundle,'
TO WHICH the soul of the righteous is attached. And all the souls of the
righteous are there. This is the "angel of Hashem," WHICH IS MENTIONED
IN THE VERSE.

368. וְהַשָּׂטָן עוֹמֵד עַל יְמִינוֹ לְשִׂטְנוֹ. דָּא יֵצֶר הָרָע, דְּאִיהוּ מְשׁוֹטֵט
וְאָזֵיל בְּעָלְמָא, לְנַטְלָא נִשְׁמָתִין, וּלְאַפָּקָא רוּחִין, וּלְמִסְטֵי לוֹן
לִבְרִיָּיתָא, לְעֵילָא וְתַתָּא. וְדָא הוּא בְּשַׁעֲתָא דַּאֲטֵיל לֵיהּ נְבוּכַדְנֶצַּר
לְאֶשָּׁא, עִם אִינוּן נְבִיאֵי הַשֶּׁקֶר, וְהַאי הֲוָה מַסְטִין לְעֵילָא, בְּגִין דְּיִתּוֹקַד
עִמְּהוֹן.

368. The phrase, "and the Satan standing at his right to prosecute him"
refers to the Evil Inclination, which roams the world snatching souls and
taking spirits FROM HUMAN BEINGS by bringing accusations against
humankind, above as well as below. This occurred when Nebuchadnezzar
cast JOSHUA, THE HIGH PRIEST, into the fire, together with all the false
prophets. At that time, the Satan brought accusations against him above, so
that he would be burned with them.

369. דְּהָכֵי הוּא אוֹרְחוֹי, דְּלָאו אִיהוּ מְקַטְרֵג, אֶלָּא בְּזִמְנָא דְּסַכָּנָה
וּבְזִמְנָא דְּצַעֲרָא שָׁרְיָא בְּעָלְמָא, וְאִית לֵיהּ רְשׁוּ, לְמִסְטֵי וּלְמֶעְבַּד דִּינָא
אֲפִילוּ בְּלָא דִּינָא, כִּדְבָר אַחֵר וְיֵשׁ נִסְפָּה בְּלֹא מִשְׁפָּט. מַהוּ לְשִׂטְנוֹ,
דַּהֲוָה אָמַר, אוֹ כֻּלְּהוּ יִשְׁתֵּזְבוּן, אוֹ כֻּלְּהוּ יִתּוֹקְדוּן. דְּהָא בְּשַׁעֲתָא
דְּאִתְיְיהֵיב רְשׁוּתָא לִמְחַבְּלָא לְחַבָּלָא, לָא אִשְׁתְּזֵיב זַכָּאָה מִן חַיָּיבַיָּא.

369. This is the way OF THE SATAN, who shows his indictment at the hour
of danger or when the world is in distress. At those times, he is allowed to
prosecute and punish, even without justice, as it is written: "but sometimes
ruin comes for want of judgment" (Mishlei 13:23). What is meant by "to
prosecute him"? IN OTHER WORDS, WHAT DID HE ACCUSE HIM OF? He
was asking that they all be saved or all be burned. When the Angel of
Destruction is granted permission to destroy, the righteous are in as much
danger as the wicked.

370. וּבְגִין כָּךְ בְּשַׁעֲתָא דְּדִינָא שָׁרְיָא בְּמָתָא, בָּעֵי בַּר נָשׁ לְעָרְקָא, עַד

לָא אִתְפַּס תַּמָּן, דְּהָא מְחַבְּלָא כֵּיוָן דְּשָׁרֵי, הָכִי נָמֵי עָבֵיד לְזַכָּאָה
כְּחַיָּיבָא. וְכָל שֶׁכֵּן דַּהֲווֹ תְּלָתֵיהוֹן כְּחַד, וַהֲוָה תָּבַע דְּיִתּוֹקְדוּן כֻּלְּהוּ, אוֹ
יִשְׁתֵּזְבוּן כֻּלְּהוּ. בְּגִין דְּכַד אִתְעֲבֵיד נִיסָא, לָא אִתְעֲבֵיד פַּלְגוּ נִיסָא,
וּפַלְגוּ דִּינָא, אֶלָּא כֹּלָּא כַּחֲדָא, אוֹ נִיסָא אוֹ דִּינָא.

370. Therefore, when Judgment hangs over a city, a man should flee before he is captured there AND FALLS INTO THE HANDS OF THE DESTROYER. Once the Angel of Destruction resides IN A PLACE, he treats the righteous the same as the wicked. All the more so, as all three of them were together. THIS REFERS TO JOSHUA, THE HIGH PRIEST, AND THE OTHER TWO FALSE PROPHETS – AHAB, THE SON OF KOLYAH, AND TZIDKIYAHU, THE SON OF MA'ASSIYAH. THE SATAN was demanded that all be burned or all be saved, because if a miracle is to occur, there cannot be half a miracle. It must be the same for all – either miracle or Judgment.

371. אָמַר לוֹ ר' יוֹסֵי, וְלָא, וְהָא בְּזִמְנָא דְּבָקַע קוּדְשָׁא בְּרִיךְ הוּא יַמָּא
לְיִשְׂרָאֵל, הֲוָה קָרַע יַמָּא לְאִלֵּין, וְאָזְלִין בְּיַבֶּשְׁתָּא, וּמַיָּיא הֲווֹ תָּבִין
מִסִּטְרָא אָחֳרָא, וְטָבְעִין לְאִלֵּין, וּמֵתִין, וְאִשְׁתְּכַח נִיסָא הָכָא, וְדִינָא
הָכָא כֹּלָּא כַּחֲדָא.

371. Rabbi Yosi said to him: That is not so. For when the Holy One, blessed be He, split the sea for Yisrael, He divided the sea only for those, NAMELY, THE CHILDREN OF YISRAEL. They walked on dry land while the waters came together again and drowned the others, NAMELY, THE EGYPTIANS who perished. So there was a miracle on one side and judgment on the other, EVEN THOUGH they both occurred together.

372. אָמַר לוֹ, וְדָא הוּא דְּקַשְׁיָא קַמֵּיהּ, דְּכַד קוּדְשָׁא בְּרִיךְ הוּא עָבֵיד
דִּינָא וְנִיסָא כַּחֲדָא, לָאו בְּאַתַר חַד, וְלָא בְּבֵיתָא חֲדָא, וְאִי אִתְעֲבֵיד,
קַשְׁיָא קַמֵּיהּ, דְּהָא לְעֵילָא, לָא אִתְעֲבֵיד כֹּלָּא, אֶלָּא בִּשְׁלִימוּ כַּחֲדָא,
אוֹ נִיסָא, אוֹ דִּינָא בְּאַתַר חַד, וְלָא בְּפַלְגוּ.

372. He said to him: This is why THE SPLITTING OF THE RED SEA was so difficult for Him. When the Holy One, blessed be He, simultaneously performs a miracle and executes His Judgment, it does not usually happen in the same place, nor even in the same house. If it occurs IN THE SAME PLACE, AS HAPPENED AT THE RED SEA, then it is difficult for Him. In Heaven, everything is done to perfection. EVERYTHING IS as one and at one place – either a miracle or doom, but not usually half and half, HALF MIRACLE AND HALF DOOM.

373. בְּגִין כָּךְ, לָא עָבֵיד קוּדְשָׁא בְּרִיךְ הוּא דִּינָא בְּחַיָּיבַיָּא, עַד דְּאִשְׁתַּלִּימוּ בְּחוֹבַיְיהוּ הה"ד כִּי לֹא שָׁלֵם עֲוֹן הָאֱמֹרִי עַד הֵנָּה. וּכְתִיב בְּסַאסְּאָה בְּשַׁלְחָהּ תְּרִיבֶנָּה. וְעַל דָּא, הֲוָה אַסְטִין לֵיהּ לִיהוֹשֻׁעַ, דְּיִתּוֹקַד בְּהוּ, עַד דַּאֲמַר לֵיהּ, יִגְעַר יי' בְּךָ הַשָּׂטָן. מַאן אֲמַר לֵיהּ, דָּא, מַלְאַךְ יי'.

373. This is why the Holy One, blessed be He, does not punish the guilty until they have all filled their measure of sin. THIS WAY, HE DOES NOT HAVE TO SAVE ANY OF THEM FROM PUNISHMENT. As it is written: "for the iniquity of the Emorites is not yet full" (Beresheet 15:16), and "You should punish it in exact measure" (Yeshayah 27:8). Therefore, THE SATAN demanded that Joshua be burned together with the rest, SO THERE WOULD NOT BE HALF MIRACLE HALF DOOM, until he said to him: "May Hashem rebuke you, Satan" (Zecharyah 3:2). AND HE ASKS: Who said to him, "May HASHEM REBUKE YOU, SATAN"? AND HE REPLIES: It was the Angel of Hashem WHO SAID SO.

374. וְאִי תֵימָא וַיֹּאמֶר יי' אֶל הַשָּׂטָן יִגְעַר יי' בְּךָ וגו'. תָּא חֲזֵי הָכֵי נָמֵי לְמֹשֶׁה בַּסְּנֶה, דִּכְתִיב וַיֵּרָא מַלְאַךְ יי' אֵלָיו בְּלַבַּת אֵשׁ. וּכְתִיב וַיַּרְא יי' כִּי סָר לִרְאוֹת. לְזִמְנִין מַלְאַךְ יי', וּלְזִמְנִין מַלְאָךְ, וּלְזִמְנִין יי'. וּבְגִין כָּךְ, אֲמַר לֵיהּ יִגְעַר יי' בְּךָ הַשָּׂטָן, וְלֹא אָמַר הִנְנִי גּוֹעֵר בָּךְ.

374. You may say that since IT IS WRITTEN: "And Hashem said to the Satan, Hashem rebuke you, Satan," THEREFORE IT IS HASHEM WHO SAYS SO, AND NOT AN ANGEL. Come and behold: the same is true of Moses in the bush, about which it is written: "And the angel of Hashem appeared to him in a flame of fire" (Shemot 3:2) and, "And when Hashem saw that he turned aside to see" (Ibid. 4). Sometimes IT IS WRITTEN: "the angel of Hashem," sometimes "an angel," and sometimes, "Hashem." THEREFORE,

26. "And the Satan standing at his right to prosecute him"

HERE AS BEFORE, "AND HASHEM SAID TO THE SATAN" MAY REFER TO AN ANGEL, AS WITH MOSES. This is why he said to him: "May Hashem rebuke you, Satan" rather than 'I hereby rebuke you, Satan.' HAD IT BEEN HASHEM WHO HAD SAID THIS, IT WOULD HAVE BEEN WRITTEN: 'I HEREBY REBUKE YOU, SATAN.' THEREFORE, WE CONCLUDE THAT THE ONE WHO SAID THIS WAS AN ANGEL.

375. תָּא חֲזֵי, כְּגַוְונָא דָא, בְּיוֹמָא דְּאִשְׁתְּכַח דִּינָא בְּעָלְמָא, וְקוּדְשָׁא בְּרִיךְ הוּא יָתֵיב עַל כָּרְסַיָיא דְּדִינָא, כְּדֵין אִשְׁתְּכַח הַאי שָׂטָן, דְּאַסְטֵי לְעֵילָא וְתַתָּא, וְאִשְׁתְּכַח אִיהוּ לְחַבָּלָא עָלְמָא, וְלִיטוֹל נִשְׁמָתִין.

375. Come and behold: the same applies when Judgment hangs over the world, and the Holy One, blessed be He, sits upon the Throne of Judgment. Then the Satan, who accuses above and below, comes to destroy the world and snatch away the souls OF HUMAN BEINGS, BECAUSE THE SATAN IS ALSO THE ANGEL OF DEATH, AS IS ALREADY KNOWN.

27. "And the elders of that city
shall break the heifer's neck in the ravine"

A Synopsis
When someone is murdered and the killer is not brought to justice for whatever reason, the soul of the dead person remains in this realm as a negative force and influence upon the community. In ancient times, the Elders of the town performed a ritual slaughter on a Heifer [calf] to remove this negativity.

The Relevance of this Passage
Situations in life unexpectedly turn negative for no apparent reason. Whatever can possibly go wrong does so to the detriment of our well being. . There are no coincidences in life, no random events of chaos. It is our inability to perceive the metaphysical influences that manifest in our environment, that creates the illusion of disorder. The spiritual energy of this passage eliminates unseen negative forces and influences from our life.

376. רַבִּי שִׁמְעוֹן הֲוָה יָתֵיב וְלָעֵי בְּאוֹרַיְיתָא, וַהֲוָה מִשְׁתַּדֵּל בְּהַאי קְרָא. וְלָקְחוּ זִקְנֵי הָעִיר הַהִיא עֶגְלַת בָּקָר וְגוֹ'. וְעָרְפוּ שָׁם אֶת הָעֶגְלָה בַּנָּחַל. וְדִינָא אִיהוּ בְּקוּפִּיץ לְעָרְפָּא לָהּ. אָמַר לֵיהּ רַבִּי אֶלְעָזָר הַאי לְמַאי אִצְטְרִיךְ.

376. While studying Torah, Rabbi Shimon examined the meaning of the verse: "And the elders of that city shall bring down the heifer to a rough ravine...and shall break the heifer's neck in the ravine" (Devarim 21:4). According to the law, its head should be severed with a hatchet, THAT IS, WITH AN AX. Rabbi Elazar asks him why.

377. בָּכָה ר' שִׁמְעוֹן וַאֲמַר, וַוי לְעָלְמָא, דְּאִתְמְשַׁךְ בָּתַר דָּא, דְּהָא מִן הַהוּא יוֹמָא, דְּהַהוּא חִוְיָא בִּישָׁא, דְּאִתְפַּתָּה בֵּיהּ אָדָם, שַׁלִּיט עַל אָדָם וְשַׁלִּיט עַל בְּנֵי עָלְמָא, אִיהוּ קָאִים לְמִסְטֵי עָלְמָא, וְעָלְמָא לָא יָכִיל לְנָפְקָא מֵעוֹנְשֵׁיהּ עַד דְּיֵיתֵי מַלְכָּא מְשִׁיחָא, וְיוֹקִים קוּדְשָׁא בְּרִיךְ הוּא לִדְמִיכֵי עַפְרָא, דִּכְתִיב בִּלַּע הַמָּוֶת לָנֶצַח וְגוֹ'. וּכְתִיב וְאֶת רוּחַ הַטּוּמְאָה אַעֲבִיר מִן הָאָרֶץ. וְאִיהוּ קָאִים עַל עָלְמָא דָּא, לְמֵיטַל נִשְׁמָתִין דְּכָל בְּנֵי נָשָׁא.

377. Rabbi Shimon wept and said: Woe to the world that has been lured after this, REFERRING TO THE HEIFER. BECAUSE OF THIS, THEY HAVE TO BREAK ITS NECK. Ever since the day that Adam was enticed by that evil Serpent, it obtained control over Adam and all the people in the world. And so the Serpent persecutes humankind, who cannot evade its inflictions – NAMELY THE PUNISHMENT OF DEATH – until King Messiah appears. Then the Holy One, blessed be He, will revive those who sleep in the dust, as it is written: "He will swallow up death for ever" (Yeshayah 25:8), and, "I will cause the unclean spirit to pass out of the land" (Zecharyah 13:2). But until then, He remains to seize the souls from all human beings WHO LIVE IN THIS WORLD.

378. וְתָא חֲזֵי, הָא כְּתִיב כִּי יִמָּצֵא חָלָל וגו', תָּא חֲזֵי כָּל בְּנֵי עָלְמָא, ע"י מַלְאַךְ הַמָּוֶת נָפְקָא נִשְׁמָתַיְיהוּ, אִי תֵימָא דְּבַר נָשׁ דָּא, עַל יְדָא דְּהַהוּא מַלְאַךְ הַמָּוֶת, נְפַק נִשְׁמָתֵיהּ, לָאו הָכֵי, אֶלָּא מַאן דְּקָטֵיל לֵיהּ, אַפֵּיק נִשְׁמָתֵיהּ, עַד לָא מָטָא זִמְנֵיהּ, לְשַׁלְטָאָה בֵּיהּ הַהוּא מַלְאַךְ הַמָּוֶת.

378. Come and behold. It is written: "If a corpse is found slain..." (Devarim 21:1) The souls of all human beings are taken away by the Angel of Death. But if you say that the Angel of Death took away the soul of this person, WHO WAS FOUND SLAIN, you would be in error. He who killed him has taken his soul away before it was time for the Angel of Death to rule.

379. וּבְגִין כָּךְ וְלָאָרֶץ לֹא יְכֻפַּר וגו', וְלָאָרֶץ דִּילָן. וְלָא דִּי לוֹן, דְּקָאִים אִיהוּ לְמִסְטֵי עָלְמָא לְמַגָּנָא, וּלְקַטְרְגָא תָּדִיר, כ"ש דְּגַזְלִין מִינֵיהּ, מַה דְּאִית לֵיהּ לְנַטְלָא, וְקוּדְשָׁא בְּרִיךְ הוּא חָיֵיס עַל בְּנוֹי, וּבְגִין כָּךְ, קָרְבִּין עַל הַאי עֶגְלָא, בְּגִין לְתַקָּנָא עִמֵּיהּ, מַה דְּאִתְנְטֵיל, הַהִיא נִשְׁמָתָא דְּבַר נָשׁ מִנֵּיהּ, וְלָא יִשְׁתְּכַח מְקַטְרְגָא עַל עָלְמָא.

379. This is why it is written: "and the land cannot be cleansed" (Bemidbar 35:33). THE KILLERS are not satisfied that THE EVIL SERPENT inflicts punishments on the world without reason, and falsely accuses them constantly of sins so that they have to take away that which he is entitled to receive. But the Holy One, blessed be He, has Mercy on His children. This is why they sacrifice a heifer. In so doing, they correct TWO THINGS: (a) that the soul of the man was taken from him, REFERRING TO THE MAN FOUND SLAIN, AND (b) they prevent him from prosecuting the world.

380. וְרָזָא עִלָּאָה תְּנִינָן הָכָא, שׁוֹר, פָּרָה, עֵגֶל, עֶגְלָה, כֻּלְּהוּ בְּרָזָא עִלָּאָה אִשְׁתְּכָחוּ, וּבְגִין כָּךְ, בְּדָא מְתַקְּנִין לֵיהּ, וְדָא הוּא דִּכְתִיב יָדֵינוּ לֹא שָׁפְכָה אֶת הַדָּם הַזֶּה וְגוֹ', לֹא שָׁפְכָה, וְלָא גָרֵימְנָא מִיתָתֵיהּ וּבְדָא לָא אִשְׁתְּכַח מְקַטְרְגָא עֲלַיְיהוּ, וּבְכֹלָּא יָהֵיב קוּדְשָׁא בְּרִיךְ עֵיטָא לְעָלְמָא.

380. We have here a deep and sublime secret, because a bull, a cow, calf, and a heifer all follow a supernal and secret pattern. Therefore, with the heifer, everything is properly atoned for. As it is written: "Our hands have not shed this blood..." (Devarim 21:7) Thus, we "have not shed" this blood, nor have we caused his death. As a result, they are free from any accusations. Thus, the Holy One, blessed be He, provides a solution for every problem in the world.

28. Rosh Hashanah and Yom Hakippurim

A Synopsis

Through the Zohar, various mysteries about Rosh Hashanah and Yom Kippur are revealed. The penetrating sound of the Shofar has the power to confuse the negative angel called Satan, who acts as prosecutor during these days of judgment and repentance. The ten days that fall between Rosh Hashanah and Yom Kippur are likened to a great gift. This time frame provides us with the chance to remove all the negativity and decrees of judgment that we have brought down upon ourselves through our wrongful actions over the prior year. The prerequisite for accomplishing this goal is accountability and genuine permanent change in our character.

The Relevance of this Passage

The act of repentance is a profound tool available to each of us anytime we truly choose to change our ways. The energy radiating from the verses revealing the hidden mysteries of Rosh Hashanah and Yom Kippur, allow us to continually draw upon the forces of purification throughout the entire year.

381. תָּא חֲזֵי, כְּגַוְונָא דָא, בְּיוֹם ר"ה, וְיוֹם הַכִּפּוּרִים, דְּדִינָא אִשְׁתְּכַח בְּעָלְמָא, אִיהוּ קָאֵים לְקַטְרְגָא, וְיִשְׂרָאֵל בָּעְיִין לְאִתְעָרָא בְּשׁוֹפָר, וּלְאִתְעָרָא קוֹל, דְּכָלִיל בְּאֶשָׁ"א וּמַיָּ"א וְרוּחָ"א, וְאִתְעֲבִידוּ חָד, וּלְאַשְׁמָעָא הַהוּא קוֹל, מִגּוֹ שׁוֹפָר.

381. Come and behold: the same applies for Rosh Hashanah and Yom Hakippurim, when Judgment hovers over the world and the Satan is there to prosecute. The children of Yisrael should be aroused by the Shofar, to create a voice (also: 'sound') that is a combination of water, fire, and wind, WHICH ARE CHESED, GVURAH, AND TIFERET, which become one in it, and sound that voice from whithin the Shfar.

382. וְהַהוּא קוֹל, סָלְקָא עַד אֲתָר, דְּכָרְסְיָּיא דְּדִינָא יָתְבָא, וּבָטַשׁ בָּהּ, וְסָלְקָא, כֵּיוָן דְּמָטָא הַאי קוֹל מִתַּתָּא, קוֹל דְּיַעֲקֹב אִתַּתְּקַן לְעֵילָּא, וְקוּדְשָׁא בְּרִיךְ הוּא אִתְעַר רַחֲמֵי, דְּהָא כְּגַוְונָא דְיִשְׂרָאֵל מִתְעָרֵי לְתַתָּא, קוֹל חַד, כָּלִיל בְּאֶשָׁ"א וְרוּחָ"א וּמַיָּ"א, דְּנָפְקֵי כַּחֲדָא, מִגּוֹ שׁוֹפָר, הָכֵי נָמֵי אִתְעַר לְעֵילָּא שׁוֹפָר, וְהַהוּא קוֹל דְּכָלִיל בְּאֶשָׁ"א וּמַיָּ"א וְרוּחָ"א

אִתְתַּקַּן, וּנְפַק דָּא מִתַּתָּא, וְדָא מֵעֵילָּא, וְאִתְתַּקַּן עָלְמָא, וְרַחֲמֵי אִשְׁתְּכָחוּ.

382. And this voice rises up to the Throne of Judgment, strikes it, and rises further. And after this voice has reached above, then the voice of Jacob is established on high and the Holy One, blessed be He, is aroused with Mercy. Just as Yisrael uses the Shofar to release a voice from below, which includes fire, water, and air, so a voice is released from on high from the supernal Shofar, WHICH IS BINAH. THE POWER TO BLOW THE SHOFAR IS FIRE, AND THE VOICE IS FORMED BY THE AIR. THE AIR IS MINGLED WITH SWEAT AND HOT BREATH, WHICH ARE THE SECRET OF WATER, AND THESE AROUSE THE THREE UPPER COLUMNS OF BINAH, FROM WHERE THE MOCHIN ARE DRAWN DOWN TO ZEIR ANPIN AND MALCHUT. And this voice, which consists of fire, water, and air, AND HAS RISEN FROM BELOW; it is established and appears from below, and another appears from above. So the world, WHICH IS MALCHUT, is established and Mercy prevails.

383. וְהַהוּא מְקַטְרְגָא אִעַרְבַּב, דַּחֲשִׁיב לְשַׁלְטָאָה בְּדִינָא, וּלְקַטְרְגָא בְּעָלְמָא, וְחָמֵי דְּמִתְעָרֵי רַחֲמֵי, כְּדֵין אִעַרְבַּב, וְאִתְשַׁשׁ חֵילֵיהּ, וְלָא יָכִיל לְמֶעְבַּד מִדֵּי, וְקוּדְשָׁא בְּרִיךְ הוּא דָּאִין עָלְמָא בְּרַחֲמֵי, דְּאִי תֵּימָא דְּדִינָא אִתְעֲבֵיד, לָאו הָכֵי, אֶלָּא אִתְחַבָּרוּ רַחֲמֵי בְּדִינָא, וְעָלְמָא אִתְדָן בְּרַחֲמֵי.

383. Now the prosecutor is confused, because he thought that by executing Judgment, he would punish the world. But when he realizes that Mercy was aroused, he is perplexed, his strength fails, and he is unable to do anything. Then the Holy One, blessed be He, judges the world with Mercy. You may say that Judgment has been executed, but it is not so. Judgment and Mercy are joined, and the world is judged Mercifully.

384. תָּא חֲזֵי, כְּתִיב תִּקְעוּ בַחֹדֶשׁ שׁוֹפָר בַּכֶּסֶה לְיוֹם חַגֵּנוּ דְּאִתְכַּסְיָא סִיהֲרָא, דְּהָא כְּדֵין, שַׁלְטָא הַאי חִוְיָא בִּישָׁא, וְיָכִיל לְנַזְקָא עָלְמָא, וְכַד מִתְעָרֵי רַחֲמֵי, סַלְּקָא סִיהֲרָא, וְאִתְעֲבַרַת מִתַּמָּן, וְאִיהוּ אִתְעַרְבַּב, וְלָא יָכִיל לְשַׁלְטָאָה, וְאִתְעֲבַר, דְּלָא יִתְקְרַב תַּמָּן, וְעַל דָּא, בְּיוֹם ר"ה, בָּעֵי

לְעַרְבְּבָא לֵיהּ, כְּמַאן דְּאִתְעַר מִשִּׁנְתֵּיהּ, וְלָא יָדַע כְּלוּם.

384. Come and behold. It is written: "Blow the Shofar at the new moon, at the time appointed (lit. 'when the moon is covered') on our solemn feast day" (Tehilim 81:4), when the moon, WHICH IS MALCHUT, is covered, because at that time, AS A RESULT OF THE ILLUMINATION OF THE LEFT, that evil Serpent prevails and may bring harm to the world. But when Mercy is aroused BY BLOWING THE SHOFAR, the moon rises and moves away FROM THE ILLUMINATION OF THE LEFT. THUS, THE SATAN is confused and loses control. Then he is removed FROM THE MOON and never comes near again. This is why on Rosh Hashanah, THE SATAN IS dumbfounded, as is a person who has just been awakened and is still half asleep.

385. בְּי"ה בָּעֵי לְנַיְיחָא, וּלְמֶעְבַּד לֵיהּ נַיְיחָא דְּרוּחָא, בְּשָׂעִיר דְּקָרְבִין לֵיהּ, וּכְדֵין אִתְהַפַּךְ סַנֵּיגוֹרְיָא, עֲלַיְיהוּ דְיִשְׂרָאֵל, אֲבָל בְּיוֹמָא דְּר"ה, אִתְעַרְבַּב, דְּלָא יָדַע וְלָא יָכִיל לְמֶעְבַּד כְּלוּם. חָמֵי אִתְעֲרוּתָא דְּרַחֲמֵי סָלְקִין מִתַּתָּא, וְרַחֲמֵי מִלְּעֵילָא, וְסִיהֲרָא סָלְקָא בֵּינַיְיהוּ, כְּדֵין אִתְעַרְבַּב וְלָא יָדַע כְּלוּם, וְלָא יָכִיל לְשַׁלְטָאה.

385. On Yom Hakippurim, we should pacify and appease THE SATAN by offering him a scapegoat. BY SENDING IT TO THE DESERT, WHICH IS HIS PLACE, then he will become a defender for Yisrael. But on Rosh Hashanah, he is confused, and loses his abilities. He does not know, nor is he able to do anything, as he sees Mercy aroused from below and endowed from on high. And the moon, WHICH IS THE MALCHUT, rises in between them. This is when he is perplexed and no longer knows anything. Thus, he loses his power.

386. וְקוּדְשָׁא בְּרִיךְ הוּא דָּן לְהוּ לְיִשְׂרָאֵל בְּרַחֲמֵי, וְחָיֵיס עֲלַיְיהוּ, וְאַשְׁתְּכַח לְהוּ זִמְנָא כָּל אִינוּן י' יוֹמִין, דְּבֵין ר"ה לְיוֹם הַכִּפּוּרִים, לְקַבְּלָא כָּל אִינוּן דְּתָיְיבִין קַמֵּיהּ, וּלְכַפְּרָא לוֹן מֵחוֹבַיְיהוּ, וְסָלֵיק לוֹן לְיוֹמָא דְכִפּוּרֵי.

386. Then the Holy One, blessed be He, judges Yisrael with Mercy. He has pity on the children of Yisrael and gives them time – the ten days between Rosh Hashanah and Yom Hakippurim – to accept those who repent before

Him, and atone for their sins. Then He raises them up to THE SANCTITY OF Yom Hakippurim.

387. וְעַל דָּא, בְּכֹלָּא קוּדְשָׁא בְּרִיךְ הוּא פַּקִּיד לוֹן לְיִשְׂרָאֵל, לְמֶעְבַּד עוֹבָדָא, בְּגִין דְּלָא יִשְׁלוֹט עֲלַיְיהוּ, מַאן דְּלָא אִצְטְרִיךְ, וְלָא יִשְׁלוֹט עֲלַיְיהוּ דִּינָא, וִיהוֹן כֻּלְּהוֹן זַכָּאִין בְּאַרְעָא, כְּרַחֲמוּ דְּאַבָּא עַל בְּנִין, וְכֹלָּא בְּעוֹבָדָא וּבְמִלִּין תַּלְיָא, וְהָא אוּקִימְנָא מִלִּין.

387. From that day forward, to keep all in order, the Holy One, blessed be He, commanded Yisrael to perform the precept OF 'THE BLOWING OF THE SHOFAR' so that the Satan would not have dominion over them. THIS MEANS TO ABOLISH THE SATAN AND HIS PERSECUTION, so that Mercy, and not Judgment, will prevail, and so they will be worthy on earth OF THE MERCY OF THE HOLY ONE, BLESSED BE HE, which is like the Mercy of a father towards his children. All this depends on THE AROUSAL OF THE LOWER BEINGS by action and words. And all this has already been explained.

29. "And Hashem visited Sarah"

A Synopsis
A beautiful discussion takes place between the great sages concerning the mysteries of the resurrection of the dead and the events that will unfold at the End of Days. The End of Days will see the dawning of an abundance of spiritual energy, unprecedented in human history. The determining factor as to who will harness this energy and generate a radiance of Light and who will short-circuit and suffer, will be based upon one parameter: treating our fellow man with human dignity. Whereas in the past, the consequences of our intolerant behavior were delayed for years or even lifetimes, the End of Days will see the distance between cause and effect contract and the repercussions of our actions, positive or negative, will be felt immediately. Judgment and mercy will co-exist side-by-side.

The Relevance of this Passage
According to the wisdom of Kabbalah, it is the behavioral interactions of mankind that drive the cosmos, establishing the positive and negative conditions of our global and personal existence. We arouse compassion and mercy towards our fellow man in order to ensure that we connect to a positive manifestation of the End of Days.

מִדְרָשׁ הַנֶּעְלָם

388. וַה' פָּקַד אֶת שָׂרָה כַּאֲשֶׁר אָמָר. ר' יוֹחָנָן פָּתַח, בְּהַאי קְרָא, רֹאשֵׁךְ עָלַיִךְ כַּכַּרְמֶל וְדַלַּת רֹאשֵׁךְ כָּאַרְגָּמָן מֶלֶךְ אָסוּר בָּרְהָטִים. עָשָׂה קוּדְשָׁא בְּרִיךְ הוּא שִׁלְטוֹנִים לְמַעְלָה, וְשִׁלְטוֹנִים לְמַטָּה, כְּשֶׁנּוֹתֵן קוּדְשָׁא בְּרִיךְ הוּא מַעֲלָה לַשָּׂרִים שֶׁל מַעְלָה נוֹטְלִים מַעֲלָה הַמְּלָכִים שֶׁל מַטָּה, נָתַן מַעֲלָה לְשָׂרוֹ שֶׁל בָּבֶל, נָטַל מַעְלָה נְבוּכַדְנֶצַר הָרָשָׁע, דִּכְתִּיב בֵּיהּ, אַנְתְּ הוּא רֵאשָׁה דִּי דַּהֲבָא, וְהָיוּ כָּל הָעוֹלָם, מְשׁוּעְבָּדִים תַּחַת יָדוֹ, וּבְנוֹ וּבֶן בְּנוֹ, הה"ד רֹאשֵׁךְ עָלַיִךְ כַּכַּרְמֶל, זֶהוּ נְבוּכַדְנֶצַר הה"ד תְּחֹתוֹהִי תַּטְלֵל חֵיוַת בָּרָא. וְדַלַּת רֹאשֵׁךְ כָּאַרְגָּמָן, זֶהוּ בֵּלְשַׁאצַר, דַּאֲמַר אַרְגְּוָנָא יִלְבַּשׁ. מֶלֶךְ אָסוּר בָּרְהָטִים, זֶהוּ אֱוִיל מְרוֹדַךְ, שֶׁהָיָה אָסוּר, עַד שֶׁמֵּת אָבִיו נְבוּכַדְנֶצַר, וּמָלַךְ תַּחְתָּיו.

Midrash Hane'elam (Homiletical interpretations on the obscure)

388. "And Hashem visited Sarah as He had said..." (Beresheet 21:1). Rabbi Yochanan opened the discussion with this verse: "Your head upon you is like Carmel, and the hair of your head like purple; the king is held in the galleries" (Shir Hashirim 7:6). The Holy One, blessed be He, placed governors on high and down below. When the Holy One, blessed be He, raises the governors on high, He grants the same elevation to the kings below. Thus, because He gave the governor of Babylon rise, Nebuchadnezzar the Wicked also received it, as it is written about him: "You are this head of gold" (Daniel 2:38). And the entire world was enslaved by him, by his son, and by the son of his son. It is written, "Your head upon you is like Carmel," which applies to Nebuchadnezzar. And it is also written: "the beasts of the field had shadow under it" (Daniel 4:9). The phrase, "and the hair of your head like purple" applies to Belshatzar, who said: "shall be clothed with scarlet (purple)" (Daniel 5:7). "The king is held in the galleries" refers to Evil Merodach (the king of Babylon), who was imprisoned until the death of his father, and then ruled in his place.

389. אָמַר ר' יְהוּדָה, לְמַאי אָתָא, הַאי טַעַם בְּשִׁיר הַשִּׁירִים. אֶלָּא אָמַר ר' יְהוּדָה, שִׁבְעָה דְבָרִים נִבְרְאוּ, קוֹדֶם שֶׁנִּבְרָא הָעוֹלָם, וְאֵלוּ הֵן וְכוּ', כִּסֵּא הַכָּבוֹד, שֶׁנֶּאֱמַר נָכוֹן כִּסְאֲךָ מֵאָז מֵעוֹלָם אָתָּה. וּכְתִיב, כִּסֵּא כָבוֹד מָרוֹם מֵרִאשׁוֹן. שֶׁהוּא הָיָה רֹאשׁ, הַנִּקְדָּם לַכֹּל, וְנָטַל, הַקוּדְשָׁא בְּרִיךְ הוּא, אֶת הַנְּשָׁמָה הַטְּהוֹרָה, מִכִּסֵּא הַכָּבוֹד, לִהְיוֹת מְאִירָה לַגּוּף, הֲדָא הוּא דִכְתִיב, רֹאשֵׁךְ עָלַיִךְ כַּכַּרְמֶל, זֶהוּ כִּסֵּא הַכָּבוֹד, שֶׁהוּא רֹאשׁ עַל הַכֹּל. וְדַלַּת רֹאשֵׁךְ כָּאַרְגָּמָן, זוֹ הִיא הַנְּשָׁמָה, הַנִּטֶּלֶת מִמֶּנּוּ. מֶלֶךְ אָסוּר בָּרְהָטִים, זֶהוּ הַגּוּף, שֶׁהוּא אָסוּר בַּקֶּבֶר, וְכָלָה בֶּעָפָר, וְלֹא נִשְׁאָר מִמֶּנּוּ, אֶלָּא כִּמְלֹא תַרְוָוד רֶקֶב, וּמִמֶּנּוּ יִבָּנֶה כָּל הַגּוּף. וּכְשֶׁפּוֹקֵד הַקָּדוֹשׁ בָּרוּךְ הוּא אֶת הַגּוּף, הוּא אוֹמֵר לָאָרֶץ, שֶׁתַּפְלִיט אוֹתוֹ לַחוּץ, דִּכְתִיב וְאֶרֶץ רְפָאִים תַּפִּיל.

389. Rabbi Yehuda asks: Why does this description appear in the Song of Songs? Then he continued to explain that seven items were created before the creation of the universe. The first is the Throne of Glory, as it is written: "Your throne is established of old, You are from everlasting" (Tehilim 93:2) and "A glorious high throne from the beginning" (Yirmeyah 17:12). Hence, this was the beginning; it preceded everything else. And the Holy One, blessed be He, took the pure soul from the Throne of Glory, so it would shine on the body. This is as it is written: "Your head upon you is like Carmel," which refers to the Throne of Glory, which is the "head" over everything. And the phrase, "the hair of your head like purple" refers to the soul that is taken from it. "...the king is held in the galleries" is the body imprisoned in the grave and consumed in the dust. Nothing remains of it except for a scrap of rot, but from this, the entire body will be rebuilt. And when the Holy One, blessed be He, visits the body, He will tell the earth to cast it out, as it is written: "and the earth shall cast out the dead" (Yeshayah 26:19).

390. אָמַר רַבִּי יוֹחָנָן, הַמֵּתִים שֶׁבָּאָרֶץ, הֵם חַיִּים תְּחִלָּה, הֲדָא הוּא דִּכְתִיב יִחְיוּ מֵתֶיךָ, נְבֵלָתִי יְקוּמוּן, אֵלּוּ שֶׁבְּחוּצָה לָאָרֶץ. הָקִיצוּ וְרַנְּנוּ שׁוֹכְנֵי עָפָר, אֵלּוּ הַמֵּתִים שֶׁבַּמִּדְבָּר. דְּאָמַר רַבִּי יוֹחָנָן, לָמָה מֵת מֹשֶׁה, בְּחוּצָה לָאָרֶץ. לְהַרְאוֹת לְכָל בָּאֵי עוֹלָם, כְּשֵׁם שֶׁעָתִיד הַקָּדוֹשׁ בָּרוּךְ הוּא, לְהַחֲיוֹת לְמֹשֶׁה, כָּךְ עָתִיד לְהַחֲיוֹת לְדוֹרוֹ, שֶׁהֵם קִבְּלוּ הַתּוֹרָה. וַעֲלֵיהֶם נֶאֱמַר, זָכַרְתִּי לָךְ חֶסֶד נְעוּרַיִךְ אַהֲבַת כְּלוּלוֹתָיִךְ לֶכְתֵּךְ אַחֲרַי בַּמִּדְבָּר בְּאֶרֶץ לֹא זְרוּעָה.

390. Rabbi Yochanan said: The dead of the land (of Yisrael) shall be the first to live, as it is written: "Your dead men shall live..." (Yeshayah 26:19); "dead bodies shall arise," refers to those who have died away from the land (of Yisrael). "Awake and sing, you who dwell in dust" refers to those who have died in the desert. As Rabbi Yochanan asks: Why did Moses die away from the land (of Yisrael)? It was to show the entire world that just as the Holy One, blessed be He, shall resurrect Moses in the future, so shall He resurrect his generation, who received the Torah. And of them it is written: "I remember in your favor, the kindness of your youth, the love of your espousals, when you went after me in the wilderness, in a land that was not sown" (Yirmeyah 2:2).

391. דָּבָר אַחֵר, הָקִיצוּ וְרַנְּנוּ שׁוֹכְנֵי עָפָר, אֵלּוּ הֵם הָאָבוֹת. וְהַמֵּתִים בְּחוּצָה לָאָרֶץ, יִבָּנֶה גוּפָם, וּמִתְגַּלְגְּלִים תַּחַת הָאָרֶץ, עַד אֶרֶץ יִשְׂרָאֵל, וְשָׁם יְקַבְּלוּ נִשְׁמָתָם, וְלֹא בְּחוּצָה לָאָרֶץ, הֲדָא הוּא דִכְתִיב, לָכֵן הִנָּבֵא וְאָמַרְתָּ אֲלֵיהֶם הִנֵּה אָנֹכִי פוֹתֵחַ אֶת קִבְרוֹתֵיכֶם וְהַעֲלֵיתִי אֶתְכֶם

מִקִּבְרוֹתֵיכֶם עַמִּי וְהֵבֵאתִי אֶתְכֶם אֶל אַדְמַת יִשְׂרָאֵל. מַה כְּתִיב אַחֲרָיו,
וְנָתַתִּי רוּחִי בָכֶם וִחְיִיתֶם.

391. Another explanation of the verse, "Awake and sing, you that dwell in
dust" is that it refers to the Patriarchs. And the bodies of those who died
away from the land (of Yisrael) will be rebuilt, and they shall roll under the
ground until they reach the land of Yisrael. There, and not away from the
land (of Yisrael), they shall receive their souls. As it is written: "Therefore
prophecy, and say to them: Thus says Hashem Elohim, Behold, my people, I
will open your graves, and cause you to come up out of your graves, and
bring you into the land of Yisrael" (Yechezkel 37:12), which is followed by:
"And I shall put my spirit in you, and you shall live..." (Ibid. 14)

392. רַבִּי פִּנְחָס אָמַר, הַנְּשָׁמָה נִטְלָה מִכִּסֵּא הַכָּבוֹד, שֶׁהוּא הָרֹאשׁ,
כְּדְקָאָמַר רֹאשֵׁךְ עָלַיִךְ כַּכַּרְמֶל. וְדַלַּת רֹאשֵׁךְ כָּאַרְגָּמָן. זוֹ הִיא הַנְּשָׁמָה
שֶׁהִיא דַלַּת הָרֹאשׁ. מֶלֶךְ אָסוּר בָּרְהָטִים, הוּא הַגּוּף, שֶׁהוּא אָסוּר
בַּקְּבָרִים, זֶהוּ הַגּוּף, וְזֶהוּ שָׂרָה, וְזֶהוּ מֶלֶךְ. וְקוּדְשָׁא בְּרִיךְ הוּא פּוֹקְדָהּ,
לַמּוֹעֵד אֲשֶׁר דִּבֶּר אֵלָיו, הה"ד וַה' פָּקַד אֶת שָׂרָה כַּאֲשֶׁר אָמַר. פּוֹקֵד
אֶת הַגּוּף, לַזְּמַן הַיָּדוּעַ שֶׁבּוֹ יִפְקוֹד הַצַּדִּיקִים.

392. Rabbi Pinchas said: The soul is taken from the Throne of Glory, which
is the "head," as it is written: "Your head upon you is like Carmel." "...and
the hair of your head like purple" means the soul that is the hair of the head.
Finally, "the king is held in the galleries" means the body that is held in the
grave. This refers to the body, Sarah, and the King. So the Holy One,
blessed be He, shall visit it at the appointed time, as it is written: "And
Hashem visited Sarah as He had said." He shall visit the body at the
appointed time, when He shall visit upon the righteous."

393 אָמַר רַבִּי פִּנְחָס, עָתִיד הַקוּדְשָׁא בְּרִיךְ הוּא, לְיַפוֹת לְגוּף
הַצַּדִּיקִים לֶעָתִיד לָבֹא, כְּיוֹפִי שֶׁל אָדָם הָרִאשׁוֹן כְּשֶׁנִּכְנַס לַגַּן עֵדֶן,
שֶׁנֶּאֱמַר וְנָחֲךָ ה' תָּמִיד וְגו' וְהָיִיתָ כְּגַן רָוֶה. אָמַר רַבִּי לֵוִי, הַנְּשָׁמָה
בְּעוֹדָהּ בְּמַעֲלָתָהּ, נִיזוֹנֶת בְּאוֹר שֶׁל מַעֲלָה, וּמִתְלַבֶּשֶׁת בּוֹ, וּכְשֶׁתִּכָּנֵס
לַגּוּף לֶעָתִיד לָבֹא, בְּאוֹתוֹ הָאוֹר מַמָּשׁ תִּכָּנֵס, וַאֲזַי הַגּוּף יָאִיר, כְּזוֹהַר

הָרָקִיעַ, הה״ד, וְהַמַּשְׂכִּילִים יַזְהִירוּ כְּזוֹהַר הָרָקִיעַ, וְיַשִּׂיגוּ בְּנֵי אָדָם
דֵּעָה שְׁלֵימָה, שֶׁנֶּאֱמַר כִּי מָלְאָה הָאָרֶץ דֵּעָה אֶת ה'. מנ״ל הָא, מִמַּה
דִּכְתִיב, וְנָחֲךָ ה' תָּמִיד וְהִשְׂבִּיעַ בְּצַחְצָחוֹת נַפְשֶׁךָ. זֶה אוֹר שֶׁל מַעֲלָה.
וְעַצְמוֹתֶיךָ יַחֲלִיץ, זֶה פְּקִידַת הַגּוּף. וְהָיִיתָ כְּגַן רָוֶה וּכְמוֹצָא מַיִם אֲשֶׁר
לֹא יְכַזְּבוּ מֵימָיו. זֶהוּ דַעַת הַבּוֹרֵא יִתְבָּרַךְ, וַאֲזַי יֵדְעוּ הַבְּרִיּוֹת,
שֶׁהַנְּשָׁמָה הַנִּכְנֶסֶת בָּהֶם, שֶׁהִיא נִשְׁמַת הַחַיִּים, נִשְׁמַת הַתַּעֲנוּגִים,
שֶׁהִיא קִבְּלָה תַּעֲנוּגִים מִלְמַעְלָה, וּמַעֲדַנּוֹת לַגּוּף, וְהַכֹּל תְּמֵהִים בָּהּ,
וְאוֹמְרִים מַה יָּפִית וּמַה נָּעַמְתְּ אַהֲבָה בַּתַּעֲנוּגִים. זוֹ הִיא הַנְּשָׁמָה,
לע״ל.

393. Rabbi Pinchas said: In the future, the Holy One, blessed be He, will make the bodies of the righteous as beautiful as Adam was when when he entered the Garden of Eden, as it is written: "And Hashem shall guide you continually...and you shall be like a watered garden" (Yeshayah 58:11) Rabbi Levi then said: As long as the soul remains in its exalted position, it is nourished by the Light from above and is enclothed with It. And when it enters the body in the future, it shall enter with that same Light. Then the body will shine as the brightness of the firmament. This is as it is written: "And they that are wise shall shine as the brightness of the firmament..." (Daniel 12:3) And people will attain full knowledge, as it is written: "for the earth shall be full of the knowledge of Hashem" (Yeshayah 11:9). How do we reach this conclusion? From the verse: "And Hashem shall guide you continually, and satisfy your soul in drought" (Yeshayah 58:11). This is the Light of above. "...and make fat your bones" is the visiting of the body, while "and you shall be like a watered garden, and like a spring of water, whose waters fail not" is the knowledge of the Blessed Creator. Then all creatures shall know of the soul that entered them – that it is the soul of Life, the soul of Delight, which has received all pleasures and delights for the body from above. And all are amazed by it, saying: "How fair and how pleasant are you, love, in delights" (Shir Hashirim 7:3), all of which refers to the soul.

394. אָמַר רַבִּי יְהוּדָה תָּא חֲזֵי שֶׁכָּךְ הוּא, דִּכְתִיב מֶלֶךְ אָסוּר בָּרְהָטִים.
וּכְתִיב בַּתְרֵיהּ מַה יָּפִית וּמַה נָּעַמְתְּ. וְאָמַר ר' יְהוּדָה, בְּאוֹתוֹ זְמַן, עָתִיד
הַקּוּדְשָׁא בְּרִיךְ הוּא לְשַׂמֵּחַ עוֹלְמוֹ, וְלִשְׂמוֹחַ בִּבְרִיּוֹתָיו, שֶׁנֶּאֱמַר יִשְׂמַח

ה' בְּמַעֲשָׂיו. וַאֲזַי יִהְיֶה שְׂחוֹק בָּעוֹלָם, מַה שֶּׁאֵין עַכְשָׁיו, דִּכְתִיב אָז
יִמָּלֵא שְׂחוֹק פִּינוּ וגו'. הה"ד וַתֹּאמֶר שָׂרָה צְחוֹק עָשָׂה לִי אֱלֹהִים.
שֶׁאֲזַי עֲתִידִים בְּנֵי אָדָם לוֹמַר שִׁירָה, שֶׁהוּא עֵת שְׂחוֹק. רַבִּי אַבָּא אָמַר,
הַיּוֹם שֶׁיִּשְׂמַח הַקוּדְשָׁא בְּרִיךְ הוּא עִם בְּרִיּוֹתָיו, לֹא הָיְתָה שִׂמְחָה
כְּמוֹתָהּ, מִיּוֹם שֶׁנִּבְרָא הָעוֹלָם, וְהַצַּדִּיקִים הַנִּשְׁאָרִים בִּירוּשָׁלַיִם, לֹא
יָשׁוּבוּ עוֹד לַעֲפָרָם, דִּכְתִיב וְהָיָה הַנִּשְׁאָר בְּצִיּוֹן וְהַנּוֹתָר בִּירוּשָׁלַםִ
קָדוֹשׁ יֵאָמֶר לוֹ. הַנּוֹתָר בְּצִיּוֹן וּבִירוּשָׁלַםִ דַּיְיקָא.

394. Rabbi Yehuda said: Come and behold. It is indeed so. It is written: "the king is held in the galleries," and then, "How fair and how pleasant are you..." Rabbi Yehuda continued: At that time, the Holy One, blessed be He, will make His world happy, and rejoice in His created beings, as it is written, "Hashem shall rejoice in his works" (Tehilim 104:31). And then there will be laughter in the world, which we do not see now, as it is written: "Then will our mouth be filled with laughter..." (Tehilim 126:2) This is according to the verse: "And Sarah said, 'Elohim has made for me to laugh..." (Beresheet 21:6). So at that time, people will chant songs, as it is a time of laughter. Rabbi Aba added that on the day when the Holy One, blessed be He, will rejoice together with His created beings, there will be joy such as has not existed since the world was created. And the righteous that remain in Jerusalem shall return no more to dust, as it is written: "And it shall come to pass, that he that is left in Zion, and he that remains in Jerusalem, shall be called holy" (Yeshayah 4:3), precisely "he that is left in Zion, and he that remains in Jerusalem."

395. אָמַר רַבִּי אַחָא, אִם כֵּן זְעֵירִין אִינּוּן, אֶלָּא כָּל אִינּוּן דְּאִשְׁתְּאָרוּ
בְּאַרְעָא קַדִּישָׁא דְיִשְׂרָאֵל, דִּינָא דִלְהוֹן, כִּירוּשָׁלַם, וּכְצִיּוֹן לְכָל דָּבָר,
מְלַמֵּד דְּכָל אֶרֶץ יִשְׂרָאֵל בִּכְלַל יְרוּשָׁלַם הִיא, מִמַּשְׁמַע דִּכְתִיב וְכִי
תָבֹאוּ אֶל הָאָרֶץ, הַכֹּל בִּכְלָל.

395. Rabbi Acha asks: Then there will only be a few? Rather, the rule that applies to Jerusalem and Zion applies to all those who remained in the holy land of Yisrael. This teaches us that the whole land of Yisrael is included within Jerusalem, based on what is written: "And when you shall come into the land..." (Vayikra 19:23) – the entire land as a whole.

396. ר' יְהוּדָה בַּר' אֶלְעָזָר, שָׁאַל לְרַבִּי חִזְקִיָּה, אָמַר לוֹ, מֵתִים שֶׁעָתִיד
הַקּוּדְשָׁא בְּרִיךְ הוּא לְהַחֲיוֹתָם, לָמָּה לָא יָהֵיב נִשְׁמַתְהוֹן, בַּאֲתַר
דְּאִתְקְבָרוּ תַּמָּן, וְיֵיתוּן לְאַחֲיָיא בְּאַרְעָא דְיִשְׂרָאֵל. אָמַר לוֹ, נִשְׁבַּע
הַקּוּדְשָׁא בְּרִיךְ הוּא, לִבְנוֹת יְרוּשָׁלַם, וְשֶׁלֹּא תֶּהֱרֵס לְעוֹלָמִים, דְּאָמַר ר'
יִרְמְיָה, עָתִיד הַקּוּדְשָׁא בְּרִיךְ הוּא לְחַדֵשׁ עוֹלָמוֹ, וְלִבְנוֹת יְרוּשָׁלַם,
וּלְהוֹרִידָהּ בְּנוּיָה מִלְמַעְלָה, בְּגִין שֶׁלֹּא תֶּהֱרֵס, וְנִשְׁבַּע שֶׁלֹּא תִּגְלֶה עוֹד
כְּנֶסֶת יִשְׂרָאֵל, וְנִשְׁבַּע שֶׁלֹּא יֵהֱרֵס בִּנְיַן יְרוּשָׁלַם, שֶׁנֶּאֱמַר לֹא יֵאָמֵר לָךְ
עוֹד עֲזוּבָה וּלְאַרְצֵךְ לֹא יֵאָמֵר עוֹד שְׁמָמָה. וּבְכָל מָקוֹם, שֶׁאַתָּה מוֹצֵא
לֹא לֹא, הִיא שְׁבוּעָה, הה"ד וְלֹא יִכָּרֵת כָּל בָּשָׂר עוֹד מִמֵּי הַמַּבּוּל. וְלֹא
יִהְיֶה עוֹד מַבּוּל וגו'. וּכְתִיב אֲשֶׁר נִשְׁבַּעְתִּי מֵעֲבֹר מֵי נֹחַ. מִכָּאן שֶׁלֹּא
לֹא שְׁבוּעָה, וּמָן לָאו אַתָּה שׁוֹמֵעַ הֵן. וְעָתִיד הַקּוּדְשָׁא בְּרִיךְ הוּא לְקַיֵּים
עוֹלָמוֹ, קִיוּם שֶׁלֹּא תִגְלֶה כְּנֶסֶת יִשְׂרָאֵל, וְלֹא תֶּהֱרֵס בִּנְיַן בֵּית הַמִּקְדָּשׁ,
לְפִיכָךְ, אֵין מְקַבְּלִין נִשְׁמָתָן, אֶלָּא בְּמָקוֹם קַיָּים לְעוֹלָמִים, כְּדֵי שֶׁתִּהְיֶה
הַנְּשָׁמָה קַיֶּימֶת קַיָּים בַּגּוּף לְעוֹלָמִים, וְדָא הוּא דִכְתִיב, הַנִּשְׁאָר בְּצִיּוֹן
וְהַנּוֹתָר בִּירוּשָׁלַם קָדוֹשׁ יֵאָמֵר לוֹ וגו'.

396. Rabbi Yehuda, the son of Rabbi Elazar, asks Rabbi Chizkiyah about the dead that the Holy One, blessed be He, shall resurrect: Why does He not give them back their souls in the places where they were buried and let them come to live in the land of Yisrael? Rabbi Chizkiyah responded: The Holy One, blessed be He, took an oath to build Jerusalem and to see that it shall never be destroyed. As Rabbi Yirmeyah said, The Holy One, blessed be He, shall renew His world, and build Jerusalem. He shall bring it down from above completely built, so that it may never be destroyed. And he took a solemn oath that the Congregation of Yisrael shall never be exiled again and that Jerusalem shall never be destroyed, as it is written: "You shall no more be termed Forsaken, neither shall your land any more be termed Desolate..." (Yeshayah 62:4). Everywhere you find a double negative, there is an oath, as it is written: "neither shall all flesh be cut off any more by the waters of the flood; neither shall there any more be a flood to destroy the earth" (Beresheet 9:11), and it is written: "for as I have sworn that the waters of Noah should no more go over the earth" (Yeshayah 54:9). From this we conclude that a double negative is a solemn oath, and from that negative, we can hear an affirmative. So the Holy One, blessed be He, shall reestablish

His world in the future in such a manner that the Congregation of Yisrael shall never be exiled and the Temple will never be destroyed. Therefore, they shall not be given back their souls except in a place that is forever established, so that the soul will forever dwell in the body. Thus, it is written: "he that is left in Zion, and he that remains in Jerusalem, shall be called holy."

397. אָמַר רָבִּי חִזְקְיָּה, מֵהָכָא, הוּא קָדוֹשׁ, יְרוּשָׁלַם קָדוֹשׁ, הַנּוֹתָר בָּהּ קָדוֹשׁ, הוּא קָדוֹשׁ, דִּכְתִיב קָדוֹשׁ ה' צְבָאוֹת. וּכְתִיב בְּקִרְבְּךָ קָדוֹשׁ. יְרוּשָׁלַם קָדוֹשׁ, דִּכְתִיב וּמִמְּקוֹם קָדוֹשׁ יְהַלֵּכוּ. הַנּוֹתָר בָּהּ קָדוֹשׁ, דִּכְתִיב וְהָיָה הַנִּשְׁאָר בְּצִיּוֹן וְהַנּוֹתָר בִּירוּשָׁלַם קָדוֹשׁ יֵאָמֶר לוֹ. מַה קָדוֹשׁ הָרִאשׁוֹן קַיָּים, אַף הַשְׁאָר קָדוֹשׁ קַיָּים.

397. Rabbi Chizkiyah said: Thus, He is holy, Jerusalem is holy, and he who remains in it is holy. He is holy, as it is written: "holy is Hashem Tzva'ot" (Yeshayah 6:3), and "the Holy One in your midst" (Hoshea 11:9); Jerusalem is holy, as is written: "had gone from the holy place" (Kohelet 8:10); and he that remains in it is holy, as it is written: "And it shall come to pass, that he that is left in Zion, and he that remains in Jerusalem, shall be called holy" (Yeshayah 4:3). So as the first holy one is established, so are the other two holy ones.

398. אָמַר רָבִּי יִצְחָק, מַאי דִכְתִיב, עוֹד יֵשְׁבוּ זְקֵנִים וּזְקֵנוֹת בִּרְחוֹבוֹת יְרוּשָׁלַם וְאִישׁ מִשְׁעַנְתּוֹ בְּיָדוֹ מֵרוֹב יָמִים. מַאי טִיבוּתָא דָא לְמֵיזַל כְּדֵין, דִּכְתִיב וְאִישׁ מִשְׁעַנְתּוֹ בְּיָדוֹ. אֶלָּא אָמַר רָבִּי יִצְחָק, עֲתִידִים הַצַּדִּיקִים לֶעָתִיד לָבֹא, לְהַחֲיוֹת מֵתִים כֶּאֱלִישַׁע הַנָּבִיא, דִּכְתִיב וְקַח מִשְׁעַנְתִּי בְּיָדְךָ וָלֵךְ. וּכְתִיב וְשַׂמְתָּ מִשְׁעַנְתִּי עַל פְּנֵי הַנַּעַר. אָמַר לוֹ קוּדְשָׁא בְּרִיךְ הוּא, דָּבָר שֶׁעֲתִידִים לַעֲשׂוֹת הַצַּדִּיקִים, לֶעָתִיד לָבֹא, אַתָּה רוֹצֶה עַכְשָׁיו לַעֲשׂוֹת, מַה כְּתִיב וַיָּשֶׂם אֶת הַמִּשְׁעֶנֶת עַל פְּנֵי הַנַּעַר וְאֵין קוֹל וְאֵין עֹנֶה וְאֵין קָשֶׁב. אֲבָל הַצַּדִּיקִים לֶעָתִיד לָבֹא, עָלָה בְּיָדָם, הַבְטָחָה זוֹ, דִּכְתִיב וְאִישׁ מִשְׁעַנְתּוֹ בְּיָדוֹ, כְּדֵי לְהַחֲיוֹת בּוֹ אֶת הַמֵּתִים, מֵהַגֵּרִים שֶׁנִּתְגַּיְירוּ מֵאוּ"ה, דִּכְתִיב בְּהוּ כִּי הַנַּעַר בֶּן מֵאָה שָׁנָה יָמוּת וְהַחוֹטֵא בֶּן מֵאָה שָׁנָה יְקוּלָל. אָמַר רָבִּי יִצְחָק, סוֹפֵיהּ דִּקְרָא מוֹכִיחַ, דִּכְתִיב מֵרוֹב יָמִים.

398. Rabbi Yitzchak asks: What is meant by the verse: "Once again old men and old women will dwell in the streets of Jerusalem, and every man with his staff in his hand because of old age" (Zecharyah 8:4)? What is the good in phrasing it thus: "and every man with his staff"? Rabbi Yitzchak replies that the righteous shall revive the dead in the future as did Elisha the prophet, as it is written: "and take my staff in your hand, and go your way..." "and lay my staff upon the face of the child" (II Melachim 4:29). The Holy One, blessed be He, said to him: 'What the righteous are to perform in the future which is to come, you wish to accomplish now.' And what is written? "...and he laid the staff upon the face of the child; but there was neither voice nor sound" (Ibid. 31). But the righteous in the future shall succeed in accomplishing this promise, as it is written: "and every man with this staff in his hand" will use it to revive the dead, those who have converted from among the nations of the world, as it is written of him: "for the child shall die a hundred years old; and the sinner being a hundred years old shall be deemed cursed" (Yeshayah 65:20). Rabbi Yitzchak said that the end of this passage confirms this, as it is written: "because of old age."

399. דָּבָר אַחֵר, וַתֹּאמֶר שָׂרָה צְחוֹק עָשָׂה לִי אֱלֹהִים. כְּתִיב שִׂמְחוּ אֶת יְרוּשָׁלַם וְגִילוּ בָה כָּל אֹהֲבֶיהָ שִׂישׂוּ אִתָּה מָשׂוֹשׂ כָּל הַמִּתְאַבְּלִים עָלֶיהָ. אָמַר רַבִּי יְהוּדָה, לֹא הָיְתָה שִׂמְחָה, לִפְנֵי הַקָּדוֹשׁ בָּרוּךְ הוּא, מִיּוֹם שֶׁנִּבְרָא הָעוֹלָם, כְּאוֹתָהּ שִׂמְחָה, שֶׁעָתִיד לִשְׂמוֹחַ עִם הַצַּדִּיקִים, לֶעָתִיד לָבוֹא. וְכָל אֶחָד וְאֶחָד, מַרְאֶה בָּאֶצְבַּע, וְאוֹמֵר הִנֵּה אֱלֹהֵינוּ זֶה קִוִּינוּ לוֹ וְיוֹשִׁיעֵנוּ זֶה ה' קִוִּינוּ לוֹ נָגִילָה וְנִשְׂמְחָה בִּישׁוּעָתוֹ. וּכְתִיב זַמְּרוּ ה' כִּי גֵאוּת עָשָׂה מוּדַעַת זֹאת בְּכָל הָאָרֶץ.

399. A different explanation of the verse: "And Sarah said: Elohim has made for me to laugh," is that it is written: "Rejoice you with Jerusalem, and be glad with her, all you who love her, rejoice for joy with her, all you who mourn for her" (Yeshayah 66:10). Rabbi Yehuda said that since the world was created, there is no greater joy for the Holy One, blessed be He, as the joy in rejoicing with the righteous in the future. Each and every one shall point his finger and say: "This is our Elohim: we have waited for Him, we will be glad and rejoice in His salvation" (Yeshayah 25:9), and "Sing to Hashem; for He has done wonders: this is known in all the earth" (Yeshayah 12:5).

400. רַבִּי יוֹחָנָן אָמַר, לֹא חָזֵינָן מַאן דְּפָרֵישׁ הַאי מִלָּה כְּדָוִד מַלְכָּא, דְּאָמַר תַּסְתִּיר פָּנֶיךָ יִבָּהֵלוּן וְגו'. מִכָּאן שֶׁאֵין הַקּוּדְשָׁא בְּרִיךְ הוּא עוֹשֶׂה רָעָה לְשׁוּם אָדָם, אֶלָּא כְּשֶׁאֵינוּ מַשְׁגִּיחַ בּוֹ, הוּא כָּלָה מֵאֵלָיו, דִּכְתִיב תַּסְתִּיר פָּנֶיךָ יִבָּהֵלוּן תּוֹסֵף רוּחָם יִגְוָעוּן וְגו'. וְאַחַר כָּךְ תְּשַׁלַּח רוּחֲךָ יִבָּרֵאוּן וְגו'. וְאַחַר כָּךְ יְהִי כְבוֹד ה' לְעוֹלָם יִשְׂמַח ה' בְּמַעֲשָׂיו. וַאֲזַי הַשְּׂחוֹק בָּעוֹלָם, דִּכְתִיב אָז יִמָּלֵא שְׂחוֹק פִּינוּ וּלְשׁוֹנֵנוּ רִנָּה. הה"ד, וַתֹּאמֶר שָׂרָה צְחֹק עָשָׂה לִי אֱלֹהִים לְשָׂמוֹחַ בִּישׁוּעָתוֹ.

400. Rabbi Yochanan said that we have not seen a person who has explained this term better than King David, who said: "You hide your face, they are troubled" (Tehilim 104:29). According to this, the Holy One, blessed be He, never harms anyone. But if He does not supervise a person, he simply dies on his own, as it is written: "You hide your face, they are troubled: You take away their breath (spirit), they die and return to their dust" (Ibid.), then, "You send forth Your spirit, they are created..." and finally, "The glory of Hashem shall endure for ever, Hashem shall rejoice in His works" (Ibid. 30-31). Then shall there be laughter in the world, as it is written: "Then will our mouth be filled with laughter, and our tongue with singing." This is as we read "And Sarah said: Elohim has made for me to laugh," to rejoice in his salvation.

401. רַבִּי חִיָּיא אָמַר, תָּא חֲזֵי, עַד שֶׁהַגּוּף עוֹמֵד בָּעוֹלָם הַזֶּה, הוּא חָסֵר מִן הַתַּשְׁלוּם, לְאַחַר שֶׁהוּא צַדִּיק, וְהוֹלֵךְ בְּדַרְכֵי יוֹשֶׁר, וּמֵת בְּיוֹשְׁרוֹ, נִקְרָא שָׂרָה בְּתַשְׁלוּמוֹ, הִגִּיעַ לִתְחִיַּית הַמֵּתִים הוּא שָׂרָה, כְּדֵי שֶׁלֹּא יֹאמְרוּ שֶׁאַחֵר הוּא שֶׁהֶחֱיָה קוּדְשָׁא בְּרִיךְ הוּא. לְאַחַר שֶׁהוּא חַי, וְשָׂמֵחַ עִם הַשְּׁכִינָה, וּמַעֲבִיר הַקּוּדְשָׁא בְּרִיךְ הוּא, הַיָּגוֹן מִן הָעוֹלָם, דִּכְתִיב בִּלַּע הַמָּוֶת לָנֶצַח וּמָחָה ה' אֱלֹהִים דִּמְעָה מֵעַל כָּל פָּנִים וְגו'. אֲזַי נִקְרָא יִצְחָק, בִּשְׁבִיל הַצְּחוֹק וְהַשִּׂמְחָה, שֶׁיִּהְיֶה לַצַּדִּיקִים לֶעָתִיד לָבֹא.

401. Rabbi Chiya said: Come and behold. When the body exists in this world, it has not yet reached perfection. After it becomes righteous, walks the paths of honesty, and dies in its righteousness, then it is called 'Sarah' (lit. 'provided what is necessary'), as it has been perfected. When it reaches the Resurrection of the Dead, it is still called Sarah, so that nobody will say that the Holy One, blessed be He, has revived a different body. And after it becomes alive and rejoices with the Shechinah, and the Holy One, blessed be He, has wiped all distress from the world, as it is written: "He will swallow up death forever; and Hashem Elohim will wipe away tears from off all faces" (Yeshayah 25:8). Then it shall be called Isaac (lit. 'be laugh'), because of the laughter and happiness of the righteous in the future.

402. רַבִּי יְהוּדָה אָתָא לְהַהוּא אֲתַר דִּכְפַר חָנָן, שָׁדְרוּ לֵיהּ תִּקְרוֹבְתָּא, כָּל בְּנֵי מָאתָא, עָאל לְגַבֵּיהּ ר׳ אַבָּא, אָמַר לוֹ אֵימָתַי לֵיזִיל מַר, אָמַר לוֹ, אֶפְרַע מַה דְּיָהֲבוּ לִי בְּנֵי מָאתָא וְאֵיזִיל, אָמַר לֵיהּ, לָא לֵיחוּשׁ מַר לְהַאי תִּקְרוֹבְתָּא, לְאוֹרַיְיתָא הוּא דַּעֲבָדוּ, וְלָא יְקַבְּלוּ מִנָּךְ כְּלוּם, אָמַר לֵיהּ, וְלָא מְקַבְּלֵי מִלֵּי דְאוֹרַיְיתָא, אָמַר אֵין. אָתוּ כָּל בְּנֵי מָאתָא. אָמַר לוֹ רַבִּי יְהוּדָה, כֻּלְּהוֹן מָארֵי מְתִיבְתָּא, אָמַר לֵיהּ, וְאִי אִית מַאן דְּלָא יָאוֹת לְמֵיתַב הָכָא לֵיקוּם וְלֵיזִיל. קָם רַבִּי אַבָּא, וְאַבְדֵּיל מִנַּיְיהוּ עֲשָׂרָה, דִּי יְקַבְּלוּן מִנֵּיהּ, אָמַר לְהוּ, תִּיבוּ בַּהֲדֵי גַבְרָא רַבָּא דְּנָא, וַאֲנָא וְאִינּוּן נְקַבֵּל לְמָחָר, וּנְתִיב עִמֵּיהּ. אָזְלוּ. וְאִינּוּן עֲשָׂרָה דְּאִשְׁתְּאָרוּ עִמֵּיהּ, יְתִיבוּ, וְלָא אָמַר כְּלוּם, אָמְרוּ לֵיהּ, אִי רְעוּתֵיהּ דְּמַר, נְקַבֵּל אַפֵּי שְׁכִינְתָּא. אָמַר לְהוּ, וְהָא רַבִּי אַבָּא לֵית הָכָא, שָׁדְרוּ בַּהֲדֵיהּ וַאֲתָא.

402. Rabbi Yehuda arrived at the village of Chanan, and all the inhabitants sent him a gift. Rabbi Aba came to him and asks: Sir, when are you leaving? He replies: I shall pay for what the people of the village have given me and be on my way. He said to him: Sir, do not feel troubled because of the gift. It was offered for (in honor of) the Torah, so they will not accept anything from you. He responded: Will they accept words of Torah? He said: Yes. All the people of the village came. Rabbi Yehuda said: Are they all Yeshivah deans? He then said: If there is anyone who does not attend the Yeshivah, let him get up and leave. Rabbi Aba stood up and separated ten men from them all to receive the leanings from Rabbi Yehuda. Rabbi Aba said to them: Be seated here you masters (teachers), while the rest of us will sit with him tomorrow and receive the learnings. They went, and the ten who stayed sat down. But he said nothing. They said to him: If it pleases Sir, let us welcome the Shechinah. He said to them: While Rabbi Aba is not here? So, they sent for him, and he came.

403. פָּתַח וַאֲמַר, וַה' פָּקַד אֶת שָׂרָה כַּאֲשֶׁר אָמָר. מַאי שִׁנּוּיָא הֲוָה הָכָא, הֲוָה לֵיהּ לְמֵימַר וַה' זָכַר אֶת שָׂרָה. כְּמָה דְאָמַר וַיִּזְכֹּר אֱלֹהִים אֶת רָחֵל. דְּאֵין פְּקִידָה, אֶלָּא עַל מַה דַּהֲוָה בְּקַדְמֵיתָא. אֶלָּא בְּקַדְמֵיתָא הֲוָה, דִּכְתִיב שׁוֹב אָשׁוּב אֵלֶיךָ כָּעֵת חַיָּה, וְעַל אוֹתוֹ עִנְיָן נֶאֱמַר, שֶׁפָּקַד עַבְשָׁיוּ, מַשְׁמַע דִּכְתִיב כַּאֲשֶׁר אָמָר, דְּאִלְמָלֵא לֹא נֶאֱמַר כַּאֲשֶׁר אָמָר, לֵימָא זְכִירָה, אֲבָל פָּקַד הַהִיא מִלָּה דַּאֲמַר, לַמּוֹעֵד אָשׁוּב אֵלֶיךָ.

403. He opened the discussion with the verse: "And Hashem visited Sarah as He had said." Why is it written this way? It should have been written: 'And Hashem remembered Sarah,' as he said, "And Elohim remembered Rachel" (Beresheet 30: 22). This is because there is no visiting unless it was previously mentioned, but it was previously written: "I will certainly return to you this season" (Beresheet 18:10). And, in relation to this issue, it is now said that He visited. This we derive from the words, "as He had said," because had it not been said, "as He had said," it would have said 'He remembered'. So the visiting is connected to the phrase, "He said, 'At the time appointed I will return to you'" (Ibid. 14).

404. לְבָתַר אָמַר הָכֵי, הַאי צַדִּיק, דְּזָכֵי לְמֵיסַק, לְהַהוּא יְקַר עִלָּאָה, דְּיוֹקְנֵיהּ מִתְפַּתַּח בְּכֻרְסֵי יְקָרֵיהּ, וְכֵן לְכָל צַדִּיק וְצַדִּיק, דְּיוֹקְנֵיהּ לְעֵילָא, כַּד הֲוָה לְתַתָּא, לְאַבְטָחָא לְהַהִיא נִשְׁמָתָא קַדִּישָׁא.

404. Afterward he said: The image of this righteous man, who has merited to be elevated up to that Glory on high, is engraved on the Throne of Glory. And each and every righteous person has his image above, IN THE GARDEN OF EDEN, just as it was down below IN THIS WORLD. This secures the holy soul AND ENSURES ITS RESURRECTION IN A BODY IN THIS WORLD.

405. וְהַיְינוּ דְּאָמַר רַבִּי יוֹחָנָן, מַאי דִּכְתִיב שֶׁמֶשׁ יָרֵחַ עָמַד זְבֻלָה, דְּזָהֲרָן גּוּפָא וְנִשְׁמָתָא, דְּקַיְימִין בְּאִדְרָא קַדִּישָׁא עִלָּאָה דִּלְעֵילָא, כְּדִיוֹקְנָא דַּהֲוָה קָאִים בְּאַרְעָא, וְהַהִיא דִּיוֹקְנָא מִמֶּזּוֹנָה הֲנָאַת נִשְׁמָתָא, וְהַהִיא, עֲתִידָה לְאִתְלַבָּשׁ, בְּהַאי גַּרְמָא, דְּאִשְׁתָּאַר בְּאַרְעָא, וְאַרְעָא מִתְעֲבַר מִנֵּיה, וּפָלַט טִינֵיה לְבָרָא, וְדָא הוּא דְּאִתְקְרֵי קְדוּשָׁה.

405. This is what Rabbi Yochanan said that the verse: "The sun and moon stood still in their habitation" (Chavakuk 3:11), TEACHES US that the body and the soul are in the Holy Supernal Chamber above, and shine in the same image there as they had on the earth in this world. And the sustenance of this image, OF THIS WORLD, comes from the pleasure of the soul. And it shall enter into this bone, WHICH IS CALLED *LUZ* that remains intact in the earth UNTIL THE DEAD SHALL RISE. The earth is conceived by it and throws out its refuse. This IMAGE is called 'Holy'.

406. וְכַד קַיְימָא דְּיוֹקְנָא הַהִיא דִּלְעֵילָא, אָתָא בְּכָל יַרְחָא לְסָגְדָּא, קַמֵּי מַלְכָּא קַדִּישָׁא בְּרִיךְ הוּא, דִּכְתִיב וְהָיָה מִדֵּי חֹדֶשׁ בְּחָדְשׁוֹ. וְהוּא מְבַשֵּׂר לֵיהּ, וְאָמַר לַמּוֹעֵד אָשׁוּב אֵלֶיךָ, לְהַהוּא זְמַן דְּעָתִיד לְאַחֲיָא מֵיתַיָּא, עַד דְּאִתְפַּקְדַת לְהַהוּא זִמְנָא, כְּמָה דְּאִתְבַּשַּׂר, הה"ד וַה' פָּקַד אֶת שָׂרָה כַּאֲשֶׁר אָמָר. וְהַהוּא יוֹמָא, דְּחָדֵי קוּדְשָׁא בְּרִיךְ הוּא בְּעוֹבָדוֹי, הה"ד יִשְׂמַח ה' בְּמַעֲשָׂיו.

406. So when this image OF THIS WORLD exists above, it then comes on every first day of the month to bow before the Holy One, blessed be He, as it is written: "And it shall come to pass, that from one new moon to another..." (Yeshayah 66:23). And He, THE HOLY KING, says to it: "At the time appointed I will return to you," REFERRING to the time when He shall resurrect the dead in the future, when it will be visited, as was promised. And this is why it is written: "And Hashem visited Sarah, as He had said." This is the day when the Holy One, blessed be He, shall rejoice with His creations, as it is written: "Hashem shall rejoice in His works" (Tehilim 104:31).

407. אָמַר לוֹ ר' אַבָּא, לֵימָא לָן מַר, עַל פָּרְשָׁתָא, לְבָתַר אָמַר, יָאוֹת לְכוֹן לְמִפְתַּח פָּרְשָׁתָא דָא. פָּתַח וַאֲמַר, וַיְהִי אַחַר הַדְּבָרִים הָאֵלֶּה וְהָאֱלֹהִים נִסָּה אֶת אַבְרָהָם וגו'. וַיֹּאמֶר קַח נָא אֶת בִּנְךָ אֶת יְחִידְךָ אֲשֶׁר אָהַבְתָּ וגו'. הָכָא אִית לְאִסְתַּכְּלָא הַאי אוּמָנָא, דְּאַפֵּיק כַּסְפָּא, מִמְּקוֹרָא דְּאַרְעָא, מַאי עֲבַד, בְּקַדְמֵיתָא, מְעַיֵּיל לֵיהּ בְּנוּר דָּלִיק, עַד דְּנָפֵיק מִנֵּיהּ כָּל זוּהֲמָא דְּאַרְעָא, וְהָא אִשְׁתְּאָרַת כַּסְפָּא, אֲבָל לָא כַּסְפָּא שְׁלֵימָתָא, לְבָתַר מַאי עָבֵיד, מְעַיֵּיל לֵיהּ בְּנוּרָא, כְּדִבְקַדְמֵיתָא,

וּמַפִּיק מִנֵּיהּ סְטַיְיפֵי, כִּדְבַר אַחֵר הָגוֹ סִיגִים מִכָּסֶף וגו'. וּכְדֵין, הוּא כַּסְפָּא שְׁלֵימָתָא, בְּלָא עִרְבּוּבְיָא.

407. Rabbi Aba said to him, AS HE HEARD HIM BEGIN WITH THE VERSE, "HASHEM SHALL REJOICE IN HIS WORKS": May Sir speak and tell us his explanation of THE VERSES IN this portion, AND NOT OF THE VERSES OF TEHILIM. RABBI YEHUDA said to them: It is appropriate for you to open with this passage. He said: "And it came to pass after these things, that the Elohim did test Abraham...And He said, Take now your son, your only son, whom you love..." (Beresheet 22:1-2). We should study this verse carefully. THIS IS SIMILAR TO a craftsman who takes silver from the earth. What does he do with it? First he puts the raw material into the burning fire until all the dirt of the earth is removed and only the silver remains. But even this is not yet pure silver. So what does he do next? He puts it into the fire again and extracts the dross, as we may read: "Take away the dross from the silver" (Mishlei 25:4). And then the silver is pure.

408. כָּךְ הַקּוּדְשָׁא בְּרִיךְ הוּא, מְעַיֵּיל הַאי גוּפָא תְּחוֹת אַרְעָא, עַד דְּמִתְרְקַב כּוּלֵיהּ, וְנָפִיק מִנֵּיהּ כָּל זוּהֲמָא בִּישָׁא, וְאִשְׁתְּאַר הַהוּא תַּרְוָוד רֶקֶב, וְאִתְבְּנֵי גוּפָא מִנֵּיהּ, וְעַד כְּעַן הוּא גוּפָא לָא שְׁלִים.

408. So does the Holy One, blessed be He, put the body under the ground until it is completely petrified and all the rotten defilement completely leaves it. And a handful of rot is all that is left. Then the body is rebuilt from this, but it is still an incomplete body.

409. לְבָתַר, הַהוּא יוֹמָא רַבָּא, דִּכְתִיב וְהָיָה יוֹם אֶחָד הוּא יִוָּדַע לַה' לֹא יוֹם וְלֹא לַיְלָה. מִתְטַמְּרָן כֻּלְּהוּ בְּעַפְרָא כְּדְבְקַדְמֵיתָא, מִן קֳדָם דְּחִילוּ וְתַקִּיפוּ דְּקוּדְשָׁא בְּרִיךְ הוּא, הַהֲ"ד וּבָאוּ בִּמְעָרוֹת צֻרִים וּבִמְחִלּוֹת עָפָר מִפְּנֵי פַּחַד ה' וּמֵהֲדַר גְּאוֹנוֹ וגו'. וְנָפִיק נִשְׁמָתַיְיהוּ, וּמִתְעַכַּל הַהוּא תַּרְוָוד רֶקֶב, וְאִשְׁתְּאַר גּוּפָא דְּאִתְבְּנֵי תַּמָּן נְהוֹרָא, דִּילֵיהּ כִּנְהוֹרָא דְּשִׁמְשָׁא, וּכְזֹהֲרָא דִּרְקִיעָא, דִּכְתִיב וְהַמַּשְׂכִּילִים יַזְהִירוּ כְּזֹהַר הָרָקִיעַ וגו'. וּכְדֵין כַּסְפָּא שְׁלִים, גּוּפָא שְׁלֵימָא, בְּלָא עִרְבּוּבְיָא אַחֲרָנִיתָא.

409. This is after that Great Day, as it is written: "But it shall be one day which shall be known to Hashem, not day nor night..." (Zecharyah 14:7). This is the day when everyone shall hide in the earth as they did in the beginning, THAT IS, AS THEY WERE IN THE GRAVE BEFORE THE RESURRECTION, because of the fear and the mighty power of the Holy One, blessed be He. As it is written: "And they shall go into the holes of the rocks, and into the caves of the earth, for fear of Hashem, and for the glory of His majesty..." (Yeshayah 2:19). And their souls shall leave and the handful of rot shall be digested there. The body that is rebuilt shall remain there as the light of the sun and the splendor of the firmament. As it is written: "And they who are wise shall shine as the brightness of the firmament" (Daniel 12:3). And then the silver is pure, WHICH MEANS THAT the body is pure without any other mixture.

410. דְּאָמַר ר' יַעֲקֹב, גּוּפָא דְּנָהֵיר, יַרְמֵי קוּדְשָׁא בְּרִיךְ הוּא מִלְּעֵילָא, דִּכְתִיב כִּי טַל אוֹרוֹת טַלֶּיךָ. וּכְתִיב הִנֵּה ה' מְטַלְטֶלְךָ וְגוֹ'. וּכְדֵין יִתְקְרוּן, קַדִּישִׁין עִלָּאִין, דִּכְתִיב קָדוֹשׁ יֵאָמֶר לוֹ. וְדָא הוּא, דְּאִתְקְרֵי תְּחִיַּית הַמֵּתִים דִּבְתְרַיְיתָא, וְדָא הוּא נִסְיוֹנָא בַּתְרַיְיתָא, וְלָא יִטְעֲמוּן עוֹד טַעֲמָא דְּמוֹתָא, דִּכְתִיב בִּי נִשְׁבַּעְתִּי נְאֻם ה' כִּי יַעַן אֲשֶׁר עָשִׂיתָ וְגוֹ' כִּי בָרֵךְ אֲבָרֶכְךָ וְגוֹ'. וּבְהַהוּא זִמְנָא, מְצַלּוֹ צַדִּיקַיָּיא. דְּלָא יִתְנַסּוּן בְּדָא יַתִּיר.

410. As Rabbi Ya'akov said, the Holy One, blessed be He, shall cast down a shining body from above, as it is written: "for your dew is as the dew (Heb. *tal*) of the herbs..." (Yeshayah 26:19) and, "Behold Hashem will carry you away (Heb. *metaltelcha*)" (Yeshayah 22:17). And then they shall be called Celastial Holy Ones, as it is written: "and he...shall be called holy" (Yeshayah 4:3). This is what is called the last resurrection of the dead, as they shall never taste death anymore, as it is written: "By Myself I have sworn, says Hashem, because you have done this thing...that I will exceedingly bless you..." (Beresheet 22:16-17). During that period, the righteous pray that they may never experience this again.

411. מַה כְּתִיב וַיִּשָּׂא אַבְרָהָם אֶת עֵינָיו וַיַּרְא וְהִנֵּה אַיִל וְגוֹ'. אִלֵּין שְׁאָר חַיָּיבֵי עָלְמָא. דְּאִתְקְרוּן אֵילִים, כְּדָבָר אַחֵר אֵילֵי נְבָיוֹת יְשָׁרְתוּנֶךְ וּמִתַּרְגְּמִינָן רַבְרְבֵי נְבָיוֹת. אַחַר נֶאֱחַז בַּסְּבַךְ וְגוֹ'. כְּדָבָר אַחֵר וְכָל קַרְנֵי

רְשָׁעִים אֲגַדֵּעַ וַיֵּלֶךְ אַבְרָהָם וַיִּקַּח אֶת הָאַיִל וְגו'. דְּאִינוּן מְזוּמָּנִין,
לְאִתְנַסָּאָה בְּכָל נִסְיוֹנָא בִּישָׁא, וְיִשְׁתָּאֲרוּן הַצַּדִּיקִים, לְעָלְמָא דְּאָתֵי,
כְּמַלְאָכִין עִלָּאִין קַדִּישִׁין, לְיַחֲדָּא שְׁמֵיהּ, וּבְגִין כָּךְ כְּתִיב, בַּיּוֹם הַהוּא
יִהְיֶה ה' אֶחָד וּשְׁמוֹ אֶחָד וְגו'.

411. What is then written? "And Abraham lifted up his eyes and looked, and behold behind him a ram..." (Beresheet 22:13) WHICH ALLUDES TO the other wicked people of the world who are called 'rams,' as it is written: "the rams of Nevayot shall minister to you" (Yeshayah 60:7). And this PHRASE is translated INTO ARAMAIC as: "the high ranks (also: 'the proud people') of Nevayot..." "caught in a thicket..." This is as you may read: "All the horns of the wicked also will I cut off" (Tehilim 75:11). The phrase: "and Abraham went and took the ram," means that they are about to go through all kinds of bad experiences. But the righteous, in the future, shall remain as the holy supernal angels, to bring about the unison of His Name. Therefore it is written: "in that day Hashem shall be one, and His Name One" (Zecharyah 14:9).

412. אָמַר לוֹ רַבִּי יְהוּדָה מִכָּאן וּלְהָלְאָה, אַצְלָחוּ פִּתְחָא. עָאל יוֹמָא
אָחֳרָא, עָאלוּ קַמֵּיהּ כָּל בְּנֵי מָתָא, אֲמָרוּ לֵיהּ, לֵימָא לָן מַר, מִלַּיָּיא
דְּאוֹרַיְיתָא, בְּפָרְשָׁתָא דְּקָרֵינָן בָּהּ יוֹמָא דְּשַׁבַּתָּא, וַה' פָּקַד אֶת שָׂרָה.
קָם בֵּינֵי עַמּוּדֵי, פָּתַח וְאָמַר וַה' פָּקַד אֶת שָׂרָה וְגו'. ג' מַפְתְּחוֹת בְּיָדוֹ
שֶׁל הַקּוּדְשָׁא בְּרִיךְ הוּא, וְלֹא מְסָרָם לֹא בְּיַד מַלְאָךְ, וְלֹא בְּיַד שָׂרָף,
מַפְתֵּחַ שֶׁל חַיָּה, וְשֶׁל גְּשָׁמִים, וְשֶׁל תְּחִיַּית הַמֵּתִים. בָּא אֵלִיָּהוּ, וְנָטַל
הַשְּׁנַיִם, שֶׁל גְּשָׁמִים וְשֶׁל תְּחִיַּית הַמֵּתִים. וְאָמַר רַבִּי יוֹחָנָן, לֹא נִמְסַר
בְּיַד אֵלִיָּהוּ, אֶלָּא אַחַת. דְּאָמַר ר' יוֹחָנָן, כְּשֶׁבִּקֵּשׁ אֵלִיָּהוּ, לְהַחֲיוֹת בֶּן
הַצָּרְפִית, אָמַר לוֹ קוּדְשָׁא בְּרִיךְ הוּא, לָא יָאוּת לָךְ, לְמֵיסַב בִּידָךְ, שְׁתֵּי
מַפְתְּחוֹת, אֶלָּא תֵּן לִי מַפְתֵּחַ הַגְּשָׁמִים, וּתְחַיֶּה הַמֵּת. וְהַיְינוּ דִּכְתִיב לֵךְ
הֵרָאֵה אֶל אַחְאָב וְגו'. וְאֶתְּנָה מָטָר. לֹא אָמַר, וְתֵן מָטָר, אֶלָּא וְאֶתְּנָה.

412. Rabbi Yehuda said to him: From here on, open up the gate, WHICH MEANS THAT FROM NOW ON, WHOEVER WANTS TO ENTER MAY DO SO, BECAUSE HE HAS FINISHED REVEALING ALL THE MOST SUBLIME

MYSTERIES. All the people of the village came to him. They said: May Sir tell us a few words of the Torah about the portion of the week that we read on the day of Shabbat, "and Hashem visited Sarah." He stood up between the pillars, opened, and said: "And Hashem visited Sarah..." – The Holy One, blessed be He, has three keys in His hands, which He did not hand over to any angel. They are: the Key of Life, the Key of Rain, and the Key of Resurrecting the Dead. Elijah came and took two: the one of rain and the one of resurrecting the dead. Rabbi Yochanan disagreed and said: Elijah was handed only one. Rabbi Yochanan explained: When Elijah wanted to revive the son of the woman of Tzarfat, the Holy One, blessed be He, said to him: It is not proper for you to take two keys and hold them in your hands. So give Me the key of rain, and go and and revive the dead. This is as it is written: "Go, show yourself to Ahab, and I will send rain upon the earth" (I Melachim 18:1). He did not say, 'and send rain,' but rather, "and I will send rain."

413. וְהָא אֱלִישָׁע הֲוָו לֵיהּ. אֵין. לְקַיֵּם פִּי שְׁנַיִם בְּרוּחוֹ שֶׁל אֵלִיָּהוּ, אֶלָּא, שְׁלָשְׁתָּם לֹא מְסָרָם הַקּוּדְשָׁא בְּרִיךְ הוּא, בְּיַד שָׁלִיחַ, דְּאָמַר רַבִּי סִימוֹן, בֹּא וּרְאֵה כֹּחוֹ שֶׁל הַקּוּדְשָׁא בְּרִיךְ הוּא, בְּפַעַם אַחַת מְחַיֶּה מֵתִים, וּמוֹרִיד שְׁאוֹל וַיָּעַל, מַזְרִיחַ מְאוֹרוֹת, וּמוֹרִיד גְּשָׁמִים, מַצְמִיחַ חָצִיר, מְדַשֵּׁן יְבוּלִים, פּוֹקֵד עֲקָרוֹת, נוֹתֵן פַּרְנָסוֹת, עוֹזֵר דַּלִּים, סוֹמֵךְ נוֹפְלִים, זוֹקֵף כְּפוּפִים, מְהַעֲדֵא מַלְכִין, וּמְהָקֵם מַלְכִין, וְהַכֹּל בִּזְמַן אֶחָד, וּבְרֶגַע אֶחָד, וּבְבַת אַחַת, מַה שֶּׁאֵין שָׁלִיחַ, לְעוֹלָם יָכוֹל לַעֲשׂוֹתוֹ.

413. And then Elisha had to establish a double portion of Eliyahu's spirit. Nevertheless, the Holy Once, blessed be He, did not hand three of them over to any messenger. As Rabbi Simon said: Come and behold the might of the Holy One, blessed be He. Simultaneously He resurrects the dead, He "brings down to the grave and brings up" (I Shmuel 2:6), He makes the luminaries shine, brings down rain, "causes the grass to grow" (Tehilim 104:14), fertilizes the crop, visits barren women, supplies food, helps the needy, supports those who have fallen, makes those who are bent down stand erect, removes kings, and raises kings. He does all this at the same time and at the same moment, a task no messenger can ever accomplish.

414. תַּנְיָא אָמַר רַבִּי יוֹסֵי, כָּל מַה שֶּׁעוֹשֶׂה הַקּוּדְשָׁא בְּרִיךְ הוּא, אֵינוֹ

צָרִיךְ לַעֲשׂוֹת, אֶלָּא בְּדִבּוּר, דְּכֵיוָן דְּאָמַר, מִמְּקוֹם קְדוּשָׁתוֹ יְהֵא כָךְ, מִיָּד נַעֲשֶׂה. בֹּא וּרְאֵה כֹּחַ גְּבוּרָתוֹ שֶׁל הַקוּדְשָׁא בְּרִיךְ הוּא, דִּכְתִיב בִּדְבַר ה' שָׁמַיִם נַעֲשׂוּ. דְּאָמַר ר' יוֹחָנָן מַאי דִכְתִיב וְעָבַרְתִּי בְּאֶרֶץ מִצְרַיִם אֲנִי וְלֹא מַלְאָךְ וְגו'.

414. We have learned, as Rabbi Yosi said: All that the Holy One, blessed be He, does, He can do by a word. As soon as He says from the place of His Holiness 'let this be done', it immediately occurs. Behold the power of the Holy One, blessed be He, and His might, as it is written: "By the word of Hashem were the heavens made" (Tehilim 33:6). Rabbi Yochanan then asks: Why is it written: "For I will pass through the land of Egypt, I and not an angel" (Shemot 12:12)?

415. אִי הָכֵי, יְקָרָא סַגִּיאָה הוּא לְמִצְרָאֵי, דְּלָא דָמֵי מַאן דְּתָפַשׂ מַלְכָּא, לְמַאן דְּתָפַשׂ הֶדְיוֹטָא. וְעוֹד אֵין לְךָ אוּמָה מְזוּהֶמֶת בְּכָל טוּמְאָה, כְּמוֹ הַמִּצְרִים, דִּכְתִיב בְּהוֹ אֲשֶׁר בְּשַׂר חֲמוֹרִים בְּשָׂרָם וְגו'. שֶׁהֵם חֲשׁוּדִים עַל מִשְׁכַּב זָכוּר, וְהֵם בָּאִים מֵחָם, שֶׁעָשָׂה מַה שֶׁעָשָׂה לְאָבִיו, וְקִלֵּל אוֹתוֹ, וְלִכְנַעַן בְּנוֹ. וְכִי לֹא הָיָה לְהַקוּדְשָׁא בְּרִיךְ הוּא, מַלְאָךְ, אוֹ שָׁלִיחַ, לְשַׁגֵּר לַעֲשׂוֹת נִקְמָה בְּמִצְרַיִם, כְּמוֹ שֶׁעָשָׂה בְּאַשּׁוּר, שֶׁהָיָה בְּנוֹ שֶׁל שֵׁם, דִּכְתִיב וּבְנֵי שֵׁם עֵילָם וְאַשּׁוּר. וְשָׁם הָיָה כֹּהֵן גָּדוֹל וְנִתְבָּרֵךְ, שֶׁנֶּאֱמַר בָּרוּךְ ה' אֱלֹהֵי שֵׁם. וְהָיָה לְשֵׁם הַגְּדוּלָה וְהַבְּרָכָה עַל אֶחָיו. וּכְתִיב בָּם, וַיֵּצֵא מַלְאַךְ ה' וַיַּכֶּה בְּמַחֲנֵה אַשּׁוּר. וְעַל יְדֵי שָׁלִיחַ נַעֲשָׂה, כְּמַ"שׁ הַמִּצְרִים, שֶׁהֵם מְזוּהָמִים, יוֹתֵר מִכָּל אוּמָה, וְאָמַר אֲנִי וְלֹא מַלְאָךְ.

415. If so, it is a great honor for Egypt, because it is not the same to be caught by a king and as to be caught by a simple man. Even more so, as there is no nation that is as defiled with all sorts of impurity as Egypt, of which it is written: "whose flesh is as the flesh of donkeys," (Yechezkel 23:20) because they are suspected of sodomy. And they issue from Ham, who did what he did to his father, who then cursed him and his son Canaan. Did not the Holy One, blessed be He, have an angel or a messenger to send to take revenge on Egypt, as he had done to Ashur who was the son of Shem, as it is written: "The children of Shem, Elam and Ashur..."

(Beresheet 10:22)? And Shem was a High Priest who was blessed, as it is written: "Blessed be Hashem, the Elohim of Shem" (Beresheet 9:26). Thus, Shem received blessings and attained superiority over his brothers. Of them, it is written: "Then the angel of Hashem went forth and smote in the camp of Ashur" (Yeshayah 37:36). So this revenge was accomplished by a messenger. So much more so with Egypt, the most impure of all nations. Nevertheless, He said, "I and not an angel."

416. אֶלָּא אָמַר רַבִּי יְהוּדָה, מִכָּאן לָמַדְנוּ כֹּחַ גְּבוּרָתוֹ שֶׁל הַקּוּדְשָׁא בְּרִיךְ הוּא, וּמַעֲלָתוֹ, שֶׁהוּא גָּבוֹהַּ עַל הַכֹּל. אָמַר הַקָּדוֹשׁ בָּרוּךְ הוּא, אוּמָה זוֹ שֶׁל מִצְרַיִם, מְזוּהֶמֶת וּמְטוּנֶּפֶת, וְאֵין רָאוּי לְשַׁגֵּר מַלְאָךְ, וְלֹא שָׂרָף, דָּבָר קָדוֹשׁ בֵּין רְשָׁעִים אֲרוּרִים מְטוּנָּפִים, אֶלָּא אֲנִי עוֹשֶׂה, מַה שֶׁאֵין יָכוֹל לַעֲשׂוֹת מַלְאָךְ, וְלֹא שָׂרָף, וְלֹא שָׁלִיחַ. שֶׁאֲנִי אוֹמֵר מִמְּקוֹם קְדוּשָׁתִי, יְהֵא כָּךְ, וּמִיָּד נַעֲשָׂה, מַה שֶׁאֵין הַמַּלְאָךְ יָכוֹל לַעֲשׂוֹתוֹ. אֲבָל הַקּוּדְשָׁא בְּרִיךְ הוּא, מִמְּקוֹם קְדוּשָׁתוֹ, אוֹמֵר יְהֵא כָּךְ, וּמִיָּד נַעֲשָׂה, מַה שֶׁהוּא רוֹצֶה לַעֲשׂוֹת. וּלְפִיכָךְ לֹא נַעֲשֵׂית נְקָמָה זוֹ, ע״י מַלְאָךְ וְשָׁלִיחַ, בִּשְׁבִיל קְלוֹן הַמִּצְרִים, וּלְהַרְאוֹת גְּדוּלָתוֹ שֶׁל מָקוֹם, שֶׁלֹּא רָצָה שֶׁיִּכָּנֵס בֵּינֵיהֶם דָּבָר קָדוֹשׁ, וְעַל הַדֶּרֶךְ הַזֶּה נֶאֱמַר, אֲנִי וְלֹא מַלְאָךְ, אֲנִי יָכוֹל לַעֲשׂוֹתוֹ וְלֹא מַלְאָךְ.

416. Rabbi Yehuda said that from this we learn the great might of the Holy One, blessed be He, and His exaltedness, which is high above all. The Holy One, blessed be He, said: This nation of Egypt is impure and full of filth, so it is not proper to send an angel or anything holy among filthy, impure, and cursedly wicked people. So I will perform what cannot be done by an angel or a messenger or a Seraph. From the place of My holiness I announce, Let this be done. And immediately what cannot be done by an angel is done. So the Holy One, blessed be He, from His place of holiness, announces: Let thus happen so! And all that He wanted done occurs immediately. Therefore, this revenge was not accomplished by an angel or a messenger, for the dishonor of the Egyptians, and to display the greatness of the Creator, who did not want anything holy to enter among them. According to this, it is written: "I and not an angel"; I alone am able to perform this.

417. כַּיּוֹצֵא בּוֹ אָמַר רַבִּי יְהוּדָה, מַאי דִכְתִיב וַיֹּאמֶר ה׳ לַדָּג. וְכַמָּה

צַדִּיקִים וַחֲסִידִים מִיִּשְׂרָאֵל, שֶׁלֹּא דִּבֵּר עִמָּהֶם הַקוּדְשָׁא בְּרִיךְ הוּא, וּבָא לְדַבֵּר עִם הַדָּג, דָּבָר שֶׁאֵינוֹ מַכִּיר וְיוֹדֵעַ. אֶלָּא אָמַר ר' יְהוּדָה, כֵּיוָן שֶׁעָלְתָה תְּפִלָּתוֹ שֶׁל יוֹנָה, לִפְנֵי הַקוּדְשָׁא בְּרִיךְ הוּא, מִמְּקוֹם קְדוּשָּׁתוֹ אָמַר, בִּשְׁבִיל שֶׁיָּקִיא הַדָּג אֶת יוֹנָה אֶל הַיַּבָּשָׁה, לְמַ"ד לַדָּג, כְּמוֹ בִּשְׁבִיל, כְּלוֹמַר, וַיֹּאמֶר ה' בִּשְׁבִיל הַדָּג, שֶׁיָּקִיא אֶת יוֹנָה אֶל הַיַּבָּשָׁה, מִמְּקוֹם קְדוּשָּׁתוֹ אָמַר הַקוּדְשָׁא בְּרִיךְ הוּא יְהֵא כָךְ, וּמִיָּד נַעֲשָׂה, מַה שֶׁאֵין שָׁלִיחַ, יָכוֹל לַעֲשׂוֹתוֹ.

417. Rabbi Yehuda continued by asking: Why is it written: "And Hashem spoke to the fish..." (Yonah 2:11)? How many righteous and pious men of Yisrael did the Holy One, blessed be He, never speak to, while He came to speak to the fish, who does not know or recognize Him? Rabbi Yehuda continued: Because Yonah's prayers reached to the Holy One, blessed be He, He spoke, from the place of His holiness, so that the fish would vomit Jonah out and cast him ashore. So why did He speak to the fish? Hashem spoke to the fish, so that Jonah would be thrown back to the shore. So from the place of His Holiness, the Holy One, blessed be He, said: Let this happen. And immediately it was done, something that no messenger was able to do.

418. תַּנְיָא אָמַר רַבִּי שִׁמְעוֹן, מַפְתֵּחַ שֶׁל חַיָּה, בְּיָדוֹ שֶׁל הַקוּדְשָׁא בְּרִיךְ הוּא הִיא, וּבְעוֹד שֶׁהִיא יוֹשֶׁבֶת עַל הַמַּשְׁבֵּר, הַקָּדוֹשׁ בָּרוּךְ הוּא, מְעַיֵּן בְּאוֹתוֹ הַוָּלָד, אִם רָאוּי הוּא לָצֵאת לָעוֹלָם, פּוֹתֵחַ דַּלְתוֹת בִּטְנָהּ וְיוֹצֵא, וְאִם לָאו סוֹגֵר דַּלְתוֹתֶיהָ, וּמֵתוּ שְׁנֵיהֶם. אִי הָכִי, לֹא יֵצֵא רָשָׁע לָעוֹלָם. אֶלָּא הָכִי תָּנִינָן, עַל שָׁלֹשׁ עֲבֵירוֹת נָשִׁים מֵתוֹת וְכוּ'. וְאָמַר רַבִּי יִצְחָק, לָמָּה אִשָּׁה מַפֶּלֶת פְּרִי בִטְנָהּ. אֶלָּא אָמַר רַבִּי יִצְחָק, הַקָּדוֹשׁ בָּרוּךְ הוּא רוֹאֶה אוֹתוֹ הָעוּבָּר, שֶׁאֵינוֹ רָאוּי לָצֵאת לָעוֹלָם, וּמַקְדִּים לַהֲמִיתוֹ בִּמְעֵי אִמּוֹ, שֶׁנֶּאֱמַר הַנְּפִלִים הָיוּ בָאָרֶץ בַּיָּמִים הָהֵם. הַנְּפִלִים כְּתִיב, בְּלֹא יוּ"ד רִאשׁוֹנָה. וְלָמָּה, בִּשְׁבִיל שֶׁאַחֲרֵי כֵן, בָּאוּ בְּנֵי הָאֱלֹהִים אֶל בְּנוֹת הָאָדָם, וְיָלְדוּ לָהֶם בִּזְנוּת, וַיִּרְבּוּ מַמְזֵרִים בָּעוֹלָם.

418. We learned as Rabbi Shimon said: The key of Life is in the hands of the Holy One, blessed be He. So while the mother still lies in labor, the

Holy One, blessed be He, examines the newborn. If he is worthy of emerging and coming into this world, then He opens the gates of her womb and he comes out. If not, then He shuts the gates and they both die. If so, an evil person will never come into the world. Rather we have learned that women die because of three transgressions. Rabbi Yitzchak asks: Why should any woman have a miscarriage and lose the fruit of her womb? Rabbi Yitzchak responded: The Holy One, blessed be He, examines that fetus that is not fit to come into the world and kills it while it is still in the womb of its mother, as it is written: "there were giants (Heb. *nefilim*) on the earth in those days..." (Beresheet 6:4) Nefilim is spelled without the first *Yud* (Heb. *nefalim* or: 'miscarriages'). And why? Because later, "the sons of Elohim came onto the daughters of men, and they bore children to them," by prostitution. And so the number of bastards grew in the world.

419. הֵמָּה הַגִּבּוֹרִים אֲשֶׁר מֵעוֹלָם. שֶׁאֵין גִּבּוֹר וּפָרִיץ וְעָרִיץ, כְּמוֹ הַמַּמְזֵר. אַנְשֵׁי הַשֵּׁם, שֶׁהַכֹּל יַכִּירוּ, לְקרוֹתוֹ הַשֵּׁם הַיָּדוּעַ מַמְזֵר, דְּכֵיוָן שֶׁרוֹאִים מַעֲשָׂיו, שֶׁהוּא פָּרִיץ וְעָרִיץ וְגִבּוֹר, הַכֹּל יִקְרָאוּהוּ אוֹתוֹ שֵׁם. וּמַה דְּאָמַר רַבִּי שִׁמְעוֹן הַקּוּדְשָׁא בְּרִיךְ הוּא מְעַיֵּין בְּאוֹתוֹ הַוָּלָד. אֵין לְךָ רָשָׁע בָּעוֹלָם, מֵאוֹתָם הָרְשָׁעִים הַיּוֹצְאִים לָעוֹלָם, שֶׁאֵין הַקּוּדְשָׁא בְּרִיךְ הוּא מְעַיֵּין בּוֹ, וְרוֹאֶה אִם אוֹתוֹ הַגּוּף, יַנִּיחַ בֵּן צַדִּיק וְכָשֵׁר, אוֹ שֶׁיַּצִּיל לְאָדָם מִיִּשְׂרָאֵל מִמִּיתָה מְשׁוּנָּה, אוֹ שֶׁיַּעֲשֶׂה טוֹבָה אַחַת, וּבִשְׁבִיל כָּךְ הַקָּדוֹשׁ בָּרוּךְ הוּא מוֹצִיאוֹ לָעוֹלָם.

419. "...they were the men of renown which were of old..." (Beresheet 6:4) because there is no greater tyrant, robber, or mighty man than a bastard. They were recognized as "...men of renown (lit. 'men of the name')" by all, and called by that known brand, 'bastard'. Because they all see by his actions that he is a tyrant, a robber, and mighty man, they call him by that name. And Rabbi Shimon said that the Holy One, blessed be He examines the newborn. There is no wicked person in the world who is not examined by the Holy One, blessed be He. And He checks whether that person will ever beget a righteous son or save somebody from Yisrael from a cruel death or do even one good deed. And if the answer is yes, the Holy One, blessed be He, allows him to come out into the world.

420. בְּיוֹמוֹי דְּרַבִּי יוֹסֵי, הֲווֹ אִינּוּן פְּרִיצֵי, דַּהֲווֹ מְשַׁדְּדֵי בְּטוּרַיָּיא, עִם

פְּרִיצֵי אוּמוֹת הָעוֹלָם, וְכַד מַשְׁכְּחֵי בַּר נָשׁ, וְתָפְשֵׂי לֵיה לְקַטְלֵיה, הֲווֹ
אָמְרִין לֵיה, מַה שְׁמָךְ, אִי הֲוָה יוּדָאי, הֲווֹ אָזְלִין עִמֵּיה, וּמַפְּקִין לֵיה מִן
טוּרַיָּיא, וְאִי הֲוָה בַּר נָשׁ אַחֲרִינָא, קַטְלֵי לֵיה, וַהֲוָה אָמַר רַבִּי יוֹסֵי,
אִתְחֲזוּן אִינּוּן, בְּכֹל הַאי, לְמֵיעַל לְעָלְמָא דְאָתֵי.

420. In the days of Rabbi Yosi, there were bandits who robbed people in the mountains, along with bandits from other nations of the world. When they found someone, they seized him for the purpose of killing him. They said to him: What is your name? If he was a Jew, they accompanied him, bringing him out and away from the mountains. But if he was not a Jew, they killed him. Rabbi Yosi said: Nevertheless, they are yet suitable to enter the World to Come and attain its life.

421. ת״ר, ג׳ דְּבָרִים הַלָּלוּ, אֵינָן בָּאן לְעוֹלָם אֶלָּא בְּקוֹלוֹת, קוֹל חַיָּה,
דִּכְתִיב בְּעֶצֶב תֵּלְדִי בָנִים. וּכְתִיב וַיִּשְׁמַע אֵלֶיהָ אֱלֹהִים. קוֹל גְּשָׁמִים,
דִּכְתִיב, קוֹל ה׳ עַל הַמָּיִם. וּכְתִיב כִּי קוֹל הֲמוֹן הַגָּשֶׁם. קוֹל תְּחִיַּית
הַמֵּתִים, דִּכְתִיב קוֹל קוֹרֵא בַּמִּדְבָּר. מַאי בָּעֵי הָכָא קָלָא בְּמִדְבְּרָא. אֶלָּא
אָמַר רַבִּי זְרִיקָא אִלֵּין אִינּוּן קָלַיָּיא, לְאַתְעָרָא מֵתֵי מִדְבָּר, וּמִכָּאן
דְּהוּא הַדִּין לְכָל הָעוֹלָם. אָמַר רָבִּי יוֹחָנָן, הָא תְּנָן, כְּשֶׁנִּכְנַס אָדָם
לַקֶּבֶר, נִכְנָס בְּקוֹלוֹת. כְּשֶׁיָּקוּמוּ בִּתְחִיַּית הַמֵּתִים, אֵינוּ דִין שֶׁיָּקוּמוּ
בְּקוֹלֵי קוֹלוֹת.

421. The sages taught that the following three things do not come into the world except through voices: the voice of a woman giving birth, as it is written: "in sorrow shall you bring forth children" (Beresheet 3:16), and "and Elohim hearkened to her" (Beresheet 30:22); the voice of the rains, as it is written: "The voice of Hashem is upon the waters" (Tehilim 29:3) and, "a sound of the rumbling of the rainstorm" (I Melachim 18:41); the voice of the resurrection of the dead, as it is written: "A voice cries...in the wilderness" (Yeshayah 40:3). What is the purpose of the voice in the wilderness? Rabbi Zrika says this voice came to raise the dead of the wilderness. From this we derive that it is true for the whole world. Rabbi Yochanan says we learned that when a man enters the grave he does so with voices. And when they rise at the resurrection of the dead, should they not also rise with great voices?

422. אָמַר רִבִּי יַעֲקֹב, עֲתִידָה בַּת קוֹל, לִהְיוֹת מִתְפּוֹצֶצֶת, בְּבָתֵּי קְבָרוֹת, וְאוֹמֶרֶת, הָקִיצוּ וְרַנְּנוּ שׁוֹכְנֵי עָפָר, וַעֲתִידִים לִחְיוֹת, בְּטַל שֶׁל אוֹר גָּדוֹל שֶׁל מַעְלָה, דִּכְתִיב כִּי טַל אוֹרוֹת טַלֶּךָ וְאֶרֶץ רְפָאִים תַּפִּיל, אכי"ר.

(ע"כ מִדְרָשׁ הַנֶּעֱלָם).

422. Rabbi Ya'akov said that a divine voice will burst in the graveyards, saying: "Awake and sing, you who dwell in dust" (Yeshayah 26:19), and they will live by the dew of a great supernal light from above, as it is written: "for your dew is as the dew of the herbs ('lights'), and the earth shall cast out the dead" (Yeshayah 26:19). Amen, may it be so.

End of Midrash Hane'elam

423. וַיְיָ' פָּקַד אֶת שָׂרָה כַּאֲשֶׁר אָמַר, דִּכְתִיב, לַמּוֹעֵד אָשׁוּב אֵלֶיךָ כָּעֵת חַיָּה וּלְשָׂרָה בֵן. וְתָנִינָן פָּקַד אֶת שָׂרָה, פְּקִידָה לְנוּקְבָא, זְכִירָה לִדְכוּרָא וּבְגִין כָּךְ, וַיְיָ' פָּקַד אֶת שָׂרָה כַּאֲשֶׁר אָמַר, דִּכְתִיב שׁוּב אָשׁוּב אֵלֶיךָ כָּעֵת חַיָּה וגו', מֵהָכָא מַשְׁמַע דְּאָמַר, וַיֹּאמֶר שׁוּב אָשׁוּב אֵלֶיךָ, וַיֹּאמֶר סְתָם, דְּאִיהוּ הֲוָה, וְלָא שְׁלִיחָא אַחֲרָא.

423. "And Hashem visited Sarah, as He had said..." This is IN ACCORDANCE WITH what is written: "I will certainly return to you, at this season, and Sarah shall have a son." And we have learned in relation to "visited Sarah," that visitation is related to the female, while remembrance is related to the male. Therefore, IT IS WRITTEN ABOUT SARAH: "And Hashem visited Sarah." AND HASHEM (VAV-YUD HEI VAV HEI) IS THE SECRET OF THE NUKVA, NAMELY HIM AND HIS COURT OF JUDGMENT. The words, "as He had said" REFER TO WHAT is written: "As the time appointed I will return to you..." From this we learn THAT THE VERSE: "And he said: As the time appointed I will return to you..." IS WRITTEN AS "He said," in a general way. Thus, it was he, NAMELY THE NUKVA, WHO "HAD SAID" and not any other messenger. OTHERWISE, HOW COULD IT BE WRITTEN HERE: "AND HASHEM (VAV-YUD HEI VAV HEI) VISITED SARAH, AS HE HAD SAID." WHERE ELSE DID HE SAY THIS?

30. "And Hashem did to Sarah"

A Synopsis
Children help their parents earn and enhance a connection to the Light of the Creator when they pursue a spiritual path in life.

The Relevance of this Passage
A spiritual umbilical cord between parent and child remains in place for all eternity. Hence, the actions of a parent influence the child, and the actions of the child bear spiritual consequences for the parents. We arouse and bestow tremendous Light upon our children that will help motivate and guide them towards a spiritual lifestyle and existence.

424. וַיַּעַשׂ יי' לְשָׂרָה וגו'. כֵּיוָן דַּאֲמַר וַיי' פָּקַד אֶת שָׂרָה, מַהוּ וַיַּעַשׂ יי' לְשָׂרָה. אֶלָּא הָכֵי תָּנִינָן דְּאִיבָּא דְּעוֹבָדוֹי דְּקוּדְשָׁא בְּרִיךְ הוּא, מֵהַהוּא נָהָר דְּנָגִיד וְנָפִיק מֵעֵדֶן אִיהוּ, וְאִיהוּ נִשְׁמַתְהוֹן דְּצַדִּיקַיָּיא, וְאִיהוּ מַזָּלָא, דְּכָל בִּרְכָאן טָבָאן, וְגִשְׁמֵי בִרְכָאן, נָזְלֵי מְנֵיהּ, וּמִתַּמָּן נָפְקֵי, דִּכְתִיב לְהַשְׁקוֹת אֶת הַגָּן, דְּאִיהוּ מַזִּיל, וּמַשְׁקֶה מֵעֵילָא לְתַתָּא, בְּגִין דִּבְנֵי בְּהַאי מַזָּלָא תַּלְיָין, וְלָא בַּאֲתַר אָחֳרָא.

424. "And Hashem did to Sarah..." (Beresheet 21:9). HE ASKS: It is said, "And Hashem visited Sarah." Why, then, DO WE ALSO NEES "And Hashem did to Sarah"? AND HE REPLIES: We have learned that the 'fruits' of the works of the Holy One, blessed be He, come from the river that flows and issues from Eden, WHICH IS ZEIR ANPIN, and are the souls of the righteous. IN OTHER WORDS, HIS WORKS ARE THE SOULS OF THE RIGHTEOUS. And this is Mazal (lit. 'Flow') from where all the good blessings and blessed rains flow. And from there they issue, as it is written: "to water the garden" (Beresheet 2:10), as it flows and irrigates from above downward, because (bearing) children depends on Mazal and no other place.

425. וְעַל דָּא כְּתִיב, וַיי' פָּקַד אֶת שָׂרָה, פְּקִידָה בִּלְחוֹדוֹי. וַיַּעַשׂ יי' לְשָׂרָה. עֲשִׂיָּיה אִיהוּ, לְעֵילָא מֵהַאי דַּרְגָּא, כְּמָה דְּאִתְּמַר דְּהָא בְּמַזָּלָא תַּלְיָיא, וְעַל דָּא, כָּאן פְּקִידָה, וְכָאן עֲשִׂיָּיה. וּבְגִין כָּךְ אָמַר יי' וַיי', וְכֹלָּא חַד.

-459-

425. So in reference to this, it is written: "And Hashem visited Sarah," IN WHICH "visit," only WHICH IS THE SECRET OF NUKVA, IS MENTIONED. In the phrase, "And Hashem did to Sarah," THIS 'doing,' WHICH IS THE SECRET OF CHILDREN AND THE SOULS OF THE RIGHTEOUS, WHICH ARE THE FRUITS OF HIS HANDIWORK, is higher than the grade OF THE "VISIT," which depends on Mazal, as previously explained. This is why IT IS DESCRIBED here AS a "visit," WHICH IS RELATED TO THE NUKVA, and there as a 'doing,' WHICH IS RELATED TO ZEIR ANPIN. And therefore it is said, "And Hashem," and again, "And Hashem," both being the same. OF THE "VISIT," IT IS WRITTEN: "AND HASHEM (*VAV*-YUD HEI VAV HEI) VISITED," WHICH IS THE SECRET OF HIM AND HIS COURT OF JUDGMENT, WHICH IS THE NUKVA – WHILE IN THE 'DOING,' IT IS WRITTEN: "HASHEM (YUD HEI VAV HEI) DID," WHICH RELATES TO ZEIR ANPIN.

426. רַבִּי אֶלְעָזָר, פָּתַח וַאֲמַר, הִנֵּה נַחֲלַת יי' בָּנִים שָׂכָר פְּרִי הַבָּטֶן. הִנֵּה נַחֲלַת יי', אַחְסַנְתָּא לְאִתְאַחֲדָא בֵּיי', דְּלָא יִתְעֲבַר מִינָהּ לְעָלְמִין, דְּבַר נָשׁ דְּזָכֵי לְבָנִין בְּהַאי עָלְמָא, זָכֵי בְּהוֹ לְמֵיעַל לְפַרְגּוֹדָא, בְּעַלְמָא דְּאָתֵי. בְּגִין, דְּהַהוּא בְּרָא דְּשָׁבֵיק בַּר נָשׁ, וְזָכֵי בֵּיהּ בְּעַלְמָא דָא, אִיהוּ יְזַכֵּי לֵיהּ לְעַלְמָא דְּאָתֵי וְזָכֵי לְאַעֲלָא בֵּיהּ, לְנַחֲלַת יי'.

426. Rabbi Elazar opened the discussion with the verse: "For children are the heritage of Hashem, and fruit of the womb is a reward" (Tehilim 127:3). "For children are the heritage of Hashem" MEANS "a heritage" by which one can cleave to Hashem and never turn away from Him, because a person who merits the virtue of having children in this world shall, as a result of those children, deserve to join the company OF THE HOLY ONCE, BLESSED BE HE, in the World to Come. Thus, that child, whom that person merited and left behind in this world, shall in return bring him merit in the World to Come. Thereby, he shall merit to enter the "heritage of Hashem."

427. מַאן נַחֲלַת יי', דָּא אֶרֶץ הַחַיִּים. וְהָכִי קָרָא לָהּ לְאֶרֶץ יִשְׂרָאֵל, דְּאִיהִי אֶרֶץ הַחַיִּים. דָּוִד מַלְכָּא, קָרָא לֵיהּ נַחֲלַת יי' דִּכְתִיב כִּי גֵּרְשׁוּנִי הַיּוֹם מֵהִסְתַּפֵּחַ בְּנַחֲלַת יי' לֵאמֹר לֵךְ עֲבֹד אֱלֹהִים אֲחֵרִים, וּבְגִין כָּךְ, הִנֵּה נַחֲלַת יי' בָּנִים. מַאן אַזְכֵּי לֵיהּ, לְבַר נָשׁ. בְּנִין. אִי זָכֵי בְּהוֹ בְּהַאי

עָלְמָא, שָׂכָר פְּרִי הַבֶּטֶן, אַגְרָא וְחוּלָקָא טָבָא, בְּהַהִיא עַלְמָא, בְּהַהוּא
אִיבָּא דְּמֵעוֹי, אִיהוּ דְּזָכֵי בַּר נָשׁ, בְּהַהוּא עַלְמָא, בְּהוּ.

427. HE ASKS: What is the "heritage of Hashem?" AND HE ANSWERS: This is the 'Land of the Living', NAMELY THE NUKVA. And King David called the land of Yisrael, which is the 'Land of the living,' also, the "heritage of Hashem," as it is written: "for they have driven me out this day from abiding in the heritage of Hashem, saying, Go, serve other Elohim" (I Shmuel 26:19). And this is why THE SCRIPTURE SAYS, "For children are the heritage of Hashem." Who enables a person to inherit THE HERITAGE OF HASHEM? Children ENABLE HIM. So if he has the merit of BEGETTING CHILDREN in this world, "the fruit of the womb is a reward," because they are the reward and good portion in that ETERNAL world. So because of this "fruit of the womb," a person deserves to enter the Eternal World.

428. תָּא חֲזֵי הִנֵּה נַחֲלַת יי' בָּנִים. יְרוּתָא וְאַחֲסַנְתָּא, דְּאִיבִּין דְּעוֹבָדוֹי
דְּקוּדְשָׁא בְּרִיךְ הוּא מִלְעֵילָא, אִיהוּ מֵאִילָנָא דְחַיֵּי, דְּהָא מִתַּמָּן זָכֵי בַּר
נָשׁ לִבְנִין, כד"א מִמֶּנִּי פֶּרְיְךָ נִמְצָא. מַה כְּתִיב, אַשְׁרֵי הַגֶּבֶר אֲשֶׁר מִלֵּא
אֶת אַשְׁפָּתוֹ מֵהֶם לֹא יֵבוֹשׁוּ וְגו'. אַשְׁרֵי בְּעָלְמָא דֵין, וְאַשְׁרֵי בְּעָלְמָא
דְאָתֵי.

428. Come and behold: "For children are the heritage of Hashem." THIS REFERS TO the inheritance and heritage of the fruit of the handiwork of the Holy One, blessed be He – NAMELY, the 'Tree of Life', AS THE HOLY ONE, BLESSED BE HE, IS CALLED THE 'TREE OF LIFE', because a person merits his children from there. As it is written: "From me is your fruit found" (Hoshea 14:9). What is written? "Happy is the man that has his quiver full of them, they shall not be ashamed..." (Tehilim 127:5). Happy is he in this world, and happy is he in the World to Come.

429. לֹא יֵבוֹשׁוּ כִּי יְדַבְּרוּ אֶת אוֹיְבִים בַּשָּׁעַר. מַאן אוֹיְבִים בַּשָּׁעַר. אִלֵּין
מָארֵיהוֹן דְּדִינִין, דְּכַד נִשְׁמָתָא נָפְקַת מֵהַאי עַלְמָא, כַּמָּה אִינוּן מָרֵיהוֹן
דְּדִינִין, דְּזַמִּינִין קַמֵּיה, עַד לָא יֵיעוֹל לְדוּכְתֵּיה, בַּשָּׁעַר. בְּהַהוּא תַּרְעָא,
דְּיֵיעוֹל תַּמָּן, בְּגִין דְּמַשְׁכּוֹנִין, שָׁבֵיק בְּהַאי עַלְמָא, וּבְגִינַיְהוֹן יִזְכֵּי
בְּהַהוּא עַלְמָא, וְעַל דָּא, לֹא יֵבוֹשׁוּ כִּי יְדַבְּרוּ אֶת אוֹיְבִים בַּשָּׁעַר.

429. Of the verse: "they shall not be ashamed when they shall speak with the enemies at the gate" (Ibid.) HE ASKS: Who are the 'enemies at the gate"? AND HE ANSWERS: These are the accusers, because when the soul departs from this world many accusers are standing ready before it, as it enters into its place. "The gate" is the gate through which it enters TO REACH ITS PLACE, AND THERE THEY WAIT. BUT IT IS SAVED FROM THEM, because he has left offspring in this world, REFERRING TO HIS CHILDREN. And because of them, he shall merit the world OF ETERNITY. This is why: "they shall not be ashamed when they shall speak with the enemies at the gate."

430. רַבִּי יְהוּדָה וְרַבִּי יוֹסֵי, הֲווֹ אָזְלֵי בְּאָרְחָא, אָמַר לוֹ רַבִּי יְהוּדָה לְרַבִּי יוֹסֵי, פְּתַח פּוּמָךְ, וְלָעֵי בְּאוֹרַיְיתָא, דְּהָא שְׁכִינְתָּא אִשְׁתַּכְּחַת גַּבָּךְ, דְּכָל זְמַן דִּבְמִלֵּי דְאוֹרַיְיתָא לָעָאן, שְׁכִינְתָּא אַתְיָא וּמִתְחַבְּרָא וְכָל שֶׁכֵּן בְּאוֹרְחָא, דִּשְׁכִינְתָּא קַדְמָא וְאַתְיָא וְאָזְלָא קַמַּיְיהוּ דִּבְנֵי נָשָׁא, דְּזָכָאן בִּמְהֵימְנוּתָא דְקוּדְשָׁא בְּרִיךְ הוּא.

430. While walking together, Rabbi Yehuda said to Rabbi Yosi: Open your mouth and delve into the teachings of Torah, for the Shechinah dwells upon you. Whenever a person delves into the study of Torah, the Shechinah joins him, and even more so when walking along the road. Then the Shechinah comes and welcomes him and goes in front of those who have merited the Faith in the Holy One, blessed be He.

31. "Your wife shall be as a fruitful vine"

A Synopsis

The importance of modesty and spiritual behavior for the wife of a man is examined through the teachings of the holy Zohar. A woman corresponds to the Sfirah of Malchut, which is the receptacle and vessel for the Light of the Creator in this physical realm. A woman plays the same role in the physical world of family, manifesting spiritual energy for the entire household. The more pure her vessel is, the more Light she generates for her loved ones.

The Relevance of this Passage

The letters that form these mystical texts arouse a greater sense of appreciation for the dynamic role that a woman's virtue plays in the family. This appreciation helps to purify a woman's vessel, making her a more effective channel of energy for her family.

431. פָּתַח רַבִּי יוֹסֵי וַאֲמַר, אֶשְׁתְּךָ כְּגֶפֶן פֹּרִיָּה בְּיַרְכְּתֵי בֵיתֶךָ בָּנֶיךָ כִּשְׁתִילֵי זֵיתִים סָבִיב לְשֻׁלְחָנֶךָ. אֶשְׁתְּךָ כְּגֶפֶן פֹּרִיָּה, כָּל זִמְנָא, דְּאִתְּתָא בְּיַרְכְּתֵי בֵיתָא, וְלָא נָפְקָא לְבַר, הִיא צְנוּעָה, וְאִתְחֲזֵי לְאוֹלָדָא בְּנִין דְּכַשְׁרָן. כְּגֶפֶן, מַה גֶּפֶן, לָא אִתְנַטְעָא אֶלָּא בְּזִינָהּ, וְלָא בְּזִינָא אַחֲרָא. כָּךְ אִתְּתָא דְּכַשְׁרָא, לָא תֶּעֱבַד נְטִיעָן בְּבַר נָשׁ אַחֲרָא. מַה גֶּפֶן, לָא אִית בֵּיהּ רְכִיבָה מֵאִילָנָא אַחֲרָא, אוֹף הָכֵי אִתְּתָא דְּכַשְׁרָא הָכֵי נָמֵי.

431. Rabbi Yosi began the discussion with the verse: "Your wife shall be as a fruitful vine by the sides of your house, your children like olive plants round about your table" (Tehilim 128:3). "Your wife shall be as a fruitful vine" MEANS THAT as long as the woman remains by the sides of the house and does not go outside, she is modest and worthy of bearing worthy children. "As a fruitful vine" means that just as a vine is always planted with its own kind, so shall an honorable wife never grow any sprouts, NAMELY CHILDREN, from another man. And just as a vine is never grafted with another kind of tree, so an honorable wife NEVER MATES WITH ANOTHER MAN.

432. חֲמֵי מָה אַגְרָהּ, בָּנֶיךָ כִּשְׁתִילֵי זֵיתִים. מַה זֵיתִים לָא נָפְלֵי טַרְפַּיְיהוּ, כָּל יוֹמֵי שַׁתָּא, וְכֻלְּהוּ קְשׁוּרִין תָּדִיר. אוֹף הָכֵי בָּנֶיךָ כִּשְׁתִילֵי זֵיתִים סָבִיב לְשֻׁלְחָנֶךָ.

432. What is her reward? It is "your children like olive plants." Just as the leaves of the olive plants never fall, but are attached to the tree all the time, so "the children like olive plants round about your table" SHALL ALWAYS BE ATTACHED TO YOU.

433. מַה כְּתִיב בַּתְרֵיהּ, הִנֵּה כִי כֵן יְבֹרַךְ גֶּבֶר יְרֵא יי'. מַאי הִנֵּה כִי כֵן יְבֹרַךְ גָּבֶר. הִנֵּה כֵן מִבָּעֵי לֵיהּ. אֶלָּא לְאַסְגָּאָה מִלָּה אָחֳרָא, דְּאוֹלִיפְנָא דָא מִנָּהּ, דְּכָל זִמְנָא דִּשְׁכִינְתָּא הֲוָה צְנִיעָא בְּאַתְרָהּ, כְּדְקָא חֲזֵי לָהּ, כִּבְיָכוֹל, בָּנֶיךָ כִּשְׁתִילֵי זֵיתִים, אִלֵּין יִשְׂרָאֵל כַּד שָׁרָאן בְּאַרְעָא. סָבִיב לְשֻׁלְחָנֶךָ. דְּאַכְלֵי וְשָׁתָאן, וּקְרֵבִין קָרְבָּנִין וְחָדָאן קַמֵּי קוּדְשָׁא בְּרִיךְ הוּא, וּמִתְבָּרְכָן עִלָּאִין וְתַתָּאִין בְּגִינַיְיהוּ.

433. What is written next? "Behold, that thus shall the man be blessed, that fears Hashem" (Tehilim 128:4). AND HE ASKS: What is MEANT BY "Behold, that thus shall the man be blessed." SHOULD IT NOT BE WRITTEN: 'BEHOLD – THUS'? AND HE REPLIES: This is another issue that is learned from her. As long as the Shechinah was kept modestly in Her place, as is properly suited for Her, then it is as though "your children like olive plants." These are the children of Yisrael living in the land OF YISRAEL "round about your table," as they eat, drink, offer sacrifices, and rejoice before the Holy One, blessed be He. And the upper and lower beings are blessed because of them.

434. לְבָתַר דִּשְׁכִינְתָּא נָפְקַת, אִתְגְּלוּ יִשְׂרָאֵל, מֵעַל פְּתוֹרָא דַּאֲבוּהוֹן, וַהֲווֹ בֵּינֵי עַמְמַיָּא, וְצַוְוחִין כָּל יוֹמָא, וְלֵית דְּאַשְׁגַּח בְּהוֹ, בַּר קוּדְשָׁא בְּרִיךְ הוּא, דִּכְתִיב וְאַף גַּם זֹאת בִּהְיוֹתָם בְּאֶרֶץ אוֹיְבֵיהֶם וגו'. וְחָמֵינָן, כַּמָּה קַדִּישִׁין עִלָּאִין, מִיתוּ בִּגְזֵרִין תַּקִּיפִין, וְכָל דָּא, בְּגִין עוֹנָשָׁא דְאוֹרַיְיתָא, דְּלָא קַיְימוּ יִשְׂרָאֵל, כַּד הֲווֹ שָׁרָאן בְּאַרְעָא קַדִּישָׁא.

434. After the Shechinah departed FROM HER PLACE, the children of Yisrael were exiled from the table of their Father and dispersed among the nations. And they cry out all day long, but there is no one who takes heed except the Holy One, blessed be He, as it is written: "And yet for all that, when they are in the land of their enemies..." (Vayikra 26:44) And we do see how many holy and saintly men did perish under harsh decrees, all this being a punishment of the Torah, which Yisrael did not observe when they lived in the Holy Land.

435. חֲמֵי מַה כְּתִיב, תַּחַת אֲשֶׁר לֹא עָבַדְתָּ אֶת יי' אֱלֹהֶיךָ בְּשִׂמְחָה וּבְטוּב לֵבָב מֵרֹב כֹּל. הַאי קְרָא, אִיהוּ רָזָא תַּחַת, אֲשֶׁר לֹא עָבַדְתָּ בְּשִׂמְחָה בִּזְמַן דְּכֹהֲנֵי הֲווֹ קְרֵבִין קָרְבָּנִין וַעֲלָוָון, וְדָא הִיא בְּשִׂמְחָה. וּבְטוּב לֵבָב, אִלֵּין לֵיוָאֵי. מֵרֹב כֹּל, אֵלּוּ יִשְׂרָאֵל, דַּהֲווֹ אֶמְצָעִיִּים בֵּינַיְיהוּ, וְנָטְלֵי בִּרְכָאן מִכָּל סִטְרִין.

435. As it is written: "Because you do not serve Hashem your Elohim with joyfulness and with gladness of heart, for the abundance of all things" (Devarim 28:47). There is a secret in this verse. The verse "Because you serve not Hashem your Elohim with joyfulness" refers to when the priests offered sacrifices and burned offerings, which is done "...with joyfulness." "And with gladness of heart..." refers to the Levites. And "for the abundance of all things" refers to Yisrael, who are positioned in the middle, between THE PRIESTS AND THE LEVITES, and receive blessings from both sides – FROM THE RIGHT AND THE LEFT.

436. דִּכְתִיב הִרְבִּיתָ הַגּוֹי לוֹ הִגְדַּלְתָּ הַשִּׂמְחָה. אִלֵּין כַּהֲנֵי. שָׂמְחוּ לְפָנֶיךָ כְּשִׂמְחַת בַּקָּצִיר, אֵלּוּ יִשְׂרָאֵל, דְּקוּדְשָׁא בְּרִיךְ הוּא בָּרֵיךְ לוֹן, עֲבוּרָא דְחַקְלָא, וְיַהֲבֵי מַעַשְׂרָא מִכֹּלָּא. כַּאֲשֶׁר יָגִילוּ בְּחַלְּקָם שָׁלָל. אִלֵּין לֵיוָאֵי, דְּנָטְלָא מַעַשְׂרָא, מִגּוֹ אִדְרָא.

436. As it is written: "You have multiplied the nation, and increased its joy" (Yeshayah 9:2). This refers to the priests. "Yisrael rejoiced before You as the joy in harvest" refers to Yisrael, who are blessed by the Holy One, blessed be He, with the harvest OF the fields, as they offer a tenth of everything. "...and as men rejoice when they divide the spoil" refers to the Levites, who receive a tenth from the threshing floor.

437. דָּבָר אַחֵר הִרְבִּיתָ הַגּוֹי. אִלֵּין יִשְׂרָאֵל דִּמְהֵימְנוּתָא דְקוּדְשָׁא בְּרִיךְ הוּא עֲלַיְיהוּ, כִּדְקָא חֲזֵי. לוֹ הִגְדַּלְתָּ הַשִּׂמְחָה. דָּא אִיהוּ דַרְגָּא, רֵישָׁא עִלָּאָה דְּאַבְרָהָם דְּאִתְדַּבַּק בָּהּ, דְּאִיהוּ גָּדוֹל, וְחֶדְוָה בֵּיהּ אִשְׁתְּכַח.

437. A different meaning of "You have multiplied the nation" is that it refers to Yisrael, who properly keep Faith in the Holy One, blessed be He. THIS IS THE SECRET OF THE CENTRAL COLUMN, WHICH INCLUDES THE RIGHT AND LEFT COLUMNS, AS WAS SAID BEFORE. The words "and increased its joy" mean the grade of the supernal Head, REFERRING TO CHESED THAT HAS BECOME CHOCHMAH, to which Abraham has cleaved, because it is called 'Great' and joyfulness can be found in it. THIS IS THE SECRET OF THE RIGHT COLUMN, WHICH IS CHESED.

438. שָׂמְחוּ לְפָנֶיךָ בְּשַׁעֲתָא דְסָלְקִין לְאִתְדַּבְּקָא בָּךְ. כְּשִׂמְחַת בַּקָּצִיר. דָּא כְּנֶסֶת יִשְׂרָאֵל, דְּשִׂמְחַת בַּקָּצִיר דִּילֵיהּ הֲוָה. כַּאֲשֶׁר יָגִילוּ בְּחֶלְקָם שָׁלָל. כַּאֲשֶׁר יָגִילוּ, אִלֵּין שְׁאָר חֵילִין, וּרְתִיכִין לְתַתָּא, בְּזִמְנָא דִּמְחַלְּקֵי שָׁלָל, וְטַרְפֵי טַרְפָּא, בְּרֵאשִׁיתָא דְכֹלָּא.

438. "They rejoiced before You" refers to the time when they rose to cleave to You "as the joy in harvest," which is the Congregation of Yisrael, NAMELY THE NUKVA, which rejoiced in His harvest. THIS IS THE SECRET OF THE LEFT COLUMN, BECAUSE THE REAPING OF THE CROP OF A FIELD COMES FROM THE ILLUMINATION OF THE LEFT. AND THE "HARVEST" IS THE DESIRED RESULT OF WORKING THE FIELDS. SO WHEN IT IS SAID, "THE JOY IN HARVEST," THIS IS THE SECRET OF HER HUSBAND BEING CROWNED BY HER, WHILE SHE IN RETURN IS NOT CROWNED BY HER HUSBAND. "...as men rejoice when they divide the spoil" refers to rejoicing by the other hosts and Chariots, THOSE BENEATH THE NUKVA, while they divide among themselves the spoil and fall upon the prey before everyone else. THIS REFERS TO THE SUPERNAL HEAD, WHICH ABRAHAM CLEAVED TO AND WHICH IS THE SECRET OF THE RIGHT COLUMN, WHICH IS CHESED.

32. The reckoning of the Messianic era

A Synopsis
The Zohar reveals two potential ways in which the Messiah will appear in our world: one is the path of mercy, the other is the path of harsh judgment. When we facilitate this process through our own proactive initiative towards self-transformation, we can usher in the age of Messiah through the path of mercy. If, however, [Heaven forbid] man remains in his self-indulgent ways, it will be through a path of judgment that the Messiah will appear.

The Relevance of this Passage
Kabbalistically, the Messiah is not a righteous individual who will emancipate the world, performing all the spiritual work on our behalf. Rather, the concept of Messiah refers to both a personal state of existence and a global happening. The toil of our own spiritual work will produce personal peace through a merciful path. Global turmoil will force change upon those who reject transformation. As people change, a critical mass will eventually be met and the global Messiah will appear to signify a new world. A proactive desire for self-transformation is awakened within us so that our spiritual development occurs within a framework of mercy and positivity.

439. ר' יְהוּדָה פָּתַח וְאָמַר, עֵת לַעֲשׂוֹת לַיי' הֵפֵרוּ תוֹרָתֶךָ. עֵת לַעֲשׂוֹת לַיי' מַהוּ. אֶלָּא, הָא אוֹקְמוּהָ. אֲבָל עֵת: דָּא כְּנֶסֶת יִשְׂרָאֵל, דְּאִקְרֵי עֵת. כְּמָה דְּאַתְּ אָמֵר, וְאַל יָבֹא בְכָל עֵת אֶל הַקֹּדֶשׁ. מַאי וְאַל יָבֹא בְכָל עֵת. כְּמָה דְּאַתְּ אָמֵר, לְשָׁמְרֶךָ מֵאִשָּׁה זָרָה. וְדָא הוּא וַיַּקְרִיבוּ לִפְנֵי יי' אֵשׁ זָרָה וְגו'. מַאי טַעֲמָא עֵת. בְּגִין, דְּאִית לָהּ עֵת וּזְמַן לְכֹלָּא, לְקָרְבָא, לְאִתְנַהֲרָא, לְאִתְחַבְּרָא כִּדְקָא יָאוֹת. כד"א וַאֲנִי תְפִלָּתִי לְךָ יי' עֵת רָצוֹן.

439. Rabbi Yehuda opened with the verse: "It is time to work for Hashem, for they have made void Your Torah" (Tehilim 119:126). AND HE ASKS: What is the meaning of "It is time to work for Hashem"? AND HE REPLIES: This has already been explained. Nevertheless, "time" alludes to the Congregation of Yisrael, NAMELY THE NUKVA, which is called "time." As it is written: "that he come not at all times into the holy place" (Vayikra 16:2). And what is MEANT BY "that he come not at all times?" The meaning is

similar to what is written: "That they may keep you from a strange woman" (Mishlei 7:5). And this also relates to the verse: "and offered strange fire before Hashem" (Vayikra 10:1). IN OTHER WORDS, THE NUKVA OF THE KLIPOT IS ALSO CALLED 'TIME', WHICH IS A STRANGE WOMAN, A STRANGE FIRE. THIS IS WHY IT IS WRITTEN: "THAT HE COME NOT AT ALL TIMES INTO THE HOLY PLACE," BUT ONLY AT THE TIMES OF HOLINESS. AND HE ASKS: Why is THE NUKVA CALLED 'Time'? AND HE REPLIES: Because there is a time and a period for everything. THIS REFERS TO THE 28 PERIODS OF TIME THAT APPEAR IN THE BOOK OF KOHELET IN ORDER to come closer to shine from and cleave TO ZEIR ANPIN properly, as it is written: "But as for me, my prayer is to You, Hashem, in an acceptable time" (Tehilim 69:14).

440. לַעֲשׂוֹת לַיי'. כְּמָה דִכְתִיב, וַיַּעַשׂ דָּוִד שֵׁם. דְּכָל מַאן דְּאִשְׁתַּדַּל בְּאוֹרַיְיתָא, כְּאִילוּ עָבֵיד וְתַקֵּן, הַאי עֵת, לְחַבְּרָא לָהּ בְּקוּדְשָׁא בְּרִיךְ הוּא. וְכָל כָּךְ לָמָּה, בְּגִין דְּהֵפֵרוּ תוֹרָתֶךָ, דְּאִילוּ לֹא הֵפֵרוּ תוֹרָתֶךָ, לָא אִשְׁתַּכַּח פֵּרוּדָא דְּקוּדְשָׁא בְּרִיךְ הוּא מִיִשְׂרָאֵל לְעָלְמִין.

440. "To work (or make) for Hashem" is similar to what is written: "and David made himself a name" (II Shmuel 8:13), WHICH MEANS THAT HE AMENDED THE NUKVA THAT IS CALLED "A NAME." AND IN THE SAME MANNER, whoever studies Torah, it is as though he "made" and prepared the "time," WHICH IS THE NUKVA, to attach Her to the Holy One, blessed be He. And why do all that? WHY SHOULD ANYONE HAVE TO WORK AND PREPARE THE NUKVA? Because "they have made void Your Torah." Had they not "made void Your Torah," then there would not have ever been a separation of the Holy One, blessed be He, from Yisrael, BECAUSE THE UNION OF THE HOLY ONE, BLESSED BE HE, AND HIS SHECHINAH WOULD NEVER HAVE BEEN INTERRUPTED.

441. אָמַר ר' יוֹסֵי, כְּגַוְוֹנָא דָא כְּתִיב, אֲנִי יי' בְּעִתָּהּ אֲחִישֶׁנָּה. מַהוּ בְּעִתָּהּ. בְּעֵת ה' דְּתָקוּם מֵעַפְרָא, כְּדֵין אֲחִישֶׁנָּה. אָמַר רַבִּי יוֹסֵי, וְעִם כָּל דָּא, יוֹמָא חַד, אִיהִי כְּנֶסֶת יִשְׂרָאֵל, גּוֹ עַפְרָא וְלָא יַתִּיר.

441. Rabbi Yosi said that the same applies to the verse: "I Hashem will hasten it in its time" (Yeshayah 60:22). What does "in its time (Heb. *itah*)"

mean? IT MEANS at the time (*et*) when *Hei*, WHICH IS THE NUKVA, shall rise up from Her dust – then I "will hasten it." IN OTHER WORDS, BY MY POWER, NOT BY HER OWN STRENGTH, SHE SHALL RISE FROM THE DUST OF EXILE. Rabbi Yosi said that in spite of all this, the Congregation of Yisrael lies only for one day in the dust OF EXILE, and no more. THIS REFERS TO THE ONE DAY OF THE HOLY ONE, BLESSED BE HE, WHICH LASTS A THOUSAND YEARS, AS IT IS WRITTEN: "FOR A THOUSAND YEARS IN YOUR EYES ARE BUT AS YESTERDAY..." (TEHILIM 90:4) AND THIS ALLUDES TO THE FIFTH MILLENNIUM, AS IS FURTHER EXPLAINED, BECAUSE THE FOURTH MILLENNIUM WAS NOT FULL, AS IT LACKED 172 YEARS BECAUSE THE DESTRUCTION OF THE TEMPLE OCCURRED IN THE YEAR 3828.

442. אָמַר ר' יְהוּדָה, הָכֵי אָמְרוּ. אֲבָל תָּא חֲזֵי, רָזָא דְּאוֹלִיפְנָא, בְּשַׁעֲתָא דִּכְנֶסֶת יִשְׂרָאֵל אִתְגַּלְיָיא מֵאַתְרָהּ, כְּדֵין אַתְוָון דִּשְׁמָא קַדִּישָׁא, כִּבְיָכוֹל אִתְפָּרְשׁוּ. דְּאִתְפָּרְשָׁא ה"א, מִן וא"ו, וּבְגִין דְּאִתְפָּרְשׁוּ, מַה כְּתִיב, נֶאֱלַמְתִּי דוּמִיָּה, בְּגִין דְּאִסְתַּלַּק, וא"ו מִן ה"א, וְקוֹל לָא אִשְׁתְּכַּח, כְּדֵין דִּבּוּר אִתְאַלָם.

442. Rabbi Yehuda then said: So it has been said. Nevertheless, come and behold the secret that I learned. At the time when the Congregation of Yisrael was exiled from Her place, it was as if the letters of the Holy Name were separated from one another. *Hei* was seperated from *Vav* IN THE NAME YUD HEI VAV HEI. As a result of this separation, it is written: "I was dumb with stillness" (Tehilim 39:3). Because the *Vav* departed from the *Hei*, the voice disappeared. As a result, Speech was silenced.

443. וּבְגִין כָּךְ, הִיא שְׁכִיבַת בְּעַפְרָא, כָּל הַהוּא יוֹמָא דְּה"א. וּמַאן אִיהוּ, אֶלֶף חֲמִשָּׁאָה, וְאַף עַל גַּב דְּאַקְדֵּימַת בְּגָלוּתָא, עַד לָא יֵיעוֹל הַהוּא אֶלֶף חֲמִשָּׁאָה, רָזָא דְּה"א.

443. And because of this, She lies in the dust OF EXILE during all that day of the *Hei*. And when is this? It is during the fifth millennium, even though She was exiled before it began – BECAUSE THE TEMPLE WAS DESTROYED DURING THE FOURTH MILLENNIUM, IT WAS NOT A FULL MILLENNIUM AND WE DO NOT COUNT IT.

444. וְכַד יֵיתֵי אֶלֶף שְׁתִיתָאָה דְּאִיהוּ רָזָא דְּוָא"ו, כְּדֵין וָא"ו יוֹקִים לְה"א. בְּזִמְנָא שִׁית זִמְנִין עֶשֶׂר, וָא"ו סַלְקָא בִּי', וָא"ו נַחֲתָא בְּה"א.

444. And when the sixth millennium arrives, which is the secret of the *Vav* – NAMELY THE YESOD, SPELLED WITH THE *VAV*, WHICH IS ZEIR ANPIN – then the *Vav* shall elevate the *Hei*, WHICH IS THE NUKVA, at the time of "six multiplied by ten", as the *Vav* (= 6) rises up to the *Yud* (= 10) OF YUD HEI VAV HEI, WHICH IS CHOCHMAH. AND THEN the *Vav* descends to the *Hei*, AND BRINGS TO IT ABUNDANCE.

445. אִשְׁתְּלִים וָא"ו גּוֹ עֶשֶׂר, שִׁית זִמְנִין, כְּדֵין הֲווֹ שִׁתִּין, לְאָקְמָא מֵעַפְרָא, וּבְכָל שִׁתִּין וְשִׁתִּין, מֵהַהוּא אֶלֶף שְׁתִיתָאָה, אִתְתַּקַּף ה"א, וְסַלְקָא בְּדַרְגּוֹי, לְאִתְתַּקְּפָא. וּבְשִׁית מְאָה שְׁנִין לִשְׁתִיתָאָה, יִתְפַּתְּחוּן תַּרְעֵי דְחָכְמְתָא לְעֵילָא, וּמַבּוּעֵי דְחָכְמְתָא לְתַתָּא, וְיִתְתַּקַּן עָלְמָא, לְאַעֲלָא בִּשְׁבִיעָאָה. כְּבַר נָשׁ, דְּמִתְתַּקַּן בְּיוֹמָא שְׁתִיתָאָה, מֵכִי עֶרֶב שִׁמְשָׁא, לַאֲעֲלָא בְּשַׁבַּתָּא. אוּף הָכִי נָמֵי. וְסִימָנֵיךְ בִּשְׁנַת שֵׁשׁ מֵאוֹת שָׁנָה לְחַיֵּי נֹחַ וְגוֹ'. נִבְקְעוּ כָּל מַעְיָינוֹת תְּהוֹם רַבָּה.

445. And when the *Vav*, WHICH IS THE SECRET OF ZEIR ANPIN, reaches completion by reaching sixty (by multiplying six times ten), THE NUKVA is raised from the dust. So every sixty years during the sixth millennium, the *Hei* is strengthened and rises up through its own grades to become firm. And in the year 600 of the sixth millennium, the gates of Wisdom of above and the fountains of Wisdom below shall be opened. And the world shall be prepared to enter the seventh MILLENNIUM, as a person who prepares himself on the sixth day (Friday), as the sun sets, to enter the Shabbat. And as a mnemonic for this, we take the verse: "in the six hundredth year of Noach's life...all the fountains of the great deep were broken open" (Beresheet 7:11)

446. אָמַר לוֹ רַבִּי יוֹסֵי, כָּל דָּא, אֲרִיכוּ זִמְנָא יַתִּיר, מִכְּמָה דְאוֹקְמוּהָ חַבְרַיָּיא, דְּאִיהוּ יוֹמָא חַד, גָּלוּתָא דִכְנֶסֶת יִשְׂרָאֵל, וְלָא יַתִּיר, דִּכְתִיב נְתָנַנִי שׁוֹמֵמָה כָּל הַיּוֹם דָּוָה. אָמַר לוֹ, הָכִי אוֹלִיפְנָא מֵאַבָּא, בְּרָזִין דְּאַתְוָון דִּשְׁמָא קַדִּישָׁא, וּבְיוֹמֵי דִּשְׁנֵי עַלְמָא, וּבְיוֹמֵי דִבְרֵאשִׁית, וְכֹלָּא

רָזָא חֲדָא אִיהוּ.

446. Rabbi Yosi said to him: This is more time than the friends have said – the exile of the Congregation of Yisrael is only for one day and no more, as it is written: "he has made me desolate and faint all the day" (Eichah 1:13). THIS IS THE SECRET OF "ONE DAY" OF THE HOLY ONE, BLESSED BE HE, WHICH IS 1000 YEARS, AS EXPLAINED ABOVE. He said to him: I have learned so from my father among the secrets of the letters of the holy name, YUD HEI VAV HEI, and in the years of the world, and the days of Creation, all is one secret.

447. וּכְדֵין יִתְחֲזֵי קַשְׁתָּא בַּעֲנָנָא, בִּגְוָונֵי נְהִירִין, כְּאִתְּתָא דְמִתְקַשְּׁטָא לְבַעֲלָהּ, דִכְתִיב וּרְאִיתִיהָ לִזְכֹּר בְּרִית עוֹלָם. וְהָא אוֹקְמוּהָ וְשַׁפִּיר הוּא. וּרְאִיתִיהָ: בִּגְוָונִין נְהִירִין כַּדְקָא יָאוֹת.

447. And then the rainbow will be seen in the clouds in shining colors, as a woman who adorns herself for her husband – BECAUSE THE RAINBOW IS THE MYSTERY OF THE NUKVA. As it is written: "and I will look upon it, that I may remember the everlasting covenant" (Beresheet 9:16). And this has already been carefully explained. HOWEVER, "and I will look upon it" MEANS in its shining colors, as should properly be.

448. וּכְדֵין לִזְכֹּר בְּרִית עוֹלָם. מַאן בְּרִית עוֹלָם. דָא כְּנֶסֶת יִשְׂרָאֵל וְיִתְחַבַּר וא"ו בְּה"א, וְיֵיקִים לָהּ מֵעַפְרָא, כד"א וַיִּזְכֹּר אֱלֹהִים אֶת בְּרִיתוֹ. דָא כְּנֶסֶת יִשְׂרָאֵל. דְאִיהִי בְּרִית, כד"א וְהָיְתָה לְאוֹת בְּרִית וְגו'.

448. And then IT SHALL BE SAID, "that I may remember the everlasting covenant." And what is the "everlasting covenant"? It is the Congregation of Yisrael, NAMELY THE NUKVA, WHICH IS THE COVENANT. And the *Vav* will join the *Hei* and raise it from the dust, as it is written: "and Elohim remembered his covenant" (Shemot 2:24). This is the Congregation of Yisrael, which is the covenant, as it is written: "and it shall be for a sign of a covenant" (Beresheet 9:13).

449. כַּד יִתְעַר וא"ו, לְגַבֵּי ה"א, כְּדֵין אָתִין עִלָּאִין, יִתְעָרוּן בְּעָלְמָא. וּבְנוֹי דִרְאוּבֵן, זְמִינִין דְיִתְעָרוּן קָרְבִין, בְּכָל עָלְמָא, וּכְנֶסֶת יִשְׂרָאֵל

יוֹקִים לָה מֵעַפְרָא, וְיִדְכַּר לָה קוּדְשָׁא בְּרִיךְ הוּא.

449. When the *Vav*, WHICH IS ZEIR ANPIN, is aroused toward the *Hei*, WHICH IS THE NUKVA, then signs from above shall reach the world. The children of Reuben shall wage war throughout the world and the Holy One, blessed be He, shall remember the Congregation of Yisrael, and raise Her up and out from the dust of exile.

450. וְיִשְׁתַּכַּח קוּדְשָׁא בְּרִיךְ הוּא לְגַבָּה, גּוֹ גָּלוּתָא בְּחוּשְׁבַּן וא״ו, שִׁית זְמְנִין י׳. עֲשַׂר זִמְנִין שִׁית שְׁנִין, וּכְדֵין תֵּיקוּם, וְיִתְפַּקַּד עַלְמָא, לְמֶעְבַּד נוּקְמִין, וּמַאן דְּאִיהוּ מָאִיךְ יִתְרְמֵי.

450. And the Holy One, blessed be He, shall be with Her in exile, DURING THE SIXTH MILLENNIUM, according to the count of *Vav*: *Vav* (= 6) times *Yud* (= 10) EQUALS SIXTY, and ten (*Yud*) times sixty EQUALS 600, NAMELY, THE YEAR 600 OF THE SIXTH MILLENNIUM. And then He shall rise and visit the world, WHICH IS THE NUKVA, to execute vengeance. And whoever is humble shall be elevated.

451. אָמַר לוֹ ר׳ יוֹסֵי, שַׁפִּיר קָאֲמַרְתְּ, בְּגִין דְּאִיהוּ גּוֹ רָזָא דְּאַתְוָון. וְלֵית לָן לְאִתְעָרָא, חוּשְׁבַּן וְקִצִּין אַחֲרָנִין, דְּהָא בְּסִפְרָא דְּרַב יֵיבָא סָבָא אַשְׁכְּחָן, חוּשְׁבַּן דָּא, דִּכְתִיב אָז תִּרְצֶה הָאָרֶץ. וְהוּא רָזָא דְּוא״ו, דִּכְתִיב, וְזָכַרְתִּי אֶת בְּרִיתִי יַעֲקוֹב. וְדָא הוּא ו״ו, כֹּלָּא כַּחֲדָא, וְעַל דָּא אֶזְכּוֹר, וּלְבָתַר וְהָאָרֶץ אֶזְכּוֹר, דָּא כְּנֶסֶת יִשְׂרָאֵל. תִּרְצֶה: תִּתְרְעֵי אַרְעָא, לְגַבֵּי קוּדְשָׁא בְּרִיךְ הוּא.

451. Rabbi Yosi said to him: You have spoken well, because YOU HAVE EXPLAINED the secret of the letters OF THE NAME YUD HEI VAV HEI. And we should not delve into the other calculations and 'end of times,' WHICH ARE NOT RELATED TO THE SECRET OF THESE LETTERS, for we have found AN ESSAY SIMILAR IN CONTENT TO this calculation OF YOURS in the book of Rav Yeba Saba (the elder.) As it is written: "Then shall the land enjoy (or desire) HER SHABBATS" (Vayikra 26:34). And this is the secret of the *Vav*, WHICH MEANS THAT THIS DESIRE SHALL NOT BE REVEALED TO THE LAND, WHICH IS THE NUKVA, EXCEPT WHEN THE *VAV* HAS

REACHED COMPLETION, AS RABBI YEHUDA HAS EXPLAINED. And it is written: "And I will remember My covenant with Jacob" (Vayikra 26:42). OBSERVE THAT JACOB IS SPELLED WITH A VAV. This is Vav, fully spelled as Vav-Vav, BECAUSE WHEN THE LETTER VAV IS PRONOUNCED, WE HEAR ANOTHER VAV. THE FIRST VAV ALLUDES TO JACOB, WHO IS TIFERET, AND THE SECOND VAV ALLUDES TO THE YESOD OF ZEIR ANPIN, WHICH IS THE SECRET OF THE VAV THAT APPEARS IN THE NAME JACOB. And all is one, WHICH MEANS THAT IN THE NAME JACOB SPELLED WITH VAV, TIFERET AND YESOD ARE UNITED AS ONE. And this is why the verse is written: "I will remember," and later, "I will remember the land" (Ibid.), which is the Congregation of Yisrael, NAMELY THE NUKVA. "Enjoy" (or 'be appeased') MEANS THAT the land shall be appeased by the Holy One, blessed be He, AS HE SHALL RAISE HER. ENJOY IS READ AS PASSIVE "BE APPEASED," FOR DESIRE DOES NOT DEPEND ON THE NUKVA HERSELF, BUT ON THE WILL OF ZEIR ANPIN.

452. אֲבָל יוֹמָא חַד, דַּאֲמָרוּ חַבְרַיָּיא, וַדַּאי כֹּלָּא הוּא גָּנִיז, קַמֵּי קוּדְשָׁא בְּרִיךְ הוּא, וְכֹלָּא אִשְׁתְּכַח בְּרָזָא דְאַתְוָון, דִּשְׁמָא קַדִּישָׁא, דְּהָא גָלוּתָא, בְּאִינּוּן אַתְוָון, גָּלֵי לוֹן רַבִּי יֵיסָא הָכָא, וְהַשְׁתָּא בְּאִינּוּן אַתְוָון אִתְגַּלְיָין, וְגָלֵי לוֹן.

452. As for that "one day," which our friends have mentioned IN RELATION TO THE TIME OF EXILE, it is certain that everything is hidden and concealed before the Holy One, blessed be He. And everything is revealed through the secret of the letters of the Holy Name. Thus the exile, WHICH IS THE SECRET OF CONCEALMENT, has been revealed to us by Rabbi Yesa through these letters. And now, through these letters, THE SECRET OF REDEMPTION is revealed to us, WHICH MEANS THAT IT DEPENDS ON THE VAV OF THE NAME YUD HEI VAV HEI ACHIEVING COMPLETION.

453. אָמַר לוֹ תָּא חֲזֵי, דַּאֲפִילוּ כַּד אִתְפַּקְדָא שָׂרָה, מֵהַאי דַּרְגָּא, לָא פַּקִּיד לָהּ, אֶלָּא בְּרָזָא דְוא"ו, דִּכְתִיב וַיְיָ' פָּקַד אֶת שָׂרָה וְגוֹ'. בְּגִין דְּכֹלָּא בְּרָזָא דְוא"ו אִיהוּ, וּבְהָא כָּלֵיל כֹּלָּא, וּבֵיהּ אִתְגַּלְיָא כֹּלָּא, בְּגִין דְּכָל מִלָּה דְּאִיהִי סְתִימָא, אִיהִי גָּלֵי כָּל סָתִים, וְלָא אָתֵי מַאן דְּאִיהוּ בְּאִתְגַּלְיָא, וִיגַלֵּי מַה דְּאִיהוּ סָתִים.

453. He said to him: Come and behold. Even when Sarah was visited, she was not visited by this grade OF VISITATION, WHICH IS THE NUKVA, THE LOWER *HEI* OF YUD HEI VAV HEI, but by the secret of the *Vav*, as written: "And Hashem visited Sarah..." – BECAUSE "AND HASHEM (*VAV* - YUD HEI VAV HEI)" REFERS TO HIM AND HIS COURT OF JUDGMENT. 'HIM' IS THE SECRET OF ZEIR ANPIN, NAMELY THE *VAV*, WHILE HIS COURT OF JUDGMENT IS THE NUKVA. THEREFORE, EVEN THE VISITATION OF SARAH WAS BY THE LETTER *VAV* OF YUD HEI VAV HEI, because everything is according to the secret of the *Vav* and everything is included within it. THAT IS, EVERYTHING IS CONCEALED WITHIN THE LETTER *VAV* and everything is revealed there as well. IN OTHER WORDS, EVERYTHING BECOMES REVEALED BY THE COMPLETION OF THE LETTER *VAV*. For everything that is concealed may reveal all that is concealed, but nothing that is revealed may come and reveal what is concealed.

‫454. אָמַר רָבִּי יוֹסֵי, כַּמָּה אִית לָן לְאִתְמַשְׁכָא גּוֹ גָּלוּתָא, עַד הַהוּא‬
‫זִמְנָא, וְכֹלָּא תָּלֵי לֵיהּ קוּדְשָׁא בְּרִיךְ הוּא, כַּד יְתוּבוּן בִּתְיוּבְתָּא, אִי‬
‫יִזְכּוּ, וְאִי לָא יִזְכּוּ כְּמָה דְאִתְּמַר בְּהַאי קְרָא, דִּכְתִיב אֲנִי יְיָ' בְּעִתָּהּ‬
‫אֲחִישֶׁנָּה. זָכוּ אֲחִישֶׁנָּה, לָא זָכוּ בְּעִתָּהּ.‬

454. Rabbi Yosi said: How long do we have to endure the exile until we reach that time? And the Holy One, blessed be He, made everything depend on whether they atone for their sins and repented, whether they merited REDEMPTION or not, WHETHER THEY REPENTED OR NOT. As it is written: "I Hashem will hasten it in its time" (Yeshayah 60:22). If they are worthy, THAT IS, IF THEY REPENT, "I...will hasten it," but if they are unworthy, THAT IS, THEY DO NOT REPENT, then, "in its time."

‫455. אַזְלוּ עַד דַּהֲווֹ אָזְלֵי, אָמַר רָבִּי יוֹסֵי, אַדְכַּרְנָא הַשְׁתָּא, דְּהָא‬
‫בַּאֲתַר דָּא יָתֵיבְנָא, יוֹמָא חַד עִם אַבָּא, וַאֲמַר לִי בְּרִי, זַמִּין אַנְתְּ, כַּד‬
‫מָטוּן יוֹמָךְ, לְשִׁיתִּין שְׁנִין, לְאַשְׁכְּחָא בְּהַאי אֲתַר סִימָא, דְּחָכְמְתָא‬
‫עִלָּאָה, וְהָא זָכֵינָא לְאִינוּן יוֹמִין, וְלָא אַשְׁכַּחְנָא, וְלָא יָדַעְנָא, אִי הֲנֵי‬
‫מִלִּין דְּקָאֲמָרָן, אוֹ הַהִיא חָכְמְתָא, דְּאִיהוּ אֲמַר.‬

455. As they walked on, Rabbi Yosi said: I have just remembered that I once sat in this place with my father. He said to me: My son, when you are sixty years old, you will find in this place a treasure of sublime Wisdom. And I have just reached this age, yet I have still found nothing. And I do not know if these new explanations are that Wisdom that he told me I SHALL FIND.

456. וַאֲמַר לִי כַּד יִמְטוּן קוּלְפִין דְּנוּרָא, גּוֹ טְהִירֵי יְדָךְ, אִתְאֲבֵיד מִינָךְ. אֲמִינָא לֵיהּ אַבָּא בַּמֶּה יְדַעְתְּ. אָמַר לוֹ, בְּהַנֵּי תְּרֵין צִפּוֹרִין, דְּאַעֲבָרוּ עַל רֵישָׁךְ יְדַעְנָא.

456. And he further said to me: When strikes of fire shall reach the palms of your hands, then the wisdom shall disappear from you. I said to him: My father, how do you know this? He replies: I know this by these two birds that have passed over your head.

457. אַדְהֲכֵי, אִתְפְּרַשׁ ר' יוֹסֵי, וְעָאל גּוֹ מְעַרְתָּא חֲדָא, וְאַשְׁכַּח סִפְרָא חַד, דַּהֲוָה נָעִיץ גּוֹ נוּקְבָא דְּטִנָּרָא, בִּסְיָיפֵי מְעַרְתָּא, נָפַק בֵּיהּ.

457. In the meantime, Rabbi Yosi left RABBI YEHUDA and entered a cave where he found a hidden book in a cleft of a rock at the far end. HE TOOK IT AND left with it.

458. כֵּיוָן דְּפָתַח לֵיהּ, חָמָא שַׁבְעִין וּתְרֵין גְּלִיפִין דְּאַתְוָון, דְּאִתְמְסָרוּ לְאָדָם הָרִאשׁוֹן, וּבְהוֹ הֲוָה יָדַע, כָּל חָכְמְתָא דִּעֵלָּאִין קַדִּישִׁין, וְכָל אִינוּן דְּבָתַר רֵיחַיָא, דְּמִתְגַּלְגְּלָן בָּתַר פָּרוּכְתָּא, גּוֹ טְהִירִין עֵלָּאִין, וְכָל אִינוּן מִלִּין, דְּזַמִּינִין לְמֵיתֵי לְעָלְמָא, עַד יוֹמָא, דִּיקוּם עֲנָנָא, דְּבִסְטַר מַעֲרָב, וְיַחְשִׁיךְ עָלְמָא.

458. As he opened the book, he saw 72 forms of letters that were handed down to Adam. By these letters, Adam knew the entire Wisdom of the Holy Supernal Beings and all the Klipot that abide "behind the millstones," which revolve around behind the veil THAT COVERS the supernal Lights, together with all the things that are destined to come upon the world until the day when a cloud will rise from the west and the world will be darkened.

459. קָרָא לְרַבִּי יְהוּדָה, וְשָׁרוֹ לְמִלְעֵי, בְּהַהוּא סִפְרָא, לָא סְפִיקוּ

לְמִלְעֵי, תְּרֵי אוֹ תְּלָתָא סִטְרִין, דְּאִינּוּן אַתְוָון, עַד דַּהֲווֹ מִסְתַּכְּלִין, בְּהַהִיא חָכְמָה עִלָּאָה, כֵּיוָן דְּמָטוּ, לְמִלְעֵי בְּסִתְרִירוּ דְּסִפְרָא, וּמִשְׁתָּעוּ דָּא עִם דָּא, נְפַק שְׁבִיבָא דְּאֶשָׁא, וְעַלְעוּלָא דְּרוּחָא, וּבָטַשׁ בִּידֵיהוֹן, וְאִתְאָבֵיד מִנַּיְיהוּ. בָּכָה ר' יוֹסֵי וַאֲמַר דִּילְמָא ח"ו, חוֹבָה אִיהוּ גַּבָּן, אוֹ דְּלָאו אֲנָן זַכָּאִין, לְמִנְדַּע לֵיהּ.

459. He called to Rabbi Yehuda and they both started to study the book. After examining only two or three pages, they were already contemplating the supernal Wisdom. As soon as they read further and spoke with each other, a flame and a strong wind struck their hands, and the book vanished. Rabbi Yosi wept and said: It could be that we have sinned, or we are not worthy of knowing this.

460. כַּד אָתוּ לְגַבֵּי דר' שִׁמְעוֹן, אִשְׁתָּעוּ לֵיהּ עוֹבָדָא דָּא, אֲמַר לוֹן, דִּילְמָא בְּקֵץ מְשִׁיחָא דְּאִינּוּן אַתְוָון, הֲוֵיתוּן מִשְׁתַּדְּלֵי, אַמְרוּ לֵיהּ, דָּא לָא יַדְעִינָן, דְּהָא כֹּלָּא אִתְנְשֵׁי מִינָן. אֲמַר לוֹן רַבִּי שִׁמְעוֹן. לֵית רְעוּתָא דְּקוּדְשָׁא בְּרִיךְ הוּא בְּדָא, דְּיִתְגַּלֵי כָּל כָּךְ לְעָלְמָא, וְכַד יְהֵא קָרֵיב לְיוֹמֵי מְשִׁיחָא, אֲפִילוּ רַבְיֵי דְּעָלְמָא, זְמִינִין לְאַשְׁכָּחָא טְמִירִין דְּחָכְמְתָא, וּלְמִנְדַּע בֵּיהּ קִצִּין, וְחוּשְׁבְּנִין, וּבְהַהוּא זִמְנָא, אִתְגַּלְיָא לְכֹלָּא, הה"ד, כִּי אָז אֶהְפֹּךְ אֶל עַמִּים וגו'. מַהוּ אָז. בְּזִמְנָא דְּתֵיקוּם כְּנֶסֶת יִשְׂרָאֵל מֵעַפְרָא, וִיוֹקִים לָהּ קוּדְשָׁא בְּרִיךְ הוּא, כְּדֵין אֶהְפֹּךְ אֶל עַמִּים שָׂפָה בְרוּרָה לִקְרֹא כֻלָּם בְּשֵׁם יי' וּלְעָבְדוֹ שְׁכֶם אֶחָד.

460. When they told Rabbi Shimon the story, he said: Maybe you delved into those letters that deal with the Days of Messiah? They answered: We do not know, because we have forgotten everything. Rabbi Shimon continued: The Holy One, blessed be He, does not wish that too much be revealed to the world. But when the Days of Messiah are near, even infants in the world will discover the secrets of Wisdom and, through them, know how to calculate THE TIME OF THE REDEMPTION and figure the End of Days. At that time, it will be revealed to everyone. Therefore, it is written: "For then will I turn to the peoples a pure language..." (Tzefanyah 3:9). What is meant by "then"? It means at the time when the Congregation of Yisrael shall rise from the dust, and the Holy One, blessed be He, shall raise

Her up. Then, "I will turn to the peoples a pure language that they may all call upon Hashem and serve Him with one consent" (Ibid.).

461. תָּא חֲזֵי, אַף עַל גַּב דְּאַבְרָהָם כְּתִיב בֵּיהּ, וַיִּסַּע אַבְרָם הָלוֹךְ וְנָסוֹעַ הַנֶּגְבָּה. וְכָל מַטְלָנוֹי, הֲווֹ לְדָרוֹמָא. וְאִתְקַשַּׁר בֵּיהּ, לָא סָלֵיק לְדוּכְתֵּיהּ כַּדְקָא יָאוֹת, עַד דְּאִתְיְלֵיד יִצְחָק, כֵּיוָן דְּאִתְיְלֵיד יִצְחָק, אִסְתַּלַּק לְאַתְרֵיהּ, וְאִיהוּ אִשְׁתַּתַּף בַּהֲדֵיהּ, וְאִתְקַשָּׁרוּ דָּא בְּדָא.

461. Come and behold. Even though it is written of Abraham: "And he journeyed still toward the south" (Beresheet 12:9), and all his journeys were southward, WHICH IS THE RIGHT COLUMN, OR CHESED, to which he was attached, he did not rise to his proper place until Isaac was born. As soon as Isaac was born, he immediately rose to his place, THAT IS, TO THE NORTH, THE LEFT COLUMN. And Abraham joined him, and they became united. THROUGH THEIR JOINING AND INCLUSION IN EACH OTHER, THEY BOTH REACHED COMPLETION.

462. בְּגִין כָּךְ, אִיהוּ קָרֵי לֵיהּ יִצְחָק, וְלָא אָחֳרָא, בְּגִין לְשַׁתְּפָא מַיָּא בְּאֶשָּׁא, דִּכְתִיב וַיִּקְרָא אַבְרָהָם אֶת שֵׁם בְּנוֹ הַנּוֹלַד לוֹ אֲשֶׁר יָלְדָה לוֹ שָׂרָה יִצְחָק, מַאן הַנּוֹלַד לוֹ, אֵשׁ מִמַּיִם.

462. This is why ABRAHAM called him Isaac, and not any other NAME, so as to join fire with water, AS THE ATTRIBUTE OF ABRAHAM IS WATER AND THAT OF ISAAC IS FIRE, as it is written: "And Abraham called the name of his son that was born to him, whom Sarah bore to him, Isaac" (Beresheet 21:3). AND HE ASKS: Why DOES THE VERSE EMPHASIZE "that was born to him?" AND HE REPLIES: Fire from water.

33. "The son of the Hagar the Egyptian"

A Synopsis

Sarah, the wife of the Patriarch Abraham, banishes one of her husband's concubines from her home, a woman called Hagar. Hagar is the mother of Ishmael, who signifies the force of negativity. The banishment of Hagar pertains to the removal of man's *desire to receive for the self alone.*

The Relevance of this Passage

The first step in transformation involves a recognition and admittance of our self-indulgent desires. This self-acknowledgment is 90% of the battle. The Light of the Creator is then free to enter and eradicate the dark recesses of our nature. Towards that end, this passage arouses self-awareness, thus banishing our own Evil Inclinations and negative attributes from our character.

463 וַתֵּרֶא שָׂרָה אֶת בֶּן הָגָר הַמִּצְרִית אֲשֶׁר יָלְדָה לְאַבְרָהָם מְצַחֵק. אָמַר רַבִּי חִיָּיא, מִיּוֹמָא דְּאִתְיְלֵיד יִצְחָק, וַהֲוָה יִשְׁמָעֵאל בְּבֵיתָא דְּאַבְרָהָם, לָא אִסְתַּלַּק יִשְׁמָעֵאל בִּשְׁמָא, בַּאֲתַר דְּדַהֲבָא שַׁרְיָא, סוֹסְפִיתָא לָא אִדְכַּר קַמֵּיה, וּבְגִין כָּךְ אֶת בֶּן הָגָר הַמִּצְרִית, גְּבַר דְּלָא יִתְחֲזֵי לְאַדְכְּרָא, קַמֵּיה דְּיִצְחָק.

463. "And Sarah saw the son of Hagar the Egyptian, which she had born to Abraham, mocking" (Beresheet 21:9). Rabbi Chiya said: From that day when Isaac was born, Ishmael was not mentioned by his name as long as he was still present in the house of Abraham. This is because in the presence of gold, refuse cannot be mentioned. Why is it written: "the son of Hagar the Egyptian" AND NOT "ISHMAEL THE SON OF HAGAR"? Because his name should not be mentioned in the presence of Isaac.

464. אָמַר רַבִּי יִצְחָק, וַתֵּרֶא שָׂרָה, בְּעֵינָא דְּקִלְנָא, חָמַאת לֵיה שָׂרָה דְּלָא חָמַאת לֵיה בְּעֵינָא, דְּאִיהוּ בְּרָא דְּאַבְרָהָם, אֶלָּא דְּאִיהוּ בְּרָא, דְּהָגָר הַמִּצְרִית, וּבְגִין כָּךְ וַתֵּרֶא שָׂרָה: דְּשָׂרָה חָמַאת לֵיה בְּעֵינָא דָא, וְלָא אַבְרָהָם, דְּאִילּוּ בְּאַבְרָהָם, לֹא כְּתִיב אֶת בֶּן הָגָר, אֶלָּא אֶת בְּנוֹ.

464. Rabbi Yitzchak said: "And Sarah saw." She looked at him disdainfully,

as she did not look at him as the son of Abraham, but rather as the son of Hagar the Egyptian. Thus, it is written: "And Sarah saw," because only Sarah saw him this way, not Abraham. So with Abraham, it is not written: 'the son of Hagar,' but "his son."

465. תָּא חֲזֵי לְבָתַר מַה כְּתִיב, וַיֵּרַע הַדָּבָר מְאֹד בְּעֵינֵי אַבְרָהָם עַל אוֹדוֹת בְּנוֹ. וְלָא כְתִיב, עַל אוֹדוֹת בֶּן הָגָר הַמִּצְרִית. בְּגִין כָּךְ, וַתֵּרֶא שָׂרָה אֶת בֶּן הָגָר הַמִּצְרִית. וְלָא חָמָאת דְּאִיהוּ בְּרֵיה דְּאַבְרָהָם.

465. Come and behold. After this, it it written: "And the thing was very grievous in Avraham's eyes because of his son" (Beresheet 21:11). It is not written: 'because of the son of Hagar the Egyptian.' And in contrast to this, it is written: "And Sarah saw the son of Hagar the Egyptian," as she did not see him as the 'son of Abraham.'

466. רַבִּי שִׁמְעוֹן אָמַר, הַאי קְרָא, תּוּשְׁבַּחְתָּא דְּשָׂרָה אִיהוּ, בְּגִין דְּחָמָאת לֵיה, דְּקָא מְצַחֵק לְכוּ"ם, אָמְרָה, וַדַּאי לָאו בְּרָא דָא, בְּרָא דְּאַבְרָהָם, לְמֶעֱבַד עוֹבָדוֹי דְּאַבְרָהָם, אֶלָּא בְּרָא דְּהָגָר הַמִּצְרִית אִיהוּ, אֲהַדַר לְחוּלָקָא דְּאִמֵּיה, בְּגִין כָּךְ, וַתֹּאמֶר לְאַבְרָהָם גָּרֵשׁ הָאָמָה הַזֹּאת וְאֶת בְּנָהּ כִּי לֹא יִירַשׁ בֶּן הָאָמָה הַזֹּאת עִם בְּנִי עִם יִצְחָק.

466. Rabbi Shimon said: This passage shows that Sarah is praiseworthy. Because she saw him participating in idolatrous practices, she said: This boy is definitely not the son of Abraham, who shall follow the example of Abraham. Rather, he is the son of Hagar the Egyptian, as he has returned to his mother's way of life. Because of this, "she said to Abraham, 'Cast out this bondwoman and her son: for the son of this bondwoman shall not be heir with my son, with Yitzchak'" (Ibid. 10).

467. וְכִי ס"ד, דְּקַנֵּי לָהּ שָׂרָה, אוֹ לִבְרָהּ, אִי הָכִי, לָא אוֹדֵי קוּדְשָׁא בְּרִיךְ הוּא עִמָּהּ, דִּכְתִיב כֹּל אֲשֶׁר תֹּאמַר אֵלֶיךָ שָׂרָה שְׁמַע בְּקוֹלָהּ. אֶלָּא, בְּגִין דְּחָמָאת לֵיה בְּכוּ"ם, וְאַמֵּיה אוֹלְפָא לֵיה נִמוּסֵי דְּכוּ"ם, בְּגִין כָּךְ, אָמְרַת שָׂרָה, כִּי לֹא יִירַשׁ בֶּן הָאָמָה הַזֹּאת, אֲנָא יָדַעְנָא, דְּלָא יָרֵית לְעָלְמִין, חוּלָקָא דִּמְהֵימְנוּתָא, וְלָא יְהֵא לֵיה, עִם בְּרִי חוּלָקָא, לָא

בְּעָלְמָא דֵין, וְלָא בְּעָלְמָא דְאָתֵי, וּבְגִין כָּךְ אוֹדֵי עִמָּה קוּדְשָׁא בְּרִיךְ הוּא.

467. Now Sarah was not jealous or envious of her or her son. If she were, the Holy One, blessed be He, would not have supported with the words, "in all that Sarah says to you, hearken to her voice" (Beresheet 21:12). In fact, it was only because she saw him indulging in idolatrous practices and his mother teaching him the laws of idol worshipping that she said, "for the son of this bondwoman shall not be heir." I know that he shall never inherit a portion of the Faith, and he shall have no share with my son, not in this world and not in the World to Come. And this is why the Holy One, blessed be He, supported her.

468. וְקוּדְשָׁא בְּרִיךְ הוּא, בָּעָא לְאַפְרָשָׁא בִּלְחוֹדוֹי, זַרְעָא קַדִּישָׁא כִּדְקָא יָאוֹת, דִּבְגִין כָּךְ, בָּרָא עָלְמָא, דְּהָא יִשְׂרָאֵל, סָלִיק בִּרְעוּתָא דְּקוּדְשָׁא בְּרִיךְ הוּא, עַד לָא יִבְרֵי עָלְמָא, וּבְגִין כָּךְ, נָפַק אַבְרָהָם לְעָלְמָא, וְעָלְמָא מִתְקַיֵּים בְּגִינֵיה, וְאַבְרָהָם וְיִצְחָק קַיְימוּ, וְלָא אִתְיַישְׁבוּ בְּדוּכְתַּיְיהוּ, עַד דְּנָפַק יַעֲקֹב לְעָלְמָא.

468. And the Holy One, blessed be He, wanted the Holy Seed separated, for that was why He created the world. Yisrael was already in the mind of the Holy One, blessed be He, even before He created the world. This is why Abraham appeared in the world, which continued to exist because of him. So Abraham and Isaac remained insecurely in their places, until Jacob appeared in the world.

469. כֵּיוָן דְּנָפַק יַעֲקֹב לְעָלְמָא אִתְקַיְימוּ, אַבְרָהָם וְיִצְחָק, וְאִתְקַיַּים כָּל עָלְמָא, וּמִתַּמָּן נָפַק עַמָּא קַדִּישָׁא לְעָלְמָא, וְאִתְקַיַּים כֹּלָּא, כְּגַוְונָא קַדִּישָׁא, כִּדְקָא יָאוֹת, וּבְגִין כָּךְ, אָמַר לוֹ קוּדְשָׁא בְּרִיךְ הוּא, כֹּל אֲשֶׁר תֹּאמַר אֵלֶיךָ שָׂרָה שְׁמַע בְּקוֹלָה כִּי בְיִצְחָק יִקָּרֵא לְךָ זָרַע, וְלֹא בְּיִשְׁמָעֵאל.

469. As soon as Jacob came into the world, Abraham and Isaac were established, as was the whole world. From there, FROM JACOB, the Holy Nation was born in a holy way. This is why the Holy One, blessed be He, said to him, "in all that Sarah says to you, hearken to her voice, for in Isaac shall your seed be called" – and not in Ishmael.

470. מַה כְּתִיב לְבָתַר, וַתֵּלֶךְ וַתֵּתַע בְּמִדְבַּר בְּאֵר שָׁבַע. כְּתִיב הָכָא וַתֵּתַע וּכְתִיב הָתָם הֶבֶל הֵמָה מַעֲשֵׂה תַּעְתֻּעִים. וְקוּדְשָׁא בְּרִיךְ הוּא, בְּגִינֵיהּ דְּאַבְרָהָם, לָא שָׁבֵיק לָהּ, וְלִבְרָהּ.

470. After this, it is written: "and she departed and wandered in the wilderness of Beer Sheva" (Beresheet 21:14). It is written here, "and wandered (Heb. *vateta*) in the wilderness," and elsewhere it is written: "They are vanity, and the works of delusion (Heb. *ta'atu'im*)" (Yirmeyah 10:15). FROM THIS WE LEARN BY ANALOGY THAT BECAUSE IT REFERS TO IDOL WORSHIPPING IN THE LATTER VERSE, SO IT REFERS TO IDOL WORSHIPPING IN THE FORMER. And for the sake of Abraham, the Holy One, blessed be He, did not abandon her and her son, BUT SAVED THEM FROM THIRST, EVEN THOUGH SHE INDULGED IN IDOL WORSHIPPING.

471 תָּא חֲזֵי, בְּקַדְמֵיתָא כַּד אַזְלַת מִקַּמָּהּ דְּשָׂרָה, מַה כְּתִיב, כִּי שָׁמַע יְיָ' אֶל עָנְיֵךְ. וְהַשְׁתָּא דְּטָעָאת בָּתַר כּוּ"ם, אַף עַל גַּב דִּכְתִיב, וַתִּשָּׂא אֶת קוֹלָהּ וַתֵּבְךְּ. מַה כְּתִיב, כִּי שָׁמַע אֱלֹהִים אֶל קוֹל הַנַּעַר. וְלָא כְתִיב כִּי שָׁמַע אֱלֹהִים אֶת קוֹלֵךְ.

471. Come and behold. In the beginning, when she ran away from Sarah, it is written: "because Hashem has heard your affliction" (Beresheet 16:11). Now, however, that she went astray and followed idolatrous practices, even though it is written: "and she lifted up her voice, and wept" (Beresheet 21:16), "Elohim heard the voice of the lad" (Ibid. 17), instead of: 'And Elohim heard your voice.'

472 בַּאֲשֶׁר הוּא שָׁם. הָא אוּקְמוּהָ, דְּלָאו בַּר עוֹנָשָׁא הוּא, לְגַבֵּי בֵּי דִּינָא דִּלְעֵילָּא, דְּהָא בֵּי דִּינָא דִלְתַתָּא, עָנְשִׁין מִתְּלֵיסַר שְׁנִין וּלְעֵילָּא, וּבֵי דִּינָא דִלְעֵילָּא, מֵעֶשְׂרִים שְׁנִין וּלְהָלְאָה. וְאַף עַל גַּב דְּחַיָּיבָא הֲוָה, לָאו בַּר עוֹנָשָׁא אִיהוּ. וְהָא אוּקְמוּהָ, וְדָא הוּא דִכְתִיב, בַּאֲשֶׁר הוּא שָׁם.

472. The words, "where he is" (Ibid.) have already been explained.

ISHMAEL was not yet punishable by the heavenly Court of Judgment. At the earthly Court of Judgment, a person can be punished after the age of thirteen, but at the heavenly Court of Judgment, a person must be at least twenty years of age to be punished. AS A RESULT, even though he was wicked, he was too young to be punished. This is why it is written: "where he is," WHICH MEANS THAT BECAUSE HE WAS YOUNGER THAN TWENTY YEARS OF AGE, THE HOLY ONE, BLESSED BE HE, SPARED HIS LIFE.

473. אָמַר רְבִּי אֶלְעָזָר, אִי הָכֵי, מַאן דְּאִסְתַּלַּק מֵעַלְמָא, עַד לָא מָטוֹן יוֹמוֹי, לְעֶשְׂרִין שְׁנִין, מֵאָן אֲתַר אִתְעֲנַשׁ, בְּגִין דְּהָא מִתְּלֵיסַר שְׁנִין וּלְתַתָּא, לָאו בַּר עוֹנָשָׁא אִיהוּ, אֶלָּא בְּחֶטְאוֹי דַּאֲבוֹי, אֲבָל מִתְּלֵיסַר שְׁנִין וּלְעֵילָא מַהוּ. אָמַר לוֹ, קוּדְשָׁא בְּרִיךְ הוּא חָס עֲלֵיה, דְּלֵימוּת זַכָּאי, וְיָהִיב לֵיה אֲגַר טַב, בְּהַהוּא עָלְמָא, וְלָא לֵימוּת חַיָּיב, דְּיִתְעֲנַשׁ בְּהַהוּא עָלְמָא, וְאוֹקְמוּהָ.

473. Rabbi Elazar asks: If this is so, then why punish anyone before he reaches the age of twenty? Under the age of thirteen years, even though he is not yet punishable, he can be sentenced to death because of the sins of his father, BECAUSE HE IS UNDER HIS FATHER'S AUTHORITY. But after the age of thirteen, why does this happen? AS HE IS NO LONGER SUBJECT TO HIS FATHER'S AUTHORITY, COULD IT BE THAT HE IS PUNISHED AND SENTENCED TO DEATH WHILE HE IS STILL TOO YOUNG AND THEREFORE UNPUNISHABLE? He replies: The Holy One, blessed be He, has Mercy on him, so that he may die as a righteous person. And He gives him a good reward in the World OF ETERNITY, so that he may not die as a wicked person and be punished in that world. This has already been explained.

474. אָמַר לוֹ אִי חַיָּיבָא הוּא, וְלָא מָטוֹן יוֹמוֹי, לְעֶשְׂרִין שְׁנִין, מַהוּ, כֵּיוָן דְּאִסְתַּלַּק מֵעַלְמָא, בְּמַאי הוּא עוֹנְשֵׁיה. אָמַר לוֹ בְּדָא אִתְקַיַּים וְיֵשׁ נִסְפֶּה בְּלֹא מִשְׁפָּט. דְּכַד עוֹנָשָׁא נָחִית לְעָלְמָא, אִיהוּ אַרְעָא בְּלָא כַּוָּנָה, לְעֵילָא וְתַתָּא, בְּהַהוּא מְחַבְּלָא, וְיִתְעֲנַשׁ, כַּד לָא אַשְׁגָּחוּ עֲלֵיה מִלְעֵילָא.

474. He said to him: If he is a wicked person who has not yet reached the age of twenty years, how is this resolved? If he departs from this world,

where is he punished? YOU CAN NOT SAY THAT HE MAY DIE A RIGHTEOUS PERSON, BECAUSE HE IS A WICKED PERSON AND A NOT RIGHTEOUS ONE. He responded: In this case THE VERSE, "But sometimes ruin comes for want of judgment" (Mishlei 13:23) is fulfilled. HE IS PUNISHED WITHOUT JUDGMENT, because when a punishment descends into the world, he, REFERRING TO THE PERSON UNDER TWENTY YEARS OF AGE, meets the Angel of Destruction, WHO PUNISHES HIM without it being intended from above or below. THIS MEANS THAT WITHOUT ANY EXPRESS INTENTION FROM THE HEAVENLY COURT OF JUDGMENT above or EARTHLY COURT OF JUDGMENT below, he is punished, for the sole reason that he was not protected FROM THE ANGEL OF DESTRUCTION from above. ONCE HE MEETS THE ANGEL OF DESTRUCTION, HE NO LONGER DISTINGUISHES BETWEEN GOOD AND BAD.

475. וַעֲלֵיהּ כְּתִיב עֲווֹנוֹתָיו יִלְכְּדֻנוֹ אֶת הָרָשָׁע. א"ת לְאַסְגָּאָה, מַאן דְּלָא מָטוֹן יוֹמוֹי, לְאִתְעֲנָשָׁא, עֲווֹנוֹתָיו יִלְכְּדֻנוֹ וְלָא בֵּי דִינָא דִלְעֵילָא, וּבְחַבְלֵי חַטָּאתוֹ יִתָּמֵךְ, וְלָא בֵּי דִינָא דִלְתַתָּא בְּגִין כָּךְ כְּתִיב כִּי שָׁמַע אֱלֹהִים אֶל קוֹל הַנַּעַר בַּאֲשֶׁר הוּא שָׁם.

475. Of him it is written: "His own iniquities shall trap the wicked man" (Mishlei 5:22). Here, the particle *Et* ('the') is written to include those who are not of punishable age. "His own iniquities shall trap the wicked man," and not the heavenly Court of Judgment; "and he shall be caught fast in the cords of his sins," and not by the earthly Court of Judgment. This is why it is written: "For Elohim has heard the voice of the lad where he is," AS HE WAS NOT YET OLD ENOUGH TO BE PUNISHED FOR HIS SINS. THEREFORE, ELOHIM HEARD HIS VOICE, EVEN THOUGH HE WAS EVIL.

34. The signs heralding Messiah

A Synopsis
There are various windows of opportunity during a 6000-year period of transformation where we can bring about world peace through a proactive change of our nature. The Zohar expounds upon these opportunities and the signs that signal their arrival.

The Relevance of this Passage
Often times, hardships and obstacles appear to provide us with an opportunity to grow and evolve spiritually. If we are not cognizant of this truth, our tendency is to react in despair and with distress. Consciousness creates our reality; therefore, our negative thoughts and doubts become akin to self-fulfilling prophecies. The Light of this passage helps us recognize and connect to positive transformational opportunities when they appear throughout our life. This ensures a life filled with meaning, as opposed to the illusion of random chaos.

476. רִבִּי שִׁמְעוֹן פָּתַח וְאָמַר וְזָכַרְתִּי אֶת בְּרִיתִי יַעֲקוֹב, מָלֵא בְּוא"ו, אֲמַאי. אֶלָּא, בִּתְרֵין סִטְרִין אִיהוּ, רָזָא דְחָכְמְתָא, חָדָא, דְּאִיהוּ רָזָא דַּרְגָּא דְחָכְמְתָא אֲתַר דְּשָׁרֵי בֵּיה יַעֲקֹב. אֲבָל הַאי קְרָא, עַל גָּלוּתָא דְיִשְׂרָאֵל אִתְּמָר, דְּכַד אִינוּן גּוֹ גָּלוּתָא, הַהוּא זִמְנָא דְיִתְפַּקְדוּן, יִתְפַּקְדוּן בְּרָזָא דְוא"ו. וְאִיהוּ בְּאֶלֶף שְׁתִיתָאָה.

476. Rabbi Shimon opened the discourse with the verse: "And I will remember my covenant with Jacob" (Vayikra 26:42). THE NAME JACOB IS WRITTEN in full; it includes the *Vav*. HE ASKS: Why? AND HE ANSWSERS: It appears from two sides. The first is the secret of Wisdom, NAMELY THE VAV, which is the secret of the grade of Chochmah where Jacob dwells. THE SECOND IS BECAUSE this passage refers to the exile of the children of Yisrael. While in captivity, they will be visited (also: 'redeemed') by the power of the letter *Vav*, which symbolizes the sixth millenium. Through the letter *Vav*, their exile is ended. THIS IS WHY JACOB IS SPELLED WITH VAV. THE CHILDREN OF YISRAEL SHALL BE REDEEMED FROM EXILE BY THE VAV (= 6), WHICH REPRESENTS THE SIXTH MILLENNIUM.

477. וּפְקִידָה בְּרָזָא דְוא"ו, שִׁית רַגְעֵי, וּפְלַג עִידָן. וּבְזִמְנָא דְשִׁתִּין שְׁנִין, לַעֲבוּרָא דְרַשָּׁא, בְּאֶלֶף שְׁתִיתָאָה, יָקִים אֱלָה שְׁמַיָא, פְּקִידוּ

לִבְרַתֵּיה דְּיַעֲקֹב. וּמֵהַהוּא זִמְנָא, עַד דִּיהֵא לָהּ זְכִירָה, שִׁית שְׁנִין וּפַלְגָּא. וּמֵהַהוּא זִמְנָא, שִׁית שְׁנִין אָחֳרָנִין, וְאִינּוּן שַׁבְעִין וּתְרֵין וּפַלְגָּא.

477. And the visitation, according to the secret of the *Vav*, occurs at six and one half moments. After the sixtieth year to the bar on the door of the sixth millenium – THE *VAV*, NAMELY TIFERET, WHICH IS THE SECRET OF THE MIDDLE BAR (OF THE TABERNACLE) THAT RUNS THROUGH THE BOARDS FROM ONE END TO THE OTHER, AND IS THEREFORE DESCRIBED AS THE "BAR OF THE DOOR" – shall Elohim of heaven visit the "Daughter of Jacob." And after six and a half years have passed, she shall be remembered. THIS IS THE DURATION OF THE VISITATION. And from that time, another six years shall pass, WHICH IS THE DURATION OF THE REMEMBRANCE. This totals 72 and a half years.

478. בְּשִׁיתִּין וְשִׁית, יִתְגְּלֵי מַלְכָּא מְשִׁיחָא בְּאַרְעָא דְּגָלִיל, וְכַד כֹּכָבָא דִּבְסְטַר מִזְרָח, יִבְלַע שֶׁבַע כֹּכְבַיָּא מִסְטַר צָפוֹן, וְשַׁלְהוֹבָא דְּאֶשָּׁא אוּכְמָא, תְּהֵא תַּלְיָא בִּרְקִיעָא שִׁיתִּין יוֹמִין, וּקְרָבִין יִתְעָרוּן בְּעָלְמָא, לִסְטַר צָפוֹן, וּתְרֵין מַלְכִין יִפְּלוּן, בְּאִינּוּן קְרָבִין.

478. In the year 66, the King Messiah will appear in the land of Galilee, AND HE IS CALLED MESSIAH BEN JOSEPH HE WILL THEREFORE APPEAR IN THE GALILEE, IN THE POSSESSION OF JOSEPH. A star from the east will swallow up seven stars from the north, and a flame of black fire will be suspended from the heavens for sixty days. Wars will be begun in the world from the north, and two kings will fall in these wars.

479. וְיִזְדַּוְּוגוּן כֻּלְּהוֹן עַמְמַיָּא, עַל בְּרַתֵּיה דְּיַעֲקֹב, לְאַדְחֲיָיא לָהּ מֵעָלְמָא. וְעַל הַהוּא זִמְנָא כְּתִיב, וְעֵת צָרָה הִיא לְיַעֲקֹב וּמִמֶּנָּה יִוָּשֵׁעַ, וּכְדֵין, יִסְתַּיְּימוּן נַפְשִׁין מִגּוּפָא, וּבָעְיָין לְאִתְחַדְּשָׁא, וְסִימָנֵיךְ כָּל הַנֶּפֶשׁ הַבָּאָה לְיַעֲקֹב מִצְרַיְמָה וגו', כָּל נֶפֶשׁ, שִׁשִּׁים וָשֵׁשׁ.

479. And all the nations will be united against the Daughter of Jacob, in order to drive her out of this world. And of that time it is written: "And it is a time of trouble for Jacob, but out of it he shall be saved" (Yirmeyah 30:7). Then all the souls shall be gone from the body; they will have to come back and be renewed. And your proof is the verse: "All the souls of the house of

Jacob that came into Egypt...were 66" (Beresheet 46:26).

480. בְּשַׁבְעִין וּתְלַת, כָּל מַלְכֵי עָלְמָא, יִתְכַּנְשׁוּן לְגוֹ קַרְתָּא רַבְּתָא דְּרוֹמִי, וְקוּדְשָׁא בְּרִיךְ הוּא, יִתְעַר עֲלַיְיהוּ, אֶשָּׁא וּבַרְדָא, וְאַבְנֵי אַלְגְּבִישׁ, וְיִתְאַבְּדוּן מֵעָלְמָא, בַּר אִינוּן מַלְכִין, דְּלָא יִמְטוֹן לְתַמָּן, וִיהַדְרוּן לְאַגָּחָא קְרָבִין אַחֲרָנִין. וּמֵהַהוּא זִמְנָא, מַלְכָּא מְשִׁיחָא, יִתְעַר בְּכָל עָלְמָא, וְיִתְכַּנְשׁוּן עִמֵּיה, כַּמָּה עַמִּין, וְכַמָּה חַיָּילִין, מִכָּל סְיָיפֵי עָלְמָא, וְכָל בְּנֵי יִשְׂרָאֵל, יִתְכַּנְשׁוּן בְּכָל אִינוּן אַתְרֵי.

480. In the 73rd year, THAT IS, SEVEN YEARS AFTER MESSIAH BEN JOSEPH WAS REVEALED, all the kings of the world shall assemble in the great city of Rome. And the Holy One, blessed be He, will shower fire and hail and meteoric stones upon them, until they are wiped out from the world. And only those kings who did not go to Rome will remain in the world. And they shall return and wage other wars. During this time, the King Messiah will declare himself throughout the whole world, and many nations will gather around him together with many armies from all corners of the world. And all the children of Yisrael will assemble together in their places.

481. עַד דְּאִשְׁתַּלִּימוּ אִינוּן שְׁנִין לְמֵאָה, כְּדֵין, וא"ו יִתְחַבַּר בְּה"א, וּכְדֵין וְהֵבִיאוּ אֶת כָּל אֲחֵיכֶם מִכָּל הַגּוֹיִם מִנְחָה לַיי' וְגו'. וּבְנֵי יִשְׁמָעֵאל זְמִינִין בְּהַהוּא זִמְנָא לְאִתְעָרָא עִם כָּל עַמִּין דְּעָלְמָא, לְמֵיתֵי עַל יְרוּשָׁלֵם, דִּכְתִיב וְאָסַפְתִּי אֶת כָּל הַגּוֹיִם אֶל יְרוּשָׁלַם לַמִּלְחָמָה וְגו'. וּכְתִיב יִתְיַצְּבוּ מַלְכֵי אֶרֶץ וְרוֹזְנִים נוֹסְדוּ יָחַד עַל יי' וְעַל מְשִׁיחוֹ. וּכְתִיב יוֹשֵׁב בַּשָּׁמַיִם יִשְׂחָק יי' יִלְעַג לָמוֹ.

481. When the century is completed, the *Vav* will join the *Hei*. And "they shall bring all your brethren out of all the nations for an offering to Hashem" (Yeshayah 66:20). THIS IS WHEN THEY SHALL BE GATHERED FROM THE DIASPORA. The children of Ishmael – WHO ARE THE HEAD (ALSO: LEADERS) OF ALL THE FORCES OF THE KLIPAH FROM THE RIGHT, AS ROME IS FOR THE LEFT – shall join together at that time with all the nations of the world WHO HAVE NOT GONE TO ROME and come to Jerusalem to wage war, as it is written: "For I will gather all nations against Jerusalem to battle" (Zecharyah 14:2); "The kings of the earth stand up and the rulers take counsel together, against Hashem and against his anointed" (Tehilim 2:2); and, "He that sits in heaven laughs, Hashem has them in derision" (Tehilim 2:4).

482. לְבָתַר וא"ו זְעִירָא, יִתְעַר, לְאִתְחַבְּרָא, וּלְחַדְּשָׁא נִשְׁמָתִין, דַּהֲווֹ עַתִּיקִין, בְּגִין לְחַדְתָּא עָלְמָא, כְּמָה דִכְתִיב, יִשְׁמַח יי' בְּמַעֲשָׂיו. וּכְתִיב יְהִי כְבוֹד יי' לְעוֹלָם. לְאִתְחַבְּרָא כִּדְקָא יָאוֹת. יִשְׁמַח יי' בְּמַעֲשָׂיו, לְנַחֲתָא לוֹן לְעָלְמָא, וּלְמֶהֱוֵי כֻּלְּהוֹן בִּרְיָין חַדְתִּין, לְחַבְּרָא עָלְמִין כֻּלְּהוּ כַּחֲדָא.

482. After ALL THE FORCES OF THE OTHER SIDE, THE RIGHT AND THE LEFT, ARE WIPED OUT OF THE WORLD, the small *Vav*, WHICH IS YESOD OF ZEIR ANPIN, will join THE *Hei* and renew old souls – NAMELY ALL THE SOULS THAT WERE IN A BODY SINCE THE CREATION OF THE WORLD – in order to renew the world, WHICH IS MALCHUT. As it is written: "let Hashem rejoice in His works," and: "May the glory of Hashem endure forever" (Tehilim 104:31), WHICH MEANS THAT in order FOR THE *Hei* to join THE *VAV* properly, "let Hashem rejoice in His works." Let Him bring HIS WORKS down, REFERRING TO THE RENEWED SOULS, into the world, so they all become new creatures and all the worlds are united.

483. זַכָּאִין אִינוּן, כָּל אִינוּן, דְּיִשְׁתָּאֲרוּן בְּעָלְמָא בְּסַיְיפֵי אֶלֶף שְׁתִיתָאָה, לְמֵיעַל בְּשַׁבַּתָּא, דְּהָא כְּדֵין, אִיהוּ יוֹמָא חַד לְקוּדְשָׁא בְּרִיךְ הוּא בִּלְחוֹדוֹי לְאִזְדַּוְּוגָא כִּדְקָא יָאוֹת, וּלְמִלְקַט נִשְׁמָתִין חַדְתִּין, לְמֶהֱוֵי בְּעָלְמָא, עִם אִינוּן דְּאִשְׁתָּאֲרוּ בְּקַדְמֵיתָא, דִּכְתִיב וְהָיָה הַנִּשְׁאָר בְּצִיּוֹן וְהַנּוֹתָר בִּירוּשָׁלַם קָדוֹשׁ יֵאָמֶר לוֹ כָּל הַכָּתוּב לַחַיִּים בִּירוּשָׁלָם.

483. Happy are all those who shall remain in the world at the end of the sixth millennium and enter the Shabbat, WHICH IS THE SEVENTH MILLENNIUM – Because that is a "day" for Hashem alone to join THE *Hei* properly, and cull new souls IN ORDER TO BRING THEM into the world. THIS REFERS TO THE SOULS THAT HAVE NOT YET COME INTO THE WORLD, together with THE RENEWED SOULS that have been there from the beginning, as it is written: "And it shall come to pass, that he that is left in Zion, and he that remains in Jerusalem, shall be called holy, everyone that is written for life in Jerusalem" (Yeshayah 4:3).

35. "And Elohim tested Abraham"

A Synopsis
The Zohar explores the story of the binding of Isaac. The biblical character of Isaac is a code referring to the Left Column energy, our reactive, self-centered nature. Abraham corresponds to the Right Column, our positive sharing attributes. The story is a metaphor for man's spiritual work, which is to bind and transform his selfish, reactive desires into positive and sharing qualities that embody care and concern for others.

The Relevance of this Passage
Repeatedly, something in our nature provokes us to indulge in negative behavior, even though it goes against our very will. Likewise, we're compelled to forsake positive actions despite our best intentions to follow through. This uniquely human idiosyncrasy is a depiction of the ongoing conflict between the body's *desire to receive* and the soul's desire to share. We arouse the inner strength and willpower to bind our own Evil Inclination and negative impulses, known Kabbalistically, as the *desire to receive for the self alone.*

484. וַיְהִי אַחַר הַדְּבָרִים הָאֵלֶּה וְהָאֱלֹהִים נִסָּה אֶת אַבְרָהָם וַיֹּאמֶר אֵלָיו אַבְרָהָם וַיֹּאמֶר הִנֵּנִי. רַבִּי יְהוּדָה, פָּתַח וְאָמַר, אַתָּה הוּא מַלְכִּי וְגוֹ' דָּא הוּא שְׁלִימוּ, דְּכָל דַּרְגִּין כַּחֲדָא, דָּא בְּדָא.

484. "And it came to pass after these things, that Elohim tested Abraham and said to him, 'Abraham,' and he replies, 'Behold, here I am'" (Beresheet 22:1). Rabbi Yehuda began the discussion with the verse: "You are my king, Elohim" (Tehilim 44:5). This symbolizes the complete unification of all the grades as one; they ARE ATTACHED to one another. THIS IS BECAUSE IN THIS VERSE ARE THE SFIROT – CHESED, GVURAH, TIFERET AND MALCHUT – WHICH REPRESENT ALL THE GRADES, BECAUSE "YOU" ALLUDES TO CHESED, ACCORDING TO THE MYSTERY OF THE VERSE, "YOU ARE A PRIEST FOR EVER" (TEHILIM 110:4); "ELOHIM" IS GVURAH; "ARE" IS TIFERET; AND "MY KING" IS MALCHUT.

485. צַוֵּה יְשׁוּעוֹת יַעֲקֹב, כָּל אִינּוּן שְׁלִיחָן, דְּעָבְדֵי שְׁלִיחוּתָא בְּעָלְמָא דְּלֶיהֱוֵי כֻּלְּהוּ, מִסִּטְרָא דְּרַחֲמֵי, וְלָא לֶהֱווֹ מִסִּטְרָא דְּדִינָא, בְּגִין דְּאִית

מָארֵי שְׁלִיחָן, מִסִּטְרָא דְרַחֲמֵי, וּמִסִּטְרָא דְדִינָא קַשְׁיָא. אִינוּן שְׁלִיחָן, דְּאַתְיָין מִסִּטְרָא דְרַחֲמֵי, לָא עַבְדֵי שְׁלִיחוּתָא דְדִינָא בְּעַלְמָא כְּלָל.

485. "...command deliverances for Jacob..." (Tehilim 44:5) MEANS THAT all the messengers who accomplish their missions in the world shall be from the side of Mercy and not from the side of Judgment. There are emissaries from both sides – some from the side of Mercy and some from the side of harsh Judgment. Those messengers who come from the side of Mercy never take on themselves a mission of Judgment in the world.

486. וְאִי תֵימָא, הָא מַלְאָכָא, דְּאִתְגְּלֵי לֵיה לְבִלְעָם, הָא תָּנֵינָן, שְׁלִיחָא דְרַחֲמֵי הֲוָה, וְאִתְהַפַּךְ לְדִינָא. לָא. לְעוֹלָם לָא אִשְׁתַּנֵּי, אֶלָּא שְׁלִיחָא דְרַחֲמֵי הֲוָה, לַאֲגָנָא עֲלַיְיהוּ דְיִשְׂרָאֵל, וּלְמֶהֱוֵי סַנֵּיגוֹרְיָא עֲלַיְיהוּ, וּלְקִבְלֵיה, הוּא דִינָא, וְכָךְ אוֹרְחוֹי דְקוּדְשָׁא בְּרִיךְ הוּא, כַּד אוֹטִיב לְדָא, הַהוּא טִיבוּ, דִּינָא לְדָא. כָּךְ הָא שְׁלִיחָא דְרַחֲמֵי, הֲוָה לְהוֹ לְיִשְׂרָאֵל, וּלְבִלְעָם אִתְהַפַּךְ לְדִינָא. בְּגִין כָּךְ צַוֵּה יְשׁוּעוֹת יַעֲקֹב, אָמַר דָּוִד, פַּקִּיד עַל עָלְמָא, כַּד יִשְׁתַּלְּחוּן שְׁלִיחָאָה, דִּי לֶהֱוֵיָין מִסִּטְרָא דְרַחֲמֵי.

486. You might say: But we have learned that the angel that was revealed to Bilaam was a messenger of Mercy who changed to a messenger of Judgment, THEREBY SHOWING THAT A MESSENGER OF MERCY CAN EXECUTE JUDGMENT. HOWEVER, THE ANSWER IS no. He never changed TO EXECUTE JUDGMENT. Rather, he was a messenger of Mercy who came to protect Yisrael and to be in their favor. But toward Bilaam, he was a messenger of Judgment. So these are the ways of the Holy One, blessed be He, when He does good to someone. We can see that this benefit to one person may be a punishment for another person. And so first, he was a messenger of Mercy for Yisrael. But for Bilaam he was a messenger of Judgment. Because of this, HE PLEADED, "Command deliverances for Jacob." Thus, David said, "Command this for the world so that when a messenger will be sent, he will be from the side of Mercy."

487. רַבִּי אַבָּא אָמַר, צַוֵּה יְשׁוּעוֹת יַעֲקֹב, דְּאִינוּן גּוֹ גָּלְוָותָא, וְיִשְׁתַּכַּח פּוּרְקָנָא לְהוֹן, גּוֹ גָּלוּתְהוֹן. תָּא חֲזֵי, תוּשְׁבְּחָן דַּאֲבָהָן, יַעֲקֹב הֲוָה,

וְאִלְמָלֵא יִצְחָק, לָא אָתָא יַעֲקֹב לְעָלְמָא, וּבְגִין כָּךְ, צַוֵּה יְשׁוּעוֹת יַעֲקֹב דָּא יִצְחָק, דְּכֵיוָן דְּאִשְׁתְּזֵיב יִצְחָק, יְשׁוּעוֹת יַעֲקֹב הֲווֹ.

487. Rabbi Aba said: "command deliverances for Jacob" MEANS THAT HE PRAYED FOR JACOB, prayed for those in exile, that they might receive salvation. Come and behold: Jacob was the glory of the Patriarchs. Had it not been for Isaac, Jacob would not have appeared in the world. For this reason, "command deliverances for Jacob" alludes to Isaac, WHO IS THE DELIVERER OF JACOB, because when Isaac was saved DURING THE BINDING OF ISAAC, this was the deliverance of Jacob.

488. וַיְהִי אַחַר הַדְּבָרִים הָאֵלֶּה, ר' שִׁמְעוֹן אָמַר, הָא תָּנִינָן, וַיְהִי בִּימֵי, עַל צַעֲרָא אִתְּמָר, וַיְהִי אַף עַל גַּב דְּלָא כְּתִיב בִּימֵי, טַפְסֵי דְצַעֲרָא אִית בֵּיה. וַיְהִי אַחַר, בָּתַר דַּרְגָּא תַּתָּאָה, דְּכָל דַּרְגִּין עִלָּאִין, וּמַאן אִיהוּ, דְּבָרִים, כִּדְבָר אַחֵר, לֹא אִישׁ דְּבָרִים אָנֹכִי.

488. "And it came to pass after these things…" Rabbi Shimon said: We have learned that the words "And it came to pass (Heb. *vayehi*) in the days" are said concerning trouble. Thus, even though it is not written 'in the days of,' there is still a certain tinge of distress, as it says, "Vayehi." "And it came to pass after" MEANS that it happened after the lowest of the supernal grades OF ATZILUT. And what is it? IT IS "these things (Heb. *d'varim*)," NAMELY MALCHUT, as it is written: "I am not a man of words (Heb. *d'varim*)" (Shemot 4:10).

489. וּמַאן הֲוָה בָּתַר דַּרְגָּא דָא, וְהָאֱלֹהִים נִסָּה אֶת אַבְרָהָם. דְּאַתְיָא יֵצֶר הָרָע, לְקַטְרְגָא קַמֵּי קוּדְשָׁא בְּרִיךְ הוּא. הָכָא אִית לְאִסְתַּכְּלָא, וְהָאֱלֹהִים נִסָּה אֶת אַבְרָהָם. אֶת יִצְחָק מִבָּעֵי לֵיה. דְּהָא יִצְחָק, בַּר תְּלָתִין וְשֶׁבַע שְׁנִין הֲוָה, וְהָא אֲבוֹי, לָאו בַּר עוֹנָשָׁא דִילֵיה הֲוָה, דְּאִלְמָלֵא אָמַר יִצְחָק, לָא בָּעֵינָא, לָא אִתְעֲנַשׁ אֲבוֹי עֲלֵיה, מַאי טַעְמָא, וְהָאֱלֹהִים נִסָּה אֶת אַבְרָהָם, וְלָא כְּתִיב נִסָּה אֶת יִצְחָק.

489. And what is "after" this grade, THAT IS, AFTER MALCHUT? THIS IS A REFERENCE TO THE WORDS, "that Elohim tested Abraham," which mean that the Evil Inclination came from there to lay accusations before the Holy One, blessed be He. THEREFORE, "ELOHIM TESTED ABRAHAM." This phrase should be studied carefully. It should have been written, 'tested Isaac,' because Isaac was already 37 years old and his father could no longer be punished for his sins. So if Isaac had said, 'I refuse to obey,' his father would not have been punished because of him. So then why is it written: "that Elohim tested Abraham," rather than, 'tested Isaac?'

490. אֶלָּא, אֶת אַבְרָהָם וַדַּאי, דְּבָעֵי לְאִתְכְּלָלָא בְּדִינָא, דְּהָא אַבְרָהָם, לָא הֲוָה בֵּיהּ דִּינָא כְּלַל, מִקַּדְמַת דְּנָא, וְהַשְׁתָּא אִתְכְּלִיל מַיָּי״א בְּאֶשָׁ״א. וְאַבְרָהָם, לָא הֲוָה שְׁלִים, עַד הַשְׁתָּא, דְּאִתְעַטַּר לְמֶעְבַּד דִּינָא, וּלְאַתְקְנָא לֵיהּ בְּאַתְרֵיהּ.

490. AND HE REPLIES: IT SHOULD definitely BE WRITTEN: "tested Abraham," because he was supposed to be included within Judgment, as there was no judgment in Abraham previously – HE HAD CONSISTED ENTIRELY OF CHESED. Now water was mixed with fire; CHESED WAS MIXED WITH JUDGMENT. So Abraham did not achieve perfection until he crowned (prepared) himself to execute Judgment and establish it in its place.

491. וְכָל יוֹמוֹי, לָא הֲוָה שְׁלִים, עַד הַשְׁתָּא דְּאִתְכְּלִיל מַיָּ״א בְּאֶשָׁ״א, וְאֶשָׁ״א בְּמַיָּ״א, וּבְגִין כָּךְ וְהָאֱלֹהִים נִסָּה אֶת אַבְרָהָם, וְלָא אֶת יִצְחָק, דְּאַזְמִין אַבְרָהָם, לְאִתְכְּלָלָא בְּדִינָא, וְכַד עָבֵיד דָּא, עָאל אֶשָׁ״א בְּמַיָּ״א, וְאִשְׁתְּלִים דָּא עִם דָּא. וְדָא עָבֵיד דִּינָא, לְאִתְכְּלָלָא דָּא בְּדָא, וּכְדֵין יֵצֶר הָרָע, אָתָא לְקַטְרְגָא עֲלֵיהּ דְּאַבְרָהָם, דְּלָא אִשְׁתְּלִים כְּדְקָא יָאוֹת, עַד דְּיַעֲבֵיד דִּינָא בְּיִצְחָק, דְּיֵצֶר הָרָע, אַחַר הַדְּבָרִים אִיהוּ, וְאָתָא לְקַטְרְגָא.

491. So all his life, he did not reach perfection until now, until water mixed with fire – RIGHT MIXED WITH LEFT – and fire with water – LEFT WITH RIGHT. This is why: "Elohim tested Abraham" and not Isaac. Because THE HOLY ONE, BLESSED BE HE, invited Abraham to be included with Judgment ACCORDING TO THE SECRET OF THE LEFT. So when he performed THE ACT OF BINDING ISAAC, the fire entered the water, THAT IS, JUDGMENT ENTERED CHESED, and they were perfected by each other, AS

WAS SAID BEFORE. This is what the act of Judgment accomplished: it included one within the other. This is also the reason why the Evil Inclination came and accused Abraham of not being properly perfected until he performed the act of Judgment by BINDING Isaac. THE PLACE of the Evil Inclination is "after" (beyond) these "things," WHICH ALLUDES TO MALCHUT ACCORDING TO THE SECRET OF THE VERSE, "SIN CROUCHES AT THE DOOR" (BERESHEET 4:7). And so he came to persecute.

492. וְתָא חֲזֵי, רָזָא דְמִלָה, אַף עַל גַב דְקָאֲמָרָן דְאַבְרָהָם כְּתִיב, וְלָא יִצְחָק, יִצְחָק נָמֵי אִתְכְּלֵיל בֵּיהּ, בְּהַאי קְרָא, רָזָא דִכְתִיב, וְהָאֱלֹהִים נִסָּה אֶת אַבְרָהָם. נִסָּה לְאַבְרָהָם, לָא כְּתִיב, אֶלָּא אֶת אַבְרָהָם, אֶת דַּיְיקָא, וְדָא יִצְחָק. דְּהָא בְּהַהִיא שַׁעֲתָא, בִּגְבוּר"ה תַּתָּאָה שַׁרְיָא, כֵּיוָן דְאִתְעֲקַד, וְאִזְדַּמַּן בְּדִינָא, עַל יְדָא דְאַבְרָהָם, כִּדְקָא יָאוֹת, כְּדֵין אִתְעַטַּר בְּאַתְרֵיהּ, בַּהֲדֵיהּ דְאַבְרָהָם, וְאִתְכְּלִילוּ אֶשָׁ"א בְּמַיָ"א, וּסְלִיקוּ לְעֵילָא, וּכְדֵין אִשְׁתַּכַּח מַחֲלוֹקֶת כִּדְקָא יָאוֹת, מַיָא בְּאֶשָׁא.

492. Come and behold: observe the mystery behind this issue. Even though it is written: "Abraham" and not Isaac, Isaac is still included in the passage. It is written: "Elohim tested (*et*) Abraham," rather than 'tested Abraham.' Instead of a dative particle, it uses *Et*. *Et* is accurate and ALLUDES TO Isaac, because at that time ISAAC resided in lower Gvurah, WHICH REFERS TO THE NUKVA. And as he was bound and underwent the trial of Judgment performed by Abraham, ISAAC was crowned in his place together with Abraham, and the fire combined with the water and rose upward. AND ABRAHAM WITH CHESED ROSE UP TO CHOCHMAH, AND ISAAC WITH GVURAH ROSE UP TO BINAH. Then the dispute was settled properly, BECAUSE THEY MADE PEACE BETWEEN THEMSELVES, AS fire and water WERE COMBINED AND BECAME INCLUSIVE OF EACH OTHER.

493. מַאן חָמָא אַבָּא רַחֲמָנָא, דְּאִתְעֲבֵיד אַכְזָר. אֶלָּא, בְּגִין לְאִשְׁתַּכְּחָא מַחֲלוֹקֶת מַיָא בְּאֶשָׁא, וּלְאִתְעַטְּרָא בְּאַתְרַיְיהוּ, עַד דְּאָתָא יַעֲקֹב, וְאִתְתַּקַּן כֹּלָּא, כִּדְקָא יָאוֹת, וְאִתְעֲבִידוּ תְּלָתָא אַבָּהָן שְׁלֵמִין, וְאִתְתַּקְנוּ עִלָּאֵי וְתַתָּאֵי.

493. Who has ever seen a merciful father do a cruel thing TO HIS SON? It is

only to settle the dispute and combine water with fire. THIS REFERS TO THE ATTRIBUTE OF CHESED OF ABRAHAM WITH THE FIRE OF ISAAC, and each one is properly crowned in its place. AND THIS REMAINED SO until Jacob appeared, WHO WAS THE SECRET OF THE CENTRAL COLUMN. Then, everything was properly established, and all three Patriarchs achieved perfection, WHICH MEANS THAT THEY BECAME A CHARIOT FOR THE UPPER THREE COLUMNS, and so the upper and lower beings were properly established.

494. וַיֹּאמֶר קַח נָא אֶת בִּנְךָ. וְכִי הֵיאַךְ יָכִיל אַבְרָהָם, דְּאִיהוּ סָבָא. אִי תֵימָא, בְּגִין דְּיִצְחָק, לָא נָפֵיק מֵרְשׁוּתֵיהּ כְּלַל, יָאוֹת. אֲבָל, כִּדְבָר אַחֵר קַח אֶת אַהֲרֹן וְאֶת אֶלְעָזָר בְּנוֹ. אֶלָּא, בְּגִין לְאַמְשָׁכָא לוֹן בְּמִלִּין, וּלְאַדְכְּרָא לוֹן, לִרְעוּתָא דְּקוּדְשָׁא בְּרִיךְ הוּא, אוּף הָכָא קַח בְּמִלִּין. אֶת בִּנְךָ אֶת יְחִידְךָ אֲשֶׁר אָהַבְתָּ. הָא אוֹקִמוּהָ. וְלֶךְ לְךָ אֶל אֶרֶץ הַמּוֹרִיָּה, כִּדְבָר אַחֵר אֵלֵךְ לִי אֶל הַר הַמּוֹר. לְאַתְקָנָא בְּאַתְרָא דְּיִתְחֲזֵי.

494. Of the verse, "And He said, Take now your son" (Beresheet 22:2), HE ASKS: How could Abraham HAVE TAKEN ISAAC, HIS SON, by force, when he was old? If you say THAT Isaac was still under his authority AND THEREFORE HAD TO OBEY HIS FATHER'S COMMANDMENTS, IT WOULD BE a good explanation. But this is similar to: "take Aaron and Elazar his son" (Bemidbar 20:25), WHERE THE MEANING IS only to convince them with words and remind them THAT THEY SHOULD FULFILL the will of the Holy One, blessed be He. So here as well, WITH ABRAHAM, THE MEANING IS to "take," by verbal persuasion, "your son, your only son, whom you love, Isaac, and go to the land of Moriah," as it is written: "I will go to the mountain of myrrh (Heb. mor)" (Shir Hashirim 4:6), to be established in a proper place.

36. "And he saw the place afar off"

A Synopsis
As Abraham walks with Isaac to the place of sacrifice, Abraham is granted a crystal clear vision of his future grandson, Jacob, the predestined son of Isaac. Abraham perceives the important role that Jacob will play in the world; nonetheless, he remains true to his commitment to sacrifice his son, despite his compelling vision. Abraham surrenders total control, placing all his trust in the Creator's words.

The Relevance of this Passage
Man's nature is to succumb to the temptations of the material world, to give in to the lure of immediate gratification at the expense of long-term fulfillment. The wisdom and strength to place our trust in the spiritual laws of life and relinquish control to the Creator are granted to our soul. This portion allows the radiance of the Creator to enlighten and direct us along the darkened corridors of life.

495. בַּיּוֹם הַשְּׁלִישִׁי וַיִּשָּׂ"א אַבְרָהָ"ם אֶ"ת עֵינָיו וַיַּרְא אֶת הַמָּקוֹם מֵרָחוֹק. בַּיּוֹם הַשְּׁלִישִׁי, הָא אוּקְמוּהָ, אֶלָּא, כֵּיוָן דְּאִתְּמָר, וַיָּקָם וַיֵּלֶךְ אֶל הַמָּקוֹם אֲשֶׁר אָמַר לוֹ הָאֱלֹהִים, מַאי טַעְמָא, בַּיּוֹם הַשְּׁלִישִׁי וַיַּרְא אֶת הַמָּקוֹם מֵרָחוֹק. אֶלָּא, בְּגִין דִּכְתִיב, כִּי בְיִצְחָק יִקָּרֵא לְךָ זָרַע. וְדָא הוּא יַעֲקֹב, דְּנָפַק מִנֵּיהּ. וְהַאי הוּא בַּיּוֹם הַשְּׁלִישִׁי.

495. "On the third day, Abraham lifted up his eyes and saw the place afar off" (Beresheet 22:4). The meaning of "on the third day" has already been explained, but since it has already been stated: "and he rose up and went to the place of which the Elohim had told him" (Ibid. 3), ONE SHOULD ASK why does it then say, "On the third day...and he saw the place afar off"? WHAT DO WE LEARN FROM THIS REPETITION? HE REPLIES: It is written, "for in Isaac shall your seed be called" (Beresheet 21:12), because Jacob came from him. ISAAC IS THE SECRET OF THE LEFT COLUMN, WHICH HAS NO EXISTENCE WITHOUT THE CENTRAL COLUMN, WHICH IS JACOB. And, he is called "the third day," BECAUSE ABRAHAM, ISAAC, AND JACOB ARE THE SECRET OF CHESED, GVURAH AND TIFERET, WHICH ARE CALLED 'THREE DAYS.' THUS, JACOB, WHO IS TIFERET, IS EQUIVALENT TO THE THIRD DAY. THIS IS WHY HE LOOKED FOR JACOB, WHO IS THE CAUSE OF THE EXISTENCE OF ISAAC.

496. וַיַּרְא אֶת הַמָּקוֹם מֵרָחוֹק. כְּדָבָר אַחֵר מֵרָחוֹק יי' נִרְאָה לִי. וַיַּרְא
אֶת הַמָּקוֹם. דָּא הוּא יַעֲקֹב, דִּכְתִיב וַיִּקַּח מֵאַבְנֵי הַמָּקוֹם. אִסְתַּכַּל
אַבְרָהָם, בַּיּוֹם הַשְּׁלִישִׁי דְּאִיהוּ דַּרְגָּא תְּלִיתָאָה, וְחָמָא לֵיהּ לְיַעֲקֹב,
דְּזַמִּין לְמֵיפַק מִנֵּיהּ. מֵרָחוֹק, כְּמָה דַאֲמָרָן, מֵרָחוֹק, וְלָא לִזְמַן קָרִיב.

496. The words, "and saw the place afar off," are similar to: "from afar off
has Hashem appeared to me" (Yirmeyah 31:3), WHICH IS THE SECRET OF
THE CENTRAL COLUMN. The phrase, "and he saw the place" refers to
Jacob, of whom it is written: "and he took of the stones of that place"
(Beresheet 28:11). SO Abraham looked into the "third day," which is the
third grade, NAMELY TIFERET, and there he saw Jacob, who was to issue
from him. BUT "afar off" MEANS at some distant time, as we have already
explained, rather than in the near future.

497. אָמַר לֵיהּ רִבִּי אֶלְעָזָר, מַאי שְׁבָחָא אִיהוּ לְאַבְרָהָם, כַּד אִסְתַּכַּל,
וְחָמָא דְּזַמִּין לְמֵיפַק, מִנֵּיהּ יַעֲקֹב. דְּהָא כַּד אָזִיל לְמֶיעְקַד לֵיהּ לְיִצְחָק,
לָאו שְׁבָחָא כָּל כָּךְ אִיהוּ דִילֵיהּ.

497. Rabbi Elazar said to him: What is Abraham praised for, as he already
saw that Jacob was destined to issue from him? Since he was on his way to
sacrifice Isaac, this cannot be such a great praise for him. THIS IS
PARTICULARLY TRUE BECAUSE THIS MUST HAVE BROUGHT SOME DOUBT
INTO HIS MIND ABOUT THE HOLY ONE, BLESSED BE HE. IF HE IS ABOUT
TO OFFER HIM AS A SACRIFICE, HOW THEN WILL JACOB BE BORN?

498. אָמַר לוֹ וַדַּאי חָמָא לֵיהּ לְיַעֲקֹב, דְּהָא מִקַּדְמַת דְּנָא, יָדַע אַבְרָהָם
חָכְמְתָא, וְאִסְתַּכַּל הַשְׁתָּא, בַּיּוֹם הַשְּׁלִישִׁי, דְּאִיהוּ דַּרְגָּא תְּלִיתָאָה,
לְמֶעְבַּד שְׁלִימוּ, וּכְדֵין חָמָא לֵיהּ לְיַעֲקֹב, דִּכְתִיב וַיַּרְא אֶת הַמָּקוֹם.
אֲבָל הַשְׁתָּא, קַיְימָא לֵיהּ מִלָּה מֵרָחוֹק, בְּגִין דְּאָזִיל לְמֶיעְקַד לֵיהּ
לְיִצְחָק, וְלָא בָּעָא לְהַרְהֵר אֲבַתְרֵיהּ דְּקוּדְשָׁא בְּרִיךְ הוּא.

498. He said to him: It is certain that he saw Jacob, because even before
THE SACRIFICE, Abraham had knowledge of wisdom. THIS MEANS THAT
HE HAD ALREADY ATTAINED THE SUPERNAL MOCHIN THAT FLOW OVER

THE THREE COLUMNS, THE THIRD COLUMN OF WHICH IS JACOB. So now he looked into the "third day," which is the third grade, TIFERET, to draw perfection from it – THAT IS, TO COMPLETE HIS MOCHIN, BECAUSE PERFECTION CANNOT BE REACHED EXCEPT THROUGH THE CENTRAL COLUMN. Then THE SCRIPTURES SAY THAT he saw Jacob, as it is written: "and he saw the place," MEANING HE SAW THE CENTRAL COLUMN, WHICH IS CALLED JACOB. But this still remained "afar off" from him, AS HE COULD NOT ACHIEVE IT NOW. He was on his way to bind Isaac and did not wish to have any doubts about the Holy One, blessed be He, WHO TOLD HIM TO OFFER ISAAC AS A SACRIFICE. AND THEREFORE, HE DID NOT ACHIEVE THE CENTRAL COLUMN COMPLETELY, AS IS FURTHER EXPLAINED.

499. מֵרָחוֹק: חָמָא לֵיה, גּוֹ אַסְפָּקְלַרְיָאה דְּלָא נָהֲרָא בִּלְחוֹדוֹי, וּבְגִין כָּךְ, חָמָא לֵיה, וְלָא אִתְגְּלֵי כֹּלָּא, דְּאִלּוּ אַסְפָּקְלַרְיָאה דְּנַהֲרָא, הֲוָה שְׁכִיחַ, עַל הַאי אַסְפָּקְלַרְיָאה דְּלָא נַהֲרָא, אִתְקַיֵּים עֲלֵיה אַבְרָהָם, כִּדְקָא יָאוֹת, אֲבָל מֵרָחוֹק בִּלְחוֹדוֹי הֲוָה, מֵרָחוֹק.

499. The words "afar off" MEAN THAT he only saw him through a clouded mirror, which is why he did not see him clearly. If the illuminating mirror had been over the opaque mirror, then Abraham would have grasped him properly, BUT THIS WAS NOT THE CASE. THUS, ABRAHAM SAW HIM only from "afar off."

500. מַאי טַעֲמָא אִסְתַּלָּק, מֵהַאי מֶלָּה, אַסְפָּקְלַרְיָאה דְּנַהֲרָא בְּגִין דְּהַאי, דַּרְגָּא דְּיַעֲקֹב הֲוָה, וּבְגִין דְּיַעֲקֹב עַד לָא אִתְיְילִיד, לָא אִשְׁתַּכַּח הַשְׁתָּא עַל הַאי דַרְגָּא. וְתוּ, בְּגִין דְּיֵיהַךְ וִיקַבֵּל אַגְרָא. וַיַּרְא אֶת הַמָּקוֹם מֵרָחוֹק. דָּא יַעֲקֹב, כְּמָה דְאִתְּמַר מֵרָחוֹק, דְּלָא זָכָה בֵּיה.

500. AND HE ASKS: Why did the clear shining mirror disappear? AND HE REPLIES: Because this is the grade of Jacob, and as Jacob was not yet born, his aspect was not yet present over this grade. Furthermore, it disappeared so that Abraham could go AND BIND HIS SON and receive his reward. SO ACCORDINGLY, "he saw the place afar off" MEANS THAT HE SAW Jacob, as is explained, "afar off," MEANING THAT he did not reach him.

501. וַיָּבֹאוּ אֶל הַמָּקוֹם אֲשֶׁר אָמַר לוֹ הָאֱלֹהִים וְגוֹ'. רְמִיז הָכָא, דְּאַף עַל גַּב דְּאָתוּ לְהַהוּא רְאִיָּיה, וְחָמָא לְיַעֲקֹב, אָמַר אַבְרָהָם, וַדַּאי קוּדְשָׁא בְּרִיךְ הוּא יָדַע בְּגַוְונָא אָחֳרָא דְּאִתְחֲזֵי, מִיָּד וַיִּבֶן שָׁם אַבְרָהָם אֶת הַמִּזְבֵּחַ וְגוֹ'.

501. The verse: "And they came to the place which the Elohim had told him of" (Beresheet 22:9) implies that even though he had the ability to "see" Jacob, Abraham said that the Holy One, blessed be He, WHO TOLD HIM TO BIND ISAAC, certainly knows another way to achieve this end. So immediately, "Abraham built an altar there," WHICH MEANS THAT EVEN THOUGH HE SAW THAT ISAAC WOULD BEAR JACOB, HE HAD NO DOUBTS ABOUT THE COMMANDS OF THE HOLY ONE, BLESSED BE HE. AND BECAUSE OF HIS TRUST IN THE HOLY ONE, BLESSED BE HE, HE BUILT AN ALTAR.

502. מַה כְּתִיב לְעֵילָא, וַיֹּאמֶר יִצְחָק אֶל אַבְרָהָם אָבִיו וַיֹּאמֶר אָבִי, הָא אוֹקְמוּהָ. אֲבָל מַאי טַעְמָא, לָא אָתִיב לֵיהּ מִיָּד. אֶלָּא, בְּגִין דְּהָא אִסְתַּלַּק, מֵרַחֲמֵי דְּאַבָּא עַל בְּרָא, וּבְגִין כָּךְ, כְּתִיב הִנֶּנִּי בְנִי, הִנֶּנִּי דְּאִסְתַּלָּקוּ רַחֲמֵי, וְאִתְהַפָּךְ לְדִינָא.

502. But before this, it is written: "And Isaac spoke to Abraham his father, and said, 'My father...'" (Ibid. 7) which has already been explained. But why did he not reply to him at all? AND HE REPLIES: Because Abraham ceased to have the mercy of a father towards his son. INSTEAD, THE ATTRIBUTE OF JUDGMENT CAME UPON HIM. THIS IS THE REASON WHY HE DID NOT ANSWER HIM THE FIRST TIME. Thus, it is written: "Here I am, my son." "Here I am," AS IF TO SAY – the Mercy has gone and changed into Judgment.

503. וַיֹּאמֶר אַבְרָהָם, וְלָא כְּתִיב, וַיֹּאמֶר אָבִיו. דְּהָא לָא קָאִים עֲלֵיהּ כְּאַבָּא, אֶלָּא בַּעַל מַחֲלוֹקֶת, הֲוָה בֵּיהּ. אֱלֹהִים יִרְאֶה לוֹ הַשֶּׂה. יִרְאֶה לָנוּ מִבְּעֵי לֵיהּ, מַאי יִרְאֶה לוֹ. אֶלָּא, אָמַר לוֹ אֱלֹהִים יִרְאֶה לוֹ לְגַרְמֵיהּ, כַּד אִיהוּ יִצְטְרִיךְ, אֲבָל הַשְׁתָּא בְּנִי, וְלָא אָמְרָא. מִיָּד וַיֵּלְכוּ שְׁנֵיהֶם יַחְדָּו.

503. Note that it is written: "And Abraham said," rather than 'And his father said.' This is because he was no longer like a father; but had become an adversary. Of the verse: "Elohim will provide himself a lamb," HE SAID: It should have been written, 'will provide us' and not "Himself." AND HE REPLIES THAT he said to him: Elohim will provide for His own needs at the time when He shall need it. But now my son, and not the lamb, IS THE OFFERING. Immediately, it is written: "they went both of them together," WHICH MEANS THAT ISAAC FOLLOWED THE WILL OF HIS FATHER.

504. רִבִּי שִׁמְעוֹן, פָּתַח וְאָמַר, הֵן אֶרְאֶלָּם צָעֲקוּ חוּצָה מַלְאֲכֵי שָׁלוֹם מַר יִבְכָּיוּן. הֵן אֶרְאֶלָּם, אִלֵּין מַלְאֲכֵי עִלָּאֵי. צָעֲקוּ, בְּהַהִיא שַׁעֲתָא, וּבְעוֹ לְקַיָּימָא, עַל הַהִיא מִלָּה, דִּכְתִיב, וַיּוֹצֵא אוֹתוֹ הַחוּצָה. בְּגִין כָּךְ, צָעֲקוּ חוּצָה.

504. Rabbi Shimon began with the verse: "Behold, the mighty ones shall cry outside, ambassadors of peace shall weep bitterly" (Yeshayah 33:7). In this verse, "the mighty ones (also: 'angels')" are the celestial angels who cried out at the time WHEN ISAAC WAS BOUND UPON THE ALTAR and wanted the Holy One, blessed be He, to remember and fulfill the promise in the verse, "And He took him outside" (Beresheet 15:5), WHICH ALLUDES TO THE BLESSING OF HIS OFFSPRING. Therefore, they "shall cry outside" IS WRITTEN.

505. מַלְאֲכֵי שָׁלוֹם. אִלֵּין אִינוּן מַלְאָכִין אָחֳרָנִין, דַּהֲווֹ זְמִינִין, לְמֵיהַךְ קַמֵּיהּ דְּיַעֲקֹב, וּבְגִינֵיהּ דְּיַעֲקֹב, אַבְטַח לוֹן שְׁלִימוּ קוּדְשָׁא בְּרִיךְ הוּא, דִּכְתִיב וְיַעֲקֹב הָלַךְ לְדַרְכּוֹ וַיִּפְגְּעוּ בוֹ מַלְאֲכֵי אֱלֹהִים. וְאִלֵּין אִקְרוּן מַלְאֲכֵי שָׁלוֹם, כֻּלְּהוּ בָּכוּ, כַּד חָמוּ לֵיהּ לְאַבְרָהָם, דְּעָקִיד לֵיהּ לְיִצְחָק, וְאִזְדַּעְזָעוּ עִלָּאֵי וְתַתָּאֵי, וְכֻלְּהוּ עֲלֵיהּ דְּיִצְחָק.

505. "...ambassadors of peace" are other angels, who were destined to walk in front of Jacob. For Ya'akov's sake, the Holy One, blessed be He, promised them perfection, as it is written: "And Jacob went on his way, and the angels of Elohim met him" (Beresheet 32:2). These are called the 'Angels of Peace,' and they all wept as they saw Abraham binding Isaac. The upper and lower beings trembled and shook for the sake of Isaac.

37. "Abraham, Abraham"

A Synopsis
During the binding of Isaac, an angel calls out the name of Abraham twice. Kabbalistically, Isaac corresponds to man's negative and selfish *desire to receive*, the root of all egotistic and self-centered behavior. Abraham is a metaphor for the positive sharing attributes of man. Avraham's willingness to sacrifice his son Isaac, is a code signifying the complete subjugation of Avraham's negative *desire to receive*. The second utterance of Avraham's name by the angel indicates the complete transformation of Avraham's nature into the *desire to share*.

The Relevance of this Passage
Avraham's extraordinary actions and faith created a reservoir of spiritual energy for all future generations to draw upon in their effort to completely transform their nature. The change in Avraham's name and its appearance in this text of Zohar is the portal through which the energy flows. These metaphysical forces arouse an awareness of our own negative attributes and generates the desire and strength to subjugate our ego, transforming all our wanton desires into positive attributes that embody care and compassion for others.

506. וַיִּקְרָא אֵלָיו מַלְאַךְ יי' וגו', פְּסִיק טַעֲמָא בְּגַוַויְיהוּ, דְּלָאו אַבְרָהָם בַּתְרָאָה, כְּקַדְמָאָה, בַּתְרָאָה שְׁלִים, קַדְמָאָה לָא שְׁלִים, כְּגַוְונָא דָא, שְׁמוּאֵל שְׁמוּאֵל, בַּתְרָאָה שְׁלִים, קַדְמָאָה לָא שְׁלִים. בַּתְרָאָה נָבִיא, קַדְמָאָה לָא נָבִיא. אֲבָל מֹשֶׁה מֹשֶׁה, לָא פְּסִיק, בְּגִין דְּמִיּוֹמָא דְּאִתְיְלִיד, לָא אַעֲדֵי מִנֵּיהּ שְׁכִינְתָּא. אַבְרָהָם אַבְרָהָם: רַבִּי חִיָּיא אָמַר, בְּגִין לְאַתְעָרָא לֵיהּ, בְּרוּחָא אָחֳרָא, בְּעוֹבָדָא אָחֳרָא, בְּלִבָּא אָחֳרָא.

506. "And the angel of Hashem called to him...ABRAHAM, ABRAHAM" (Beresheet 22:11). There is a disjunctive mark between the two Avrahams, WHICH MEANS THAT the second "Abraham" is not the same as the first. Abraham AFTER THE BINDING has achieved perfection, BECAUSE HE HAS BEEN INCLUDED WITH ISAAC, while the first "ABRAHAM" HAS not yet achieved perfection, BECAUSE HE WAS NOT YET INCLUDED WITHIN ISAAC. Similarly, "Samuel, Samuel" (I Shmuel 3:10) ALSO HAS A DISJUNCTIVE MARK BETWEEN THE TWO NAMES, WHICH MEANS THAT the latter is perfected while the first is not. WHY? BECAUSE the latter was already a prophet, while the former had not yet achieved that grade. But in "Moses Moses" (Shemot 3:4), there is no pause BETWEEN THE NAMES, because ever since the day Moses was born, the Shechinah never left him. THUS, THERE IS NO DIFFERENCE BETWEEN THE LATTER AND THE FORMER. "Abraham, Abraham," Rabbi Chiya said. The reason WHY HE CALLED HIS NAME TWICE was to arouse him with a different spirit, a different action, and a different heart.

507. ר' יְהוּדָה אָמַר, אִתְבְּרִיר יִצְחָק, וְאִסְתַּלֵּיק בִּרְעוּתָא, קַמֵּי קוּדְשָׁא בְּרִיךְ הוּא, כְּרֵיחָא דִקְטֹרֶת בּוּסְמִין, דְּקַרְבִין כַּהֲנַיָּא קַמֵּיה, תְּרֵין זִמְנִין בְּיוֹמָא, וְאִשְׁתְּלִים קָרְבָּנָא. דְּהָא צַעֲרָא דְּאַבְרָהָם הֲוָה, בְּשַׁעֲתָא דְּאִתְמַר לֵיה, אַל תִּשְׁלַח יָדְךָ אֶל הַנַּעַר וְאַל תַּעַשׂ לוֹ מְאוּמָה. חָשִׁיב דְּקָרְבְּנֵיה לָא אִשְׁתְּלִים, וּלְמַגָּנָא עָבַד וְסַדַּר כֹּלָּא, וּבְנָה מִזְבֵּחַ. מִיָּד וַיִּשָּׂא אַבְרָהָם אֶת עֵינָיו וַיַּרְא וְהִנֵּה אַיִל אַחַר וְגו'.

507. Rabbi Yehuda said: Isaac was purified and elevated properly before the Holy One, blessed be He, BY BEING BOUND UPON THE ALTAR, like the odor of the incense of spices which the priests offered before Him twice a day. Thus, the sacrifice was perfected AS IF IT WERE OFFERED AND BURNED AS A SWEET SAVOR BEFORE HASHEM. Abraham felt sorry when he was told: "Lay not your hand upon the lad, neither do anything to him" (Beresheet 22:12), BECAUSE he thought it meant that his offering was not perfect – that all his preparations and the building of the altar were in vain. But immediately, it is written: "And Abraham lifted up his eyes, and looked, and behold behind him a ram caught in a thicket" (Ibid. 13); AND HE OFFERED IT INSTEAD OF ISAAC, AND SO ACHIEVED PERFECTION.

508. הָא תָּנִינָן הוּא אַיִן דְּאִתְבְּרִי בֵּין הַשְּׁמָשׁוֹת הֲוָה. וּבֶן שְׁנָתוֹ הָיָה, כִּדְבָר אַחֵר כֶּבֶשׂ אֶחָד בֶּן שְׁנָתוֹ. וְהָכֵי אִצְטְרִיךְ, וְאַתְּ אֲמָרְתְּ בֵּין הַשְּׁמָשׁוֹת. אֶלָּא אִתְפַּקַּד חֵילָא, לְאִזְדַּמְּנָא הַהוּא אִימְרָא, בְּשַׁעֲתָא דְּאִצְטְרִיךְ לֵיה לְאַבְרָהָם. כְּמָה דְּכָל אִינוּן מִלִּין, דַּהֲווֹ בֵּין הַשְּׁמָשׁוֹת, אִתְמַנָּא חֵילָא, לְאִזְדַּמְּנָא הַהוּא מִלָּה בְּשַׁעֲתָא דְּאִצְטְרִיךְ לֵיה. הָכֵי נָמֵי, הַאי אַיִל, דְּאִתְקְרִיב תְּחוֹתֵיה דְּיִצְחָק.

508. We have learned that this ram was the one that was created at twilight. But he was one year old, as it is written: "one he-lamb a year old" (Bemidbar 7:63). It was required FOR HIM TO BE ONE YEAR OLD, JUST AS THE DAILY OFFERING. If so, how can you say that the ram was born at twilight? AND HE REPLIES: It was predestined THEN, AT TWILIGHT ON SHABBAT EVE, that the ram would be at hand for Abraham when he should be in need of it. SO IT WAS REALLY BORN AT TWILIGHT, AND WHEN IT WAS ONE YEAR OLD, IT CHANCED UPON ABRAHAM. It was like all the other things created on Shabbat eve at twilight, WHICH MEANS THAT THEY WERE predestined to actually appear at the time of need. And so was that ram, which was sacrificed instead of Isaac.

38. "In all their affliction He was afflicted"

A Synopsis

In the same way that a parent suffers when his or her child is hurting, the Zohar reveals that the Creator equally suffers when anyone in this world undergoes pain.

The Relevance of this Passage

The conventional religious view of the Creator is of a deity who metes out punishments and rewards. In reality, the Creator is an infinite force of sharing whose essence is only goodness, whose sole desire is to bestow unending pleasure upon the souls of man. The Creator neither punishes nor rewards. It is man's actions that determine which path to endless fulfillment he will journey. The gifts of the Torah and the Zohar were revealed so that man could choose the path of mercy and fulfillment. When we suffer or hurt, it is the inherent nature of the Creator to feel and experience this pain along with us. Awareness of this profound truth connects our soul to the Creator helping to quickly dissipate any darkness that is causing pain in our life. We create the consciousness that the Creator is always with us, feeling our pain whenever we hurt.

509. פָּתַח וְאָמַר בְּכָל צָרָתָם לֹא צָר וּמַלְאַךְ פָּנָיו הוֹשִׁיעָם וְגוֹ'. תָּא חֲזֵי, בְּכָל צָרָתָם דְּיִשְׂרָאֵל, כַּד אִזְדַּמַּן לוֹן עָאקָן, כְּתִיב לֹא בְּאל"ף, וּקְרִי בּוא"ו, בְּגִין דְּקוּדְשָׁא בְּרִיךְ הוּא עִמְּהוֹן בְּעָקוּ. לֹא בְּאל"ף, אֲתַר עִלָּאָה יַתִּיר, אַף עַל גַּב, דְּלָאו בְּהַהוּא אֲתַר, רוֹגְזָא וְעָקוּ, לְהָתָם לְעֵילָא, מָטָא עַקְתָּא דְּיִשְׂרָאֵל. לֹא בְּאל"ף, כִּדְבָר אַחֵר הוּא עָשָׂנוּ וְלֹא אֲנַחְנוּ. כְּתִיב בְּאל"ף, וּקְרִי בּוא"ו.

509. He opened the discussion with the verse: "In all their affliction He was (Heb. *lo*) afflicted, and the angel of His presence saved them" (Yeshayah 63:9). Come and behold: during the time when Yisrael are afflicted with troubles, "*lo* ('not')" is spelled with the letter *Aleph,* but pronounced "LO ('HE WAS')" with the letter *Vav,* because the Holy One, blessed be He, is distressed by their affliction. So *lo* with an *Aleph,* WHICH MEANS THAT HE WAS NOT DISTRESSED, refers to a higher place. Even though there is no sorrow or grief up there at the place DESCRIBED BY THE WORDS, "STRENGTH AND GLADNESS ARE IN HIS PLACE" (I DIVREI HAYAMIM 16:27), NEVERTHELESS, the afflictions of Yisrael reach this high place.

The term "*lo*" with an *Aleph* is used similarly in "it is He that has made us and not (Heb. *lo*) ourselves" (Tehilim 100:3), where "*lo*" is written with an *Aleph,* but pronounced with a *Vav,* WHICH LITERALLY MEANS 'AND WE BELONG TO HIM (Heb. *LO*).'

510. וּמַלְאַךְ פָּנָיו הוֹשִׁיעָם. וְהָא אִיהוּ עִמְּהוֹן, בְּהַהוּא עָקוּ, וְאַתְּ אֲמַרְתְּ הוֹשִׁיעָם. אֶלָּא מוֹשִׁיעָם לֹא כְּתִיב אֶלָּא הוֹשִׁיעָם, מִקַּדְמַת דְּנָא, דְּאִיהוּ זַמִּין, בְּהַהוּא עָקוּ, לְמִסְבַּל עִמְּהוֹן. תָּא חֲזֵי, בְּכָל זִמְנָא דְיִשְׂרָאֵל אִינוּן בְּגָלוּתָא, שְׁכִינְתָּא עִמְּהוֹן בְּגָלוּתָא, וְהָא אוֹקְמוּהָ, דִּכְתִיב וְשָׁב יְיָ' אֱלֹהֶיךָ אֶת שְׁבוּתְךָ וְרִחֲמֶךָ וְגו'.

510. Of the verse, "and the angel of His presence saved them" (Yeshayah 63:9), HE ASKS: But He is together with them in their affliction, AS THE BEGINNING OF THE VERSE STATES. Now you are saying that He "saved them." IF HE IS STILL TOGETHER WITH THEM IN THEIR AFFLICTION, THEN He HAS NOT YET "SAVED THEM." AND HE REPLIES: It is not written, 'saves them,' but "saved them," IN THE PAST TENSE, meaning that they had already been saved. THIS MEANS THAT HE "SAVED THEM" by staying together with them in the same affliction and suffering with them. Come and behold: every time the children of Yisrael are in exile, the Shechinah is with them; this has already been explained, as it is written: "Then Hashem your Elohim will return your captivity, and have compassion upon you" (Devarim 30:3). THE VERSE 'WILL RETURN YOUR CAPTIVITY,' LITERALLY MEANS 'WILL RETURN' USING THE INTRANSITIVE, MEANING TO INFORM US THAT THE SHECHINAH IS WITH THEM IN EXILE NAMLY 'WILL SIT'.

511. דָּבָר אַחֵר וּמַלְאַךְ פָּנָיו הוֹשִׁיעָם, דָּא שְׁכִינְתָּא, דְּאִיהִי עִמְּהוֹן בְּגָלוּתָא וְאַתְּ אֲמַרְתְּ דְּאִיהוּ הוֹשִׁיעָם. אֶלָּא הָכֵי הוּא וַדַּאי, דְּאִלֵּין אִינוּן, מַשְׁכְּנוֹתָיו דְּקוּדְשָׁא בְּרִיךְ הוּא בְּגָלוּתָא, וּבְגִין דִּשְׁכִינְתָּא עִמְּהוֹן, קוּדְשָׁא בְּרִיךְ הוּא אַדְכַּר לוֹן, לְאוֹטָבָא לוֹן, וּלְאַפָּקָא לוֹן מִן גָּלוּתָא, דִּכְתִיב וָאֶזְכֹּר אֶת בְּרִיתִי, בְּקַדְמֵיתָא, וּלְבָתַר וְעַתָּה הִנֵּה צַעֲקַת בְּנֵי יִשְׂרָאֵל בָּאָה אֵלָי.

511. A different explanation of the verse: "and the angel of His presence saved them" is that it refers to the Shechinah, which is with them in exile,

AS IS STATED IN THE BEGINNING OF THE VERSE. You claim that He "saved them," BUT IF HE IS TOGETHER WITH THEM IN EXILE, THEN HE HAS NOT YET "SAVED THEM." AND HE REPLIES: IT is certainly true that the residing places of the Holy One, blessed be He, in exile are WHEREVER THE AFFLICTIONS OF YISRAEL ARE – MEANING THAT THE HOLY ONE, BLESSED BE HE, IS PRESENT IN EVERY SINGLE AFFLICTION AND SORROW BROUGHT UPON YISRAEL. And because the Shechinah resides with them, the Holy One, blessed be He, remembers to benefit them and draw them out of exile, as it is first written: "and I have remembered my covenant" (Shemot 6:5), WHICH REFERS TO THE SHECHINAH. Later, it is written: "and now, behold, the cry of the children of Yisrael has come to me" (Shemot 3:9). SO HE ACTUALLY "SAVED THEM" BY BEING WITH THEM IN THEIR AFFLICTION. AND EVEN THOUGH THE FORMER VERSE APPEARS AFTER THE LATTER, THERE IS NO CONTRADICTION HERE, BECAUSE THERE IS NO CHRONOLOGICAL SEQUENCE IN THE TORAH.

512. וְגַם רָאִיתִי. לְאַסְגָּאָה רְאִיָּה אָחֳרָא, דְּאִיהוּ קַדְמָאָה דְכֹלָּא, וּכְתִיב וַיִּזְכֹּר אֱלֹהִים אֶת בְּרִיתוֹ, דָּא שְׁכִינְתָּא. אֶת אַבְרָהָם, לְאַבְרָהָם מִבָּעֵי לֵיהּ, אֶלָּא אֶת אַבְרָהָם, דָּא הוּא, חַבְרוּתָא וְזִוּוּגָא דִילָהּ, בַּאֲבָהָן. אֶת אַבְרָהָם, דָּא הוּא, מַעֲרָבִית דְּרוֹמִית. אֶת יִצְחָק, דָּא הוּא, צְפוֹנִית מַעֲרָבִית. וְאֶת יַעֲקֹב, דָּא הוּא, זִוּוּגָא חֲדָא, כְּלָלָא חֲדָא, זִוּוּגָא שְׁלִים, כִּדְקָא יָאוֹת.

512. The phrase, "moreover I have seen" includes another 'seeing,' which is the first among all, as it is written: "And Elohim remembered His covenant" (Shemot 2:24), which is the Shechinah. THIS VERSE APPEARS BEFORE THE VERSE: "AND I HAVE REMEMBERED MY COVENANT...with (*et*) Abraham." HE ASKS: It should have been written 'REMEMBERED HIS COVENANT for Abraham's sake'? AND HE ANSWERS: "with Abraham" alludes to the unison and joining OF THE SHECHINAH with the Patriarchs, BECAUSE THE PARTICLE "*ET*", WRITTEN BEFORE "ABRAHAM", IS THE NAME OF THE SHECHINAH. SO "with Abraham" means the Southwest, THAT IS, THE "EMBRACING" OF THE RIGHT, BECAUSE THE SOUTH IS THE SECRET OF THE RIGHT AND OF CHESED, WHICH IS ABRAHAM. THE WEST IS THE SECRET OF THE SHECHINAH, WHICH IS CALLED *ET* AND WHICH ABRAHAM 'EMBRACES' WITH CHASSADIM. "...with Isaac..." refers to the Northwest, NAMELY THE 'EMBRACING' OF THE LEFT, BECAUSE THE

NORTH IS THE SECRET OF THE LEFT AND OF GVURAH, WHICH IS CALLED ISAAC. AND THE WEST IS THE SECRET OF THE SHECHINAH, WHICH IS CALLED "*ET*" AND WHICH ISAAC 'EMBRACES' WITH HIS GEVUROT. "...and with Jacob..." means One Union, One Whole – a perfect and complete union, as should properly be. THIS ALLUDES TO THE MATING OF ZEIR ANPIN, WHICH IS CALLED JACOB, WITH THE SHECHINAH, WHICH IS CALLED "*ET*." AND THE MATING CANNOT BE COMPLETED WITHOUT THE CENTRAL COLUMN, WHICH IS JACOB. SO WITH ABRAHAM AND ISAAC, THERE WAS ONLY 'EMBRACING'. THEREFORE, IT IS WRITTEN OF JACOB: ONE UNION. THUS THE PHRASE "AND WITH (HEB. *VE-ET*) JACOB" CONSISTS OF THEM BOTH, AS ONE WHOLE. SO THE EXTRA LETTER *VAV* IN "*VE-ET*" ALLUDES TO THE PERFECTION OF THIS MATING, WHICH IS A PERFECT AND COMPLETE MATING.

513. כְּגַוְונָא דָא, אֶת הַשָּׁמַיִם, דָּא הוּא, כְּלָלָא מִדַּת לַיְלָה בַּיּוֹם. וְאֶת הָאָרֶץ, דָּא מִדַּת יוֹם בְּלַיְלָה כַּחֲדָא. אוֹף הָכָא, בְּכֻלְּהוּ אֶת, וּבְיַעֲקֹב וְאֶת, לְמֶהֱוֵי כֹלָּא, זִוּוּגָא חֲדָא, דְּלָא מִתְפָּרְשִׁין דְּכַר וְנוּקְבָּא לְעָלְמִין. וְזַמִּין קוּדְשָׁא בְּרִיךְ הוּא, לְאַכְרְזָא בְּכָל עָלְמָא, וּלְאַשְׁמָעָא קָל, דְּיֵימָא, וַיֹּאמֶר אַךְ עַמִּי הֵמָּה בָּנִים לֹא יְשַׁקֵּרוּ וַיְהִי לָהֶם לְמוֹשִׁיעַ.

513. Similarly, IT IS WRITTEN: "(*et*) the heavens" (Beresheet 1:1), which is the quality of the night, WHICH IS THE NUKVA, with day, WHICH IS ZEIR ANPIN. "...and the (*ve'et*) earth..." refers to the union of the quality of the day with THE QUALITY OF the night as one. THIS REFERS TO THE INCLUSION OF ZEIR ANPIN IN THE NUKVA, BECAUSE THE LETTER *VAV* IN "*VE'ET* ('AND THE')" ALLUDES TO UNION OF THE MALE WITH THE FEMALE. So the term "*et*" ('the')" appears in them all, AS IN WITH (*ET*) ABRAHAM AND WITH (*ET*) ISAAC. However, in reference to Jacob it is written: "and with (*ve-et*)," WHICH SHOWS THAT they are in complete unison, for the Male and Female never depart from each other. And the Holy One, blessed be He, in the future shall make His voice heard and announce to all the world, "For He said, Surely, they are My people, children that will not deal falsely; so He was their savior" (Yeshayah 63:8).

בָּרוּךְ י' לְעוֹלָם אָמֵן וְאָמֵן.

Blessed be Hashem for evermore. Amen and Amen.

NOTES

NOTES

NOTES

NOTES

NOTES

NOTES

NOTES

NOTES

NOTES